Praise and Condemnation
for
The Illusion of an Islamic State

"People who are convinced that they know more than anyone else about Islam, and yet are full of hatred towards any of God's creatures who do not travel the same path as they; and those who claim to be in possession of the absolute truth, and for that reason entitled to act as God's vice-regents on earth (caliphs) and to dictate how everyone else must live—clearly, their words and behavior will not lead us into the presence of God. Their dream of an Islamic state is merely an illusion, for the true islamic state is not to be found in the structure of any government, but rather, in hearts which are open to God and all His creatures."

> ~ Former Indonesian President Kyai Haji Abdurrahman Wahid,
> from his introduction to *The Illusion of an Islamic State*

"The goal [of this book] is to raise our awareness, and counter the spread of extremist ideology in a peaceful and responsible manner. Although its title is challenging and some Muslims may not like it, LibForAll has published this book not to create enemies, but to facilitate a positive, constructive dialogue, both among Muslims and between Muslims and those of other faiths."

> ~ Dr. Syafii Maarif, Former Chairman of
> the Muhammadiyah Organization

"*The Illusion of an Islamic State* conveys an extremely firm and clear message. The hidden danger that lies at the heart of extremist attempts to establish an Islamic state consists of the unconscious juxtaposition of profound ignorance regarding Islam's true nature, and a false conviction that they possess perfect knowledge of the same.... Perhaps all would agree that ignorance is highly dangerous. Yet not everyone is aware of the hidden dangers of ignorance, which dwell within."

~ Kyai Haji A. Mustofa Bisri
Deputy Chairman, Nahdlatul Ulama Supreme Council

"A path-breaking new report by the LibForAll Foundation."

~ *Wall Street Journal*, "Indonesia Rejects Extremism,"
by Sadanand Dhume

"Throwing a gauntlet down at the feet of radical Islam, a group of mainstream Muslim leaders led by former President Abdurrahman Wahid on Thursday announced the release of a book asserting that Indonesia is being infiltrated by foreign-funded extremists bent on turning the country into an Islamic state."

~ *The Jakarta Globe*

"Just days before Indonesians go to the polls, a study has been released charging that an Islamic party is spreading radical and extremist ideology—undermining the country's moderate Islamic tradition.... [T]he findings will certainly have some bearing on the country's politics."

~ *Channel News Asia*

"LibForAll has been exceptional in a regional context for issues involving innovative forms and communicating the message of anti-extremism. One guiding star in these efforts has been selecting methods with maximum impact and that reach the largest possible audience.... LibForAll's coordinated media strategy has had a decisive political effect in terms of curbing political parties with an extremist agenda. Exposing the true nature of the parties has enabled marginalization of corrosive, subversive forces."

~ *Preventing Violent Radicalization and Terrorism: The Case of Indonesia*
by Dr. Magnus Ranstorp, Director of Research
The Center for Asymmetric Threat Studies
at Sweden's National Defense College

"The LibForAll Foundation is one of the rare success stories of an initiative in which moderate and liberal Muslims—too often the silent and disorganized majority—have organized effectively to counter radical Islamist groups by promoting democracy and tolerance."

~ *Democracy Digest*,
published by the National Endowment for Democracy

"C. Holland Taylor doesn't look like a man radical Muslims should fear.... He possesses no arsenal of weapons, holds no government post and operates no intelligence service. Yet he runs the world's most potent and innovative anti-extremist network and may hold a key to defusing the ticking bomb of Islamist terrorism."

~ *The Weekly Standard*, "In Defense of Moderation,"
by Jennifer Rubin

"LibForAll Foundation, an NGO which cares deeply about Islam and Muslims... strives to express, clarify and widely disseminate a true understanding of Islam not only to non-Muslims, but also to Muslims in general. LibForAll aims to present the moderate and tolerant face of Islam, and explain the importance of [Muslims] returning to the essence of Islamic teachings which, until now, have been poorly understood by many groups [both in Islam and the West]."

~ *Al-Ahram* (one of the oldest & most widely-read newspapers in
the Arab world) "Extremism is Alien to Islam," by Alaa Amer

"The [Muslim Brotherhood-affiliated] PKS has accused the authors of *The Illusion of an Islamic State: The Expansion of Transnational Islamist Movements to Indonesia* of being agents of former American President George W. Bush. But the various researchers involved in the book take said accusations in stride, and joke about them."

~ *Inilah.com*, a popular Indonesian website that
closely monitors the PKS

"A researcher from LSI, Burhanudin Muhtadi, explained that if the Wahhabi rumors are believed by the public, it will curtail the acceptability of a vice-presidential candidate put forward by the

PKS.... According to Burhan, who also wrote a thesis on the PKS and Social Movements at the Australian National University, the Wahhabi rumors are in fact true...."

~ *Inilah.com*

"*The Illusion of an Islamic State* really scourged Wahhabism.... The Justice and Prosperity Party (PKS) fell victim and was gravely wounded [by the book's publication]."

~ Abu Rusdan, former commander of al-Qaeda-affiliated terrorist group Jemaah Islamiyah's Military Region III (Borneo, Sulawesi and the southern Philippines), quoted in *Sabili* ("*The Path*") magazine

"Here is the book from that accursed Satanic network. Read, Study and Anticipate. This is the link (to download *The Illusion of an Islamic State*)."

~ *al-Jamaah*, website affiliated with the terrorist organization Jemaah Islamiyah and its founder, Abu Bakr Ba'asyir

"Infidels may not be killed if they do not oppose [radical] Islam. We can live alongside them. But people who are involved in movements that oppose Islam, even on the level of thought, not only may be killed, but should and must be."

~ Abu Bakr Ba'asyir, as reported in *Tempo* magazine, following release of *The Illusion of an Islamic State*, which linked terrorism to the spread of Islamist ideology

"Since the explosion of the bombs in Kuningan [Jakarta] in July of 2009, the terms Wahhabism and transnationalism have suddenly been on everyone's lips. Many national television stations and other mass media outlets have been quoting a number of leading national figures about the relationship between terrorist bombs and Wahhabism.

"Whether this is intentional or not, one thing is certain: the assistance of media (especially TV) has caused the term Wahhabi to become a new stigma that is terrorizing many [extremist] Muslim organizations. It may be that those behind the spread of this stigma hope to divide Indonesian Muslims and turn them against each other....

THE ILLUSION OF AN ISLAMIC STATE

How an Alliance of Moderates Launched a
Successful Jihad Against Radicalization and Terrorism
in the World's Largest Muslim-Majority Country

THE ILLUSION OF AN ISLAMIC STATE

How an Alliance of Moderates Launched a Successful Jihad Against Radicalization and Terrorism in the World's Largest Muslim-Majority Country

Editor
H.E. Kyai Haji Abdurrahman Wahid

Prologue & Preface
Prof. Dr. Ahmad Syafii Maarif
C. Holland Taylor

Epilogue
Kyai Haji A. Mustofa Bisri

Principal Authors/Editorial Team
Kyai Haji Hodri Ariev, Prof. Dr. Ratno Lukito
and C. Holland Taylor

The WAHID Institute
Seeding Plural and Peaceful Islam

LIBFORALL
FOUNDATION

ΛΛAARif

LibForAll Foundation Press publishes works that further LibForAll's mission to promote a pluralistic, tolerant and spiritual understanding of Islam, at peace with itself and the modern world.

The Illusion of an Islamic State:
How an Alliance of Moderates Launched a Successful Jihad Against Radicalization and Terrorism in the World's Largest Muslim-Majority Country

Originally published in Indonesian as *Ilusi Negara Islam: Expansi Gerakan Islam Transnasional di Indonesia* (*The Illusion of an Islamic State: The Expansion of Transnational Islamist Movements in Indonesia*)

Editor: Kyai Haji Abdurrahman Wahid
Principal Authors/Editorial Team: Hodri Ariev, Ratno Lukito and C. Holland Taylor
English Translation: C. Holland Taylor
Cover Design and Interior Layout: Widhi Cahya
Printed by CV A Sembilan Mathba'ah Utama

First Indonesian Edition: April 2009
First English Edition: May 2011

Published with The Wahid Institute (www.wahidinstitute.org)
and Maarif Institute (www.maarifinstitute.org)

ISBN 978-0-9834629-0-3
ISBN 978-0-9834629-1-0 (ebook)
1. Islam, Extremism.   2. Islam, Counter-Extremism.   3. Islam, Spirituality.   4. Indonesia, Contemporary.   5. Wahhabism.   6. Muslim Brotherhood.
I. Abdurrahman Wahid, Kyai Haji

LIBFORALL
FOUNDATION

Jakarta • Winston-Salem • Cairo • Leiden
www.libforall.org

Table of Contents

Preface to the English Edition

FIGHTING FIRE WITH WATER
By C. Holland Taylor

The Illusion of an Islamic State represents a landmark achieve-ment in the field of counter-radicalization, which demonstrates how an alliance of moderate Muslim leaders can effectively isolate, and discredit, the ideology of religious hatred, supremacy and vio-lence that underlies and animates terrorism. As such, it warrants serious study—as well as the wide dissemination, and application, of its findings—by public policy makers, journalists and people of good will of every faith and nation, who care about the threat to humanity posed by Islamist ideology, terrorism and a rising tide of Islamophobia in the West.

If the Muslim world, including the contemporary Middle East, is to navigate a path between the Scylla and Charybdis of temporal and religious authoritarianism—and, at long last, provide its inhabitants with the kinds of civil liberty, and rule of law, that people in the West have come to take for granted—it can only do so by applying the principles articulated in this visionary work. For the renowned Muslim theologians who authored *The Illusion of an Islamic State* have issued a stirring *theological* defense of freedom, grounded in a profoundly spiritual understanding of Islam that is capable of deepening and broadening, rather than destroying, Muslims' faith. As such, it represents a unique contribution from Indonesia to the world, offered in the spirit of love, compassion and respect.

For Muslim societies in the midst of intense political transfor-mation, this book offers a model for dealing responsibly with the threat of both violent and non-violent extremists, including the

Muslim Brotherhood, by using democratic methods rather than those of a brutal police state. In Europe and North America, *The Illusion of an Islamic State* may help to illuminate the increasingly polarized and strident debate on Islam that has paralyzed Western societies, and led to institutional deadlock in the face of a profound threat that jeopardizes the prospects of a peaceful and harmonious future for Muslims and non-Muslims alike.

An immediate publishing phenomenon upon its "hard launch" in May of 2009 in Indonesia—the country with the world's largest Muslim population and democracy—*The Illusion of an Islamic State* exposed extremist ideology to public ridicule and rejection, and decisively influenced the outcome of Indonesia's national elections that year.

Active participation by the most respected Muslim leaders in Indonesia was crucial to the project's success. Former president Kyai Haji Abdurrahman Wahid (1940 - 2009)—whom Bret Stephens of the *Wall Street Journal* once called "the single most influential religious leader in the Muslim world," and "easily the most important ally the West has in the ideological struggle against Islamic radicalism"—served as the book's editor. In this capacity, he wrote an extensive introduction ("The Enemy Within") that served both as an executive summary of the report, and a dramatic appeal for Indonesians "to restore honor and respect to Islam, which the extremists have desecrated," and to "restore the majesty of Islamic teachings as *rahmatan lil-'âlamîn*—a blessing for all creation—[which] represents a vital key to building a peaceful world."

The Illusion of an Islamic State also includes contributions by Kyai Haji Mustofa Bisri, a renowned leader of the world's largest Muslim organization (the 40-million-member Nahdlatul Ulama, which President Wahid himself once led), and Dr. Syafii Maarif, the immediate past chairman of the 30-million-member Muhammadiyah organization, and 2008 recipient of the Ramon Magsaysay Award, Asia's equivalent of the Nobel Prize. The fact that the book was co-published with two widely known and respected NGOs—The Wahid Institute and Maarif Institute—further strengthened the dramatic impact of its launch.

Western journalists quickly identified *The Illusion of an Islamic*

State as "a path-breaking new report" (*Wall Street Journal*) that exposed "Islamist groups... systematically infiltrating Indonesian mosques, institutes, universities and government, posing an even greater threat to the country than regional terrorist groups" (*International Herald Tribune*), "rais[ing] concerns that Indonesia's moderate form of Islam and its secular ideology are under siege" (*Sydney Morning Herald*).

Yet except for Channel News Asia, which reported that "the [study's] findings will certainly have some bearing on the country's politics," the international press generally overlooked a far more significant angle to the story, which was immediately evident to the Indonesian media and public alike. Backed by Abdurrahman Wahid, Syafii Maarif and Mustofa Bisri—the most prominent spiritual leaders associated with "the country's two major Muslim organizations, the traditionalist Nahdlatul Ulama and the modernist Muhammadiyah... [which] together command the allegiance of 70 million people" (*Jakarta Globe*)—*The Illusion of an Islamic State* did not passively "report" on the phenomenon of Wahhabi/Muslim Brotherhood infiltration of Indonesian institutions.

Instead, as Indonesia's largest web portal, with over 10 million visitors a day, was quick to proclaim following the book's launch: "*The Illusion of an Islamic State* is the NU and Muhammadiyah's Response to the [Muslim Brotherhood-affiliated) PKS and Hizb ut-Tahrir" (*Detik.com*). "Throwing a gauntlet down at the feet of radical Islam, a group of mainstream Muslim leaders led by former President Abdurrahman Wahid on Thursday announced the release of a book asserting that Indonesia is being infiltrated by foreign-funded extremists bent on turning the country into an Islamic state" (*Jakarta Globe*).

The Nahdlatul Ulama prominently featured the book on its website, as did the NU's 10-million-member youth wing, Ansor. Within weeks of its launch, *The Illusion of an Islamic State* went from zero results on Google to over 556,000, and dramatically influenced Indonesia's 2009 national elections: helping to prevent the Muslim Brotherhood-linked Justice and Prosperity Party (PKS) from merging its political platform with that of incumbent president (and 2009 winner) Susilo Bambang Yudhoyono (SBY); derailing PKS ambitions to nominate its cadre as Yudhoyono's vice presidential candidate, and thereby obtain the legitimacy required to secure the presidency in 2014; facilitating the nomination of Javanese nationalist Boediono as SBY's vice president; and providing a robust theological justification and defense of Indonesia's largely secular constitution, which rejects the notion of an "Islamic" state.

Unlike anything previously published on the subject of counter-radicalization—either in the Muslim world, or the West—*The Illusion of an Islamic State* seamlessly incorporated four distinct elements to achieve its unprecedented results:

- Field research, during which a team of 27 academicians from a network of Islamic State Universities and Institutes traveled to 24 districts in 17 provinces of Indonesia, and interviewed 591 extremist agents, in order to ascertain their ideology, agenda and affiliation with various transnational and domestic Islamist movements;

- Consultative research, in which the book's editorial team met with dozens of top Muslim clerics, educators, political leaders, high ranking government officials, military officers, businessmen and media professionals, in order to obtain first-hand information regarding extremist infiltration of Indonesian society from moderate Muslim leaders who have direct, personal knowledge of these developments, and also to request said leaders' advice regarding the issues covered by this book;

- Literature research, concerning the origins, ideology and spread of Islamist extremism in the Middle East and Indonesia, and the reaction of moderate Muslim organizations, such as the Nahdlatul Ulama and Muhammadiyah, to this threat;

- Theological refutation of the ideology articulated, and generally shared, by the 591 extremist agents interviewed by the project's field research team, and widely propagated not only in Indonesia, but among Muslim communities throughout the world, including Europe and North America. This theological refutation was written under the direct supervision of Kyai Haji Abdurrahman Wahid by his disciple, the Muslim theologian and *'alim* (scholar) Kyai Haji Hodri Ariev, who is LibForAll Foundation's Director of Programs for Southeast Asia, and head of Pondok Pesantren Bahrul Ulum ("Ocean of Knowledge Madrasa") in Jember, East Java.

Launched in September of 2006, the project required more than two and a half years to complete. The project team confronted numerous difficulties, ranging from the mundane to significant—including implicit and explicit threats of character assassination, and/or violence, directed towards those involved with the project. I recall discussing the latter with President Wahid, after informing him that a prominent Muslim figure involved with one phase of the project had suggested we not publish *The Illusion of an Islamic State*, "to avoid being attacked by extremists." President Wahid immediately replied, "Let them attack us! Then at least people will hear about the controversy, and can decide whether or not they agree with us. If we remain silent, only the extremists will be heard."

On another occasion, I informed President Wahid of the advice of a sympathetic but fearful Muslim leader, who knew of the book's imminent release, and asked that we not speak up (by publishing it). When asked his opinion, President Wahid laughed and replied loudly, "Holland, I made that decision forty years ago. Should we speak up? YES!!!!"

Historical Background

President Wahid was referring to the brutal massacre of half a million to a million Indonesians in 1965/'66, in the wake of an abortive communist coup attempt. Because General Suharto's troops were insufficient in number to comb the Javanese countryside, his subordinates enlisted Muslim militias (including many members of the Nahdlatul Ulama, which Abdurrahman Wahid's grandfather had established in 1926) to help exterminate the Indonesian Communist Party (PKI). In 1965, PKI had been the third largest communist party in the world, its membership rolls exceeded only by those of China and the Soviet Union. By the end of 1966, the PKI had been virtually annihilated.

Abdurrahman Wahid—whose father and paternal grandfather played key roles in Indonesia's independence struggle, and establishing the new nation as a pluralistic and largely secular state—was twenty-five at the time, and enrolled at Egypt's famed al-Azhar University in Cairo. During this period, he also worked part-time at the Indonesian embassy. There, the young Wahid was privy to diplomatic cables that described the bloody massacres underway back home, engendering a period of introspection that led to his fateful decision: never to remain silent in the face of injustice.

Upon his return to Indonesia, Wahid (popularly known as "Gus Dur") became prominent in intellectual circles and the Nahdlatul Ulama (NU), assuming the role of general chairman of the mass-based Islamic organization in 1984. A lifelong devotee of freedom, Wahid promptly mobilized the NU to oppose President Suharto's authoritarian regime, and lay the foundation for Indonesia's eventual transition to democracy.

As one Indonesian activist told *Wall Street Journal* columnist Bret Stephens in April of 2007, "Gus Dur was the only person in Indonesia who, having dared to oppose Suharto at the height of his power, was never broken (by Suharto's regime)... Anyone who could do that must be very, very *sakti* (possessed of immense spiritual power)... And one who is that *sakti* must be very close to being *wali allah* (i.e., a saint)."

The massacres of 1965/'66, which eviscerated the PKI, also had the unforeseen consequence of altering the balance of socio-religious forces within Indonesia. For hundreds of years, rural Javanese society in particular was divided between *santri* (observant) and *abangan* (non-observant) Muslims, the latter generally adhering to a syncretic, mystical set of beliefs referred to as *kejawen* (or "Javaneseness"). Like Sufism (Islamic mysticism), *kejawen* maintains that Truth is universal, with many paths leading to the divine goal of human existence: i.e., union with God. Unlike Sufism, *kejawen* practitioners often disavow the need to observe Islamic law (or any other formal religious teaching/dogma) in order to attain to the Truth, which they maintain is synonymous with the inner state of enlightenment.

"The people behind this are identical to those who were behind the book *The Illusion of an Islamic State*.... I can't stop thinking about LibForAll, which financed and published this project, and how it claims to be liberal and promoting liberalism, but in reality is extremely conservative, sectarian and exclusive, unwilling to tolerate differences [i.e., extremist interpretations of Islam]."

~ *Hidayatullah* (*Allah's Guidance*) magazine

"Through its book *The Illusion of an Islamic State*, LibForAll has backed [radical] Islam into a corner."

~ *Swara Muslim* (*The Voice of Muslims*), a website whose slogan is "Jihad never sleeps; holy warriors never die"

"The authors of this book are intolerant of their fellow Muslims, as evidenced by their unrelenting attacks, stigmatizing their fellow Muslims as close-minded literalists, in addition to other pejorative abuse. On the other hand, while they themselves are incapable of behaving in a tolerant manner towards their fellow Muslims, they call for tolerance towards infidels.... Indeed, they reinterpret Qur'anic verses and sayings of the Prophet Muhammad which command [us] to wage war against them...."

~ *Syabab* (*Youth*), a webzine and media production company affiliated with the transnational extremist group Hizb ut-Tahrir

"*The Illusion of an Islamic State*: Screams of the Syphilitic Crowd.... There is a new book from the Syphilitic [secularism, religious pluralism and liberalism] School of Thought that perhaps has not yet found its way into your hands.... In order to save Muslims the trouble of reading the book (and indeed, perhaps there is no need to read it at all), nahimunkar.com has summarized everything you need to know about this book."

~ *Nahimunkar* (*Forbidding Evil*), Islamist website

"The enemies of Islam never cease in their efforts to destroy the Muslim community. They use not only physical methods, but ideological warfare as well. They regard this methodology as more inexpensive and effective. Just look at what happened before the bombing of the J.W. Marriott and Ritz Carlton hotels. A couple months earlier we were 'treated' to the book *The Illusion of an Islamic State*, which attacks political Islam."

~ *Sabili* (*The Path*) magazine

"[In 2004], Indonesia's best-selling magazine was an Islamic weekly called *Sibili* [i.e., *Sabili*], which offered a mix of wild anti-American conspiracy theories and cheerleading for jihad.... Today the tide seems to have turned.... *Sibili*, meanwhile, has toned down its anti-Western rhetoric. 'We now see bigger potential for sales among moderate Muslims,' said Lufti Tamimi, the magazine's editor and part-owner. In January [2010], Tamimi ditched *Sibili's* hard-line editor and commissioned a series of articles denouncing Salafism, a purist strain of Islam that underpins extremist ideology."

~ *Washington Post*, "Indonesia steps up pressure on Islamist militants,"
by Pulitzer Prize-winning journalist Andrew Higgins

"*The Illusion of an Islamic State*... has given rise to enormous polemics, which is precisely what [its authors] intended. All kinds of people are now following the lead of Gus Dur and Syafii Maarif, [criticizing Wahhabism and transnational Islamist movements]. But what is clear is that this book was created by LibForAll.... They are attacking "transnational Islam," using deep-rooted local power structures."

~ *Hidayatullah* (*Allah's Guidance*) magazine

As President Wahid—the leader of Indonesia's *santri* population—once said to me, "The reason Indonesian Islam is so tolerant is not because of *santris*. It's because of *kejawen*, and the fact that *santris* have always had to live alongside the *kejawen*."

The 1965/'66 rural massacres—which specifically targeted *abangan* Javanese—disrupted the historic balance between Islam and *kejawen*. Although few *abangan* were familiar with the details of Marxist-Leninist ideology, or the geopolitical stakes involved in the struggle between capitalism and communism, the PKI had managed to build a mass movement by infiltrating *abangan* villages, and networking *abangan* communities throughout Central and East Java. Thus, destruction of the PKI resulted in the wholesale massacre of thousands of *abangan* communities.

In 1968, President Suharto issued a decree that required all Indonesian citizens to list one of five state-sanctioned religions on their identity cards: Muslim, Catholic, Protestant, Hindu or Buddhist. Because of the *abangan* link to PKI, *kejawen* and other indigenous belief systems (*kepercayaan*) were not an option. Disgusted by the massacres they had just witnessed, millions of *abangan* and *priyayi* (Javanese aristocrats) chose to convert to Christianity, or revert to Hinduism. However, the vast majority of *abangan* Muslims listed Islam on their identity cards. Haunted by the recent holocaust, which had transformed vast areas of Java into a killing field, many felt it wise to inoculate their children against future risk (i.e., massacre) by teaching them to observe the formal practices of Islam, while neglecting their *kejawen* roots.

Suharto, himself a *kejawen* Muslim and nationalist—but above all, a brilliant opportunist—promptly cracked down on Islamist extremism, as he consolidated power in the late '60s. Yet when confronted by Abdurrahman Wahid's, Nurcholish Madjid's and other Muslim leaders' mobilization of the Nahdlatul Ulama, Muhammadiyah and civil society in general to promote democracy in the late '80s and '90s, Suharto cynically mobilized Islamist ideologues to counter his opponents.

Establishment of the Suharto-backed Indonesian Association of Muslim Intellectuals (ICMI)—which advocated the social, political and economic dominance of Muslims—and of a "green generals" faction in the military, occurred in tandem with the rise of a Saudi-funded *da'wa*, or proselytism movement on university campuses, whose Muslim Brotherhood-affiliated alumni were quick to establish political parties when Abdurrahman Wahid and his democracy-movement allies finally toppled the Suharto regime in 1998.

The reform era launched by Suharto's downfall brought dramatic changes to Indonesia, such as freedom of the press; the revocation of state-sanctioned discrimination against ethnic minorities, including the Chinese; and the subordination of military to civilian authority, which constitute three of Abdurrahman's Wahid's greatest achievements during his brief tenure as President (1999 – 2001), before remnants of the Suharto regime managed to impeach and remove him from office, on the alleged grounds of "incompetence." Yet the very freedom that liberated Indonesians from the arbitrary dictates of Suharto's regime also permitted the blossoming of religious extremism, as Wahhabi/Muslim Brotherhood ideology and Arab petrodollars encouraged indigenous extremists to revive the dream of an Islamic state, which Indonesia's founding fathers (including President Wahid's own father and grandfather) had firmly rejected.

Few people, today, recall the fact that Kyai Haji Hasyim Asyari and other traditional religious scholars founded the Nahdlatul Ulama in January of 1926, in direct response to the Wahhabi conquest of Mecca and Medina approximately sixteen months before. After a delegation of Indonesian *ulama* failed to persuade the new Saudi rulers to allow Muslims freedom of worship in the Haramain (the sacred cities of Mecca and Medina), President Wahid's grandfather and other Indonesian Muslims called for a spiritual "awakening of the *ulama*" (literally, *nahdlatul ulama*), to prevent the spread of Wahhabi influence to the East Indies. Within a few years, the organization they established had become the world's largest Muslim organization, whose followers currently number well over 40 million.

The historical antecedents of the NU—which traces its spiritual heritage to the saints who propagated Islam in Java, and one in particular known as Sunan Kalijogo—are also significant. For the sixteenth century was a time of great upheaval and bloodshed on the Indonesian island of Java, as newly Muslim city-states along its northern coast destroyed local Hindu-Buddhist kingdoms, and extended their power to the island's interior.

Flush with victory, fanatical adherents of the new religion—many of Arab or Chinese descent—spread terror as they sought to eradicate the island's ancient cultural heritage, and obtain a monopoly on economic and political power, under the pretext of serving the One True God. Opposing them were indigenous Javanese—now led by Islamic saints and political figures, such as Sunan Kalijogo—who sought continuity and a common ground between religions, based on the precepts of tolerance and mysticism.

For nearly a hundred years, the opposing forces struggled for the soul of Java—and, ultimately, for that of Islam—in a war whose decisive engagements occurred not only on the field of battle, but in the hearts and minds of countless individuals scattered across its lush, tropical landscape. For in this conflict between orthodox, self-described "jihadists" and Sufi (mystically-inclined) Muslims, the Sufis' profound spiritual ideology—popularized among the masses by storytellers and musicians—played a role even more vital than that of economics or pure military force, in defeating religious extremism in Java.

In the end, a new dynasty arose, founded on the principle of "the throne for the people," which established religious tolerance as the rule of law, and guaranteed freedom of conscience to all Javanese—two centuries before the Virginia Statute of Religious Freedom and Bill of Rights separated church and state in America. The founder of that dynasty was a Javanese Sufi Muslim and disciple of Sunan Kalijogo named Senopati ing Alogo. The basis of Senopati's victory was the popular appeal of his message of freedom, justice and profound inner spirituality, in contrast to the fanaticism and tyranny of his political opponents.

Today, more than four centuries later, Kalijogo's and Senopati's legacy remains, in the form of Java's distinctly tolerant and pluralistic culture. Their ideological descendants continue to resist the tide of religious extremism, now funded by Gulf petrodollars and entrenched local elites, who use radical Islam for personal advancement, or to attack and undermine the process of reform in Indonesian society.

Contemporary leaders—including those who produced *The Illusion of an Islamic State*—are not alone in their efforts, but supported by tens of millions of Indonesians, who wish to preserve their culture's enlightened embrace of religious tolerance and diversity.

Muslim extremists generally hate and fear Indonesian Islam, just as they despise and denounce other forms of Sufism throughout the Islamic world. The fact that the largest Muslim population in the world (Indonesia's) does not share the radicals' intolerant Wahhabi/Salafi views is a constant source of irritation to many Saudis and other Islamists. As a result, Indonesia is in the crosshairs: the target of a sustained militant Islamist campaign to destroy the most liberal and tolerant form of Islam on earth, by: 1) trying to rewrite and/or reinterpret the Indonesian constitution, to incorporate Islamic law; 2) funding terrorism; 3) instituting piecemeal legislative change; and 4) domination of towns and provinces where the militants can impose their views through local support or by intimidation.

In many ways, Indonesia resembles Britain in World War II. Hitler's failure to seize the UK cost him that war, as Britain transformed itself into an "unsinkable aircraft carrier," and the base from which the liberation of Europe was launched. Similarly—given its rich spiritual traditions, and extensive population of *ulama* (Muslim religious scholars) who possess a profound knowledge of both the exoteric and esoteric dimensions of Islam—Indonesia can serve as a launching pad for an intellectual and cultural assault upon extremist ideology throughout the Muslim world.

Muslim extremists are determined to prevent this from happening. For decades, the Wahhabis have been quietly promoting strict Islam in Indonesia: financing educational institutions; providing scholarships to study at Saudi universities; funding radical Islamist groups to wage jihad against Christians, Westerners and even Muslims whose understanding and practice of Islam differs from their own; building mosques and hiring Islamist imams (religious leaders); churning out translations of militant Islamist texts from Arabic to Indonesian and subsidizing their distribution to millions; and attempting to discredit spiritual and progressive Islamic leaders.

As Paul Marshall of Hudson Institute's Center for Religious Freedom has written, "The struggle against extremist Islam is not only military and diplomatic, it is also a war of ideas. In this battle there are few more important countries than Indonesia, whose 230 million people make it by far the largest Muslim country and democracy. It is also the home of the largest concentration of Muslims developing an understanding of Islam at home in a democratic and diverse world, and committed to resisting the reactionary versions being exported from Saudi Arabia."

The enormous popularity, controversy and impact of *The Illusion of an Islamic State*—upon the fourth most populous country in the world, after China, India and the U.S.—suggests its relevance to the world at large, where Muslims and non-Muslims alike continue to grapple with issues concerning the nature of Islam and its proper role in society, as well as the ongoing threat of terrorism.

Project Objectives and Overview

When President Wahid and I conceived and designed the project in the fall of 2005, it was in the context of this global struggle for the "soul of Islam," and with four distinct objectives in mind, as articulated soon thereafter in LibForAll's business plan (*cf.* Appendix 3, "Project Description"):

- Help stem the tide of radical Islam in Indonesia and use it as a "launching pad" from which to stimulate opposition to the Wahhabi/Salafi agenda in the rest of the Islamic world;
- Mobilize traditional Muslim leadership and masses, who are not yet radicalized, to consciously oppose the spread of militant Islam;
- Expose and discredit Wahhabi/Salafi proselytism activities, which are a crucial factor in the spread of Islamist extremism worldwide; and
- Establish a proven template for discrediting Wahhabi/Salafi extremism, which can be effectively replicated in other parts of the Muslim world.

In order to document the project's impact—and enable read-ers to evaluate the extent to which it has, and has not, achieved the goals outlined above—this English language edition includes not only the complete text of the original, translated from Indonesian, but several new appendices that contain over 150 pages of selected media/internet coverage of *The Illusion of an Islamic State* and its impact, which appeared in the weeks, months and years following its launch.

In the interest of providing a brief overview of the book's con-tents for those who may not have time to read the entire docu-ment, the work opens with a prologue by Dr. Syafii Maarif, whose pointed reference to "fundamentalist Christian groups" as the "pri-mary supporters" of "President George W. Bush's... neo-imperialist regime" reflects the diversity of views held by the Muslim leaders who joined in making this project successful.

What united President Wahid, Mustofa Bisri and Syafii Maarif was not their political views (which differ dramatically), but rather, their resolute opposition to Islamist movements and their "totalitarian-centralistic" ideology, based on a harsh, narrow and rigid understanding of Islam. The fact that President Wahid (who deeply appreciated the American founders' ideal of limited government); Kyai Haji Mustofa Bisri (who is apolitical) and Dr. Syafii Maarif (whose views incline towards a European social-demo-cratic model) could set aside these differences so readily, provides an implicit rebuke to those in the West who allow their disdain for political opponents to lead them into a misbegotten alliance with Wahhabi/Muslim Brotherhood activists, whose "civilizational jihad" against the West parallels the infiltration of Indonesian soci-ety documented by this book.

President Wahid's introduction to *The Illusion of an Islamic State* constitutes an executive summary of the work as a whole; a theological rejection of Islamist ideology, by one of the world's lead-ing Muslim scholars, who was trained in the classical traditions of Islam; and a ringing call to action, to "[h]alt in its tracks and elimi-nate—using responsible methods—the vicious cycle of radicalization that spreads extremist ideology and doctrine." Significantly, Presi-dent Wahid singles out and condemns the insidious link between extremist movements and opportunistic politicians and political parties, which have "joined the extremists in driving our nation towards a deep chasm, which threatens destruction and national disintegration... [due to] the fact that radical movements have already succeeded in infiltrating to the heart of government institutions, and are using these to accomplish their goals."

Chapter I ("A Study of Transnational Islamist Movements and Their Accomplices in Indonesia") describes the study's purpose and methodology, and highlights a number of its key findings. These include the fact that—far from leading a socially or economically marginalized existence—the overwhelming majority of the 591 extremists interviewed for the study were "'white collar' professionals, and included government employees, university professors, university students, teachers, businessmen, regional legislators (DPRD), college deans and local chairmen of political parties."

> Another prominent characteristic of respondents that should be noted is that of *dual membership*, whereby a respondent maintained simultaneous memberships in both a moderate and an extremist group. Nearly all of the field researchers encountered this *dual membership* phenomenon, which was especially prevalent in the Muhammadiyah community. This demonstrates that extremist groups have already engaged in systematic infiltration of the Muhammadiyah and NU. They are conducting guerrilla-style campaigns to transform the Muhammadiyah and NU from moderate Islamic organizations into radical movements, remade in the image of the extremist organizations that are infiltrating them.

Chapter II ("The Origins and Global Spread of Wahhabi/Muslim Brotherhood Ideology") provides extensive background regarding the ideology and history of these movements in the Middle East, and as "transplanted" to Indonesia over the past 40 years, as part of a "global Wahhabization" campaign heavily funded by Arab petrodollars. Among its notable findings:

The primary factors that induce local extremist leaders and activists to affiliate themselves with one of the above-mentioned transnational Islamist movements are: financial opportunism; a desire for power; social environment and/or social dislocation; and/or a weak understanding of religious teachings, especially in regard to spiritual matters... However, the most important causal factor leading to infatuation with extremist movements is a shallow understanding of religion (i.e., Islamic teachings)....

Anyone who is unfamiliar with the complexity of ta'wil (exegesis of religious texts), as widely practiced by Sunni Muslim theologians, may have difficulty confronting the theological claims asserted by extremist groups, which base their interpretations on a literal reading of the texts in question. Even those with a conventional university education can be easily deceived to support the radicals' political agenda, as proven by this study, which found that a disproportionate number of college students and professionals not only sympathize with, but have become active cadres in the PKS and Hizb ut-Tahrir Indonesia... *Significantly, it is spirituality, more than any other aspect of life, that extremist groups reject.*

Chapter III ("The Ideology and Agenda of Extremist Movements in Indonesia") begins with an essay, written by Nahdlatul Ulama theologian Kyai Haji Hodri Ariev under President Wahid's supervision, which dissects and refutes the extremist understanding of *shari'a*, and instead positions *shari'a* as

a path to attain the level of actually knowing, and fulfilling, God's will (*ridlâ*) through spiritual apprehension... Every attempt to formalize religion [through the imposition of Islamic law, and the establishment of an Islamic state, and/or caliphate] has a pure political objective: viz., to seize power. When extremists claim that their actions are based on the fact that God—Pure and Exalted is He!— dictates every aspect of human life, this constitutes a blatant theological error that must be refuted and rejected. No specific form of government, nor the formalization of religion, are needed to create a good *muslim*. All that is actually required is self-transcendent spiritual awareness, so that one may constantly feel the presence of God (*ihsân*). Thus, extremist claims that they will create an "Islamic society" by implementing *shari'a* or establishing an Islamic state or caliphate are nothing more than political maneuvers employed to justify the seizure of power.

Chapter IV ("The Infiltration of Indonesian Islam by Extremist Agents") examines the success radicals have achieved infiltrating the Muhammadiyah; the Nahdlatul Ulama; the quasi-governmental Indonesian Council of Religious Scholars (MUI); schools and universities; government institutions and businesses. Among its many trenchant observations, the chapter describes how:

> The combination of a virulent ideology, backed by enormous financial resources deployed in a systematic manner, has enabled extremist infiltration to become increasingly broad, deep and threatening to the people and nation of Indonesia....

> In an official document published by the PKS itself, the Justice and Prosperity Party explicitly talks about spreading its cadres [throughout Indonesian society] through a three-stage process: *first*, the spread of *da'wa* (proselytism) cadres to organizations/institutions in the various fields of life, with these cadres focusing their efforts on reaching the respective organizations'/institutions' centers of power and policy; *second*, to ensure these *da'wa* cadres have a successful career within the target organizations/institutions; and third, for these *da'wa* cadres to play a key role influencing, formulating, interpreting and implementing these organizations'/institutions' public

policies, to ensure they are consistent with Islamic *man-haj* (methods).

Chapter V ("Conclusion and Recommendations") summarizes the study's findings, and provides twelve strategic recommendations to the Indonesian public, to "prevent extremist groups from dominating Indonesia, and guarantee that moderate Muslims once again 'color' the life of our people, and government, in such a way as to protect the rights of minorities, and ensure that religion truly functions as a blessing for all sentient beings."

In his concluding essay, "Never Cease Learning," Kyai Haji A. Mustofa Bisri writes:

> If Muslims were all driven by a passion to learn, and to listen to others, their understanding of Islam would become progressively more wise and complete. As a consequence, they would not seek to reduce Islam to a mere ideology or rule of state. They would realize that Islam is too great to be boxed into a narrow ideology, or confined by the limits of state laws. For that reason, the vital insight contained in this book is the struggle (*jihad*) to constantly inspire every person to learn without ceasing; to oppose ignorance; to inspire all people to open their hearts and minds to humanity; and the struggle (*jihad*) to free every man, woman and child on earth from ideological and dogmatic strictures which have long prevented them from understanding the glorious teachings of religion, and instead confined their comprehension to those elements of the message that they can squeeze into a narrow box of their own or others' construction.

> To repeat: we may overcome our ignorance by seeing, listening and paying close attention; that is, by constantly learning. What halts this process dead in its tracks, and poses a threat to oneself and others, is when people feel that their knowledge is already perfect, and consider themselves to be in possession of the absolute Truth, and

thus no longer in need of learning, or seeking the truth. Perhaps all would agree that ignorance is highly dangerous. Yet not everyone is aware of the hidden dangers of ignorance, which dwell within.

WaLlâhu A'lam. God alone knows the truth of all things.

Appendix 1 ("Policy of the Muhammadiyah Central Board Concerning the Consolidation of Organizations and Charitable Enterprises within Muhammadiyah") reproduces the text of a Muhammadiyah Central Board Decree banning the Muslim Brotherhood-affiliated PKS from the Muhammadiyah, and warning its members to

> adopt a critical attitude which recognizes that every political party in this nation—including those that claim to represent '*da'wa*' or Islamic proselytism activities, such as Partai Keadilan Sejahtera (PKS)—are in fact mere political parties. Every political party is focused on the acquisition of political power. For that reason, in dealing with any political party, we must always remain committed to the true Path of the Muhammadiyah and must free ourselves from, and never engage ourselves with, the mission, interests, activities or goals of the above-mentioned political parties.

Appendix 2 ("Documents from the Nahdlatul Ulama Central Board Rejecting Transnational Extremist Movements and Their Ideology") reproduces the text of an NU *fatwa* regarding whether or not Muslims have a religious duty to establish a caliphate and/or formalize *shari'a*, or Islamic jurisprudence, as the basis of a nation's legal system. Readers may be especially interested in the theological argument presented by *ulama* (religious scholars) from the world's largest Muslim organization, in rejecting extremist demands to establish a caliphate—which has no basis either in the Qur'an, or the life of the Prophet Muhammad—and their citation of over a thousand years of Islamic jurisprudence in support of their position.

As mentioned previously: the remaining appendices in this book were assembled especially for the English language edition of *The Illusion of an Islamic State*, and did not appear in the original Indonesian edition. When read in conjunction with the rest of the book, Appendix 3 ("Project Description from LibForAll Foundation's 2006 Business Plan") demonstrates the remarkable extent to which this ambitious project was able to achieve its original objectives. Appendix 4 ("PKS Derailed by Wahhabi Issue") contains selected news coverage of the sequence of events that led to PKS being denied the Vice Presidential nomination by incumbent Indonesian president Susilo Bambang Yudhoyono in the 2009 national election. Instead, President Yudhoyono appointed a Javanese nationalist/technocrat, with a profoundly tolerant understanding of Islam, to this vital position. The election of Vice President Boediono—who received his doctorate from the Wharton School of Business at Pennsylvania University—was a profound disappointment to the PKS and its cadres, who continue to roil Indonesia's parliament in their efforts to undermine this widely-respected economist and former governor of the Bank of Indonesia.

Appendix 5 ("Selected Indonesian Media/Internet Coverage of *The Illusion of an Islamic State* as the Book Went Viral") provides a sampling of articles about the book that appeared between 16 May and 4 June 2009, and following terrorist attacks on the Marriott and Ritz-Carlton Hotels in Jakarta on 17 July 2009, as well as the book's continuing impact. Of particular note is the explosive coverage of *The Illusion of an Islamic State* on the internet, where a Google search for the three word string "Ilusi Negara Islam" turned up virtually no results prior to the book's publication, and soared dramatically—to over 556,000 results (i.e., individual webpages containing these three words, in sequence)—within three weeks of the book's hard launch in Jakarta.

Also noteworthy was the turbo-charged "second wind" the book received in the wake of the July 2009 terrorist bombings mentioned above. Citing President Wahid and *The Illusion of an Islamic State*, the former head of Indonesia's national intelligence agency (BIN), A.M. Hendropriyono, immediately declared, in print and on national television, that "Wahhabi ideology" lay behind the attacks carried out by al-Qaeda's Indonesian affiliate, Jemaah Islamiyah.

Following on the heels of the book's enormous success in May/June of 2009, this unleashed a second firestorm of controversy, to the extent that the two most widely-circulated extremist publications in Indonesia (*Sabili* and *Hidayatullah*) each devoted an entire issue to *The Illusion of an Islamic State* and the ensuing "Wahhabi controversy," as they sought to defend extremist ideology from widespread public revulsion. Indeed, the general reaction was so strong that by May of 2010, Pulitzer Prize-winning journalist Andrew Higgins was able to report, in the *Washington Post*, that *Sabili* itself had undergone a profound transformation: "*Sibili* [sic], meanwhile, has toned down its anti-Western rhetoric. 'We now see bigger potential for sales among moderate Muslims,' said Lufti Tamimi, the magazine's editor and part-owner. In January [2010], Tamimi ditched *Sibili's* hard-line editor and commissioned a series of articles denouncing Salafism, a purist strain of Islam that underpins extremist ideology."

Finally, Appendix 6 ("Excerpts from *Preventing Violent Radicalization and Terrorism: The Case of Indonesia*") provides further documentary evidence of the project's success, from a study conducted by the Center for Asymmetric Threat Studies at Sweden's National Defense College, at the behest of the Swedish international development agency, or SIDA. This report has found a home in government libraries from Brussels (the European Union) to the White House, and has been widely cited by news media and governments alike, including Indonesia's foreign minister, as evidence of the positive contribution Indonesian civil society can make, to overcoming the ideology that underlies and animates terrorism.

Yet for all these indications of success, it is critical to note that *The Illusion of an Islamic State* represents merely a single battle on a single front in what is actually a global conflict, whose outcome will profoundly influence the future not only of Muslim-majority nations, but the entire world.

Even in Indonesia itself, *The Illusion of an Islamic State* has by no means led to the defeat of Islamic extremism. Stunned by public revelations of its Wahhabi/Muslim Brotherhood origins, at the height of the 2009 election season, the PKS "fell victim and was gravely wounded" (*Sabili* magazine), yet managed to cling to its alliance with Yudhoyono's Democrat Party, and secure four key cabinet positions in his second term administration.

The spotlight which *The Illusion of an Islamic State* focused on the PKS and its systematic infiltration of the Muhammadiyah, did force the PKS to suspend its efforts to gain control of the mass organization, and provided the Muhammadiyah with sufficient breathing room to cleanse its leadership of many Islamist radicals associated with the PKS and Hizb ut-Tahrir. Extremists notably failed to achieve their goal of dominating the Muhammadiyah's 2010 Congress, and LibForAll associates within the Muhammadiyah report that the organization is now systematically vetting potential leaders to weed out those who adhere to extremist ideology.

Yet PKS efforts to penetrate the Nahdlatul Ulama, and its traditional redoubts in rural communities, is proceeding apace. While rebranding itself as an "open and inclusive" political party and adopting a new slogan transparently inspired by LibForAll Foundation, "*PKS untuk semua*" ("PKS for All"), the party continues to infiltrate Indonesian society, and prepare for the 2014 elections.

At the Nahdlatul Ulama's 2010 Congress, LibForAll senior advisor Kyai Haji A. Mustofa Bisri was appointed Deputy Chairman (and functional day-to-day head) of the NU's Supreme Council. In that position, he is seeking to "mobilize the NU to help stop extremist infiltration of government, the MUI and other strategic fields; help develop Indonesia into a more just and prosperous nation; and position the NU to assume the lead in efforts to free the world from the crisis of misunderstanding about Islam, and thus rescue humanity from the dangers of religious extremism" (Chapter V, Strategic Recommendation # 5). Yet he and his allies face an enormous uphill battle. As the largest single voting bloc in Indonesia, the NU must grapple with systematic infiltration not only by extremist movements, but also by opportunistic political parties and politicians that seek to prevent the NU from uniting to speak with a single voice, and thereby hold the government accountable for its policies.

To cite just one example: in February of 2011, I was visiting

Kyai Haji Mustofa Bisri in his home in Rembang, Central Java, when two gentlemen from an Islamic institution arrived to seek his advice, in conjunction with a project funded by a major government ministry in Jakarta.

The head of the ministry is affiliated with an Islamist political party that is involved in the extremists' prolonged and intense campaign to ban the Ahmadiyah sect, which mainstream Muslims often regard as heretical. Following the death of President Wahid—who tirelessly defended the Ahmadiyah for decades, along with Christians, Confucians, Bahais and other religious and ethnic minorities—extremist attempts to ban the Ahmadiyah appear to be on the verge of success in Indonesia.

Asked about their funding, the visitors explained, with embarrassment, that the ministry in question had provided 3.5 billion rupiah (close to US$400,000), of which 50% had to be disbursed, off the top, to local cadres affiliated with the Minister's political party. Sources within the Nahdlatul Ulama indicate that these cadres, in turn, are systematically using the funds generated by this and other Ministry grants to mobilize support within the NU, and obstruct its leadership from coalescing around the vision of pluralism, tolerance and moral responsibility espoused by Kyai Haji Mustofa Bisri and his allies.

The fact that this one grant, to a single institution, provided extremists with nearly half the funds LibForAll spent on the entire project described in this book, provides some idea of the enormous scale of funding that is available to political opportunists and their extremist allies. As President Wahid warned in his article "Right Islam vs. Wrong Islam," which the *Wall Street Journal* published in December of 2005: "Islamic fundamentalism has become a well-financed, multi-faceted global movement that operates like a juggernaut in much of the developing world, and even among immigrant Muslim communities in the West."

With an unfailing instinct for the critical role played by finance in any organized movement, extremists not only seek to maximize the resources available to themselves, but also to starve their opponents of funding. A well-coordinated media campaign conducted by extremists—which portrayed the Asia Foundation and

Ford Foundation as Zionist/CIA agents—was apparently enough to frighten both foundations, and the U.S. embassy/USAID in Jakarta, away from funding so-called "liberal" Muslims, as reported by Andrew Higgins in another front-page story in the *Washington Post*, "As Indonesia Debates Islam's Role, U.S. Stays Out" (28 October 2009).

Just before *The Illusion of an Islamic State's* hard launch in May of 2009, Indonesia's largest print media conglomerate, which owns the nation's largest newspaper and a chain of approximately 300 bookstores, purchased every copy of the book's first print run, other than a few hundred required for distribution at the launch itself. The group's head of retail asked for an immediate reprint, and estimated that their bookstores would sell over 100,000 copies in the weeks ahead. Less than 24 hours later, this same man called me personally to apologize, and asked to return the books from his company's warehouse, where they had been delivered. His frank explanation: his office had already received credible threats that bookstores would be burned down, if they stocked *The Illusion of an Islamic State*.

Prior to these developments, LibForAll had prepared an electronic version of the book, and set up a website (www.bhinnekatunggalika.org) where it could be downloaded for free. In the weeks following the book's hard launch, nearly 45,000 copies were indeed downloaded from this site, with hundreds of thousands of additional copies of *The Illusion of an Islamic State* apparently downloaded from other websites that posted the pdf file online, including 12 sites advertising such downloads (e.g., "Download Gratis Buku Ilusi Negara Islam") whose rank, on Google, consistently exceeded our own.

Ironically, when some of the largest media outlets in Indonesia reported that the book's unavailability in stores was due to the threat of terrorism, extremist publications responded that this was merely a clever pretext, to "slander Islam" and justify LibForAll giving away hundreds of thousands of copies for free on the internet.

Another issue arose when three members of the "Yogya Team" that conducted field research for this project (out of 27), and one of their six supervisors, held a press conference at the height of the controversy surrounding the book. At this press conference, they protested the inclusion of their names in the book (in a table that specifically identified, by name, those who conducted the field research in each of 24 districts in Indonesia). The gentlemen also stated that the book included material beyond the scope of their own research/findings, and objected to not having been consulted prior to its publication.

There was some element of truth to these complaints. Inclusion of the field researchers' names in the first Indonesian edition of the book apparently exposed at least one of the protestors to death threats from members of the extremist group he had interviewed. And as explained in Chapter I, the research contained in this book was conducted by two separate teams, managed by a "Jakarta Team" operating under the direct supervision and authority of President Wahid. This Jakarta Team (whose key members are identified in the English edition of this book as "Principal Authors/Editorial Team") exercised provisional control over the book's contents, subject to President Wahid's review and approval as chief editor.

The Yogya Team's field research, including its interviews with 591 Muslim extremists, was only one of three research components contained within the book. And while the Jakarta Team extensively reviewed and revised the final product in consultation with the chairman of the Yogya Team (Dr. Abdul Munir Mulkhan) and other prominent Muhammadiyah and Nahdlatul Ulama figures, individual researchers and supervisors from the Yogya Team were not involved in reviewing the final product, other than one supervisor (Dr. Ratno Lukito) who belonged to both the Jakarta and Yogya Teams, and played a key role in integrating their respective findings.

As it turned out, this protest by four ideological allies cast the only real (though minor) shadow on the book, whose heavily-documented findings could not be refuted by the extremists themselves, however much they tried to obfuscate the matter. *The Illusion of an Islamic State* nailed its case shut by reprinting an official decree of the Muhammadiyah Central Board—banning the PKS from its organization—as Appendix 1; and also reprinting fifty-five pages of official NU documents that warned, in no uncertain terms, about the threat posed by transnational Islamist movements and their ideology to Indonesia, and Islam ("Appendix 2").

Rather than refute the book's theological arguments and/or its academic findings, the extremists—unaccustomed to being on the defensive—were reduced to expedients such as denying their ties to Wahhabism (*cf.* Appendix 4, "PKS Derailed by Wahhabi Issue") or hurling baseless and humorous accusations such as, "My guess is that funding for the book's research came from Bush. It represents Bush's final project, before his fall from power" (PKS Vice Secretary Fahri Hamzah, quoted by *inilah.com*, in the wake of the book's "soft launch" on 2 April 2009).

In fact, the money for this project (except for the book's printing and subsequent hard launch) was provided by a single high net worth donor from the U.S., who has no affiliation with any government or government agency. The printing and launch itself was financed by a grant from the Security Policy Department of Sweden's Ministry for Foreign Affairs, as part of a project entitled "The Smiling Face of Islam," whose goal was to facilitate "the spread of pluralistic and tolerant ideas between Indonesia and other parts of the Islamic world."

To cite one more example of the extremists' response (many more of which may be read in Appendix 5): shortly after the July 2009 terrorist bombings in Jakarta—and the ensuing "anti-Wahhabi" firestorm that swept through Indonesia's mainstream media, and much of the general public—*Sabili* magazine sought to deflect criticism of Wahhabi ideology. It did so by claiming that "foreign intelligence agencies" and other "enemies of Islam" are "deliberating maintaining terrorist groups," so that "whenever the plans of those who wish to destroy Muslims and Indonesia are ripe, they simply click their fingers and launch a deadly terrorist strike," in conjunction with the "ideological warfare" represented by "the book *The Illusion of an Islamic State*, which attacks political Islam... [and] is more powerful, and dangerous, than bombs." (*Sabili*, 12 August 2009).

Far more serious than the reactive and generally delusional response of extremists, was President Wahid's own ill health during and after the book's launch. On the day of the launch itself, the major figures associated with *The Illusion of an Islamic State* gathered in Jakarta to establish a movement (Gerakan Bhinneka Tunggal Ika, or the Oneness Amid Diversity Movement) to systematically implement the book's strategic recommendations, contained in Chapter 5 ("Summary and Recommendations").

When the meeting ended and everyone else had left the boardroom to rest prior to the launch that evening, I remained behind with President Wahid, and sat alone with him for about 45 minutes, in complete silence. Finally, he said, "You know, Holland, my entire body is wracked with pain." When I expressed sympathy for his condition, he replied, "Every time I undertake something really important, I feel pain throughout my body." We were silent again for a few moments, and he added, "I know from the tremendous pain I feel right now, that what we're doing today will be enormously successful." Then President Wahid called his assistant Sulaiman, who was waiting outside with several of his bodyguards, to take him upstairs in his wheelchair, to rest prior to the launch.

Perhaps the single greatest disappointment, amid the project's otherwise remarkable success, was LibForAll's (i.e., *my*) failure to immediately organize and set in motion the widespread civil society movement we discussed that day in Jakarta. Having exhausted LibForAll's financial resources in bringing the book to market, I returned to the U.S. immediately after the launch, to engage in fundraising. And while we did secure the resources necessary to keep LibForAll afloat, and drive forward another, potentially far more significant program (LibForAll's International Institute of Qur'anic Studies), we were unable to simultaneously exploit the unique opportunity at hand. Severe time, personnel and monetary constraints prevented us from following up on the success of *The Illusion of an Islamic State*, to organize the millions of Indonesians who spontaneously voiced agreement with its denunciation of religious extremism, into a systematic movement for social and political change (i.e., the Bhinneka Tunggal Ika Movement).

As the Greek historian Polybius wrote in the 2nd century BCE, "Those who have won victories are far more numerous than those who have used them to their advantage." The British military historian B.H. Lidell Hart made a similar point, when he observed about the Roman general and consul, Scipio Africanus (who defeated Hannibal and ended the Carthaginian threat to Rome): "Masterly as were his battle tactics, still more remarkable perhaps were the decisiveness and rapidity of their exploitation, which find no parallel in military history until Napoleon came to develop the pursuit as the vital complement of battle and one of the supreme tests of generalship."

Failure to exploit strategic advantage, to systematically isolate and discredit Islamist extremists and sever their relationship with opportunistic political allies, allows the extremists precious time to recuperate and regain their momentum, as can be clearly seen in Indonesia today. To use a military analogy: among the many valuable lessons that can be derived from this "path-breaking" project—for anyone who seeks to discredit Islamist ideology—is the necessity of having sufficient "troops" in reserve (i.e., trained personnel and resources) to ensure the determined pursuit of a defeated and demoralized opponent, in order to secure lasting victory.

A single battle rarely determines the outcome of any widespread conflict, and history is replete with generals who "won a major battle, but lost the war."

This, in turn, sheds light on the enormous confusion that has prevailed in the West ever since 9/11, regarding how best to confront (or *not* confront) Islamist extremism. As President Wahid warned in his 2005 article "Right Islam vs. Wrong Islam":

All too many Muslims fail to grasp Islam, which teaches one to be lenient towards others and to understand their value systems, knowing that these are tolerated by Islam as a religion. The essence of Islam is encapsulated in the words of the Quran, "For you, your religion; for me, my religion." That is the essence of tolerance. Religious fanatics—either purposely or out of ignorance—pervert Islam into a dogma of intolerance, hatred and bloodshed. They justify their brutality with slogans such as "Islam is above everything else." They seek to intimidate and subdue anyone who does not share their extremist views, regardless of nationality or religion. While a few are quick to shed blood themselves, countless millions of others sympathize with their violent actions, or join in the complicity of silence.

This crisis of misunderstanding—of Islam by Muslims themselves—is compounded by the failure of governments, people of other faiths, and the majority of well-intentioned Muslims to resist, isolate and discredit this dangerous ideology. The crisis thus afflicts Muslims and non-Muslims alike, with tragic consequences. Failure to understand the true nature of Islam permits the continued radicalization of Muslims world-wide, while blinding the rest of humanity to a solution which hides in plain sight.

The most effective way to overcome Islamist extremism is to explain what Islam truly is to Muslims and non-Muslims alike. Without that explanation, people will tend to accept the unrefuted extremist view—further radicalizing Muslims, and turning the rest of the world against Islam itself.

Accomplishing this task will be neither quick nor easy. In recent decades, Wahhabi/Salafi ideology has made substantial inroads throughout the Muslim world. Islamic fundamentalism has become a well-financed, multifaceted global movement that operates like a juggernaut in much of the developing world, and even among immigrant Muslim communities in the West. To neutralize the virulent ideology that underlies fundamentalist terrorism and threatens the very foundations of modern civilization, we must identify its advocates, understand their goals and strategies, evaluate their strengths and weaknesses, and effectively counter their every move. What we are talking about is nothing less than a global struggle for the soul of Islam....

Only by recognizing the problem, putting an end to the bickering within and between nation-states, and adopting a coherent long-term plan (executed with international leadership and commitment) can we begin to apply the brakes to the rampant spread of extremist ideas and hope to resolve the world's crisis of misunderstanding before the global economy and modern civilization itself begin to crumble in the face of truly devastating attacks.

Muslims themselves can and must propagate an understanding of the "right" Islam, and thereby discredit extremist ideology. Yet to accomplish this task requires the understanding and support of like-minded individuals, organizations and governments throughout the world. Our goal must be to illuminate the hearts and minds of humanity, and offer a compelling alternate vision of Islam, one that banishes the fanatical ideology of hatred to the darkness from which it emerged.

Having lived three years in Iran as a child (from 1965 – '68); traveled extensively in Afghanistan and Pakistan prior to the Soviet invasion; and spent much of the past 12 years in Java, I have enjoyed the good fortune of having been surrounded, for much of my life, by the "right" Islam President Wahid described so well in his many writings, and through the example of his life.

One day, while reviewing the manuscript of this book shortly before its publication, President Wahid said, "You know, Holland, I often tell Muslims: 'It's impossible to understand Islam, if you don't understand other religions.'" We both knew that he was not referring to dogma, but rather, the spiritual essence of religion, which is to reunite with the Source—the Alpha and Omega of all existence.

Or as a Christian friend said to me, after meeting President Wahid when he visited the U.S. in May of 2008, to accept the Simon Wiesenthal Center's Medal of Valor for his role in the Bali Holocaust conference, at which he had publicly branded Mahmud Ahmadinejad a liar: "Holland, I keep asking myself: how do these

Muslim leaders you introduce me to, know what I know?"

"What do you mean?" I asked, hoping that she would be more explicit, although I understood her question full well.

"It's obvious that President Wahid is filled with the Holy Spirit."

"How do you explain that?" I asked.

"Well," my Pentecostal friend replied, "I wouldn't be comfortable saying this to anyone at church... but the only explanation that makes sense to me, is that Jesus is far, far greater than I ever realized."

I mention these conversations for a specific reason. More than seven years after President Wahid and I established LibForAll, it has become painfully obvious that one of the primary challenges faced by the West, in dealing with Islamist extremism, is a profound lack of understanding about Islam and the actual dynamics of the Muslim world. By and large, Westerners and Muslims live in "parallel universes," which few can navigate at ease. Those who can readily traverse this enormous gap are often Wahhabi/Muslim Brotherhood agents, who seek to achieve an end state completely inimical not only to the West, but also the spiritual traditions of Islam itself.

Westerners who study the ideology of al-Qaeda and the Muslim Brotherhood have developed an increasingly acute, and accurate, awareness of its key elements. Yet for a variety of reasons, this very insight often leads Westerners (whether Christian, Jewish or atheist) to conflate said ideology with Islam itself, as if the religion were monolithic (with only one "true" expression), and to overlook those elements within Islam and the Muslim world which—if effectively mobilized—are capable of dismantling extremist movements and their underlying ideology.

In August of 2009, I visited President Wahid at his home in Cijangur, a suburb of Jakarta, to wish him a happy birthday. As I entered the spacious grounds of his home, which is flanked by a mosque and *pesantren* (*madrasa*), I heard the beautiful yet mournful sound of his students reciting Surah Yasin from the Qur'an, which Muslims often read in supplication to God, including on behalf of one who is near death. In doing so, they ask God to restore the person to health, or accept his or her soul in paradise. At that moment, in hundreds if not thousands of mosques and *pesantren* throughout Indonesia, Muslims were gathered to recite the Surah Yasin for President Wahid, aware of his grave illness.

I entered his home to find the furniture in the reception room cleared away, and my friend lying on the floor, covered by a loose sarong and surrounded by visitors and family. His adjutants asked me to come close, and President Wahid whispered in my ear, in a barely audible voice, "You know, Holland. It's very important if you can describe how America can help Islam." Even on the threshold of death, his heart and mind were filled with compassion for humanity.

I thought deeply about his statement for the next two weeks, and when President Wahid experienced a remarkable recovery— which lasted for some time prior to his death on 30 December 2009—we discussed a new project at length, based on the idea he whispered to me that day. We decided to write a new book called *How the West Can Help Islam*, and outlined its key elements together. Given that many Westerners, to the extent they even think about Islam, are primarily concerned with defending themselves from it, President Wahid's concept was both counter-intuitive and profoundly insightful.

Never, for an instant, did President Wahid "buy" the notion— widely propagated by Islamists, and many in the West—that European or American support for Muslim moderates, in their struggle with Islamist extremism, will somehow discredit the former. He considered LibForAll's track record of success—including with *The Illusion of an Islamic State*—to be proof positive thereof. When asked whether the name LibForAll should appear on the cover of the original Indonesian edition of this book, he replied, "No. But I'll describe what LibForAll is in the opening paragraph of my introduction, so that when people see the name, they'll also realize who's involved with the organization, and what our purpose is."

Confident of his own "Islamicity," and revered as a saint by tens of millions, from the East Indies archipelago to the Middle East, President Wahid knew that moderate/spiritual Muslims alone (and, by the same token, Westerners acting alone) can no more derail the Islamist juggernaut than the Russians, Chinese or even Americans could have defeated the combined forces of Nazism and Japanese militarism in World War II, acting alone and without allies. Thus, although this book describes in great detail how to "fight fire with water"—i.e., how to marginalize and discredit Islamist ideology by drawing on universal spiritual principles deeply rooted within Islam itself—it does not ignore the practical dimensions of this challenge.

Nor should readers fall into the trap of assuming that Muslims who embrace the spiritual principles articulated in this book are pacifists or religious quietists, unable to address the threat of violence, or engage effectively with the world at large. While nonviolent extremists (who seek to use the repressive apparatus of the state to impose their views on others) felt the intense heat of public opprobrium generated by this book, their ideological brethren from Jemaah Islamiyah and other terrorist groups were being hunted night and day, with dozens captured or killed by Indonesia's elite counter-terrorist task force, Detachment 88. In the fall of 2009, former Muhammadiyah chairman and LibForAll advisor Dr. Syafii Maarif—who was also advising Indonesia's security officials, in the wake of the July attacks—informed me that the top leadership of Indonesia's police and military hierarchy viewed *The Illusion of an Islamic State* as an invaluable tool for understanding, and countering, terrorists and the ideology they share with a far broader spectrum of society, on which they rely for recruitment and support.

Upon hearing of the book's dramatic impact in Indonesia, a former chairman of Pakistan's armed forces—who is part of LibForAll's counter-extremist *rahmatan lil-'âlamîn* network—dispatched a similar message to us: "This is a great achievement, and I wish you all success as you move on in this direction."

Since the attacks of 9/11, America and the West have played into al-Qaeda's hands, by focusing the overwhelming preponderance of their energy on "fighting fire with fire," while merely talking about, pretending to address or actively ignoring the hate-filled supremacist ideology that underlies and animates Islamist terrorism. All too often, Western governments and civil society institutions have been infiltrated by, or aligned themselves with, the Wahhabi/Muslim Brotherhood lobby, which seeks to prevent the West from establishing an alliance with truly moderate and progressive Muslim leaders, who espouse a loving, merciful and compassionate vision of Islam.

Soon after Indonesia's presidential election in July of 2009, a key figure from the *istana*, or presidential palace, asked to meet with me to discuss *The Illusion of an Islamic State*. Over dinner she remarked, "*Para pejabat menganggap LibForAll sebagai sebuah yayasan yang luar biasa kuat dan sakti.*" ("Many government officials regard LibForAll as a remarkably powerful foundation, possessed of sacred, and supernatural, abilities"—like those of a magical *keris*, or dagger, that can fly through the night and strike its opponents to the quick.)

To use language more familiar to those living in the West, what she was saying was simple yet profound: LibForAll's success is directly attributable to the selfless Muslim leaders who form the backbone of its global network, and their heart-felt desire to work in a spirit of mutual cooperation and respect with others—whether Christian, Hindu, Buddhist, Jewish, Muslim or atheist—who share a common love for humanity, and a desire to see Islamic teachings reconciled with the modern world of freedom, democracy and human rights. Current upheavals in the Middle East—and the escalating controversy about Islam and Islamophobia roiling North America and Europe—demonstrate the urgent need for such a process to occur.

Those who are uncomfortable with talk about God, or with any conception of God that differs from their own, may find *The Illusion of an Islamic State* a challenge to their settled notions of reality. Yet those who seriously read and reflect upon the message of this book may find themselves rewarded with the unique ability to cross over the vast gulf that separates Islam and the West, and make common cause with what President Wahid liked to call the vast, silent majority of Muslims, so that together we may strive "to illuminate the hearts and minds of humanity... and banish the fanatical ideology of hatred to the darkness from which it emerged."

Jakarta, 16 March 2011

Prologue

THE FUTURE OF ISLAM IN INDONESIA
By Ahmad Syafii Maarif

From a purely numerical perspective, there is no need to fear about the future of Islam in Indonesia. The 2000 census recorded that 88.22% of Indonesia's inhabitants are Muslim, which is very high. Others need not worry about this statistic, either, because the two great pillars of the Muslim community, the Nahdlatul Ulama and Muhammadiyah, have from the outset worked hard to develop an Islam that is warm and friendly towards all, even towards those with no religious faith, as long as everyone respects each others' differences of opinion. However, disaster may occur when a religion's adherents lose the ability to reason, and begin to condemn everyone who does not agree with their monolithic line of thought. It's not difficult to find examples of such behavior, stemming from a monopolization of truth, in various civilizations throughout history. Rivers of blood have flowed as a result of one group condemning another, because of religious or ideological differences.

Nor is it difficult to trace, within the history of Islam, groups that have proclaimed themselves to be the most pure and genuine in their faith. To the extent that individuals or groups feel this way without condemning others, it may not be too dangerous. Yet danger will certainly arise the moment those who claim to speak in the name of God condemn, and then seek to eliminate, beliefs different from their own. Insofar as I have read and understood the Qur'an, it is far more tolerant, for the most part, than that distinct minority of Muslims who refuse to accept or tolerate differences.

The phenomenon of religious intolerance may be encountered in many nations—those that are economically developed and those that are not—and not simply in the Muslim world. Fundamentalist movements, of whatever religion, often fall into this camp. For example, in America during the era of President George W. Bush, fundamentalist Christian groups became the primary supporters of his neo-imperialist regime. In recent decades, fundamentalist tendencies have been highly visible in many parts of the Muslim world. The most radical of these groups easily fall into the trap of terrorism.

Various theories have been advanced to explain the rise of fundamentalism in the Islamic world. The one most often cited is the Muslim community's failure to successfully confront the tide of modernity, which many claim is "boxing Islam into a corner." Because they are unable to deal with the swift tide of modernity, fundamentalist groups seek a religious pretext to comfort themselves with the dream of [recapturing] a world they imagine to have been pure and uncontaminated [i.e., that of early Islam].

To the extent this is limited to providing them with comfort or solace, it may not give rise to many problems. But when fundamentalists seek to employ the repressive apparatus of government to oppose modernity in various ways, it's impossible to avoid conflict with other Muslim groups that do not agree with their methods or beliefs. This does not mean that Muslims who don't agree with the fundamentalists' approach are all fully at ease with modernity. Many who oppose fundamentalist groups are no less critical of modern trends, but the methods they use in confronting the problems posed by modernity are guided by the power of reason and calm deliberation, although of course they do not always succeed in their efforts.

Another theory holds that the rapid growth of fundamentalist groups in many Muslim countries is driven primarily by a feeling of loyalty towards their suffering brothers in Palestine, Kashmir, Afghanistan and Iraq. In fact, this feeling of solidarity is shared by Muslims throughout the world. But what differentiates fundamentalists from others is that the majority of Muslims studiously avoid violence as much as possible and continue to display the banner of peace, even when the suffering of those in conflict regions is more than one can bear. When linked to conditions in Indonesia, which are relatively peaceful and secure, the emergence of fundamentalist forces that run the gamut from mild to the most extreme (terrorism), appears completely irrational. Take, for example, the murderous practice of suicide bombing (as in the case of the Bali, Marriott and other attacks), which is absolutely incomprehensible. Indonesia is not Palestine, Kashmir, Afghanistan or Iraq. So why is this barbaric practice occurring here?

A third theory, especially for Indonesia, holds that fundamentalism stems from our nation's failure to realize the goals of independence in the form of social justice and prosperity for all people. The corruption that is so deeply ingrained in our society is proof of this failure. Everyone acknowledges this bitter reality. But because fundamentalist groups have an extremely weak grasp of Indonesia's sociological makeup, which is truly complex, they seek short-cuts on the path to achieving justice: namely, to implement Islamic law through the exercise of political power. If this is not yet possible to do on a national level, then they attempt to institute *shari'a* through regional regulations. Fundamentalists imagine that through this implementation of *shari'a*, God will bless Indonesia. The strange thing is, most fundamentalist groups are anti-democratic, and yet they manipulate democratic state institutions in order to achieve their political goals. This fact alone demonstrates one ugly reality: for Islamic fundamentalists, a conflict between theory and practice does not pose any moral dilemma. In other words, they are dishonest in the practice of politics. In theory, democracy is *haram*, or forbidden; yet in practice, it is useful and exploited as a means to achieve extremist goals.

Finally, I must acknowledge that I share the fundamentalists' concern regarding the condition of Indonesia, which is far from just. Yet the methods they employ cannot possibly bring this nation closer to the noble goals of independence. Rather, they will strangle these aspirations on the very path to realization. The problems of Indonesia, which has the largest Muslim population on earth, cannot be solved by simplistic minds that choose to adopt shortcuts, often in the form of compulsion or violence. I am fully aware that

Indonesia's current form of democracy is not yet healthy, and if not soon improved, may quickly give rise to disaster. But for the long term there is no other way to achieve the goals of independence, except through a democratic system that is strong and healthy, and a moderate and inclusive Islam which will lead Indonesia into the future.

Yogyakarta, 18 February 2009

THE ENEMY WITHIN
By Kyai Haji Abdurrahman Wahid

The book you are reading is the result of over two years' research conducted by LibForAll Foundation, a non-governmental organization inspired by Indonesia's rich traditions and culture, and whose mission is to encourage the growth of peaceful, free and tolerant societies throughout the world. I established LibForAll Foundation in 2003 with American businessman and author C. Holland Taylor, and serve as a member of its board of directors and as an advisor, along with Kyai Haji A. Mustofa Bisri, Prof. Dr. Ahmad Syafii Maarif, Prof. Dr. M. Amin Abdullah, Prof. Dr. Azyumardi Azra, Prof. Dr. Nasr Hamid Abu-Zayd, Shaykh Musa Admani, Prof. Dr. Abdul Munir Mulkhan, Dr. Sukardi Rinakit, and Father Franz Magnis-Suseno, S.J. In addition, the Grand Shaykh of al-Azhar University in Cairo—Sayyid Muhammad Tantawi—expressed his desire to advise LibForAll Foundation in its efforts to present Islam as a blessing for all creation (*rahmatan lil-'âlamîn*), during the visit of LibForAll CEO C. Holland Taylor to Egypt in May of 2008. And in reality, those whose hearts are filled with sincerity and goodwill, and who strongly embrace efforts to achieve peace, freedom and tolerance, are, in a cultural sense, members of LibForAll Foundation's global family.

To accomplish its mission, LibForAll Foundation employs a spiritual approach, to raise individual and social consciousness and thereby transform individuals and society for the better. This approach is predicated upon the fact that the innate struggle between the spiritual (higher) and animalistic (base) natures of humanity exerts a major impact upon the external world. The tension between spiritual and carnal impulses frequently ignites conflict, within both individuals and society at large. In this context, it is vital that we contemplate what the noble Prophet Muhammad, may God bless him and grant him peace, told his companions following their triumph in the battle of Badr: "*Raja'nâ min jihâd al-ashghar ilâ jihâd al-akbar*" ("We have returned from the lesser *jihad* to the greater").[1] Hearing his words, the companions were surprised. They asked, "What kind of war (*qitâl*) could possibly be greater than the one we just fought, against overwhelming odds?" When the Messenger of God, may God bless him and grant him peace, replied, "the war

---

1. This hadith (saying of the Prophet Muhammad) is extremely popular among traditional *ulama* (religious scholars) and Sufis, although various parties regard it as weak (*dlâ'if*), and members of the Wahhabi sect reject it altogether. In terms of its line of transmission (*riwâyah*), this hadith is indeed regarded as weak. But in terms of its meaning and content (*dirâyah*), it is consistent with Islam's highest teachings regarding *jihad*. This is clear from other hadith which differ slightly in terms of redaction, but are consistent with the above-quoted hadith's message in terms of meaning (*ma'nâwi*), such as those conveyed by Ahmad ibn Hanbal in hadith numbers 24678, 24692 and 24465, "*Al-Mujâhid man jâhada nafsahu li-Llâh atau fi Allâh 'azz wa jall*" ("A mujahid (holy warrior) is one who wages jihad against himself for the sake of Allah," or, in a different version, "in (the path which leads to) God the Most Noble and Great") [read in: Abu 'Abdillah Ahmad ibn Muhammad ibn Hanbal, *Masnad Ahmad*, (Cairo: Mauqi' Wizârat al-Auqâf al-Mishriyyah, undated)]. One may also consult a hadith found in *Fath al-Qadîr* by al-Syaukânî, "*Al-Mujâhid man jâhada nafsah fi thâ'at Allâh*" (A mujahid is one who wages jihad against himself, in order to be obedient to God), conveyed by Ibn Jarîr and confirmed by al-Hakim as being valid; conveyed also by Ibn Mardawaih from 'Aisyah [al-Syaukânî, *Fath al-Qadîr* (Cairo: Mauqi' al-Tafâsir, undated), Vol. 5, p. 142]. An important point to stress in this context is that jihad greatly emphasizes efforts to control and subdue one's own carnal nature, in the form of ego and its attendant lusts. Al-Razy, for example, even states that jihad in the context of war (*qitâl*) must first and foremost be preceded by victory over oneself, so as not to engage in the actions of a hypocrite, or one who seeks praise, glory, profit or other benefits for himself. All must be conducted in a completely self-less manner, after having tamed oneself, so that one's actions are not dictated by egotism or personal desire (read in: Fakhruddin al-Râzî, *Mafâtih al-Ghaib* (Cairo: Mauqi' al-Tafâsir, undated), vol. 7, p. 474). In summary, the hadith *Raja'na min jihâd al-ashghar ilâ jihâd al-akbar* ("We have returned from the lesser to the greater jihad") is accepted by traditional *ulama* and Sufis because, in terms of meaning and content, it is consistent with other hadith which are fully valid in terms of their transmission.

against one's own carnal nature," his companions fell silent, recognizing how difficult it is to overcome this enemy within. Besides being difficult to identify, the struggle against internal enemies requires tenacity and emotional steadfastness, since base and carnal impulses constitute an inseparable part of every human being.

Base instincts are a powerful force which always harbor a destructive potential, rendering individuals discontented and incapable of experiencing peace. Islamic scholars often compare this lust (for power, wealth, sexual satisfaction, etc.) to a wild beast. Whoever succeeds in taming his carnal nature achieves inner peace, and can employ his vital energies to achieve far-reaching, lofty and noble goals. On the other hand, whoever is still dominated by egotism and lust is in a state of constant, restless anxiety/desire, and is a danger to himself and others.

From this perspective, there are two categories of human beings: *First*, those who have tamed their carnal nature, and act in a manner beneficial to others and to society at large. These calm and peaceful souls (*al-nafs al-muthmainnah*) are the embodiment of spirituality: the true vice-regents of God on earth (i.e., caliphs). Within the context of the ancient *Mahabarata* epic, these are the Pandavas. *Second*, those who are dominated by egotism and various forms of lust, and are thus a source of constant dissension, creating problems for others and society at large. These discontented souls (*al-nafs al-lawwâmah*) give rise to countless social upheavals and strife, and represent the embodiment of selfish lust. They are the true polytheists.[2] Within the context of the *Mahabarata*, they

---

2. "Experts on Qur'anic exegesis say that a polytheist is one who performs ritual worship, or gives charity, for reasons other than devotion to God. Thus the verse, '*Wa lam yusyrik bi 'ibâdati Rabbihi ahada*' ('and does not associate anything whatsoever in worship of his God'). For example, if one says that he is fighting for Islam, but in reality, his motivation is selfish and egotistical, then he has already associated (himself) with God." "Don't be trapped by worldly temptations, or the sparkle of material existence; for example, the flattery of women. Don't be tempted by status or power and become arrogant, forgetting yourself.... Don't allow yourself to be entrapped by snares that give the appearance of devotion to God, humanity or jihad ("strenuous effort on the Divine path"), when in reality they're not. These are snares that truly mire us (in forgetfulness of God) and doom us (to separation from God). For example, arrogance may emerge after one has already become a (religious) leader, giving countless sermons to

are the Kuravas.[3] These two types of people are present, in varying degrees, in our every day lives and at every social and economic level of society—local, national, and international; and in the realms of education, religion, business and politics.

In reality, this conflict between tranquil and discontented souls informs and colors the history of every corner of the earth, including the struggle between the Prophet Muhammad, may God bless him and grant him peace, and the infidels/polytheists in the Hijaz. Yet one thing unique about Nusantara (the East Indies) is that every time this epic struggle has repeated itself, since the days of our ancient ancestors, the spiritual teachings and sublime values of tranquil souls have emerged triumphant in our beloved archipelago. For example, Mpu Tantular's principle of *Bhinneka Tunggal Ika* ("Oneness Amid Diversity")[4] has inspired the rulers of these

---

wide applause, and with people everywhere respecting you. The snares of ego and self-importance mire us (in forgetfulness of God), and those who fall prey to this are called, in Arabic, hidden polytheists." "The antidote to polytheism is self-transcendence. A polytheist is one who is not self-transcendent; who is motivated by ego and self-interest, or the interests of his group, rather than engaging in actions moment by moment (guided by and) purely for the sake of the Divine." (In sequence, statements by Prof. Dr. Jalaluddin Rakhmat, Prof. Dr. Kyai Haji Said Aqil Siraj, and Kyai Haji Masdar F. Mas'udi in: *Ocean of Revelations: Understanding Islam as a Blessing for All Creation*, Episode 4: "People of Faith," Program Supervisor: Kyai Haji Mustofa Bisri, ©LibForAll Foundation 2009).

3. [Translator's note: As in India, the *Mahabarata* and *Ramayana* represent two of the great national epics of Java, and are deeply embedded in Javanese and Indonesian awareness. The *Mahabarata* tells of the struggle between two sets of cousins, the Pandavas and Kuravas, who represent the forces of *dharma* (virtue or right action, which arises from spiritual awareness) and *adharma* (lack of virtue or sinful action, which arises from egotism and lust).]

4. [Translator's note: Indonesia's state motto, *Bhinneka Tunggal Ika*, literally means, "(Although) different, yet simultaneously One." Emerging from Java's Hindu-Buddhist past, the phrase references not only social and political unity amid diversity, but also a spiritual apprehension regarding the Unicity of Being, or the emergence of all creation from a Divine Source from which it is inseparable, and to which it shall inevitably return (as individual waves arise from, and return to, the ocean). This principle is also a key tenet of Sufism, or Islamic mysticism. The Old Javanese verse by Mpu Tantular in which this phrase appears, reads as follows: "The diverse forms of the universe are expressions of the One Buddha/Shiva; They are indeed different (bhinneki), yet it is impossible to

islands from Hindu-Buddhist times until the present; and the
Muslim saint and mystic Sunan Kalijogo—who is famed for having
accommodated local traditions—taught indigenous rulers a peaceful, tolerant and spiritual understanding of Islam. Through his
disciples, including Sultan Adiwijoyo, Juru Martani and Senopati
ing Alogo, Sunan Kalijogo succeeded in rescuing and preserving
these sublime values which, thanks to his efforts, we can still enjoy
today.[5]

In the history of modern Indonesia, we also witness the presence of tranquil souls (al-nafs al-muthmainnah) during the birth and
evolution of our national awareness—especially in the dialogue between Islam and Indonesian nationalism. In fact, not many people
know about one of the key factors in the conceptual development
of Indonesian nationalism.[6] In 1919, three cousins began intensive
weekly discussions concerning the relationship between Islam, as
a set of religious teachings, and nationalism. They were H. O. S.
Tjokroaminoto, Kyai Haji Hasjim Asy'ari[7] and Kyai Haji Wahab
Chasbullah. In addition, the future son-in-law of Tjokroaminoto,
Sukarno—who at the time was just 18 years old—was soon actively

perceive them as *fundamentally* different, when one apprehends the underlying
Unity of existence; for the Truth of Buddha and the Truth of Shiva is One (tunggal); (the diverse forms of the universe) are indeed different, yet simultaneously
One (bhinneka tunggal ika)."]
5. [Translator's note: Kyai Haji Abdurrahman Wahid was directly descended
from both the last Hindu-Buddhist kings of Java, and from Sunan Kalijogo and
Sultan Adiwijoyo. The story of their successful efforts to preserve a pluralistic,
tolerant and spiritual understanding of religion in the face of radical Muslim
attempts to annihilate indigenous Javanese culture (in the 16th century) is told in
the national epic, *Babad Tanah Jawi*, or *History of the Land of Java*.]
6. The seed of awareness of Indonesian nationalism is generally traced to 20 May
1908 with the establishment of Boedi Oetomo, the first indigenous political
society in the Dutch East Indies.
7. [Translator's note: Kyai Haji Hasjim Asy'ari (the grandfather of K.H. Abdurrahman Wahid) founded the Nahdlatul Ulama in 1926, in order to stimulate a
spiritual awakening among ulama, and defend traditional Sunni Muslim teachings in the face of contemporary developments, including the Wahhabi conquest of Mecca and Medina and the spread of extremist ideology, which rejects
Sufism (Islamic spirituality) and the accommodation of local cultural practices.
The Nahdlatul Ulama, or NU, has since grown to become the largest Muslim
organization in the world.]

involved in the weekly meetings, which occurred for many years. This national awareness was inherited by the following generation, including such figures as Abdul Wahid Hasjim (the son of Kyai Haji Hasjim Asy'ari), Kyai Haji Kahar Muzakkir from Yogyakarta (a leading Muhammadiyah figure), and Haji Ahmad Djoyo Sugito.

During a Nahdlatul Ulama (NU) congress held in Banjarmasin, Borneo in 1935, the NU decided not to support the formation of an Islamic state. Rather, it urged Muslims to practice Islamic teachings, so as to establish a truly islamic (i.e., virtuous and enlightened) populace within the framework of a pluralistic nation state. Ten years later, East Indies Muslim leaders who were involved in the Independence struggle accepted the concept of a Pancasila state presented by Sukarno, as did most heads of Islamic organizations at the time.[8] Based upon a concept of nationality enriched by the religious and cultural values of our people, on 17 August 1945 Sukarno and Muhammad Hatta proclaimed Indonesia's independence in the name of its people, establishing a nation whose basic constitution and state ideology acknowledge and protect the traditions of cultural and religious pluralism that have long been integral to the lives of Indonesia's inhabitants.

The idea to create this Pancasila nation state [as opposed to an explicitly Islamic state] was the fruit of bitter experience garnered from the history of the East Indies archipelago itself. On the one hand, the long history of the East Indies—which has given birth

---

8. [Translator's note: Pancasila is the official philosophical foundation of the Indonesian state. Pancasila consists of two Sanskrit words, "panca," meaning five, and "sila," meaning principle(s). It comprises five principles held to be inseparable and interrelated: belief in the one and only God; a just and civilized humanity; the unity of Indonesia; democracy guided by inner wisdom, and arising out of deliberations by elected representatives; and social justice for all the people of Indonesia. In adopting the term pancasila to describe the newly-independent state of Indonesia's official ideology, the nation's primarily Muslim founders established a conscious link with the past. In Buddhism, pancasila (the Five Precepts) refers to the basic Buddhist code of ethics, undertaken by lay followers of Gautama Buddha in the Theravada and Mahayana traditions. The Five Precepts are commitments to abstain from killing, stealing, sexual misconduct, lying and intoxication. They are not formulated as imperatives, but as training rules that lay people undertake voluntarily to facilitate practice on the path to spiritual liberation.]

to many great Hindu, Buddhist and Islamic civilizations, during the Sriwijaya, Sailendra, first Mataram, Kediri, Singosari, Majapahit, Demak, Aceh, Makasar, Goa, second Mataram and other kingdoms—has created a strong awareness of the need to preserve the rich and diverse culture and traditions of our people. On the other hand, the continuous dialogue between Islam as a system of religious teachings, and nationalism—which dialogue is deeply rooted in the experience of the Indonesian people—strengthened our founders' awareness that a nation state which accepts and protects the diverse beliefs, cultures and traditions of Indonesia represents the best foundation upon which to build the life of our nation and people. Mpu Tantular's saying ("Oneness Amid Diversity"), the teachings and religious-cultural-political movement led by Sunan Kalijogo, as well as other such examples, aptly express the profound spiritual awareness which ultimately became the foundation of modern Indonesia, and has preserved it from disintegration since the proclamation of independence in 1945.

This was not an easy process, given the fluctuating relationships that have occurred between religion and nationalism. The difficulties which have arisen constitute historical facts that we must recognize and understand. A number of periods in the history of the East Indies are drenched in blood because of conflicts that occurred, often in the name of religion. Muslim religious scholars such as Abikusno Tjokrosujoso, Kyai Haji A. Kahar Muzakkir, Haji Agus Salim, Kyai Haji A. Wahid Hasjim, Ki Bagus Hadikusumo, Kasman Singodimejo, Teuku Mohammad Hassan, and other founders of Indonesia, understood that the country they struggled to create and defend was not based upon a single religion, but instead was a nation state which acknowledged and protected all the various religions, cultures and traditions that have always been an integral part of life for the people of Indonesia.

Our founding fathers recognized that Pancasila does not contain a single principle that conflicts with religious teachings. On the contrary, its principles reflect the highest values of all religions, including that which, in Islam, is known as maqâshid al-sharî'ah, (the purpose of shari'a) namely, the common good (al-mashlahat al-'âmmah). With this insight and awareness, Indonesia's founders renounced the formal establishment of religion, and instead emphasized its spiritual essence. They positioned the state as an institution which acknowledges pluralism, protects all interests, and guards all beliefs, cultures and traditions within Indonesian society. In other words, they instituted Pancasila so as to foster religion as the manifestation of God's blessing for all creation (rahmatan lil-'âlamîn) in its true sense. In the idealized context of Pancasila, everyone may assist everyone else in achieving worldly prosperity; and everyone is free to worship in whatever way he or she considers best suited to attain eternal prosperity in the hereafter, without sacrificing the former.

As previously mentioned, there has been a fluctuating relationship between religion (i.e., Islam) and nationalism (Pancasila) throughout the history of Indonesia as a nation state. There have been groups that sought to establish an Islamic state through constitutional means (e.g., the 1950s' Constitutional Assembly), and others through force of arms (such as Darul Islam/TII).[9] And yet the majority of Indonesians, Muslim and non-Muslim alike, have always agreed with Pancasila and struggled to realize the vision of our founding fathers. This tumultuous history provides invaluable lessons concerning how to build our nation state. The behavior of mass religious organizations such as the NU and Muhammadiyah, as well as nationalist political parties—all of which strongly affirm that the Unitary State of the Republic of Indonesia (NKRI), based on Pancasila and the 1945 Constitution (which rejected the establishment of an Islamic state), represent the final form and consensus for the building of our nation state—does not represent opportunistic political behavior, but rather, a mature and genuine awareness based on historical reality, the culture and traditions of our people, and the substance of religious teachings of whose truth

---

9. [Translator's note: From 1949 – 1962, the Darul Islam guerilla movement waged an armed struggle to overthrow the Indonesian state and replace it with a theocratic Islamic state, based upon a fundamentalist understanding of the Qur'an and Sunnah. Offshoots of the Darul Islam rebellion include the contemporary terrorist group Jemaah Islamiyah (JI), which has been responsible for dozens of bombings in Indonesia since the fall of Suharto, including the notorious attack in Bali that killed over 200 in October of 2002, and led to the establishment of LibForAll Foundation.]

we are certain.

This nationalistic approach serves to assure our nation's future, so that developments will remain consistent with our own culture and traditions, as well as with the substantive teachings of the various religions which have long been an integral part of Indonesian national life. The stand adopted by nationalist-religious figures, who have struggled to maintain the structure of our national unity based on Pancasila and the Basic Constitution of 1945 (UUD 1945), may be likened to the incarnation of tranquil souls (al-nafs al-muthmainnah)—individuals who constantly seek to assist others, regardless of any difference in their religious or cultural beliefs. In doing so, they ardently strive to share God's infinite love and compassion (rahmat) with all sentient beings.

Such behavior is not reflected in various mass organizations and political parties that have appeared in Indonesia since shortly before, and after, the collapse of Suharto's New Order regime. These new organizations remind us of the Darul Islam (DI) movement since, like DI, they seek to transform Indonesia into an explicitly religious state, replacing the state ideology of Pancasila with their own version of Islam, or even to eliminate NKRI and replace it with an Islamic caliphate.

Concerning the implicit claim of hardline activists that they completely understand the meaning of holy scripture and are therefore entitled to become God's vice-regents (caliphs) and rule this world, compelling others to follow their "perfect" understanding—this claim is totally unacceptable and must be rejected, both theologically and politically. The extremists are correct that power belongs to God alone (lâ hukm illâ li Allâh), but not a single human being completely grasps or comprehends God's power. That is why the Prophet once said, "You do not understand what is truly God's law."[10] In brief, although based upon the Qur'an and Sunnah, Islamic jurisprudence (fiqh)—which extremists generally cite, to theologically justify their rule—is actually the product of human

---

10. Khaled Abou El Fadl, *Atas Nama Tuhan: dari Fikih Otoriter ke Fikih Otoritatif (In the Name of God: From Authoritarian Islamic Jurisprudence to Authoritative Islamic Jurisprudence)*, translated from *Speaking in God's Name: Islamic Law, Authority and Women* (Jakarta: Serambi, 2003), p. 48.

understanding and efforts which are constrained by time, place and the respective abilities of the *fiqh* authors of such jurisprudential texts.

Unaware of these facts, or consciously disregarding them for the sake of power, hardline activists are striving to transform Islam from a religion into an ideology. In their hands, Islam becomes a weapon to attack and discredit anyone who holds political views or religious beliefs different from their own. In other words, their call to "struggle for Islam" masks the reality that they are in fact struggling for a specific political agenda, and employing Islam as a lethal weapon to advance their worldly ambitions. This strategy is highly effective, since anyone opposing them can be accused of being an enemy of Islam itself, even when such statements are blatantly false.

Under the pretext of "promoting and defending" Islam, extremists are simultaneously hard at work to displace expressions of local culture and tradition that form an integral part of Indonesians' daily lives. They wish to replace these with foreign culture and traditions from the Middle East—especially Wahhabi and Muslim Brotherhood practices—due to their inability to distinguish between religion and the culture of the land in which Islam was revealed. The extremists adopt a harsh and violent demeanor, and refuse to compromise with other viewpoints—as if Islam had no tradition or command to create peace (*islah*), but rather, merely commanded its followers to employ compulsion and violence. Because of such attitudes and behavior, Islamist radicals are frequently referred to as "hardliners."[11]

We must be aware that whenever Islam is transformed into an ideology, it becomes narrow and restricted, constrained by ideological limits and political platforms. Any contrary view of Islam, not to mention those that directly conflict with the extremists' narrow understanding, will readily be cast as inimical to Islam itself, because the fundamental nature of an ideologically-driven inter-

---

11. [Translator's note: The terms "hardliner," "extremist" and "radical" are used interchangeably in this book. In Indonesia, the term "hardliner" (*garis keras*) has a derogative connotation, describing someone who has a coarse and superficial understanding of Islam, as opposed to a deep and nuanced understanding based upon wisdom and experience.]

pretation of Islam is to eliminate opposition and justify political supremacy and power. It is in this context that extremists often accuse their opponents of being infidels and/or apostates. This transformation of Islam into an ideology clearly amputates, and emasculates, the supreme teachings of Islam, by attempting to stuff a religion that embodies compassion and tolerance into a narrow and rigid ideological framework.

In general, the aspirations of hardline movements in Indonesia—especially those that have a Wahhabi or Muslim Brotherhood view of Islam, or a mixture of the two—are strongly influenced by transnational Islamist movements from the Middle East. Indonesian extremist movements, including political parties, thus pursue an agenda that differs markedly from those of moderate Islamic mass organizations such as the Muhammadiyah, NU and nationalist political parties. Since their appearance after the fall of Suharto, extremist movements have begun to succeed in changing the face of Indonesian Islam to become more aggressive, furious, intolerant and full of hate.[12] This, despite the fact that Indonesian Islam has long been known as gentle, tolerant and peace-loving (the international magazine *Newsweek* once called it "Islam with a smiling face").

Hardliners seek to obtain the sympathy and support of Muslims by employing jargon which claims to promote and defend Islam; by using the subterfuge of "Islamic" education; and through what they call *da'wa amar ma'rûf nahyi munkar* (proselytism by commanding the good deed and forbidding evil). Such rhetoric misleads even those who are highly educated in the modern sense of that term, but unaccustomed to thinking about spirituality and the essence of Islamic teachings. Such people are easily hooked by extremists, since they may be fascinated and attracted by the hardliners' use of religious symbols.[13] In fact, the extremists themselves

12. For instance, read the Wahid Institute's 2008 annual report on *Religious Pluralism in Indonesia*, "Contemplating a Nation that is Increasingly Fractured" (*Pluralisme Beragama/Berkeyakinan di Indonesia*, "Menapaki Bangsa yang Kian Retak").
13. [Translator's note: Extremists often make a show of their supposed devoutness, employing religious symbols such as beards and so-called "Muslim" clothing (long, white shirts or robes for men), quoting the Qur'an, ostentatiously

"grasp" Islam without comprehending the essence of its teachings, as understood by saints, religious scholars and Indonesia's founding fathers. Their understanding of Islam is framed by narrow ideological definitions and political agendas, which render them incapable of grasping any truth that is opposed to their narrow viewpoint, literal interpretation and/or political agenda. This inability to comprehend the truth drives them to accuse anyone who holds a different view of Islam, or does not support their agenda, of being an infidel or apostate.

With regard to rank and file extremists, many people associate with and support radical movements because they're genuninely attracted to, and fascinated by, the religious symbols bandied about by extremist leaders. On the other hand, there are those who deliberately mobilize and manipulate the public by shouting religious formulae, when their actual goal is to satisfy their own egotistical and materialistic agenda. In order to short-circuit this process of radicalization, we must strive to encourage and inspire the public to be humble, to constantly raise their level of knowledge about Islam and to be open-minded, so that they may understand the spirituality and essence of Islamic teachings, and themselves become tranquil souls.

In addition, we must realize—as a nation—that what hardline activists are doing, and seeking to accomplish, not only conflicts with and threatens Pancasila and the Basic Constitution of 1945, but may ultimately destroy the Unitary State of the Republic of Indonesia (NKRI). Anarchistic actions, proclaiming others to be infidels and/or apostates, and other forms of character assassination in which extremists often engage, are in reality attempts to destroy our national unity.

I have often been accused of being an infidel or apostate, but remain tranquil in the face of such baseless accusations. Extremist movements measure the truth of religious understanding in terms of ideology and politics, while we [traditional Muslims] base our understanding and practice of religion on an enthusiasm for love, mercy and compassion, and a spirituality that leaves one open to

---

praying and fasting, etc., in order to appear "Islamic" and thereby don a mantle of religious authority.]

all sentient beings. We who produced this study/report base our Islamic teachings on the understanding of *ahlussunnah wal-jamâ'ah*, the great traditions of Sunni Islam, while radicals have inherited the extreme practices of the *Khawârij*,[14] who blithely condemned all who disagreed with them as infidels and apostates—an evil and corrupt practice that is still propagated today by many Wahhabis and their accomplices.[15]

Because hardline movements consider every Muslim who is different from them as less Islamic, or even an infidel or apostate, they are engaged in systematically infiltrating mosques, institutes, educational establishments, government, businesses, and moderate Islamic mass organizations, especially the Muhammadiyah and Nahdlatul Ulama (NU), in order to transform the various institutions of Indonesian society, and Islam itself, into their own harsh and rigid likeness. The extremists claim to be promoting and defending Islam, yet what they actually promote and defend is a narrow understanding of Islam trapped within the boundaries of their own political platform and ideology, *not* Islam itself. They are engaged in strenuous efforts to seize control of the Muhammadiyah and NU, because these two powerful organizations have more followers than any other Islamic mass organization, either in Indonesia or the world. In addition, these hardline groups regard the Muhammadiyah and NU as the primary obstacles in the path of

---

14. [Translator's note: The Khawârij, or Kharijites, were an early Islamic splinter group that sought to annihilate everyone who did not agree with their views. The most notorious of their terrorist acts was the assassination of the fourth Caliph, the Prophet Muhammad's son-in-law, 'Ali.]

15. "Furthermore, there are those who understand faith in a monopolistic fashion, so that anyone whose understanding is different from theirs, is considered unfaithful. In reality this is an old phenomenon, not just contemporary. At the time of Sayadina Ali, may God give him honor and praise, there was a group called the Khawârij who denounced everyone outside their narrow sect as infidels. This phenomenon has now reincarnated once again, to the point where someone like (the terrorist) Azhari comes to Indonesia setting off bombs and imagines that he'll be rewarded in heaven for such actions." ~ Kyai Haji Hasyim Muzadi, Chairman of the Nahdlatul Ulama Executive Board, in *Ocean of Revelations: Understanding Islam as a Blessing for All Creation*, Episode 3: "Faith Communities," Program Supervisor: Kyai Haji A. Mustofa Bisri, ©LibForAll Foundation 2009).

achieving their political agenda, because both have long promoted
the essence of Islamic values while rejecting the formalization of
Islam through the establishment of an Islamic state, or the implementation of *shari'a* as positive law.

Extremist infiltration has already provoked a great deal of
upheaval within both of the afore-mentioned Islamic mass organizations. In this context, we recall the never-ending struggle that
occurs within human beings themselves, and society at large (*insân
shaghîr*), i.e., the struggle between tranquil souls (*al-nafs al-muthmainnah*) and those that are selfish and discontented (*al-nafs al-lawwâmah*), or the struggle between the Pandavas and Kuravas, which
lies at the heart of the *Mahabarata*. While the former strive to create peace and tranquility for all, the latter constantly give rise to
trouble and disturbances for others.

Transnational extremist movements and their accomplices in
Indonesia have long been engaged in infiltration of the Muhammadiyah. This came to a head at the July, 2005 Muhammadiyah
Congress in Malang, East Java, when extremist agents, including
PKS and Hizb ut-Tahrir cadres,[16] dominated many forums and succeeded in having a number of hardline movement sympathizers
elected to the Muhammadiyah's central board. But it was only after Professor Abdul Munir Mulkhan visited his native village of
Sendang Ayu in Lampung Province, Sumatra, that the problem
of radical infiltration of the Muhammadiyah grew into a major
controversy, whose ramifications were observed even at an international level.[17]

A Muhammadiyah mosque in the small, remote village of Sendang Ayu, which had long been calm and tranquil, was suddenly
thrown into chaos when a visiting PKS activist (in the form of an
itinerant imam) introduced political issues into the mosque—de-

16. [Translator's note: The Justice and Prosperity Party (Partai Keadilan Sejat-
erah, or PKS) is an Indonesian political party inspired by the Muslim Brotherhood, while Hizb ut-Tahrir is a subversive organization that seeks to establish a
global caliphate. For more on both organizations, see Chapter II, "The Origins
and Global Spread of Wahhabi/Muslim Brotherhood Ideology."]
17. Read Bret Stephens, "The Exorcist: Indonesian man seeks to create an Islam
that will make people smile," at http://www.libforall.org/news-WSJ-the-exorcist.
html.

faming other organizations, including the Muhammadiyah itself—and began denouncing his opponents as infidels. When Professor Munir visited Sendang Ayu to celebrate the end of Ramadan with his mother and other relatives, he took the opportunity to explain to his fellow villagers the Muhammadiyah way of addressing differences of opinion, without questioning others' faithfulness. As a result, the villagers no longer allowed PKS members to deliver sermons in their mosque. Dr. Munir subsequently described his experience, and expressed his wider concern, in *Suara Muhammadiyah* (*The Voice of Muhammadiyah*), the organization's official magazine.[18] This article evoked a serious discussion within the Muhammadiyah about extremist infiltration of the organization that had already occurred in many regions of Indonesia, using methods both subtle and blunt, even to the point of force.

Professor Munir's article inspired Farid Setiawan—General Chairman of the Regional Board of Directors of the Muhammadiyah Student Movement, in the province of Yogyakarta—to discuss radical infiltration of the Muhammadiyah more widely, in two articles that also appeared in *Suara Muhammadiyah*. In the first, "Ahmad Dahlan [founder of the Muhammadiyah] in Tears (Reflections on the Writing of Abdul Munir Mulkhan),"[19] Farid advised the Muhammadiyah to immediately amputate the extremist "virus" which, in his opinion, had already reached the critical stage of a category 4 cancer. He warned that if moderate Muhammadiyah members remained silent, "it's entirely possible that the Muhammadiyah will not outlive its current leadership. And it's also possible that if Kyai Haji Ahmad Dahlan could rise from his tomb, he would be shocked and in tears seeing the condition of the Muhammadiyah's membership and cadres,"[20] which are in the process of being taken over by extremist movements.

---

18. Abdul Munir Mulkhan, "Sendang Ayu: Pergulatan Muhammadiyah di Kaki Bukit Barisan," ("Sendang Ayu: Muhammadiyah Battle at the Foot of Barisan Mountain,") *Suara Muhammadiyah*, 2 January 2006.
19. Farid Setiawan, "Ahmad Dahlan Menangis (Tanggapan terhadap Tulisan Abdul Munir Mulkhan)," *Suara Muhammadiyah*, 20 February 2006.
20. Ibid.

In the second article, "Three Actions (to Improve the Muhammadiyah's) Male and Female Teachers Schools," Farid wrote
that "the 'Tarbiyah virus'[21] produces cadres who have an extreme
and radical understanding of Islam. And the systematic effort to
produce such cadres has already spread far and wide in the Muhammadiyah. This phenomenon has led to great disappointment
among the Muhammadiyah's leadership and wider family. The sons
and daughters who, they hoped, would drive the Muhammadiyah's
future developments have, in fact, been transformed into enemies
of the Muhammadiyah itself."[22]

Recognizing just how far this Tarbiyah virus had infiltrated
the Muhammadiyah, Farid recommended three steps to save the
organization from extremist domination. *First,* to dissolve the
schools which train Muhammadiyah cadres, because these have already been thoroughly corrupted by the Tarbiyah virus; *second,* to
discard the system and curriculum employed in these schools, and
expel all Muhammadiyah leaders and teachers who are involved
in non-Muhammadiyah ideological movements and political agendas; and *third,* to re-energize all autonomous organizations within
the Muhammadiyah movement.[23]

---

21. "At the time of its birth in the 1970s and '80s, the Tarbiyah movement was
a campus proselytism movement that used the Tarbiyah system of education
employed by the Muslim Brotherhood in Egypt. This militant group represented
a new direction, as an ideological Islamic movement, that was entirely different from the major streams of Indonesian Islam represented by the Muhammadiyah and the Nahdlatul Ulama, which are moderate and culturally-oriented
Islamic movements. Activists from the Tarbiyah movement established the Justice Party (Partai Keadilan, or PK) in 1998, which changed its name to become
the Justice and Prosperity Party (PKS) in 2004. The PKS established Tarbiyah
a la the Muslim Brotherhood as a system for the education and recruitment
of its party members. Thus, the Tarbiyah movement cannot be divorced from
the PK/PKS, as both derive the breath of their ideological inspiration from the
Muslim Brotherhood, while Tarbiyah serves as the medium/vital instrument of
the PKS, which is famed for combining *da'wa* (proselytism) and politics." (from
the back cover of Haedar Nashir's book, *Manifestations of the Tarbiyah Movement:
How Should the Muhammadiyah Respond?*, 5th printing, Yogyakarta: Suara Muhammadiyah, 2007).
22. Farid Setiawan, "Tiga Upaya Mu'allimin dan Mu'allimat," *Suara Muhammadiyah,* 3 April 2006.
23. Ibid.

Munir's and Farid's articles provoked a bitter controversy and polemic between Muhammadiyah leaders who agreed with their criticisms, and those who did not. A primary concern of those who did agree was that the Muhammadiyah's institutions, facilities, membership and resources were being used by extremist movements to promote the interests and goals of groups other than the Muhammadiyah. In the midst of this heated polemic concerning the Tarbiyah virus, a member of the Muhammadiyah's central board, Dr. Haedar Nashir, clarified the various issues in a thin book entitled *Manifestations of the Tarbiyah Movement: How Should the Muhammadiyah Respond?*[24]

Less than three months after the book's publication, the Muhammadiyah's central board issued Muhammadiyah Central Board Decree Number 149/Kep/I.0/B/2006, in order to "rescue the Muhammadiyah from various activities that are damaging the organization" and free it "from the influence, mission, infiltration and interests of a political party which is engaged in religious proselytizing, and (thus flies on) the wings of *da'wa* (religious proselytism)," because said party is exploiting the Muhammadiyah to achieve its own political goals, which conflict with the supreme vision and mission of the Muhammadiyah as a moderate Islamic organization:

> "The Muhammadiyah has a right to be respected by others, and to be free of all agendas, interference and influence by other parties which may disrupt the unity and progress of its movement" (Preamble, Point 4). "All Muhammadiyah members need to be aware, understand and adopt a critical attitude which recognizes that every political party in this nation—including those that claim to represent '*da'wa*' or Islamic proselytism activities, such as Partai Keadilan Sejahtera (PKS)—are in fact mere political parties. Every political party is focused on the acquisition of political power. For that reason, in dealing with any political party, we must always remain commit-

---

24. Haedar Nashir, *Manifestasi Gerakan Tarbiyah: Bagaimana Sikap Muhammadiyah?* 5th printing (Yogyakarta: Suara Muhammadiyah, 2007).

ted to the true Path of the Muhammadiyah and must free ourselves from, and never engage ourselves with, the mission, interests, activities or goals of the above-mentioned political parties (Decree, Point 3).[25]

The issuance of this decree is understandable, because in fact the PKS does not merely "provoke problems and conflict within other Islamic organizations, including the Muhammadiyah,"[26] but according to political experts, represents a greater threat than [the terrorist group] Jemaah Islamiyah to Pancasila, the Basic Constitution of 1945 and the Unitary State of the Republic of Indonesia (NKRI). In the words of Sadanand Dhume, an expert on Indonesian politics and extremist movements:

> Despite the Justice Party's social work, little separates its thinking from Jemaah Islamiyah's. Like Jemaah Islamiyah, in its founding manifesto, the Justice Party called for the creation of an Islamic caliphate. Like Jemaah Islamiyah, it has placed secrecy—facilitated by the cell structure both groups borrowed from the Brotherhood—at the heart of its organisation. Both offer a selective vision of modernity—one in which global science and technology are welcome, but un-Islamic values are shunned. The two groups differ chiefly in their methods: Jemaah Islamiyah is revolutionary; the Justice Party is evolutionary.

> Of the two, the Justice Party is by far the larger threat to Indonesia. With its suicide bombings Jemaah Islamiyah has set itself up for a confrontation with the government that it cannot hope to win. In contrast, the Justice Party uses its position in parliament and its metastasizing network of cadres to advance the same goals incrementally, one vote at a time.... Ultimately, Indonesians alone will decide whether their future lies with the rest of Southeast

---

25. Muhammadiyah Central Board Decree Number 149/Kep/I.0/B/2006. To read the full text of the decree, see Appendix 1.
26. Ibid, Haedar Nashir, p. 66.

Asia, or with a backward-looking movement cloaked in religious fundamentalism. The Justice Party remains on the march. How far it goes may well determine Indonesia's future.[27]

As demonstrated by the research published in this book, although the Muhammadiyah central board's Decree was issued in December of 2006, it has not been effectively implemented to this date. Transnational Islamist movements (Wahhabi, Muslim Brotherhood and Hizb ut-Tahrir) and their Indonesian accomplices have succeeded in deeply infiltrating the Muhammadiyah, and establishing alliances with other radicals who have long found harbor inside the organization itself. Both groups are actively recruiting other Muhammadiyah leaders and members to follow their extreme ideology, as occurred when the entire leadership of the Bantul branch of Nasyiatul Aisyiyah, the Muhammadiyah women's movement, joined the PKS en masse.

While Farid Setiawan expressed concern that the Muhammadiyah might not outlive its current leadership, extremist organizations are busy attempting to seize control of the Muhammadiyah and employ it as a vehicle to achieve their goals in Indonesia for countless years to come. Many moderate Muhammadiyah figures are worried that extremists may dominate the next Muhammadiyah Congress in 2010, because radical activists within the Muhammadiyah have become progressively more strong and numerous.

Precisely because of this increasingly deep infiltration, moderate Muhammadiyah leaders regard the situation as profoundly dangerous, both for the Muhammadiyah itself and the Indonesian nation. In confronting such problems, wherever they exist, we must be honest, transparent and direct, so that our actions may serve to educate all Muslims, helping them to become mature in their faith and good citizens.

One finding which shocked those engaged in the field research component of this study was the phenomenon of dual member-

---

27. Sadanand Dhume, "Indonesian Democracy's Enemy Within: Radical Islamic party threatens Indonesia with ballots more than bullets," in the *Far Eastern Economic Review*, May 2005.

ship, especially between the Muhammadiyah and extremist movements. In fact, the field research team estimated that up to 75% of the radical leaders interviewed for this study had ties with the Muhammadiyah.

Besides the Muhammadiyah, extremist infiltration of the Nahdlatul Ulama is also systematically underway. The strategic function of mosques within Muslim society leads radical groups to constantly attempt to seize control of them, using every possible method, including many which no one could possibly imagine other than the infiltrators themselves. Kyai Haji Mu'adz Thahir, Regional Chairman of the Nahdlatul Ulama in Pati, Central Java, informed our researchers that radicals were successfully infiltrating NU mosques in his area using the stratagem of providing a free cleaning service.

According to Kyai Thahir, the process works as follows: at first, a group of youths come and voluntarily clean the mosque, not just once but many times. Attracted by their apparent religious sincerity, the mosque board gives them an opportunity to issue the call to prayer, and eventually involves them as members of the board itself. These new members cleverly and conscientiously discharge their responsibilities, because in reality they're extremist agents tasked with the job of seizing control of the mosque. As their position becomes increasingly powerful, they begin to invite other friends to join the board, and eventually control who may or may not serve as imam, deliver the Friday sermon, or provide religious education to attendees at the mosque. Slowly but surely, the mosque falls into the hands of radicals, until local religious leaders who once gave sermons and lectures at the mosque are denied the opportunity to teach Islam to their own congregations, and in fact lose control of the mosque and the local people, unless they prove willing to accept and promote the extremists' ideology.

This case from Pati is only one of countless instances in which radicals have seized control of NU mosques. If this particular example were portrayed in film, viewers would likely assume it was merely the director's wild imagination at work. But in fact, it is the logical manifestation of *a virulent ideology, backed by immense funding, and operating in a systematic manner*, as transnational Islamist movements and their local accomplices work nonstop to undermine and ultimately seize control of our nation. The research contained in this book demonstrates that the groups most often involved in the infiltration and seizure of NU mosques are the PKS and Hizb ut-Tahrir.

After realizing that many of its mosques and congregations had already been seized by extremist groups, the NU launched a campaign to consolidate and tighten the structure of its organization, both in mosques and other locations. The Nahdlatul Ulama's central board firmly proclaimed that transnational Islamist movements such as al-Qaeda, the Muslim Brotherhood (represented in Indonesia by the PKS) and Hizb ut-Tahrir are dangerous political movements which threaten Sunni teachings and have the potential to destroy the nation.[28] The radicals' ability to dissimulate and pretend to accept NU teachings and tradition makes them even more dangerous, because this enables them to infiltrate anywhere, anytime. While in regard to the issue of a caliphate, the NU's official forum for discussing Islamic law, the Majlis Bahtsul Masa'il, formally declared that there is no theological basis for an Islamic caliphate, either in the Qur'an or the hadith [the sayings of the Prophet Muhammad].[29]

Although in some places the NU has succeeded at reclaiming its mosques from extremists, the radical infiltration and capture of mosques and NU congregations continues to accelerate. As demonstrated by this study, in general the infiltration of extremists is far more dynamic than NU efforts to drive them out. If this situation is allowed to persist, it is very possible that the NU will lose a significant percentage of its mosques and followers, and itself be transformed into an organization that is less spiritual, and more extreme.

---

28. The NU Central Board has pressed Indonesia's government to halt the infiltration of transnational ideology. Much earlier, the respected NU leader Kyai Haji Yusuf Hasjim asked the NU Central Board to cut off the flow of transnational ideology because of its danger to the NU and to Indonesia itself. (Memorial speech delivered 100 days after the death of KH. Yusuf Hasjim in Jombang, East Java; see NU Online, "PBNU Desak Pemerintah Cegah Ideologi Transnasional," Ahad, 29 April 2007, which appears in Appendix 2 of this book).
29. See Appendix 2 of this book.

Radical infiltration of NU environs, and the failure of the world's largest Muslim organization to halt extremist infiltration of Indonesia's government, the Indonesian Council of Religious Scholars (MUI) and other strategic fields in general, is due in large part to the widespread phenomenon of "materialistic kyais," or religious leaders.[30] Materialistic kyais are more interested in their personal well-being than the interests of the NU's followers or the nation as a whole. The forty million NU followers, who are concentrated in specific villages and districts, represent the largest single group of voters in Indonesia. Their votes can determine who is elected to regional or national legislatures, and who becomes a regent, governor or even president of Indonesia. This demographic reality tempts many political parties to manipulate the NU and exploit their relationships with materialistic kyais to achieve their own political interests. Because of human nature, there are kyais who long to receive cash-filled envelopes from political operatives, or elected office, and thus seek to fulfill their personal ambitions by acquiring a leadership position in the NU, whether at a local, regional or national level. Membership in the NU's formal leadership structure thus serves as a bridge to exploiting, and being exploited by, certain political parties and politicians.

At the same time, many spiritual kyais have withdrawn from the above-mentioned arena of egotism and self-interest, and share their wisdom only with those who come, without self-interest, seeking God rather than worldly position. With a following of about 40 million, the NU—together with the Muhammadiyah—can truly serve as a pillar capable of supporting and maintaining Indonesia's national integrity. However, in order to fulfill this vital role, the

---

30. [Translator's note: The original etymological meaning of the Javanese term *kyai* was "lord," referring to nobles, aristocrats and/or landed gentry who exerted political, military, economic and religious authority in a specific region. During the Dutch colonial era, the military and political aspects of this authority waned, and the term kyai evolved to refer specifically to Muslim leaders who exert religious authority within a given geographic region. The term is in many ways similar to the Arabic "shaykh," which can refer either to a tribal leader/elder, or to a religious figure. Historically, the top leadership of the Nahdlatul Ulama consisted of kyais who were descended from Javanese nobility, but increasingly this is no longer the case.]

NU must conduct a spiritual revitalization and return to its highest values. In this manner, its *ulama* (religious scholars) may guide those in power, and not permit themselves to be manipulated or exploited in return. Our ancestors proclaimed such a relationship between spiritual and worldly leaders to be the path of *dharma*, and that is why *wayang kulit* always portrays kings acting not only with respect, but also obedience towards *rishis*, and not the reverse.[31]

These days, *wayang* culture—which is distinctly Indonesian and full of sublime values—is rapidly being shunted aside by foreign culture. The unwise adoption of foreign culture is causing the Indonesian people to lose their own identity as a nation. One example of this process may be glimpsed through an event that occurred in Cairo in the middle of 2004. A Nahdlatul Ulama Vice Chairman had been invited to deliver a paper to an international seminar on the topic of "Education and an Emancipatory Islamic Law-giving Body," in conjunction with professors Hassan Hanafi and Youhanna Qaltah. One day before the paper was to be delivered, the President of the Egyptian chapter of the Association of Indonesian High School and University Students (PMII) and his companions barged into the Sonesta hotel, where the event was to be held, and demanded that the NU Vice Chairman withdraw from the event. They threatened that if he failed to do so, the students would take any step necessary to prevent him from delivering his paper, even to the point of murder. "If you go forward [and participate], I'll kill you myself," threatened Limra Zainuddin, the President of PPMI.[32] Subsequent research revealed that the students in question were PK (PKS) activists in Cairo.[33]

---

31. [Translator's note: Prior to the spread of television, *wayang kulit*, or shadow puppet performances, were the most popular form of public entertainment in Java. The extensive repertory of *wayang kulit* tales—which are primarily derived from the ancient Hindu epics the *Ramayana* and *Mahabharata*—seek to educate viewers about the nature of good and evil, and life's ultimate Truth. Kings and *rishis* (enlightened sages) appear in most *wayang kulit* performances, with the latter imparting the knowledge required for good governance, and spiritual liberation, to the former.]

32. See "Gertak Mati Pengawal Akidah (Threatening to Murder in the Name of Islamic Morality)" in *Gatra*, edition 14, published on 13 February 2004.

33. Interview with an Indonesian alumnus of al-Azhar University in Cairo, who began his study at al-Azhar in the year 2000.

As Muslims, those students were obliged to behave humbly (*tawâdlu'*), respecting elders while acting with love and kindness towards those who are younger (*laisa minnâ man lam yukrim kibârana wa lam yarham shighârana*). However, this did not occur, because the students in question had neither understood nor internalized the teachings of Islam that are full of spirituality, and instead had already adopted a foreign culture, in a manner that was foolish and unwise. Both an immature grasp of Islam, and the adoption of Wahhabi/Muslim Brotherhood culture, can easily trap one in a narrow and rigid understanding of Islam. Anyone who lacks a profound understanding of Islam, especially those elements which concern ultimate Truth/Reality (*haqiqa*) and Gnosis (*ma'rifa*, or mystical knowledge of, and union with, the Divine), will tend to think that what extremist groups proclaim is identical to that which is understood and believed by the majority of Muslims worldwide. Radicals employ the same language as Muslims in general, such as *da'wa* (proselytism), *amar ma'rûf nahy munkar* (enjoining the good and forbidding evil) or *Islam rahmatan lil-'âlamîn* (Islam as a blessing for all creation), but in reality they understand these terms differently.[34]

In their hands, *amar ma'rûf nahy munkar* becomes a formula for legitimizing compulsion, violence and attacks against anyone who differs from them. They excuse themselves by claiming to promote the good and forbid evil every time they commit such acts of violence or defame others. As for the concept of *rahmatan lil-'âlamîn:* in the mouths of extremists, it becomes an excuse to

---

34. "Because ideological movements are often neither felt nor recognized by those who are infiltrated by them, they can systematically penetrate organizations and grow quite large. All the more so when the ideological movements in question convey a puritanical and militant Islamic ideology, so that whoever views them as problematic will himself be accused of causing problems. To oppose them means to be Islamophobic, or opposed to religious unity. In this way such ideological movements become ever more deeply rooted and expand systematically, until by the time they are finally recognized as a serious problem, it's too late and they can no longer be halted or controlled, because they have already developed a mass base of followers. Ideological movements' mode of infiltration is truly broad and systematic, something which is seldom realized by most people." (Haedar Nashir, *Manifestasi Gerakan Tarbiyah: Bagaimana Sikap Muhammadiyah?* Fifth printing [Yogyakarta: Suara Muhammadiyah, 2007], p. 59).

formalize Islam; to force others to agree with their interpretation of Islam; and to accuse everyone who thinks differently, or rejects their interpretation, of rejecting the concept of *rahmatan lil-'âlamîn*, as a prelude to finally branding them as infidels and apostates. And with regard to proselytism: the fundamental spirit of *da'wa* is to provide information and to gently invite, for Islam guarantees freedom of religion (*lâ ikrâh fi al-dîn*).[35] Here we see the fundamental contradiction between the activities of extremist groups and the teachings of Islam, which are full of love, tolerance and openness.

This use of a common religious language makes radicals extremely dangerous, because it enables them to easily deceive many Muslims and to infiltrate almost anywhere, anytime. Through this strategy, combined with militancy and strong financial support from abroad and within our country, extremist movements have deeply infiltrated most sectors of Indonesian society and are seeking to influence the majority of Muslims to follow their understanding of Islam. Until now, the Muslim community at large, and the government of Indonesia, have been deceived and/or permitted the activities of extremist movements, to the point that radical groups are increasingly large and powerful, and more and more easily force their agendas not only upon Islamic mass organizations but also upon the government, political parties, the mass media, the business world and educational institutions.

The militant behavior and truth claims asserted by radical groups often leaves the majority of Muslims, including opportunistic politicians, confused how to respond, because any rejection will be construed as opposing Islamic *shari'a*, although in fact this is not the case.[36] Thus it is not surprising that many government authori-

35. "The proper role of government, concerning (extremists' use of force and calling it) *da'wa* is to have the ulama and intellectuals advise and correct those who are wrong. If (the extremists) fail to immediately accept this advice, the government must enforce the law by arresting and sentencing them to prison, in accordance with their wrongdoing." ~ The Grand Shaykh of al-Azhar, Muhammad Sayyid Tantawi, in *Ocean of Revelations: Understanding Islam as a Blessing for All Creation*, Episode 5: "Da'wa" ("Proselytism,") Program Supervisor: KH. A. Mustofa Bisri, ©LibForAll Foundation 2009).
36. [Translator's note: for a detailed discussion of *shari'a*, see Chapter III of this book ("The Ideology and Agenda of Extremist Movements in Indonesia"), especially the section entitled "Prefatory Remarks."]

ties and opportunistic political parties prefer to simply follow the dictates of extremist groups. One common example is the issuance of unconstitutional regional *shari'a* regulations, which in fact are jurisprudential (*fiqh*) regulations that do not convey the true message or teachings of *shari'a* itself. Their issuance is characterized by intolerance, and they violate both universal civil rights and the rights of religious minorities. Because they are derived from a jurisprudential understanding of Islam that is narrow and time-bound, they also fail to reflect the essence of religious teaching, which is full of spirituality, tolerance and love for all humanity.

In short, opportunistic politicians who work with extremist political parties or groups are also highly dangerous. They have joined the extremists in driving our nation towards a deep chasm, which threatens destruction and national disintegration. They care nothing about, and indeed, are actively engaged in sacrificing the future of our multi-religious and multi-ethnic nation. It appears that they place importance only upon their private political ambitions, in order to acquire wealth and power.

The hardline movement in Indonesia consists of various groups that support one another in achieving their common agenda, whether outside or within the institutions of government. Two extremely clear and present dangers are their persistent efforts to identify Islam with Wahhabi/Muslim Brotherhood ideology, and their attempt to annihilate our nation's culture and traditions and replace them with foreign culture and traditions that reek of Wahhabism, but are claimed to represent the culture and traditions of Islam. Extremist success in either or both of these endeavors will place the Indonesian nation and its people beneath the thumb of the global Wahhabi/Muslim Brotherhood ideological network. And what is most disturbing about their activities, is the fact that radical movements have already succeeded in infiltrating to the heart of government institutions, and are using these to accomplish their goals.

Extremist agents have also infiltrated the Indonesian Council of Religious Scholars (Majelis Ulama Indonesia, or MUI), which knowledgeable observers have identified as a bunker of fundamentalist and subversive movements.[37] This quasi-governmental organization, which was established by Suharto's New Order regime in order to control Indonesia's Muslim community, has largely fallen into the grip of radicals, and is now dictating to, and in many ways controlling, the actions of government. Thus it is not surprising that *fatwas* originating with the MUI are counter-productive and provoke controversy, such as those banning secularism, pluralism and liberalism, and branding as deviant certain groups within society, thus provoking violent actions in the name of Islam.

Numerous acts of violence committed by radical groups such as the Front for the Defense of Islam (FPI)—which injure and destroy the property of those proclaimed "deviant" by the MUI—and the support by MUI's leadership of those linked to such actions, confirms that the MUI is now playing a key role among extremist movements in Indonesia. At present, there is even a Hizb ut-Tahrir member of MUI, although Hizb ut-Tahrir explicitly aims to establish a global Islamic caliphate, which ideologically conflicts with Pancasila and necessarily entails the destruction of the Unitary State of the Republic of Indonesia (NKRI).

The low degree of attention and concern paid to the extremist phenomenon is not confined to radical ideology, movements and infiltration. The flow of Wahhabi money—which not only subsidizes terrorism, but also the spread of extremist ideology through global Wahhabization efforts—also goes largely unmentioned.[38]

---

37. See "MUI Bunker Islam Radikal," posted on the Wahid Institute's website at http://www.wahidinstitute.org/Program/Detail/?id=47/hl=id/MUI_Bunker_Islam_Radikal.

38. In his book *The Two Faces of Islam: Saudi Fundamentalism and its Role in Terrorism*, Stephen Sulaiman Schwartz clearly and convincingly describes the flow of Wahhabi money to finance global Wahhabization efforts and acts of international terrorism committed in the name of Islam. During the Balkan conflict, for example, Wahhabis used the pretext of defending Bosnian Muslims from ethnic cleansing, to spread their ideology by building infrastructure for education and worship. The Wahhabis specifically employ education (*tarbiyah*) and worship (*ubûdiyah*) as ideological camouflage to spread their narrow and rigid understanding of religion. While in the case of the World Trade Center, it is already clear who was the mastermind behind that tragedy. (Stephen Sulaiman Schwartz (2002). *The Two Faces of Islam: Saudi Fundamentalism and Its Role in Terrorism*. New York: Doubleday. Published in Indonesian as: *Dua Wajah Islam: Mod-*

Until now, the flow of Wahhabi money to Indonesia has not attracted serious public attention, although the phenomenon of extremist infiltration is backed by extraordinary financial support, to the point that radicalism has become a major business that delivers profit to many of its agents.

Some people are aware that huge amounts of Wahhabi petrodollars are flowing into Indonesia, but it's difficult to prove the details in the field, because those who receive the funds in question are highly sensitive to this issue and generally refuse to speak about it. It appears that extremists refuse to discuss the issue of Wahhabi funding because they're ashamed to have it known that they've made a business out of religion, and are serving Wahhabi goals, and also in order to conceal Wahhabi and Muslim Brotherhood infiltration of Indonesian Islam. On the other hand, Indonesian government authorities responsible for supervising the flow of funds in and out of the country also do not publicize this issue, although high-ranking officials responsible for state security privately admit that they are extremely concerned about this phenomenon.

To cite one example of Wahhabi funding, it has long been an open secret among experts that the Wahhabi proselytism group *Rabita al-'Alam al-Islami* (the Muslim World League), financed by Saudi Arabia, directs large sums of money to radical movements in Indonesia, via Dewan Dakwah Islamiyah Indonesia (the Indonesian Council for Islamic Proselytism, or DDII).[39] Numerous campus *da'wa* activities conducted by the organization known as Lembaga Dakwa Kampus (the Institute for Campus Proselytism, or LDK)—which gave birth to the Tarbiyah movement, which in turn gave birth to the political party PKS—enjoy Saudi funding, and have been responsible for spreading the Tarbiyah virus throughout Indonesia.

In Central Java, one of our researchers obtained information from a former Muhammadiyah executive from a local sub-regency in Magelang that PKS was currently seeking mosques that needed

eratisme vs Fundamentalisme dalam Wacana Global. Jakarta: LibForAll Foundation, the Wahid Institute, the Center for Islamic Pluralism, and Blantika.)
39. Noorhaidi Hasan, "Islamic Militancy, *Sharia*, and Democratic Consolidation in Post-Soeharto Indonesia," Working Paper No. 143, S. Rajaratnam School of International Studies (Singapore, 23 October 2007).

renovation, and villages that needed new mosques. The PKS activist responsible for this project openly admitted to the former Muhammadiyah executive that all the funding for this project came from Saudi Arabia. If a mosque was to be built or renovated, the local inhabitants were merely requested to support the PKS electorally. According to the activist, "In 2008, 11 mosques are already scheduled for renovation or construction with Saudi money" in Magelang Regency alone. Nearly all the mosques in Magelang that are infiltrated by the PKS using this strategy are attended by NU followers.[40] If the Saudis and PKS are working on 11 mosques in one regency alone (out of more than 400 regencies in Indonesia), imagine how much Wahhabi money is going to build mosques in all of Indonesia, motivated by political calculations!

After a PKS candidate unexpectedly triumphed in the West Java gubernatorial election in July of 2008, a Nahdlatul Ulama vice chairman informed our researchers that this victory was marked by PKS success in capturing numerous NU mosques and their congregations. Although the NU vice chairman was shocked by this occurrence, the PKS success in capturing NU mosques and congregations should not surprise anyone. A virulent ideology—supported by vast sums of foreign money, deployed in a systematic manner—can infiltrate nearly anywhere, and overcome disorganized opposition. In other words, as *ulama* often state: *al-haqq bi lâ nizhâm tughlab al-bâthil bi al-nizhâm* (truth which is not organized may be readily defeated by evil that is).

Extremist agents often shout that foreigners, including Western foundations and governments, employ their money to destroy Islam in Indonesia, and hurl accusations that a Zionist/Christian conspiracy lurks behind such efforts. In reality, Western governments and foundations such as Ford Foundation and the Asia Foundation openly publicize the programs they conduct, so that the public may know what they are actually doing, and how much money they're spending on the projects in question.[41] Although

---

40. Research interview conducted in Magelang Regency in August, 2008.
41. The United States government heavily funds training to build human resources capacity in conjunction with democracy, throughout the developing world. The National Democratic Institute, a quasi-governmental institute from the United States that seeks to promote democracy in Indonesia, "typically works

LibForAll Foundation's funding is extremely small, and the majority of its board members, advisors and management are native Indonesians, it too reports its programs in an open and transparent
manner.

This is completely different from foreign Wahhabi/Muslim
Brotherhood movements and their various accomplices in Indonesia. The research contained in this book clearly demonstrates that
while extremists scream that foreigners are coming to Indonesia
with vast sums of money to destroy Islam.... of course that is *true*,
because the foreigners are activists from transnational movements
from the Middle East, who spend fantastic sums of petrodollars to
Wahhabize and destroy an Indonesian Islam that is polite, tolerant and spiritual, and to transform Indonesia in accordance with
their utopian dream of an ideal Islamic state which does not exist
anywhere in the world, including the Middle East.[42]

Wrapped in Arab-looking turbans, baggy white robes and
beards, which several Indonesian figures have described as the garb

---

with parties from across the ideological spectrum to foster a genuine multiparty
political system. However, in most countries, resource limitations and other considerations prevent the Institute from working with all registered political parties. In such cases, the Institute typically selects its partners based on their commitment to democratic principles and non-violence rather than by their political
beliefs. In addition, as appropriate, NDI considers objective criteria such as: political viability and base of popular support, as evidenced by legitimate election
results; level of grassroots organization; [and] the ability to absorb assistance....
NDI continues to support reform efforts within Indonesia's major political parties. In response to issues parties face—such as training of activists and members,
direct election campaigns, policy development, leadership selection, analysis of
voter attitudes and political party development and reform—NDI continues to
provide comparative global expert advice, information, and skills-building training to party leaders and instructors at national, provincial, and local levels." (See:
http://www.ndi.org/indonesia). Interviews with key NDI officials in March of
2008 indicate that the party which most actively participates in, and benefits
from, the NDI's Political Party Development program in Indonesia is the PKS.
42. Saudi activities in Indonesia represent only a small fraction of a more than
US$70 billion campaign (from 1979 to 2003, and still rising) to spread the fun-
damentalist Wahhabi sect throughout the world. These constantly intensifying
Wahhabi proselytization efforts constitute "the largest worldwide propaganda
campaign ever mounted—dwarfing the Soviets' propaganda efforts at the height
of the Cold War." (See: "How Billions in Oil Money Spawned a Global Terror
Network," in *US News & World Report*, 7 December 2003).

of robed thugs, they wish to convince others that the extremist views they scream at the top of their lungs and try to force on everyone else represent the true message of Islam, for which all must struggle. Yet in reality they are damaging the religion of Islam, and are responsible for countless acts of violence which they and their allies have committed in the name of Islam, both in Indonesia and throughout the world. And the rest of us, as Muslims, should be deeply ashamed of their actions.

The primary reason we must oppose hardline movements is to restore honor and respect to Islam, which the extremists have desecrated, while at the same time preserving Pancasila and the Unitary State of the Republic of Indonesia. Victory in the struggle against extremists will restore the majesty of Islamic teachings as *rahmatan lil-'âlamîn*—a blessing for all creation—and this represents a vital key to building a peaceful world.

We have conducted and published this study in order to raise awareness among all components of Indonesian society, particularly the elite and mass media, concerning the dangers of extremist ideology and doctrine with which Middle Eastern transnational movements are flooding our nation, and which have sprouted like mushrooms in the rainy season over the past decade, during our democratic era. This work is also intended as a call to defend and preserve Pancasila, which reflects the essence of *shari'a* and transforms Islam into a true blessing for all creation.

In chapter five, this study recommends a number of strategic steps to guard and preserve Pancasila, the Basic Constitution of 1945 and the Unitary State of the Republic of Indonesia, and our nation's glorious cultural and spiritual heritage and traditions. These strategic steps include:

- Encourage and inspire the public, including Indonesia's elites, to be open-minded, humble and devoted to constant learning, so that they may comprehend the spirituality and essence of religious teachings, and thus become tranquil souls.
- Halt in its tracks and eliminate—using responsible methods—the vicious cycle of radicalization that spreads extremist ideology and doctrine, by promoting enlightened educa-

tion (in the broadest sense of the term), and by teaching and practicing the sublime commands of Islam, which foster an awareness of the need to become a humble, tolerant and peaceful servant of God.

Working together, while reminding each other of the truth (*wa tawâshau bil-haqq*) and always being patient (*wa tawâshau bil-shabr*), are vital keys in this endeavor. We must be polite, tolerant, open-minded and transparent in our efforts to preserve the glorious vision of our ancestors and founding fathers. A noble purpose should not be disgraced by the use of unethical methods, hatred towards others or harsh actions. Exalted goals must be accomplished using methods that are truthful, sincere, resolute, wise and responsible, without the slightest admixture of arrogance, compulsion or the like.

In this context, it's appropriate that we recall Shaykh Ibn 'Atail-lah al-Iskandari's advice, from his opus *Hikam*: "Do not closely associate with anyone whose spiritual state does not inspire you, and whose speech does not lead you to God" (*lâ tash-hab man lâ yunhid-luka ilâ Allah hâluhu, wa la yahdîka ilâ Allâh maqâluhu*). People who are convinced that they know more than anyone else about Islam, and yet are full of hatred towards any of God's creatures who do not travel the same path as they; and those who claim themselves to be in possession of the absolute truth, and for that reason entitled to act as God's vice-regents on earth (caliphs) and to dictate how everyone else must live—clearly, their words and behavior will not lead us into the presence of God. Their dream of an Islamic state is merely an illusion, for the true Islamic state is not to be found in the structure of any government, but rather, in hearts which are open to God and all His creatures.

Truth and falsehood are abundantly clear. Extremists wish to compel the entire Indonesian people to prostrate before their extreme and rigid doctrines concerning Islam. The history of our nation—including the *Babad Tanah Jawi*, the Padri War, the Darul Islam rebellion and other such bloody eruptions—clearly demonstrates that restless, discontented souls will constantly shove our nation towards the brink of destruction until they succeed in acquiring total power, or we stop them, as earlier generations of tranquil souls—i.e., *our ancestors*—have done so many times before. Now it is *we* who must decide the fate of our nation.

Jakarta, 8 March 2009

Chapter I

A Study of Transnational Islamist Movements and Their Accomplices in Indonesia

Rationale Behind the Study

Hard-line activists are fully aware that they are engaged in a "war of ideas," as they strive to convince Muslims throughout the world that their extreme ideology is the one and only true interpretation of Islam. They embrace a monolithic understanding of Islam, and reject local and spiritual variants of the religion, as practiced by Muslims in general—condemning these variants as erroneous and heretical, on the basis of their being "contaminated" and no longer pure expressions of Islam, as defined by the radicals themselves.

The primary strategy adopted by transnational Islamist movements, in their efforts to radicalize the world's Muslim population, is to: a) establish, mold and support local groups that will serve as their accomplices in propagating Wahhabi/Salafi ideology, while b) simultaneously working to isolate and destroy other, more tolerant forms of Islamic practice, which have a far longer history and a dominant presence in most parts of the Muslim world. In this way, Islamist radicals strenuously engage in systematic efforts to infiltrate virtually all key sectors of Muslim life, employing methods that range from the subtle to those which are crude and spectacularly violent, as evidenced by daily newspaper headlines around the world.

In regions such as Saudi Arabia, Sudan, Gaza and Taliban-dominated areas of Afghanistan and Pakistan, the Islamists have already succeeded in forcing the local population to pay obeisance to their extreme ideology. Meanwhile, in the rest of the Muslim world, there is virtually no systematic and serious effort underway to expose and discredit extremist movements, and to mobilize support for pluralistic and tolerant forms of Islam that are consistent with life in the modern world. However, the situation is different in Indonesia, for spiritual Islam retains a powerful, deeply rooted presence in the East Indies, and renowned Indonesian Muslim leaders are not only aware of the threat posed by hard-line movements, but also have the courage to directly confront them, before it's too late.

In our vast archipelago, a reaction against extremist infiltration and subversion—including the propagation of Wahhabi/Salafi ideology and its political agenda—can be seen in the publication of Muhammadiyah Central Board Decree Number 149/Kep/I.O/B/2006 and the *fatwa*, or religious edict, issued by the Nahdlatul Ulama's Majlis Bahtsul Masa'il rejecting the alleged theological necessity of an Islamic caliphate, as well as in numerous statements issued by prominent Muslim clerics and national figures regarding the danger of transnational Islamist movements.[1] In fact, a former commander-in-chief of the Indonesian armed forces told one of this book's researchers that "When I was young, extremist threats to the Constitution and Pancasila were posed by non-government actors, such as the Darul Islam/Negara Islam Indonesia [guerilla movements]. But now, radicals have succeeded in infiltrating our government itself, including parliament, and are far more dangerous than before."[2]

These official declarations by the Muhammadiyah and Nahdlatul Ulama (NU), together with detailed information conveyed to our research team by renowned Muslim clerics and national figures, provide a clear indication of just how widespread the extremists'

---

1. The full text of the Muhammadiyah decree, the NU Majlis Bahtsul Masa'il fatwa and other public statements referenced herein are contained in Appendices 1 and 2.
2. Consultative interview conducted on 17 September 2008.

infiltration has become in recent years, and how powerfully their influence has grown. Hopefully, these official decrees—as well as the private and public statements by renowned Indonesian figures presented in this study—will serve as a positive example for Muslims in Indonesia and throughout the world, to mobilize opposition to the Wahhabi/Salafi agenda, and elicit support from leaders and the Muslim community at large, who have not yet been contaminated by Wahhabism, to consciously and deliberately oppose the spread of Islamist movements and their ideology. Simultaneously, this opposition may initiate systematic efforts to publicly expose and discredit the activities of transnational extremist movements, both in Indonesia and throughout the world.

The Subject of This Study

The main issues examined by this study are the origins, ideology, agenda, activities and agents of Islamic movements in Indonesia that may be identified as hard-line or extremist groups; the strategies these groups use in promoting their ideology and agenda; and their successful infiltration of Indonesian society at large, including other, more moderate Islamic groups.

This study also examines whether extremist infiltration of Indonesian Islam has re-awakened the concept of, and sentiment for, the formalization of Islam, which was truly and deeply buried by most Indonesians after the Nahdlatul Ulama, the Muhammadiyah and other Muslim mass organizations embraced Pancasila—together with the non-sectarian Unitary State of the Republic of Indonesia (NKRI)—as the foundation of the Indonesian nation state, and the final consensus regarding the form of government adopted by the multi-religious and multi-ethnic population of the Indonesian archipelago. Acting on the advice of top officials at BIN (Indonesia's State Intelligence Agency) and other experts, moderate Islamic groups were included as subjects in this study, in order to ascertain to what extent these mass organizations have been infiltrated, and influenced, by extremist agents.

Operational Definitions

For the purposes of this study, we have created operational definitions of both extremist and moderate Islam, as follows:

Extremist Islam: classified as either an individual, or organization.

- Individual extremists are those who have an absolutist understanding of religion; are intolerant of differing religious views and beliefs; either personally act to compel, or justify the use of force to compel, others to act in accordance with their belief system; hate and/or view as enemies those who hold different religious views; support the use of government authority and/or private force to restrict the religious freedom of others; justify the use of violence against those who believe or worship differently; reject Pancasila as the ideological basis of the Indonesian state; and/or, wish to establish an Islamic state or caliphate.
- Extremist organizations are those consisting largely of individuals who have the above-mentioned characteristics, and an organizational mission and vision that shares these characteristics and is intolerant of differences, whether explicitly stated or implicit/hidden.

Moderate Islam: classified as either an individual, or organization.

- Moderate individuals are those who accept and value differing beliefs as a blessing to life; do not want to force others to adopt their personal beliefs, whether directly or through government compulsion; reject any and all use of violence in the name of God; believe that religious freedom is guaranteed by Indonesia's constitution; and accept Pancasila and the Unitary State of the Republic of Indonesia as the final consensus and foundation of national life, in order to protect the variety of cultural and religious expressions that exist in the Indonesian archipelago.
- Moderate organizations are those consisting largely of individuals who share the above-mentioned characteristics, and

an organizational mission and vision that accept Pancasila and the Unitary State of the Republic of Indonesia (NKRI) as the final consensus and foundation of national life.

Purpose of the Study

The threat that Islamist movements pose to the Unitary State of the Republic of Indonesia (NKRI), and Pancasila, is the responsibility not merely of government officials, but also the Indonesian people as a whole, especially in our current era of democracy and reform. Political freedom has given us the power, and responsibility, to directly confront the afore-mentioned threat.

Academically, the purpose of this study was to ascertain, highlight and provide demonstrable evidence regarding the origins, ideology and activities of extremist groups in Indonesia, and to identify and understand the views held by agents of these extremist groups regarding specific social, political and religious issues.

In terms of practical objectives, it is hoped that the results of this study will serve as a major stepping stone in the struggle against transnational Islamist movements and their totalitarian agenda, in Indonesia and throughout the world—mobilizing both opinion leaders and Muslims in general, who have not yet been contaminated by Wahhabi/Salafi ideology, to consciously oppose the continued spread of extremist doctrine.

At the same time, this study aims to highlight the activities of extremist movements, which represent a critical factor in the spread of Wahhabi/Salafi ideology in Indonesia and throughout the world.

Issues Examined By the Study

Given the background described above, we designed this study in order to map out and answer a number of questions, as follows:

1. What are the actual views of extremist agents regarding current social, political and religious issues in Indonesia?
2. What is the current "map" of transnational Islamist movements and their accomplices operating in Indonesia?
3. What agendas do these extremist groups promote, and how

are their agendas related to Indonesia's current problems?

4. What strategies do radical groups employ in promoting their agendas, and infiltrating their agents into other Muslim organizations and society at large?

5. What relationship exists between local extremist groups and transnational Islamist movements from the Middle East?

6. What is the relationship between extremist groups and moderate Islamic organizations?

7. Have extremist groups succeeded in influencing the two largest Islamic organizations in Indonesia, i.e., the Nahdlatul Ulama and the Muhammadiyah?

8. Is it true that numerous mosques and educational institutions have been infiltrated and employed by radical groups to propagate their ideology?

9. What are the relationships between various radical groups, and how are their networks structured?

Methodology

Two distinct but integrated teams of researchers performed the investigation and analysis contained in this study, which they conducted separately. We refer to these as the "Jakarta Team" and the "Yogya Team," respectively.

The Jakarta Team consulted with moderate Muslim clerics, intellectuals and prominent national figures from a variety of fields, concerning domestic, social, political and religious issues, and especially matters pertaining to the activities of extremist movements within their particular field of expertise. The Jakarta Team also conducted extensive research of existing literature in the field of Islamist radicalism, in order to ascertain the ideological and practical relationships that exist among various extremist movements in Indonesia and the rest of the world, and the Nahdlatul Ulama's and Muhammadiyah's response to extremist infiltration. The Jakarta Team was formally designated as the Consultative and Literature Research Team. Members of this team included C. Holland Taylor, Kyai Haji Hodri Ariev, Dr. Ratno Lukito, Niluh Dipomanggolo, and Ahmad Gaus AF., all acting under the direction of His Excellency Kyai Haji Abdurrahman Wahid, the former president of Indonesia and long-time chairman of the Nahdlatul Ulama (1984 – 99).

The Yogya Team consisted of researchers who conducted a series of in-depth interviews with 591 radical activists and their sympathizers in 24 districts and 17 provinces throughout Indonesia (see map at the end of this chapter). The Yogya Team was formally designated as the Field Research Team. Its members included Dr. Ratno Lukito, Dr. Zuly Qodir, Dr. Agus Nuryatna, and Dr. Rizal Panggabean, who supervised an additional 27 other field researchers, many of them professors and/or lecturers at a network of Islamic State Universities and Institutes throughout Indonesia. The 31 members of this Field Research team acted under the direction of Prof. Dr. Abdul Munir Mulkhan, who served as Chairman of the Yogya Team, and Dr. Sukardi Rinakit, who served as an adviser.

In brief, the "respondents" interviewed by the Yogya Team were all hardline activists, or sympathizers who had been strongly influenced by radical movements. On the other hand, the "sources" with whom the Jakarta Team consulted were primarily moderate figures opposed to the spread of Islamist ideology. Although the Yogya and Jakarta teams interviewed entirely different classes of respondents (i.e., extremists, and key figures opposed to extremism), their research combined to produce an unparalleled portrait of Islamist infiltration of Indonesian society.

The primary role of the Jakarta Team was to augment and complete the field research conducted by the Yogya Team, through consultation with top *ulama* (religious scholars), intellectuals and high-ranking government officials who are deeply concerned by the threat Islamist movements pose to Pancasila, the Basic Constitution of 1945 and the Unitary State of the Republic of Indonesia. However, it should be noted that because the field research represents only a portion of this entire study, the Yogya team is "academically responsible" only for the results of its field investigations, which constitute a significant portion of chapters III and IV of this book, "The Ideology and Agenda of Extremist Movements in Indonesia" and "The Infiltration of Indonesian Islam by Extremist Agents."

Overall responsibility for the study lies with the Jakarta Team, acting under the supervision of Kyai Haji Abdurrahman Wahid, who is LibForAll Foundation's patron, co-founder and a member of its board of directors.

a. Consultative and Literature Research
For this study, the Jakarta Team collected extensive data connected to the issue of extremist agents' infiltration of society from a variety of sources, both written and unwritten.

- Written sources include the product of past research on similar topics; relevant books and articles; and documents related to this issue, whether published or unpublished, including those produced by the Nahdlatul Ulama and Muhammadiyah.
- Unwritten sources: consultations with Muslim clerics, leaders of moderate Islamic organizations such as the NU and Muhammadiyah, educators, leaders of political parties, high ranking government officials, military officers, businessmen and the press.

The purpose of studying various written materials concerning this subject was to enrich the information obtained from field and consultative research; verify the accuracy of data and information received from other sources; and to observe patterns of continuity and change in the development of extremist movements.

Meanwhile, the consultative phase of research was conducted in order to obtain first-hand information regarding extremist infiltration of Indonesian society from moderate Muslim leaders who have direct, personal knowledge of these developments, and also to request said leaders' advice and recommendations regarding the issues covered by this book. Major figures from virtually every sector of Indonesian society share similar concerns about the ongoing infiltration of extremist ideology and agents within Indonesian Islam, and agree that this infiltration has become a thorn in our sides, disrupting social harmony and threatening to destroy not only Pancasila, but also the Basic Constitution of 1945 and the Unitary State of the Republic of Indonesia (NKRI) itself.

b. Field Research
The Yogya Team conducted its field research using qualitative methods. This qualitative gathering of data occurred by means of in-depth interviews with individual respondents, each of whom were interviewed as many as 3 to 5 times by the researcher assigned to their district. These in-depth interviews were conducted in order to obtain the necessary level of detailed information desired from respondents. In order to verify and augment the results of its field research, the Yogya Team also employed secondary data, consisting of previously-conducted research whose topics correlated with the primary themes of this investigation.

After obtaining data from their interviews with extremist agents and sympathizers, researchers transcribed this data and sent the resulting transcripts to the management team's office in Yogyakarta. The management team analyzed this information, and also specifically invited other analytical experts to review and assess the results. To further enrich their analysis, the monitoring team—which consisted of university scholars, activists and experts on radical Islam—also conducted direct field observation, in order to verify each of the individual researchers' activities in their respective regions, and to observe the research as it actually occurred in the field.

Field Research
a. The Yogya Team and Field Research Locations
In order to analyze the rather complex issues researched in this study, we engaged 27 field researchers from a network of Islamic State Universities and Institutes, the substantial majority of whom had either Masters degrees or PhDs. These researchers' activities were coordinated by a team of experts,

which consisted of six people including the head of the Field Research Team, Prof. Dr. Abdul Munir Mulkhan of Sunan Kalijaga Islamic State University in Yogyakarta, who is also a member of Indonesia's National Commission for Human Rights (Komnas HAM). Dr. Sukardi Rinakit, a prominent public intellectual affiliated with the Soegeng Sarjadi Syndicate, served as advisor. Field research was conducted in 24 cities/regions spread across 17 of Indonesia's 33 provinces, on the islands of Sumatra, Java, Madura, Kalimantan, Sulawesi, Ambon and Lombok, with 591 respondents deliberately chosen for the purposes of this study (purposive sampling).

The various cities/regions were selected based upon the known presence and activities of radical movements within their respective geographic bounds. Extremist groups were found to be active not only in conflict-prone areas like Poso, Ambon and Aceh,[3] but also in areas that appear stable and secure, such as the capital city of Jakarta, Bogor, Bandung, Pekalongan, Yogyakarta, Malang, Pamekasan, Medan and numerous other regions.

b. Respondents' Characteristics

The respondents interviewed in this field research were selected based upon their functional positions in their respective extremist groups. A number of them held positions such as chairman, secretary or public relations (official spokesman) within a particular organization or group; others were "ordinary" members of an extremist group, but had close emotional ties with their leaders and were trusted members of the organization in question.

The extremist agents who became participants of this field re-

---

3. [Translator's note: Poso, in Central Sulawesi, was the scene of violent Muslim-Christian conflict for a number of years after the fall of Suharto. Ambon, in the fabled Spice Islands, was the center of a vicious Muslim-Christian conflict that cost approximately 10,000 lives, and left another 500,000 homeless, between 1999 and 2002. The restive province of Aceh was the site of a decades-long separatist rebellion, which ended only with the devastating tsunami of 2005.]

search were, in general, "white collar" professionals, and included government employees, university professors, university students, teachers, businessmen, regional legislators (DPRD), college deans and local chairmen of political parties. In all, the 591 respondents were actively involved in 58 local and national organizations, either as leaders or as members that exert influence upon the policies of their respective organizations. These 58 organizations include several moderate Islamic mass organizations that have been heavily infiltrated by extremist agents.

The extremist agents interviewed for this study maintain continuous communication with society at large, utilizing every form of mass media that they can exploit to propagate their ideology. The propagation of this ideology can be observed in some detail, through the successful infiltration of hard-line agents in traditionally moderate Islamic organizations such as the Muhammadiyah and Nahdlatul Ulama, and in schools, universities, mosques, government ministries, private workplaces, etc.

The Field Research Team reported that 63% of respondents functioned as core leaders within the extremist organization(s) where they were currently active as members, and only 7% had the status of "average member." Viewed from the perspective of their location and wider network, the organizations with which respondents were involved may be divided into either local or national organizations. We define a local organization as one without branches or networks in other regions, and thus confined to the area where the respondent resided, or nearby areas. We define a national organization as one with headquarters in a particular city, and far-flung branches in other regions.

Another prominent characteristic of respondents that should be noted is that of *dual membership*, whereby a respondent maintained simultaneous memberships in both a moderate and an extremist group. Nearly all of the field researchers encountered this *dual membership* phenomenon, which was especially prevalent in the Muhammadiyah community. This demonstrates that extremist groups have already engaged in systematic infiltration of the Muhammadiyah and NU. They are conducting guerrilla-style campaigns to transform the Muhammadiyah and NU from moderate

Islamic organizations into radical movements, remade in the image of the extremist organizations that are infiltrating them.

c. List of Organizations

The names of the 58 Islamic organizations in which extremist respondents were actively involved are as follows:

- DDI (Darul Dakwah wal-Irsyad) [The wal-Irsyad Mission]
- DDII (Dewan Dakwah Islamiyah Indonesia) [Indonesian Council for Islamic Proselytism]
- FKUB (Forum Kerukunan Umat Beragama) [Harmony of Religious Communities Forum]
- FPMI (Front Pembela Masyarakat Islam) [Front for the Defense of Islamic Society]
- FORMIS (Forum Mahasiswa Islam) [Islamic Students Forum]
- FPI (Front Pembela Islam) [Front for the Defense of Islam]
- FSPUI (Forum Silaturrahmi Perjuangan Umat Islam) [The Friendship Forum (to Support) the Muslim Community's Struggle]
- FSRMP (Forum Silaturrahmi Remaja Masjid Panggungharjo) [The Friendship Forum of Panggungharjo Mosque Youths]
- FTPS (Forum Tokoh Peduli Syariat) [Forum of Leaders Who Care About Shari'a]
- FUI (Forum Umat Islam) [Muslim Community Forum]
- FUI (Forum Ukhuwah Islamiyah) [Islamic Brotherhood Forum]
- FUUI (Forum Ulama Umat Islam) [Muslim Community Clerics Forum]
- FUUU (Forum Ulama Untuk Umat) [The Clerics' Forum for the Islamic Community]
- GERPI (Gerakan Pemuda Perti) [Indonesian Youth Educational Movement]
- GMM (Gerakan Muslim Minangkabau) [Minangkabau Muslim Movement]
- GPI (Gerakan Pemuda Islam) [Islamic Youth Movement]
- HIDMI (Himpunan Dai Muda Indonesia) [Association of Young Indonesian Proselytizers]
- HIMA PUI (Himpunan Mahasiswa Persatuan Umat Islam) [Association of United Muslim Students]
- HIMA (Himpunan Mahasiswa) [Male University Students Association]

- HIMI   (Himpunan Mahasiswi) [Female University Students Association]
- HMI   (Himpunan Mahasiswa Islam) [Islamic Students Association]
- HPI   (Himpunan Pemuda Insafuddin) [Insafuddin Youth Association]
- HTI   (Hizbut Tahrir Indonesia) [The Indonesian Party of Purity]
- HUDA   (Himpunan Ulama Dayak Aceh) [Dayak Aceh Clerics Association]
- ICMI   (Ikatan Cendikiawan Muslim Indonesia) [Association of Indonesian Muslim Intellectuals]
- IKADI   (Ikatan Dai Indonesia) [Association of Indonesian Muslim Proselytizers]
- IMM   (Ikatan Mahasiswa Muhammadiyah) [Muhammadiyah College Students Association]
- IPM   (Ikatan Pelajar Muhammadiyah) [Muhammadiyah Grade School Students Association]
- IRM   (Ikatan Remaja Muhammadiyah) [Muhammadiyah Youth Association]
- JMAF   (Jamaah Masjid AR Fachruddin) [Congregation of AR Fachruddin Mosque]
- JMF   (Jamaah Masjid Fisipol) [Congregation of Fisipol Mosque]
- KAMCI   (Keluarga Mahasiswa Cimahi) [Cimahi Student Family]
- KAMMI   (Kesatuan Aksi Mahasiswa Muslim Indonesia) [Unified Action of Indonesian Muslim Students Association]
- KNPI   (Komite Nasional Pemuda Indonesia) [Indonesian National Youth Committee]
- KPPRA   (Komite Persiapan Partai Rakyat Aceh) [The Aceh People's Party Preparation Committee]
- KPPSI   (Komite Persiapan Penegakan Syariat Islam) [Committee to Prepare for the Establishment of Islamic Law]
- KPSI   (Komite Penegakan Syariat Islam) [Committee to Establish Islamic Law]
- LDII   (Lembaga Dakwah Islam Indonesia) [Institute for Islamic Proselytism in Indonesia]
- LDK   (Lembaga Dakwah Kampus) [Institute for Campus Proselytism]
- LDM   (Lembaga Dakwah Mahasiswa) [Institute for College Student Proselytism]

- LPIK   (Lembaga Pengembangan Ilmu dan Kajian) [Institute for the Development of Science and Study]
- MMI   (Majelis Mujahidin Indonesia) [Indonesian Council of Holy Warriors]
- Muhammadiyah
- MUI   (Majelis Ulama Indonesia) [Council of Indonesian Religious Scholars]
- NU   (Nahdlatul Ulama)
- PBB   (Partai Bulan Bintang) [Crescent Moon and Star Party]
- PBR   (Partai Bintang Reformasi) [Star of Reformation Party]
- PERSIS   (Persatuan Islam) [Islamic Unity]
- PI   (Partai Islam) [Party of Islam]
- PII   (Pelajar Islam Indonesia) [Indonesian Muslim Students]
- PKPUS   (Pos Keadilan Peduli Ummat Sumatera Barat) [Justice Association for Those Concerned about West Sumatran Society]
- PKS   (Partai Keadilan Sejahtera) [Justice and Prosperity Party]
- PMII   (Pergerakan Mahasiswa Islam Indonesia) [Indonesian Islamic Students Movement]
- PSII   (Partai Sarikat Islam Indonesia) [Indonesian Islamic Union Party]
- PUSAKA   (Pusat Studi Antar Komunitas) [Center for Inter-Communal Study]
- RTA   (Rabithah Thaliban Aceh) [Aceh Taliban Federation]
- SI   (Sarekat Islam) [Islamic Union]
- UKMI   (Unit Kegiatan Mahasiswa Islam) [Unit for Islamic Student Activity]

Table 1. Research Locations & the Corresponding Number of Respondents

No.	Region	Number of Respondents
1	Aceh	33
2	Medan	34
3	Padang	33
4	Palembang	16
5	Lampung Timur	33

No.	Region	Number of Respondents
6 & 7	Tangerang and Jakarta	42
8	Bogor	24
9	Bandung	33
10	Pekalongan	25
11	Solo	30
12	Klaten	2
13	Yogyakarta	48
14	Lamongan	30
15	Kediri	24
16	Malang	26
17	Banyuwangi	6
18	Madura	7
19	Lombok	20
20	Balikpapan	26
21	Makasar	24
22	Poso	27
23	Gorontalo	24
24	Ambon	24

Field Research Locations

Chapter II

THE ORIGINS AND GLOBAL SPREAD OF WAHHABI/MUSLIM BROTHERHOOD IDEOLOGY

Wahhabism

The Honorable Prophet Muhammad (saw.)[1] once mentioned that his followers would be divided into 73 groups, of which all but one will go to hell.[2] Those who will be saved are "the ones who adhere to my *Sunnah* (example) and the followers of my companions" (*mâ ana 'alaih wa ash-hâbî*). This group later became known as *ahlussunnah wal-jamâ'ah* (*aswaja*), or Sunni Muslims—i.e., those who hold firm to the Prophet's wisdom and the community of the Prophet's companions. Ever since the time of the Prophet, Muslim clerics have earnestly strived to identify the character of this *aswaja*, or Sunni Islam. Over time, the fundamental character of Sunni Islam—in the context of social interaction—came to be summarized as *al-tawassuth wal-i'tdâl*, i.e., moderate and consistent behavior.

This prophetic *hadith* is immensely popular, because it addresses the issue of salvation in the afterlife. This is also why two entirely different versions of the hadith emerged, concerning whether only

---

1. [Translator's note: when Muslims say or write the name of Muhammad, they usually follow his name with the phrase *sall Allahu `alayhi wa sallam* (Arabic: صلى الله عليه وسلم), which means, "May God bless him and grant him peace." This is often abbreviated as "SAW." or "saw."]

2. Another version states: "All will be saved, except one." However, this statement is considered weak (*dla'îf*). Read in: *Nazhm al-Mutanâtsir*, volume 1, p. 47; compare with: Abû Nu'ain Ahmad ibn 'Abdillah al-Isbahânî, *Hilyat al-Auliyâ'* (Beirut: Dâr al-Kutub al-'Arabî, 1405 H [2003 C.E.]), volume IX, p. 242.

one of the 73 groups would be saved, or condemned. In conjunction with this issue of salvation, some groups claim that they alone grasp the truth, and will be saved in the hereafter. In asserting their claim to exclusive possession of the truth and salvation, their members readily brand others as infidels, in order to emphasize that they and they alone are in possession of the real truth—the most faithful, the most Islamic, and the most assured of eternal salvation. They forget that salvation is not determined by such claims, but rather, by self-transcendence and religious sincerity... i.e., by completely surrendering oneself and one's ego to the Divine, and thus living a life devoted only to God—Pure and Exalted is He![3] To express this in negative terms, salvation stems not from asserting exclusive truth claims, but from dissolving the bonds of attachment to one's own ego and carnal desires, through Divine grace.

On another occasion, the Prophet Muhammad (saw.) told his followers that "Anyone who proclaims his brother to be an infidel, without offering a true and compelling explanation for his statement, is himself an infidel[4] (*man kaffara akhâhu bi-ghairi ta'wîl—fa-huwa kamâ qâla*)."[5] Or as conveyed in a different tradition, "If anyone proclaims his brother to be an infidel, then surely one of

---

3. [Translator's note: when Muslims speak or write the name of God, they usually follow this with the phrase *subhanahu wa-ta'ala* (Arabic: سبحانه وتعالى), which means, "Pure and Exalted is He (Allah)." The phrase is often abbreviated as "swt."]

4. "An infidel is anyone whose heart is dead. Etymologically, the word infidel means "closed," in the sense of disavowing or denying. For that reason, what is meant by infidel is to deny the Truth and seal your heart against It, claiming that you are right and the truth resides with you. So if anyone disavows the Truth and shuts their heart against It, they are an infidel. To lie is to deny what exists; what we know exists; to disavow reality. For that reason, it's inaccurate to refer to most people who do not embrace Islam as "infidels," because infidelity means to disavow the good (which all people acknowledge, whatever their religion), and to deliberately close oneself off from embracing it. And what actually covers the Truth, according to Islam, is sin, arrogance and qualities which prevent people from seeing anything but themselves." ~ Maryam Ishaq al-Khalifa Sharief, Shadhili Sufi figure from Omdurman, Sudan, speaking in: *Ocean of Revelations: Understanding Islam as a Blessing for All Creation*, Episode 3: "Faith Communities," Program Supervisor: Kyai Haji Mustofa Bisri, ©LibForAll Foundation 2009).

5. Hadith conveyed by Imam Bukhari, *Shahih al-Bukhari*, Volume XX, Chapter 73 (Egypt: Mauqif Wizarat al-Auqaf, undated), p. 259.

the two is indeed an infidel" (*man kaffara akhâhu—fa-qad bâ'a bihâ ahaduhâ*).[6] Thus, from whichever point of view one considers these two sayings of the Prophet, one who is a true muslim,[7] within and without, will never proclaim another Muslim to be an infidel.

In the history of Islam, the first occasion on which Muslims systematically accused their fellow Muslims of being infidels was when members of the *Khawârij* sect deserted the Prophet's son-in-law and Caliph, 'Ali ibn Abi Thalib, in conjunction with his accepting a truce in the Shiffin war against Mu'awiyah. Disagreeing with the truce, the Khawârij condemned as infidels anyone and everyone whose opinion differed from their own—whether they were supporters of 'Ali or of Mu'awiyah—and proceeded to massacre any of the accused "infidels" they could touch.[8] Their slogan, "the law belongs to God alone," negates the role of human reason in comprehending divine revelations, while simultaneously conflating the Khawârij's own limited, superficial understanding with the Truth itself.[9]

---

6. Hadith conveyed by Ahmad ibn Hanbal, *Masnad Ahmad*, Volume XIII, Chapter Masnad 'Abdullah ibn 'Umar, (Egypt: Mauqif Wizarat al-Auqaf, undated), p. 455.

7. [Translator's note: Kyai Haji Abdurrahman Wahid, like most Muslim clerics grounded in the spiritual traditions of Islam, distinguishes between a "muslim" (i.e., one who is truly surrendered to the Divine, in a state of complete self-transcendence) and a "Muslim" (one who professes the formal religion of Islam, but who may or may not have realized, and lived, its essence). Similarly, President Wahid and Muslims like him throughout the world distinguish between "islam" (the actual state of ego annihilation and moment-by-moment awareness of, and surrender to, Divine Will) and the formal religion known as Islam. According to this definition, muslims who practice islam may or may not actually profess the formal religion of Islam. Significantly, the Qur'an itself uses the terms "muslim" and "islam" primarily in this sense, and not to refer to the followers of Muhammad, or the formal religion of Islam.]

8. [Translator's note: the Khawârij assassination of 'Ali—while he was at prayer in a mosque—is known to virtually all Muslims, producing intense aversion for the *Khawârij* among traditional Sunni and Shi'a Muslims alike.]

9. The Khawârij and their ideological successors throughout history have mistakenly believed that their understanding of religious teachings—and their inevitably flawed, human interpretation of holy scriptures—are endowed with an Absolute Truth that in fact pertains only to the religious teachings and scriptures themselves. The Khawârij and their contemporary successors are thus afflicted by an epistemological illness that renders differences of opinion counterproduc-

The actions of the Khawârij established an appalling precedent for future generations of Muslims. Their cruel and destructive behavior not only created political instability, but also undermined the Muslim community's ability to engage in logical reasoning, which corrupt inheritance has been transmitted from generation to generation, up to the present day. Contemporary Muslim clerics generally label anyone who exhibits the abominable behavior of the Khawârij as "neo- Khawârij."

The various depraved characteristics of the Khawârij/neo-Khawârij include: understanding the Qur'an and hadith in a strictly narrow, literal and close-minded way; eagerly condemning as infidels all whose views or behavior differ from their own; and not hesitating to butcher anyone they regard as an infidel. Each of these appalling characteristics became prominent features of the Wahhabi movement, which appeared in the Arabian Peninsula in the 18th century. Admittedly, Wahhabism cannot be categorized as an historical continuation of the Khawârij. As a matter of fact, Wahhabism was a new phenomenon in the history of Islam, without precise theological precedent.[10] This is due to the fact that in the 1400-year history of Islamic thought, Wahhabism does not hold a position of importance, and indeed is clearly marginal, from an intellectual perspective. (Wahhabism became regionally—and then globally—significant not because of any theologically profound or valuable insights contained within its ideology, but rather, because of the political power of Ibn Saud and the enormous wealth of his modern successors.) In addition, scholarly researchers and historians of Islam view Wahhabism as a unique phenomenon that is divorced from the great streams of Islamic thought, and movements, that preceded it. In fact, early Sunni Muslim leaders who encountered Wahhabism flatly proclaimed that Wahhabi ideology and its accompanying military/political movement were not part of *ahlussunnah wal-jamâ'ah* (the Sunni Muslim community).[11]

Wahhabism is a rigid and violent religious sect, which devotes

tive. Whereas in fact, a famous saying of the Prophet (saw.) states that "Differences of opinion among my people are a blessing" (*ikhtilâfu ummatî rahmah*).
10. Hamid Algar, *Wahhabism: A Critical Essay*, New York: Islamic Publications International, 2002, p. 10.
11. Ibid., pp. 2-3.

itself to the teachings of Muhammad ibn 'Abdul Wahab. His father, 'Abdul Wahab, was a judge (*qâdî*) in the town of 'Uyaynah,
who adhered to the *madzhab*, or Islamic school of law, established
by Ahmad ibn Hanbal. Ibn 'Abdul Wahab was born in 1703/1115
in 'Uyaynah, which lies in the Najd region, a vast desert area in the
eastern portion of current Saudi Arabia. Comparing it to Yemen
and Syria, the Prophet once said that nothing would emerge from
Najd, except *fitnah* (false accusations) and Satan (*al-zalâzil wal-fitan
wa qarn al-syaitân*). Perhaps the Prophet's statement had nothing to
do with Wahhabism; however, it is clear that the Najd was one of
the last areas on the Arabian Peninsula to accept Islam, and also
was home to Musailamah al-Kadzdzab, a false prophet and enemy
of early Islam.

'Utsman ibn 'Abdullah ibn Bisyr, a standard Saudi historian,
praised Ibn 'Abdul Wahab as a man who received God's blessing,
which enabled him to perceive the truth amid complex problems,
and to guide others to the true path. On the other hand, Ibn 'Abdul Wahab's own father and elder brother detected something sus-
piciously wrong in the founder of Wahhabism's religious thought
right from the beginning. According to historians, 'Abdul Wahab
was fired from his position as a judge and ordered to depart from
'Uyaynah in the year 1726/1139 because of his son's odd and dangerous behavior. 'Utsman avoids relating the details of a heated argument that occurred among Ibn 'Abdul Wahab, his father and his
older brother, by diplomatically stating that it was merely a "conversation among them" (*waqa'a bainahu wa baina abîhi kalâm*)[12], but
Sulaiman ibn 'Abdul Wahab, the founder of Wahhabism's elder
brother, later criticized his younger sibling and wrote a long document rejecting his ideology—*al-Shawâ'iq al-Ilâhiyyah fî al-radd 'alâ
al-Wahhâbiyyah* (*A Strong Warning from Allah to Reject Wahhabi Ideology*).[13]

12. *'Utsman ibn 'Abdullah ibn Bisyr, Unwân al-Majd fî Târîkh al-Najd*, (undated) p. 8.
13. The latest edition of *al-Shawâ'iq al-Ilâhiyyah fî al-radd 'alâ al-Wahhâbiyyah* (*A
Strong Warning from Allah to Reject Wahhabi Ideology*) has been printed as a single
book with a similar document written by Sayyid Ahmad ibn Zaini Dahlan, the
Grand Mufti of Mecca at the time, entitled *Al-Durar al-Sunniyyah fî al-Radd 'alâ
al-Wahhâbiyyah* (*The Sunni Diamond's Rejection of Wahhabi Ideology*), which can be read
in: 'Abdullah al-Qashimi, *Al-Tsaurah al-Wahhâbiyyah* (*The Wahhabi Rebellion*), Köln,

Ibn 'Abdul Wahab's extreme, rigid and violent ideology—
which has been preserved and propagated by his followers (known
as Wahhabis) up to the present day—is the product of a crude and
literalistic understanding of the sources of Islamic teaching. This
caused him to reject rationalism, Islamic tradition and the rich and
varied treasures of Islamic thought. In regards to polemic, Christians, Shi'ites, Sufis and Mu'tazilah (a school of thought within
Islam that emphasizes rational thought) were Wahab's primary
targets. However, this does not imply that those unaffiliated with
any of above-mentioned groups were safe from harsh critiques and
threats, based on the Wahhabis' literalistic interpretation of Holy
Scriptures (i.e., the Qur'an and Sunnah).

Wahhabi fundamentalism transformed Holy Scripture into a
closed *corpus*, by forbidding any forms of interpretation other than
the literalistic one favored by Ibn 'Abdul Wahab. This crude understanding divorced the Holy Scriptures from the context of the
time of their revelation, as well as from the current age in which
they are read. As a result, the scriptures, and ultimately Islam itself,
became divorced and no longer communicative with the lives of
their believers. In the hands of Ibn 'Abdul Wahab, Islam—which
in its origins was extremely sensitive to, and appreciative of, the
needs of its followers—was transformed into an unfeeling, violent
and merciless religion.

From the perspective of Ibn 'Abdul Wahab, the primary goal
of this literalism may have been to avoid having to address the
complex ideas and practices associated with Islamic law, theology
and mysticism, which had continued to evolve ever since Muhammad's death. However, to imagine that every individual or society
throughout the world can or will practice Islam in accordance with
a literal reading of the holy book and hadith, with virtually no
influence from the vast scholarly traditions of Islam, or from local
cultures, is completely unrealistic, and represents nothing but a
wild dream. Close-minded literalism stems, in most cases, from a
reader's inability to grasp the complex nature of social reality, and
integrate this with the equally complex and sublime messages contained within religious teachings. As a result, everything is adjusted

Germany: Al-Kamel Verlag, 2006.

downwards, to accord with a reader's own ability (or lack thereof) to understand and absorb what is written in scripture. In other words, the vast and sublime message of religion founders upon the shoals of a reader's limited ability to comprehend, and his psychological/emotional rigidity.

Ibn 'Abdul Wahab's close-minded literalism cannot not be equated with—for example—Ibn 'Arabi's open-minded literalism. Close-minded literalism isolates and divorces the meaning of a text or texts from various other interpretations that may be equally correct, and this represents not only a reduction, but also a distortion of the text's original message.[14] Meanwhile, open-minded literalism represents a search for the meaning of a text or texts in the broadest sense possible, while continuing to recognize and acknowledge its literal meaning, without ever being constrained by one's own rigidity.[15]

Closed-minded literalism, a la Wahhabism, is actually afflicted by an acute epistemological deviation. A Wahhabi can never

---

14. [Translator's note: for a Christian view similar to that of Ibn Arabi, see St. Bonaventura (1221 – 1274; Italian Scholastic philosopher, cardinal, mediaeval writer and contemplative, known as 'the Seraphic Doctor'): "Now that which is one according to the literal sense, is however three according to the mystical and spiritual sense. For in all the books of Holy writ in addition to the literal sense, which the words express outwardly, there is a conception of the threefold spiritual sense, namely the allegorical, whereby we learn what we should believe concerning Godhead and manhood; the moral, whereby we learn how we should live; and the anagogical, whereby we learn in what manner we must cling to God. Whence the Holy Writ teaches these things, namely the eternal begetting and incarnation of Christ, the order of living, and the union of God and the soul."]

15. To illustrate this point, Ibn 'Abdul Wahab's concept of a *kâfir*, or infidel, is completely different from that of Ibn 'Arabi. For Wahab, the infidel is an enemy of devout Muslims, and thus permissible to kill. While for Ibn 'Arabi, infidelity is the condition of being closed to or refusing the truth, or even the Source of Truth itself. This refusal may be caused by arrogance, or by ignorance. For this reason, Ibn Arabi maintains that infidels may not be branded as enemies, much less prescribed or killed. According to Ibn 'Arabi, infidel may also mean to be "closed off to" anything but Allah (swt.). In this context, infidel actually represents one of the highest levels of sainthood. There is a well-known joke in the Sufi tradition that whoever has been branded an infidel by 41 people, and yet remains patient and does not resist, let alone accuse others of being infidels, is a true saint.

see, let alone understand, any form of truth other than the "literal truth" that he or she has discovered, and still remain a Wahhabi. The very fact of such understanding would begin to release the Wahhabi from his mental prison. Yet in the absence of this release, Wahhabis can never understand the immense subtlety and complexity of Holy Scriptures, let alone their relationship to the complexities of social reality. As an epistemological disease, this kind of close-mindedness often gives rise to one-sided truth claims, accompanied by rejection and condemnation of anything and anyone that differs from the individual who perceives himself to be in exclusive possession of the truth.

In reality, one-sided truth claims that rely on theological assertions—accompanied by the condemnation of others as infidels—represent immature religious behavior, and evidence a profound lack of humility (islâm). One possessed of mature religious faith, and humility, is never disturbed by the fact that others hold different beliefs. Indeed, such people are prepared to exchange views with others in an open-minded way, in the search for ultimate truth. The Qur'an itself emphasizes that differences are a test, and need not be rendered uniform. The rejection of differences is a direct manifestation of the epistemological disease and deviation caused by closed-minded literalism.

Every conclusion derived from the use of an unsound methodology will surely give rise to unhealthy actions as well. In the case of Wahhabism, the distortion and reduction of Islam's sublime message has led to actions highly destructive of the spiritual and intellectual traditions of Islam itself. This, in turn, has produced distortions and social and cultural barbarity directed not only towards Muslim societies, but global society as a whole, and indeed evoked violence directed against the very teachings of Islam itself.

In his development, Ibn 'Abdul Wahhab grew impatient with the process of dialogue for bringing about change, and concluded that mere words were not enough (lâ yughnî al- qaul).[16] He then attempted to produce change through direct action.[17]

16. 'Utsman ibn 'Abdullah ibn Bisyr, Unwân al-Majd fî Târîkh al-Najd (undated), p. 7.
17. In this regard, Wahhabis base their actions on the hadith concerning amr

When his father died in 1740/1153, Ibn 'Abdul Wahab returned to 'Uyaynah and received support from 'Utsman ibn Mu'ammar, the local ruler. This support gave him the freedom and power to employ more than words against those he considered to deviate from the "true" teaching of Islam (one must emphasize that in reality, the deviation in question was from Ibn 'Abdul Wahab's rigid *understanding* of Islam). Mu'ammar provided 600 soldiers to escort Ibn 'Abdul Wahab and his followers while conducting their "actions." Wahab also strengthened his support from 'Uyaynah's ruler by marrying Mu'ammar's aunt, al-Jauhara.

The first act of Wahhabi violence consisted of destroying the tomb of Zaid ibn al-Khaththab, a companion of the Prophet and a blood relative of 'Umar ibn al-Khaththab. Before that, Ibn 'Abdul Wahab had also begun to accuse people of being infidels and apostates, as a prelude to violence directed against them. However, Wahab's enjoyment of patronage from the chief of the local tribe did not last long, because Mu'ammar sensed danger in the expanding Wahhabi movement. For this reason, Ibn 'Abdul Wahab abandoned 'Uyaynah and moved to Dir'iyah where he acquired a new patron, Muhammad ibn Sa'ud, who proved to be a permanent ally. This enduring alliance between the Wahab and Sa'ud families ul-

---

ma'rûf, i.e., *Man ra'â minkum munkaran, fal-yughayyir biyadih, fa-inlam yasthathi' fa-bilisânih, fa-inlam yasthathi' fa-biqalbih, wa dzâlik min adl'âf al-îmân* (If any of you witnesses the commission of evil deeds, he should prevent these with his "hands"; if unable, then with his "tongue"; if incapable of this as well, then he should reject and regret the commission of evil in his heart. This is considered the weakest level of faith.") Wahhabis interpret this hadith literally, and teach that anyone who witnesses the commission of "evil," as they understand this term, must take direct physical action to prevent it; if that's impossible, verbal condemnation and hindrance are sufficient; and if too weak for that, they must regret the evil in their heart. Unlike Wahhabis, Sunni Muslim clerics in general interpret the above hadith as restricting the exercise of physical authority/repression to the ruler/government, and reject the notion that individuals may legitimately engage in vigilante violence. Sunni clerics teach that the second level of obstructing evil, through the apt use of words (which they also interpret to mean "writings"), lies within the purview of wise individuals who possess a depth of religious knowledge. An inability to inspire others to abjure evil, through oral or written means, evidences a weakness in one's own faith. This is because such individuals are either too stupid or foolish to acquire the requisite knowledge, or simply lazy and unconcerned about the well-being of society at large.

timately led to the creation of the modern Wahhabi Kingdom of Saudi Arabia.

Muhammad Ibn Sa'ud was a brilliant politician. He did not squander this invaluable opportunity to achieve his political ambitions, by supporting Ibn 'Abdul Wahab. At first, he asked Wahab not to disrupt the Saudis' habitual collection of annual tribute from the people of Dir'iyah. But instead, Wahab convinced Ibn Sa'ud that *jihad* would produce far greater profit than the tribute he desired. Thus, based on the alliance between Sa'ud and Wahab, the stage was set for wholesale charges of infidelity and apostasy, and widespread acts of violence that would soon bathe the entire Arabian Peninsula in blood.

In the year 1746/1159, Wahab/Sa'ud officially proclaimed jihad against anyone whose understanding of *tauhid* [the Oneness of God] differed from their own. This campaign was launched with accusations of polytheism, apostasy and infidelity. Every Muslim whose understanding or practice of Islam differed from Wahhabism was labeled an apostate, and open warfare not only permitted, but actively required against them, as a religious duty imposed by Wahhabi teachings. Raids, surprise attacks and robberies committed against neighboring "infidels" and "apostates" soon became widespread. According to Wahhabis, the term "Muslim" referred exclusively to themselves, as written in *'Unwân al-Majd fi Târikh al-Najd* (*Resolute Grandeur in the History of Najd*), an official Wahhabi history book.

Approximately 15 years after this proclamation of jihad, Wahhabis had occupied much of the Arabian Peninsula, including Najd, Central Arabia, 'Asir, and Yemen. Muhammad ibn Sa'ud died in 1766/1187 and was succeeded by 'Abdul 'Aziz, who seized Riyadh in 1773/1187, and seventeen years later launched a campaign to conquer the Hijaz region, the site of Mecca and Medina. Muhammad ibn 'Abdul Wahab died in 1791/1206, soon after the war against the rulers of the Hijaz began. Little more than a decade later, Wahhabi teachings were imposed by force of arms upon the inhabitants of the Haramain (Mecca and Medina). Although this initial Wahhabi occupation of the holy sites of Islam was brief, it exerted a great influence not only upon the Hijaz, but also other regions of the Muslim world, including the East Indies.

In the year 1802/1217, the Wahhabis attacked the Shi'ite holy city of Karbala and massacred the majority of its population, including women and children. They also destroyed the tomb of the Prophet Muhammad's grandson, Hussein, and robbed it of all the gold, jewelry and other treasures stored in its sacred precincts. In 1803/1217 the Wahhabis invaded the Hijaz once again, with Ta'if being the first city they attacked. In 1805/1220 they conquered Medina, and in 1806/1220 captured Mecca for the second time. As usual, the Wahhabis forced Muslim clerics to swear loyalty at the point of a sword.

The Haramain occupation lasted approximately six and a half years. This period of unbridled cruelty was characterized by indiscriminate slaughter, and the people of the Haramain were compelled to profess Wahhabi teachings, or face death. The Wahhabis destroyed historical buildings and cemeteries linked to the Prophet and his companions;[18] burned virtually all books other than the Qur'an and Hadith; prohibited the celebration of the Prophet Muhammad's birthday, *Barzanji* (Sufi musical poetry, recited in praise of Muhammad) and the reading of various *mau 'izhah hasanah* hadith before Friday prayers. They also forbade the smoking of tobacco, and even banned coffee.

All this Wahhabi cruelty came to an end when Muhammad 'Ali Pasha, the Ottoman Governor of Egypt, liberated the Haramain under orders from the Sultan in Istanbul. In 1811/1226, 'Ali Pasha landed in Yanbu port, along the Red Sea. By the end of the

18. "Regarding the history of Islamic civilization, it is well known that in recent centuries the Wahhabis have been behind movements that use violence to "command good and forbid evil." When the Wahhabis seized control of Arabia, they destroyed every building or structure that they considered evil. That's why all of Saudi Arabia's Islamic heritage has been wiped out, to the point where there's nothing left. The house where the Prophet lived with his wife Khadijah vanished. The Prophet's place of birth was also destroyed, and there's no trace of it today. But the strange thing is, the palaces and housing complexes of King Abdul Aziz (the founder of modern Saudi Arabia) are still beautifully preserved in Riyadh." ~ Kyai Haji M. Tolchah Hasan, Senior Advisor to the Nahdlatul Ulama and Indonesia's former Minister of Religion, speaking in *Ocean of Revelations: Understanding Islam as a Blessing for All Creation*, Episode 5: "Da'wa (Proselytism)," Program Supervisor: Kyai Haji Mustofa Bisri, ©LibForAll Foundation 2009).

following year he had freed Medina from the Wahhabis, and three months later, he liberated Mecca. The Wahhabis retreated to Najd, where they gathered their forces, but Muhammad 'Ali Pasha continued his campaign against them until he captured Dir'iyah, the Saudi/Wahhabi capital, in 1819/1234. Unfortunately, this Ottoman victory buried Wahhabism for only a few years. In 1832/1248, the Wahhabi cult rose from its tomb to launch a new military expedition against Oman, and forced the Sultan of Muscat to pay annual tribute to Riyadh. The Wahhabis recognized that Mecca and Medina were not only religious centers, but also a never-ending source of revenue, because of Islam's annual pilgrimage and the Haramain's irresistible attraction for Muslims worldwide. Thus, after conquering adjacent regions, the Wahhabis renewed their efforts to control the two holy cities, and in 1925 they finally conquered Mecca and Medina once again—this time, supported by a "treaty of friendship and cooperation" the Saudi ruler had recently signed with the British.

The history of Wahhabism has never been free of doctrinal, cultural and social violence. During the Saudi/Wahhabi conquest of the Arabian Peninsula in the 1920s, as many as 400,000 Muslims—including countless women and children—were either killed outright, executed in public or suffered the amputation of limbs.[19] In addition, their opponents' wives, daughters and property were widely confiscated during war, and every Muslim living in regions conquered by the Wahhabis forced to conform to their ideology, at least outwardly. Wahhabism thus became the new "religion" not only of the Saudi state, but of the holy cities of Islam as well.

In short, from the very outset of the Wahhabi movement, Muhammad ibn Abdul Wahab's followers have joyfully engaged not only in robbery, murder and the abduction of women, but also in the systematic destruction of tombs and historical buildings, and the banning of traditional Muslim practices such as *tawassul* (intercessory prayers directed to Muhammad or various saints), *isti'ana* (prayers for Divine aid, offered by one perceived to be close to God, on behalf of others in attendance); *istighâtsah* (communal prayers led by one perceived to be pure of heart), *syafâ'a* (the successful

---

19. Hamid Algar, op. cit., p. 42.

outcome of intercessory prayers), *tabarruq* (the giving of blessings by one perceived to be close to God), and the visitation of tombs to pray and honor deceased saints. Wahhabis also ban or destroy books that do not support their virulent ideology, and condemn those whose religious practices differ from their own—even though, in reality, these practices are not forbidden by Islam—as polytheists, infidels and apostates.

It is true that whenever they lack the power to force their ideology on others, Wahhabis generally restrict their violence to doctrinal, intellectual and psychological assaults, by accusing others of polytheism, infidelity and apostasy, without actually killing them. However, as soon as they acquire sufficient power, these accusations are followed by physical attacks ranging from beatings to amputations and murder. The Wahhabis refer to their violent acts as *da'wa* (proselytism), *amr ma'ruf nahy munkar* (commanding the good and forbidding evil) and *jihâd*, although these terms, properly understood, lack any violent connotations.[20]

---

20. The term jihad literally means "wholehearted and serious effort" in performing a noble activity, or discharging a duty. In its generic sense the term is neutral. It assumes a connotative meaning only when placed side by side with specific activities. Serious study may be considered jihad, but only because of the seriousness and sincerity of one's effort, and not because of the act of study itself. When the word jihad appears in the context of war, it likewise refers to seriousness and sincerity, rather than to the act of war. In this context, the Prophet Muhammad (saw.) once said, "*Raja'nâ min jihâd al-ashghar ilâ jihâd al-akbar*" ("We have returned from acting seriously (jihad) in a lesser field (i.e., war), and will now turn our attention to acting seriously (jihad) in a far greater field (i.e., striving to overcome the ego and carnal desires)." The Prophet's statement should not be understood as returning from the "lesser war" to the "greater war," but rather, from the "lesser effort" to the "greater effort." Physical struggles such as war require sincere and earnest effort, but not so serious and earnest as the inner, spiritual struggle to control one's lower nature, if one is to triumph in this latter struggle. As the Sufi poet Jalaluddin Rumi wrote, "Deem of small account the lion who breaks the ranks of the enemy; the lion is he who breaks himself." The struggle to promote human rights, the rule of law and justice also represent forms of jihad, when performed with an attitude of complete sincerity. In Islam, as reflected in the hadith quoted above, efforts to subdue one's lower nature are regarded as the "greater jihad" because they require a remarkable degree of self-discipline and awareness. It is in this context that *amr ma'ruf nahy munkar* (enjoining the good and forbidding evil) should be performed. Jihad and *amr ma'ruf nahy munkar* have acquired a filthy and disreputable image in recent years,

In recent years a similar phenomenon has appeared in Indonesia, and it is difficult to deny that there is a causal relationship between this phenomenon and Wahhabism, which is the Kingdom of Saudi Arabia's official state ideology. For a number of years now, this ideology has been systematically propagated throughout Indonesia by Wahhabi agents, backed by enormous financial support from the Saudi Kingdom itself.

The Repudiation of Wahhabism

Before the attacks of 9/11 on the World Trade Center and the Pentagon, the government of Saudi Arabia was actively engaged in financing al-Qaeda, a group that employs armed violence in order to provoke chaos and achieve its destructive aims. Following the events of 9/11, and especially after al-Qaeda unleashed its fury upon the Saudi Kingdom itself, it appears that the Saudi government stopped financing this terrorist movement. However, Saudi Arabia continues to finance the spread of Wahhabi ideology throughout the world (global Wahhabization). Terrorist violence committed through bombings and similar acts are indeed extremely dangerous. However, Wahhabi ideology, with its theological, psychological and intellectual violence—and its goal of committing cultural genocide and dominating other nations—is far more dangerous than bombs.

The Wahhabis' consistent pattern of theological, psychological, cultural and physical violence has caused many *ulama* (religious scholars), and Muslims in general, to realize that what the Wahhabis are striving to promote is *not* Islam. The most favorable interpretation of their actions—which we may derive from Ibn 'Abdul Wahab's original point of view—is that the Wahhabis are striving to propagate a specific *understanding* of Islam that is remarkably violent and extreme. It represents a close-minded and literal understanding of the Truth, and precisely because of this close-mindedness, Wahhabis are convinced that their narrow, superficial grasp

---

because these terms have been appropriated as political jargon and closely linked with the cruel and violent actions/agenda of immature souls who must strive to control themselves, and learn to overcome their own base nature, before they can serve as a noble example for others.

of Islam *is* the Truth itself.

One's opinion of the Wahhabi movement will be far different, of course, if seen from the perspective of Ibn Sa'ud. Ibn 'Abdul Wahab's cruel and violent religious views were—for Ibn Sa'ud—a highly effective and strategic (i.e., *deadly*) political weapon. Anyone who is unaccustomed to studying scripture and the various teachings of Islam in a mature, rational, highly sensitive and compassionate manner would naturally have difficulty refuting the Wahhabis' theological claims and accusations. Others' inability to resist these theological claims and accusations is precisely what enabled Ibn Sa'ud to acquire enormous wealth and power. The mutually synergistic benefits of this theological/political alliance may be clearly observed from the fact that for over 250 years the male and female descendants of Ibn Sa'ud and Ibn 'Abdul Wahab have intermarried, with the male descendents of Ibn 'Abdul Wahab exercising continuous control over religious authority in the Saudi Kingdom, while Ibn Sa'ud's male descendents have exercised exclusive political authority.

This bargain between Saud and Wahab led to a marriage between politics and religion, although in fact—perhaps subconsciously—religion itself became subordinated to this arrangement, and the means to not only legitimize Saudi power, but also victimize every Muslim whose view of Islam differed from that of the official state hierarchy. Over time this union has proved to be completely worldly in nature, although—and perhaps for just this reason—the two parties have yet to divorce. The hypocritical nature of the Saudi regime was on full display during the rebellion of Wahhabi militants who seized control of the Haram (the holy sanctuary in Mecca) in 1979, causing enormous loss of life and extensive damage to the Haram Mosque. The fanatical militants rebelled in protest against the Sa'ud family's lifestyle, which deviated from Wahhabi teachings. And yet the Sa'ud family continued to enjoy the support of Wahhabi clerics, despite their morally corrupt behavior.

In general, Wahhabism conflicts with the spirit of Islam itself. The violent tendencies of its adherents; their pleasure in condemning fellow Muslims as polytheists, infidels and apostates; and their passion for destructive behavior are all proofs that are difficult to deny. Their conduct as a whole conflicts with the established view of Sunni *ulama* expressed in the *fiqh* (Islamic jurisprudence) principle which states that avoiding destruction, disorder, cruelty and the like (*mafsâdah*) must assume priority over attempts to achieve greater well-being (*dar' al-mafâsid muqaddam 'alâ jalb al-mashlâlih*). Turning this key theological principle on its head, Wahhabis delight in committing *mafsâdah* (disorder, destruction and cruelty) for the sake of achieving what they proclaim to be *mashlâhah* (the common welfare).

Even supposing that the Wahhabis' actions were acceptable, they nonetheless contradict another basic principle of *fiqh* (Islamic jurisprudence), which serves as a common guideline for Sunni clerics: when facing a major danger, one must overcome it by embracing the least dangerous solution available (*yudfa'u asyaddu al-dlarûrain bi tahammuli akhaffihimâ*). Wahhabis, on the other hand, typically address problems by adopting highly problematic "solutions," which inevitably give rise to larger and more numerous problems in the future.

While they delight in condemning their fellow Muslims as infidels, it is clear that this practice directly contradicts the words of the Honorable Prophet Muhammad, may God bless him and grant him peace, who said that "Anyone who accuses his muslim brother of being an infidel, is himself an infidel." The widespread current phenomenon of Muslims accusing other Muslims of being polytheists, infidels and apostates clearly arises from the global dissemination of Wahhabi ideology. From this it is obvious that Wahhabism has assumed the form of a "religion" within a religion.

These facts concerning Wahhabi brutality have caused Muslims who understand *ahlussunnah wal-jamâ'ah*, and who firmly embrace Sunni Islam's credo—that one must behave with tolerance and moderation, and prioritize peace and harmony with all—to repudiate Wahhabi ideology. That is why the Ottoman Sultan, more than two centuries ago, felt a religious obligation to halt the spread of the Wahhabi movement, and attempt to bury it once and for all.

The Ottoman Sultan's decision was based not only upon political calculations, but precise religious considerations as well.

When Muhammad 'Ali Pasha captured a number of Wahhabi leaders, they were invited to engage in religious debate, in order to ascertain the truth among themselves. The dialogue failed, however, because the Wahhabi leaders were so obstinate that they could not accept the existence of views that differed even slightly from their own, let alone those that were totally opposite. This story demonstrates that Wahhabis regard their understanding as the one and only truth, which virtually amounts to conflating their views with "religion" itself. And it is precisely for this reason that those who adhere to Wahhabi doctrine consider non-Wahhabi Muslims to be infidels.

During the formative period of Wahhabism, Muslims who lived in the Hijaz and its surroundings consistently rejected and repudiated the virulent new ideology. They did so because Wahhabi doctrine clearly violated the teachings of Islam, as practiced by Muslims in that region. The radicalism and terror perpetrated by the Wahhabis, not to mention their close-minded and literal interpretation of Islamic holy texts, made other Muslims realize the enormous danger posed by Wahhabism. The quarrels that erupted between Ibn 'Abdul Wahab and his father; the repudiation of Wahab by his elder brother Sulaiman; and his denunciation by Sayyid Ahmad ibn Zaini Dahlan, the Grand Mufti of Mecca during this formative period, offer solid proof of contemporary Muslims' repudiation of Wahhabism.

However, since the Wahhabi conquest of Mecca and Medina, and their success at erecting the modern Kingdom of Saudi Arabia, Muslims in the region no longer dare to openly repudiate Wahhabism. For generations, Muslims living in the holy cities of Islam have had no choice but to embrace Wahhabism, remain silent, or face imprisonment, torture and possible death. The Wahhabis do not permit criticism of their beliefs, despite the fact that they are extremely vocal in directing criticism towards others. Open repudiation of Wahhabi ideology can thus occur only in regions free of Wahhabi control.

Another, more contemporary example of the repudiation of Wahhabism occurred among Bosnian Muslims several years ago. Seeking to exploit the chaotic situation in the former Yugoslav territories, Wahhabis appeared in the midst of the conflict between Serbs and Muslims, offering to deliver humanitarian aid, build schools and mosques, and distribute religious texts. After observing the architecture of the new Wahhabi mosques (which were devoid of the beautiful ornamentation characteristic of Turkish and Bosnian mosques); the new schools' curricula; and the donated books, which were filled with Wahhabi doctrine, Bosnian Muslims realized that the offer of aid was merely a pretext, camouflaging efforts to convert Balkan Muslims into Wahhabis. The majority of Bosnian Muslims rejected Saudi aid, realizing that it would undermine and could eventually destroy their religious traditions and culture, which for centuries have been renowned as civilized and tolerant.

Long before the Balkan conflict, Ayatollah Khomeini of Iran had also voiced a strong critique of Saudi Arabia, following his rise to power in 1979. The Sa'ud family's immoral practices, such as gambling, drinking, womanizing, etc., were the primary targets of Khomeini's criticism of the Kingdom's ruling family, who claimed to be servants of the Two Holy Cities (*Khadim al-Haramain*). At the time, Khomeini broached an important idea—namely, to free Mecca and Medina from the grip of Wahhabis and place them under international management and supervision. As Iran's new ruler, Khomeini undoubtedly had his own political agenda. Nevertheless, his suggestion was highly significant, and worthy.

The armed occupation of al-Haram mosque by Juhayman al-Utaybi and his followers on 1 Muharram 1400/20 November 1979—combined with Ayatollah Khomeini's blistering criticism and strategic vision of freeing Mecca and Medina from the Wahhabis—alerted the Saudi rulers to the fact that their dirty laundry was now exposed to the world. These developments threatened and disgraced the Saudi royal family, by damaging their reputation as *Khâdim al-Haramain*. In response, the Wahhabi/Saudi rulers launched a massive propaganda campaign to defend themselves from such criticism, and avoid the loss of power—spending as much as US $90 billion over the next 30 years to "Wahhabize" the entire Sunni Muslim world. Key channels for the distribution of these funds have been the Muslim World League (*Rabîthat al-'Alam al-*

Islâmî), the International Islamic Relief Organization (IIRO), al-Haramain and other Saudi-financed and -dominated foundations active throughout the entire world.[21] In Indonesia, the Muslim World League and IIRO have distributed their funds through organizations such as Dewan Dakwah Islamiyah Indonesia (DDII—the Indonesian Council for Islamic Proselytism), LIPIA,[22] MMI (the Council of Indonesian Holy Warriors), Kompak and many others.[23]

A non-Wahhabi *sayyid* and *'alim* (descendant of the Prophet Muhammad, and religious scholar), whose family has lived for many generations in the Hijaz, told one of this book's researchers that "Mecca and Medina resemble the heart. If a heart is healthy, it will pump a healthy flow of blood and nutrition throughout the body. But if it's diseased, it will spread its disease to every 'nook and cranny' of the body. That is why the heart should always be clean and healthy. Since the earliest days of Islam, renowned Muslim scholars have been visiting Mecca and Medina, and then returning home to disseminate the religious influences they absorbed in the holy land."[24]

Before the Wahhabis conquered Mecca and Medina, these two holy cities were centers of religious activity and study for every school of Islamic jurisprudence, and Sufi brotherhoods. For well over a thousand years, different schools of thought engaged in open and mature dialogue, enjoying the freedom to pursue truth, and perform the various religious practices to which each of them adhered. During that era, theologians (*mutakallim*), experts in Islamic law (*fuqahâ*), Sufi scholars (*mutashawwifîn*), and experts from numerous other scholarly disciplines met in the holy cities to exchange views.

21. The Saudi government itself is on record acknowledging that it had spent approximately US $70 Billion to promote (Wahhabi) Islam throughout the world, as of 2003 (see: "How Billions In Oil Money Spawned a Global Terror Network," in *US News & World Report*, 15 December 2003).
22. Noorhaidi Hasan, "Islamic Militancy, Sharia, and Democratic Consolidation in Post-Soeharto Indonesia," Working Paper No. 143, S. Rajaratnam School of International Studies (Singapore, 23 October 2007).
23. Zachary Abuza, "Jemaah Islamiyah Adopts the Hezbollah Model," in *Middle East Quarterly*, Winter 2009
24. Consultative interview conducted on 6 June 2007.

Wide-ranging discussions and debates deepened their knowledge and strengthened their religious practice. Many remained in Mecca or Medina for years, to worship and acquire wisdom in these holy cities. In addition, countless pilgrims extended their stay after the *haj*, benefiting from the opportunity to study with *ulama* from various schools of jurisprudence, and return home with the knowledge of Islam they acquired during their pilgrimage.

Many of the greatest figures in Islamic thought, including Abû Hanîfah, Anas ibn Malik, Muhammad ibn Idrîs al-Shafi'î, Ahmad ibn Hanbal, Abu Yazid al-Bistami, Junaid al-Baghdadi, Abû Mansûr al-Hallâj, al-Ghazâlî, ibn Rusyd, ibn 'Arabî, and even Kyai Haji Ahmad Dahlan and Kyai Haji Hasyim Asy'ari had the opportunity to study, discuss and share their knowledge with others in the holy land.[25]

---

25. [Translator's note: Abû Hanîfah (699 – 765), Anas ibn Malik (c. 711 – 795), Muhammad ibn Idrîs al-Shafi'î (767 – 820) and Ahmad ibn Hanbal (780 – 855) were the founders of the four primary schools of Sunni jurisprudence.

Abu Yazid al-Bisthami (804 – 874), from Persia, was one of the first great Sufi mystics, renowned for his spiritual ecstasy and annihilation of the self in God (*fana fi Allah*): "I stood with the pious and didn't find any progress with them. I stood with the warriors in the cause (of Islam) and didn't find a single step of progress with them. Then I said, 'O Allah, what is the way to You?' and Allah said, 'Leave yourself and come.' Junaid al-Baghdadi (830 – 910) was a Persian Sufi who laid the foundation for "sober" mysticism—restraining the outward expression of Divine intoxication and the spiritual insights arising therefrom—whose teachings have played a vital role for over a thousand years, in defending Sufism from attack by Muslim fundamentalists.

Abû Mansûr al-Hallâj (c. 858 – 922) was a Persian Sufi mystic who acquired numerous enemies for sharing his spiritual insights with the masses. This enmity was exacerbated by occasions when he would fall into trances that he attributed to being in the presence of God, and was heard to utter the words, "*Anâ al-Haqq* (I am the Truth)," which is one of the ninety-nine names of Allah. After a long trial and eleven years of imprisonment, al-Hallâj was tortured and publicly crucified in Baghdad. As the great Sufi mystic and poet Jalaluddin Rumi wrote of al-Hallâj's claim to be God, three centuries later: "People imagine that it is a presumptive claim, whereas it is really a presumptive claim to say "I am the slave of God," while "I am God" is an expression of great humility. The man who says "I am the slave of God" affirms two existences, his own and God's, but he that says "I am God" has made himself non-existent and has given himself up and says "I am God," that is, "I am naught, He is all; there is no being but God's."

K.H. Ahmad Dahlan and K.H. Hasyim Asy'ari returned to Indonesia profoundly influenced by their time in Mecca and Medina, which influence helped to shape the mass organizations they established. Although the Muhammadiyah and NU are very different organizations, both have a history of tolerance and mutual respect, acknowledging diversity as one of the treasures of Islam's great intellectual tradition. This is in stark contrast to the Padri movement founded by Haji Miskin, Haji Abdurrahman and Haji Muhammad Arif, who made the pilgrimage to Mecca during the Wahhabi occupation at the turn of the 19th century. The Wahhabi virus infected all three religious leaders, who brought it back with them to West Sumatra, triggering a civil war amongst Mingankabau Muslims that raged for many years, and is truly a dark, tragic period in the history of Indonesian Islam.

Not only Muslims repudiate Wahhabism. Many non-Muslims, especially in the West, hate and reject Islam itself, because of ter-

---

This is the extreme of humility and self-abasement." (Van Cleef, Jabez L. (2008). *The Tawasin Of Mansur Al-Hallaj, In Verse: A Mystical Treatise On Knowing God, & Invitation To The Dance.*)

Abû Hâmid Muhammad al-Ghazâlî (1058 – 1111) was a renowned theologian, jurist, philosopher and mystic of Persian origin, who contributed significantly to the development of a systematic view of Sufism and its integration and acceptance in mainstream Islam. Ibn Rushd (known as Averroes in the West: 1126 – 1198) was a Spanish-born master of Islamic philosophy, theology and jurisprudence, whose powerful influence on Thomas Aquinas, Maimonides and other medieval thinkers—along with his rational and theological justification for the emancipation of science and philosophy from official Ash'ari theology—has led him to be described as the founding father of secular thought in Western Europe (Majid Fakhry) and "one of the spiritual fathers of Europe" (Alain de Libera).

The Spanish-born mystic, philosopher, poet and sage Muhammad b. 'Ali ibn 'Arabî (1165 – 1240) is widely regarded in Muslim circles as the greatest master of gnostic and philosophical mysticism. "Man must first of all know his own soul before he can know his Lord; for his knowledge of the Lord is as the fruit of his knowledge of himself."

Kyai Haji Ahmad Dahlan (1868 – 1923) and Kyai Haji Hasyim Asy'ari (1875 – 1947) were the founders of the Muhammadiyah and the Nahdlatul Ulama, the world's two largest Muslim organizations. All of the historical figures mentioned above are well known to Indonesian Muslim readers, which is why the text does not elaborate on their identity.]

rorist activities perpetrated in the name of Islam. This, despite the fact that non-Wahhabi Muslims also reject and abhor such terrorist activities. If Westerners understood the subtle complexities of Islam, and realized that those committing terrorist acts are Wahhabis and their allies, they would be far less likely to despise or fear Islam itself. Thus, once again, we see that Islam has fallen victim to the global spread of Wahhabism.

The occasional repudiation of their ideology and agenda has not induced Wahhabis to give up, or caused them to lose grip of their senses. Explicit repudiation has merely resulted in their adopting more secretive and covert ways to infiltrate the rest of the Muslim world. This includes Indonesia, the nation with the largest Muslim population and democracy. In the case of Indonesia, foreign Wahhabis do not operate alone. Rather, numerous local groups act as their paid accomplices, or share the same general orientation and goals: namely, the formalization of Islam [through the imposition of Islamic law, and the establishment of an Islamic state, and/or caliphate]. These groups serve as agents in the spread of Wahhabi teachings to Indonesia.

Transnational Islamist Movements in Indonesia

The relationship between Wahhabis and local extremist groups cannot be fully demonstrated, from a structural and organizational perspective, because radical groups are generally ashamed to be identified as Wahhabi accomplices.[26] In addition to direct contact

26. [Translator's note: The extent of this shame and denial was on dramatic display during the 2009 Indonesian presidential election campaign, when the Muslim Brotherhood-affiliated political party, PKS, attempted to secure the vice presidential nomination for its cadre, Hidayat Nur Wahid (HNW), to serve as the popular incumbent president Susilo Bambang Yudhoyono's (SBY's) running mate. Public revelations that HNW and the PKS were linked to transnational Islamist movements, and to Wahhabism in particular, were met with furious denials by HNW and the PKS. Concerned about a public backlash should he nominate a PKS cadre to stand a heartbeat away from the presidency, Yudhonoyo rejected HNW as his running mate, and instead selected the Javanese nationalist Governor of the Bank of Indonesia, Boediono, who received his Ph.D. from Wharton Business School in Philadelphia, Pennsylvania. Together, SBY and Boediono went on to win the election in a landslide. For detailed media coverage of this controversy, see Appendix 4.]

with transnational extremist leaders, the relationship between local and foreign movements is also grounded in a common orientation, ideology and goals. Numerous extremist groups cooperate in their various activities. As a general rule, most of these local groups have some relationship with transnational Islamist organizations that are believed to be dangerous and represent a threat to Pancasila, NKRI (the Unitary State of the Republic of Indonesia), and the Basic Constitution of 1945. In addition, they pose a serious threat to the polite and tolerant traditions of Indonesian Islam.

Among the various transnational Islamist movements that operate in Indonesia are: 1) the *Ikhwanul Muslimin*, or Muslim Brotherhood, founded by Hasan al-Banna in Egypt, which first appeared in Indonesia as a campus-based *da'wa* (proselytism) institution, and later evolved into the Tarbiyah (Islamic Education) Movement. This group eventually gave birth to the Justice and Prosperity Party (PKS);[27] 2) Hizb ut-Tahrir Indonesia (HTI), with its goal of establishing an Islamic caliphate throughout the world, and subsuming Indonesia within it; and 3) Wahhabism, whose "global Wahhabization" agenda necessarily entails the radicalization of Muslim populations throughout the world. Of these three transnational movements, which are a primary focus of this study, Wahhabism is perhaps the strongest, by virtue of its being funded by Saudi Arabia's immense oil wealth. However, these three transnational movements often cooperate in seeking to achieve their goals [in Indonesia], which include transforming Indonesia into an Islamic State; imposing their concept of *shari'a* upon Indonesia's population in the form of positive law; and (in the case of Hizb ut-Tahrir and the terrorist group Jemaah Islamiyah) establishing an Islamic caliphate.

The Wahhabi presence in modern Indonesia has been inextricably linked to the role of Dewan Dakwah Islamiyah Indonesia (DDII, or the Indonesian Council for Islamic Proselytism).[28]

---

27. For more information about the Muslim Brotherhood and PKS, see Haedar Nashir's book, *Manifestasi Gerakan Tarbiyah: Bagaimana Reaksi Muhammadiyah?* (*Manifestations of the Tarbiyah Movement: How Should the Muhammadiyah Respond?*) Yogyakarta: Suara Muhammadiyah (official Muhammadiyah publishing house), 5th edition, 2007.

28. [Translator's note: DDII was founded in 1967 by Muhammad Natsir (1908

With significant financial support from Jama'ah Salafi (the Salafi Community, or "Those Who Follow the Righteous Ancestors," i.e., Muhammad and his companions)—which is how Wahhabis describe themselves in Indonesia and much of the Muslim world, to avoid the stigma of being labeled Wahhabis—DDII sent students to study in the Middle East. Many of these students subsequently become agents for the spread of Wahhabi/Muslim Brotherhood ideology in Indonesia. Later, with full financial support from the Wahhabis/Saudi government, DDII established LIPIA—The Institute for Arab and Islamic Knowledge—a majority of whose students became agents of the Tarbiyah movement and Jama'ah Salafi following their graduation. The Wahhabis enjoy a far closer relationship with the Muslim Brotherhood than with HTI.[29] This intimate relationship between the Wahhabis and Muslim Brotherhood began in the 1950s and '60s, when Gamal Abdel Nasser banned the extremist Ikhwanul Muslimin and all their activities in Egypt. Many key Muslim Brotherhood leaders fled Egypt at the time, with far-reaching consequences for the world.

The Muslim Brotherhood

A young teacher named Hasan al-Banna founded the Muslim Brotherhood in 1928, in Egypt. At the time, Palestine and Egypt were occupied by the British; Syria and the Maghreb (Morocco, Algeria and Tunisia) colonized by France; while Italy controlled Libya. The various European nations colonizing the Middle East embraced widely varying ideological principles at home. The British tended towards liberalism (although socialism was on the rise), while Italy—ruled by Mussolini—embraced fascism. The term fascism itself is derived from the Latin word *fasces* (*fascio* in Italian), a device that was a symbol of authority in ancient Rome. The *fasces* consisted of many wooden rods bound together, which were weak individually, but impossible to break when united as a whole. In

– 1993), a prominent Islamist political figure whose life-long goal was the establishment of an Islamic state as Indonesia's official form of government.]

29. [Translator's note: In Indonesia, the Wahhabis, Muslim Brotherhood and Hizb ut-Tahrir have been known to frequently cooperate in achieving tactical and/or strategic objectives. Internationally, Hizb ut-Tahrir is generally at odds with the Saudi government and the Muslim Brotherhood.]

other words, the *fasces* symbolized strength through unity.

Hasan al-Banna's goals in establishing the Muslim Brother-hood were to oppose colonialism, reverse the decline of Islamic civilization, and to bring Muslims back to what he considered to be the pure teachings of Islam. Unfortunately, al-Banna and his followers apparently believed that the ideology and organizational structure/tactics employed by Mussolini's fascism and Soviet com-munism would be more useful in helping to achieve these goals than classical liberalism, which allows every individual to search for the truth, and to practice his or her religion freely. Besides his Eu-ropean influences, al-Banna was also familiar with Wahhabi ideol-ogy, and from the very beginning the Muslim Brotherhood's orga-nizational DNA contained the centralistic and totalitarian thought patterns of fascist, communist and Wahhabi ideology.

One may state factually that the Muslim Brotherhood was a "child" of western ideologies, which from the outset exhibited in-tense hostility towards its "parents" in the West. From Mussolini's fascism, the Muslim Brotherhood adopted a centralistic and to-talitarian ideology, but rejected nationalism. From Soviet Com-munism, the Brotherhood adopted totalitarianism, systems for infiltrating the institutions of civil society and government; a cell system for recruiting new members; movement strategy and inter-nationalism, but rejected the atheism characteristic of Marxism/ Leninism. Because of these historical facts, some experts refer to the Muslim Brotherhood and other Islamist groups as "Islamofas-cist," which is to say, political movements that aim to concentrate absolute power in the hands of governments which they themselves control, based on their interpretation of the Qur'an.[30]

In developing his political movement, Hasan al-Banna tapped into an immensely popular network of Sufi Brotherhoods (*tariqa*) that had flourished in Egypt for over a thousand years. This strat-egy was so critical to the explosive growth of the Muslim Brother-

---

30. As a general rule, Islamic revivalist movements, including the Muslim Broth-erhood and others, wish to restore the "golden age" of Islam, which they define as the era of the Prophet Muhammad, may God bless him and grant him peace, and the first four "rightly guided" Caliphs, when political power was centralized in the hands of a single ruler. This, in turn, inspires their desire to restore the Islamic Caliphate.

hood that one could even describe the Ikhwanul Muslimin as a *tariqa* with political, rather than spiritual, goals—unlike the Sufis' mystical fraternities. In a relatively short period, Hasan al-Banna and the Muslim Brotherhood succeeded in recruiting hundreds of thousands of members in Egypt. Indeed, one of their first objectives was to oppose British colonialism, rather than adopt a harsh attitude towards their fellow Muslims. However, because the Ikhwanul Muslimin was essentially a political movement draped in religious robes, political ambition was tightly woven into its DNA. Political motivations and the impulse to acquire power—wedded to the centralistic and totalitarian spirit of fascism and communism—caused the Muslim Brotherhood to be constantly engaged in conflict with those in power.

The end of British colonialism proved to be a disappointment rather than a golden opportunity for the Muslim Brotherhood, which failed to achieve its political goals. Convinced that they had played a decisive role in defeating colonialism, but were cheated of their just fruits, the Muslim Brotherhood's leadership turned violent and fanatical. This brought the Muslim Brotherhood into headlong conflict with the Egyptian government, culminating in the assassination of Prime Minister Mahmoud an-Nukrashi Pasha in December of 1948. In retaliation, the Egyptian government ordered the assassination of al-Banna himself.

The death of Hasan al-Banna did not destroy the Muslim Brotherhood. Instead, it grew even more fanatical and violent. Political failure led the Muslim Brotherhood to form an alliance with young military officers who sought to overthrow Egypt's ruler at the time, King Farouk. The victory of this rebellion (known as the Free Officers Movement) proved to be another disappointment for the Muslim Brotherhood, which failed to acquire political power in Egypt due to the fact that its ideology was completely inconsistent with the Arab nationalist/socialist ideology of the triumphant military officers, right from the outset. Gamal Abdel Nasser—one of the officers involved in the 1954 rebellion, who became Egypt's president in 1956—had no intention of sharing power with the Muslim Brotherhood. Instead, he pressed forward with his own secularist vision of Pan-Arabism. Once again, Muslim Brotherhood leaders felt intensely disappointed and betrayed.

Sayyid Qutb, a prominent Ikhwanul Muslimin ideologue and leader following al-Banna's death, felt that the Egyptian government's indisputably cruel and oppressive acts—particularly as directed towards the Muslim Brotherhood—were reminiscent of the ancient Pharoahs and the *jahiliyyah* (ignorant of Divine guidance) inhabitants of pre-Islamic Arabia. Political frustration led Qutb and other Ikhwanul Muslimin leaders to become even more aggressive towards their political opponents. Captured and tortured in jail, Qutb raged against the Egyptian government in his writings, and condemned any and all who opposed his extremist ideology of being infidels and apostates who should be killed. His writings were full of terms such as *takfir* (denouncing fellow Muslims as apostates), *bid'a* (innovation), Pharaohism and modern *jahiliyyah* (contemporary ignorance/refusal to follow Divine guidance—as defined by Qutb himself), which he wielded as theological weapons to bludgeon and destroy anyone who did not agree with his ideology. In addition to obvious Muslim Brotherhood, Hizb ut-Tahrir and Wahhabi influences on his writings, the presence of terms such as "revolutionary vanguard" in Qutb's manuscripts evidence a strong influence from the prevailing communist trend of the time.[31]

Qutb's writings exhort followers of his ideology to struggle for the triumph of the proletariat, the supremacy of the Islamic community and his vision of *shari'a*, or Islamic law, and the creation of an Islamic state, leading ultimately to a centralistic and totalitarian global caliphate through the efforts of a revolutionary-vanguard, which would consist of extremist leaders implementing Qutb's ideology. Sayyid Qutb's writings were intended to incite readers to commit acts of extreme violence, and thereby threatened the lives not only of Egyptian government officials, but the public at large—disrupting political stability in Egypt and ultimately the entire world.[32] In short, it may be said that Sayyid Qutb's writings

31. [Translator's note: In his 2008 article, "Four Decades After Sayyid Qutb's Execution," Muslim Brotherhood activist Ibrahim al-Houdaiby wrote, "In *Milestones*, Qutb presents a manifesto for change, one heavily influenced by Lenin's *What is to be Done*, with the clear Islamization of its basic notions."]

32. [Translator's note: Qutb's writings have been translated into virtually every major language spoken by Muslims, and have inspired the radicalization

inspire his ideological followers to employ extreme violence in the pursuit of political power.

The Marriage of Wahhabi/Muslim Brotherhood Ideologies

Qutb's incendiary writings led to his execution in Egypt in 1966. Actually, in the years following the Free Officers Revolution of 1954, Gamal Nasser imprisoned countless Muslim Brotherhood leaders in addition to Sayyid Qutb. This systematic political repression caused many Ikhwanul leaders to flee Egypt. Saudi Arabia—which at the time was engaged in intense ideological conflict with Nasser's Pan-Arab Socialism—offered haven to many of these political refugees. Among those who fled to Saudi Arabia was Said Ramadan, who subsequently helped found the Muslim World League, which has served as a primary vehicle for the Wahhabization of Muslim populations worldwide since its establishment in Mecca in 1962. The son-in-law of Hasan al-Banna, Said Ramadan later moved to Geneva to spearhead the Muslim Brotherhood's penetration of Europe, with Wahhabi financial support, and execute a long-term strategy of converting European Muslims to Wahhabi/Muslim Brotherhood ideology. Tariq Ramadan—Said's son, and thus the grandson of Hasan al-Banna on his mother's side—has since become the most famous Muslim intellectual in Europe, where he enjoys immense popularity for his deft melding of Islamist and anti-capitalist/anti-globalization ideologies, in one of the most visible expressions of the common cause which unites many contemporary European leftists and Islamists.

Another notable Muslim Brotherhood leader who fled Egypt for Saudi Arabia in the 1960s was Sayyid Qutb's brother, Muhammad Qutb, who became a professor at the recently-founded King Abdulaziz University in Jeddah, where he taught Osama Bin Laden and many other students.

These Saudi actions reflected the Wahhabi rulers' intense fear of Gamal Abdel Nasser's Pan-Arab movement, which was based on socialism and represented a clear and present danger to Wah-

---

of countless Muslims, including those involved in the assassination of Anwar Sadat, the 9/11 attacks, and terrorist massacres in Bali, Madrid, London, Beslan, Mumbai and myriad other locations around the world.]

habi ideology. By offering safe haven to Muslim Brotherhood leaders, the Saudi government sought to kill two birds with one stone. As sworn enemies of Nasser, the Brotherhood members could be trusted to serve as strategic allies in Saudi Arabia's struggle against Nasser's Pan-Arab socialism. In addition, the Ikhwanul leaders—who were far more educated and cosmopolitan than their Bedouin hosts—were eager to help the Saudis erect a system for the proselytizing of Wahhabi ideology to other Middle Eastern nations, and ultimately the entire world.

Thus the 1960s witnessed a marriage of Wahhabi and Muslim Brotherhood ideologies, which has since given birth to the majority of radical Sunni movements in the world today. Wahhabism and the Muslim Brotherhood already shared a number of characteristics, including a fanatical, supremacist ideology; centralistic political ambitions; an international outlook; a literalistic approach to Islam; and a desire to formalize religious teachings, with themselves as the ultimate arbiters of its meaning and practice. In addition, the Wahhabis enjoyed immense wealth—especially after oil prices skyrocketed in 1973—while Muslim Brotherhood leaders were highly educated and ambitious, but often impoverished. Over time, it became evident that this Wahhabi/Muslim Brotherhood union was truly strategic, for it produced an international movement that for decades has functioned like a juggernaut, systematically deploying vast financial resources in order to disseminate its virulent ideology throughout the world, up to the present day.

The end of the 1970s and early '80s were a time of great danger for Saudi Arabia's rulers. The successful Iranian revolution of 1979, and Juhayman al-Uteybi's seizure of the Haram Mosque in Mecca that same year, exerted enormous pressure on the Saudis. Soon thereafter, the Soviet Union invaded Afghanistan, and in 1981 extremists from Egyptian Islamic Jihad—an offshoot of the Muslim Brotherhood—assassinated Egyptian President Anwar Sadat. In response to these ominous developments, Saudi Arabia accelerated the systematic dissemination of Wahhabi/Muslim Brotherhood ideology throughout the world, through organizations such as the Muslim World League, Al-Haramain Foundation, the International Islamic Relief Organization (IIRO) and many others. Al-

Haramain, for one, became infamous after 9/11, when the United Nations labeled it a "terrorist-funding entity" that facilitated terrorist acts in many parts of the world, including Indonesia.

The Afghan war against the Soviet Union attracted many Islamist radicals from around the world, including, Ja'far Umar Thalib, the founder of Laskar Jihad,[33] and many members of Jemaah Islamiyah's subsequent terror network, including Hambali, Imam Samudra, and Ali Ghufron.[34] In fact, Jemaah Islamiyah, which was established by two former members of the Darul Islam guerilla movement—Abdullah Sungkar and Abu Bakar Baasyir—had a strong connection to al-Qaeda through its military commander Hambali, who served as the only non-Arab on al-Qaeda's central board, prior to his capture in Thailand in 2004.

Al-Qaeda is another offspring from the union of Wahhabi/Muslim Brotherhood ideology, as is clearly visible from the participation of Saudi and Yemeni Wahhabis led by Osama bin Laden (Muhammad Qutb's student), and the Egyptian Ayman al-Zawahiri and his followers. Al-Zawahiri joined the Muslim Brotherhood at the age of 14, and was strongly influenced by Sayyid Qutb. He became Egyptian Islamic Jihad's second leader, and was involved in the assassination of that nation's president, Anwar Sadat, in 1981.

Hizb ut-Tahrir

Disappointed with the Muslim Brotherhood, which he accused of being too moderate and accommodative of the West, Taqiuddin

---

33. [Translator's note: From 1999 – 2002, Lasker Jihad recruited thousands of Indonesian Muslims to wage war against their fellow citizens in Ambon and the Malukus, in a religious conflict that claimed approximately 10,000 lives and rendered half a million Indonesians homeless.]

34. [Translator's note: From 1999 to the present, Jemaah Islamiyah (which seeks to establish an Islamic caliphate encompassing southern Thailand, Malaysia, Singapore, Brunei, Indonesia and the southern Philippines) has been waging a terrorist campaign that has claimed hundreds of lives, including spectacular attacks on Western hotels, embassies, churches, malls, the Jakarta stock exchange, the Jakarta airport and the infamous Bali bombings, for which Imam Samudra, Ali Ghufron and Amrozi were tried and executed by the Indonesian judicial system in 2008. In order to stoke inter-communal tensions, JI even placed a small bomb in the basement of Istiqlal Mosque, the largest in Indonesia, to create the appearance of violence against Muslims in the nation's capital.]

al-Nabhani founded Hizb ut-Tahrir in 1953 in Jerusalem, which at
the time was occupied by Jordan. According to al-Nabhani, contemporary Muslims had been intellectually and emotionally contaminated by the ideologies of capitalism, socialism, nationalism
and sectarianism. Proclaiming his ambition to establish an Islamic
caliphate, he aimed to restore this caliphate in Arab territories first,
before incorporating the entire Muslim world under the umbrella
of his organization.

Following al-Nabhani's death in 1977, Hizb ut-Tahrir was led
by Abu Yusuf Abdul Qadim Zallum, who upon his death in 2003
was succeeded by Ata ibn Khalil Abu Rashta. The organization's
radicalism and aggressive behavior have continued to grow from
the time of its establishment to the present. As a result, Hizb ut-
Tahrir is banned in most Muslim nations, and the movement's
headquarters is now located in Great Britain.[35]

Hizb ut-Tahrir claims that it is struggling to promote truly Islamic ideas and values. This claim cannot be divorced from the
contemporary situation in the Middle East when Hizb ut-Tahrir
was formed, and its total rejection of anything that originates from,
or is in any way tied to, the West. And yet Ed Husain (a former Hizb
ut-Tahrir leader from the UK) states that in addition to being influenced by the 11th century Muslim jurist al-Mawardi, al-Nabhani's
thoughts were clearly influenced by Hegel, Rousseau and other
European figures. In fact, al-Nabhani's political thought—and thus
Hizb ut-Tahrir's as well—is completely derivative from earlier European political philosophy. Al-Nabhani simply replaced Western
terms with Arabic ones, in order to convey an Islamic flavor.[36]

Hizb ut-Tahrir leaders proclaim that contemporary Muslims
are living in a *jahiliyyah* era (i.e., an age of ignorance, comparable

35. Zeyno Baran, *Hizb ut-Tahrir: Islam's Political Insurgency* (Washington: Nixon
center, 2004), pp. 16-17. Interestingly, researchers for this book found Hizb ut-
Tahrir in de facto control of al-Aqsa Mosque in Jerusalem, when an Indonesian
peace delegation visited Israel and Palestine in December of 2007, and attended
Friday prayer on the Temple Mount.
36. Ed Husain, *The Islamist*, London: Penguin Books, 2007, pp. 161-164. The
book has been translated into Indonesian with the title *Matinya Semangat Jihad:
Catatan Perjalanan Seorang Islamis* (*Death of the Jihadist Spirit: Notes on the Journey of an
Islamist*). Jakarta: Pustaka Alvabet, 2008.

to that preceding the revelation of Islam), as a result of the collapse of the Ottoman caliphate in 1922. Muslims can overcome this renewed "dark age" only by ending their "submission" to the West, retrieving their collective identity, and—most importantly—re-establishing the international caliphate, with *shari'a*, or Islamic jurisprudence, serving as positive law. Unlike al-Qaeda, Hizb ut-Tahrir teaches that only a caliph has the right to declare war. For this reason, Hizb ut-Tahrir employs elaborate strategies to infiltrate Muslim societies, and is delaying the use of military action or violence until its leadership is certain that their infiltration has reached a critical mass and they will be successful in seizing power and establishing their caliphate.[37]

Hizb ut-Tahrir doctrine identifies three stages in its struggle to establish an international caliphate. *The first* is to establish a local party (*hizb*). During this stage, Hizb ut-Tahrir agents recruit new members and train them for approximately six months to three years, depending on their individual capability and progress. This step may aptly be termed brainwashing, and produces an "Islamic personality" a la Hizb ut-Tahrir. The process is usually conducted through religious seminars. At this stage, Hizb ut-Tahrir leaders and trusted members build a personal relationship with their new recruits, in order to more effectively indoctrinate them with the movement's ideology and operational methods.

The second stage entails direct interactions with society at large, with newly graduated members of the first stage forming new cells and becoming active—linking local issues with global problems—in order to inflame the masses and thus ignite social tensions between people and their government. Hizb ut-Tahrir then presents its interpretation of the Islamic path as an alternative to present circumstances, and the only way to escape the conflicts that they themselves have created. The primary target of their infiltration is government and military officials, in order to seize power,[38] although in fact Hizb ut-Tahrir tends to attract young Muslims with little understanding of Islam, and is especially popular on university campuses around the world. At present, Hizb ut-Tahrir agents are

---

37. Zeyno Baran (2004), op. cit., pp. 19-20.
38. Zeyno Baran (2004), op. cit., pp. 20-23.

active in over 40 countries, including Indonesia, where in August of 2007 they managed to pack over 80,000 people into Jakarta's Bung Karno Stadium, to call for the establishment of an Islamic caliphate and the abolition of Indonesia's state ideology (Pancasila), as well as the dissolution of the Unitary State of the Republic of Indonesia (NKRI) itself.

The third stage is the actual seizure of power. This final stage will be launched once Hizb ut-Tahrir's leadership is convinced that their coup will be successful, the indications for which will be their success in infiltrating the government and military institutions. Once they have acquired power, Hizb ut-Tahrir leaders plan to impose their rigid and extreme interpretation of Islam in every field of human life.[39]

As a result of its obsessive political ideology, Hizb ut-Tahrir is devoid of spirituality, and its movement dry and supremacist. In fact, most Hizb ut-Tahrir activists have no understanding of the profound depths of Islam, and instead pride themselves on the extremely artificial teachings they have absorbed. It is truly ironic that with virtually no understanding of Islam, they claim to be standing in the vanguard, fighting for Islam![40] Their weak grasp of Islam is the primary cause of their ignorance, and induces them to promote concepts that are shrouded in Arabic terminology, and thus assumed to be identical with Islam, when in fact their political agenda represents a supremacist and all too human "will to power." In general, the extreme rhetoric of such groups serves as a prelude to violent action. Extremist movements have manipulated religion to such an extent, that they provide theological inducement for their followers to willingly commit any act—even murder or suicide—if it will help achieve their political goals.

---

39. The Central Board of the Nahdlatul Ulama (PBNU) has warned Indonesia about the dangers posed by transnational Islamist movements (including Hizb ut-Tahrir), which stem from the fact that Islamist ideology conflicts with, and threatens the continued existence of the religious traditions and beliefs of *ahlussunnah wal-jamâ'ah* (Sunni Islam), Pancasila and NKRI. See Appendix 2 for extensive NU rulings and pronouncements in this regard.
40. Ed Husain (2007), op. cit., pp. 146-149 and 208-209.

Three Aspects of Islamist Violence

These three transnational movements (Wahhabism, the Muslim Brotherhood and Hizb ut-Tahrir) have an active presence in Indonesia, both open and surreptitious. With their rigid, extreme and violent ideology, backed by strong financial support and communist-style methods of infiltration, these transnational Islamist movements have penetrated nearly all aspects of Indonesian society. All three seek to transform the face of Indonesian Islam—which is generally well-mannered and tolerant—to become arrogant, fierce, cruel and full of hatred, like their own twisted visage. They feel it is their right to dominate and rule others. The violence they commit to achieve their goals may be categorized as follows:

First, doctrinal violence: that is, a close-minded and literalistic reading of religious texts, while rejecting all views other than their own. In this regard, closed-minded literalism has severed the concrete and actual relationship between the sublime teachings of religion, on the one hand, and historical, cultural and social reality on the other. As a result, the sublime wisdom of religion has been amputated and the living faith destroyed, so that nothing remains but organs harvested from a corpse, that match the extremists' ideology.

Second, violence committed against various traditions and cultures, which directly stems from doctrinal violence itself. Their one-sided claim to monopolize the truth renders Islamists incapable of grasping other truths. As a result, they condemn religious practices observed by other Muslims as deviant, and denounce their practitioners as polytheists, infidels and/or apostates. Extremist groups reject the vast body of Islamic tradition, of which they are generally ignorant. This often includes rejecting the various schools of Islamic jurisprudence, Sufi traditions, and numerous practices that represent the fruitful interaction of scripture or sublime Islamic teachings with the traditions and culture of Muslims living in various regions throughout history. As a result, the extremists propagate a mistaken and deluded understanding of how Islamic teachings should be practiced. Claiming to imitate the Noble Prophet, they make a great show of dressing up in Arab clothing, such as robes and turbans, and growing beards. And yet they fail to model their own behavior on the Noble Prophet's example, such as politeness, patience, humility, forgiveness, compassion, etc., etc.

Third, sociological violence, which stems from the first two forms of violence. This consists of anarchic and destructive acts directed towards others, whom the extremists accuse of being polytheists, infidels and/or apostates. This social violence causes widespread fear, instability and social anxiety, which threatens every community or nation that the extremists manage to infiltrate. The cumulative effect of these three forms of violence is to destroy Muslims' common sense and their ability to reason logically—propagating superficial and deluded interpretations of Islam that proliferate wildly as a result of the theological jargon extremists love to yell at the top of their lungs, non-stop, at anyone within hearing distance. As a consequence, more and more Muslims' perception of the truth becomes based upon theological jargon, rather than the substance of religion's sublime essence and message, which the jargon (e.g., "*Allahu akbar!*," "*shari'a*," "caliphate") merely symbolizes.

According to Indonesia's Minister of Defense, the nation does not face any serious military threat originating from outside the country. The real danger that Indonesia faces is internal (i.e., social disintegration stemming from religious conflict, provoked by extremist movements and ideology), and the weapon the government uses to counter this danger is Pancasila.[41]

The Motivations of Extremist Agents

The primary factors that induce local extremist leaders and activists to affiliate themselves with one of the above-mentioned transnational Islamist movements are: financial gain; the opportunity to acquire power; social environment and/or social dislocation; and/or a weak understanding of religious teachings, especially in regard to spiritual matters.

The financial factor represents an undercover business within extremist movements. One former Laskar Jihad leader openly told our researchers that when he was active in the group, he received an

---

41. Consultative researcher's discussion with Indonesian Minister of Defense Juwono Sudarsono on 31 July 2008.

allowance that never fell below three million rupiah[42] a month. In the midst of a prolonged economic crisis, such material temptation exerts a powerful influence on those of weaker faith. This is readily understandable, for the prospect of significant financial gain may indeed overwhelm one's faith, and transform religion into a profitable business opportunity for extremist agents. The availability of such financial rewards acts as a magnet for all sorts of adventurers, who wish to obtain instant profit without hard work.

On the other hand, those who feel they have significant ability, but lack the social roles or status they desire, often achieve "self-actualization" in extremist groups. As leaders within such groups, they obtain important roles and positions, because of their ability to recruit and direct followers, and attract widespread public attention. The more followers they have, and the more headlines they create, the more satisfied is their craving for self-importance and public recognition.[43] Media coverage often represents the fulfillment of their dreams, satisfying a thirst for fame. This was very obvious during an interview conducted by a foreign reporter with the leader of an extremist group that occurred in April of 2007, facilitated and attended by researchers from this project.[44]

However, the most important causal factor leading to infatuation with extremist movements is a shallow understanding of religion (i.e., Islamic teachings). Extremist jargon such as "defending Islam," "implementing *shari'a*," (Islamic law) or establishing an Islamic caliphate is extremely powerful and attractive to many

---

42. [Translator's note: approximately US $300, which represented a substantial sum at the time (1999 – 2001), when the average wage was less than $50 a month.]

43. [Translator's note: according to traditional Islamic doctrine, the egotistical craving for wealth, power and recognition are all de facto evidence of a lack of religious sincerity. The above text thus implies that those afflicted by such cravings (i.e., the majority of extremist leaders) are strangers to true islam, and merely manipulating religion for personal gain. Although not explicitly stated, this message is crystal clear for the majority of Muslim readers.]

44. Wall Street Journal columnist Bret Stephens' interview with Front for the Defense of Islam leader Muhammad Rizieq Shihab in Petamburan, Jakarta, published on 17 April 2007 ("The Arab Invasion: Indonesia's Radicalized Muslims aren't Homegrown." See: http://www.libforall.org/news/Wall-Street-Journal_The-Arab-Invasion.pdf).

Muslims, who lack a profound understanding of religious teachings. Simultaneously, those who reject the extremist agenda lurking behind such jargon are easily accused of rejecting Islamic law, or even repudiating Islam itself.[45] Such accusations are typically made by self-righteous (or opportunistic) individuals who imagine (or pretend) they understand everything there is to know about Islam, and who are convinced (or seek to convince others) that only *their* shallow understanding of Islam is true and righteous. Such arrogance causes them to eagerly condemn those who think differently, while simultaneously rendering it impossible for them to engage in sincere introspection. *This attitude arises from the absence of a truly islamic approach to life, and a failure to surrender oneself fully to God—Pure and Exalted is He!—for complete humility is the primary message of Islam itself.* The shallowness of such extremists' understanding gives rise to acute misinterpretations of Islam, for they are unable to differentiate between the actual source of Islamic teaching (the Qur'an and Sunnah), and their own superficial understanding of that source. They also lack the ability to discern the complex relationship that exists between religious teachings and social, cultural, economic and political reality. As a result, a religion full of sublime and glorious tidings for humanity, which emphasize the development of noble character, has been reduced to a set of heartless dicta derived from the extremists' own ideological limitations and/or political agenda.

It is tragic that so many Muslims—both the uneducated, and those with a high degree of formal education—sincerely support an extremist agenda, having become infatuated with the jargon employed by radical leaders, who are constantly seeking to build a symbiotic relationship not only with idealists or those who possess a shallow understanding of Islam, but also with rank opportunists, for the sake of personal benefit. It is no coincidence that many

---

45. [Translator's note: such accusations amount to a death threat, since according to classical Muslim jurisprudence, the penalty for "repudiating Islam" (i.e., apostasy) is death. Throughout Muslim history extremists have hurled such charges at their opponents—and frequently assassinated or executed those so accused—in order to narrow the bounds of religious discourse and maintain the dominance of their fundamentalist/political view of Islam. This phenomenon continues to the present day in many/most parts of the Muslim world.]

extremist groups, like the Muslim Brotherhood and Hizb ut-Tahrir, recruit new members using a cell system reminiscent of communism. This enables them to more easily and effectively control their followers. A cell system is the easiest medium through which to reorient a new recruit's understanding of Islam, brainwashing him or her with the movement's ideology. In addition, the closed and hierarchical nature of a cell structure is effective in avoiding unwelcome questions from new members regarding sensitive matters, including the organization's finances.

Wahhabis and local adventurers both profit by working together. Wahhabism—which cannot publicly reveal its face, or openly transplant its ideology to Indonesia, because Muslims who understand its history and teachings would reject it—are fortunate that unprincipled adventurers are willing to serve as their accomplices in spreading Wahhabi ideology. From their side, the local opportunists benefit from the mighty flow of petrodollars unleashed by Saudi Arabia.

Apart from this financial incentive, Wahhabism has joined the Muslim Brotherhood and Hizb ut-Tahrir in subverting local Muslims with their extreme ideology. Although their perspectives differ, including on various details of religious interpretation, their ultimate goal is similar: i.e., the formalization of Islam [through the imposition of Islamic law, and the establishment of an Islamic state, and/or caliphate]. To achieve this goal, radical groups employ every method at their disposal, including many that conflict with the very teachings of Islam itself. This fact alone is sufficient to reveal the true nature of such movements. If they truly wished to promote Islam, they would of course avoid doing anything that conflicts with the teachings of Islam itself. One of the most basic principles taught by *ahlussunnah wal-jamâ'ah ulama* (Sunni religious scholars) is that the end can never justify the means (*l-ghâyah lâ tubarrir al-washîlah*, or *man kâna amruhû ma'rûfan fal-yakun bi ma'rûfin*). This means that "an act does not become good simply because its stated goal is virtuous," and that "anyone who wishes to achieve a virtuous goal should obtain it using virtuous methods as well." Corrupt means, utilized in pursuit of a noble objective, will corrupt and stain the intended good itself, negating the stated objective.[46]

---

46. "*Man kâna amruhu ma'rufan fal-yakun bi ma'rûfin*," ("Anyone who wishes to

The First Infiltration of Wahhabi Ideology into Indonesia: The Padri Movement

Ever since independence, the official history lessons taught in Indonesian schools have portrayed the Padri War as a struggle against Dutch colonial occupation. Members of the Padri movement are described as heroes who bravely defended our native archipelago. The inherently violent nature of the Padri movement and its affiliation with Wahhabi ideology have been hushed up and circulated only among experts. But in order to understand the threat of Wahhabism to contemporary Indonesia, it is vital that we recognize the other, hidden side of the Padri movement's history.

The movement began with Haji Miskin, Haji Abdurrahman and Haji Muhammad Arif's introduction to Wahhabism, when they undertook the pilgrimage to Mecca at the beginning of the 19th century. At the time, the Wahhabis controlled both Mecca and Medina. Infatuated by the Wahhabi movement, Haji Miskin was determined to launch a similar purification struggle when he returned to the East Indies, and was supported by the other two Hajis.[47] Their ideology and movement was virtually identical to that of the Wahhabis. They condemned the Shattariah Sufi brotherhood, and Sufism in general—which were deeply rooted in the Minangkabau region, and had been for centuries—as heretical and intolerant deviations from Islam, because Sufi teachings harbored numerous superstitions (*takhyul*), fables and innovations (*bid'a*) that had to be corrected, with bloodshed if necessary.[48] For example, Tuanku Nan Renceh—a Minang noble who joined the

---

perform good deeds should do so in an honorable manner")—Prof. Dr. K.H. Said Aqil Siraj in *Ocean of Revelations: Understanding Islam as a Blessing for All Creation,* Episode 5: *"Da'wa"* (Proselytism). Program Supervisor: Kyai Haji A. Mustofa Bisri, ©LibForAll Foundation 2009).

47. Abdul A'la, "The Genealogy of Muslim Extremism in the East Indies: its Origins and Intellectual Characteristics, and the Padri Movement in Light of the Relationship between Religion and Political Power," commencement speech upon becoming a full professor, Sunan Ampel Islamic State Institute in Surabaya, Indonesia, May 2008 (unpublished), p. 11.

48. Oman Fathurrahman, "Syatariah Brotherhood in the Malay-Indonesian World: a Study of its Dynamics and Development Through Manuscripts from West Sumatra," dissertation from the Literature postgraduate program at the University of Indonesia, Jakarta 2003 (unpublished), p. 164, as quoted by Abdul A'la, Ibid., p.14.

Padri Movement—demonized his own guru, Tuanku Nan Tuo, because the latter elected to defend moderate Islamic teachings. Tuanku Nan Renceh also denounced his former close friend and fellow disciple, Fakih Saghir, and condemned him as "the king of infidels" and an "old monk," simply because he did not share the same religious views.[49]

In addition to adopting the Wahhabi practice of condemning people different from themselves as polytheists, infidels and apostates, Padri violence also extended to the implementation of laws that were totally alien to Islamic law itself, such as the requirement for men to grow beards or be fined 2 suku (equivalent to 1 guilder), if they shaved; a prohibition on the local custom of filing teeth, which was punishable by a fine of one water buffalo; a fine of 2 suku for men who appeared in public with a bared knee; a fine of 3 suku for women who did not veil their entire body, except the hands and eyes; a fine of 5 suku for anyone who neglected the obligatory prayers for the first time, followed by the death sentence for subsequent infractions.[50]

The Padris also practiced slavery. Tuanku Iman Bonjol, a famous Padri leader who has been canonized as a national hero, had seventy male and female slaves. Many of these slaves were acquired during raids against other Muslims, whom the Padris regarded as infidels.[51]

Other Padri violence committed against their fellow Muslims in Minangkabau included the notorious attack on Pagaruyung palace in 1809. This attack was initiated because Tuanku Lelo, a leading Padri figure, accused various members of the king's family—including Tuanku Rajo Naro, Tuanku di Talang and one of the king's sons—of practicing the Muslim faith incorrectly, and hence being infidels who must be killed. The incident resulted in the mass slaughter of members of the royal family and their supporters, including all religious leaders associated with the palace.[52] In 1815,

---

49. Suryadi, "The Padri Controversy: If Not For Tuanku Nan Renceh," as quoted by Abdul A'la, Ibid., p. 14.

50. Abdul A'la, Ibid., pp. 14-15.

51. For a full description see Abdul A'la, Ibid., pp. 15-16.

52. See Puti Reno Raudha Thaib, "Sejarah Istana Pagaruyung (The History of Pagaruyung Palace)" at http://groups.yahoo.com/group/RantauNet/mes-

WAHHABI/MUSLIM BROTHERHOOD IDEOLOGY | 95

another assault was launched under the command of Tuanku Lint-au. This time, the Padri movement butchered almost the entire royal family, which had embraced Islam since the 16th century.

Padri cruelty was not limited to these dramatic events. History records that Tuanku Nan Renceh murdered his own elderly aunt because she chewed betel leaf, which the Wahhabis prohibited. He refused to allow her burial, and instead tossed her corpse into the jungle to be devoured by wild animals.[53] These Padri actions were virtually identical to the conduct of Wahhabis during that sect's formative period in Arabia, and of Wahhabi adherents such as al-Qaeda and the Taliban until the present day.

The Padri movement finally ended not merely because of the "colonial factor," but also because Padri ideology ran directly coun-ter to the atmosphere, traditions and culture of the Indonesian people. The facts associated with the Padri movement provide con-crete evidence of how the Wahhabi virus—by infecting the heart of Islam (Mecca and Medina)—can rapidly spread its disease through-out the entire body of the Muslim world. Unfortunately, the Padri Movement's collapse did not spell the end to Wahhabi subversion of Indonesia.

Infiltration by Transnational Islamist Movements from the New Order Era[54] to the Present

Since the 1970s—when Indonesian Muslims experienced dif-ficulty financing students' overseas study—Wahhabis have provided significant financial aid through Dewan Dakwah Islamiyah Indo-nesia (DDII, or the Indonesian Council for Islamic Proselytism) to sponsor students who wish to study in various Middle East coun-tries, especially Saudi Arabia. Upon their return, a majority of this program's alumni became agents for the spread of transnational Islamist ideology from the Middle East to Indonesia. In addition, DDII helped Saudi Arabia establish LIPIA, a Wahhabi educational institution whose alumni have also played a key role as Salafi (i.e.,

---

sage/61114, as quoted by Abdul A'la, Ibid., pp. 22-23.

53. Abdul A'la, Ibid., p. 23.

54. [Translator's note: Indonesians refer to the years of the Suharto regime (1966 - 1998) as the New Order, because it followed the prior Sukarno era (1945 - 1965).]

Wahhabi) and Tarbiyah (Muslim Brotherhood) agents. DDII also laid the foundation for extremist proselytism (da'wa) movements on university campuses around the country. Like the alumni of Middle East universities, many of these homegrown extremists have also become agents through which transnational Islamist movements conduct their infiltration of Indonesia.

With Wahhabi financial support, DDII has also played a vital role in translating books and disseminating the ideas of transnational Islamist figures such as Hasan al-Banna, Sayyid Qutb, Abdul A'la Maududi, Yusuf Qaradawi and others. The magazine *Sabili*, whose weekly distribution has exceeded 100,000 copies, is widely believed to receive Wahhabi financial support.[55] It is an undeniable fact that DDII's formation followed on the heels of the political party Masyumi's liquidation, as a new vehicle through which the puritan modernists who controlled Masyumi could pursue their agenda of creating an Islamic state. It would be inaccurate to generalize and claim that all modernist figures have been agents of transnational Islamist movements. However, the Wahhabis and Muslim Brotherhood have been clever enough to exploit even the tiniest openings, to subvert modernist organizations and subsequently employ them to disseminate their ideology.

In addition to DDII, Indonesia has witnessed the rise of many local extremist groups, which have sprouted like mushrooms in the rainy season since the collapse of the New Order regime. Among these are the Front for the Defense of Islam (FPI), the Forum for

---

55. [Translator's note: Pulitzer Prize-winning journalist Andrew Higgins, writing in the *Washington Post*—"Indonesia steps up pressure on Islamist militants" (13 May 2010)—documented the impact of *The Illusion of an Islamic State* in turning the tide against hard-line, extremist ideology Indonesia, by exposing the origins and agenda of radical movements to the harsh glare of public scrutiny. "[In 2004,] Indonesia's best-selling magazine was an Islamic weekly called *Sibili*, [sic] which offered a mix of wild anti-American conspiracy theories and cheerleading for jihad.... Today the tide seems to have turned.... *Sibili*, meanwhile, has toned down its anti-Western rhetoric. 'We now see bigger potential for sales among moderate Muslims,' said Lufti Tamimi, the magazine's director and part-owner. In January [2010], Tamimi ditched *Sibili's* hard-line editor and commissioned a series of articles denouncing Salafism, a purish strain of Islam that underpins extremist ideology." For more detailed information on *Sabili's* reaction to *The Illusion of an Islamic State*, see Appendix 5.]

the Muslim Community (FUI), Laskar Jihad (Warriors of Jihad), Jemaah Islamiyah (the Islamic Community), Majelis Mujahidin Indonesia (the Council of Indonesian Holy Warriors), the Justice and Prosperity Party (PKS), the Committee to Prepare for the Establishment of Islamic Shari'a (KPPSI), etc., etc. At present, the Muslim Brotherhood (i.e., the PKS)[56] and Hizb ut-Tahrir operate openly in Indonesia, while the Saudi government generally conceals its Wahhabi proselytism activities. These activities have been so extensive that extremist movements have already spread like cancer throughout the nation's body, infiltrating from the state palace to remote mountaintops. The results of the extensive field research and consultations published in this book clearly demonstrate that extremist movements operate in a well-planned and systematic manner, with enormous financial backing.

The subversive methodologies employed by transnational Islamists and their local accomplices are extremely varied, and

---

56. As Muhammadiyah Vice Chairman Dr. Haedar Nashir has written:

"The close ties that exist between the PKS and the Muslim Brotherhood have been explicitly acknowledged by Anis Matta, a leading PKS figure and its current Secretary General. Anis Matta's declaration reads as follows:

"The Muslim Brotherhood inspiration that animates and informs the Justice and Prosperity Party, if we may delineate it here, provides two dimensions of power simultaneously. **First** is the ideological inspiration, which is based in part on the principle of **Syumuliyat Al-Islam** ("the all-encompassing nature of Islam"), which became the core principal not only of Hassan Al-Banna's struggle, but of all those who struggle in the same cause. **Second**, the historical inspiration, which seeks a model and strategy derived from the Islamic struggle that occurred after the fall of the Islamic [i.e., Ottoman] Caliphate and hence the era of Western imperialist domination of Muslim states. But what unites these two inspirations in Hassan Al-Banna and the Muslim Brotherhood is the vital "movement" aspect. While others became reformers in the field of thought, Hassan al-Banna succeeded in transforming the reform impulse from mere "talk" into a concrete movement. And it is not an exaggeration to say that the inspiration of that movement can also be felt beating in the pulse of the Justice and Prosperity Party."

Anis Matta, "Introduction" to Aay Muhammad Furkon, *Partai Keadilan Sejahtera: Ideologi dan Praksis Politik Kaum Muda Muslim Indonesia Kontemporer* (The Justice and Prosperity Party: Ideology and Political Practices of Contemporary Indonesian Muslim Youth), Bandung: Teraju, 2004, as quoted by Haedar Nashir, op. cit., pp. 33-34.

range from a straightforward financial approach, through educational projects and the "sharing" of Islamic knowledge, to almost unimaginable strategies, such as infiltrating and seizing control of mosques by offering a free cleaning service. For example, at the end of 2005, a nongovernmental organization submitted a proposal to the president of Indonesia, to cooperate in the distribution of US $500 million, which was allegedly "parked" in various foreign bank accounts. If the Indonesian government would permit these funds to enter Indonesia and agreed to establish formal collaboration, the NGO in question offered to allocate 40% of the funds, or $200 million, to be employed as the Indonesian Cabinet saw fit, while the NGO would use the remaining 60% to finance various development programs that were not associated with Indonesia's federal or provincial budgets—especially to build "the infrastructure for noble character education" in Central Sulawesi, which was just emerging from an armed religious conflict in which radical Islamic groups were clearly involved. As if this were not audacious enough, the proposal went on to state that if the Indonesian Government was attracted to the funds offered, "the NGO hopes to receive the opportunity (license) to place its personnel within the governmental Institute for State Planning and Supervision (the Republic of Indonesia's Economic Team)."

A confidential source within the palace intimately familiar with this proposal informed our researchers that the funds in question originated from Saudi Arabia and—given the fantastic sum of money involved, to be routed via several banks in Malaysia—sought a legal path of entry into Indonesia (i.e., government permission). Our source added that the proposal had suddenly "vanished" from the state palace, because concerned individuals feared the proposal's devastating impact upon Indonesian society, should it be approved.[57] This case clearly demonstrates that efforts exist to graft Wahhabi/Muslim Brotherhood ideology upon Indonesian Islam, with enormous financial backing from the Middle East.

Attempts to infiltrate Indonesian society "greased" by money are often directed towards influential figures that are deemed re-

---

57. Information derived through consultative research in 2006, including review of the proposal in question.

ceptive to bribes. Indeed, many Indonesians have gladly accepted Wahhabi funding, and become willing channels for the dissemination of extremist ideology. Yet our nation also has great leaders who deeply love their country, are convinced of the truth embodied within moderate and tolerant Islamic teachings—rather than a violent and extreme ideology—and thus firmly reject the temptation of Wahhabi funding. One striking example involves an incident that occurred at Sunan Kalijaga Islamic State University in Yogyakarta, shortly after the devastating earthquake of 2006. Two men from Saudi Arabia visited the university's rector, bringing CD-Roms that contained Wahhabi and Muslim Brotherhood books translated into Indonesian. They offered the rector a large amount of money in exchange for use of Sunan Kalijaga University's imprint in publishing the books. The rector refused their offer, because he was fully aware that the books in question were brimming with extremist ideology, and that his visitors' sole purpose was to promote Wahhabism throughout Indonesia, by means of his university.[58] Unfortunately, not all Indonesians have that rector's noble principals and steadfast character. As a result, they are willing to sell their religion, become Wahhabi agents, and sacrifice the future of our nation and its people. From this, it is once again evident that Wahhabis finance not only terrorism, but also the spread of their ideology.

The infiltration and seizure of mosques is but one example of extremist subversion. Their infiltration of academia is generally conducted by acquiring control of a university's board of trustees, administration, student body leadership, and so forth. They even establish their own grade school networks, such as the PKS's "Islam Terpadu (Integrated Islamic)" schools. Their pattern of activities makes it abundantly clear that campus proselytism groups are en-

---

58. [Translator's note: The Saudi visitors' choice of Sunan Kalijaga Islamic State University to publish the books was well-informed and deliberate. The university is named after a renowned Muslim saint who defeated radical Islam in 16th century Java, and whose cultural and spiritual disciples established the Nahdlatul Ulama approximately 350 years later (in 1926), to prevent the spread of Wahhabism to the East Indies in the wake of the Saudi conquest of Mecca and Medina. Kyai Haji Abdurrahman Wahid was not only the grandson of NU founder K.H. Hasjim Asyari, but also a descendent of Sunan Kalijaga himself.]

gaged in systematic efforts to control the field of education—and Indonesia's future—by indoctrinating students and teachers alike with their Wahhabi/Muslim Brotherhood or Hizb ut-Tahrir world view.

It has proven much easier for radicals to seize control of Muhammadiyah educational institutions than those affiliated with the Nadhlatul Ulama (NU), and easier still to assume control of those that have no affiliation with either the NU or Muhammadiyah. Muhammadiyah institutions are generally characterized by formal/structural relationships, while NU society is linked by emotional and cultural bonds. In addition, many Muhammadiyah members appear more receptive to the concepts of extremist groups because of the Muhammadiyah's own agenda to "purify" Islam, which although non-political, is something the Muhammadiyah shares in common with extremist movements, which have made the purification of Islam one of their key projects. Even more vulnerable are students who enter public schools and universities, without having any prior affiliation with either the NU or Muhammadiyah. Because they lack a profound understanding of Islam, such students have virtually no theological ability, nor reason, to reject extremist ideology.

A Danger Staring Us Right in the Face

Wahhabism, together with its equally harsh and extreme cohorts, has played a significant role in countless acts of doctrinal, cultural and social violence that have been—and continue to be—perpetrated around the world. Most Indonesian Muslims do not recognize the danger posed by extremist groups, both because of their trusting nature, and due to a strong normative assumption that anything which claims to be "Islamic" must be good. Indonesian Muslims also have a tendency to consider Islam identical with "Arab," and vice versa. For this reason, anything that comes from the Arab world, claiming to be "Islamic," tends to be readily accepted, rather than subject to normal standards of skepticism and scrutiny. This phenomenon stems from Indonesian Muslims' normative awareness, which views Arabia as the place where Islam descended from heaven. Therefore, Indonesian Muslims appear reluctant to criticize Wahhabism, which represents the official view of Islam embraced by the Kingdom of Saudi Arabia. Yet in reality, respect for others should not lead to irrational behavior, or the abandonment of one's own critical faculties.

In brief, we may state that the primary agenda of extremist groups is to seize political power, through the formalization of religion. They claim that "if only Islam becomes the foundation of our country;" "if only *shari'a* is institutionalized as positive law;" "if only an Islamic caliphate is established," then every problem will miraculously disappear. This is nothing but utopian nonsense. If only they understood 'Ali ibn Abi Talib's response to the Khawârij when Mu'âwiyah requested a truce,[59] they would realize that no matter how sublime the teachings of a religion may be, as recorded in its sacred scripture, everything depends on the state of awareness of those who read the scriptures in question, or proclaim themselves its followers. If only extremists were able to perceive 'Ali's wisdom, they would not manipulate religion for the sake of acquiring political power. However, it is widely recognized that radical movements (and especially Wahhabism) are, in fact, modern reincarnations of the Khawârij. Not surprisingly, it is virtually impossible for these neo-Khawârij to busy themselves trying to fathom the depths of 'Ali's wisdom. Instead, they viciously condemn as infidels any Muslim who differs from and/or disagrees with them, and seek to formalize religion in order to attain their political objectives.

Of course, there *are* correlations between various social problems—such as corruption, collusion, nepotism, poverty, ignorance, etc.—and the neglect of religious teachings. But the solution to these problems does not lie in formalizing religion—i.e., imposing extrem-

---

59. In that incident, the Khawârij met with 'Ali and quoted a verse from the Qur'an that reads, "the law belongs to God alone (*in al-hukm illâ liLlâh*)," claiming that truce offered by Mu'awiyah should be rejected, and the battle continued until the last enemy surrendered. 'Ali, who favored the path of compromise and peace, replied, "Holy Scripture does not lug its meaning around upon its shoulders. To convey its inner meaning, it requires readers. And those readers are human beings." As 'Ali recognized, humans have the potential to rise to the level of truth, but also to fall into error. [Translator's note: acknowledging their own human fallibility, traditional Muslim clerics generally qualify their views by stating, "God alone knows the truth"—an expression of profound humility that is notably absent in the pronouncements of many radical Muslims.]

ists' narrow understanding of Islam upon society as a whole—but rather, in improving religious adherents' morals, through a process of spiritual upliftment. Proclaiming the formalization of religion as the "solution" to the world's problems is in fact a thinly veiled excuse to achieve political power, rather than eliminate social problems. For the real problem we face is not the absence of formal religion, but rather, the deformed character of religious adherents, who fail to implement the sublime values of their own faith.

The formalization of religion poses an extreme danger to religion itself, its followers and the people of Indonesia as a whole. Formalization will amputate religion—divorcing Islam from the social and cultural context of its revelation, while also severing the faith from its own evolution throughout history... its teachings and content dictated by a rigid ideological framework, and/or political party platforms. In such circumstances, religious symbols and identity become all-important; far more so, in fact, than the substance of religion itself. People chase after symbols, while neglecting to implement the substance of religious teachings in their own lives.

One may cite any number of examples of this passion to display religious symbols, on both a personal and social level. The Prophet Muhammad—may God bless him and grant him peace—once remarked that God will love those of His servants who have a "black mark" upon their forehead. Inspired by this hadith, millions of extremists seek to bruise and blacken their foreheads in prayer, when in reality the saying is meant to inspire Muslims to engage in frequent prayer and surrender themselves fully to God—Pure and Exalted is He!—striving to love Him with all our hearts, and to elicit His love for all His creatures. Extremists think that a black mark upon their forehead will be presented to God in the hereafter, as proof of their devotion, when in reality God—Pure and Exalted is He!—examines our hearts, minds and deeds, rather than outward symbols. The same applies to beards and clothing. The most generous assumption we can make about extremists is that they lack the ability to differentiate between the substance of religious teachings and religious symbols, or Arab culture. This is only natural, because their ability to comprehend is confined to the purely literal. Nonetheless, we cannot exclude another possibility, which is that all these religious symbols are deliberately being used to generate a political identity, and differentiate the radicals from moderate and tolerant Muslims, who understand and focus upon the profound message of religion primarily in terms of substance, rather than as a collection of artificial signs and symbols.

A literalist reading of scripture and obsession with religious symbols will encourage Muslim populations to become uniform and monolithic. Hence it is no wonder extremist groups reject pluralism, both in terms of the various religions that exist in the world, and within Islam itself. This is extremely dangerous, because it denies any legitimate basis for differences. To use theological terms, everyone who deviates from the extremists' monolithic understanding of Islam will be condemned as infidels, apostates and so forth. Accusing others of infidelity—a foul habit of the Khawârij and their neo-Khawârij followers—has found fertile ground in Indonesia, and grown prolific of late. This symptom should alert us to the fact that the dangers of Wahhabism are not distant from our shores, but rather, have already snuck beneath our own blanket in the dead of night.

Concerning his relationship with other religions, the Prophet once remarked, quite beautifully: *"Nahnu abnâ'u 'allât, abûnâ wâhid wa ummunâ syattâ"* ("We (the Prophets) are the offspring of a single man by his various wives; our father is one, but our mothers are many"). All messengers of God have the same father (religion), namely islam (in the sense of self-transcendence/surrendering oneself totally to God).[60] Yet they spring from many different mothers (*syir'ah wa minhâj*, or paths to God).[61] The Prophet Muhammad's

60. "Our lives and beliefs should align with the teachings conveyed by a Sufi master on the subject of self-transcendence: 'Bury yourself (i.e., your ego) in the empty earth.' That is, completely abandon selfishness and surrender yourself totally to God, and to God's will, which emerges from the Transcendent." ~ Kyai Haji Abdurrahman Wahid, speaking in *Ocean of Revelations: Understanding Islam as a Blessing for All Creation*, Episode 1: "Islam and Faith," Program Supervisor: Kyai Haji Mustofa Bisri, ©LibForAll Foundation 2009).

61. "It is true that Islam came to strengthen other religions, and to validate some of their premises. But this does not mean that Islam is fundamentally different from the religions that came before it. In fact, just the opposite. The Prophet always said, "I am an integral part of the chain of Messengers. We Messengers are all the children of *'allat.' 'Allat* refers to a group of women who are wed to

statement is a clear and unambiguous confession of religious pluralism, which extremist groups nevertheless refuse to accept.

The formalization of Islamic law as positive law through the
promulgation of local *shari'a* regulations in various regions of Indonesia represents an extremist strategy of "isolating (and ultimately
conquering) a city, by controlling its surrounding villages." "If many
regions [throughout Indonesia] have already applied *shari'a* as positive law, then eventually there will be no basis for refusing to adopt
it nationally," a number of extremist leaders told our researchers,
in explaining their efforts to formalize Islamic law in their local areas. Unfortunately, these local *shari'a* regulations constitute a literalistic and partial application of Islamic law, and will thus certainly
distort and reduce Islam to a pale imitation of its greatness, in addition to discriminating against—and causing widespread alienation
among—both non-Muslims and Muslims alike.

As is well known, extremist groups embrace a literal understanding of religious texts, and ignore Qur'anic verses and hadith
that do not support their agenda. Thus, the profound essence
of religion is reduced to gross concepts or commands that may
be conveyed by a series of Arabic letters, and interpreted in accordance with radical ideology. Qur'anic verses and hadith that
address the topics of murder, theft and the drinking of alcoholic
beverages, for example, are used to justify a literalistic application
of legal dictates [dating from the time of the Prophet Muhammad],
with sanctions motivated by revenge. The fundamental question
arises, as to whether these Qur'anic verses and hadith were truly
revealed for the purpose of whipping everyone who drinks alcohol,
amputating the hands and feet of thieves, and executing murderers [i.e., for the purpose of punishment]? If the answer is yes, then

---

a single man. As children of *'allat*, "Our father is one; our religion is one, the
religion of *tauhid*, or Oneness. And our mothers are many." "Mothers" refers
to the many different paths to God. In Islam it is said that there are different
laws, but no (essential) differences of religion. Religious paths vary, but not the
essence of religion itself, from the time of Adam to the Last Day." ~ Maryam
Ishaq al-Khalifa Sharief, Shadhili Sufi Figure from Omdurman, Sudan, speaking in *Ocean of Revelations: Understanding Islam as a Blessing for All Creation,* Episode
4: "People of Faith," Program Supervisor: Kyai Haji Mustofa Bisri, ©LibForAll
Foundation 2009).

where does that leave the primary message of Islam as a blessing for all creation, and the Honorable Prophet Muhammad's mission to perfect human morality (may God bless him and grant him peace)? When mercy, compassion and noble morality are nowhere to be found in the application of religious teachings, then religion itself is—without a doubt—being falsely interpreted, and such a perverse understanding of faith can be neither condoned nor accepted.

A partial and literalistic reading of the Qur'an and hadith are indeed advantageous to those who wish to conform religious teachings to a particular ideology and/or political party's platform. For on the pretext of embracing the literal meaning of a religious text, an individual or group may conceal their own political agenda, while simultaneously hijacking religious teachings to accomplish their personal objectives. Anyone who is unfamiliar with the complexity of ta'wil (exegesis of religious texts), as widely practiced by Sunni Muslim theologians, may have difficulty confronting the theological claims asserted by extremist groups, which base their interpretations on a literal reading of the texts in question. Even those with a conventional university education can be easily deceived to support the radicals' political agenda, as proven by this study, which found that a disproportionate number of college students and professionals not only sympathize with, but have become active cadres in the PKS and Hizb ut-Tahrir Indonesia.

The formalization of religion is the "biological offspring" of a literal reading of religious texts, and extremely dangerous not only for religion itself, but also for those who practice the religion in question, and those who embrace other religions. The formalization of religion subordinates and subjects the sublime teachings of religion to ideological/political interests and manipulation, and a monolithic view that leads to uniformity among religious adherents, while those who believe differently are cast aside and alienated from the extremist community of believers. Pluralism appears abnormal and freakish to those who seek to formalize religion. Because of their literalistic and rigid views, extremist groups have great difficulty accepting the presence—and sometimes, even the existence—of non-Muslims, and even Muslims whose understanding of Islam differs from their own.

Indeed, according to a hadith, the Honorable Prophet Muhammad, may God bless him and grant him peace, once said, "I have been commanded to wage war against people, until they acknowledge there is no god but God, that Muhammad is the Messenger of God, perform ritual prayer and pay alms (*zakat*). If they do these things, they safeguard their lives and wealth from me, except for just cause, and their lives of selfish calculation shall instead be (completely transformed, and) surrendered to God." (*Umirtu an uqâtil al-nâs hattâ yasyhadû an lâ ilâha ill-Allâh wa anna Muhammadan RasûluLlâh wa yuqîmû al-shalâta wa yu'tû al-zakâta. Fa idzâ fa'alû dzâlik 'ashamû minnî dimâahum wa amwâlahum illâ bihaqq al-Islâm wa hisâbuhum 'alâLlâh).*[62] In the hands of extremists and radical groups, this hadith provides a clear example of how Muslims should behave—i.e., eradicating non-Muslims, and even Muslims whose views or practices differ from their own, by establishing a legal and theological rationale for annihilating them. Yet such interpretations obviously result from reading this or other hadith out of context, which causes one so-called "Islamic teaching" to collide head-on with another. For it is clear that the interpretation cited above is far from being the only possible way to interpret this hadith, and indeed, any such reading must be firmly rejected.

---

62. This hadith is transmitted in many versions, the most common of these being: "I have been commanded to wage war against people, until they bear witness that there is no god but God" (*Umirtu an uqâtil al-nâs hatta yasyhadû lâ ilâh ill-Allâh*); "I have been commanded to wage war against people, until they bear witness that there is no god but God, and have faith in me and what I have conveyed. If they do these things, they safeguard their lives and wealth from me, except for just cause, and their lives of selfish calculation shall instead be (completely transformed, and) surrendered to God." (*Umirtu an uqâtil al-nâs hattâ yasyhadû la ilâh ill-Allâh wa yu'minû bî wa bimâ ji'tu bihi. Fa idzâ fa'alû dzâlik 'ashamû minnî dimâahum wa amwâlahum illâ bihaqqihâ, wa hisabuhum 'alâLlâh*). In fact, there is one tradition that reads: "I have been commanded to wage war against polytheists, until they bear witness that there is no god but God, and Muhammad is His servant and Messenger. If they bear witness that there is no god but God, and Muhammad is His servant and Messenger; engage in ritual prayer like us; face (the Ka'aba in) Mecca like we do (when we pray); and eat the foods that we eat, then it is forbidden for us to kill them or take their wealth, except for just cause." (*Umirtu an iqâtil al-musyrikîn hattâ yasyhadû an lâ ilâha ill-Allâh wa anna Muhammadan 'abduHu wa RasûluHu. Fa idzâ syahidû an lâ ilâha ill-Allâh wa anna Muhammad 'abduHu wa RasûluHu wa shallau shalâtanâ was-taqbalû qiblatanâ wa akalû dzabîhanâ fa qad harumat 'alaina dimâuhm wa amwâluhum illâ bihaqq*).

WAHHABĪ/MUSLIM BROTHERHOOD IDEOLOGY | 107

In fact, the words of the Prophet—may God bless him and grant him peace—assume an entirely different meaning within the hearts and minds of those who are familiar with the complexities of ta'wil (exegesis of the Qur'an and Sunnah), and who focus upon the totality of Islam's teachings, and the mission of the Prophet (saw.).

If Islam indeed constitutes a blessing for all sentient beings (and not only Muslims),[63] then it is impossible that the Prophet (saw.) would have claimed to receive a Divine command to butcher non-Muslims. If the Prophet's mission was to perfect noble character,[64] then we must acknowledge that murder—from any point of view, and regardless of who should be killed—is completely immoral. Thus, the hadith in question should be read within the context of its original transmission; within the context of Islam's teachings as a whole; and within the context of the Prophet's mission, may God bless him and grant him peace. A partial, misguided and non-contextual reading will only cause religion to become a source of great confusion and misfortune to humanity.

Based on its chain of transmission, (we must accept that) this statement was indeed made by the Prophet (saw.). Following the Messenger of God's emigration to Medina, the Quraish infidels of Mecca kept trying to kill the Messenger of God and his companions, and to annihilate Islam itself. Eventually, a Qur'anic verse was revealed, which allowed Muslims to wage war in self-defense, viz., "Permission to fight is given to those against whom war is being wrongfully waged, because they have been treated unjustly— and, verily, God has indeed the power to succor them—those who have been driven from their homelands against all right, for no other reason than their saying, 'Our Sustainer is God!'" (Qur'an 22:39–40).[65]

---

63. [Translator's note: it is a fundamental tenet of Sunni Islam that the religion of Islam is meant to be a blessing for all creatures, based on the Qur'anic verse "I (God) sent you (Muhammad) to be nothing other than a blessing for all creation" (Qur'an 21:107).]

64. [Translator's note: two of the most frequently cited hadith directly address this topic, viz., "I have not been sent for any purpose other than to perfect noble character," and "The Prophet was asked, 'Which Muslim has perfect faith?' He answered, 'One who possesses the best moral character.'"]

65. Abdullah ibn 'Abbas, Mujahid, al-Dlahhak, Qatadh and other companions

Within the context of this verse, and in response to the behavior of the Quraish infidels of Mecca, who continuously threatened the existence of Islam and the tiny Muslim community, the Messenger of God affirmed that he would wage war against "people" (within the context of this statement, "the Quraish infidels of Mecca") until they affirmed the Muslim confession of faith, prayed and paid the obligatory Muslim alms. Because the Quraish infidels' goal was to annihilate Islam and Muslims,[66] it was necessary to fight them until they accepted the existence of Islam and Muslims, which was Muhammad's actual objective, rather than forcing them to become his followers, or to embrace the Islamic religion.

When they transmitted the above-mentioned hadith, many companions of the Prophet, including Jabir, made a practice of simultaneously citing chapter 88, verses 21–22 of the Qur'an: "And so, (O Prophet), exhort them; thy task is only to exhort: thou canst not compel them (to believe)." (*Fadzakkir, innamâ Anta mudzakkir, lasta 'alaihim bi-musaithir*).[67] It was not within the province of the Messenger of God (saw.), nor of his followers, to determine whether or not the Quraish infidels would recite the confession of faith. "Verily, thou canst not guide aright even those whom thou lovest; rather, it is God who guides him that wills (to be guided)" (Qur'an 28:56). The meaning of the hadith in question becomes more clear, when we understand the context of various Qur'anic verses concerning war.

In the second chapter of the Qur'an, verses 190–193—which

---

of the Prophet (saw.)—as quoted in various books of Qur'anic exegesis written by al-Tabari, Ibn Kathir, al-Razi, Jalalain and other religious scholars—are of the identical opinion that this was the first Qur'anic verse revealed concerning war. The verse was revealed in Medina. The injustice to which it refers includes the expulsion of the Prophet and his companions from their homes in Mecca; the Quraish infidels' refusal to allow them to worship freely in Mecca; the torture, abuse and murder of many of Muhammad's followers; and various other injustices.

66. The Qur'anic exegesis written by Ibn Kathir, vol. 1, pp. 523 and 526, relates that the goal and obsession of the Quraish infidels of Mecca was indeed to wage war on Islam, in order to compel Muslims to worship gods other than God, Pure and Exalted is He!

67. Read, for example, the authoritative collection of hadith, *Shahih Muslim*, vol. 1, p. 52; and Sunan Tirmidzi, vol. 5, p. 439 and vol. 12, p. 207.

were revealed after those cited above (Quran 22:39–40)—God, Pure and Exalted is He!, decrees:

> "And fight in God's path against those who wage war against you, but do not transgress boundaries (*lâ ta'tadû*)—for verily, God does not love those who commit aggression. And slay them wherever you may come upon them, and drive them away from wherever they drove you away—for oppression is even worse than killing. And fight not against them near the Inviolable House of Worship unless they fight against you there first, but if they fight against you, slay them: such shall be the recompense of those who deny the truth. But if they desist—behold, God is much-forgiving, (and) a dispenser of grace. Hence, fight against them until there is no more oppression and all worship is devoted to God alone; but if they desist, then all hostility shall cease, save against those who (willfully) do wrong." [68]

Many Qur'anic exegetes and hadith commentators have voiced the opinion that this verse circumscribes and restricts the saying of the Prophet cited above. Specifically, these four Qur'anic verses (2:190–193) contain a number of points that we should emphasize, so that the Prophet's words cited above—which may easily be misunderstood, and all-too-often are—may instead be rightly understood in accordance with the teachings of Islam in their entirety.

It is clear from the first verse (2:190) that war may only be conducted in self-defense, and may not exceed boundaries (*lâ ta'tadû*) by becoming aggressive in nature. The second verse (2:191) permits war against those who commit oppression, but may not be conducted in the Sacred Mosque of Mecca, except in self-defense. The third verse (2:192) proclaims that hostilities must immediately cease, if and when one's opponents stop attacking, while the last

---

68. According to Mujahid, if they *stop* attacking Muslims, war must immediately cease. If, thereafter, they resume their attacks on Muslims, then they are cruel oppressors, and no hostility may be directed against anyone, except those who are being cruel and oppressive (*Tafsir* ("*Exegesis of*") Ibn Kathir, vol. 1, p. 526).

verse (2:193) states that the purpose of war is to end injustice and oppression, and that hostility may not be directed towards anyone who is not engaged in committing said oppression.

During the time of the revelation, the companions obviously knew and understood that those indicated by the term "al-nâs" (people) in the above-cited hadith, were the Quraish infidels of Mecca: i.e., a specific group of individuals who were oppressing the young Muslim community and seeking to annihilate it, and to destroy the religion of Islam itself. However, subsequent generations of Muslims, who fail to understand the context of the Prophet's statement; or nurse hatred towards others within their hearts; or who understand the teaching of Islam in a literalistic and partial manner, may interpret "al-nâs" to refer to any and all non-Muslims, at all times and places. Such people cite this hadith to justify their attacks upon anyone they regard as an infidel, and to continue doing so unless and until they embrace Islam. It is obvious that this interpretation conflicts with the basic teachings of Islam, and indeed, destroys the majestic beauty of Islam itself.

The majority of *ulama* maintain that the saying of the Prophet cited above constituted a response to the intimidation and threats posed by the Quraish infidels of Mecca. Thus, this hadith cannot be severed from the controlling message that appears in Qur'an 2:190–193, which was revealed on the eve of the liberation of Mecca. In his book *Adlwa' al-Bayân fî Tafsîr al-Qur'ân bi al-Qur'ân*, ("*The Most Profound Explanation of the Meaning of the Qur'an, with the Qur'an Itself*"), Muhammad Amin al-Syanqithi wrote that the purpose (*ghâyah*) of the above-mentioned hadith was to forestall the possibility of there occurring further oppression directed against the Muslim community.[69]

The Qur'an states that it is more cruel to oppress than to kill. In this context, oppression includes acts of intimidation, torture, tyranny, expulsion from one's home (such as occurred to the Messenger of God and his followers), assassination attempts and various other acts intended to ridicule and humiliate Muslims when

---

69. Al-Syanqithi, Muhammad Amin, *Adlwa' al-Bayân fî Tafsîr al-Qur'ân bi al-Qur'ân* ("*The Most Profound Explanation of the Meaning of the Qur'an, with the Qur'an Itself*"), vol. 6, p. 181.

they voiced the confession of faith, affirming the Oneness of God—Pure and Exalted is He! (*lâ ilâha ill-Allâh*). The Qur'an permitted members of the young Muslim community to defend themselves until there was no longer oppression, that is, until freedom of worship and the undisturbed practice of religious teachings had been secured.[70]

Given this context, the saying of the Prophet (saw.)—viz., that "I have been commanded to wage war against people, until they acknowledge there is no god but God, that Muhammad is the Messenger of God, perform ritual prayer and pay alms (zakat). If they do these things, they safeguard their lives and wealth from me, except for just cause, and their lives of selfish calculation shall instead be (completely transformed, and) surrendered to God"—should be understood as meaning: "I have been commanded to wage war against people, *until* they stop attacking Muslims, cease their oppression, and there is no longer any hostility towards anyone, except those who commit oppression,[71] for the purpose of this statement by the Prophet (saw.) was to halt tyranny and oppression.

Assuming that war was permitted, it could not exceed proper boundaries (*lâ ta'tadû*) by veering into aggressive warfare, for that would signify disobedience to God's commands—Pure and Exalted is He! Ibn Katsir has quoted Hasan al-Basri's clarification of this matter:

> Wage war against them in the path of God, and do not exceed boundaries, by doing things forbidden (by religion), such as killing women, children, old people, priests and monks, people taking refuge in synagogues, animals, or destroying trees, crops or the environment, as transmitted by Ibn 'Abbas, 'Umar ibn 'Abdul Aziz, Muqatil ibn Hibban and others, from the Messenger of God (saw.).[72]

This is how the saying of the Prophet (saw.) should be under-

70. Ibn Ishaq cited in *Tafsir* ("*Exegesis of*") al-Tsa'alabi, vol. 2, p. 110.
71. Read Mujahid's statement in *Tafsir* ("*Exegesis of*") al-Thabari, vol. 1, p. 526.
72. Read in *Tafsir* ("*Exegesis of*") Ibn Katsir, vol. 1, p. 524.

stood: viz., that a defensive war may be conducted against anyone who commits violent aggression, *until* their aggression and/or oppression ceases, and not *until* they become Muslims. Besides arising from a mistaken and non-contextual interpretation, as described above, the latter reading also betrays the fundamental teachings of Islam itself, for "there is no compulsion in religion" (Qur'an 2:257), and all human beings are free to have faith or remain infidels (Qur'an 18:29). Closely connected to this issue, in regard to a specific case, the Prophet (saw.) once said: "I have not been commanded to investigate people's hearts, and I have no objection to their feeling (whatever they happen to feel)."[73] In other words, whether or not a person has faith is God's concern, not man's.

The sayings of the Prophet (saw.) and the verses of the Qur'an cannot be properly understood, if divorced from the teachings of Islam as a whole. For the Qur'an contains both primary (universal) and specific (peripheral) messages; commands that are eternal, and others that were temporal. With regard to the hadith cited above, the message concerning war was temporal in nature, and closely tied to the context of its utterance. For that reason, it may not be generalized to apply to all non-Muslims, in every time and place. The hadith's primary and universal message is to eliminate oppression, and this may only be achieved if the rules of war are observed, and war itself conducted only in self-defense, without exceeding boundaries (*lâ ta'tadu*) or becoming an act of aggression in turn. Even if the criteria permitting war have been fulfilled, any war or act of war that exceeds the proper limits thereof cannot be accepted, for it thus betrays the very teachings of Islam itself.

A pluralistic, tolerant and spiritual understanding of the hadith in question (and of the Qur'anic verses regarding war associated therewith), serve as a "guiding principle" for the vast majority of Muslims in the world today, who reject terrorism for precisely this reason. Their pluralistic, tolerant and spiritual view of Islam stands in complete opposition to that of extremists, who manipulate the Prophet's (saw.) hadith, and various Qur'anic verses, to justify horrific acts of violence. We pray that those who teach others about Islam, and interpret the Qur'an and hadith, will seek to truly and

---

73. *Masnad* Ahmad ibn Hanbal, vol. 23, p. 332.

deeply grasp the profound teachings of Islam, rather than simply use a superficial understanding of Islam to provide legal and theological support for extremist actions. A literal reading of sacred texts, and especially a partial reading thereof, has the potential to cause enormous misunderstanding in the study and application of Islamic teachings. For Islam can only serve as *a blessing for all creation (rahmatan lil-'âlamîn)*, to the extent that Muslims themselves are possessed of noble character. If not, the formal religion of Islam will tend to manifest, instead, as a curse and affliction to all sentient beings (*laknatan lil-'âlamîn*).

It is obvious that close-minded literalism and the formalization of religion are extremely dangerous, both on the level of epistemology and in practice. Thus it is vital to recognize the hidden dangers posed by extremist groups, with their close-minded literalism and their agenda to formalize religion. The formalization they seek is driven by political, rather than spiritual, motives—including the will to power, and a determination to force others to conform to their particular interpretation of religion. It is morally, spiritually and theologically unacceptable to politicize religion—or to claim that this is an intrinsic part of religious teaching—because such formalization castrates religion itself.

Extremists embrace *religion*, rather than God, as their primary objective. If they succeed in their attempt to impose this inverted understanding on society at large, religion will be stripped of its sublime essence, and all that will remain are its "hollowed-out" symbols of greatness. This represents a gross misunderstanding and perversion of religion, which has become so widespread in contemporary society that many accept it as the truth. In reality, *religion should be seen and followed as a path (shari'a) to the Divine, enabling those who embrace religion to become the living manifestations of its sublime and noble teachings.* Whenever religion becomes a goal in and of itself, God vanishes from the scene. Viewed in this light, it is crystal clear that the formalization of religion is driven by political, rather than spiritual, motivations.

The dangers posed by the formalization of religion have grown increasingly acute in the case of Indonesia, because this process of radicalization is being conducted systematically, and with enormous financial support. It is common knowledge that Wahhabi money flows freely to Indonesia, and the government appears not to care, as if the funds in question were not accompanied by a hidden agenda, that contains the seeds of a mortal danger for Indonesia. In addition to providing the financial incentive that drives the symbiotic relationship between transnational Islamist movements and their Indonesian accomplices, these funds are employed to popularize the concept of formalizing religion, and to systematize extremist infiltration of all aspects of Indonesian life, from the state palace to the smallest of villages, and within both government and civil society institutions, using methods that no one could even imagine, except those who are fully engaged in this systematic infiltration.

As previously mentioned, it is vital to recognize that many extremist movements have employed, from the time of their establishment, a communist-like cell structure for the recruitment of new members. Those who join such an organization are trained in several stages of "development programs," such as *ta'rif* (introduction to fundamental concepts and the implantation of ideology), *takwin* (formation of one's personality in accordance with the group's teachings), and *tanfidz* (the implementation of that which is taught).[74] Illustrating the profound depths of this indoctrination, our researchers obtained information from an individual whose family members are PKS supporters in Jakarta. During a heated personal quarrel between two of his aunts, one threatened to "report" her sister, and bring their private dispute to the party's leadership. This case is reminiscent of what used to occur in Maoist China or the Stalinist Soviet Union, where a centralistic communist government sought to control all aspects of people's lives.

Due to this "cell system" of recruitment and strong financial backing, radical infiltration is well-planned, systematic and dangerous. Extremist groups are busy infiltrating countless places of worship, such as mosques; the entire educational field, including college campuses and even Nahdlatul Ulama *pesantren* (Islamic boarding schools), where they often gain entry by providing books filled with the virus of extremist ideology; the mass media; the busi-

---

74. For a complete description of the various stages that constitute this system of infiltration, it is valuable to read Haedar Nashir, op. cit., pp. 7-35.

ness world; and even political parties and the government itself. Besides infiltrating established mosques and educational institutions, radicals are also engaged in building new mosques (and renovating old ones) with financial support from the Wahhabis—such as those already described in Magelang regency—and establishing their own "integrated" schools (combining religion with academic disciplines) in many areas. This systematic infiltration represents yet another concrete expression of the marriage between Wahhabism and the Muslim Brotherhood, which is occurring in Indonesia today.

Of course, financial aid for the construction of mosques is widely regarded as beneficial and honorable. But when such aid comes with a stipulation to support certain political parties or to accept certain teachings, then this represents a naked infiltration by sects promoting a particular ideology and/or political agenda. Their purpose in building mosques is not to provide places of worship, but to erect facilities from which to propagate their ideological indoctrination and facilitate their party's political campaigning. This constitutes a blatant act of manipulation—using foreign ideology and funds (provided by Saudi Arabia) to target a guileless and unsuspecting populace—in order to seize power in the Republic of Indonesia, while these very same radicals are constantly screaming about a foreign (i.e., Western) threat to Indonesia. It was for exactly this reason that the Muhammadiyah's central board issued Muhammadiyah Central Board Decree Number 149/Kep/I.0/B/2006, which sought to prevent the PKS from continuing to infiltrate the Muhammadiyah, and instructed all Muhammadiyah administrators to drive the PKS from the organization:

> "[T]he Muhammadiyah, as one of the oldest and largest Islamic movements, reveres brotherhood, collaboration, tolerance and mutual respect towards other elements in society, especially other Muslim groups, and therefore deserves the same respect from others, and has the right to be free from intervention and/or self-interested actions by other parties that might interfere with Muhammadiyah's integrity and the performance of its responsibilities; (Considerations, point 4).... All Muhammadiyah mem-

bers need to be aware, understand and adopt a critical attitude which recognizes that every political party in this nation—including those that claim to represent 'da'wa,' or Islamic proselytism activities, such as Partai Keadilan Sejahtera (PKS)—are in fact mere political parties. Every political party is focused on the acquisition of political power (for itself). For that reason, in dealing with any political party, we must always remain committed to the true Path of the Muhammadiyah and must free ourselves from, and never engage ourselves with, the mission, interests, activities or goals of the above-mentioned political parties." (Decree, point 3)

This extremist infiltration, which includes building and repairing houses of worship (mosques) for political purposes, is reminiscent of the Dutch East Indies Company's approach, when it sought to colonize Indonesia by securing the support of indigenous allies, who established a symbiotic and parasitic relationship with the foreign colonists, like lice infesting a host. Transnational Islamist movements are systematically engaged in similar activities, because they have been fully aware, from the outset, that their efforts to "colonize" Indonesia will be strongly opposed and rejected, if conducted openly. They lack confidence, and the courage to act openly, because their ideology and agenda are completely at odds with the Indonesian people's long tradition of diversity.

There is an obvious contradiction between the religious traditions and culture of Indonesia, and extremist groups whose cultural orientation (kibla) is not the East Indies archipelago, but the Middle East. The Indonesian peoples' religious traditions are rich with spiritual values bequeathed from generation to generation, a tradition that extremist groups truly hate, and wish to destroy. This tradition teaches, and emphasizes, a pattern of living in harmony and peace—whether between humans and nature; between people of the same faith; or with those of other faiths—by accepting differences as a necessary and integral part of reality, which enriches life and should thus be valued, rather than despised. Such a pattern of diversity will never be cracked by heat nor mildewed by rain;

it will always accommodate historical developments, and whatever growth or changes occur in the lives of its adherents.

Indeed, spirituality places a primary emphasis upon developing a refined sense of awareness (*dhawq*) in religion, while rationality (*'aql*) serves as a motivating force alongside it. This is the pattern of religiosity experienced by all the Prophets, such as Abraham and Moses, may God bless them and grant them peace, when they sought God (swt.) and endeavored to know Him. When explaining the *'ubûduyah* (private, vertical) relationship between humans and the Divine, the Prophet Muhammad—may God bless him and grant him peace—said, "Worship God as though you see Him, but if you cannot see Him, verily He sees you." The expression "as though" emphasizes that the sensory organs (*hiss*) and reason (*'aql*) are of value to religion, but must be transcended, and a refined sense of awareness (*dhawq*) allowed to play its vital role in apprehending the presence of God. The sublime and unbounded nature of religious teachings and messages (from God) cannot be grasped by human reason or sensory organs, much less by ideology or political platforms. The nature of the Divine—whose revelation is the content and goal of all religious teachings—can only be apprehended by a correspondingly unbounded sense of awareness experienced through an open and divinely-illumined heart. In this context, we should meditate deeply on the meaning of God's (swt.) decree in the *qudsi* verse, "Heaven and earth cannot accommodate Me, but the heart of My faithful servant (easily does)."[75] Thus, the rejection of spirituality clearly represents a form of religious arrogance. *Significantly, it is spirituality, more than any other aspect of life, that extremist groups reject.*

The ideology of radical groups not only differs from, but directly conflicts with, this spiritual religiosity and the traditions associated with it. Extremists have reduced religion to a mere skeleton, without flesh, feelings or soul. This is the result of their close-minded and literal understanding of scripture, which amputates religion from its social, cultural and historical context, from the time of revelation to the present. This approach is what makes radicals so

---

75. [Translator's note: *hadith qudsi* are sayings of the Prophet Muhammad whose meaning and authority are believed to originate directly with God.]

obsessed with letters, and oblivious to the fact that scriptures convey a far broader message than said letters could ever contain. In their universe, the vast sublimity of religion is reduced to the narrow bounds of a closed and literalistic reading of scripture. This profound lack of awareness is what prompts radicals to claim sole possession of the truth, while simultaneously condemning as erroneous and heretical anyone who does not share their view. This occurs for the simple reason that they are incapable of understanding others' inner reality. This, despite the fact that an individual's religiosity is not measured by physical or intellectual activities alone, but more importantly, by the depths of his or her heart.

The radicals' monolithic approach to religion provides no space for differences of opinion. And by asserting theological claims, they wish to emphasize that only they are correct, and thus belong to the elect who shall be saved (mâ ana 'alaih wa ash-hâbî). Accusing others of infidelity and polytheism is a blatant form of character assassination, employed for psychological recruitment and to achieve mundane political objectives. It is difficult to identify any theological rationale that would justify such accusations. For if the extremists truly possessed a sincere religious character, and faith that was broad and deep, their hearts would be more boundless than heaven and earth, and their inner tranquility unperturbed by pluralism or diversity, or even explicit contradiction of their views. A sincere religiosity allows no space for hatred—always thinking positively (husn al-zhann) of others, and guarding against the reality of one's own flaws. Thus, while the Honorable Prophet Muhammad, may God bless him and grant him peace, said that his flock would one day be divided into 73 groups, genuine Muslims do not waste their time investigating who falls outside the circle of the "elect" (mâ ana 'alaih wa ash-hâbî), so they can brand them as infidels. Instead, their thoughts are preoccupied with whether or not they themselves have fulfilled the requirements of being true muslims (i.e., completely self-transcendent, free of ego and devoted to God).

Monolithic religiosity has truly become a threat, not only to the safety and security of Indonesia, but also to the Indonesian people's diverse religious traditions and culture. Compulsion always devours its victims. One Padri tragedy was enough. Let us not allow a repetition of communism's latent dangers, which ultimately precipitated the loss of so many lives.[76] Radical groups not only claim to be the most righteous of all Muslims; they also seek to annihilate Indonesia's diverse cultures and traditions. Whether we realize it or not, their project to formalize religion is intended to culminate not only in global Wahhabization, but also the establishment of an Islamic caliphate and/or the Islamization of the Indonesian nation state, and the disappearance of the Unitary State of the Republic of Indonesia (NKRI). Thus, by opposing the formalization of Islam, we can simultaneously accomplish three noble objectives: rescue Islam from being hijacked by extremists, and reduced to a mere shadow of its true self, for the sake of the extremists' political agenda; preserve Pancasila, NKRI and the Indonesian people's spiritually-rich religious traditions and culture; and inspire Muslims throughout the world to reject the false teachings of Islamist movements, and instead return to the sublime essence and teachings of Islam, which are truly *rahmatan lil-'âlamîn* (a blessing for all creation).

---

76. [Translator's note: In the early 1960s, the Communist Party of Indonesia (PKI) was the world's third largest, after those in China and the Soviet Union. A failed communist coup attempt in September of 1965 triggered a nationwide backlash that devastated the PKI's membership, claiming anywhere from 500,000 to 1,000,000 lives. The vast majority of these victims were *abangan* or non-practicing Muslims, massacred primarily by Muslim militias recruited by the Suharto military, to "cleanse the countryside" of anyone remotely associated with the PKI.]

Chapter III

THE IDEOLOGY AND AGENDA OF EXTREMIST MOVEMENTS IN INDONESIA

Prefatory Remarks

Virtually every Muslim is convinced that the God he or she worships is the All-Knowing, Omnipotent, Loving, Merciful and Compassionate One. Nothing in this world is concealed from His knowledge, or beyond the realm of His love and authority. In brief, God knows and dictates every aspect of His creatures' lives, including humans. However, His omnipotence is tempered by His loving kindness (*al-Rahmân 'alâ al-'arsy-istawâ* [Qur'an 20:5]).[1] Given His omnipotence, Allah—Pure and Exalted is He!—could easily have made all humans members of a single community and religion (Qur'an 11:118), but this is not what He has done. Instead, He allows His creatures to choose whether or not to have faith (Qur'an 18:29), and has even decreed that there may not be any compulsion in religion (Qur'an 2:256).

For the well-being of humanity, God teaches—via His messengers—the distinction between things that are good (*haqq*) and bad (*bâthil*); that which we should do (*wâjib*) and that which is forbidden (*haram*); behavior which humans are well-advised to emulate

---

1. "The Beneficent One is firmly established on His throne." Within the exegetical traditions of Islam, and especially those with an *isyârî* orientation, this Qur'anic verse is generally considered to indicate that God tempers His omnipotence with loving kindness and mercy. Al-Rahmân [one of the ninety-nine "beautiful names of God"] is a term that explicitly means beneficent, merciful and full of loving kindness, while *'arsy* means "the throne," which is universally regarded as a symbol of power. Thus, although God (swt.) is omnipotent, His power is effectively tempered and directed by His loving kindness.

(sunnah), and that which is inadvisable (makruh); as well as that which people are free to do or not do, as they please (ibâhah). These provisions represent a first step for humans to approach God (swt.). Only by growing progressively more intimate with God may one know what He actually desires, and what one must do, moment by moment, to live in accord with His will. In this regard, the Prophet Muhammad—may God bless him and grant him peace—has narrated that God (swt.) decreed, "My servant keeps himself in a state of constant intimacy with Me by performing pleasing acts (nawâfil), so that I may love him. And when I love him, I become the ears with which he hears, the eyes with which he sees, the tongue with which he speaks, and the feet with which he walks."[2]

When God becomes His devotee's ears, eyes, tongue and feet, His humble servant's actions are naturally confined to, and focused upon, that which God Himself wills. In other words, God dictates every aspect of the true devotee's [i.e., the saint's] life. To achieve complete self-transcendence and become a genuine servant of God—Pure and Exalted is He!—should be every Muslim's highest aspiration. Strangely, however, extremist agents—who assume an air of sanctity, and behave as if they know God's will for all humanity—are consumed by a passion to dictate and control every aspect of human life, in accord with their own partial, rigid and inhumane grasp of religious teachings.

Moderate Sunni Muslims (ahlussunnah wal-jamâ'ah) understand the phrase "God dictates every aspect of human existence" in light of the profound religiosity that always and forever exists in the Divine presence (ihsân), as described above. A genuine servant of God [i.e., a saint], who has achieved a state of purity without blemish (mukhlish), is capable of fulfilling the role of caliph [God's vice-regent], to enrich the earth and act as a true blessing for all His creatures (khalîfat Allah fil-ardl). This ability is not derived from intellectual processes, nor a textual understanding of religion, nor the possession of political power. Rather, it arises from a profound

2. In Arabic, the complete hadith qudsî reads: Lâ yazâl al-'abd yataqarrabu ilayya bi al-nawâfil hatta uhibbahu. Fa-idza ahbabtuhu, kuntu sam'ahu alladzi yasma'u bihi, kuntu 'ainâhu allati yubshiru biha, kuntu lisanahu alladzi yanthiqu bihi, kuntu rijlâhu allati yabthisyu biha.

spiritual awareness, and an expansive heart that is capable of accommodating the presence of God.[3] Unlike those who proselytize merely with words, or seek to impose their understanding of Islam upon others by force, the "religious proselytizing" (da'wa) conducted by saints—who have attained an exalted state of awareness, in which good deeds arise spontaneously from pure devotion (ihsân) to God—consists of efforts to raise the spiritual awareness of others, so that they, too, may directly experience the illuminating presence of God—Pure and Exalted is He!—and spontaneously bring every aspect of their lives into conformity with Divine will, moment by moment, in a state of true and complete surrender to God (islâm) as His humble servants (muslimîn).

Those immersed in pure devotion to God (muhsinîn) realize that shari'a is not a goal, but a path. A person's level of spiritual awareness determines whether he or she will choose the path that is true (haqq), or misguided (bâthil).

The world view and religiosity of extremist groups is completely different from that of moderate Muslims. As a result of their narrow-minded and literal interpretation of Islamic teachings, they focus on the exoteric aspects of religion and ignore its inner, spiritual dimensions.[4] Symbols, identity and quantity are far more im-

---

3. Another hadith qudsî relates that God (swt.) has proclaimed, "Heaven and earth cannot accommodate Me, but the heart of my faithful servant (easily does)." Perfect faith leaves no room for anything unpraiseworthy, and all that it receives is in accord with the Divine will.

4. In this context it is important to note that extremist movements in general ignore spirituality, and even mistakenly regard it as an innovation (bid'ah) and/or occult practice (khurafat) strictly forbidden by Islam. This is a direct result of their obsession with politics and worldly power, in addition to their literal, narrow-minded and limited understanding of the sources of Islamic teaching. For example, one of the Wahhabis' primary objectives is to attack and destroy Sufism. Global Wahhabization is, in fact, a systematic effort to render Muslims' religiosity shallow and superficial. The Muslim Brotherhood, on the other hand, is primarily obsessed with implementing shari'a as positive law, and acquiring political power. As for Hizb ut-Tahrir, its primary objective is to seize power and establish an international caliphate. Of these three transnational Islamist organizations operating in Indonesia, not one is oriented towards—or devotes any effort to—raising Muslims' spiritual awareness. If they do not demonize and seek to annihilate Sufism, at a minimum they ignore and divorce it from the Muslim community's religious traditions.

portant to them, than spiritual awareness and the quality of one's
religious experience. This explains why they wish to impose their
views of Islam upon everyone else, by formalizing and implementing Islamic law, establishing an Islamic state or caliphate, and other
related goals the extremists share.

They presume that God will be satisfied if human beings exercise political power, or rule, in His name. They imagine that God—
Pure and Exalted is He!—will be pleased, if their version of Islamic
law becomes the formal law of the land. In fact, many extremists
are subconsciously convinced that God is so pitifully weak that Islam actually needs to be defended—although, of course, this may
simply be an excuse for their hidden agenda to seize power. All of
this is inextricably linked to [the extremists'] religious and spiritual
ignorance. A little bit of knowledge is indeed highly dangerous.
Ignorance often causes people to become arrogant and reject the
truth,[5] precisely because they are incapable of comprehending or
sensing its reality.[6] In this context we may grasp the significance of
the traditional sayings, "Seek knowledge, even (if you must go) to
China!" (uthlub al-'ilm walau bi al-shîn),[7] and "knowledge is light (al-

---

5. [Translator's note: one who rejects the Truth is by definition an infidel—an
obvious implication of this passage that is not lost upon Muslim readers.]
6. Jalaluddin Rumi tells the story of a bat that denies the sun's existence, because
he has never witnessed it. Once upon a time, while dozing between wakefulness
and sleep, a bat overheard a congregation of birds praising the beauty of the
Sun, the Source of Light. The bat arose and tried to find the sun, but because
of the blinding brightness of its rays, he closed his eyes and promptly went back
to sleep. At midnight, he arose again to search for food and for the sun, which
had already set. Not finding it, he sneered and yelled at the birds, "You're all
fools and liars! The Sun you praise doesn't exist. It's just an illusion. I've looked
everywhere, and there's no sign of it." Anyone who has ever known a fool realizes that they're generally unaware of their ignorance. Arrogantly convinced that
they know more than everyone else, and are always right, fools reject the truth
whenever it doesn't coincide with their own views and feelings.
7. This tradition is extremely popular, to the point of being regarded as a hadith.
It is valuable in this regard to mention another tradition associated with the act
of study: "Man thalab al-'ilm li arba'in dakhala al-nâr—au nahwa hadzih al-kalimah—:
li-yubâhiya bih al-'ulama, au liyimâriya bih al-sufahâ', au liyashrifa bih wujuh al-nâs
ilaih, au liya'khudza bih min al-umarâ" ("Those who study for four purposes will
enter hell"—or, according to a different version:—"for the sake of feeling pride
before the ulama, to be able to debate with ordinary people, to attract others'

'ilm nûr), while ignorance is darkness." There is nothing one may expect from darkness except deviation and error, and a partial and shallow understanding of reality.[8]

When formalization of religion becomes a goal, along with the nominal embrace of Islam, then formalism and religion be-come a new god and the primary object of one's efforts, to the point that there is no longer a path (shari'a) to attain the level of actually knowing, and fulfilling, God's will (ridlâ) through spiritual apprehension. This constitutes a theological error that must be cor-rected, and indeed firmly opposed if disseminated to other people for the purpose of corrupting their understanding of Islam. Every attempt to formalize religion [through the imposition of Islamic law, and the establishment of an Islamic state, and/or caliphate] has a pure political objective: viz., to seize power. When extrem-ists claim that their actions are based on the fact that God (swt.) dictates every aspect of human life, this constitutes a blatant theo-logical error that must be refuted and rejected. No specific form of government, nor the formalization of religion, is needed to cre-ate a good muslim. All that is actually required is self-transcendent spiritual awareness, so that one may constantly feel the presence of God (ihsân). Thus, extremist claims that they will create an "Islamic society" by implementing shari'a or establishing an Islamic state or caliphate are nothing more than political maneuvers employed to justify the seizure of power.

Extremist ideology, which is totalitarian and centralistic by nature, positions religion as a mere theological reference helpful in achieving worldly goals. In other words, the theological claims asserted by extremists are, in fact, blatant political maneuvers de-signed to attack and discredit whoever dares to oppose them, or refuses to go along with their agenda, while simultaneously shield-ing them from attack by their political opponents. Far from "de-fending Islam," or implementing its teachings, Muslim extremists

---

attention, or to acquire government favoritism" (Abu Muhammad 'Abdullah ibn 'Abdurrahman ibn al-Fadll ibn Bahram al-Darimi, Sunan al-Dârimî (Kairo: Mauqi' al-Wizârat al-Auqâf al-Mishriyah, undated.), vol. I, p. 410).

8. The tale "Touching an Elephant in the Dark" explicitly addresses this mat-ter, and is related in the epilogue to this book, written by Kyai Haji A. Mustofa Bisri.

shamelessly transform Islam into a tool for the acquisition of power. Extremist agents are devilishly clever at exploiting Muslims' belief that God (swt.) dictates every aspect of human life, and use this belief as an entry point through which the extremists themselves can dominate and rule the masses. Meanwhile, their true agenda is to acquire unlimited power, by becoming God's vice-regents on earth (khalîfat Allâh fil-ardl). When in reality, the only people who can truly become God's vice-regents on earth (caliphs) are those who have attained the status of muhsinîn (those of pure devotion) and mukhlishîn (those whose purity is without blemish), namely, the beloved friends of God—Pure and Exalted is He! [9]

Most Sufis regard shari'a as a path, and not a goal. Hence, they are generally tolerant and inclusive whenever they encounter those traveling along a different path. They realize that anyone who sincerely journeys along a religious path (whatever the faith involved) wishes to approach God, the Origin of all that exists. This awareness of sharing a common goal makes them tolerant of differences. Of course, artificial differences do exist—not only between those of different faiths, but also between the adherents of one and the same religion. Yet substantive commonalities also exist between, and may unite, those who truly seek God. That is why Sufis—religious believers who strongly emphasize the spiritual dimensions of faith—never think about forcing others to travel the same path as they, for no matter what path one takes, the goal remains the same. Sufis are generally convinced that every individual has his or her own path, suitable to his personal tendencies and beliefs, through which to approach God. For Sufis, shari'a constitutes not one but many paths which, if followed correctly, will lead whoever travels along them to the Source of all that exists, and the Goal of all paths, i.e., to Allah—Pure and Exalted is He!

Similarly, in reverse: if the path (shari'a) that should be followed as a tool (to aid in approaching God) is altered and regarded as a goal, travelers along that path will be treading in place, and not reach the final destination. In the midst of their confusion,

---

9. [Translator's note: the Muslim term for saint is wali Allah, which literally means God's representative, but is also understood to mean "beloved friend of God."]

they may seek to invite, or even force, those traveling on different paths to join them in transforming the path into a goal, because they wish to have many companions and not feel left behind in the journey. They do this without ever realizing that they themselves are neither advancing along the path, nor approaching their true and final destination.[10]

As can be seen from the following report—which describes extensive field research conducted by LibForAll Foundation—the rhetoric employed by extremist agents, in analyzing the problems that confront Muslims, diminishes and distorts Islam's primary message, and even its sublime nature, which is meant to be *rahmatan lil-'âlamîn*, or a blessing for all creation. For example, extremists denigrate, and even brand as infidels, anyone who does not share their understanding, beliefs or religion. In addition to overturning and mutilating the sublime majesty of Islam's teachings—a travesty that must be corrected—their actions also threaten Pancasila, and the unity and security of the Unitary State of the Republic of Indonesia (NKRI). It is vital to realize that extremist rhetoric, with its devious theological packaging, serves as a prelude to violent actions expressed in various ways.

Totalitarian/Centralistic Ideology and the Politicization of Shari'a

An ideological approach to *shari'a* that is totalitarian and centralistic in nature, will inevitably encourage the implementation of laws that are similarly totalitarian and centralistic. Those who advocate such an approach to *shari'a* maintain that the law should dictate every aspect of a religious community's life, without exception, and that government should determine and control the precise understanding and application of Islamic law. Thus, according

---

10. The literal meaning of *shari'a* is "water path," or river. Water flows in a spontaneous manner along this path in keeping with its nature, and will continue flowing until it reaches the sea, which is both its source and destination. According to this fundamental understanding of *shari'a*, all who follow a path correctly will reach their Source and Destination (*al-Awal wal-Akhir*), although not everyone is aware of their Origin and Divinely-intended Goal (for a complete explanation of this principle, see: Muhammad ibn Mukrim ibn Manzhur al-Ifriqi al-Mishri, *Lisân al-'Arab* (Beirut: Dâr al-Shâdir, undated.), vol. 8, p. 175).

to this view, *shari'a* cannot be divorced from politics. This totalitarian/centralistic ideology has become increasingly dominant of late, as evidenced by the numerous radical groups active in Indonesia, and in the politicization of *shari'a* that arises from their narrow and partial understanding of *shari'a* itself.

The politicization of *shari'a* was extremely widespread among the extremist agents ("respondents") who participated in the field research published in this book. For example, in regions where powerful movements have emerged to advocate the institutionalization of *shari'a*—such as Padang, Aceh, Makassar and Palembang—many religious events are being conducted with a dual purpose. The objectives in question include not only establishing Islamic law, but also propagating and reinforcing a specific political identity, and a corresponding set of attitudes concerning specific national issues. In Padang, for example, KPPSI has been holding massive religious events, in order to campaign for the speedy institutionalization of *shari'a* in the region's social life. In Palembang, FU3-SS energetically supports the so-called "unity of the *ulama* (religious clerics) and Muslim population," through religious events and other forums designed for this purpose. In numerous other regions and social settings, religious gatherings are being deliberately redirected from worship of God to the politicization of *shari'a*, in order to induce the public to support the formalization of Islamic law, in addition to propagating a specific political identity and set of attitudes concerning social and political issues in general.

It is clear from these activities that the so-called "need" for Islamic law does not arise from a pure longing for the rule of law, or the dictates of religious truth, but rather, from a need to reinforce identity and secure political advantage on the part of extremist groups, whose agenda is served by exploiting religious issues (i.e., *shari'a*). Opportunistic politicians who cooperate with extremist groups to politicize and institutionalize *shari'a* are not only unconcerned about the future of our nation and its people, but are effectively participating in a *coup d'etat* against our very constitution.

Within the context of regional Indonesian politics, the jargon of *shari'a* is often employed not to refer to an individual Muslim's fidelity to Islamic teachings, but rather, as a symbol and tool to resist political domination by the central government. This became obvious from many of the arguments presented by this study's respondents, which were far more often characterized by political nuance, than by issues concerning the requirements of substantive law itself. *Shari'a* is thus transformed into a political tool, used to affirm a specific identity, rather than advocated purely as a way of expressing fidelity to religious teachings. The history of Aceh clearly illustrates this point. The Free Aceh Movement (GAM) emerged from a deeply rooted complex of problems which had little if anything to do with religious issues. GAM's primary complaint, in fact, stemmed from Acehnese disappointment with the central government in Jakarta, prompting an inter-regional conflict that lasted for decades, with enormous loss of life.[11] Some of the key motivating factors behind the Darul Islam/TII (Tentara Islam Indonesia, or Islamic Army of Indonesia) rebellion were similarly mundane and personal in nature. Kartosuwirjo, the animating figure in the DI/TII rebellion, was originally a leader of PSII (Partai Sarekat Islam Indonesia), which he left because of disappointment with its policies. His subsequent rebellion against the Sukarno government stemmed from similar disappointments, which may be seen from two secret letters Kartosuwirjo wrote to Sukarno.[12]

The campaign to establish Islamic law in Aceh gained momentum only *after* the peace settlement between GAM and the Indonesian government, which followed the devastating tsunami of December, 2004. From the time of its founding in 1976, GAM itself never pursued an agenda to establish Islamic law in Aceh. Rather, it was the central government in Jakarta that first opened the door to implementation of *shari'a* in Aceh, at the height of the rebellion, while the current movement for a rigorous application of *shari'a* often involves groups disappointed by GAM's reconciliation with the Indonesian government.

Interviews conducted with Acehnese respondents revealed the emergence of puritanical groups along the coast of West Aceh

---

11. Taufik Abdullah, *Islam dan Masyarakat: Pantulan Sejarah Indonesia*, (Jakarta: LP3ES, 1987) pp. 178-197.
12. B. J. Boland, *The Struggle of Islam in Modern Indonesia*, (Leiden and The Hague: Martinus Nijhoff, 1982), pp. 55-62.

(Meulaboh), which aim to impose Islamic law ever more rigorously in the personal lives of Acehnese inhabitants, and society at large. Our research also involved a number of Acehnese respondents who strongly support the implementation of *shari'a* (Islamic law) locally and nationwide, although their ideas were for the most part still at the level of abstraction, and had not yet reached the level of practical implementation in the daily lives of Aceh's inhabitants. [13]

Consistent with this extremist agenda, the canon of Islamic law has now been officially implemented in Aceh, as a legal instrument that constitutionally controls and directs the lives of Muslim inhabitants of that region. Our researchers observed that a strong pro and contra debate appeared among Acehnese respondents, as to exactly what form *shari'a* values should assume, when concretized as specific rules to govern daily life. Yet regardless of any differences of opinion among respondents concerning the details of Islamic law, they universally affirmed that *shari'a* law must be established—not only in Aceh, but nationwide—following the reconciliation between GAM and the Republic of Indonesia.

In general, our field research also ascertained that calls to establish *shari'a* were more often based upon a sense of disappointment with the social and political situation in contemporary Indonesia, than a genuine religious (i.e., spiritual) enthusiasm. Nearly all respondents argued that *shari'a* was necessary to solve the various problems they face in life. They also argued that the prolonged crisis afflicting Indonesian society stems from a national development strategy that is excessively oriented towards Western models. As a campus activist in Yogyakarta put it: "Because capitalism and liberalism have served as the basis for our national development all these years, it's no wonder that Indonesia has fallen into crisis. In this situation, the only solution is *shari'a*."

---

13. [Translator's note: the field research in Aceh was conducted during 2007, not long after a peace agreement had been signed between GAM and the central government. Since that time, Aceh has witnessed the establishment of a religious police—like that of Saudi Arabia and the former Taliban regime in Afghanistan—to enforce Islamic law, with strict punishment for "crimes" that now include failure to attend mandatory prayers, fraternization between the sexes, and women's failure to "properly" veil themselves.]

The cause of the political crisis is our belief that there are laws that are better and more appropriate than Islamic law. As a result, Islam no longer governs society. It is operative only on the level of morality and rituals. But when it comes to solutions, Islam is kept at a distance, because people assume that shari'a law is not an appropriate solution to political, social, economic and other problems.

Another activist explained it this way:

Actually, there is only one thing we need to do, which is to teach, inform and convince the public that Islam has perfect rules to govern society. That is, Islam is the appropriate solution, and we don't need to look anywhere else for guidance.

Contrary to the assumptions underlying this statement, experts in Qur'anic exegesis, including most ulama (religious scholars), recognize that Islam is not isolated and distinct from other religions. It did not suddenly descend to earth as a totally new and distinct phenomenon. Indeed, it may be said that Islam is complementary—completing and perfecting other religions—and not an alternative that refuses to acknowledge the truth of other faiths.[14]

This study's respondents generally view the legal prescriptions of shari'a as rigid and inflexible rules, which must serve as normative guidance for society at large. "As sacred law, shari'a IS rigid," one such respondent proclaimed, "because it comes not from a worldly source, but from God, who knows every detail of human existence. Shari'a exists to improve human life, which is unruly and chaotic. That's why humans must obey Divine law, rather than imagining that God's law should conform to human desires. Divine law must be firm, because human nature is inclined to frivolity."

Of course, we may accept the notion that humans should ideally follow the teachings (i.e., the law) of their religion. The prob-

---

14. Explanation by Kyai Haji Abdurrahman Wahid in *Ocean of Revelations: Understanding Islam as a Blessing for All Creation*, Episode 4, "People of Faith," Program Supervisor: Kyai Haji A. Mustofa Bisri, © LibForAll Foundation, 2009.

lem arises when we contemplate who will interpret God's decrees, and translate these into specific regulations that carry the force of state authority, and thus become positive law. In this context, we must emphasize that this entire process represents the application of human understanding to Divine decrees, and any resulting "dictates" should not be confused with Divine law itself.[15] Yet it is precisely this gross misunderstanding—i.e., the conflation of their own rigid interpretations of the Qur'an and Sunnah, with Divine Law itself—that has propagated in extremist circles to the point of being widely accepted as the truth, giving rise to the absolutist, totalitarian and violent behavior we witness on a daily basis.

This ideological orientation produces a concept of Islamic law that emphasizes corporal punishment for the violation of *shari'a* regulations. A respondent from Padang expressed the view that:

> In order to eradicate theft, we must punish thieves in accordance with Islamic *shari'a*[16]—that is, cut off their

---

15. The founders of the various Islamic "schools of law," such as Abû Hanîfah, Malik ibn Anas, Muhammad ibn Idrîs al-Syafi'î, and Ahmad ibn Hanbal, instructed their disciples not to blindly accept their interpretations. Instead, they told their students to re-examine the product of interpretation, because although their opinions about the law were based on sacred sources that possess the authority of Truth, they themselves were merely human beings, and did not possess the authority of Truth. Abu Hanifa even told his closest disciple, "Woe to you, O Yusuf! What I've said today, I will alter tomorrow. And what I say tomorrow, I will change again the following day," because Yusuf blindly accepted and followed whatever his teacher said. Thus, how can those who are not *mujtahid* (confirmed experts in the interpretation of Islamic law) feel as if they have a right to enact laws and force others to abide by them, when even the founders of Islam's most renowned schools of jurisprudence never agreed for their *fatwas* to become official state jurisprudence, with the force of positive law?

16. [Translator's note: both the extremist leaders who participated in this study, and the moderate Muslim figures responsible for this book, frequently refer to "Islamic *shari'a*" when speaking of the legal aspects of *shari'a*, or Islamic jurisprudence. This is to distinguish Islamic law from Christian, Hindu, Buddhist or secular laws or custom. The authors of this book also deliberately and consistently appended the term "Islamic" to "*shari'a*" whenever using the term "*shari'a*" to refer to Islamic law, in order to distinguish this historically-derived and legalistic meaning of the term "*shari'a*" from its original meaning as used in the Qur'an, viz., "the path to God." Because non-Muslim English-speaking readers are generally not sensitive to these distinctions, and likely to be discomfited by

hand. If they steal again, cut off their other hand, and then both their feet, leaving them to die. Islamic law deters people from committing crimes.

This orientation towards corporal punishment is the product of a legal philosophy that seeks to severely punish criminals, and arouse fear in everyone else. The above quote illustrates how most extremists have an extremely shallow view of *shari'a* as a harsh and violent legal system, which is oriented towards institutionalized revenge. In their view, it is necessary and appropriate to punish—as harshly as possible—those who violate Islamic law, so they will not wish (or be able) to repeat the forbidden behavior. The effect of this approach is to render Islamic law inhumane, and devoid of any spirit of education. In Aceh, where local authorities routinely whip those who transgress the traditional canons of Islamic law, the stigma so often applied to *shari'a*—as a harsh, primitive and violent system of jurisprudence—is undeniably accurate, and on display for all to see.

Extremist support for a legal system characterized by physical punishment makes sense, if we realize that it is inextricably tied to a longing to return to Islam's formative era. This naturally gives rise to backward-looking thoughts—in this case, an enthusiastic desire to model the implementation of contemporary law on the practices of a by-gone era. Of course, it was only natural that the traditions of Islamic law developed in 7th century Arabia included physical punishments such as whipping, the severing of hands and so forth, since these legal methodologies were, in all probability, consistent with the uncivilized state of Arab society at the time. But

the constant juxtaposition of the terms "Islamic" and "*shari'a*" (perceiving them as redundant), we have generally omitted the word "Islamic" before "*shari'a*" in the translated text. Where the juxtaposition does still occur, it is simply meant to remind readers of the vital distinction between "*shari'a*" as the path to God, and "Islamic *shari'a*" as a system of jurisprudence developed in the centuries following Muhammad's death, by humans applying the faculty of reason to study of the Qur'an and Sunnah, in search of rules to guide the burgeoning Muslim community, which no longer consisted of a few thousand Arabs living in a primitive environment, isolated from the issues that confronted Muslims once their power expanded to the heart of the ancient civilized world.]

when people seek to revive such corporal punishments in the contemporary world, it is extremely likely that this will corrupt *shari'a* itself, and not merely because of the widespread negative attitudes this will evoke—not only towards such barbaric legal traditions, but even towards *shari'a* and Islam itself. Of the 591 extremist agents interviewed for this study, we could not identify a single one who favored contextualizing, reinterpreting and thus "modernizing" the teachings of *shari'a* (Islamic jurisprudence) in regard to the above-mentioned legal philosophy. Thus, we may conclude that methods of corporal punishment—and a desire to enforce such backward-looking interpretations of *shari'a*—remain completely "mainstream" for members of extremist movements active in the Indonesian archipelago.[17]

It is clear that extremist agents and their leaders overwhelmingly view Islamic law in terms of harsh rules and sanctions, rather than focusing upon the goal(s) of *shari'a* itself. This, despite the fact that in the 12th century, al-Ghazali (*al-Mustashfâ min 'Ilm al-ushûl*, vol. I, p. 284)—followed by al-Shatibi (*al-Muwâfaqât fî Ushûl al-Ahkam*, vol. I, p. 380)—explained the philosophical view that the purpose of the law (*maqâshid al-sharî'ah*) is not to punish transgressors, but to protect five key values in human life (*al-dlarîriyyât al-khamsah*), namely: the practice of religion, life, property, honor (or offspring),

---

17. [Translator's note: "Banda Aceh, Indonesia – A controversial bill that includes a provision for the stoning to death of adulterers is now officially law, even without the signature of the Aceh governor, a local councilor said on Thursday. The draft of the Qanun Jinayat Code, a set of bylaws that replaces elements of the Criminal Code with Shariah provisions for Muslims, was endorsed by the Aceh Legislative Council on Sept. 14. The measures call for the stoning of adulterers and 100 lashes for anyone caught engaging in premarital sex, among its other punishments. The ratification of the bill has been sharply criticized by human rights activists, and Governor Irwandi Yusuf reportedly refused to sign it into law. Moharriadi Syafari, a councilor from the Muslim-based Prosperous Justice Party (PKS), said the main reason for the law was to "save" people in Aceh from acts not approved by religion. 'Human rights activists should not see the Qanun Jinayat from a narrow-minded perspective, as though it breaches human rights, because basically Islamic law has a high respect for human rights,' Syafari said. He said the bill automatically became law 30 days after being endorsed by the council despite the governor's refusal to endorse the measure." "Stoning, Caning Are Now the Law in Aceh, Local Legislator Says" *The Jakarta Globe*, 15 October 2009.]

and mental health. From this perspective, the specific details of the law are viewed as part of an educational process, which involves criminals in a positive sense, in that they may still be taught to live a better life. For example, legal verses in the Qur'an, such as those concerning theft, were of course not revealed to humanity for the purpose of severing thieves' hands.

So what motivates extremists, and what is their reasoning, when they seek to impose shari'a with that kind of [horrific and barbaric] face? In light of the above analysis, the desire to enact corporal punishment appears to be motivated by radicals' wish to attract attention to themselves, and shari'a, as an alternative to that which we generally witness in daily life. In other words, their motivation for imposing a harsh and violent form of shari'a arises from an impulse to appear different from other Indonesians, and to build a distinct identity for themselves and their followers, amid the great variety of legal traditions that exist within the Indonesian archipelago.

Radicals may also be intentionally promoting this different understanding [of the Divine path, and criminal law] in order to offer a truly distinct commodity (shari'a) that will enhance their political standing with a public that is genuinely searching for solutions to the many problems confronting our society. It is clear why extremist groups condemn the idea of reinterpreting shari'a—which reformists advocate—and also reject the views of moderate Muslims, who place a much greater emphasis upon the humane and educational dimensions of shari'a, in their practice of Islam. From an extremist perspective, any efforts to reform Islam and shari'a are merely deceptive tactics employed by "the enemies of Islam," who deliberately seek to prevent Muslims from practicing shari'a. They are convinced that there is no need for Muslims to reform shari'a, because it is shalih li kulli zaman wa makan—that is, consistent with every form of society, and throughout the passage of time.

Of course, all [Muslims] will agree that shari'a is consistent with the needs of every time and place. However, we must realize that in this context, shari'a cannot be reduced to a set of legal fatwas that constitute the product of human interpretation, conducted by various ulama. In the case of Qur'anic verses concerning theft, for example, Sunni *ulama* agree that the perennial message (*shalih li kulli zaman wa makan*) contained within these verses is the prohibition of theft, not the severing of hands. This was abundantly clear from the behavior of 'Umar ibn al-Khathab, for example, who—when he was Commander of the Faithful—did not sever the hand of a thief who was brought before him for judgment.[18] Unfortunately, extremist agents have reduced *shari'a* to a set of *fatwas* and legal edicts—perhaps because their knowledge of Islam is so impoverished—although the former (*shari'a*) is perennial by nature, while the latter (*fatwas*) are obviously constrained by time and place.

The Obsession to Implement Shari'a

As is well known, the idea and aspiration of establishing an Islamic state in Indonesia has given rise to various responses among the general public, in both Muslim and non-Muslim circles. Some extremists maintain that the issue of an Islamic state is being deliberately propagated [by enemies of Islam], in order to discredit Muslim groups, while others not only acknowledge the existence of this agenda, but forthrightly claim that the establishment of an Islamic state is inevitable.[19]

---

18. [Translator's note: 'Umar ibn al-Khathab was a close companion of the Prophet, and second of the "rightly-guided caliphs" who led the Muslim community following Muhammad's death.]

19. Islamist political parties such as the PKS generally deny allegations that they seek to establish, or facilitate the establishment of, an Islamic state. Yet former Indonesian president Kyai Haji Abdurrahman Wahid says that the PKS does indeed wish to establish an Islamic state. (From an interview with former president Wahid that appeared in Reuters news service on 10 July 2008: "Indonesian Islamist party eyes polls and presidency"). Meanwhile, non-Islamist politicians and political parties generally act in an "objective" manner, in response to current political dynamics. Thus, if nationalist political parties continue to dominate the legislative and executive branches of government, the extremists' aspiration to establish an Islamic state will not be achieved. (See Harold Crouch, "The Recent Resurgence of Political Islam in Indonesia," in Anthony L. Smith, ed., *Islam in Southeast Asia: Analysing Recent Developments*, Singapore, ISEAS, 2002, p. 2). Nonetheless, Indonesian nationalists and/or non-Muslims generally believe that Islamist communities have never abandoned the aspiration to establish an Islamic state. See, for example, "Islamic Aspirations within a National Context," in Komaruddin Hidayat and Ahmad Gaus AF (editors), "*Menjadi Indonesia: 13 Abad Eksistensi Islam di Bumi Nusantara (Becoming Indonesia: 13 Centuries of Islam*

From an historical perspective, S. Maridjan Kartosuwirjo pro-claimed the establishment of an Indonesian Islamic State (*Negara Islam Indonesia*) or Abode of Islam (*Darul Islam*) in West Java in 1948. Later, his armed rebellion against the Indonesian govern-ment was joined by Daud Beureuh in Aceh and Kahar Mazakkar in South Sulawesi.[20] In recent years, Aceh has formally adopted Islamic law, while many districts in West Java and South Sulawesi have promulgated regional *shari'a* regulations following the decen-tralization of Indonesia's government in 1999.

Do political developments in these three regions represent not only the triumph of the idea of an Islamic state, but also serve as a harbinger for the implementation of *shari'a* in other parts of Indonesia, in a so-called "domino effect"? The answer is not yet clear. But one thing is certain: the issue of implementing *shari'a*, as seen in the promulgation of dozens of regional *shari'a* regulations, has elicited widespread public speculation about the possibility of establishing an Islamic state on a national level. Significantly, vari-ous groups now working to implement *shari'a* have demonstrable links to the former armed struggles of NII and DI, as in the case of extremist groups active in Cianjur in West Java (NII KW9) and South Sulawesi (through the Preparatory Committee for the Estab-lishment of Islamic *Shari'a*, or KPPSI, which is clearly tied to Kahar Mazakkar's rebellion from the 1950s).[21] [22]

---

in the East Indies Archipelago) (Jakarta: Mizan dan Yayasan Festival Istiqlal, 2006), p. 599.

20. Kahar Mazakkar of NII should not be confused with Kahar Muzakkir, a prominent Muhammadiyah leader who participated in the adoption and pro-motion of Pancasila as Indonesia's secular state ideology in 1945.

21. Taufik Adnan Amal and Samsu Rizal Panggabean, *Politik Syariat Islam: Dari Indonesia hingga Nigeria* (*The Politics of Islamic Shari'a: From Indonesia to Nigeria*) (Jakarta: Alvabet, 2004), pp. 83 and 89.

22. [Translator's note: "In recent years, extremists have taken advantage of re-gional autonomy to impose Shariah-based regulations in nearly 70 of Indonesia's 364 local regencies. These laws, among other things, compel women and girls to wear so-called "Muslim" clothing that reveals only the face, hands and feet, even if they are Christian; require students, civil servants and even couples applying for marriage to demonstrate an ability to read the Quran; and effectively restrict women from going out at night without a male relative.

"Mr. Dhume's description of the extremists' rise will be dispiriting to those who

The formal establishment of Islamic law represents a blatant violation of Indonesia's constitution. Yet various loopholes and strategies exist, through which extremists seek to accomplish their objective, including regional autonomy.[23] Activists from hard-line movements work closely with opportunistic politicians and government officials in regions throughout Indonesia, exploiting local autonomy in order to implement *shari'a* through regional *shari'a* regulations. On the one hand, this approach demonstrates the extreme difficulty radicals have encountered in their attempt to create an Islamic state by constitutionally implementing *shari'a* at a national level. Instead, they are employing a strategy of "encircling

---

view democracy as an antidote to radicalism. Indeed, one of the most striking facts he reports is the extent to which those leading the charge to institutionalize radicalism in Indonesia today are directly linked to post-independence rebellions and failed extremist movements from the past. Whereas their ideological forebears (and literally, in many cases, their fathers or grandfathers) were crushed by Indonesian nationalists committed to upholding Indonesia's secular constitution and pluralist state ideology, the new generation of radicals use democracy and the symbols of Islam to erode and ultimately destroy Indonesia's heritage of religious pluralism and tolerance. This phenomenon is rendered possible and dramatically accelerated by the tendency of opportunistic politicians and political parties—often corrupt and lacking in Islamic legitimacy—to engage in a 'chase to the lowest common denominator' of Islam, in a cynical attempt to prove their Muslim bona fides.

"Unfortunately, the current government in Jakarta—led by President Susilo Bambang Yudhoyono—has done little to retard the rapidly metastasizing phenomenon of political Islam. This threatens not only religious minorities such as the Muslim Ahmadiyah sect and Christians, but also the safety and security of the Indonesian nation-state itself. Just this month, in fact, religious extremists beat a group of moderates marching for religious freedom on the grounds of the national monument, in full view of onlooking police and the nearby state palace." C. Holland Taylor, "Unfriendly Fanatics," *Asian Wall Street Journal*, 24 June 2008.]

23. Regional autonomy came into effect with the enactment of Law No. 22/1999, Concerning Local Government. This legislation transferred eleven specific powers from the national government to regional governments, including: agriculture, education, culture, labor, health, environment, public works, transportation, commerce and industry, capital investments and cooperatives. Five areas were reserved as the exclusive province of the central government, namely: foreign policy, national defense and security, the judicial system, monetary and financial policy, and religion. See clause 7 of Law No. 22/1999 Concerning Local Government.

and conquering a city by controlling its surrounding villages"—i.e., by formalizing *shari'a* in local regions throughout Indonesia. When enough regions have implemented *shari'a*, the final step—i.e., the establishment of an Islamic state, and enshrining *shari'a* as national law—will be merely a question of time. This strategy is evident from the remarks of one *shari'a* proponent, who claimed that "Once the population has become truly Islamic, and is following the path of *shari'a*, Indonesia will automatically become an Islamic state."[24]

The extremists are progressing ever closer to the achievement of their goal, as evidenced by a 2008 Constitutional Court decision that regional *shari'a* regulations do not violate the constitution. This Constitutional Court ruling is being interpreted by some as formal legal proof that regional *shari'a* regulations are indeed constitutional. However, we must recognize that such regulations are fundamentally sectarian in nature, and represent neither the aspirations nor the interests of the Indonesian people as a whole. Instead, they merely accommodate the interests of a small minority within the Muslim community, while violating the rights of the vast majority of Muslims and non-Muslims in general. In addition, this Constitutional Court ruling cannot be divorced from the prevailing political atmosphere in government over the past five years [when extremists have actively participated in President Susilo Bambang Yudhoyono's coalition government]. This ruling also demonstrates that Indonesia is apparently in the process of transitioning from a Pancasila State to an Islamic State (i.e., the version of Islam embraced by extremists).

The situation in Indonesia today is like that of a frog that is slowly but surely being cooked in a pot of water, whose temperature will eventually rise to a boil. Without realizing that he's in the process of being killed, the frog quietly relaxes in the water. By the time he recognizes the danger, it will be too late for him to escape. Similarly, the infiltration of extremist ideology is often neither recognized nor even sensed by those who are the targets of said infiltration. As a result, extremist movements may systematically

---

24. Habib Rizieq Shihab, "Jika Syari'ah Islam Jalan, Maka Jadi Negara Islam" ("If Shari'a is Enacted, an Islamic State Will Come into Being"), from an interview published in the journal *Tashwirul Afkar*, Edition No. 12, 2002, p. 104.

develop and expand. By the time people begin to realize the danger they pose, it may already be too late, because the extremist ideology has become a popular movement too powerful to halt.[25]

There are a variety of reasons why demands to institutionalize *shari'a* in a formal, legal manner have become so pervasive of late. The most important of these is the belief that Islam is a perfect religion that encompasses every aspect of life, without exception. According to this view, Islam should become the one and only reference point in overcoming the nation's problems. This attitude gives birth to extremist slogans such as "Rescue Indonesia with *shari'a*" (Hizb ut-Tahrir Indonesia);[26] "Establishing *shari'a* through the institutions of government is the only way to overcome our national crisis" (MMI, or Indonesian Council of Holy Warriors);[27] "The multi-dimensional crisis will end only with the establishment of Islamic *shari'a*," (FPI, or the Front for the Defense of Islam);[28] or "Islam is the solution" (PKS, which adopted this slogan from the Muslim Brotherhood).[29]

Demands for the application of *shari'a* are also being driven by a strong desire to assert a distinct "Muslim" identity, amid the intermixture of identities so common in this era of globalization.[30] Additional factors—including corruption, absence of the rule of law, and a judicial system that is not independent, and frequently subject to manipulation by special interests—also provide extremist groups with an excuse to offer an alternative legal framework,

25. Haedar Nashir, *Manifestasi Gerakan Tarbiyah: Bagaimana Sikap Muhammadyah?* (*Manifestations of the Tarbiyah Movement: How Should the Muhammadiyah Respond?*) Fifth Printing, (Yogyakarta: Suara Muhammadiyah (The Voice of Muhammadiyah), 2007), p. 59.
26. Hizb ut-Tahrir Indonesia, *Selamatkan Indonesia dengan Syari'ah* (Jakarta, HTI Press, 2006).
27. For the views of MMI, see Jamhari and Jajang Jahroni, editors, *Gerakan Salafi Radikal di Indonesia* (Jakarta: Rajawali Press, 2004), p. 50.
28. Togi Simanjuntak, *Premanisme Politik* (*Political Thuggery*) (Jakarta: ISAI, 2000), p. 54.
29. Vision of Partai Keadilan Sejahtera (PKS), see http://www.pk-sejahtera.org, "Visi dan Misi" ("Vision and Mission").
30. Noorhaidi Hasan, *Laskar Jihad: Islam, Militancy, and the Quest for Identity in Post-New Order Indonesia*. Dissertation (Utrecht University, Netherlands, 2005), pp. 179-180.

although in reality the problems we face do not stem from the specific details of current statutes, but from a defective apparatus for the enforcement of said laws.

The rationales cited by extremists provide an extremely weak and tenuous basis for demanding the establishment of *shari'a* [Islamic law]. Virtually every Muslim will agree that Islam constitutes a perfect religion, and should be one's primary reference point in confronting and seeking to address life's problems. As a matter of fact, those who adhere to virtually every other faith consider *their* religion to be perfect, also. *Shari'a* [the path to God] has been an integral part of Indonesian Muslims' daily life for centuries, ever since the arrival of Islam in the East Indies archipelago. Thus, radicals screaming at the top of their lungs and demanding the implementation of *shari'a*, are behaving in a childish and ridiculous manner—as if, all this time, Indonesian Muslims have *not* been following *shari'a* [i.e., the Islamic path to God]! Ridiculous, that is, unless what the radicals truly mean by *shari'a* is the *fiqh* (Islamic jurisprudence) institutionalized in various countries dominated by Wahhabism, such as Saudi Arabia, Afghanistan beneath the Taliban, etc. If that is what they mean by *shari'a*, then it "makes sense" that they would issue harsh demands for the implementation of *fiqh*, because the *fiqh* they advocate is extremely rigid and violent, and requires the implementation of a similarly violent "*shari'a*," as a logical accompaniment to the centralistic/totalitarian ideology that local extremist agents have adopted from the transnational groups that serve as their inspiration.

The Wahhabi concept of Islam has been imposed in the Arabian Peninsula by the Sa'ud tribe since the 18th century, at the point of a sword and accompanied by rivers of blood. When this ideology arrived in the East Indies (i.e., West Sumatra) at the turn of the 19th century, the Padri War promptly exploded, pitting Wahhabi followers against local Muslims, including traditional rulers and Sufi shaykhs. Afghanistan's Taliban regime offers another example of imposing an extreme interpretation of Islamic law, a la Wahhabism. During its rule from 1996 – 2001, the Taliban regime established a Department for Commanding Good and Preventing Evil, which was responsible for enforcing strict observance of Wahhabi teachings. Religious police patrolled the streets of Afghanistan armed with canes and automatic weapons searching for anyone who violated Taliban *fiqh* (i.e., Taliban concepts of Islamic jurisprudence). Whenever they encountered someone violating their interpretation of *shari'a*, they beat or jailed them. The actions of the Front for the Defense of Islam (FPI), whose members patrol Indonesian city streets behaving like a religious police, are quite similar to those of the religious police in Afghanistan under Taliban rule.[31]

Are the demands to implement *shari'a* that have sprung up lately in Indonesia calls, in reality, for the establishment of Wahhabi *shari'a*? Quite possibly. Especially when we consider that nearly every extremist group demanding the establishment of *shari'a* in the Indonesian archipelago has its origins in—or close ideological ties with—transnational Islamist organizations that were born in that renowned arena of conflict, the Middle East. As a matter of fact, the majority of extremist leaders in Indonesia are either of Arab descent, or studied in Saudi Arabia or other Middle Eastern countries, where they lost their native religious traditions and became Wahhabi, Muslim Brotherhood or Hizb ut-Tahrir activists.

Thus, what they are striving to promote is not true Islamic *shari'a* [the path to God] as understood by the majority of Indonesian Muslims, but rather, a Wahhabi/Muslim Brotherhood version of Islamic *shari'a* [i.e., a harsh and violent interpretation of religious law]. That is why extremist campaigns to establish *shari'a* invariably give rise to dissension and chaos among Muslims themselves, no matter where they occur. This is completely different from the

---

31. "Regarding the history of Islamic civilization, it is well known that in recent centuries the Wahhabis have been behind movements that use violence to "command good and forbid evil." When the Wahhabis seized control of Arabia, they destroyed every building or structure that they considered evil. That's why all of Saudi Arabia's Islamic heritage has been wiped out, to the point there's nothing left. The house where the Prophet lived with his wife Khadijah vanished. The Prophet's place of birth was also destroyed, and there's no trace of it today. But the strange thing is, the palaces and housing complexes of King Abdul Aziz (the founder of modern Saudi Arabia) are still beautifully preserved in Riyadh." Indonesia's former Minister of Religion, Professor Kyai Haji M. Tolchah Hasan, speaking in *Ocean of Revelations: Understanding Islam as a Blessing for All Creation*, Episode 5: "Da'wa (Proselytism)," Program Supervisor: Kyai Haji A. Mustofa Bisri, © LibForAll Foundation 2009.

da'wa (religious proselytism) generally conducted by Sunni ulama, who convey the essential and universal message of Islam, which brings spiritual refreshment to its recipients, and never chaos or disturbance.

The mighty flow of modernization and globalization, which extremists believe to have a corrupting effect upon Muslims, also serve as justifications for demanding the formalization of Islamic law.[32] Another rationale often encountered is the need to barricade Islam, and Muslims, from the flow of globalization, although what actually emerges from such efforts is a strengthening of extremist identity, through which they distinguish and separate themselves from others. Of course, every person has a right to defend himself, or herself, from outside influences. In and of itself, this is not a problem. Yet it becomes a serious problem when conducted by manipulating the instruments of state power—which rightfully belong to society at large—to achieve the goals and agenda of a single group. A prime illustration of this phenomenon is the establishment of regional shari'a regulations, which frequently conflict with the public welfare as a whole. Thus, if other Muslims reject local shari'a regulations, this is not only a natural phenomenon, but absolutely within the scope of their rights as human beings. *In fact, it is the religious and patriotic duty of every Indonesian citizen to rescue our nation from any and all groups, acting in the name of religion, whose use of force may undermine and destroy our national unity.* Here we must stress that this in no way constitutes a rejection of Islam itself, but rather, a deliberate rejection of the extremists' use of compulsion to institutionalize their rigid and partial understanding of Islam.

Extremists are aflame with a passion to restrict the vast expanse of God's love, mercy and compassion—and even the greatness of God Himself—by confining religion to the tiny box of regional shari'a regulations. Ultimately, they intend to force everyone in this nation to submit to Wahhabi shari'a, which they are feverishly seeking to enshrine in law. Ironically, while compelling others

---

32. Sukron Kamil dan Chaider S. Bamualim (editors), *Syari'ah Islam dan HAM: Dampak Perda Syari'ah terhadap Kebebasan Sipil, Hak-hak Perempuan, dan Non-Muslim (Islamic Shari'a and Human Rights: The Impact of Regional Shari'a Regulations Upon Civil Liberty, Women's Rights and Non-Muslims)* (Jakarta: CSRC-UIN Jakarta, 2007), pp. xxiii-xxiv.

to submit to their will, they have the gall to claim that their rigid understanding of Islam is a blessing for all people (*Islam rahmatan lil-'âlamîn*), and use this as an excuse to force everyone else to embrace their views, despite the fact that compulsion is incompatible with the spirit of love, mercy and compassion. Rather than develop a more profound faith in Islam, most people will merely become cynical, while their hearts reject such blatantly false claims.

In other words, the behavior of those who have hijacked religion for their own purposes is contaminating the noble doctrine of Islam as a blessing for all creation (*Islam rahmatan lil-'âlamîn*), and rendering this claim an object of ridicule and disrepute. In reality, the extremists are nothing but petty dictators, who seek to deceive Muslims by wearing masks that conceal their human fallibility, while presenting themselves to the world as God's chosen spokesmen. Such behavior is not only subversive and treasonous to our nation, but also to the greatness and power of God, *subhânahu wa ta'âlâ*—Pure and Exalted is He!—for Allah forbids the use of any form of compulsion in the field of religion (*lâ ikrâh fid-dîn*), and never bestows a mandate for others to become his personal spokesmen.

The issuance of regional *shari'a* regulations is generally facilitated by political parties that claim to be "Islamic," working in conjunction with opportunistic politicians and political parties in regional legislatures, with either the support of, or pressure from, extremist groups. In South Sulawesi and West Sumatra, the Preparatory Committee for the Establishment of Islamic *Shari'a* (KPPSI) has formed numerous branches to coordinate the various elements mentioned above. In other regions, pressure to implement Islamic law has often come from extremist groups such as Hizb ut-Tahrir Indonesia (HTI), the Indonesian Council of Holy Warriors (MMI), the Front for the Defense of Islam (FPI) and other organized militias that appear bearing Islamic labels, such as Laskar Jihad (Warriors of Jihad), Laskar Jundullah (Warriors of God) and Laskar fi Sabilillah (Warriors on the Path of God), whose names alone are sufficient to evoke mistrust from the majority of Muslims, let alone those of other faiths. Nationalist political parties often find it difficult to oppose the establishment of regional *shari'a* regulations, either because they fear being labeled anti-Islamic, or are themselves motivated by power politics. Another reason nationalist politicians and political parties experience difficulty rejecting extremist claims and pressure, is because they lack a deep and holistic knowledge of Islam.

Extremist groups frequently accuse anyone who opposes regional *shari'a* regulations of being "anti-Islam," which constitutes a form of theological terrorism that blatantly exploits religious sentiments among the masses. Such accusations are extremely effective, because they create enormous anxiety among most Muslims. Abu Bakar Ba'asyir, the former Emir (Commander) of the Indonesian Council of Holy Warriors (MMI) and the terrorist group Jemaah Islamiyah, once threatened, "If the implementation of *shari'a* is blocked, then it's the religious duty of Muslims to wage jihad,"[33] as if all Muslims agreed with his view. Obsessed with the formal implementation of *shari'a*, Ba'asyir has repeatedly proclaimed that "Waging jihad to defeat infidels who oppose and prevent the implementation of *shari'a* is a religious duty, and the most noble of deeds."[34] Ba'asyir thus accuses anyone who opposes the implementation of regional *shari'a* regulations of being an infidel.

Local legislators and government officials who are "weak of faith" may tremble in the face of such accusations, and/or experience difficulty articulating the enormous difference between Islam itself, and the gross misunderstanding of Islam promoted by extremists. Yet virtually all *ulama* (religious scholars) who have a profound and holistic grasp of Islam, and are faithful to its truth, recognize that such accusations are nothing more than political maneuvers, with absolutely zero theological validity. Genuine *ulama* never brand others as infidels. Ferociously accusing others of being infidels, as recited above, is further proof of just how shallow and superficial the extremist understanding of Islam really is.

A graph charting the passage of regional *shari'a* regulations demonstrates a substantial rise over time. While only seven regen-

33. Statement by Abu Bakar Ba'asyir quoted by Andi Muawiyah Ramli (editor) in *Demi Ayat Tuhan: Upaya KPPSI Menegakkan Syari'ah Islam* (*For the Sake of God's Verses: The KPPSI's Efforts to Implement Islamic Shari'a*) (Jakarta: OPSI, 2006), p. 387.
34. Ibid.

cies had such regulations in 2003, by March of 2007 well over ten percent of Indonesia's 350+ regencies had passed local *shari'a* regulations, and this number continues to rise.[35] In fact, the passage of a new anti-pornography bill in 2008 has already had a negative impact in many regions.[36] For example, the newly-elected PKS governor of West Java, H. Ahmad Haryawan, promptly attempted to ban that region's traditional Jaipong dance, although a public uproar subsequently compelled the annulment of Haryawan's decree. If such abuses are permitted to continue, and a majority of Indonesia's local regencies—acting under pressure by extremist groups—implement regional *shari'a* regulations, then the path to establishing an Islamic state will lie wide and open before us. This, despite the fact that from an historical perspective, the formalization of Islam has never succeeded in resolving a nation's problems. In fact, if we realistically examine countries that loudly proclaim themselves to be "Islamic," we find that moral degradation such as corruption and other evils continue apace, while social equality, prosperity and justice remain distant goals. In other words, ethnic and tribal rivalries, political maneuvers, individual competition, speculation and corruption continue to be rampant, even after the so-called "Islamization" has occurred.[37]

Resistance to the spread of regional *shari'a* regulations does exist. The founder of the National Development Party, or PKB—former Indonesian president Kyai Haji Abdurrahman Wahid—has publicly declared that the dozens of regional *shari'a* regulations that have emerged in recent years constitute a de facto *coup d'etat*

35. *Time* magazine, 5 March 2007.
36. [Translator's note: the anti-pornography law in question criminalizes what extremists have cleverly labeled as "porno-action," which includes any form of dress, dance, art or personal behavior that ostensibly violates "social norms," and/or may result in sexual arousal. It also explicitly allows vigilante action to enforce the new legislation. Hindu and Christian regions of Indonesia have refused to implement the law, which they regard as inimical to their social and cultural traditions, and have even threatened to secede from Indonesia should the process of Islamization that gave rise to the anti-pornography law continue to proceed apace.]
37. Olivier Roy, *Gagalnya Islam Politik* (*The Failure of Political Islam*) (Jakarta: PT Serambi Ilmu Semesta, 1996), p. 32.

against Indonesia's constitution.[38] Former Muhammadiyah Chairman Prof. Dr. Ahmad Syafii Maarif has sharply criticized the discriminatory tendencies of regional *shari'a* regulations, and said that the central government must intervene and strike down such regulations, because the Constitution of 1945 guarantees freedom of religion.[39] Buya Syafii has also said that if Islamic *shari'a* were to be established as Indonesia's national law, this would lead to profound discord not only between Muslims and non-Muslims, but also between various groups of Muslims themselves.[40]

Was Buya Syafii exaggerating? Apparently not. One notable Christian reaction to the passage of regional *shari'a* regulations has been a drive to establish Manokwari, in West Papua, as a "Gospel city."[41] There have also been expressions of interest in establishing "Regional Hindu Regulations" in Bali, and "Regional Christian Regulations" in North Sulawesi and East Nusa Tenggara provinces, where the majority of the population is either Protestant or Catholic. Witnessing this proliferation of regional religious regulations, the Nahdlatul Ulama's General Chairman, Kyai Haji Hasyim Muzadi, signaled that the signs of national disintegration were already visible, as a result of efforts to compel the establishment of religious law.[42]

---

38. Statement by Kyai Haji Abdurrahman Wahid while speaking on the program, "Chatting with Gus Dur," in commemoration of National Development Day on Radio Utan Kayu, Jalan Utan Kayu No. 68 H, Jakarta, 20 May 2006. See also, http://www.gusdur.net, "Penerapan Perda Syari'ah Mengkudeta Konstitusi" ("Establishing Regional Shari'a Regulations Constitutes a Coup d'Etat Against the Constitution."

39. "Review sharia bylaws, say scholars," *The Jakarta Post*, 1 March 2008.

40. Ahmad Syafii Maarif, "Pertimbangkan Dampak yang Akan Timbul," ("Imagine the Consequences that will Ensue") in Kurniawan Zein and Saripuddin HA, *Syariat Islam Yes, Syariat Islam No: Dilema Piagam Jakarta dalam Amandemen UUD 1945 (Islamic Shari'a Yes, Islamic Shari'a No: the Dilemma of the Jakarta Charter in the Amendment of the Basic Constitution of 1945* (Jakarta: Paramadina, 2001), p. 44.

41. "Kebijakan Daerah Bernuansa Syari'ah," ("Regional Policies Have a Shari'a Nuance") *Gatra* magazine, 29 November 2007.

42. Statement by Kyai Haji Hasyim Muzadi, made during a "Dialogue Between Islam and the State" held in the Nahdlatul Ulama's headquarters building on Jalan Kramat Raya in Central Jakarta on 26 July 2007.

The world's largest Muslim organization, the Nahdlatul Ulama (NU), officially opposes the implementation of regional *shari'a* regulations. The Chairman of the NU's Supreme Council and its highest legal authority, Kyai Haji Sahal Mahfudz, has publicly declared, "We oppose the implementation of regional *shari'a* regulations, because they will lead to national disintegration. The observance of *shari'a* does not require its formalization."[43] In other words, one may follow the path to God, without its being codified into law. Speaking in the same tone, Kyai Haji Hasyim Muzadi has said that the campaign to formally establish *shari'a* threatens not only national disintegration, but also the transformation of Indonesia into an Islamic state.[44]

In 2006 the government itself—acting through Internal Affairs Minister Muhammad Ma'ruf—declared that it would inventory the various *shari'a* regulations that have appeared in regions throughout the country. These regional regulations were to have been researched and evaluated to ascertain to what extent they are consistent with, or violate, the national consensus—that is, Pancasila, the Basic Constitution of 1945, the Unitary State of the Republic of Indonesia, and Bhinneka Tunggal Ika (Oneness Amid Diversity). The Internal Affairs Minister firmly declared that any regional regulation that conflicts with these foundational principles embedded in the constitution and laws of Indonesia, or that contravenes the public interest, would be declared null and void.

However, the Muslim Brotherhood-affiliated Justice and Prosperity Party (PKS) strongly opposed the government embracing this agenda. Mahfudz Sidik, chairman of the PKS's legislative faction, said "There is no basis for the [central] government to void regional regulations that have an Islamic nuance, much less various laws that have been promulgated by regional governments, since these do not violate the constitution. Those who oppose regional *shari'a* regulations are a bunch of nervous worrywarts. These regulations will impel local residents to lead better lives. Thus, the central government shouldn't respond to anyone who objects to such regulations. There's no reason to make a big deal of all this," declared

---

43. "NU states opposition to sharia bylaws," *The Jakarta Post*, 29 July 2006.
44. Ibid.

Sidik, adding that the PKS would continue to support regional *shari'a* regulations.[45] In this context, it is clear that democracy is being manipulated to achieve undemocratic purposes. The spread of democracy is thus working hand-in-glove with a growing intolerance, and it is no exaggeration to declare that the PKS poses a greater threat to the underlying values of democracy in Indonesia, than terrorist groups such as Jemaah Islamiyah.[46]

Is it true that regional *shari'a* regulations are helping to produce a better life for Indonesians, as the PKS claims? A research report issued by the Center for the Study of Religion and Culture (CSRC) at Syarif Hidayatullah Islamic State University (UIN) in Jakarta demonstrates the exact reverse. During a public discussion of their research results held on 21-22 November 2007 in Bogor, West Java, university researchers reported that they had found no correlation between social welfare and the establishment of regional *shari'a* regulations. By all reasonable measures, people's lives did not change or improve following the establishment of said regulations. In fact, regional *shari'a* regulations have directly caused innumerable human rights violations, especially among non-Muslims and women.[47]

Non-Muslims have been forced to comply with many regional *shari'a* regulations. In Cianjur Regency in West Java, for example, it has been reported that a non-Muslim woman complained about being forced to wear a *jilbab* (a Muslim head-covering that reveals only the face) at the office every Friday. Local public school teachers and female students have reported the same. If girls do not wish to comply with school instructions to wear the *jilbab*, their parents must file an official request that they be exempted from

---

45. [Translator's note: strong PKS/Islamist influence in the legislature and the administration of Indonesian President Susilo Bambang Yudhoyono (2004 –) has, to date, blocked every attempt to overturn regional *shari'a* regulations.]

46. Sadanand Dhume, *My Friend the Fanatic: Travels with an Indonesian Islamist* (Melbourne: Text Publishing Company, 2008), pp. 264 and 269.

47. This research was published in the book, *Syari'ah Islam dan HAM: Dampak Perda Syari'ah terhadap Kebebasan Sipil, Hak-hak Perempuan, dan Non-Muslim* (*Islamic Shari'a and Human Rights: The Effect of Regional Shari'a Regulations upon Civil Liberty, Women's Rights and Non-Muslims*), Sukron Kamil dan Chaider S. Bamualim, eds. (Jakarta: CSRC-UIN Jakarta, 2007).

the requirement, and provide documentation that their daughters are not Muslim. The "jilbabization" process has also been forced upon Indonesians of Chinese descent who work at the offices of BCA Bank in Cianjur.[48] Non-Muslims were neither consulted nor involved in the decision to establish Islamic *shari'a* in Cianjur, and yet they are being forced to comply with regional *shari'a* regulations that have absolutely nothing to do with their own faith or religious practices.[49]

According to a report issued by the Wahid Institute, non-Muslim women living in Padang (West Sumatra) and Bulukumba (South Sulawesi) have also been forced to wear the *jilbab*, since the passage of regional *shari'a* regulations.[50] A Catholic parent of two girls, who were forced to wear the *jilbab* in a state-run school in Padang, tried to convince her daughters that the *jilbab* was merely a form of clothing "ethics," and that they should simply obey the rule in question. But the girls themselves were fully aware that something far more insidious was at work. They felt trapped in an environment that is openly hostile to their religion. A number of other Catholic girls in Padang have reported that their friends assume they've renounced Christianity and become Muslims, because they wear the *jilbab*. In regard to these and other cases, a prominent Catholic leader in Padang has said that regional *shari'a* regulations have already had a serious psychological impact upon non-Muslim female students.[51]

The research conducted by UIN's Center for the Study of Religion and Culture also reports that regional *shari'a* regulations generally discriminate against women. Laws requiring that women wear the *jilbab*, and especially anti-prostitution legislation, and laws forbidding women to go out at night without a close male relative, have made women afraid to engage in activities outside their homes. In Tangerang, a municipality in the Jakarta metropolitan area, a controversial case arose following the passage of Regional

48. Sukron Kamil dan Chaider S. Bamualim, eds. Ibid, p. xxviii.
49. Sukron Kamil dan Chaider S. Bamualim, eds. Ibid, p. xxvii.
50. "Govt defies calls to review sharia bylaws," *The Jakarta Post*, 16 February 2008.
51. "Catholic students forced to wear the Islamic veil," *AsiaNews.com*, accessed on 17 September 2007 at 11.39 a.m.

Regulation No. 8 in 2005. Its fourth paragraph reads: "Anyone whose appearance or behavior may arouse suspicion or the assumption that she/they are prostitute(s), is forbidden to be on public streets... or any other location." This passage has victimized honorable women who have nothing whatsoever to do with commercial sex work, but who nonetheless have been arrested, and even sentenced for prostitution. These events in Tangerang have evoked enormous controversy in Indonesia's mass media.

In Aceh, women who chose not to wear the *jilbab* have been humiliated by having their hair shaved in public. Regional laws requiring use of the *jilbab* have dishonored the good names and reputation of women who do not wear a *jilbab*, even though laws concerning the veiling of women fall into the area of theological controversy within Islam, with some *ulama* claiming that the veil is a religious obligation, while others rule that it is not.[52] In fact, the wearing of head-coverings or veils is largely a cultural phenomenon, with some Christian and Jewish women in parts of Europe and the Middle East also wearing *jilbabs* (for example, Catholic nuns).

In addition to the factors cited above, the formalization of Islamic law has become a vehicle for the pragmatic acquisition of power in various regions. The election of local Regents and legislators readily illustrates this fact. Politicians often use *shari'a* as a "selling point" for their candidacy, to attract voters. Elite politicians also employ this cynical strategy, to increase their perceived religious legitimacy.[53] For example, the head of Banjar Regency in South Kalimantan issued *shari'a* regulations at the beginning and end of his term in office. The Regent of North Hulu Sungai Regency, in South Kalimantan, implemented regional *shari'a* regulations in order to improve his image, which had been severely tarnished by criticism from local *ulama*, who disagreed with his development policies.[54] In Cianjur, a candidate for the position of Regent "sold" the issue of *shari'a* to the general public, and won the election, aided by his opportunistic appeal to religious

---

52. Sukron Kamil dan Chaider S. Bamualim, eds. Op. cit., pp. xxvi – xxvii.
53. Sukron Kamil dan Chaider S. Bamualim, eds. Op. cit., p. xxiii.
54. Sukron Kamil dan Chaider S. Bamualim, eds. Op. cit., p. xxviii.

symbols and emotion.[55]

In all these cases, *shari‘a* has served as nothing more than a political commodity. Collaboration between opportunistic politicians and extremist groups has become a new political phenomenon, which is responsible for the implementation of regional *shari‘a* regulations in so many different parts of our nation. The political self-interest that lies behind the establishment of regional *shari‘a* regulations has blinded those members of the political elite who thirst for mass support, and rendered them incapable of acknowledging or respecting the diversity of Islamic interpretations and practice embraced by the population at large. Everything within the public sphere is gradually being subordinated to a single, uniform understanding of *shari‘a*, identical to that promoted by extremist groups—i.e., Wahhabi/Muslim Brotherhood *shari‘a*. That is why most regional *shari‘a* regulations in Indonesia resemble laws established by the Saudi and Taliban regimes, which reflect a rigid, Wahhabi view of Islam. Unfortunately, many Indonesians remain oblivious to these facts, or have been intimidated by extremist groups, which are constantly brandishing their deadly ideological weapons, as captured by the phrase: "Follow us, or you are truly an infidel, and enemy of Islam!"

Such accusations constitute a blatant political maneuver. No human being ever has, or will, become an infidel merely by virtue of such accusations being leveled at him or her. Infidelity arises from the movement of one's heart (*a‘mâl al-qalb*) away from God, in opposition to religious teachings. Crude slogans such as "Islam is the solution" and "Save Indonesia with *shari‘a*" are nothing but simplistic rhetoric and a political commodity employed to psychologically recruit Muslims to support a particular party or agenda. It is no one's business but that of each and every individual—who must answer personally to God—whether he or she is an infidel, or a true believer. As the Qur'an plainly states, Allah does not impose His will upon His servants. So what excuse does any human

---

55. "Regulasi Syari‘ah di Kalimantan Selatan," in *Reform Review: Jurnal untuk Kajian dan Pemetaan Krisis* ("Shari'a Regulations in South Kalimantan," in *Reform Review: Journal for Studying and Mapping the Crisis*), Vol. I No. 1, April-June 2007, p. 59.

being have to force his will upon others, especially in the field of religion?

Shari'a as the Solution to the Multi-dimensional Crisis Facing Indonesia

The majority of respondents to this study expressed a firm belief that the crises that have afflicted Indonesia since 1997 stem from the fact that this nation has not established Islamic shari'a as the basis of public and national life, and instead employs a legal system derived from Pancasila and the 1945 Constitution. As a result, the nation keeps God's Law "at a distance," and will not allow it to serve as the primary reference point for all public policy and government decisions affecting national life. One respondent claimed that the many crises afflicting Indonesia demonstrate that "this is a nation of infidels," because Islam does not serve as its primary reference. Most respondents participating in this research sought to link the numerous crises facing Indonesia with an underlying theological cause. One respondent's comment is representative of a view expressed by many extremist leaders interviewed for this study:

> The source of the problem lies in the fact that Islamic shari'a is not being enforced. If it were, and we chopped off the hands of every thief, who would still want to steal? If every fornicator and adulterer was stoned to death, who would still want to fornicate or commit adultery?.... But if we don't chop off the hands of thieves, how many human lives will be ruined, and how much national treasure stolen, by the hands of those very thieves? And if we don't execute murderers, under the principle of an eye for an eye and a tooth for a tooth, how many lives will be lost to those very murderers?

The majority of respondents also blamed globalization for marginalizing shari'a in Indonesian life. They view globalization as synonymous with universalization, economic liberalization, Westernization or even Americanization. In regard to universalization, they believe that globalization is contributing to the spread of cultural homogenization, which in turn leads to the marginalization of religious values. The global culture that is the perennial reference point, or trend-setter, is created and developed by the West (America and Europe). That is why the respondents virtually all regard globalization as synonymous with Westernization or, to be even more specific, Americanization.

With regard to law, respondents consider the reform era (initiated by the fall of Suharto) to be characterized by the absence of legal certainty. They perceive not only the judiciary system, but also the police, to be incapable of satisfactorily enforcing the law. In fact, they blame the entire legal system for having failed to eliminate immorality, including prostitution and gambling—whether conducted openly or secretively, and on a large scale, or small—throughout Indonesia.[56]

Nearly all respondents agreed that Islamic *shari'a* is the solution for every crisis facing this nation. *Shari'a* is required to improve public morality, whose corruption results from people having distanced themselves from God. In the field of law, the deterrent effects of Islamic jurisprudence are thought to be more effective in preventing crime than the current system. These deterrent effects are profoundly needed, if the Indonesian people wish to overcome the acute and hitherto intractable problems confronting them, such as collusion, corruption and nepotism. In the field of economics, an "Islamic" system is thought to be far more effective at creating, and guaranteeing, general prosperity than a secular system built on interest.[57] They also claim that the establishment of

---

56. Extremist groups often limit their definition of immorality to gross acts such as prostitution, gambling and the like. And yet the fundamental meaning of immorality is ignorance of, rebellion against and opposition to religious certainties. Here we see, once again, how extremist groups reduce the sublime teachings of religion to a narrow outlook that conforms to their own ideology and self-interest. Or could it be that they lack a profound and complete understanding of Islam?

57. [Translator's note: both extremist and fundamentalist Muslims reject interest on loans, due to a Qur'anic prohibition of usury (*riba*). Moderate *ulama* often maintain that this Qur'anic prohibition applies not to interest per se, but to the excessive interest (i.e., usury) characteristic of loans generally made at the time of the Prophet Muhammad.]

shari'a will produce social justice, because *shari'a* is founded upon a concern for the general welfare, unlike economic systems such as capitalism, which defend the interests of an elite minority. If capitalism gives birth to social injustice, an Islamic economic system will "inevitably" give rise to social justice instead.

Many respondents said that Muslim unity is a necessary prerequisite for establishing *shari'a*. As long as Muslims are divided, reluctant to work together, and easily played off against one another [by Western and Zionist agents], it will be difficult to implement *shari'a*. According to the respondents, the fact that various extremist groups employ different strategies for establishing *shari'a* does not mean that they have no point of agreement. Virtually every radical group can agree upon at least one thing: the need to implement *shari'a*. They go about this task utilizing a variety of methods, ranging from regional *shari'a* regulations, as employed by KPPSI and similar groups; influencing public policy, as done by the Indonesian Council of Religious Scholars (MUI); entering parliament and dominating the legislative agenda, as pursued by the PKS, PBB and other political parties; and sweeping (i.e., street actions), as conducted by the FPI, FBR and other groups, in addition to a wide variety of other tactics directed to the same end.

Extremist groups have a strong tendency to view Islam as a rigid set of rules and regulations. Yet in fact, the formal religion of Islam does not consist merely of submission (*islâm*) to a fixed set of rules governing the physical dimension of life, about which there has never been universal agreement among Muslims themselves, beyond such basics as the five pillars of Islam. Islam is also deeply engaged with the spiritual and emotional dimensions of life, through faith (*îmân*) and inner and outer expressions of goodness, arising from a state of pure devotion to God (*ihsân*). Ideally, these three aspects (*islâm, îmân and ihsân*) should be properly balanced, in order to achieve a mature religiosity of the highest order. As Police Lieutenant General (ret.) I Made Mangku Pastika[58] told our

---

58. [Translator's note: General Pastika is a native Balinese Hindu, descended from Javanese nobles who fled to "the island of the Gods" in the 16th century, following the collapse of the Majapahit dynasty. He led the investigation of the first Bali bombings in October of 2002 and brought the perpetrators to justice, arresting not only the primary actors, but dozens of accomplices. General Pas-

researchers, "I have interrogated every single person we've arrested in Indonesia for the commission of terrorist acts in the name of Islam. Finally, I came to the conclusion that they idolize *shari'a* (i.e., Islamic law), and are completely ignorant of *haqiqa* (Reality/ Truth) and *ma'rifa* (Gnosis, or direct apprehension of God). Had they reached the level of *haqiqa* and *ma'rifa*, it would have been impossible for them to commit such (horrific) acts."[59]

Thus, it is no wonder that extremists seek to resolve every problem through a legalistic approach. Even when discussing the "vital issues" confronting our nation, they tend to focus on things such as theft, prostitution, alcohol and gambling. When they speak of God being distant from humanity, they do not suggest that we follow the path (*shari'a*) of spiritual awareness in order to bring ourselves closer to God, but rather, that we implement Islamic law and formalize religion, so that the Lord (or is it, "human lords"?) will come ever closer to us. In fact, it's unclear what they mean when they say that "*shari'a* is the solution to our multi-dimensional crisis." It seems they imagine that economic recovery and a better political system will naturally arise from the implementation of *shari'a* (Islamic law). Yet one thing is clear: extremist groups completely misinterpret and fail to understand the meaning of the phrase: "Islam encompasses (*syumûliyah*) every aspect of human life." They interpret the word *syumûliyah* in a purely structural, rather than spiritual, sense.

Extremists Versus the Muslim Community at Large

The findings of the research conducted for this study demonstrate significant differences of opinion between extremist groups and the majority of Muslims in general. While extremist groups appear dominant in the public sphere, in fact they clearly do not represent the views of mainstream Indonesian Islam. They simply appear to be dominant because of their militancy, and unflagging

---

tika received a Community Service Award from LibForAll Foundation and the Simon Wiesenthal Center in June of 2007 at a Holocaust conference in Bali, for successfully apprehending the terrorists who murdered over 200 in Bali, while scrupulously observing the rule of law (http://www.libforall.org/programs-religious-summit-bali.html).]

59. Consultative research interview conducted in May of 2007 in Jakarta.

chutzpah to speak loudly on every occasion. They have transformed religion into a "business," which they manipulate to acquire power, wealth and career advancement—all of which is completely at odds with the sublime values of Islamic teaching itself. Their approach to religion is thus different from the "silent majority" of Muslims, who do not commercialize their faith, but whose voices are drowned out by the enormous commotion raised by a militant and troublesome extremist minority.

Nearly all the respondents in this study, who are striving to promote regional *shari'a* regulations, proclaim that Islam is a religion that dictates every single aspect of human life. On that basis, the principles of Islam must be applied to every field of life—not only to religious worship, but also politics, economics, the law, etc. Actually, all Muslims share this view. The key difference is that extremists believe that *shari'a* must be established through the exercise of governmental authority (such as regional *shari'a* regulations). In contrast, the majority of Indonesian Muslims—who are represented by the Nahdlatul Ulama and Muhammadiyah—believe that Muslims have a personal obligation to observe Islamic *shari'a*, but that this does not need to be enforced via governmental authority, but will occur naturally by raising the spiritual awareness of each and every individual.

Extremist groups maintain that the concept of *Islam kaffah* (the complete and holistic practice of Islam) obliges Muslims to establish an Islamic government or caliphate. The majority of Muslims, on the other hand, believe that their primary obligation is to obey whatever legitimate and sovereign government rules over them, while the actual form and system of said government may vary from nation to nation.[60] These opposing perspectives have enormous practical implications regarding the position of *shari'a*, and how it should function in the public sphere, especially in a

---

60. For example, the General Chairman of the Nahdlatul Ulama's executive board, Kyai Haji Hasyim Muzadi, has said that "Whoever becomes the head of state through a legitimate process of appointment, from both a religious and state perspective, is the Caliph. There is no need to seek another model." See Hasyim Muzadi: "Khilafah Islamiyah bukan Gerakan Agama, tapi Gerakan Politik" ("The Islamic Caliphate is a Political Movement, not a Religious One"). *NU Online*, Tuesday, 5 September 2006.

pluralistic society such as Indonesia.

The respondents who participated in this study believe that *shari'a* represents an all-encompassing and complete (*syumûliyah*) system of law created by God, although they acknowledge that the Qur'an does not articulate a full set of legal procedures. This view is invariably accompanied by the belief/assertion that Islamic law must be identically observed by every Muslim throughout the world, regardless of national boundaries. In stark contrast to this view, the majority of *ulama* and Muslims believe that Islamic jurisprudence is contextual in nature—i.e., bound by space and time, and accommodative of social circumstances and development (*al-hukmu yadûr ma' al-'illah, wujûdan wa 'adâman*). A prime example of this can be seen in the legal views of Imam Shafi'i [founder of the Shafi'î school of Islamic jurisprudence], which changed after he moved from Iraq (which had given birth to *qaul qadîm*, or the "old fatwas") to Egypt (which gave birth to *qaul jadîd*, or the "new fatwas"). This is how Islamic law becomes a living entity, changing and adapting to the breath of each contemporary era.

The results of our field research also demonstrate that the legal ideology embraced by extremist groups has succeeded in producing an extremely rigid interpretation of the law. *First*, they maintain that Islamic law is capable of solving virtually every problem that exists in our modern era, and that any legal decisions reached outside the framework of a *shari'a* committee must be rejected. *Second*, the orientation of those seeking to implement Islamic law is profoundly inward-looking, to the point that they fail to pay serious attention to any issue that lies beyond the substance of Islamic law itself. This leads them to completely disregard a host of contemporary legal issues confronting the Indonesian people, such as the plurality of laws, conflicts between legal systems, and the relationship between Islamic law and other legal traditions that have long existed in Indonesia. As a result, extremists generally ignore the actual legal problems facing our nation.

Legal views such as those described above arise from an assumption that because God is the source of all life, it is inappropriate for humans to adopt any legal system that was not created by the Source of Life Himself. From this perspective, only God has the right to establish laws, because only He completely understands the needs of humanity. A respondent from Palembang, South Sumatra, succinctly expressed this view:

> The *shari'a* system is based on the Qur'an, and cannot be formed or shaped by men. No system of man-made laws can defeat the Divine system contained within the Qur'an.

Such views embrace and stress a totalitarian approach to the law. They reject anything that lies outside the system of *shari'a* [traditional Islamic jurisprudence], because they deem laws that do not originate from Islam as unworthy to serve as guidance for humanity, since they are clearly derived from human understanding. On the other hand, extremists act as if they themselves fully understand God's will, and that their own interpretations of the Qur'an are infallible. *The vast majority of Muslims most emphatically do not share this view.* Instead, they believe that any social tradition or custom that does not conflict with Islam may become law. The basis for their conviction lies within the traditions of Islamic jurisprudence itself, as expressed in the well-known phrase, "*al-'adat muhakkamah* (local customs may become law)."

The debate as to whether anyone or anything besides God may become a source of law within Islam has been raging since the beginning of Islamic history. This polemic first arose when Muslims inquired as to what role, if any, human reason could play in distinguishing between right and wrong. Those who trust in the power of reason tended to embrace a positive view. In their opinion, human reason should serve as a source of law, in determining right and wrong. In addition to Divine revelation, a clear and genuine intellect could become the judge of human actions, so that Islamic law would be based not only upon the Qur'an and Sunnah, but also upon a foundation of human reason itself. Those who opposed this view maintained that no one but God could properly judge legal issues, because God alone has the right to decide whether something is good or bad.

This simple issue about the role of the human intellect gave rise to a vigorous debate about whether Islamic law could embrace anything outside the Qur'an and Sunnah—including, for example, traditional laws or customs practiced by different societies throughout the world. The majority of Muslims believe that legal traditions embraced by local societies can indeed serve as valid legal reference points, based on the principle of Islamic jurisprudence cited above ("*al-'adat muhakkamah* / local customs may become law.")

The majority of respondents interviewed for this study expressed a contrary view: i.e., that Divine revelation is the one and only legitimate source of Islamic law. For this reason, they usually paid only lip service to the role of normative values embraced by local societies, in the creation of law. As a general rule, they also barely acknowledged the existence of any legal system outside that of Islam. For them, the "absolute perfection" of Islamic law reflects the independent nature of Islam in establishing law itself. As a consequence, they reject any and all legal "values" whose theory does not originate in revelation (i.e., the Qur'an), on the grounds that every possible case has already been addressed, and resolved, by God.[61]

This kind of ideological approach to the law has the practical effect of generating certain specific attitudes: *first*, a tendency to reject any and all normative values that originate outside the system of Islamic revelation. Local customs and legal traditions do not escape this rejection, because they are regarded as neither originating from, nor being based upon, *shari'a*. *Second*, an apathetic and/or antagonistic attitude towards the various legal traditions that currently exist within Indonesian society. This study's respondents reject the possibility of dialog between Islamic law and other legal norms, in constructing a system of national law. In other words, their view of *shari'a* produces a negative attitude that condemns and rejects the reality of legal pluralism.

It is worth mentioning a new argument articulated by certain respondents, in regard to local values and customs. This emerged

---

61. [Translator's note: this explains why Muslim extremists reject the notion of universal human rights, and tend to attack the human rights agenda as a Western conspiracy to "destroy" Islam.]

from our study's research into the Preparatory Committee for the Establishment of *Shari'a* (KPPSI) in Padang, West Sumatra. KPPSI has become an umbrella organization for various extremist groups operating in this province, including Hizb ut-Tahrir Indonesia (HTI), the Indonesian Council of Holy Warriors (MMI), Pagar Nagari and other local groups. Slogans such as "Custom (*adat*) based upon Islamic law; Islamic law based upon the Qur'an"—which were originally coined to lessen the conflict between Islamist groups and those embracing local traditions, and to bring about their reconciliation—have now been co-opted by KPPSI, and their meaning transformed, in order to undermine local customs and ensure their subordination to *shari'a*.

Such slogans no longer signify a willingness to engage in dialogue between Islam and local customs, in the process of establishing law. Rather, they have become a tool for arguing the necessity of legislating Islamic law in West Sumatra, and completely sidelining customary law. Our research uncovered such patterns of behavior not only in Padang, but also various other locations, including Gorontalo on the distant island of Sulawesi, east of Borneo.

Such an approach to the implementation of *shari'a* is, in fact, a-historical. When Islam entered the East Indies archipelago, the region was already teeming with a rich variety of religious traditions, customs and culture, including those in the field of law. Since its arrival, Islam has generally behaved in an accommodative manner (i.e., accepted local traditions), and merged with the diverse societies and cultures of the Indonesian archipelago. This was not difficult for Islam to accomplish, since its own doctrine commands that proselytizing be conducted in a manner consistent with the culture of any given society (Qur'an 14:4).[62] Islam thus melded with the diverse traditions and cultures of the East Indies, by transmitting its profound moral, spiritual and theological values. As a result, Islam spread, grew and developed in a pluralistic manner, consistent with the various cultures and societies of the East Indies archipelago, which were themselves highly pluralistic. This, in turn, gave birth

---

62. "And we have sent no Messenger save with the tongue of his people, that he might make all clear to them; then God leads astray whomsoever He will, and He guides whomsoever He will; and He is the All-mighty, the All-wise."

to the pluralistic traditions of Islamic law that remain characteristic of Indonesian society to the present day.

Islamic movements that seek to formalize religion have now turned the history of Indonesian Islam inside out. The conciliatory and accommodative attitude towards local customs, which has characterized Muslim societies in the East Indies for many centuries, is becoming thinner and thinner with the influx of foreign ideologies—such as those expounded by Wahhabis, the Muslim Brotherhood and Hizb ut-Tahrir—which are spread by extremist agents who blindly seek to "purify" religion, and reject anything they consider to be "unIslamic."

In conjunction with this ominous development, legal traditions based on local custom, which have thrived for hundreds of years in our society, are being categorically rejected. As a result, the tradition of mutual appreciation and reconciliation of different views, which underlies and embraces social diversity, is steadily diminishing. Similarly, Indonesians' long-standing positive attitude towards traditions that originate outside the formal religion of Islam, is steadily decreasing as well.

Such attitudes can easily be predicted to arise from the totalitarian/centralistic ideology of extremists, which in turn gives rise to a rigid and exclusivist view of Islamic law. According to this view, any and all traditions that originate outside Islam must be placed in a subordinate position, and *shari'a* [Islamic jurisprudence] elevated to serve as the one and only standard for evaluating the diverse normative traditions that have long thrived in Indonesia. This in turn leads to the imposition of a monolithic world view, arising from a conviction that the diverse legal traditions that actually exist in society must be altered, and made to conform to the extremists' totalitarian/centralistic and monolithic understanding of *shari'a*.

The rejection of all legal traditions originating outside *shari'a* is not only directed towards indigenous legal traditions and customs. Our researchers observed a similar attitude towards Western law among the majority of respondents, and towards the system of democracy, which they regard as having originated in the West. Nearly all respondents agreed that Islam could not possibly be equated with the West, nor Islamic values compared to Western values, because the two are not only unequal, but originate from completely different worlds. In numerous regions where the issue of implementing *shari'a* has become dominant, movements to reject anything and everything originating from the West have also emerged, and grown dominant.

In Padang, Bogor, Makassar, Aceh, Palembang and other regions, antagonism towards Western knowledge, philosophy, rationalism, etc., have simultaneously appeared alongside increasingly vigorous campaigns to implement *shari'a* in these regions. In general, respondents praised the superiority of Islam over every other system of values, and claimed that Islam does not need to adopt Western values, which they believe are antithetical to Islam, and will actually destroy the faith of Muslims exposed to said values. One respondent explained this view as follows:

> The most serious damage we have sustained is in the field of morality. And this is entirely due to the success of Jews and Christians in spreading [immorality]. We lack inner strength, and consider everything that comes from the West to be good. No, I say! No! The Qur'an provides guidance for all godly people, and only the godly will inhabit heaven.

An absolutist, *shari'a*-based ideology leads to the view that all human values originating outside Islam must be firmly rejected. The extremists' simplistic logic runs as follows: why should Muslims adopt rules or values from outside Islam, when Islam already contains and provides everything one needs to live a perfect life? This line of reasoning leads a significant portion of the study's respondents to reject democracy.

Most respondents exhibited a negative attitude not only towards the West, but also to any Muslim they believe has adopted Western modes of thought, as one respondent in Yogyakarta explained:

> A new trend emerged with the decline of Muslims. Because of faulty logic, they saw Islam in a subordinate posi-

tion and Western civilization on top. As a result, recent generations of Muslims have become blinded, and sought to achieve material advancement by imitating the West. They imagined that the only way to become developed and prosperous was to follow the West's example.

According to most respondents, Islam cannot—and will not—ever be reconciled with the West. Many also believe that it's impossible to reconcile democracy with the teachings of Islam, because democracy allocates power to the people, including the authority to create legislation, since law is understood to originate from the normative values of society. This is in direct contrast to Islam, which—the respondents maintain—teaches that God alone has the right to dictate the terms and circumstances of human life. As a respondent in Bogor stated:

> Democracy means that sovereignty rests in the hands of the people. This implies that the right to promulgate laws lies with the people, and not with God. If so, then democracy conflicts with Islam, which teaches that the right to make laws rests with God alone.

This is where the doctrine of an Islamic caliphate, as advocated by Hizb ut-Tahrir Indonesia (HTI), finds its justification. HTI regards a caliphate as Islam's answer to the Western system of democracy, whose ideological domination has deeply penetrated Muslim societies throughout the world. Although HTI is renowned for advocating the doctrine of an Islamic caliphate, many extremist groups publicly and/or privately agree with HTI's agenda, because it inherently aims to legislate Islamic law, which is an obsession shared by virtually every extremist group. The problem is, the majority of Indonesian Muslims do *not* agree with the doctrine or goal of creating an Islamic caliphate. In fact, the world's largest Muslim organization, the Nahdlatul Ulama, has officially declared that HTI's promotion of an Islamic caliphate is inextricably bound to a dangerous transnational ideology, which threatens the Indonesian people and nation state.[63]

HTI's obsession with the caliphate leads it to reject Indonesia's current system of government, which it believes is derived from Western democracy. This view accords with that of the Indonesian Council of Holy Warriors (MMI), which also rejects the system of democracy on the basis of its having been created by humans, and thus being subject to innumerable flaws. As an alternative, MMI advocates the concept of "Allah-cracy," that is, a system of government based on God's perfect laws. MMI claims that Allah-cracy, and not democracy, will bring goodness and well-being to all. In order to establish this system of Allah-cracy, MMI strives to promote an Islamic state and rejects the secular government of Indonesia, whose sole foundational principle is Pancasila.[64]

In reality, however, MMI has become deeply engaged with Indonesia's current system of government, and compromised its principles in doing so. MMI seeks to implement *shari'a* through a legislative agenda enacted by existing political institutions (i.e., the legislative and executive branches of government), rather than by flatly refusing to engage with the existing governmental structure, as HTI ostensibly does. Yet although their approaches differ, HTI and MMI share the same basic totalitarian and absolutist attitude towards the law. In that sense, their objectives are virtually identical: i.e., to gain control of the law-making process and repressive apparatus of the state, and subordinate these (and hence the public at large) to their own legal views and agenda.

In regard to abstract values and the "theological" dimensions of Islamic jurisprudence, the views of most respondents who participated in our research were nearly identical. Extensive polarization was found, however, in opinions regarding the actual application/ implementation of the law. The various (591) respondents and their

---

63. For the complete text of the Nahdlatul Ulama Bahtsul Masa'il's (law-making body's) ruling concerning an Islamic caliphate, see Appendix 2; also read: "Caliphate not part of Koran: NU," *The Jakarta Post*, 25 November 2007. See also, "PBNU Desak Pemerintah Cegah Ideologi Transnasional" ("NU Central Board Presses the Government to Halt Transnational Ideology"), *NU Online*, 29 April 2007.
64. Interview with Abu Bakar Ba'asyir in *Sabili* magazine, No. 12, Year X, January 2003, p. 25.

affiliated (50+) organizations share a theological view that *shari'a* is wholly and completely "the law of God," which was revealed in order to dictate and control virtually every aspect of individual and social life. Yet when it comes to practical matters, there is no universal agreement concerning the political processes through which the teachings of *shari'a* should be implemented in real life.[65]

This polarization exists because of a conflict between the extremists' imaginary constructs and the reality of life itself. As a result, various hard-line Islamist movements have emerged with a variety of strategies and agendas, ranging from those that seek to abolish the Unitary State of the Republic of Indonesia (NKRI) and replace it with an Islamic caliphate, while flatly rejecting democracy and not participating in elections, to others that seek to establish the supremacy of *shari'a* on the national stage through democratic mechanisms, and therefore participate in elections (such as the PKS). Other groups are striving to establish *shari'a* within a specific region, such as KPPSI in South Sulawesi and West Sumatra.

The question arises: are these campaigns to establish *shari'a* acceptable to a pluralistic Indonesian society, which has already adopted Pancasila and the 1945 Constitution as the source of our national law? And are the methods employed to establish *shari'a* consistent with the principles of *shari'a* itself?

If we examine those nations that have already implemented *shari'a*, such as Saudi Arabia, Iran, Sudan, Afghanistan, Pakistan, Nigeria and others, then *it is clear that the mere formal establishment of*

---

65. [Translator's note: this phenomenon is reminiscent of various communist movements and splinter groups during the 19th and 20th centuries, whose leaders invariably claimed to be struggling on behalf of the masses to create a "worker's paradise," but in reality led competing movements, each seeking to dominate the political landscape and eliminate its competitors. Indonesians frequently refer to the Muslim Brotherhood-affiliated political party PKS (Partai Keadilan Sejahtera, or the Justice and Prosperity Party), as Partai Kommunis Sejati (the Communist Party, in reality), because of its disciplined cadres and doctrinaire, ideological approach to politics. Research for this book indicated that several members of the PKS's innermost circle, including six of its founders, were formerly members of a communist youth movement established by Tan Malaka, a notorious member of the Communist International, who was executed by the Indonesian army in 1949, in the midst of that nation's bloody independence struggle.]

shari'a—or to be more precise, the establishment of Islamic jurisprudence, as distinguished from shari'a as the path to God—offers absolutely no guarantee of social well-being or justice. Nearly two million people have died in southern Sudan because of a civil war that erupted following the implementation of *shari'a* in 1983. In several Nigerian provinces, where *hudud* ordinances (entailing harsh corporal punishment) have been implemented, people are routinely whipped and the hands of thieves amputated, to demonstrate the rulers' "piety" in implementing "God's law." Nearly every time a bomb explodes in Afghanistan or Pakistan, it is because of someone's rigid interpretation of *shari'a*. Even in Egypt, which historically has enjoyed a strong secular tradition, extremists murdered the author Farag Foda in his office, executing a *fatwa* issued by a committee of *ulama* from al-Azhar, and the religious leaders of Egyptian Islamic Jihad, who had proclaimed Foda an apostate. Mohammed al-Ghazali, an al-Azhar scholar who defended the murderers' actions in court, claimed that if the Egyptian government failed to implement *shari'a* (including the death penalty for apostates), then every Muslim had the right to kill those who "betrayed" Islam.

The establishment of *shari'a* under the authority of *vilayat-e faqih* (the Guardianship of an Islamic Jurist) in Iran since 1979, has led millions of Shi'ite Muslims to despise and reject Islam, disgusted by the hypocrisy of their *ulama*. Far from becoming a social and spiritual paradise, Iran is plagued by one of the highest rates of drug addiction seen anywhere in the world. As for the cruel nature of Wahhabi *fiqh* (jurisprudence), as practiced in Saudi Arabia: in 2002, fifteen teenage girls died after being forced back into a burning school building by religious police, because they were not wearing veils when they fled the blazing inferno.

Recent, bloody conflicts in Nigeria have been provoked by extremist groups—inspired by Wahhabism—that have sought to implement *shari'a* in a pluralistic country with a non-religious constitution, like that of Indonesia. According to news reports, more than 6,000 people died in religious conflicts between 1999 and 2002, when *shari'a* was first implemented in northern Nigeria. Approximately 2,000 people lost their lives in the Kaduna region alone, as

a result of religious disturbances caused by the establishment of
shari'a in 2002. Similar religious rioting has also occurred in the
regions of Bauchi, Jos and Aba, claiming thousands of additional
lives.[66]

Will the regional *shari'a* regulations that have recently proliferated throughout our island nation bring true happiness to the
people of Indonesia, after having so clearly failed elsewhere? In reality, the only way to find genuine happiness and perfection in this
world and the next, is by following *shari'a* in the broadest and deep-
est sense of the word: that is, as a path leading to God—Pure and
Exalted is He! The profound spiritual realization attained by following this path may be glimpsed in the lives of tranquil souls who
utterly and completely surrender themselves—physically, emotionally and spiritually—to Him alone, and constantly guard themselves
against domination by egotism or any form of carnal desire. Happiness and perfection in life can never be achieved by compulsion,
or formalizing religion. Rather, true happiness and perfection can
only be attained by means of spiritual awareness, which spontaneously blossoms within a divinely-illumined heart. Thus, it is ironic
that virtually all radicals agree upon the need to establish *shari'a*
in the narrow sense (viz., Islamic jurisprudence), while simultaneously rejecting spirituality, which leads to the true Goal.

Exploit or Reject Democracy, While Seeking to Establish Shari'a?

Democracy has been the Indonesian people's chosen form
of government since the establishment of our republic, beginning
with Sukarno's "guided democracy" and continuing through the
"Pancasila democracy" introduced by Suharto's New Order regime.
Although Sukarno and Suharto both shamelessly exploited democracy, the vast majority of Indonesians continue to regard it as the
best form of government for our nation.

Our field research encountered two entirely different attitudes
towards democracy among the various extremist agents we studied.
Slightly more than half rejected democracy as incompatible with the

---

66. "Nigeria's Muslim-Christian Riots: Religion or Realpolitik," *The Economist*,
17 January 2003.

teachings of Islam, while forty-one percent (41%)—including most PKS supporters—accepted democracy as a valid means for achieving their objectives. However, both those who embrace and those who reject democracy agree upon their ultimate objective: i.e., to legislate Islamic law and establish an Islamic state. Democracy itself may be jettisoned once they achieve their objective, because even those respondents who support democracy universally regard it as a temporary means to achieve a desired end. A similar phenomenon may be witnessed in Palestine, where the Muslim Brotherhood-affiliated Hamas organization exploited democracy to acquire political power, but once entrenched in Gaza, proceeded to destroy rival Muslim groups (viz., Fatah). In short, extremist groups may exploit democracy to achieve undemocratic purposes.

Hardline groups that reject democracy employ specific theological and sociological arguments to explain their rejection. From a theological perspective, they regard democracy as un-Islamic, because its origins lie outside the formal religion of Islam. As a human (rather than Divine) creation, democracy is said to lack a foundation of faith in the Oneness and power of God. According to their logic, political systems should be based upon the Qur'an and Sunnah. Many extremists believe that the assumption inherent in democracy—that power lies in the hands of the people—conflicts with Islam, which regards all power as residing with God alone. In a democracy, decisions are made on the basis of majority vote, while in an Islamic system (*khilafah*), decisions must be taken through *ahl hall wal 'aqdi*, a council of experts who possess knowledge and authority. In this context, what matters is competence and knowledge of Islamic jurisprudence, not the number of votes one receives from a largely ignorant public. One respondent, a former member of Laskar Jihad, explained this reasoning as follows:

> It violates Qur'anic principles to elect a president by majority vote, especially if the voice of the people is treated like the voice of God. You can't determine the truth by counting how many votes it receives in an election. Islam requires that a leader be selected by a council, consisting of men of knowledge.

Many extremist groups reject not only democracy, but also the mechanisms through which it operates, such as elections. They regard elections as *haram* (forbidden), because their purpose is not to implement Islamic law, but rather, a secular law determined by majority vote. Respondents who share this view regard democracy as inappropriate for Indonesia, because the majority of Indonesians are Muslim. Many of this study's respondents claimed that it is completely natural to establish *shari'a* as the basis of Indonesian social and national life. They point out that democracy has failed to solve Indonesia's contemporary problems, or to produce positive change. Since democracy has proven to be an abject failure, why shouldn't Islam be given an opportunity to prove itself, as an alternative system? A large percentage of respondents expressed the view that Indonesia's democracy should be replaced by a system founded on *shari'a*, which they believe to be characterized by legal certainty of a permanent and unchanging nature, because it was created by God.[67]

Deeply influenced by the totalitarian/centralistic ideology they embrace, the agents of extremist groups invariably respond to problems in terms of dichotomy, and binary opposition. For example, they believe that God plays an active role in the political arena, and thus regard democracy as usurping God's power. Significantly, this theological position is often adopted by individuals who occupy an inferior social, economic or political status, and are thus tempted to "enlist" God to support their side of a political contest, in order to acquire power. Instead of democracy, they claim that *ahl al-hall wal 'aqd* (a council of experts) is the proper "Islamic" way to select leaders, or political rulers. They imagine that such a council will function smoothly and without problems. If they actually studied the history of Islam, and investigated why the Prophet's companion 'Umar ibn al-Khaththab appointed seven men to serve as *ahl al-hall wal 'aqd* in electing his successor, they would realize their

---

67. [Translator's note: Compare this with the view of renowned Sunni *ulama* such as Kyai Haji Abdurrahman Wahid, who wrote, "It is vital that we differentiate between the Koran, from which much of the raw material for producing Islamic law is derived, and the law itself. While its revelatory inspiration is divine, Islamic law is man-made and thus subject to human interpretation and revision." "Extremism Isn't Islamic Law," in the *Washington Post*, 23 May 2006.]

error. Perhaps they imagine that *ahl al-hall wal 'aqd* are truly perfect, because their knowledge of Islam—and of the practical issues related to its observance—is so pitifully shallow. This shallow grasp of Islam is certainly on display in their attempts to reduce *shari'a* to a mere set of legal rules, when in fact, *shari'a* encompasses the totality of every single principle in life that can help individuals fully surrender to God—Pure and Exalted is He!—in a state of complete self-transcendence, so that we may directly experience His sublime presence.

International Caliphate

The international, or Islamic, caliphate promoted by Hizb ut-Tahrir and other extremist groups is a purely political movement, with an international orientation. The Nahdlatul Ulama's Bahtsul Masa'il Council, which rules on issues of Islamic law, has firmly proclaimed that the concept of a caliphate—even when bonded to the adjective "Islam"—has no theological foundation whatsoever in the Qur'an or hadith.[68] The term "Islamic" has been appended to the word "caliphate" simply to endow it with theological weight/overtones, and thus transform it into a more effective political weapon.

The concept of an "Islamic caliphate" has become a hot topic in contemporary Indonesian Muslim discourse. HTI is the most active organization promoting this idea of a caliphate. According to one respondent, HTI has established a target date of 2015, by which time it maintains that the notion of a caliphate will have been embraced by the Indonesian public, and no longer regarded as a utopian concept.

Although many respondents (41%) believe that democracy can be effectively employed to achieve their goals, it is significant that nearly 74% of those interviewed during our field research support the goal of establishing an Islamic caliphate, which they regard as the political system most compatible with *shari'a*. The

---

68. See Appendix 2 to read the Bahtsul Masa'il *fatwa* in question. [Translator's note: the caliphate did not emerge until after Muhammad's death, and was not anticipated by either the Qur'an or the Prophet himself, who according to Sunni tradition left no instruction regarding succession, nor any theory of government to his followers.]

idea of a caliphate has already become central to many extremists' aspirations, as can be gleaned from remarks by two of our study's respondents:

> If anyone doesn't agree with [establishing] a caliphate, then we should question whether he's truly a Muslim. (Muslim Brotherhood activist at the prestigious, and secular, Gadjah Mada University in Yogyakarta).

> There are two systems in this world, Islamic [the caliphate] and infidel. Now this infidel system has many forms, such as liberalism, capitalism, communism and, in Indonesia, the Pancasila system. (MMI/Indonesian Council of Holy Warriors activist).

A significant majority of the respondents believe that Muslims throughout the world should adopt the caliphate system, so that Islamic teachings may be comprehensively implemented within their respective territories. This idealism evidences support for an "ideological" or "political" Islam—that is, for transforming the religion of Islam into a system which must be applied to, and imposed upon, virtually every aspect of life by means of the repressive apparatus of the state, on both a national level (in the form of an Islamic state) and transnationally (via an Islamic caliphate).

In a seminar on the establishment of *shari'a* held in the city of Yogyakarta on 5 September 2007, Sidiq al-Jawi of HTI and Irgan Awwas of MMI explicitly acknowledged that they share a common objective—i.e., an Islamic caliphate—although the methods they employ to achieve this goal differ. HTI seeks to directly establish a caliphate in Indonesia, while MMI is focused on incrementally establishing *shari'a* through the passage of laws.

According to al-Jawi and Awwas, God is the source of all law—thus rendering all legal statutes, other than God's law, null and void anywhere upon the face of this earth. Laws that do not issue from God are the corrupt and deviant product of infidels, and do not need to be obeyed. Humanity should submit only to God's law [i.e., to HTI's or MMI's interpretation of *shari'a*]. Thus, any

Muslim who opposes the twin goals of creating an Islamic caliphate and formalizing *shari'a* in Indonesia is a misguided heretic, who has fallen prey to a secular ideology that advocates the separation of religion and state.

HTI and MMI also reject Pancasila, which they claim is ruining Indonesia. They blame this alleged disaster upon secular nationalists such as Sukarno, Muhammad Hatta and other founding fathers, whom they despise.[69] HTI and MMI claim that the only way to save Indonesia is by establishing *shari'a* and an Islamic caliphate, because only Islam can effectively address our nation's manifold problems. They maintain that every Muslim has a solemn duty to help establish Islamic law, so that Islam will be practiced in its entirety, rather than allowing individuals to pick and choose whatever aspects of Islam they wish to observe. HTI and MMI both claim that *shari'a* can never be perfectly established or practiced, without the power of the state to enforce its implementation. That is why they insist that Indonesia become an Islamic state or caliphate, rather than a Pancasila state as at present, for a secular state "torments" countless Muslims.

Regarding the establishment of *shari'a*, respondents from Jamaah Tarbiyah affirmed that every Muslim should work towards this goal, because of the moral degradation that invariably afflicts Muslims in the absence of governmentally-imposed Islamic law. They pointed to the diverse Muslim, polytheist and Jewish community of Medina at the time of the Prophet, and said that it's obvious the majority (i.e., Muslims) should establish the governing law. In the view of these Jamaah Tarbiyah activists, Indonesia must eventually become an Islamic State, because a majority of its inhabitants are Muslim, but its non-Muslim inhabitants will be allowed to live undisturbed.

Of course, the view that the majority have a right to determine Indonesia's form of government—as exemplified by respondents

---

69. [Translator's note: The cover of this book features Sukarno and Muhammad Hatta proclaiming Indonesia's independence as a secular state, founded upon the principles of Pancasila. Visible beneath their "feet" are members of the extremist Front for the Defense of Islam, who on 1 June 2008 attacked a group of Indonesians demonstrating in favor of religious freedom and Pancasila, on the grounds of Jakarta's national monument, across from the state palace.]

referencing Medina—conflicts with the extremist argument that rejects democracy, on the grounds that decisions should not be taken
on the basis of majority vote.

Various campus proselytism groups (commonly known as
Lembaga Dakwah Kampus, or LDK) also voice firm support for
the establishment of an Islamic caliphate. They maintain that because such a caliphate is "God's promise" and must be fulfilled,
it's useless to oppose or reject it. However, the conditions necessary to establish an Islamic caliphate must be developed step by
step, through a slow but sure process of guiding and educating the
public. Hence, HTI's assertion that an Islamic caliphate may be
proclaimed in Indonesia by the year 2015.

The Islamic State and Non-Muslims

This study found that KPPSI and HTI respondents in West
Sumatra held identical views regarding the establishment of *shari'a*,
which closely resembled those of Jamaah Tarbiyah activists interviewed in Medan, North Sumatra. All agreed that regional *shari'a*
regulations should be promoted, in order to free the public from
various dangerous "illnesses." Society requires solutions to the numerous problems people encounter in their daily lives, and the
appropriate solution is Islamic law.

This belief/assumption is the common ground on which virtually every extremist group meets. Although their terminology
may differ, their goal is the same: namely, to implement regional
shari'a regulations throughout Indonesia, and thereby facilitate
their ultimate goal, which is to establish an Islamic state via constitutional means, legitimated by regional legislatures, the national
legislature in Jakarta, and the executive and judiciary branches of
government.

KAMMI (PKS student) activists in Yogyakarta view regional
shari'a regulations and an Islamic state as public necessities, especially given the crisis situation that has long threatened Indonesia. They maintain that the public must be compelled to observe
shari'a, until all Muslims eventually understand what *shari'a* is, and
acknowledge its benefits. Here we found that the goals of KAMMI,
HTI and Jamaah Tarbiyah activists were essentially identical—that

is, the establishment of *shari'a*—with only their methods differing from organization to organization. HTI seeks to directly establish a caliphate, while rejecting the existence of the present government. Jamaah Tarbiyah activists, on the other hand, wish to achieve the same goal in stages, step by step.

The views of respondents affiliated with various groups, including HTI, KAMMI, KPPSI and Jamaah Tarabiyah—concerning regional *shari'a* regulations and an Islamic caliphate—were quite similar, but distinguished by variations in the language each group of respondents employed. Significantly, they tended to speak with one voice about the need to establish regional *shari'a* regulations and an Islamic caliphate. However, KPPSI and Jamaah Tarbiyah are proceeding through political channels, while HTI hopes to seize power directly, and KAMMI is pursuing campus and legislative politics as a wing of the Muslim Brotherhood-affiliated PKS. Abu Bakar Ba'asyir, former head of both MMI (the Indonesian Council of Holy Warriors) and the terrorist group Jemaah Islamiyah, spoke of establishing *shari'a* (*tathbiq al-syari'ah*) as follows:

> The NU, Muhammadiyah and other Islamic organizations already have a significant role in guiding individuals and their families. But we feel their success has been extremely limited. That isn't the fault of the NU and other Islamic organizations, but of the government, which refuses to adopt Islamic law. Thus, I say that the government is responsible for destroying public morality. The guidance we've been providing to people all these years has been undermined and destroyed by government policy... We must take note of this, and Islamize the government itself. The government must adopt Islamic law in its entirety. This is non-negotiable.

These and other views expressed by respondents are consistent with the findings of a survey conducted in 2002 by the Islamic State University of Jakarta's Center for the Study of Islam and Society (PPIM). A full 67% of respondents to that study indicated that Indonesia needs to be governed by Islamic law, while an identical

PPIM survey conducted in 2001 found only 57% of respondents agreeing with this premise. With regard to Islamic leadership, 67% of the respondents in 2002 agreed that Indonesia should be governed on the basis of the Qur'an and Sunnah, and 70.8% agreed that Indonesia should become an Islamic State.

The Indonesian Council of Holy Warriors employs both a proselytizing and a religious reform movement to promote the establishment of *shari'a*. According to MMI respondents to this study, Islam represents an alternative ideology that must be established on earth by God's devoted servants, in accordance with His decrees. MMI respondents claim that non-Muslims will not be forced to convert to Islam in a future *shari'a* state. They may remain faithful to their respective religions, and in special cases, will not even be subject to Islamic law. They will be designated as *kafir dzimmi* (subject infidels)—that is, non-Muslims who live under the protection of an Islamic state and must pay tax to obtain the protection of their rulers. However, MMI respondents indicate that some non-Muslims will be designated as *kafir harbi* (infidels engaged in war with Islam), viz., those who are opposed to Islam.

According to MMI respondents, Indonesia is full of non-Muslims who fall into the category of *kafir harbi*, because of their hatred for Islam, which they evidence either through speech or actions. For example, such "enemies of Islam" often attempt to "trap" and "corner" Islam, and thereby prevent Islam and Muslims from obtaining their just rights. Actions cited as "opposition" to Islam included the successful rejection of extremist-backed legislation to revise the national educational curriculum, while non-Muslims who opposed this legislation were accused of wronging Islam. As a result, MMI respondents referred to such people as *kafir harb*, i.e., infidels whose blood is legitimate to shed. [70]

---

70. [Translator's note: the authors of this book ostensibly fall into this category, although all but one are Muslim. MMI, Jemaah Islamiyah and Abu Bakar Ba'asyir all reacted strongly to the publication of *The Illusion of an Islamic State*, with one website linked to these groups posting an electronic version of the book with the heading: "Here is the book from that accursed satanic network. Read, study, anticipate." (See Appendix 5 of this book.) Following the 17 July 2009 bombings of the Marriott and Ritz-Carlton hotels in Jakarta, which claimed seven victims, Ba'asyir held a press conference in which he stated, "Infidels may not be killed if

The views expressed by MMI respondents and members of other such groups demonstrate the overly simplistic nature of their approach to Islamic concepts. Their views are characterized by positioning a formalistic understanding of Islam in direct binary opposition to any substantive values of Islam that do not coincide with or support their agenda. There is a strong tendency for extremist rhetoric such as that described above to serve as a prelude to violent actions and/or terrorism, which cannot be justified from any perspective whatsoever.

This study's observation and analysis of extremist ideology and movements indicates that these are characterized by a strong tendency to reject any form of cultural compromise. Consistent with this tendency, extremists posit their own limited grasp of religion as an ideal model of reality, i.e., as the true, concrete and final form of Islam, which must be implemented via government diktat, and thus become "reality" for all. They assume they have a right to act as God's spokesmen, and arrogantly proclaim that only *their* interpretation of Islam is the truth, and must be accepted by everyone else. When they declare that "the law belongs to God alone," they are exploiting this renowned Qur'anic verse to bolster their own political position, by implicitly claiming that their all-too-human interpretation of Islam reflects God's absolute truth. In the process they reject history, and virtually every sociological development of the past thousand years. Instead of responding wisely to the circumstances of contemporary life, they seek to reverse the tide of history and drag everyone back to a bygone age that they imagine to have been ideal. This tendency generally stems from the extremists' inability to adapt creatively to modernism, and/or to adopt a critical and constructive response to Western influence.

Facing the Challenges of Modernity

In general, Indonesian Muslims embrace a positive attitude towards modernity, and face its challenges creatively, while extremists

---

they don't oppose [radical] Islam. We can live alongside them. But people who are involved with movements that oppose Islam, even on the level of thought, not only may be killed, but should and must be." *Tempo*, 11 November 2009. (See article in Appendix 5.)]

adopt a reactionary attitude that condemns and rejects modernity as a product of the West. Instead of embracing the present, they blindly idolize the past, and wish to dwell in a bygone era. Indonesians generally refer to extremist groups as "hard-line" movements, because their beliefs are characterized by harsh, narrow-minded absolutism and a refusal to compromise with others. They are "purists," in the sense that they are intolerant of other viewpoints, and even regard diversity as a dangerous contamination of the truth, which they alone monopolize.

One issue posed by modernity that has confronted the Muslim world, is that of gender equality. Most respondents maintained that women have a religious duty to be mothers and homemakers, and may not assume an active role in the public sphere. This view is very different from that of most moderate Muslims, who belong to the Muhammadiyah and NU. For example, the Muhammadiyah's Tarjih Council (which studies and rules on Islamic law) issued a declaration in 2002 that Islam does not prohibit women from being active in the public sphere, including political parties, or even from assuming the highest office in the land. In other words, men and women enjoy equal rights to be active in the public sphere.

The argument [derived from a Qur'anic verse] that men should lead and women follow, constitutes a proposition that husbands should act as responsible heads of household and provide sustenance to their families, but this verse should *not* be interpreted as an argument for limiting the public role of women, much less subordinating them to men. This view—clearly articulated by the Muhammadiyah's Tarjih Council—is completely different from the extremist view, which tends to reject any leadership role for women, including a refusal to recognize women as political leaders. This attitude was clearly expressed by a Wahdatul Islamiyah activist, as follows:

> Women should stay home and guard the morals of children, because leadership of the world, and of families, is the proper role of men. Gender equality is a Western concept that is completely incompatible with Islam. If Islam appears to curb the rights of women, that is only

to prevent defamation of the family [through female pro-
miscuity, or accusations thereof].

Respondents generally agreed that women should be confined to
a domestic role—including those who did not state outright that wom-
en should be subordinate—because men are their natural leaders.

Another issue that arises from modernization is how one
should view pluralism, and/or perspectives held by those who
embrace other faiths. The respondents generally believe that non-
Muslims are infidels who will never willingly accept the existence
f Islam, and are constantly seeking ways to destroy it.[71] Moderate

---

71. "There exists a tendency in certain (extremist) Muslim circles, which posits
a binary opposition between Islam and infidels. In their view, "muslims" (literally, one who submits to God) are only those who embrace the formal religion
of Islam, while people of other faiths are all infidels. This is a growing tendency
at present."

"Furthermore, there are those who understand faith in a monopolistic fashion,
so that anyone whose understanding is different from theirs, is considered unfaithful. In reality this is an old phenomenon, not just contemporary. At the
time of Sayadina 'Ali (Muhammad's son-in-law), there was a group called the
Khawarij who denounced everyone outside their narrow sect as infidels. This
phenomenon has now reincarnated once again, to the point where someone like
(the terrorist) Azhari comes to Indonesia setting off bombs and imagines that
he'll be rewarded in heaven for such actions."

"The term "infidel" actually refers to one who disavows or turns his back upon
Divine values, or indeed, the values of humanity. In Islam, the concept of infidel
has precisely this meaning: i.e., one who disdains or neglects the fundamental
values of morality which God enjoins all men to uphold, such as caring for others, building solidarity, etc.... The negation of such values constitutes infidelity
to God, regardless of what our religion may be."

"As far as I know, the Qur'an defines "infidel" as the opponent of one who is
thankful to God. Allah has divided humanity into only two groups: those who
are in a true state of surrender and gratitude to God, and infidels. An infidel is
one who is ungrateful to God. "When you are thankful, we pour further grace
upon you; but when you're ungrateful [i.e., trapped in egotistical resistance to
Divine decree], my torments are fierce." Or as the Prophet Solomon states in
the Qur'an: "All God's blessings are simply a test, to see whether I am truly [im-
mersed in and] thankful to the Divine, or an infidel." According to the Qur'an,
infidels are not always non-Muslims. A Muslim can be an infidel, too, if he's
ungrateful to God, or if he's unloving and ungrateful to his fellow man. Or if
he's given a reminder and pays no attention, then he is called an infidel."

Muslims, on the other hand, regard pluralism as a necessity within a society as diverse as Indonesia. The principle of pluralism represents a solid foundation for developing tolerant attitudes, and behavior, towards those of different faiths.

According to moderates, pluralism has a strong foundation within Islam, for the Qur'an itself explicitly values human diversity.[72] This is not so for most extremists, who are convinced that non-Muslims represent a threat constantly seeking to undermine and destroy Islam. They also regard pluralism as dangerous, because it weakens Islamic faith.

The spread of extremism represents a backward step for Indonesian Islam. From the time of Islam's arrival in the East Indies, local Muslims rarely took issue with pluralism (although they didn't use this precise term); indeed, they regarded Islam's ability to peacefully coexist with other religions as a significant virtue. The fact that Indonesian Islam has long enjoyed a moderate image is another indication of this pluralistic tradition. Only recently—as extremist groups characterized by a totalitarian outlook, dominated by fascist and communist tendencies, have gained strength in Indonesia—has the expression 'pluralism' become a theological issue, tarred with negative associations. Indeed, pluralism—together with secularism and liberalism—has actually been declared *haram* (forbidden) by the quasi-governmental Council of Indonesian Religious Scholars (MUI), whose "ulama" forget that Islam permits anything and everything in the realm of social interaction,

---

"I have not discovered a single phrase in the Qur'an which defines 'infidel' to mean 'non-Muslims,' like the erroneous definition that is so prevalent today, where if you ask people, they'll tell you an infidel is a non-Muslim."

In sequence, remarks by Prof. Dr. Kyai Haji Abdul A'la, Kyai Haji Hasyim Muzadi and Prof. Dr. Jalaluddin Rakhmat, speaking in *Ocean of Revelations: Understanding Islam as a Blessing for All Creation*, Episode 3, "Ummah (Faith Communities)," Program Supervisor: KH. A. Mustofa Bisri, © LibForAll Foundation, 2009.

72. [Translator's note: the Qur'anic verse underlying this statement is so well known among Muslims that the authors did not bother to quote it: "O Mankind! We have created you from a single (pair) of male and female, and made you into many tribes and nations that you may know one another (and not that ye may despise each other). Verily the most honored of you in the sight of God is (he who is) the most righteous of you. And verily God is All-Knowing, and All-Aware." (Qur'an 49:13)]

except that which is explicitly forbidden (*al-ashlu fi al-mu'âmalah al-'ibâhah*), which pluralism is not.

To briefly summarize our findings, regarding the ideology and agenda of extremist movements in Indonesia: extremist groups diminish the teachings of Islam and transform them into a tool of political ideology, which they wield as a pretext, and weapon, in the quest for power. Their rigid, narrow and shallow understanding of Islam, including their ignorance of the vast intellectual wealth produced by countless Muslims over the centuries, in so many regions and disciplines, renders them incapable of appreciating any other view of Islam. This includes a complete lack of enthusiasm for Sufism or any form of spiritual orientation. This spiritual void, combined with a totalitarian/centralistic ideology, renders extremists certain that no one's view of Islam is correct, except their own. Sadly, God Himself does not appear to play a significant role, either in their personal lives, or their ideology. All that's important (to them) is how to seize power and force others to accept their view of Islam, which is something that even God—Pure and Exalted is He!—does not wish to do.

Chapter IV

THE INFILTRATION OF INDONESIAN ISLAM BY EXTREMIST AGENTS

Introduction

The most important factor that has preserved Indonesia's unity, from the nation's founding in 1945 to the present, has been the loyalty of its elites—and the overwhelming majority of its citizens—to the traditions and culture of Indonesia itself. This entails accepting, and valuing, the existence of both commonalities and differences among the diverse peoples of the East Indies archipelago. In truth, Indonesia's heterogeneous traditions and cultures embody the wisdom conveyed by various religions. This does not mean that Indonesia gave birth to a new religion; but rather, that the unique genius of its people has been to absorb the sublime essence of every religion embraced by the inhabitants of the East Indies. This enables commonalities to serve as a "glue" to unite the nation, while differences become a source of mutual enrichment, rather than conflict.

During the pre-independence era, virtually all Indonesian leaders who cared deeply about the issue of nationalism, vis-à-vis religion, were aware of the potential for conflict in this arena. A number of these leaders held intense discussions concerning the relationship between religion, as a set of teachings, and the emerging nation-state and/or nationalism.[1] Eventually, they concluded that the nation they wished to establish must be able to guarantee the unity of the Indonesian people, while preserving their diverse

---

1. For a more complete description of this process, see Kyai Haji Abdurrahman Wahid's introduction to this book.

traditions and cultures. This in turn gave birth to the state ideology of Pancasila, which Sukarno derived from the very traditions and culture of the Indonesian people themselves.

Viewed from an historical, cultural and sociological perspective, it is obvious that Pancasila represents an integral part of most Indonesians' lives, and their philosophy. This is due to the fact that Indonesia's founders recognized the vital significance of Pancasila for the nation, and understood that it reflects the sublime essence of all religions' teachings. Not only that, but the noble values embodied in Pancasila are mirrored in the daily activities of the majority of Indonesians, who are moderate, tolerant and polite, and treat others as they themselves wish to be treated. In brief, it may be said that Indonesians' daily lives represent the *living Pancasila*.

Indeed, although the relationship between Islam as a formal religion—[as opposed to *islam* as a self-transcendent state of spiritual awareness and communion with God]—and nationalism had been the subject of intense discussion prior to independence, the issue of establishing an Islamic state did rise to the surface during the committee meetings held to establish the new nation's constitutional basis. This is perfectly understandable, given that the 1940s and 50s were a time of great ferment, with a wide variety of political ideologies competing throughout the world. However, the decision ultimately made by Indonesia's founding fathers [to reject a so-called "Islamic" state] reflected their profound, and spiritual, understanding of Islam and its practice, with an emphasis on content rather than symbolic packaging. Certain that Pancasila reflects the essence of *shari'a*, the nation's founders agreed with one voice to adopt Pancasila as the ideological basis of the new state of Indonesia.[2]

---

2. This does not negate the fact that other considerations also influenced the committee's decision, including a message conveyed by Muhammad Hatta after he had received a delegation from east Indonesia, whose members had informed Bung Hatta that their [Christian-populated] regions were willing to join the new nation, as long as it was not founded upon the formalization of any one religion (viz., Islam). The open-minded response of the various *ulama* on the committee, who readily agreed to the suggestion/stipulation conveyed by Bung Hatta, demonstrates their greatness of spirit. For they recognized that the profound majesty of Islam, and of God—Pure and Exalted is He!—is truly unbounded, and

The essence of *shari'a* is reflected in the Indonesian people's philosophy of life (i.e., Pancasila) by: acknowledging the one God (the transcendent first principle, or *sila*); embracing humane values, in the context of a just and civilized humanity (the second principle); explicitly rejecting separatism, and prioritizing a united citizenry (third principle); calling for wise leadership, to arise from deliberations by elected representatives (fourth principle); and a guarantee of well-being, justice and the rule of law for all Indonesians, without exception (fifth principle). Not one of these sublime principles conflicts with the teachings of any religion practiced by the people of Indonesia. This is what it means to state that Pancasila reflects the essence of *shari'a*, as our founding fathers knew.

It is an irrefutable fact that a profound awareness of Indonesia's traditions and culture, on the one hand—and a deeply spiritual understanding and practice of religion, on the other—are essential to preserving, and protecting Pancasila and the Unitary State of the Republic of Indonesia (NKRI). Our nation's leaders, and especially those who hold political office, should be individuals who are deeply loyal to the traditions and culture of Indonesia, and possessed of a profound—rather than superficial—understanding and practice of religion as well. For this will provide a strong incentive to fulfill the trust bestowed upon public officials, in a manner that is honest and loyal to the best interests of our nation as a whole.

Wealth and family, power and personal relations, all represent temptations that constantly assail individuals, who must choose whether to discharge their appointed responsibilities in a faithful manner, or exploit their privileged position for personal gain. Amid a massive stream of foreign (Wahhabi) money, personal honesty—or the lack thereof—often becomes the determining factor in how one responds to temptation. Amid a mighty stream of transnational ideology, loyalty to one's own traditions and culture is sorely tested as well, especially as these grow ever more threatened, and vital, to our nation's future. For precisely this reason, all elements of

---

can never be encompassed by the intrinsically narrow and restrictive formalities of political power. [Translator's note: One of the members of this constitutional committee was Kyai Haji Wahid Hasyim, the father of Kyai Haji Abdurrahman Wahid.]

society—and especially leaders on the national stage—must strive to preserve Indonesia's traditions and culture, on the one hand, and to grasp the profound depths of their own religion, and sincerely observe its tenets, on the other. Our nation's leaders should constantly strive to live according to the principle, "the throne for the people," rather than merely exploiting such concepts as political jargon, which they may interchange or combine with other commodities—including the symbols of religion—in an effort to acquire power for themselves.

These cultural and religious prerequisites are vital to safeguard our national interests, especially in the face of systematic infiltration by transnational ideologies and movements that are actively working to overthrow the Unitary State of the Republic of Indonesia (NKRI) and annihilate Pancasila. Extremists blame our founding fathers for having chosen Pancasila, rather than Islam, as the foundation for our nation. In their opinion, Pancasila is responsible for Indonesia's multidimensional crisis, including its economic collapse, moral degradation, the absence of justice and the rule of law, widespread corruption and countless other problems. By blaming Pancasila for all of our nation's ills, they wish to disgrace and ultimately destroy Pancasila. In its place, they offer a narrow and partial understanding of Islam. In other words, they wish to *formalize* Islam (by imposing Islamic jurisprudence and establishing an Islamic state), just as extremists sought to formalize religion in the 15th and 16th centuries, before their efforts were defeated by Sunan Kalijogo and his disciples.[3] Yet if we are to be truthful, the sublime values of Pancasila have never been fully realized in Indo-

---

3. [Translator's note: Sunan Kalijogo is widely regarded as the patron saint of the 40-million-member Nahdlatul Ulama, and the only indigenous Javanese among the *wali songo*, or nine saints, who are said to have brought Islam to Java. While Sunan Kalijogo taught a spiritual (Sufi) form of Islam that harmonized with pre-existing Hindu, Buddhist and animist traditions, radical Islam was generally propagated at the point of a sword, by immigrant Muslims of Arab and Chinese descent. The military, political and spiritual triumph of Sunan Kalijogo's disciples—which secured freedom of religion for the Javanese people, from the late 16th century to the present—is enshrined in the epic *Babad Tanah Jawi*, or *History of the Land of Java*, whose historical, political, religious and cultural content has strongly influenced the Javanese world view for centuries.]

nesia. In fact, Pancasila has frequently been exploited and abused, as a political weapon, by our nation's rulers.[4]

While constantly blaming Pancasila for all our nation's ills, a number of groups engage in "sweeping" operations and destroy entertainment establishments, under the pretext of *amr ma'rûf nahy munkar* (enjoining the good and forbidding evil). They also accuse others of being infidels or apostates, and threaten and/or physically assault anyone who publicly disagrees with them. The strange thing is, they don't recognize their own behavior as a form of moral degradation, or a violation of the law. In fact, many of the "street actions" performed by extremist groups are closely linked to constitutional efforts underway in the legislative and executive branches of government, and to *fatwas* issued by the Indonesian Council of Religious Scholars (Majelis Ulama Indonesia, or MUI). This demonstrates that the radicals are working in a systematic, rather than haphazard, manner to promote their ideology, which aims to control and dictate every aspect of Indonesians' lives, in accordance with the extremists' own narrow and rigid understanding of Islam. In fact, there are strong indications that this entire process receives an enormous amount of foreign (Wahhabi) funding, which flows into our country without restriction.

During the course of research conducted for this book, the Grand Shaykh of al-Azhar, Muhammad Sayyid Tantawi, unambiguously stated that any and all actions that threaten others' peace and well-being—even if performed in the name of *da'wa* (proselytism) and/or *amr ma'rûf nahy munkar* (enjoining the good and forbidding evil)—constitute false and erroneous *da'wa*, and must be condemned by all Muslims. In fact, the Grand Shaykh continued to

---

4. [Translator's note: the Suharto regime, in particular, employed Pancasila to crush political opposition, while manipulating Javanese cultural values to justify the imposition of a "neo-colonial" regime upon the non-Javanese inhabitants of Indonesia's resource-rich archipelago. Suharto's blatant abuse of Javanese cultural values, including Pancasila, fostered widespread suspicion and mistrust among other ethnic groups, and a reluctance on the part of many Javanese to assert these values in opposition to the spread of radical Islam, after the fall of Suharto. *The Illusion of an Islamic State* represents a deliberate effort to rehabilitate these values, and foster awareness of the vital role they have played in preserving Indonesia's traditions of pluralism, tolerance and spirituality over the centuries.]

say that the government has a legal responsibility to arrest all who perform such criminal acts (*jarîmah*), and sentence them in accordance with the law(s) they have violated.[5] Any form of *da'wa* that is inconsistent with the sublime message of religion [as a blessing for all creation] is erroneous *da'wa*, and must be rejected.[6]

The totalitarian ideology embraced by extremist groups aims to control every aspect of human life, while the extremists themselves aspire to become God's vice-regents (*khalîfah Allah*) on earth, and subject the rest of humanity to their all-encompassing dictates. In order to realize this ambition, they employ a wide variety of tactics to infiltrate virtually every field of life, in both the private sector and government, including education, the media, politics and business. In the course of pursuing their ambitions, the extremists invariably attack indigenous Islam and a spiritual orientation, for these are the two primary obstacles to the achievement of their goals.[7]

---

5. Interview with the Grand Shaykh of al-Azhar held in Cairo, Egypt on 25 May 2008. "The proper role of government, concerning (extremists' use of force and calling it) *da'wa* is to have the *ulama* and intellectuals advise and correct those who are wrong. If (the extremists) fail to immediately accept this advice, the government must enforce the law by arresting and sentencing them to prison, in accordance with their wrongdoing." See *Ocean of Revelations: Understanding Islam as a Blessing for all Creation*, Episode 5: "*Da'wa*," Program Supervisor: Kyai Haji Mustofa Bisri, © LibForAll Foundation 2009.

6. "The word *da'wa*, or proselytism, literally means 'to invite'.... to offer Divine Oneness, the religion of Islam, and (a path to develop) *akhlakul karima*, or noble character, to humans.... not to threaten or vilify others.... It is mistaken for (those engaged in) *da'wa* to condemn others, or brand them as heretics or infidels.... true *da'wa* is that which enlightens, educates, improves the intellect and gives people hope.... All *da'wa* that deviates from this Divine orientation, is erroneous *da'wa*." In sequence, Kyai Haji Masdar F. Mas'udi, Prof. Kyai Haji Said Aqil Siraj, Dr. Haedar Nashir, Prof. Dr. A. Syafii Maarif, and the Grand Shaykh of al-Azhar, Muhammad Sayyid Tantawi, speaking in *Ocean of Revelations: Understanding Islam as a Blessing for all Creation*, Episode 5: "*Da'wa*," Program Supervisor: Kyai Haji Mustofa Bisri, © LibForAll Foundation 2009.

7. "If we trace the origins of these radical groups, they all stem from an Arab (i.e., Wahhabi) mentality. It's obvious! Why do they have to chase us all the way to Java? Adopt Islam itself, *not* radical interpretations of religion! Arabism is not identical with Islam, nor is Arab clothing. For me, the two are completely unrelated. We're in the process of adopting a foreign culture, or subculture, in an extremely foolish manner. The Qur'an is patient only with those of faith, and who

According to Dr. Haedar Nashir, Vice Chairman of the Muhammadiyah's Central Board:

In general, ideological movements penetrate social environments by imitating the flow of water, which inundates low-lying areas at first, but if allowed to continue, slowly but surely becomes a flood. To use a different analogy, it's like people who devour a bowl of hot porridge, by slowly working from its perimeter towards the center. Ideological movements infiltrate new hosts and blossom, by following a specific process: (1) First, they approach individuals or subgroups, within the larger target organization, that share a common or similar view with the infiltrating party, so that the new ideology will be accepted and expand rapidly; (2) Initially, they conceal their views and ultimate goals, as they strive to permeate the target organization, until their alien ideology has become widely acceptable; (3) They employ agents who have a great deal of "militant energy" and perseverance (i.e., *true believers*) to promote their ideology; (4) They exploit any and all vulnerabilities within the organization or environment they are penetrating, while promoting the image of the infiltrating movement as being significantly better than its new host; (5) They employ the strategy known as "split bamboo," by supporting those who sympathize with their ideology, while eliminating those who create barriers or oppose its spread; (6) They carefully fertilize and water the seeds of anxiety, fear and dread of rival ideologies, in order to spread the virus of their own ideology as a welcome alternative; (7) They promote the use of a positive and idealized terminology to refer to their own views/ideology, while delegitimizing the ideology/ views and existence of the organization/environment they are infiltrating; (8) They do not hesitate to employ

possess true wisdom." Prof. Dr. A. Syafii Maarif, speaking in *Ocean of Revelations: Understanding Islam as a Blessing for all Creation*, Episode 3: "*Faith Communities*," Program Supervisor: Kyai Haji Mustofa Bisri, © LibForAll Foundation 2009.

taqiyah (deception), by concealing their true ideology and agenda, while presenting only those aspects thereof that superficially appeal to their target audience; (9) They present themselves as an "alternative power" and act like flowing water; if even a small space or hole opens up, their ideology and movement will immediately flow into it; (10) They spread and blossom within a target organization/environment, by forming links with people who sympathize with, share similar views and support the new movement; (11) They directly or indirectly manipulate people within the target organization who are dissatisfied with it, whether for personal or organizational reasons, and exploit these frustrated individuals to disseminate the infiltrating movement's ideology—thus promoting an atmosphere of internal conflict to conquer from without; (12) They utilize every possible means to spread the seeds of their ideology, including whatever media exist within the target organization/environment that they are infiltrating.[8]

Although Dr. Haedar wrote *Manifestations of the Tarbiyah Movement: How Should the Muhammadiyah Respond?* to rescue Kyai Haji Ahmad Dahlan's mass movement [the Muhammadiyah] from infiltration by the PKS and other hard-line movements, his booklet provides an extremely apt description of the way in which transnational Islamist movements are worming their way into all aspects of our national life.

To confront this mortal danger, Indonesia needs leaders who understand our nation's culture and traditions; have a deep understanding of religion; and faithfully observe its teachings, in a spiritual rather than superficial manner. The first characteristic will inspire loyalty to our nation's culture and traditions, while the latter inspires loyalty to the public interest—stimulating efforts to realize the sublime aspirations contained within Pancasila. Proximity to

---

8. Haedar Nashir, *Manifestasi Gerakan Tarbiyah: Bagaimana Sikap Muhammadiyah?* (*Manifestations of the Tarbiyah Movement: How Should the Muhammadiyah Respond?*) (Yogyakarta: Suara Muhammadiyah, 2007), pp. 57-59.

God [through a heightened state of spiritual awareness] will enable a leader to hear the inner voice of his or her people, for through such Divine communion he or she will live spontaneously in a state of Divine guidance, and thus fulfill the mandate every human being has received to become khilâfah [God's vice-regent, or caliph]. Moment by moment, he or she will receive Divine guidance as to what should or should not be done, for through genuine communion with God, Allah subhânahu wa ta'âlâ—Pure and Exalted is He!—will become His servant's "ears, eyes, tongue and feet," in fulfilling the Divine mandate.

The pages that follow convey the findings of our research into hard-line agents' infiltration of Indonesian Islam, including the Muhammadiyah, Nahdlatul Ulama, Majelis Ulama Indonesia (Indonesian Council of Religious Scholars, or MUI), educational institutions, the government and business sector, as well as the foreign subsidies that finance extremists' systematic infiltration of all these fields. The combination of a virulent ideology, backed by enormous financial resources deployed in a systematic manner, has enabled extremist infiltration to become increasingly broad, deep and dangerous to the people and nation of Indonesia.

Infiltration of the Muhammadiyah

In December of 2006 the Muhammadiyah mass organization issued Muhammadiyah Central Board Decree (SKPP) Number 149/Kep/I.0/B/2006, entitled "Muhammadiyah Central Board Policy Regarding Consolidation of the Muhammadiyah Organization and Its Charitable Activities." The decree was signed by the Muhammadiyah Central Board's general chairman, Prof. Dr. H. M. Din Syamsuddin, and by its General Secretary, Dr. H. A. Rosyad Sholeh.

This Central Board Decree (SKPP) was issued with the express purpose of "rescuing the Muhammadiyah from various actions that are damaging the Organization." What were these harmful activities? The Central Board Decree enumerates ten conclusions/sub-decrees, which explicitly link these damaging activities to infiltration of the Muhammadiyah by an alien organization whose views, mission and interests differ from those of the Muhammadiyah itself.

The Central Board Decree specifically identifies the Muslim Brotherhood-affiliated Justice and Prosperity Party (PKS) as responsible for infiltrating and exploiting the Muhammadiyah, in order to achieve its political objectives. For that reason, the Decree exhorts all Muhammadiyah members, and the organization's leadership in particular, to free themselves from the PKS's mission and objectives. "The Muhammadiyah must be free from the influence, mission, infiltration and agenda of political parties that seek to achieve their political goals in the name of 'da'wa' [proselytizing activities], and also from the missions and agenda of any other political organizations, as stipulated by the 'Khittah Muhammadiyah' [a declaration of "Muhammadiyah Duty" to refrain from involving the Organization in politics, first adopted in Makassar in 1971 and renewed in 2002 in Denpassar]."

To what extent have the PKS and other extremist movements "sunk their claws" into the Muhammadiyah, and how could this occur, to the point that the second-largest Muslim organization in Indonesia, and the world, clearly fears for its future? We shall delineate the various points that the Central Board Decree cites as evidence of infiltration by a political party that uses "religious proselytizing" to achieve its political objectives, exploiting the Muhammadiyah's charitable enterprises, mosques, educational institutions and other facilities for its own purposes. The Central Board Decree goes on to state that the PKS has conducted extensive activities—such as prayer meetings and religious training within the Muhammadiyah, in the name of "proselytizing"—when in fact these ostensibly religious activities are meant to serve the political interests of the PKS itself.

Not only that, but the Muhammadiyah's own mass media organs appear to have been infiltrated by extremist movements, whose agents consist both of individuals who have entered the Muhammadiyah from without, and Muhammadiyah members who have become activists for extremist groups, while remaining embedded within the Muhammadiyah. The Central Board Decree calls for all mass media organs within the Muhammadiyah to truly promote "the views, mission and interests of the Muhammadiyah," and to serve as tools to socialize "its views, decrees, policies, activities and virtues," while "distancing themselves from the views, mission and interests of other organizations and movements."

The Muhammadiyah Central Board issued its decree in order to "strengthen and consolidate" this mass organization. The promulgation of such a decree conclusively proves that alien ideologies and movements have indeed infiltrated the Muhammadiyah, and that the organization regards this infiltration as a serious problem. One proof of this conflict is the emergence of differing views within Muhammadiyah circles, as to how the major Islamic holidays of Eid al-Fitr and Eid al-Adha should be celebrated. Another is the transformation of the Muhammadiyah into a medium for political events held by the PKS, which have elicited opposition and consequently disrupted the organization's unity.

Three months prior to the issuance of this decree by the Muhammadiyah's Central Board, one of the organization's publishing arms (affiliated with its magazine *Suara Muhammadiyah*, or *Voice of the Muhammadiyah*) published a small book authored by Muhammadiyah Central Board Vice Chairman Dr. Haedar Nashir, entitled *Manifestations of the Tarbiyah Movement: How Should the Muhammadiyah Respond?*[9] This book clearly and succinctly described efforts by the Muslim Brotherhood-affiliated Tarbiyah movement (i.e., the PKS) to infiltrate and seize control the Muhammadiyah.

This book directly precipitated the issuance of the Muhammadiyah Central Board Decree targeting the PKS, because "there is unrest in many regions due to the presence and spread of alien views about Islam, disseminated by Islamist movements such as the Tarbiyah movement and PKS ideology, which are infecting both the formal Muhammadiyah organization and its charitable enterprises [such as schools, hospitals, etc.] in a manner that is factual and real, and not the figment of someone's imagination, thus requiring a firm response from the Muhammadiyah Central Board."[10]

---

9. Within five months of its initial publication in August of 2006, *Suara Muhammadiyah* reprinted Haedar Nashir's book *Manifestasi Gerakan Tarbiyah: Bagaimana Sikap Muhammadiyah?* five times, and distributed a total of 25,000 copies. The quotes excerpted herein are from the fifth printing, published in January of 2007, augmented by information obtained from an interview held with Haedar Nashir in Yogyakarta on 20 February 2008.
10. Ibid, p. 41.

Why is the Muhammadiyah so profoundly disturbed by the PKS's activities? In Haedar's opinion, this disturbance arises from deliberate PKS infiltration of the Muhammadiyah, in order to recruit members and disseminate its ideology. Haedar acknowledges that originally there was no conflict between the Muhammadiyah and the PKS. Indeed, the PKS is welcome to obtain support from Muhammadiyah members, as long as it "behaves in a sympathetic manner, preserving a harmonious relationship, and not through an expansion conducted under the guise of a proselytizing movement, which claims it has a right to enter freely anywhere."[11] This ethical failure on the part of the PKS became the primary bone of contention between the Muhammadiyah and this Muslim Brotherhood-affiliated political party, but it is far from the only source of their discord.

Fundamental differences between the Muhammadiyah and the PKS concerning their respective views of Islam, and their core missions, constitute the most important source of conflict between the two organizations. The Muhammadiyah view of Islam, and its mission, are clearly moderate. While the PKS is developing "Tarbiyah concepts that are inseparable from the Muslim Brotherhood movement, which has its own beliefs, system, methods, strategies and techniques, centered in Egypt. In fact, during the last phase of Hasan al-Banna's leadership, and then under Sayyid Qutb, the Muslim Brotherhood movement transformed into a radical party that was deeply engaged in violent political conflict, including the assassination of Egypt's Prime Minister, Mahmoud an-Nukrashi Pasha, in December of 1948, which violence ultimately led to the deaths of both afore-mentioned Muslim Brotherhood figures. The Tarbiyah [Islamic education] movement inculcates its cadres with a monolithic ideology, producing a high degree of militancy and radicalism within the Muslim Brotherhood movement.[12]

According to Haedar, "[T]he Tarbiyah movement's development in Indonesia has been fascinating. Within a decade of its birth ca. 1980, the movement had already spread to the most prestigious campuses in Indonesia, including the University of Indonesia (UI)

11. Ibid, pp. 44-45.
12. Ibid, p. 15.

in Jakarta, the Institute of Agriculture in Bogor (IPB), the Institute of Technology in Bandung (ITB), Gadjah Madah University (UGM) in Yogyakarta, Airlangga University in Surabaya, Brawijaya University in Malang, Hasanuddin University in Makassar, and so forth. Following the birth of two Tarbiyah magazines at the end of 1986, *Ummi* and *Sabili*, Muslim Brotherhood ideology spread even more quickly."[13] These two mass media publications, with a large circulation (estimates have placed *Sabili* circulation at 100,000 copies per bi-monthly edition),[14] became not only a means to train Tarbiyah cadres, but also an information and communications medium disseminating Tarbiyah ideology throughout Indonesia.

Haedar quotes Anis Matta, Secretary General of the PKS, that the Muslim Brotherhood inspired the birth of the PKS. Hasan al-Banna, founder of the Muslim Brotherhood, succeeded in transforming the [Islamic] reformation from a lecture topic to an actual movement. And it is no exaggeration, continued Matta, "to say that the inspiration of that movement can also be felt beating in the pulse of the Justice and Prosperity Party."[15] The basic concepts of Tarbiyah (the system through which the Muslim Brotherhood, and PKS, indoctrinate their cadres) obviously conflicts with the Muhammadiyah's own view of Islam, and its mission. This is especially true of Tarbiyah calls for the establishment of "**an Islamic State, with the system and laws that must be promulgated within it.**"[16] It is entirely logical that the Muhammadiyah would regard the infiltration of Muslim Brotherhood ideology as a threat not only to the Muhammadiyah itself, but also to the people and nation of Indonesia. For the Muhammadiyah clearly does not aspire to establish an Islamic state, having accepted Pancasila as the foundation of our nation state.

According to testimony provided by a number of key Muhammadiyah leaders to our study's research team, PKS infiltration of the Muhammadiyah had already become visible during the nation-

---

13. Ibid, p. 25.
14. See Arskal Salim dan Azyumardi Azra, "The State and Shari'a in the Perspective of Indonesian Legal Politics," Introduction to the book, *Shari'a and Politics in Modern Indonesia* (Singapore: ISEAS, 2003).
15. Haedar, op. cit., pp. 33-34.
16. Ibid, p. 9. The bold formatting appears in Haedar Nashir's original text.

al elections of 2004, and even more evident at the Muhammadiyah Congress held in Malang, East Java in July of 2005. One Muhammadiyah leader quoted in *Syirah* magazine, declared that PKS infiltration of the Muhammadiyah was conducted by the Muhammadiyah's own membership.[17] These systematic efforts were clearly visible in committee meetings held throughout the Congress. "Certain individuals were deliberately sent to join these committees," stated this source, who went from committee to committee, seeking an explanation for the afore-mentioned signs of infiltration. And indeed his suspicions proved valid, for the ideological nuance permeating each committee forum was nearly identical. The various committees were all discussing the same topic: namely, that the Muhammadiyah had abandoned *shari'a* (Islamic law) and *tarjih* (study of the preference of one legal opinion over another), and indeed, betrayed its own constitution.

This source also reported that the Muhammadiyah's elder statesman, Buya Syafii (Prof. Dr. Ahmad Syafii Maarif) received numerous SMS text messages from Muhammadiyah members themselves, exhorting others not to elect certain individuals to leadership positions within the Muhammadiyah, because the individuals in question needed to be "Islamized." "The infiltration of [extremist] ideology and discourse was conducted by Muhammadiyah members themselves, who had already gone over to the PKS. Although their numbers were not great at the Congress, the systematic nature of their activities allowed PKS members to color and dominate the various forums," he said.[18] The PKS did not act alone, but rather was joined by Hizb ut-Tahrir Indonesia (HTI) activists who were deliberately sprinkled throughout the Congress as attendees, acting as representatives from various regions. The PKS and HTI visibly conducted their campaign by disseminating a list of candidates for Muhammadiyah leadership positions who should, or should not, be elected, which list was distributed to the majority of those attending the Congress from Java, Jakarta, Su-

---

17. "Intervensi PKS Ke Muhammadiyah Dilakukan Secara Sistematis." ("The PKS is Systematically Intervening in the Muhammadiyah.") http://www.syirah.com/syirah_ol/online_detail.php?id_kategori_isi=1734 [Translator's note: this article no longer appears online].

18. Ibid.

lawesi, Sumatra and eastern Indonesia (East Nusa Tenggara, West Nusa Tenggara and Ambon).

A rancorous debate occurred at the Congress between moderate/progressive Muhammadiyah youth and the HTI. Muhammad al-Khathath, aka Gatot (when he became the head of HTI)[19] attended the Congress as a Muhammadiyah representative from Jakarta. Gatot sought to "annihilate" the group of Muhammadiyah youth who had established the Young Muhammadiyah Intellectuals Network (JIMM), when the committee organizing the Congress held a discussion with the theme, "JIMM: Blessing or Curse?"

When the names of female candidates for Muhammadiyah chairman were announced in the Congress, HTI activists responded frantically, screaming that leadership positions in the Muhammadiyah were unsuitable for women, because women are not leaders. HTI activists claimed that it's un-Islamic to elect women to leadership posts. And every time a woman spoke during the Congress, male HTI activists mocked her, rendering it practically impossible for the woman to proceed with her speech.

When a forum within the Congress raised the topic of infiltration by other organizations in the name of da'wa (proselytizing), a number of Muhammadiyah leaders—who were also members of the PKS and HTI—were displeased. They claimed that "the PKS and HTI are both Islamic organizations intent on helping the Muhammadiyah, so it would be illogical to forbid them from acting in and through the Muhammadiyah." However, their claim to be assisting the Muhammadiyah was rejected by Muhammadiyah Vice Chairman Haedar Nashir, who replied that if they truly wished to help the Muhammadiyah, they should "discard their clothes" (i.e., their PKS or HTI membership and loyalties).[20]

In fact, PKS and HTI infiltration of the Muhammadiyah had been continuously underway for at least two years prior to

19. Muhammad al-Khathath was subsequently fired from his position as chairman of HTI because he conducted activities forbidden by the central leadership of Hizb ut-Tahrir (international), viz., he collaborated with other Islamist organizations as described herein. See also, http://www.freelists.org/post/nasional_list/ppiindia-khathath-alias-gatot-dipecat-dari-hti.
20. Consultative interview with Haedar Nashir, held in the Muhammadiyah headquarters building in Jakarta on 20 February 2008.

the Malang Congress. That is why they and their allies within the Muhammadiyah were able to secure the revocation of several Muhammadiyah Central Board policies that threatened their ideology. These policies included cultural da'wa (a pilot project designed to encourage Muhammadiyah activists to adopt moderate attitudes and behavior), the encouragement of women's leadership, and development of Islamic thought within the Muhammadiyah's Tarjih Institute. The PKS, HTI and their allies waged an intensely negative campaign against moderate Muhammadiyah leaders who were accused of being involved in the adoption of these policies by the Muhammadiyah Central Board.[21] These individuals were smeared as being un-Islamic for adhering to a secular and liberal worldview, and even described as "syphilis" carriers, the acronym "sipilis" being coined from the terms secular, pluralist and liberal. This term was popularized by Adian Husaini—an activist from the Saudi-funded Dewan Dakwah Islamiyah Indonesia (Indonesian Council for Islamic Proselytism, or DDII)—whose writings often employ filthy language (such as "syphilis"), in order to discredit anyone whose view of Islam does not accord with his own.

With regard to the ease with which a mass organization such as the Muhammadiyah has been infiltrated by the Muslim Brotherhood's Tarbiyah movement (i.e., the PKS), Haedar Nashir attributes this to the fact that the Muhammadiyah organization tends to be lax, and not monolithic. An even more significant factor is that PKS cadres tend to be pragmatic in terms of their religious practices, and readily alter their style of worship to fit in with their targets, and thus gain acceptance. "While infiltrating Muhammadiyah circles, they worship like Muhammadiyah members, and when they're with the Nahdlatul Ulama, they worship like Nahdliyyin (NU members). This is just another form of taqiyyah (concealing

---

21. [Translator's note: The Muhammadiyah leaders subjected to this "black campaign" included Muhammadiyah Vice-Secretary Dr. Abdul Munir Mulkhan, who subsequently played a major role in exposing PKS infiltration of the Muhammadiyah and securing Central Board Decree Number 149/Kep/I.0/B/2006 banning the PKS, as described in the editor's introduction to this book (http://www.libforall.org/news-WSJ-the-exorcist.html). Dr. Munir also led the Yogyakarta team that conducted field research for this book.]

one's identity–*editor*)," said Haedar Nashir,[22] or in other words, *ni-faq* (hypocrisy).

Ultimately, this infiltration led to the promulgation of the Muhammadiyah Central Board Decree discussed above. This decree infuriated extremist groups. HTI demanded that the decree also be applied to moderate and progressive groups within the Muhammadiyah–although in reality, most moderates and progressives had already been sidelined within the Muhammadiyah leadership structure as a result of the extremists' own maneuverings. And the group most profoundly affected by the issuance of this decree was of course the PKS, which was explicitly named in the decree. The PKS felt compelled to issue an official explanation, which denied that the PKS had ever tried to gain control of mosques, Friday sermons, hospitals, schools, campuses, or charitable foundations belonging to other organizations.[23]

Fourteen months after the promulgation of the Muhammadiyah Central Board Decree, the PKS held a National Consultative Assembly from 1 - 4 February 2008 in Bali. This assembly may be read as another PKS response to the Muhammadiyah decree and Haedar Nashir's book.[24] This is evident from the recommendations adopted by the Assembly, which included a formal PKS embrace of "pluralism" and "the spirit of nationalism." "The PKS accepts Pancasila and the 1945 Constitution as the final basis of the

---

22. Interview, op. cit.
23. "PKS Treatise to Strengthen the Fraternity of Believers and Achieve Reconciliation," issued on 27 September 2007.
24. [Translator's note: despite the enormous upheaval in Muhammadiyah circles caused by the infiltration of extremist groups, and the Muhammadiyah decree banning the PKS, Indonesia's mass media barely took notice of these events. Neither the Muhammadiyah Central Board, nor the PKS, wished to display their "dirty laundry" to the public, as reflected in Muhammadiyah Chairman Din Syamsuddin's attempts to minimize and downplay the significance of the decree in the few Indonesian media reports that mentioned the story. In fact, the first major report of the decree appeared not in an Indonesian newspaper, but rather the *Wall Street Journal*, after foreign columnist Bret Stephens tracked the story from the remote village of Sendang Ayu in Lampung Province, Sumatra, to the Muhammadiyah headquarters in Yogyakarta in April of 2007. Ultimately, publication of *The Illusion of an Islamic State*–in the midst of national elections in 2009–brought the decree to the attention of a mass audience within Indonesia, with devastating consequences to the PKS.]

Indonesian nation state, and the national constitution."[25] At this Bali assembly, the PKS also proclaimed itself to be a transparent and open-minded political party, which would accept non-Muslim legislative candidates. The decision to hold this national assembly in Bali (the Hindu "Island of the Gods") was meant to symbolize the "fact" that the PKS leopard had truly changed its spots. This impression was further reinforced by the party heads attending the event wearing *udeng-udeng*, the cloth head-covering traditionally worn by Balinese Hindus whenever they enter a temple or attend a religious ceremony.

Why, ten years after its founding [as a Muslim Brotherhood-inspired political party] did the PKS suddenly talk about embracing pluralism, the spirit of nationalism, and accepting Pancasila and the 1945 Constitution [which established Indonesia as a secular, rather than Islamic, state] as the nation's final consensus? The obvious explanation, of course, is political calculations in the run-up to the 2009 legislative and presidential elections. The PKS recognizes that it cannot appeal to a constituency of Muslim voters—many of whom are affiliated with the Muhammadiyah and NU—who truly embrace nationalism and pluralism, and accept Pancasila and the 1945 Constitution as the final basis of the Indonesian nation state. Thus, the PKS could not afford to ignore the Muhammadiyah Central Board Decree [which, if widely publicized, could mortally wound the PKS's electoral prospects].

However, the PKS's decision—or pretense—to follow the path of an open and inclusive political party, and to accept Pancasila as the basis of the Indonesian nation state, immediately encountered severe internal resistance [from its core constituency of Muslim extremists determined to establish *shari'a* and an Islamic state]. Two days after this Bali assembly, the PKS was compelled to issue a clarification to party members who objected to the policies articulated in Bali. In the face of this internal rebellion, on 6 February 2008

---

25. Statement by Mahfudz Siddiq, chairman of the PKS legislative fraction in Indonesia's national assembly (DPR), and chairman of the PKS Media Operation Team at the Bali Congress. See, "PKS Mukernas Recomendasikan Tiga Agenda" ("PKS Congress Recommends Three Agendas") in *Republika*, 4 February 2008, p. 3. See also, "PKS Serukan Bangkitkan Semangat Kebangsaan" ("PKS Encourages Raising the Spirit of Nationalism") in *Kompas*, 4 February 2008, p.3.

the PKS issued "A Clarification Regarding the Issue of an Open Party and Non-Muslim Candidates," which it distributed to various mass media outlets to ensure a wide distribution.

This "clarification" stated that in accordance with decisions reached by the Seventh PKS Governing Council meeting held in Jakarta, and strengthened by the Ninth Party Governing Council meeting just held in Bali, the PKS was committed to the principles of clean, caring and professional governance. The clarification also addressed the issue of the PKS becoming an "open" political party. In this regard, the clarification stated that the term "open" was never adopted in any formal party resolution, whether at a meeting of the PKS Governing Council, its highest Party Leadership Council, or any decision made regarding the direction of leadership. It went on to state that the PKS remained an Islam-based da'wa party, possessed of Islamic morals, and committed to the observance of shari'a as a legal and religious obligation incumbent upon all Muslims, and especially PKS cadres. The document went on to request that the entire structure of the PKS, including its leadership and cadres, not discuss the issue of an "open party" any further, in order to avoid problems far greater than the benefits that could be expected to arise from such discussion.

The PKS's own membership base so vehemently rejected any movement towards the PKS becoming an "open" party, that the PKS promptly resumed its identity as a "closed" party, which represents only Muslims and is committed to the establishment of shari'a [and, hence, an Islamic state]. Why did the PKS so quickly and easily abandon the policies it presumably adopted and announced at the Bali assembly? It appears that the PKS wishes to pursue a two-faced style of politics: to appeal to the general public, they need to adopt an identity that is open-minded and characterized by a nationalist vision, employing the rhetoric of accepting Pancasila and the 1945 [secular] constitution as the final basis of the Indonesian nation state. However, the PKS continues to tell its own constituents that it remains a da'wa party, committed to the observance of shari'a as a legal and religious obligation incumbent upon all Muslims (i.e., the "Jakarta Charter," which Indonesia's founders rejected in favor of Pancasila and a secular nation state).

Yet if that's true, doesn't it mean that party rhetoric about accepting Pancasila and the 1945 Constitution is nothing but a political shield [to deflect criticism of the PKS as a threat to Indonesia's constitution and secular state]?

It is obvious that the Muhammadiyah decree has severely discomfited the PKS, as evidenced by its strenuous efforts to escape political fallout from the decree, which is locked onto the PKS like a heat-seeking missile. One method they've employed is to place "protective shields" around the PKS. Just as in a chess match, when one's king has been placed in check, the safest way to respond is by deploying another chess piece. In this case, the PKS is employing Pancasila and the 1945 Constitution as chess pieces (i.e., shields to deflect an opponent's attack). And this in turn gives rise to a greater danger. The infiltration of the Muhammadiyah, which resulted in the issuance of a decree banning the PKS, is being used by the PKS to infiltrate even deeper into the hearts and minds of Indonesians, by claiming that the PKS has now embraced Pancasila and the 1945 Constitution. If it succeeds in this effort, not only will the Muhammadiyah decree "become irrelevant"; public suspicions that the PKS's ultimate goal is to establish an Islamic state will also be discredited as "lacking foundation." As the Malay proverb states, "The most dangerous viper is one that can change its color!"

From the time of its promulgation to the very present, the Muhammadiyah decree has not been effectively implemented. This proves just how deeply extremists have penetrated the Muhammadiyah. They continue to wage an ideological war and "black campaign" against anyone who disagrees with their ideology, or obstructs their efforts to dominate the Muhammadiyah. Moderate Muhammadiyah leaders interviewed for this study have expressed deep concern that extremist groups have grown increasingly powerful within the Muhammadiyah, to the point that they could succeed in controlling the organization after the next Muhammadiyah Congress in 2010.[26] Should this occur, the Indonesian people

---

26. [Translator's note: according to high-level sources within the Muhammadiyah, the enormous publicity generated by The Illusion of an Islamic State forced the PKS to "strategically retreat" from its attempts to infiltrate and control the

would not only lose an asset in the form of a moderate mass Muslim organization, and the Muhammadiyah become a new "bunker" occupied by extremist movements; Indonesia would also lose one of the key pillars upholding Pancasila, the 1945 Constitution and NKRI (the Unitary State of the Republic of Indonesia).

Infiltration of the Nahdlatul Ulama

As the largest Muslim organization in Indonesia, the Nahdlatul Ulama (NU) is naturally concerned by a number of developments that it perceives as threatening both the nation and the NU itself, and especially the *ahlussunnah wal-jamâ'ah* (Sunni Muslim) view of Islam embraced by NU followers. Extremist movements have already succeeded in infiltrating the NU via mosques, Islamic study group councils and *pesantren* (Islamic boarding schools), which constitute the foundation of the NU and its membership.

The NU's general chairman, Kyai Haji Hasyim Muzadi, has publicly stated that countless mosques built and operated by NU members, and which previously observed NU religious rituals and practices, have been seized by extremist Islamic groups. In his opinion, this is done because the groups in question, which frequently accuse *Nadhliyin* (NU followers) of committing *bid'ah*, "[A]re unable to build their own mosques, and seize other people's mosques to use them as a base for constantly delivering radical sermons, in order to politicize those who pray there. That's their goal. And it's the NU that finally pays the price," said Hasyim Muzadi, who identified the extremist groups as including those that promote the concept of an Islamic caliphate, such as Hizb ut-Tahrir Indonesia.[27]

Hasyim instructed NU leaders throughout Indonesia to guard their mosques, and prevent them from being seized by extremist groups. He also warned that the NU should keep a close eye on

---

Muhammadiyah in the run-up to that organization's July, 2010 Congress. As a result, the PKS was not a major factor in the Muhammadiyah Congress, which elected a leadership slate containing a cross-section of progressive/moderate, opportunistic and extremist candidates to its Central Board.]

27. Hasyim Muzadi: "Khilafah Islamiyah bukan Gerakan Agama, tapi Gerakan Politik" ("Islamic Caliphate is a Political, Not Islamic, Movement"). See *NU Online,* Tuesday, 5 September 2006, reprinted in Appendix 2 of this book.

extremist groups, whose ideology is antithetical to the NU's Sunni beliefs. "Those groups seek to establish an Islamic state," he warned firmly.[28]

In fact, the issue of extremist groups infiltrating the NU has long been a topic of discussion within NU circles. One reason extremist groups accuse NU mosques of teaching heresy and deviant practices, is in order to justify the radicals seizing control of said mosques. Of course, this accusation has outraged many NU leaders. On 27 February 2007, the central leadership council of the Nahdlatul Ulama's Proselytism Institute (LDNU) issued a declaration that called upon all [40 million] *nahdliyyin* to tenaciously uphold the teachings and practices of *ahlussunnah wal-jamâ'ah* [Sunni Islam]. Eight regional LDNU chairman from throughout Indonesia signed the declaration, which constitutes a response to [extremist] accusations of religious deviance and heresy directed towards NU teachings and religious practices. The declaration reads as follows:

> [W]e recognize from the depths of our hearts that in recent years, ideological tendencies have developed and spread among Islamic movements (*al-harakah al-islami-yyah*), via religious practices that can eclipse the values of *ahlussunnah wal-jamâ'ah* (Sunni Islam), a la NU, and thus solemnly declare: ...To faithfully observe the charitable religious practices of *ahlussunnah wal-jamâ'ah* a la NU, and preserve the religious practices and traditions of our righteous predecessors, such as *salat sunnat* (optional prayers that may be performed by Muslims at almost any time of day), *salat tarawih* (an optional prayer performed during the month of Ramadan), with 20 *raka'ah* (prescribed cycles), *wirid* (invocations of the Divine), *salawat* (beeseeching God to bless the Prophet, conducted in the form of musical chants), *qunut* (special supplications), *talqin* (a special prayer recited for the deceased, at funerals), *ziarah qubur* (pilgrimage to the tombs of prophets, saints or

---

28. "Hasyim Imbau Takmir Masjid NU Waspada" ("Hasyim Warns Those Who Manage NU Mosques to be on Guard"). See *NU Online*, Tuesday, 28 November 2006, reprinted in Appendix 2 of this book.

other revered figures), *tahlil* (recitation of the phrase, "*la ilaha illallah*/There is no god but God"), *manaqib* (praising the virtues of Muhammad), *ratib* (a form of *dhikr*, or devotional act, performed in remembrance of God), *maulid Nabi* (celebration of the Prophet Muhammad's birth and life), *haul* (anniversary commemoration, generally for a renowned saint), and *istighâtsah* (communal prayers led by one perceived to be pure of heart); along with tolerance of cultural traditions that are compatible with Islamic values, as an integral part of *ahlussunnah wal-jamâ'ah da'wa* (proselytism) a la NU.[29]

This declaration represents but a single element of a concerted NU response to extremist groups, which have targeted the NU and are seeking to infiltrate the organization with their radical ideology, which is antithetical to the moderate, Sunni Muslim views held by the NU. According to the general chairman of the LDNU, Kyai Haji Nuril Huda, "The NU feels compelled to immediately establish a concerted movement to rescue and defend the [Sunni] beliefs that [our ancestors] have embraced all these centuries. If the NU neglects this task... there is no guarantee that in ten years moderate Sunni teachings won't disappear, and be replaced by another [i.e., extremist] ideology."[30]

According to NU Vice Chairman Kyai Haji Masdar F. Mas'udi, "The number of NU mosques that have been infiltrated and seized by extremist groups claiming to represent the 'true' Islam is already in the hundreds. They justify their actions by claiming that the NU is expert in *bid'ah*, and represents a deviant stream of Islam. The method through which they gain control of these mosques is by replacing the board members who manage them—a position formerly held by NU members. Then they eliminate the religious rituals and

---

29. "NU Layani Tantangan Kelompok Islam Garis Keras" ("The NU Will Stand Up and Face the 'Challenge' Posed by Hard Line Islamic Groups"). See *NU Online,* Tuesday, 27 February 2007, reprinted in Appendix 2 of this book.

30. "Rebut Kembali Masjid Nahdliyyin: LDNU Kumpulkan Majelis Ta'lim se-Jabotabek," ("Take Back Nahdliyyin (NU) Mosques: LDNU Assembles Islamic Study Group Councils from Throughout the Greater Jakarta Area"). See *NU Online* 24 August 2006, reprinted in Appendix 2 of this book.

traditions observed in NU mosques," Masdar explained.[31] Extremist groups are infiltrating not only NU mosques, but also NU youth organizations, *pesantren* (boarding schools) and Islamic study group councils.

The Association of Nahdlatul Ulama Students (IPNU) is one organization within the NU that has become a target of extremist infiltration. The head of the IPNU central board, Muhammad Asyhadi, is quoted as saying "A substantial number of NU youth have already joined forces with hardline Islamic movements. Once they go over to the extremists, they usually lose their NU and IPNU identity. In order to address this problem, IPNU is working with other student organizations to stem the influence of extremist movements in our respective environments, by conducting motivational and training exercises targeting students."[32]

Extremist groups also infiltrate *pesantren*. It is no exaggeration to say that many *pesantren* leaders are feeling sick to their stomachs, because of this infiltration. That is why from 18 – 21 May 2007, Rabithath al-Ma'âhid al-Islamiyah Nahdlatul Ulama[33] (RMI NU) gathered the heads of *pesantren* from throughout Indonesia at Pondok Gede Haji Dormitory in Jakarta. A key item on the agenda of this meeting of the NU's nationwide *pesantren* association was to address the threat posed by transnational Islamist ideology to the educational and religious traditions of *pesantren*.

RMI NU Vice Chairman Abdul Adhim told reporters that transnational ideology, or "imported" ideology, constitutes a serious threat to national unity and to *pesantren*. This is because most of these ideologies are incompatible with local culture and social conditions. "Indonesian Islam, which was spread by the Wali

---

31. "Dianggap Sesat, Masjid-masjid NU Diambilalih" ("Viewed as Deviant, NU Mosques Confiscated"). See *NU Online*, Thursday, 25 May 2006, reprinted in Appendix 2 of this book. [Translator's note: this quote from Masdar Mas'udi is derived from two separate *NU Online* articles, the second of which (24 August 2006) references the first (25 May 2006) in attributing this statement to Kyai Masdar.]

32. Antara (Indonesia's national news wire service), 15 October 2006.

33. A branch of the NU responsible for addressing the interests of 14,000 NU-affiliated *pesantren* (Islamic boarding schools, or madrasas), which at any given time enroll approximately 3 million students.

Songo [nine Muslim saints who are regarded as having converted Java to Islam] is imbued with the spirit of tolerance and courtesy. Transnational Islamist ideology, on the other hand, arrives uninvited and without the least bit of courtesy, screaming 'Allahu Akbar' while shattering glass," explained Adhim.[34] He went on to state that this is why the organization—which encompasses 14,000 NU *pesantren* throughout Indonesia—feels responsible for helping to stop the infiltration of transnational ideology, which threatens the integrity and stability of the Unitary State of the Republic of Indonesia (NKRI).

Islamic study groups operating under the authority of the NU (for women, men and teenagers) have also not been immune to infiltration by extremist groups, seeking to disseminate a transnational ideology imported from the Middle East (Wahhabi/Muslim Brotherhood and Hizb ut-Tahrir). In order to confront the onslaught of these extremist groups, the NU has sought to coordinate its members to revitalize and strengthen the Sunni Muslim worldview embraced by its members, so that *nadhliyyin* communities cannot easily be incited by extremist groups. In August of 2006, the LDNU held a conference attended by 162 chairpersons of Islamic study groups from throughout the "Jabotabek" metropolitan area (Jakarta, Bogor, Tangerang, Bekasi). According to LDNU General Chairman Kyai Haji Nuril Huda, this Jabotabek metropolitan area meeting was only the beginning of a nationwide effort. Later it would spread to other regions, especially those outside Java. For the phenomenon of extremist infiltration is not occurring in the Jabotabek region alone, but throughout Indonesia.[35]

The NU considers extremist groups to be dangerous not only to the NU, but also to Indonesia as a whole. For that reason, the NU has called upon the government to halt the spread of transna-

---

34. "RMI Kumpulkan Pimpinan Ponpes se-Indonesia Bahas 'Ancaman' Ideologi Transnasional" ("RMI Assembles Pesantren Heads from Throughout Indonesia to Discuss the 'Threat' of Transnational Ideology"). See *NU Online*, Wednesday, 16 May 2007, reprinted in Appendix 2 of this book.
35. "Rebut Kembali Masjid Nahdliyyin: LDNU Kumpulkan Majelis Ta'lim se-Jabotabek" ("Take Back Nahdliyyin (NU) Mosques: LDNU Assembles Islamic Study Group Councils from Throughout the Greater Jakarta Area"). See *NU Online* 24 August 2006, reprinted in Appendix 2 of this book.

tional extremist ideology in Indonesia, although this call is still being ignored by the government. The NU's General Chairman, Kyai Haji Hasyim Muzadi, explains that he has traveled both to Western nations, and Asian countries, in order to promote an understanding of Islam as a religion, not ideology, and to convey that all the violence in the Middle East stems not from Islam as a religion, but from Islamist ideology. "Islamist ideological movements in the Middle East include the Muslim Brotherhood, Islamic Jihad, al-Qaeda and so forth, but their Islamist ideology is *not* Islam itself, because Islam as a religion does not have the characteristics of a self-interested movement, much less political characteristics," said Hasyim.[36]

The NU regards the idea of an Islamic caliphate, or an Islamic state—both of which are being promoted by hardline Islamist groups in Indonesia—as a threat to the unity of the Indonesian nation state. Even more significant, according to the NU, is the fact that the concepts of an Islamic caliphate, and Islamic state, have no theological basis within the Qur'an or hadith. This view was expressed in a formal NU ruling issued as a result of a *Bahtsul Masa'il* (forum to address religious problems) held at Zainul Hasan Pesantren in Genggong, East Java for three days in November of 2007, which was attended by approximately 500 NU *kyais* (i.e., *ulama*, or religious scholars).

In addition to researching the texts of the Qur'an and hadith in regards to the concept of an Islamic state, the *Bahtsul Masa'il* forum also researched a number of references within the body of Muslim intellectual works that are acknowledged and accepted as being authoritative (*mu'tabar*), such as *Attasyrî' al-Jinâ'î al-Islâmî, al-Qaish al-Hâmî' al-Asyarqi, Jâm'ul Jawâmi', Ad-Dîn Waddaulah wa Tatbîqis Syarî'ah,* and *al-Fiqhul Islâmî.* In summary, the *Bahtsul Masa'il* forum determined that there is no theological basis for the concept of establishing an Islamic state or Islamic caliphate.[37] "Thus, efforts to replace the Unitary State of the Republic of Indonesia with

---

36. "PBNU Desak Pemerintah Cegah Ideologi Transnasional" ("PBNU Presses the Government to Halt the Spread of Transnational Ideology"). See *NU Online,* 29 April 2007, reprinted in Appendix 2 of this book.
37. See Appendix 2 of this book for the *Bahtsul Masa'il* forum's official finding.

an Islamic state are clearly forbidden [according to Islamic law], particularly when such efforts will bring more problems for this nation," reads one of the recommendations issued by the *Bahtsul Masa'il*.[38]

In conclusion, the 500 NU leaders attending the event agreed to reject the concept of an Islamic state. Not only that, but they also called upon the government and all religious leaders to be on guard against transnational [Islamist] ideology, which threatens the unity of our nation, its state ideology (Pancasila) and the Unitary State of the Republic of Indonesia (NKRI). "This (extremist) movement has attacked us far too often. It's now time for us to counter-attack," said Kyai Haji Ali Maschan Moesa, Chairman of the NU's East Java chapter, during the *Bahtsul Masa'il* forum.[39]

For the NU, the concept of an Islamic state represents an erroneous theological interpretation of the term Islam *kaffah* (comprehensive, or "complete," Islam), which is then erroneously converted into a religious obligation to establish an Islamic government. While it is true that *shari'a* or Islamic law should be observed, this does not require worldly power or an Islamic government. Muslims do indeed have a religious duty to practice the teachings of Islam. However, these duties do not extend to efforts to establish an Islamic government. "A genuine commitment to and practice of Islam does not require an Islamic caliphate. In fact, Muslims have a religious duty to acknowledge and obey whatever legitimate and sovereign government exists [ruling over them]," said NU General Chairman Kyai Haji Hasyim Muzadi, while explaining that the two largest Muslim powers in Indonesia, the NU and Muhammadiyah, have never intended that this nation be built upon the foundation of any one religion's teachings, including Islam.[40]

The NU has focused a spotlight not only upon the infiltra-

---

38. "Caliphate not part of Koran: NU," See *Jakarta Post*, 25 November 2007.
39. See Appendix 2 of this book, and also the article published in the *Jakarta Post*, ibid.
40. "PBNU: Khilafah Islamiyah Celakakan Muslim Minoritas di Negara Lain" ("PBNU: An Islamic Caliphate Would Bring Disaster to Muslim Minorities in Other Countries"). See *NU Online*, Thursday, 26 July 2007, reprinted in Appendix 2 of this book.

tion of the Hizb ut-Tahrir's ideology of an Islamic caliphate, but also the infiltration of Wahhabi and Muslim Brotherhood ideology, which similarly threaten the unity of the Indonesian Republic, due to their efforts to replace Pancasila and the Basic Constitution of 1945 [with an Islamic state]. Vice Chairman of the NU's *Bahtsul Masa'il* Institute (LBM NU), Kyai Haji Imam Ghozalie Said, has pointed out that most of the hardline groups that have sprouted up in recent years adhere to a Wahhabi worldview. "These groups dislike the religious traditions practiced by the NU, such as *tahlil* (recitation of the Islamic confession of faith)," he said.[41]

These groups' political views, continued Said, stem from the saying of the Prophet: "Whosoever dies without having sworn allegiance to the caliph, is like one who has died in a state of spiritual ignorance!" (*man mât wa lam yabi' fa-qad mâta mîtatal-jâhiliyyah*).[42] The Muslim Brotherhood uses a similar argument: "*Waman la yahkum bima anzalallah, faulaaika humul kaafiruun.*" ("Whoever does not observe the law that God revealed, is one of the infidels.")[43] "This is very intense from a theological perspective. They consider us to be infidels, because we don't follow their ideology,"

---

41. KH. Imam Ghozalie Said: "Ideologi Transnasional Sukses, Indonesia Berubah Total" ("If Transnational Ideology Succeeds, Indonesia Will be Completely Transformed"). See *NU Online*, Friday, 22 June 2007, reprinted in Appendix 2 of this book.

42. This hadith was conveyed in the context of one's duty to obey a legitimate sovereign, and has nothing to do with a supposed religious duty to establish an Islamic state. Only a spiritually blind and ignorant people [like those inhabiting Arabia at the time of the Prophet] live in a barbaric society without leaders and government. The hadith generally quoted in this context is the saying of the Prophet: "Whosoever amongst you, whether one or many, who wish to go, is obliged to choose a leader."

43. This Qur'anic verse criticizes those who observe religious teachings in a partial and selective manner, choosing to practice only those elements that conform to their personal interests and tendencies, or even distort religious teachings for the sake of personal gain, or group interests. Such people are condemned as tyrannical and godless infidels. The Prophet once explained that previous religious communities had been destroyed because their observance of religious teachings was based on self-interest and the interests of their group, rather than a genuine obedience to the teachings of religion. In the hands of extremist groups, this Qur'anic verse is turned on its head, and misinterpreted to impose a religious duty to formalize a system of law and government.

Said explained. Furthermore, he said, the doctrines of the Muslim Brotherhood movement stem from Sayyid Qutb, who wrote in his famous book Ma'alim fi at-Tariq (Mileposts) that if a country does not implement shari'a, it's a nation of infidels, lost in jahiliyyah (ignorance of Divine guidance).

The NU's strong reaction to extremist groups has already discredited the myth that the silent majority are unwilling to speak up and confront a vocal and aggressive radical minority. Although extremism directly threatens the NU's world-view, and its very existence, the NU is convinced that extremism also threatens the people and nation of Indonesia. Because the NU's religious traditions coincide with those practiced by the majority of Indonesian Muslims, it may be said that NU followers and the people of Indonesia constitute a unified whole that cannot be divided. The NU realizes that anything which threatens Pancasila and the integrity of the Unitary State of the Republic of Indonesia (NKRI), threatens the NU as well. The NU also understands that every threat to itself, ultimately threatens NKRI. As an indigenous form of Islam, which has merged with the cultural heartbeat of Indonesian society, the NU regards transnational movements and their ideology as incompatible with Indonesian culture and social conditions, which emphasize peaceful and harmonious relationships. "Islamic groups that promote transnational ideology are constantly embroiled in conflict, even in their countries of origin. Thus, if Indonesians join such movements, we will become embroiled in their conflicts, not to mention the fact that their ideology is incompatible with our local culture."[44]

Like the Muhammadiyah, the NU regards Pancasila and the Basic Constitution of 1945 as the "final consensus" regarding the structure of national life and our system of government. The NU also considers NKRI to be the final form of the Indonesian nation state. As the world's largest Muslim organization, the NU feels responsible for the unity, stability and peace of the Indonesian people and nation. Viewed in this light, the NU's firm attitude

---

44. "PBNU Minta Bangsa Indonesia tak Ikuti Ideologi Transnasional" ("PBNU Requests Indonesians not to Adopt Transnational Ideology"). See NU Online, Tuesday, 15 May 2007, reprinted in Appendix 2 of this book.

and vigorous response to hardline groups—which seek to promote the ideology of an Islamic state—is readily understandable. For any threat to the NU also represents a threat to the people and nation of Indonesia, and vice versa.

In confronting the threat posed by the many extremist groups that have emerged in recent years, the NU and Muhammadiyah—as the two largest Muslim organizations in Indonesia—are trying to defend their movements from further infiltration by extremists, and to continue their respective policies, which promote a moderate understanding of Islam. In the midst of their difficulties warding off extremist infiltration, these two mass organizations are signaling the world that extremist movements do not represent Islam. Rather, the extremists have hijacked Islam to serve their own political and worldly interests.

Infiltration of the Indonesian Council of Religious Scholars (Majelis Ulama Indonesia, or MUI)

The increasingly powerful role played by the MUI in Indonesian society deserves special attention. Its outspoken advocacy of specific views and demands is occurring in parallel with the coarsening of Indonesian Islam. What makes the MUI more powerful than other mass organizations is the fact that this religious institute, established by Suharto's New Order regime, has a direct relationship with the government. From the time of its founding, the MUI was designed to serve as the instrument of an authoritarian government, in order to buttress its power and trample underfoot any religious movement that opposed the government. As a result, its financial resources and facilities are enormous. For example, it has local branches throughout Indonesia—formally, at the level of provinces and regencies, but informally, its structure extends to the level of sub-regencies as well. This entire organizational structure receives financial support from the government. In addition, the MUI can augment its finances by creating religious projects that are free of government or public control, such as projects to certify food as halal (i.e., "kosher"); by occupying remunerative positions in shari'a banks, and other banks that have shari'a programs; as well as specific political projects financed by the government, such as laws that are related to religious issues.[45]

Any Islamic organization whose doctrine and beliefs the MUI judges to be true, is free to join the MUI and have representatives within its council, without regard to proportional representation, or how many members the organization in question may have. As a result, representatives from large, moderate organizations such as the NU and Muhammadiyah are outnumbered at the MUI by those of extremist groups, despite the fact that membership in each of these groups may number only in the tens of thousands, compared to the 40 million followers of the NU, and the 30 million said to be affiliated with the Muhammadiyah. The MUI has the sole right to determine which Muslim group is legitimate and which is not, which is "true" and which is deviant, and thus allowed, or not allowed, to join the MUI. For example, because the MUI regards the Ahmadiyah movement as deviant, it is not only denied a position at MUI, but the MUI itself is engaged in a strenuous campaign to have the Ahmadiyah formally outlawed (MRIRI-WI No.4).

On the other hand, regardless of how politically subversive a group may be, if the MUI regards it as "within the fold of Islam," it will be accommodated within this quasi-governmental body. The most disturbing example of this phenomenon is Hizb ut-Tahrir Indonesia (HTI). HTI doctrine explicitly acknowledges it to be a political organization that is anti-democratic; or to use religious terminology, HTI proclaims democracy to be *haram* (forbidden) and strives to create an Islamic caliphate. HTI further acknowledges that it strives to eliminate Pancasila and overthrow the Unitary State of the Republic of Indonesia (NKRI). Thus, HTI is an explicitly subversive movement, and yet the MUI accommodates its existence, and in fact HTI members have spread like the tentacles of an octopus, infiltrating the structure of the MUI from its headquarters to the most isolated of regions.[46] It is terrifying to imagine what will happen if HTI's membership ever becomes truly signifi-

45. Ahmad Suaedy et al. Introduction to: "Fatwa MUI dan Problem Otoritas Keagamaan" ("MUI Fatwas and the Problem of Religious Authoritarianism") in *Kala Fatwa Jadi Penjara* (*When Fatwas Become a Prison*) (Jakarta: The Wahid Institute, 2006), pp. x-xxv.
46. Ibid.

cant, for it will most certainly pose a mortal threat to the existence of the Indonesian nation state.

The MUI's membership system, with its feeble orientation towards, and observance of, Islam's spiritual traditions—as reflected in the orientation of the vast majority of its members—gives rise to products and *fatwas* that are consistent with the flow of extremist movements [e.g., "*shari'a*" finance and the labeling of bottled water as *halal*, when water is, by its very nature, *halal*]. This is occurring because NU and Muhammadiyah representation within the MUI is relatively tiny, despite the fact that their actual membership is enormous. This dynamic has caused the MUI to become a primary target for infiltration by extremist agents, and transformed the council into a tool used by extremists to promote their ideology and achieve their political agenda.

Because any Islamic organization, regardless of its doctrines—including anti-democratic and anti-Pancasila fundamentalist organizations and movements, except for those that are engaged in actual terrorism, such as Jemaah Islamiyah—can become members and dominate the MUI, it is fair to say that the MUI has become a "bunker" for fundamentalist and subversive organizations and movements in Indonesia.[47] Moreover, because the MUI is government-financed, fundamentalist organizations and movements are actually receiving government subsidies, to finance their goal of destroying our nation's constitutional underpinnings. The government is thus engaged in providing "capacity building" to fundamentalist and radical movements, which are opposed to Pancasila, the Basic Constitution of 1945 and the Unitary State of the Republic of Indonesia.

The MUI's proposal to legally require the segregation of *halal* and *haram* products in food stores would be a major step towards blatantly and publicly identifying who "is" and who "is not" a Muslim, which could be "seen" whenever people go shopping for food. With regards to the labeling of food products as *halal* and *haram*, the MUI's logic contradicts that of the Qur'an and hadith. The

---

47. The Wahid Institute: "MUI Bunker Islam Radical" ("MUI as a Bunker of Islamic Radicalism"), 4 May 2008. See http://www.wahidinstitute.org/Program/Detail/?id=47/hl=id/MUI_Bunker_Islam_Radikal.

Qur'an and hadith stipulate only those things that are *haram*, not the reverse, as expressed in the theorem often cited by *fuqaha* (legal scholars) that *kull syai'in halâl illâ ma hurrima* (everything is *halal* except that which has been forbidden). Maybe the MUI[48] is unaware of this fact, or is aware, but also conscious that it is far more profitable to label foods as *halal* than *haram* [since relatively few foods are actually forbidden by Islam].

Over the past five years, problems caused by the MUI have grown exponentially, because Indonesia's current ruler[49] appears to have close ties to extremist political parties that loyally support him, such as the Justice and Prosperity Party (PKS) and the Crescent Moon and Star Party (PBB). Whether the ruler's proximity to extremist groups stems from opportunism, or because he truly shares their agenda, is known only to God—Pure and Exalted is He! Assuming it stems from opportunism or a failure to understand the threat these problems pose to our nation, may God (swt.) inspire our political leaders to place the interests of the Indonesian people above their own, in this transitory and perishable world.

The ties between the ruler these past five years and extremist political parties—which both openly and secretly aim to transform the basis of our nation, [from Pancasila] to Islamic *shari'a*—has been strengthened by the selection of Ma'ruf Amin—the MUI's

48. [Translator's note: Ironically, most of the MUI's members are not actual *ulama*, or religious scholars, despite the organization's grand-sounding name, i.e., the "Indonesian Council of Religious Scholars." This profound discrepancy between self-proclaimed image and substance derives from the organization's original purpose, viz., to serve as a vehicle for strengthening and legitimizing the Suharto regime, which could not control the Nahdlatul Ulama—with its tens of thousands of *kyais*, or genuine *ulama*, who were devoutly supported by a following that in turn numbered in the tens of millions. In the 1980s and '90s, the NU helped to prepare Indonesia for democracy, and engineer Suharto's downfall, under the leadership of its General Chairman, H. E. Kyai Haji Abdurrahman Wahid.]

49. [Translator's note: for the sake of decorum, the Indonesian text does not identify the "current ruler" by name, and indeed, Indonesian grammar renders the original text ambiguous, as to whether the noun employed is singular or plural (i.e., "ruler" or "rulers"). However, the book's Indonesian readers are perfectly aware that the primary reference is to Indonesian President Susilo Bambang Yudhoyono, while the following admonition extends to his cabinet and advisors as well.]

vice chairman and spokesman, who is extremely vocal in opposing pluralism, freedom of religion and freedom of conscience in
general—as a member of the President's Council of Advisors in
the field of religion. This appointment clearly reveals the direction of government views and policy in the fields of religion and
freedom of conscience.[50] The clamor that accompanies accusations
of heresy [against fellow Muslims] and violence against those of
other faiths has become a deafening uproar, but one virtually never
hears the president's steadfast voice instructing the state apparatus
to act firmly and justly towards those who commit violence in the
name of religion, nor to defend the victims of religiously-motivated
violence, or those accused of heresy. Indeed, one never hears the
president express his "indomitable intent" to guard human rights
or uphold our constitutional guarantee of freedom of religion and
belief.

On the contrary, the president is explicitly demonstrating his
support for, and intention to follow, MUI *fatwas*, although these
neither reflect nor represent the views of the moderate majority of
Indonesian *ulama*, or Muslims at large. This quasi-governmental
body—which the New Order regime established in order to control
Indonesia's Muslim population—now appears to be dictating to,
and actually controlling, the government itself. At a recent national
conference of MUI, the council issued a *fatwa* listing ten characteristics of "heretical streams" [of Islam], to serve as a guideline
for Muslims engaged in vigilante "observation" of such allegedly
heretical movements. The result is already clear: intra- and inter-
religious conflict is careening out of hand, and growing ever more
wild and dangerous.[51]

Infiltration of Educational Institutions

A fourth-grade student in a state-run elementary school in the
Jakarta suburb of Bekasi denounced his parents as infidels, because
they continued to sit watching television when the *azan*, or call to

50. Van Zorge Report, 29 January 2008.
51. [Translator's note: A primary target and victim of MUI has been the Ahmadiyah sect, which attracts the ire of Muslim extremists, and fundamentalists, throughout the world, due to Ahmadiyah belief in the prophethood of its
founder, Mirza Ghulam Ahmad.]

prayer, issued from the loudspeaker of a nearby mosque. Of course the parents were shocked, and wondered where their beloved child had learned not only to talk that way, but to accuse his own parents of being infidels.[52] In the Jakarta suburb of Ciputat, a junior high school student told her mother that she was "destined for hell," because the mother didn't wear a *jilbab* (head covering), as the young student's teacher said was obligatory for all Muslim women.

A number of respondents who participated in the consultative research portion of this study indicated that their children have become hard-line in their religious views, such as being quick to label others as "infidels." "As a parent, of course I would like my child to be virtuous and devout, but I don't want him to turn into a fanatic, programmed to hate other people, and especially his own parents, just because of their religious views."[53]

Indonesian Muslims generally regard expressions such as "infidel" and "going to hell" as crude and vulgar language, which is inappropriate and rarely used in daily life. Historically, such expressions were directed only towards [Dutch] colonialists, in order to provide moral legitimacy to the struggle to evict the foreign colonialists from the land of Ibu Pertiwi [the Mother Earth, i.e., Indonesia]. During the formative era of Islam in Arab lands, those who enthusiastically accused fellow Muslims of being infidels were members of the *Khawârij* sect, which branded the Prophet's son-in-law Sayyidina 'Ali, Mu'awiyah and the many companions of the Prophet who supported them, as infidels. Although the *Khawârij* no longer exist as a distinct sect, their corrupt practice has been ideologically bequeathed to numerous hardline movements that employ it to discredit anyone who refuses to support them. The Wahhabis and their allies, in particular, are the true modern-day heirs to this corrupt practice.

Is it possible that our own children have now been anointed "heirs" to this *Khawârij* (Wahhabi) teaching, which so readily demonizes and denounces other people as infidels? If so, how did

52. Consultative interview held on 11 February 2008 with a respondent in Bekasi, West Java.
53. Consultative interview held on 20 November 2007 with a respondent in Ciputat, Tangerang Regency, Banten.

this radical theology from Saudi Arabia, and other extremist movements from the Middle East, succeed in infiltrating our educational system, and brainwashing our children? This is a vital issue, which has attracted a great deal of attention over the past ten years, ever since extremist groups linked to the Middle East began to pop up, and sought to force their uncompromising agenda on everyone else, by heaping insults, conducting terrorist attacks, and in general going after anyone and everyone they regard as "infidels." Apparently they have forgotten the saying of the Prophet, may God bless him and grant him peace, that "Anyone who proclaims his brother to be an infidel, without offering a true and compelling explanation for his statement, is himself an infidel[54] (*man kaffara akhâhu bi-ghairi ta'wîl—fa-huwa kamâ qâla*)."[55] Or as conveyed in a different tradition, "If anyone proclaims his brother to be an infidel, then surely one of the two is indeed an infidel" (*man kaffara akhâhu—fa-qad bâ'a bihâ ahaduhâ*).

With regard to the process through which children and the younger generation in general have been theologically contaminated, the cases cited above are reminiscent of a similar phenomenon that occurred in the 1980s, when many parents were pained to see their children suddenly become devout in worship, yet simultaneously isolate themselves from normal social interaction. Their daughters wore closed head coverings that differed from those typical of Malay Muslims; some even veiled their entire bodies with a long, black cloth, revealing only their eyes, and others veiled even their eyes with a fine mesh cloth. The boys grew beards and darkened their foreheads [i.e., bruised their foreheads by hitting them to the ground in prayer five times a day]. This phenomenon coincided with the arrival and spread of the Muslim Brotherhood's *usroh* or *tarbiyah* movement on university campuses, which offered its adherents a fanatical view of religion, accompanied by the notion that somehow they were more pious and obedient to God than

---

54. Hadith conveyed by Imam Bukhari, *Shahih al-Bukhari*, Volume XX, Chapter 73 (Egypt: Mauqif Wizârat al-Auqâf, undated), p. 259.
55. Hadith conveyed by Ahmad ibn Hanbal, *Masnad Ahmad*, Volume XIII, Chapter "Masnad 'Abdullah ibn 'Umar," (Egypt: Mauqif Wizarat al-Auqaf, undated), p. 455.

everyone else around them.[56]

At present, the symptoms of religious radicalization are no longer confined to university campuses, but have spread even to elementary and middle schools. The stories related above—of children who branded their parents infidels—are only tiny examples of the extent to which extremist agents have already succeeded in molding the religious views of elementary school students and teenagers. Just as college campuses are dotted with Campus Proselytism Institutes (LDK), which belong to the Muslim Brotherhood Tarbiyah movement and still serve to funnel new recruits to the Muslim Brotherhood/PKS, the movement conducts its grade school recruitment through Badan Rohani Islam, or Rohis, which represents the *only* Islamic student organization that is legally allowed to be active in state/public schools.

Public school students generally do not possess a deep knowledge of religion, like extremist agents themselves, whose understanding of Islam is actually quite superficial. As a result, public school students have a tendency to be easily attracted by "*Islam harakah*," or the "Islamic movement" offered by the Muslim Brotherhood's Tarbiyah group. This same phenomenon occurs on secular university campuses, where students easily fall in love with the Brotherhood's "Islamic movement" (*Islam harakah*). State/secular high school and university students possess substantially less profound knowledge of Islam than do *pesantren* [Nahdlatul Ulama Islamic boarding school] students. *Pesantren* students receive a comprehensive religious education whose goal is the pursuit of knowledge; as a result, *santris* (*pesantren* students) tend to have a broad religious perspective, and not easily fall into the trap of seeing things in terms of black and white. "*Islam harakah*," on the other hand, teaches a one-dimensional, ideologically-blinded view of religion, because its purpose is political [rather than communion with God]. To use the language of [renowned NU leader] Kyai Haji A. Mustofa Bisri, the only chapter in the book of Islam such groups have studied is *bab al-ghadlab*, or the Book of Anger. This, despite the fact that

---

56. Ali Said Damanik, *Fenomena Partai Keadilan: Transformasi 20 Tahun Gerakan Tarbiyah di Indonesia* (*The Justice Party Phenomenon: Transformation Through 20 Years of the Tarbiyah Movement in Indonesia*) (Jakarta: Teraju, 2002), p. vi.

religious instruction contains many other chapters, such as *bab al-shabr* (the Book of Patience), *bab al-tawâdlu'* (the Book of Humility), *bab al-qanâ'ah* (the Book of Asceticism), *bab al-tasâmuh* (the Book of Moderation), etc., etc.[57]

Extremist agents utilize a dual strategy to infiltrate educational institutions at all levels, namely, disseminating their ideology, and building cadres. The first element of this strategy entails organizing programs on the observance of religious duties, such as offering basic training on Islam to schools ("Islamic Training for Beginners"), study guides, courses for grade school and university-level students, the provision of "*Islam harakah*" books to students, and the gratis provision of *da'i* (proselytizers), including the free service of preachers to deliver Friday prayer sermons to students. The second element of their strategy involves the recruitment and caderization of students. The Tarbiyah movement conducts intensive training classes for young children, teenagers and college students, to prepare them for grooming to become movement (PKS) cadres. Special programs, such as "Intensive Study of Islam" classes, and "Practice to Become a Holy Warrior Engaged in Proselytism and Guidance" classes, are conducted in a carefully-prepared, step-by-step and highly-focused manner.

Extremist groups have already succeeded in preparing and training their cadres to become activists in various fields, and sent them out to work among the public at large, which includes deliberately infiltrating educational institutions, which the extremists regard as highly strategic and vital to their development of future cadres. Several patterns of activity can be readily discerned, including the organization of various forms of religious study and general study lessons for students and the public at large. It is easy to recognize these patterns, because they all feature the unique characteristics of the *tarbiyah* method employed by the Muslim Brotherhood movement in the Middle East.

To the general public, they offer trained cadres such as *khatib* (to deliver Friday prayer sermons), *guru ngaji* (to lead Islamic prayer sessions), lecturers and doctors, whose activities are all coordinat-

57. Kyai Haji A. Mustofa Bisri, from a discussion held at The Wahid Institute in Jakarta on 28 January 2008.

ed by a central command. This movement also dispatches trained personnel to conduct educational classes in home-making, such as cooking skills, and operates by moving systematically from house to house and neighborhood to neighborhood. They even offer a free cleaning service to mosques. Generally, once this movement's agents have been entrusted with control of an institution such as a mosque, an Islamic prayer group or school, they promptly move to cleanse the institution in question of any and all individuals who refuse to support their views and ideology, and invite their movement comrades to fill the administrative vacancies produced by this "housecleaning."[58]

Countless mosques and Islamic schools ranging from kindergarten to college have been successfully infiltrated by these extremist agents. In cities throughout Indonesia one encounters pamphlets or newspaper advertisements offering the services of *ustadz* (religious teachers) who are ready to meet the public's need for preaching, lecturing and family guidance. They also offer personnel to provide religious (Islamic) guidance to grade school and college students, as well as to the general public.

Besides outreach to formal institutions that existed long before the Tarbiyah movement was established, the PKS is also working to establish its own network of Islamic schools that have a unique brand and style of education, which are generally referred to as Sekolah Islam Terpadu (Integrated Islamic Schools). The PKS has succeeded in establishing such schools in numerous Indonesian cities, in order to completely mold the education provided to students from the age of kindergarten through senior high school. In recent years, the PKS's Integrated Islamic kindergartens, which

---

58. [Translator's note: This PKS/Muslim Brotherhood practice generated enormous unrest in the Muhammadiyah, and helped precipitate the Central Board Decree banning the PKS from the organization. With approximately 10,000 schools, 187 colleges and universities, and 345 hospitals and clinics scattered throughout Indonesia, the Muhammadiyah is a major employer. Knowledge that Muhammadiyah hospital staff and school teachers were being forced to join the PKS, or lose their jobs (once PKS cadres assumed administrative control of such institutions), created a special sense of urgency, when Muhammadiyah board members reviewed Dr. Haedar Nashir's book *Manifestasi Gerakan Tarbiyah: Bagaimana Sikap Muhammadiyah*, and had to decide whether or not to issue a decree banning the PKS from the Muhammadiyah.]

number in the hundreds, have been able to successfully compete with the NU's and Muhammadiyah's respective kindergarten networks. In 2006, a kindergarten belonging to the Muhammadiyah Women's auxiliary (Aisyiyah-Muhammadiyah) in Prambanan, which had a 20-year history, was nearly transformed into a PKS Islam Terpadu kindergarten, with the full support of the Speaker of the People's Consultative Assembly, PKS leader Hidayat Nur Wahid, acting through the Board of Regents of the Islamic Centre Foundation, which is a PKS affiliate. Naturally, the leadership of the Muhammadiyah's Central Java chapter vigorously opposed this maneuver, which occurred in the context of the PKS foundation's plan to build an Islamic Center. PKS acquisition of the site fell through, amid much rancor, and it remains an Aisyiyah-Muhammadiyah kindergarten to this day.

The presence of Muslim Brotherhood Tarbiyah groups (PKS) within Muhammadiyah educational institutions began to attract widespread notice when Farid Setiawan—General Chairman of the Regional Board of Directors of the Muhammadiyah Student Movement, in the province of Yogyakarta—published an opinion piece in the magazine *Suara Muhammadiyah* (*Voice of the Muhammadiyah*). In that article, entitled "Three Actions (to Improve the Muhammadiyah's) Male and Female Teachers Schools," Farid exposed extremist agents' infiltration of twin Muhammadiyah madrasas (for male and female students) in Yogyakarta, which help train future teachers for the Muhammadiyah's network of nearly 10,000 grade schools nationwide. These twin educational institutions are known as centers for the caderization of Muhammadiyah *ulama*, and operate under the direct control of the Muhammadiyah's central leadership.

As Farid Setiawan wrote:[59]

...the ideology of these two madrasas slowly began to change... because of the "tarbiyah virus" that spread like the tentacles of an octopus, coursing through the veins

---

59. Farid Setiawan, "Tiga Upaya Mu'allimin dan Mu'allimat" ("Three Actions (to Improve the Muhammadiyah's) Male and Female Teachers Schools"), *Suara Muhammadiyah*, 3 April 2006.

and arteries of the madrasas' leadership structure, from teachers to dormitory counselors, who are commonly known as musyrif and musyrifah.

It is true that this virus cannot be clearly "seen" with naked eyes, but the "political genes" that come from affiliation with an outside political party and its manhaj (method) steadily transformed the madrasas' administrators, teachers, and counselors into clones of a [political] movement distinct from the Muhammadiyah itself. They tend to focus their energies, and enthusiasm, to facilitate the growth of a non-Muhammadiyah political movement and to promote its interests.

In regards to the indoctrination of new cadres, they tend to use a system entirely different from that of the Muhammadiyah, characterized by frequent use of the terms Daurah (seminar), Liqa' (circle, or meeting), Usrah (family), Daulah Islamiyah (Islamic state) and the doctrine of Jihad fi Sabililllah (jihad in the path of God), which they employ as "holy jargon" to inflame the spirits of their young cadres. These "tarbiyah virus" functionaries engage in remarkably intense training and indoctrination of all madrasa students, for the purpose of recruiting new party cadres.

How does the Tarbiyah movement (PKS) succeed in recruiting and training the Muhammadiyah's elite cadres, and what differences do their attitudes reveal between the PKS and the Muhammadiyah, which is traditionally moderate? Farid continued his analysis:

Cadres indoctrinated with this "tarbiyah virus" methodology have an extreme and radical view of Islam. As a result there naturally arises an "internal contradiction" and paradox, due to the conflict between their views and the dynamics of the Muhammadiyah, which is known to be moderate. This conflict between radical and moderate views of Islam is increasingly visible [in Muhammadiyah circles], and is growing more acute, in parallel with the spread of the tarbiyah virus.

By now, this pattern of [the PKS] forming cadres within the Muhammadiyah has spread to every corner of the Muhammadiyah organization. This has caused enormous disappointment among Muhammadiyah members in general, and its leadership, in many parts of the country. Their sons and daughters, who they hoped would become Muhammadiyah cadres, leading the organization into the future, have instead turned 180 degrees, and now view the moderate Muhammadiyah organization as an adversary. This phenomenon also caused outside observers of the Muhammadiyah to join in grieving and expressing condolences for the untimely "death" of these twin training grounds for elite Muhammadiyah cadres, which had brought pride and honor to the organization for so many years.

Voice of Muhammadiyah published a series of opinion pieces related to extremist infiltration of the elite Muhammadiyah madrasas that were the subject of Farid Setiawan's article. However, a number of Muhammadiyah leaders influenced by extremist views and ideology were angered by the publication of these articles in *Voice of Muhammadiyah*. A polemical war raged for many months within the Muhammadiyah, ultimately leading to the adoption of Central Board Decree No. 149 regarding Consolidation of the Muhammadiyah Organization, which was distributed throughout the Muhammadiyah nationally, and directly forbid its members from using Muhammadiyah facilities to serve political interests, with the PKS identified in particular.

Farid Setiawan's article thus helped the Muhammadiyah organization confront, and begin to address, a problem that had been plaguing it for years. This occurred because Farid was honest and brave enough to speak without mincing words, and reveal developments that he had personally witnessed, which were extremely damaging to the Muhammadiyah. Ideally, this should inspire others to do likewise, to rescue the Muhammadiyah from infiltration and destruction by extremists.

For a number of years, the Muslim Brotherhood Tarbiyah movement has also been developing an Arab model of education sponsored by Middle East donors, especially Saudi Arabia. For example, they have established a number of Ma'had (institutes for courses in religious education) in various cities, with ties to Muhammadiyah universities. In fact, a number of study programs at these universities provide all their students with full scholarships, and professors who come directly from Saudi Arabia.

The Muhammadiyah University of Yogyakarta (UMY), for example, has opened a special Ma'had Abu Bakar, whose funding comes entirely from Saudi Arabia, with Saudi/Wahhabi professors augmented by Indonesian alumni who studied in the Middle East. Many UMY professors in the faculties of political science, engineering, economics and law are Hizb ut-Tahrir activists. They have structured a program that is called "the Islamization of the Muhammadiyah University of Yogyakarta," with a curriculum called "Islamic Education and Muhammadiyahness," which may only be taught by specific individuals, most of whom are alumni of study in the Middle East.

The UMY professors who exert the greatest influence upon the Ma'had Abu Bakar program are two vice chairmen of the Muhammadiyah Central Board, both of whom are alumni of Ibn Saud University in Riyadh, Saudi Arabia. As Professor Khaled Abou El Fadl has written, the Saudi government has deliberately created and financed a network of Ibn Saud students and alumni in order to spread Wahhabi ideology throughout the world, including Indonesia, so that Wahhabism may ultimately become the majority view among Muslims. Fadl also points out that a majority of professors at al-Azhar University in Cairo have embraced the Wahhabi school of orthodox/conservative Islam, and follow in the footsteps of radical Muslim Brotherhood leaders such as Hasan al-Bana and Sayyid Qutb. According to Fadl, since the 1990s, Wahhabism has become the dominant system of thought in the Muslim world.[60] (Cf. the

60. Khaled Abou El Fadl, *Melawan "Tentara Tuhan"* (*Fighting "God's Soldiers"*), (Jakarta: Serambi, 2001), p. 22.

extensive description of Wahhabi/Muslim Brotherhood ideology provided in chapter 2 of this book, *The Infiltration of Wahhabi/Muslim Brotherhood Ideology in Indonesia.*)

Our researchers discovered an even greater degree of extremist infiltration on the Muhammadiyah University of Surakarta (UMS) campus. There, Wahhabi/Muslim Brotherhood infiltration is particularly strong, especially in the faculties of engineering, Islam and the Master's Degree program in the Study of Islam, whose chairman is PKS Advisory Board member Dr. Muinudinillah, a graduate of King Abdul Aziz University in Jeddah, Saudi Arabia. In that program, three successive classes have now received full scholarships from the government of Saudi Arabia, and Saudi-provided textbooks constitute the program's obligatory reading material. Also noteworthy is the fact that approximately three quarters of the students enrolled in the Master's Degree program in the Study of Islam are PKS cadres selected by the program director, who receive full scholarships from the Kingdom of Saudi Arabia.

As an indication of just how extensive extremist infiltration of university campuses has become, our researchers discovered that approximately 60% of the UMS faculty belong to the PKS, distributed throughout the various academic disciplines. Many of these PKS faculty members hold tenured positions, and/or constitute part of the university administration, rendering it extremely difficult if not impossible for the UMS rector to implement the Muhammadiyah Central Board's Decree banning the PKS. Should the rector fire all PKS faculty members, UMS itself would collapse, having lost a majority of its faculty. The same is true of its student body, half of whom are close to the PKS, due to domination of the UMS campus by the Group Action Unit of the Indonesian Muslim Students Association (KAMMI), which is a branch of the PKS. In addition, many students are also alumni of the Ngruki Pesantren (Islamic Boarding School) led by Abu Bakar Ba'asyir, former Emir of the terrorist group Jemaah Islamiyah, and of the Indonesian Council of Holy Warriors (Majelis Mujahidden Indonesia).

This data is shocking, because it demonstrates that a majority of students attending a Muhammadiyah University campus belong to KAMMI (PKS), rather than to the traditionally-dominant Association of Muhammadiyah Students (IMM). This has occurred, despite the fact that the Chairman of the UMS Board of Trustees is Dr. Dahlan Rais—younger brother of Amien Rais, who served as the Muhammadiyah's General Chairman from 1995 to 1998—who is himself currently a Vice Chairman of the Muhammadiyah's Central Board. And the Vice Chairman of the UMS Board of Trustees is Dr. Marpuji Ali, Chairman of the Muhammadiyah's Central Java chapter.

By now it has become general knowledge that the PKS and HTI virtually "occupy" many campus mosques in Yogyakarta,[61] including those of Gadjah Mada University (UGM), Sunan Kalijaga Islamic State University (UIN), the Muhammadiyah University of Yogyakarta (UMY), the historic Syuhada mosque, and the postgraduate mosque at UGM, among others. Campus mosques serve as the Muslim Brotherhood/Tarbiyah movement's nexus point, for socializing and disseminating its ideology on college campuses. There is very little most universities can do to prevent this from happening, because many of their top administrators have already come to sympathize with the Muslim Brotherhood/Tarbiyah movement.

A number of conflicts have occurred on university campuses in Yogyakarta, as a result of this extremist infiltration. At Ahmad Dahlan University (UAD) and Sunan Kalijaga Islamic State University, students and professors often collide with, and reject, Muslim Brotherhood/Tarbiyah attempts to disseminate its ideology through Friday prayer sermons and student religious study sessions, especially the lectures delivered during Ramadan. UAD faculty and students' refusal to tolerate these practices recently led to upheaval and the abrupt cancellation of such meetings midstream. At the UIN campus mosque in Yogya, the mosque's board of trustees and Indonesian Muslim Students' Movement (PMII, a branch of the Nahdlatul Ulama) canceled Friday prayer sermons and public lectures because the Muslim Brotherhood's Tarbiyah group was refusing to accommodate students and UIN faculty who think dif-

---

61. [Translator's note: Yogyakarta is a royal city that lies at the heart of traditional Javanese culture, and also the educational center of Indonesia, with numerous universities that attract students from throughout the archipelago.]

ferently from themselves.

Educational institutions have long served as a focal point for infiltration by extremist movements, especially since these groups control networks and place their trained cadres within the organizational structure of the educational institutions in question. Prestigious campuses such as the University of Indonesia, the Bandung Institute of Technology, the Bogor Institute of Agriculture, Universitas Gadjah Mada, Universitas Padjadjaran and large campuses outside the island of Java have become fertile grounds for the propagation of extremist ideology. In Islamic Studies programs, for example, all students are required to have mentoring. If they refuse, they cannot hope to receive a good grade in their Islamic Studies classes. The mentors themselves are specially-trained cadres directed by Lembaga Dakwah Campus (LDK, or Campus Proselytism Institute), which has also fallen under the control of extremist groups.

In Medan, North Sumatra, our researchers interviewed 34 LDK student activists, of whom 31 rejected democracy and supported the establishment of an Islamic caliphate in Indonesia (the main goal of Hizb ut-Tahrir). At the Bandung Institute of Technology (ITB), 4 of the 32 students interviewed for this study were LDK activists. All 4 rejected democracy and embraced the establishment of an Islamic caliphate. By way of comparison, 5 KAMMI (PKS) student activists interviewed at ITB agreed with democracy, yet at the same time supported an Islamic caliphate. At the Bogor Institute of Agriculture, 5 KAMMI activists who participated in this study also agreed with democracy, while simultaneously supporting the establishment of an Islamic caliphate. These results are not surprising, because KAMMI represents a key element of the PKS infrastructure, which accepts democracy. But it is also clear that the Hizb ut-Tahrir agenda of establishing an Islamic caliphate in Indonesia has successfully penetrated educational circles, and is supported by LDK and KAMMI activists.

Infiltration of Government and Private Institutions

These days we often hear expressions such as, "No one dreams of establishing an Islamic state anymore," or "Anti-Islamic groups deliberately stigmatize the concept of an Islamic state."[62] However, the consultative research portion of this study uncovered a great deal of worry among experts in the field, due to many indications that point towards the formalization of religion through the establishment of an Islamic state, ranging from demands to return to the Jakarta Charter [which would have founded Indonesia as an Islamic state in 1945], to the appearance of regional *shari'a* regulations in many parts of our island nation. If anyone points out that these phenomena are leading us in the direction of an Islamic state, he or she will quickly be accused of suffering from Islamophobia. Yet in reality, such people are merely expressing the truth, as proven by this study.

Defense Minister Juwono Sudarsono fell victim to such accusations in 2006, when he publicly stated that radical movements are infiltrating Islam-based political parties, in order to establish an Islamic state and impose *shari'a*. In his opinion, these radical movements are waiting until the time is right to accomplish their objective. The Minister of Defense added that the establishment of an Islamic state and imposition of *shari'a* would lead to conflict between various Islam-based political parties themselves, because different parties have different interpretations of *shari'a*. Finally, Juwono Sudarsono asked Islamic political parties to be on guard against such infiltration. [63] [64]

A storm of protest from political party activists greeted the Minister's remarks. The General Chairman of the Justice and Prosperity Party (PKS), Tifatul Sembiring, said that the Defense Minister's remarks merely stigmatized all Islamic political parties. Such

---

62. [Translator's note: both of these expressions are intended to deflect criticism of the extremist agenda, either by denying its objective of establishing an Islamic state, or by discrediting anyone who objects to the establishment of such a state.]

63. *Republika*, 7 October 2006.

64. [Translator's note: although the PKS and PBB are extremist political parties, other Islam-based parties—including PAN (created by former Muhammadiyah Chairman Amien Rais), PPP (a legacy party formed during the Suharto era, which was originally supported by many NU as well as Muhammadiyah members) and PKB (established by NU General Chairman H.E. Kyai Haji Abdurrahman Wahid in 1998)—each have their own views of Islam, distinct from the Muslim Brotherhood-affiliated PKS and the Masyumi-inspired PBB.]

accusations, he said, resembled the methods used by Suharto's New Order regime. The Vice Secretary General of PPP, Lukman Hakim Saifuddin, also reacted harshly. In his opinion, it was inappropriate for the Defense Minister to make such accusations. Especially, he added, in light of the fact that Islam-based parties had long since abandoned any aspiration to establish an Islamic state.

These criticisms leveled at Juwono represent a political backlash, stemming from the short-term interests of those concerned. Actually, the Defense Minister's public remarks should be understood as reflecting his love of the Unitary State of the Republic of Indonesia (NKRI) and Islam. Extremist infiltration is not merely the subject of idle rumor and gossip. In fact, a former Chairman of the Indonesian Armed Services told one of our researchers, "Before, the extremist threat to NKRI and Pancasila lay outside of government, [in the form of armed rebellions] such as Darul Islam/NII. But now extremists have managed to infiltrate the government, including parliament, and have become far more dangerous than in the past."[65]

At present, a former chairman of the PKS occupies the strategic position of Chairman (Speaker) of the Republic of Indonesia's upper legislative body, the People's Consultative Assembly.[66] Three other PKS leaders serve as cabinet ministers, whose portfolios include the Agriculture Department, which is extremely strategic, due to its having local branches in every sub-regency throughout Indonesia, from Sabang to Merauke, and control of virtually every resource provided by the government to farmers [who constitute more than forty percent of Indonesia's workforce]. According to the head of a large Nahdlatul Ulama *pesantren* (Islamic boarding school) in Central Java, "The PKS has managed to infiltrate all the way to the village level in Central Java, using the Department of Agriculture's facilities."[67]

---

65. Consultative research interview conducted on 17 September 2008.
66. [Translator's note: the reference is to PKS leader Hidayat Nur Wahid (HNW). Publication of *The Illusion of an Islamic State* helped derail PKS/HNW's aspirations to secure Indonesia's vice presidency in the 2009 national elections, as described by media coverage reprinted in Appendix 4 of this book.]
67. Consultative research interview conducted in March of 2008.

Indonesia is now witnessing the fruits of a coalition of extremist parties with opportunistic politicians and political parties. On a macro level, in recent years the Indonesian government has received considerable international praise because of the improvement in economic conditions, and the government's "success" in capturing and bringing to trial a large number of terrorists who have acted in the name of Islam. This has created an image of stability. In reality, however—beyond the field of vision of the international press corps and politicians, and indeed, the majority of Indonesians themselves—social conditions in regard to religion have deteriorated significantly, due to collaboration between opportunistic politicians and political parties and extremist movements. This collaboration has allowed the spread of extremist ideology, agents and their agenda to virtually every field of life in Indonesia.

A professor at a prominent Islamic State University, who actively studies the education of *imams* (prayer leaders) and *khatib* (preachers), and the religious views they disseminate during Friday prayer services, visibly trembled as he told our researchers, "When I listen to the Friday sermons delivered in many Jakarta mosques, I fear for the future of our country." He added, "Many of these Friday sermons are full of angry criticism directed towards others, which is completely inappropriate behavior in a mosque."[68] [69]

---

68. Consultative research interview conducted in August of 2007.

69. [Translator's note: a fundamental distinction between traditional, spiritually-oriented Muslims on the one hand, and Wahhabi/Salafi extremists on the other, is the latter's frequent use of religious sermons to promote hatred and violence towards so-called "enemies of Islam." Kyai Haji Hodri Ariev—a key author of this report—tells of a memorable incident from his youth, when his grandfather (a renowned Nahdlatul Ulama *kyai* from Jember, East Java) rose to interrupt a Friday sermon, in which a visiting *khatib* was inciting hatred of others. In a thunderous voice imbued with authority, Hodri's grandfather ordered the visiting *khatib* to get down from the pulpit and leave the mosque immediately. The fact that Muslims never interrupt a Friday sermon, under normal circumstances, merely served to emphasize the point that the renowned spiritual kyai from Jember was making—not only to those present, but to all who would subsequently hear of the incident—viz., that no Muslim should indulge in, nor tolerate from others, the dissemination of hatred in the name of Islam. The translator witnessed a similar incident in East Java in April of 2004, when Kyai Haji Abdurrahman Wahid struck to the ground, and publicly humiliated, the head of an extremist *pesantren*, whose followers were threatening non-Muslims. President Wahid went

Ustadz A.R. is an alumnus of al-Azhar University in Cairo, Egypt, who has a moderate/progressive view of Islam. He admires the Grand Shaykh of al-Azhar, Muhammad Sayyid Tantawi, because of his moderate religious views. Many of his fellow al-Azhar alumni who have returned to Indonesia share these views. In 2002, Ustadz A.R. began routinely delivering religious education sermons at a number of offices in Jakarta, both government and private sector. But in 2004, Ustadz A.R. received the bitter news that he had been "fired" from his position delivering sermons for a courier company in South Jakarta, and a government customs office in East Jakarta.

Ustadz A.R. was unaware of what personal fault had led to this sudden termination. After investigating the circumstances behind his firing, he learned that the Islamic Spiritual Training Council in both offices had fallen into the hands of the Tarbiyah movement (PKS). A number of Ustadz A.R.'s friends have experienced the same treatment. Once the Tarbiyah movement controls an Islamic education forum, it is their standard operating procedure to take over completely. This includes determining what written materials will be distributed and who may or may not teach at these forums. They quickly replace the teaching staff with people who share their views, and use the forums they now control to socialize their ideology and political agenda.

B.M., an Islamic activist who was previously involved with the al-Azhar Youth Islamic Study Club in Kebayoran Baru, Jakarta, relates a similar story. Full of idealism and working with a network of al-Azhar alumni, B.M. and his friends often coordinated Islamic study sessions at the offices of major corporations in Jakarta. Those who delivered the sermons included top intellectuals holding PhDs from the West and the Middle East, who taught at Syarif Hidayatullah Islamic State University in Jakarta or Paramadina University, and other well-known Muslim intellectuals. Within 5 years of launching their program, said B.M., he and his friends had

---

on to tell the man's students, and thousands of startled villagers who witnessed the event, that Islam forbids Muslims to believe that they are in exclusive possession of the truth, or have any right to frighten, much less terrorize, those of another faith.]

succeeded in organizing dozens of religious forums for major corporate offices in Jakarta. However, since 2003, every proposal B.M. has submitted to continue these events has been rejected by the very same offices and businesses. After investigating the situation, it turned out that the Islamic Spiritual Training Council overseeing these offices and businesses had indeed fallen into the hands of the Tarbiyah movement. Realizing they had been out-maneuvered, he and his friends withdrew.

What is the nature and content of Islamic study sessions held by the Tarbiyah movement? The following information conveyed by a source with the initials A.T. may help paint a useful picture. A.T. is a senior executive at a telecommunications firm headquartered on Jenderal Sudirman Avenue in Jakarta [the city's most prestigious business address]. In his opinion, the Islamic study sessions attended by his office staff have completely changed, since falling under the control of the Tarbiyah movement. Whereas the sessions used to emphasize spirituality, intellectual rigor, morality and a sound work ethic, today the Islamic study sessions held for his employees tend to be harsh and grating, full of the stench of politics and talk of jihad. The person delivering the sermon will often address a controversial topic, and not hesitate to vilify and curse other groups in society, that hold a different view. "To tell you the truth, I'm worried about these developments," said A.T. "But because I have no expertise in the field of religion, there's nothing I can do about it."

A controversy surrounding the infiltration of extremist ideology into Islamic study forums in government offices has rocked the city government of Depok in Bogor Regency [a Jakarta suburb that is home to the University of Indonesia], whose mayor is the former president of PKS, Nur Mahmudi Ismail. Hasbullah Rahmad, head of the National Mandate Party faction in Depok, brought this controversy to light in 2006. Hasbullah cited an example, in which routine Islamic study sessions held for Depok government employees, and supervised by the PKS, constituted forced indoctrination in PKS ideology. "Anyone who wants to advance in his or her career must attend these PKS Islamic study sessions. This is actually happening," said Hasbullah, who added that the actions of Nur Mahmudi and the PKS are profoundly disturbing to Depok government employees. Hasbullah says that if he were the mayor, he would not convene such Islamic study sessions. "It's enough to ensure a bureaucrat's efficiency at discharging his responsibilities. For example, can you issue a building permit within a week? If not, we'll replace you. That's the important thing, to improve public service," he explained.[70]

The PKS's network of *ustadz* (preachers) scattered in government offices and businesses is nothing new. Alumni of the 1980s *usroh* (family) or Muslim Brotherhood/Tarbiyah movement, who were once activists conducting Islamic study sessions on campuses, entered the work force after graduation, and joined various businesses. Thus, Muslim Brotherhood/Tarbiyah alumni are now working in numerous offices and businesses not only in Jakarta, but in large firms scattered throughout Indonesia. Through this ever-widening network of college graduates, Islamic study groups a la Tarbiyah are being formed in work places throughout the nation. Thus, the network formed through their campus proselytism activities has now blossomed into a network infiltrating many of the largest businesses in Indonesia.[71]

In an official document published by the PKS itself, the Justice and Prosperity Party explicitly talks about spreading its cadres [throughout Indonesian society] through a three-stage process: *first*, the spread of *da'wa* (proselytism) cadres to organizations/institutions in the various fields of life, with these cadres focusing their efforts on reaching the respective organizations'/institutions' centers of power and policy; *second*, to ensure these *da'wa* cadres have a successful career within the target organizations/institutions; and third, for these *da'wa* cadres to play a key role influencing, formulating, interpreting and implementing these organizations'/institutions' public policies, to ensure they are consistent with Islamic *manhaj* (methods).[72]

---

70. "Fraksi PKS Diingatkan Tak Paksakan Ideologi Partai" ("PKS Faction Reminded Not to Impose Party Ideology"), *Kompas*, 18 December 2006.
71. Ali Said Daminik, op. cit., p. 161.
72. See, Platform Kebijakan Pembangunan Partai Keadilan Sejahtera (Policy Platform [to Ensure] Development of the Justice and Prosperity Party) (Jakarta:

As a *da'wa* party, the PKS naturally has a right to play a role in promoting Islam within society as a whole. But when this *da'wa* is conducted in a manner completely integrated with a political goal of mobilizing support to win elections, Muslims who do not belong to the PKS have every right to reject association with the PKS and to fortify themselves and their organizations from PKS infiltration. In the words of Muhammadiyah Vice Chairman Haedar Nashir:

> Fraternity with a fellow Muslim group, or with any other component of our nation, does not require sacrificing the Muhammadiyah's own organizational interests. In fact, just the opposite. If an Islamic movement truly wishes to promote fraternity, it should be careful not to disturb others, much less regard itself as "Divinely anointed" and position all other Muslim groups/communities as [deviant and thus] in need of being infiltrated and "re-Islamized." Such an attitude is not only arrogant and destructive of the ethical code that should guide Muslims' relationships with each other, but indeed is likely to spread the seeds of enmity and conflict among Muslims far and wide. If the Muhammadiyah is now erecting a defensive wall, its actions are neither inimical to Muslim fraternity, nor "reactionary." Examine problems upstream [close to their source], rather than downstream. After all, where there is smoke, there is also fire. The Muhammadiyah is merely reacting [to a threat] and defending itself. If [the PKS] wishes to enjoy Muslim fraternity, let it behave with mutual understanding and respect, and not regard itself as more Islamic, and thus a necessary alternative to other groups.

Islamic political parties inevitably have their own mission and self-interest, which is not identical with Islam itself. Political parties that bear the "label" of Islam or *da'wa* are, in reality, still political parties, whose primary goal is the acquisition of power. For this reason they

Majelis Pertimbangan Pusat PKS, 2007), p. 20.

should not be regarded as representing Islam, or Muslims, in their entirety.[73]

Closing

In this context, it is readily understandable that Indonesian Muslims have reacted strongly to the proliferation of PKS cadres, and regard their spread as a form of extremist infiltration. That is why the Muhammadiyah issued Central Board Decree No. 149 in November of 2006, which explicitly forbids its members from using the Muhammadiyah and its facilities to serve political interests. Similarly, the NU has issued a number of *fatwas* encouraging its members to guard against, and actively oppose, transnational Islamist ideology and movements. In recent years, [extremist] threats to the Unitary State of the Republic of Indonesia (NKRI), Pancasila and Islam itself have grown progressively more significant and dangerous. For the extremists' combination of virulent ideology, financial strength and systematic deployment of these resources has enabled extremist agents to successfully infiltrate many sectors of Indonesian life.

As the largest element of Indonesian society, and indeed, the most populous Muslim community in the world, Indonesian Muslims have a religious duty and a profound moral responsibility not only to defend NKRI and Pancasila from every threat, but also to rescue Islam from those who have hijacked this great religion, and turned its sublime and noble values upon their head, rendering Islam itself an object of fear and disdain throughout much of the world. All this may be accomplished by recognizing the limits of our own understanding and knowledge; constantly learning in a spirit of open-mindedness and humility; and faithfully observing the teachings of religion, which are full of spirituality and God's divine love. By doing so, we will behave in a tolerant manner that is respectful of differences and of others' freedom, while firmly opposing the efforts of all those who seek to use Islam as a vehicle for self-aggrandizement and the acquisition of power.

---

73. Haedar Nashir, *Kristalisasi Ideologi & Komitmen Bermuhammadiyah* (*The Crystallization of Muhammadiyah Ideology and Commitment*) (Yogyakarta: Suara Muhammadiyah, 2007), pp. 8-9.

Chapter V

CONCLUSION AND RECOMMENDATIONS

The East Indies archipelago constitutes a region that is extremely rich in spiritual heritage and open-minded traditions that readily acknowledge and accept differences. This attitude stems from the awareness that such differences are merely extrinsic, and that the infinite variety of creation arises from the common ground of a single, substantive reality (i.e., God), in which all may meet. When Muslim saints—who deeply valued the substantive aspects of religion, without dismissing its formal elements—brought Islam to the East Indies, they encountered the spiritually rich atmosphere and traditions of this region. And because of the saints' own profound grasp of religion, inhabitants of the East Indies archipelago naturally and appropriately embraced the august spiritual messages of Islam, which acknowledged the existence and reality of diverse traditions, which had already become an integral part of their lives.

As we are often reminded, religion is a path and a means to a goal (*syir'ah wa minhaj*). Two principles inherent in religion are selfless devotion to God (*ikhlash al-'ibâdah ilâ Allâh*) and adorning oneself with noble and praiseworthy morals (*al-tahallî bi makârim al-akhlâq*). Service to God occurs not only in the performance of pure worship (*ibâdah mahdlah*), such as prayer, almsgiving, fasting and pilgrimage to Mecca, but also in helping and serving God's creatures. This means that there is always a dimension of devotion and service to God in every activity of those who have religious faith—its depth a reflection of the purity, and intent, with which such activities are performed. And noble morals specifically ensure that the diverse forms of one's service and devotion to God are conducted in a virtuous and praiseworthy manner, without harming anyone.

Although not always formulated in the same theoretical manner, the religiosity of those inhabiting the East Indies archipelago is virtually identical to that described above. Concern for, and assistance and service to others, is performed with an awareness of creating good karma, by Hindus; in order to share the dharma and free humanity from suffering in this world of illusion, by Buddhists; in order to please God, by Muslims; and as an expression of God's love for one's fellow man, by Christians. Pancasila precisely and appropriately reflects these sublime teachings of religion: the existence of One (Transcendent) Divinity; humane values; a feeling of unity with others; consultation in leadership; and justice.

Extremist groups have lately denounced and blasphemed these majestic teachings as the cause of Indonesia's moral degradation and collapse, both in the fields of politics and economics. Their purpose is clear: by discrediting Pancasila, they are attempting to formalize religion, which is to say: their shallow, narrow, partial and rigid understanding of Islam. This, in spite of the obvious reality, that our nation's moral degradation and collapse have occurred because those in power are disloyal to our nation's founding principles and constitution. From 1945 until the present date, the principles of *shari'a* so clearly reflected in Pancasila have not yet been fully realized. Thus, moral degradation and national collapse are only pretexts designed to replace Pancasila with a state based on the extremists' version of Islam, and/or to replace the Unitary State of the Republic of Indonesia (NKRI) with an international caliphate.

In reality, the seeds of extremist movements have been present in modern Indonesia since the 1970s, although at the time they appeared sweet-faced and did not yet reveal their true goal, since they lacked sufficient power. Following the collapse of Suharto's New Order regime, these seeds sprouted as rapidly as mushrooms during the rainy season, by exploiting the atmosphere of freedom and democracy for purposes that are not only anti-democratic, but intended to shackle freedom itself. Extremist groups include some that prefer "street action" as a means to impose their ideology on society, while other extremist groups choose the path of practical politics and government. This phenomenon has attracted the attention, and concern, of many Indonesians, especially moderate Muslims and nationalists, who smell something strange and disturbing in the actions of such groups.

This study was designed to ascertain, demonstrate and prove whether or not the above-mentioned movements represent a profound hidden danger not only to Indonesia, but to Islam itself. In point of fact, the study revealed that these movements have a close relationship with transnational Islamist movements that originate from the Middle East, especially Wahhabism, the Muslim Brotherhood and Hizb ut-Tahrir. Their goal is to dictate every aspect of life in Indonesia. In other words, they adhere to a totalitarian and centralistic ideology that uses religion to provide theological justification for their own political ambitions, while their primary agenda is to become God's vice-regents on earth. Despite the obvious limitations and shallowness of their grasp and practice of Islamic teachings, they nonetheless feel entitled to represent God, and exercise absolute authority over their fellow man.

Radicals cleverly exploit the Muslim community's belief that God directs every aspect of human life. This is indeed true, but the political doctrines expounded by extremist movements constitute a gross misunderstanding that stems from their shallow and narrow view of Islam. Moderate *ulama* understand this belief (in God's direction of human affairs) as most profoundly expressed in islamic behavior that is rooted in self-transcendence, and reflected in the performance of good deeds solely for the purpose of pleasing God, to the extent that He manifests His presence to such enlightened souls, and becomes the ears with which they hear; the eyes with which they see; the tongue with which they speak, and the feet with which they walk; i.e., until the five senses and the bodily organs perform only that which is indeed the will of God.[1] God does not

---

1. The complete text of this *hadith qudsi* reads: "*Lâ yazâl al-'abd yataqarrabu ilayya bi al-nawâfil hatta uhibbahu. Fa-idza ahbabtuhu, kuntu sam'ahu alladzi yasma'u bihi, kuntu 'ainâhu allati yubshiru biha, kuntu lisanahu alladzi yanthiqu bihi, kuntu rijlâhu*

control every aspect of human life through the direct exercise of politics and power, but rather, through spirituality and love. To practice Islam in a self-transcendent and profound manner means to submit oneself only to God, and not to the base will of beasts, including that which is wrapped in political rhetoric by people who claim the right to represent God, and who manipulate religion as a tool to dominate every aspect of other people's lives.

In order to achieve their political ambitions, extremists are infiltrating nearly every field of Indonesian society: from the presidential palace to the mountains; through a legislative track and street actions; by seizing control of mosques and educational institutions, even to the point of offering free cleaning services to accomplish that objective; and moderate Islamic mass organizations.

All these actions are being conducted in a systematic and mutually supportive manner. For example, violent street actions receive justification and support in parliament, and are legitimized by *fatwas* issued by the Indonesian Council of Religious Scholars (Majelis Ulama Indonesia, or MUI). MUI *fatwas* have similarly been supported by street violence and parliamentary action. And political issues, in parliament, obtain visibility and support through street actions and the MUI. All this cannot be viewed as simply an accident.

These mutually supportive actions are enabled by two basic factors. First, the extremist groups involved in these actions share a common ideology, and are generally affiliated with either Wahhabism, the Muslim Brotherhood and/or Hizb ut-Tahrir. Of course, this does not mean there are no differences between extremist groups. For the time being they can still unite, because they confront a common enemy: i.e., the moderate Muslim community, which rejects formalization of religion, and instead adheres to substantive religiosity and spirituality. In the future, should extremists succeed in defeating moderate groups, they will battle among themselves to seize absolute power in our beloved archipelago.

---

allati yabthisyu biha" ("My servant constantly draws close to me by practicing that which pleases Me (*nawâfil*) until I love him. And when I love him I become the hearing with which he hears, the two eyes with which he sees, the tongue with which he speaks, and the two feet with which he walks."

The second reason extremists can cooperate so readily is that the global phenomenon of Wahhabization has become a tempting business, which allows many radicals to profit from the actions they perform. The fusion of ideology, massive financial support and a systematic approach to infiltrating Indonesian society has enabled extremist movements to pose a dreadful threat to Indonesia's traditions of diversity, and to Pancasila and the integrity of NKRI.

Another aspect of this threat requires serious attention. Extremist movements—which, during the Sukarno and Suharto eras (from 1945 to 1998), were locked outside of government—have now succeeded at deeply infiltrating the government. This makes them increasingly bold and dangerous, because their efforts to discard Pancasila and transform NKRI can be spearheaded through legislative channels, at both a regional and national level. Even illegal and unconstitutional actions performed by extremist groups receive protection and support from government. Radical activists have been successful at infiltrating government not only because of their virulent ideology, financial support and systematic approach, but also because their efforts to infiltrate are facilitated by opportunistic politicians who care only about their personal interests and those of their allies, and thus sacrifice the future of our people and nation without remorse.

This phenomenon appears to have accelerated during the past five years, to the point where various departments in the national government clearly side with extremist groups. Only God knows whether or not the rulers who allow this to occur are opportunists. Assuming they are not fully aware of the dangers that threaten Indonesia, may God inspire such rulers to prioritize the interests of our nation and people, and courageously refuse to cooperate with extremist groups, which use them to achieve their political goals. But if their close association with hardline groups is due to opportunism, the public should be aware in choosing leaders who will prioritize the interests of our nation and people as a whole.

Opportunistic politicians are just as dangerous as hardline activists themselves. They are two-faced hypocrites who assume whatever appearance is best suited to promoting their own interests, and acquiring the benefits they pursue. The same is true of opportunistic political parties. While extremist groups aim to seize power and dictate every aspect of human life in the name of the God, opportunists wish to acquire and preserve political power and wealth for themselves and their allies. The interests of our nation and people, as well as the sublime majesty of religious teachings, have no place in their agenda. There isn't the slightest hope for the future, or anything we can expect to obtain, from extremist movements and/or opportunistic politicians and political parties, other than subservience, prohibitions and an interlocking mass of rules which will extinguish everyone else's freedom and creativity, and which they blithely impose in order to guarantee the fulfillment of their political ambitions.

In addition to opportunistic politicians and political parties, the involvement of transnational extremist movements and foreign (i.e., Wahhabi) money has rendered the phenomenon of extremist movements, in Indonesia, progressively more large and complex. The Nahdlatul Ulama and Muhammadiyah's rejection of their agenda has made extremist movements focus on these two mass organizations as primary targets of infiltration. In addition to their loyalty to the Indonesian people's tradition of a courteous and tolerant diversity, the NU and Muhammadiyah have long since accepted Pancasila and NKRI as our nation's final consensus regarding state ideology and structure.

Moderate Muslim leaders regard extremist movements as arising from a shallow understanding and practice of Islam. This is precisely why radicals reject and attack spirituality—which they do not comprehend—as a deviation from the teachings of Islam. Thus efforts to preserve Pancasila and the integrity of NKRI, and to realize Islam as a blessing for all creation, must be conducted in a peaceful, responsible manner, through the path of education—in the widest sense of the word—which truly enlightens. Such efforts are not merely the responsibility of the NU and Muhammadiyah, but rather, of all components of our nation, in accordance with their respective abilities and capacity. In the context of this era of reform and democracy, it is vital that we recall the advice of Syeikh Ibn 'Athaillah al-Iskandari from his opus *Hikam*: "Do not closely associate with anyone whose state does not inspire you and whose speech does not lead you to God" (*lâ tash-hab man lâ yunhid-luka ilâ Allah hâluhu, wa la yahdîka ilâ Allâh maqâluhu*). The speech and behavior of both radical activists and opportunistic politicians clearly leads the Muslim community further from God. The Indonesian public should recognize this fact, and maintain a strict guard against such dangers.

The Muhammadiyah Central Board's Decree No. 149/Kep/I.0/B/2006,[2] and the NU's Bahtsul Masa'il decree concerning an Islamic caliphate,[3] represent structural attempts to create an awareness of the dangers of extremist ideology and infiltration within these organizations, and the Indonesian public in general. At present, a number of Muhammadiyah and NU board members have taken strong steps to check radical infiltration within their respective organizations. These two Islamic mass organizations have attempted to warn Indonesia's elite, and public, that radical groups are dangerous because they promote a foreign, transnational ideology that threatens the pluralistic traditions and culture of Indonesia, as well as Pancasila and NKRI. According to the Muhammadiyah decree and NU *fatwas*, radical organizations are not engaged in *da'wa* (proselytism); rather, they are political movements whose goal is to seize power.

Strategic Recommendations

The extremists' ideology and agenda—through which they have manipulated the beliefs of the Muslim community—causes them to frequently speak and behave brutally towards anyone who does not support, not to mention those who actively reject, their views. For this reason, efforts to overcome the threat of radicalism cannot succeed without the involvement of those who possess a courageous and noble character—who fear nothing, and no one, but God Himself.

We know from the history of the East Indies archipelago that there have always been saints, *rishis* (enlightened sages), noble warriors and other heroes who stepped forward to defend the truth and struggle for justice, at the risk of their own comfort and safety.

---

2. See Appendix 1 of this book.
3. See Appendix 2 of this book.

The example of their noble and courageous behavior has constantly inspired one generation after the next, including the founders
of our nation. Today, there are still many Indonesians who have
inherited, and cultivate, such noble qualities. They struggle for
truth and justice in a manner faithful to the philosophy of life embraced by our ancestors, and to our national unity. Unfortunately,
because they're not organized, such heroes often feel isolated and
alone, while radical activists constantly attack anyone who teaches
and conserves our ancestors' glorious religious and philosophical
values.

In order to vanquish the threat of religious extremism, we
need to build a movement that will inspire, mobilize, encourage
and support the vast, silent majority of Indonesians to voice the
religious truths, and traditions, of our ancestors. By doing so, we
will prevent extremist groups from dominating Indonesia, and
guarantee that moderate Muslims once again "color" the life of
our people, and government, in such a way as to protect the rights
of minorities, and ensure that religion truly functions as a blessing
for all sentient beings.

In order to safeguard Pancasila, the Basic Constitution of
1945, the Unitary State of the Republic of Indonesia (NKRI) and
our nation's majestic cultural and spiritual heritage, and traditions,
organized efforts should be made to implement a number of strategic steps, such as the following:

1. Encourage and inspire the public, including Indonesia's
   elites, to be open-minded, humble and devoted to constant
   learning, so that they may comprehend the spirituality and
   essence of religious teachings, and thus become tranquil
   souls.
2. Halt in its tracks and eliminate—using responsible methods—the vicious cycle of radicalization that spreads extremist ideology and doctrine, by promoting enlightened education (in the broadest sense of the term), and by teaching
   and practicing the sublime message of Islam, which fosters
   an awareness of the need to become a humble, tolerant and
   peaceful servant of God.

3. Help Indonesia's public and elite to recognize that the radical ideology and doctrines brought by transnational Islamist movements from the Middle East, and spread by their local agents, conflict with Islam and with Indonesia's traditions, culture and pluralistic religious environment, which has long been tolerant, courteous and moderate by nature.

4. Struggle to preserve and realize the highest ideals of Pancasila, which reflect the essence of shari'a, while assuring Indonesia's elites and general public that this will serve to manifest Islam as a true and Divine blessing for all sentient beings, as our founding fathers intended.

5. Work with spiritual kyais (religious leaders) to revitalize the Nahdlatul Ulama (NU) in accordance with the understanding of ahlussunnah wal-jamâ'ah (Sunni Islam), and also request and support such spiritual kyais to lead the NU. Success in this endeavor will make it difficult for extremist agents and groups to infiltrate or influence this moderate mass organization; will mobilize the NU to help stop extremist infiltration of government, the MUI and other strategic fields; help develop Indonesia into a more just and prosperous nation; and position the NU to assume the lead in efforts to free the world from the crisis of misunderstanding about Islam, and thus rescue humanity from the dangers of religious extremism.

6. Work with ulama, intellectuals and cultural figures from various disciplines and areas of expertise, belonging to moderate Islamic mass organizations, to provide alternative information concerning MUI fatwas which do not fully express the true message of Islam; and in this context, militate so that the creation of Islamic law in MUI environs is conducted in a transparent manner involving ulama outside the membership structure of the MUI, from various disciplines and areas of expertise, so that the creation of Islamic law is not conducted in an opaque and narrow manner by people from the same stream of thought, as is common in Wahhabi circles and among fanatical sects.

7. Work with and support educational practitioners, at all levels of education, to teach and familiarize students with the richness, nobility and significance of Indonesia's cultural heritage and traditions; encourage and support educational authorities and educational practitioners, as well as parents and foster parents, to adopt a critical attitude towards various activities in their environment—including the teaching of religion—which are often used as a means to infiltrate extremist ideology; and encourage life-long study in order to overcome ignorance, especially in comprehending and practicing religious teachings.

8. Work with businessmen to support the realization of justice, security, order and social stability, so as to develop a national life that is just and prosperous, through the institutions of government and civil society; encourage businessmen to use their wealth wisely, and never support extremist groups, radical political parties, and/or opportunistic politicians who work with radicals to achieve their political agenda. Radical groups are terrified that Indonesia's business community may one day decide to oppose and put a stop to their activities.

9. Work to ensure that the institutions of government are clean and just (characterized by good governance and the rule of law), and prioritize efforts to raise the level of general prosperity, so that the people and nation of Indonesia can truly develop, and so that the rhetoric of justice and prosperity is no longer a political commodity used by extremist groups in their efforts to achieve their political goals and agenda.

10. Develop public understanding and awareness of Islam's glorious message as a blessing to all sentient beings, and mobilize Indonesian figures who are living embodiments of our nation's spiritual heritage, in order to help humanity overcome the current crisis of misunderstanding about Islam that Middle Eastern extremists have spread from East to West, giving rise to a serious threat to non-Muslims, and Muslims, throughout the world.

11. Develop a network of those who love the Red and White [Indonesia's national colors], which will inspire the younger generation to learn the valuable lessons of their forebears' history, traditions and culture, and develop understanding of our nation's culture within the context of a complete, holistic and profound religiosity. By doing so, foreign ideology and movements such as Wahhabism, the Muslim Brotherhood and Hizb ut-Tahrir will not find cracks through which to infiltrate and brainwash our nation's youth.

12. Develop faith and pride that our nation's culture and traditions are fully consistent with the religious teachings held by the Indonesian people, despite the fact that the religions in question were originally revealed elsewhere; support efforts to understand religion, traditions and culture in an integral, profound and complete manner, so that our children do not foolishly adopt shallow foreign traditions and culture, propagated by those who hunger to commit cultural genocide against our own.

Ultimately, it is we who shall decide (through our actions, or lack thereof) whether our grandchildren will inherit an Indonesia that remains steadfastly courteous, tolerant, peaceful, civilized and spiritual.

Epilogue

NEVER CEASE LEARNING
By Kyai Haji A. Mustofa Bisri

This book, *The Illusion of an Islamic State*, may be read from the perspective of both politics and religion. In terms of politics, it constitutes a reminder to the Indonesian nation concerning the hidden dangers of attempts to transform our country into a theocratic state. This danger threatens not only the inhabitants of Indonesia, but Islam itself. For the people of Indonesia, such a change would inevitably diminish cultural richness and religious freedom—not only for non-Muslims, but also for Muslims—and grossly distort Islam itself. For non-Muslims, this change would likely cause them to experience psychological and social alienation from a country whose official belief system differed from their own. While for Muslims, this change would lead to narrow restrictions and the vanished opportunity to interpret religious teachings in accord with the social and cultural context of Indonesia. Every reading that differs from the official state interpretation of Islam will be declared subversive and forbidden.

Formalization will transform Islam itself from a religion into an ideology, whose boundaries are determined by political interests. Islam, which was broad and open-minded at the outset, and lives like an organism that is communicative and directly interactive with the situation and condition of its followers, will be stuffed into an ideological box and transformed into a lifeless monument, which is praised without reference to the true and supreme purposes of religion itself. Ultimately, religion will become viewed as *ghâyah*, or the final goal, rather than the path to God (*shari'a*) as originally revealed. God's blessing, which (accompanies a state of self-transcendent awareness and) represents the final goal, will lie increasingly far in the distance.

Efforts to transform Islam into an ideology, and to create an Islamic state, are generally prompted by an excess of religious enthusiasm unsupported by sufficient knowledge of Islam itself. Excessive enthusiasm may lead a person to "absolutize" the knowledge that he or she has attained, despite its being quite limited and partial. As a result, he or she brands other forms of knowledge as erroneous and rejects them. It is interesting to compare this partial understanding of religion with the Sufi parable conveyed by Jalaluddin Rumi, "Touching an Elephant in the Dark."

It concerns five people who argue about the nature of elephants, because they have each rubbed a different part of the giant beast in the dark, thus obtaining partial knowledge in the absence of light (*hidâyah*, or Divine guidance).

Anyone who has a full understanding of elephants' physiognomy may find it hilarious to hear the five men argue violently, as each tries to compel the others to accept his definition of an elephant, which is based on having explored, by touch, just a small fraction of the animal's body. The situation grows more unfortunate when, lacking confidence in the knowledge they have achieved, some of the men try to formalize their concept of the elephant into official schools of law (*madzhab*), while proclaiming that their comrades' divergent perceptions—which represent a threat to the newly "official" view—are subversive and must be silenced.

The mischief doesn't stop there. Swept away by enthusiasm and convinced that they're implementing the Prophet's saying, "Convey my words, even if only a single verse," there are those who—to return once again to the parable of the elephant—perpetrate acts of violence, and coerce others into admitting that an elephant is like a tree, or a pendulum, or a wall, or a whip, or a fan. Which is to say that in the real world of socio-religious interaction, Islam is reduced to an ideology and a mere set of legal conclusions, which represent only a tiny aspect of Islamic teachings as a whole.

Too great an enthusiasm often results in people misunderstanding or twisting the afore-mentioned saying of the Messenger of God, may God bless him and grant him peace, as if it were "Convey *only* a single verse from me." And this situation becomes even more serious when the person in question regards the single verse that he possesses as the One and Only Truth—which must be conveyed anywhere and everywhere—while demonizing all other verses.

Assuming that people constantly learn, and listen to others, their knowledge will of course become more beneficial, accurate and complete. Because in fact, what we regard today as truth may be false; while the manifest "error" of others may indeed be the truth. Whoever has shut the eye of his heart—convinced that he is more intelligent, and correct, than anyone else—will not be able to grasp views that differ from his own. The natural result of such an attitude is arrogance (*takabbur*) and rejection of other people. When arrogance begins; when listening to others and learning ends; then ignorance and stupidity begin—a state that is extremely dangerous not only for the person or people in question, but for humanity at large.

Ignorance is a hidden danger that lurks within every human being; the way to overcome it is to constantly learn and listen to other people. Because of ignorance, many people try to please the Prophet Muhammad by adopting his supposed physical appearance, while neglecting his inner nature. There are also those who wish to please God by erecting a so-called religious state, yet in the process transform religion itself from a path (*shari'a*) into the ultimate goal.

They imagine that the noble Prophet Muhammad, may God bless him and grant him peace, will somehow be delighted if his religious community wears clothes identical to those which he himself wore in the Arab desert fourteen centuries ago. They imagine that God will somehow be delighted if Islam becomes a formal state ideology, and His servants erect a religious state, an Islamic state. In holding these views, they completely forget that the noble Prophet Muhammad, may God bless him and grant him peace, explained that he was sent to perfect noble morals (*innamâ bu'itstu li utammima makârim al-akhlâq*). They also forget that the sole principle and goal of his having been sent as the Messenger of God was to serve as a blessing and a mercy for all sentient beings (*wa mâ arsalnâka illâ rahmatan lil-'âlamîn*). Indeed, under the pretext of "establishing" that blessing, some try to terrorize and compel others to enter into whatever they personally consider to be a blessing; a perverse form of behavior which, from whatever perspective, conflicts with the spirit of blessing and mercy itself.

In the context of education, and of the supreme values of this primary message of Islam (as a blessing for all creation), this book *The Illusion of an Islamic State* conveys an extremely firm and clear educational message. The hidden danger that lies at the heart of extremist attempts to establish an Islamic state consists of the unconscious juxtaposition of profound ignorance regarding Islam's true nature, and a false conviction that they possess perfect knowledge of the same.

If Muslims were all driven by a passion to learn, and to listen to others, their understanding of Islam would become progressively more wise and complete. As a consequence, they would not seek to reduce Islam to a mere ideology or rule of state. They would realize that Islam is too great to be boxed into a narrow ideology, or confined by the limits of state laws. For that reason, the vital insight contained in this book is the struggle (*jihad*) to constantly inspire every person to learn without ceasing; to oppose ignorance; to inspire all people to open their hearts and minds to humanity; and the struggle (*jihad*) to free every man, woman and child on earth from ideological and dogmatic strictures which have long prevented them from understanding the glorious teachings of religion, and instead confined their comprehension to those elements of the message that they can squeeze into a narrow box of their own or others' construction.

To repeat: we may overcome our ignorance by seeing, listening and paying close attention; that is, by constantly learning. What halts this process dead in its tracks, and poses a threat to oneself and others, is when people feel that their knowledge is already perfect, and consider themselves to be in possession of the absolute Truth, and thus no longer in need of learning, or seeking the truth. Perhaps all would agree that ignorance is highly dangerous. Yet not everyone is aware of the hidden dangers of ignorance, which dwell within.

WaLlâhu A'lam. God alone knows the truth of all things.

Rembang, 26 January 2009

Appendix 1

Muhammadiyah Central Board Decree (SKPP)
No. 149/KEP/I.0/B/2006,

to cleanse the Muhammadiyah of Interference by the Muslim Brotherhood-affiliated Justice and Prosperity Party (PKS)

PIMPINAN PUSAT MUHAMMADIYAH

SURAT KEPUTUSAN PIMPINAN PUSAT MUHAMMADIYAH
Nomor: 149/KEP/I.0/B/2006

Tentang:

KEBIJAKAN PIMPINAN PUSAT MUHAMMADIYAH MENGENAI
KONSOLIDASI ORGANISASI DAN AMAL USAHA MUHAMMADIYAH

MENIMBANG
: 1. Bahwa Muhammadiyah sebagai Gerakan Islam sejak kelahirannya hingga saat ini tetap istiqamah dan terus bergerak tidak mengenal lelah dalam melaksanakan dakwah dan tajdid melalui berbagai usaha (amal usaha, program, dan kegiatan) yang dilakukannya dengan maksud dan tujuan menjunjung tinggi Agama Islam sehingga terwujud masyarakat Islam yang sebenar-benarnya;

2. Bahwa Muhammadiyah merupakan organisasi (persyarikatan) Islam yang memiliki prinsip-prinsip, sistem, dan kedaulatan yang mengikat bagi segenap anggotanya dan harus dihormati oleh siapapun sebagaimana hak-hak organisasi yang bersifat independen dan memiliki hak hidup di negeri ini;

3. Bahwa Muhammadiyah sebagai organisasi dalam menjalankan misi dan usahanya harus bergerak dalam satu barisan yang kokoh sebagaimana perintah Allah dalam Al-Quran Surat Ash-Shaf (61) ayat 4, yang artinya "Sesungguhnya Allah menyukai orang yang berperang dijalan-Nya dalam barisan yang teratur seakan-akan mereka seperti suatu bangunan yang tersusun kokoh";

4 Bahwa Muhammadiyah sebagai Gerakan Islam yang cukup tua dan besar sangat menghargai ukhuwah, kerjasama, toleransi, dan sikap saling menghormati dengan seluruh kekuatan/kelompok lain dalam masyarakat, lebih-lebih dengan sesama komponen umat Islam, karena itu Muhammadiyah pun berhak untuk dihormati oleh siapapun serta memiliki hak serta keabsahan untuk bebas dari segala campur-tangan, pengaruh, dan kepentingan pihak manapun yang dapat mengganggu keutuhan serta kelangsungan gerakannya;

MENGINGAT
: 1. Al-Quran dan As-Sunnah sebagai sumber Ajaran Islam;

2. AD/ART Muhammadiyah serta aturan-aturan lainnya yang berlaku dalam Persyarikatan sebagai landasan konstitusional;

3. Keputusan Tarjih, Muqaddimah AD Muhammadiyah, Kepribadian Muhammadiyah, Matan Keyakinan dan Cita-cita Hidup Muhammadiyah, Khittah Muhammadiyah, Pedoman Hidup Islami Warga Muhammadiyah, dan prinsip-prinsip ideal lainnya dalam Muhammadiyah;

4. Keputusan Muktamar Muhammadiyah ke-45 tahun 2005;

MEMPERHATIKAN   : Keputusan Rapat Pleno Pimpinan Pusat Muhammadiyah yang dilaksanakan pada hari Senin tanggal 22 Syawwal 1427 H / 13 November 2006 M

MEMUTUSKAN :

MENETAPKAN   : KEPUTUSAN PIMPINAN PUSAT MUHAMMADIYAH TENTANG KEBIJAKAN PIMPINAN PUSAT MUHAMMADIYAH MENGENAI KONSOLIDASI ORGANISASI DAN AMAL USAHA MUHAMMADIYAH sebagai berikut:

1. Muhammadiyah dengan seluruh anggota, pimpinan, amal usaha, organisasi otonom, majelis dan lembaga, sekretariat/kantor, dan berbagai lini/struktur organisasi serta segala usaha yang berada di dalamnya harus bebas dari berbagai paham, misi, dan kepentingan pihak lain yang secara langsung maupun tidak langsung, terbuka maupun terselubung, dapat merugikan dan merusak Persyarikatan Muhammadiyah.

2. Secara khusus seluruh anggota dan lini organisasi Persyarikatan termasuk di lingkungan amal usaha Muhammadiyah harus bebas dari pengaruh, misi, infiltrasi, dan kepentingan partai politik yang selama ini mengusung misi dakwah atau partai politik bersayap dakwah, di samping bebas dari misi/kepentingan partai politik dan organisasi lainnya sebagaimana kebijakan Khittah Muhammadiyah. Hal tersebut karena seiain telah menjadikan kegiatan dakwah dengan institusi/pranata umat Islam seperti masjid dan lain-lain sebagai alat/sarana politik, juga secara nyata-nyata telah menimbulkan sikap mendua di sebagian kalangan Muhammadiyah, termasuk dalam melaksanakan Hari Raya Idul Fitri/Idul Adha, serta menjadikan Muhammadiyah sebagai sarana politik partai yang bersangkutan dan lebih jauh lagi dapat menimbulkan pengeroposan dan mengganggu keutuhan organisasi.

3. Segenap anggota Muhammadiyah perlu menyadari, memahami, dan bersikap kritis bahwa seluruh partai politik di negeri ini, termasuk partai politik yang mengklaim diri atau mengembangkan sayap/kegiatan dakwah seperti Partai Keadilan Sejahtera (PKS) adalah benar-benar partai politik. Setiap partai politik berorientasi meraih kekuasaan politik. Karena itu, dalam menghadapi partai politik mana pun kita harus tetap berpijak pada Khittah Muhammadiyah dan harus membebaskan diri dari, serta tidak menghimpitkan diri dengan misi, kepentingan, kegiatan, dan tujuan partai politik tersebut.

4. Seluruh anggota Muhammadiyah di seluruh lini Persyarikatan, termasuk yang berada di Amal Usaha, dituntut komitmen, integritas, loyalitas, pengkhidmatan, dan kiprah yang penuh dan optimal dalam menjalankan usaha-usaha, menjaga dan berpedoman pada prinsip-prinsip, membela kepentingan, serta memajukan dan memperjuangkan Muhammadiyah menuju pada pencapaian tujuannya. Jika memiliki kelebihan materi/harta, pikiran, tenaga, relasi/hubungan, jaringan, dan rizki Allah lainnya maka kerahkan/jariyahkan secara maksimal untuk membesarkan, mengembangkan, dan menyempurnakan gerakan Muhammadiyah serta seluruh amal usaha, program, dan kegiatannya sehingga semakin mendekati pencapaian tujuan Muhammadiyah.

5. Seluruh institusi dalam Muhammadiyah termasuk amal usaha, masjid/mushalla, fasilitas milik Persyarikatan, dan kegiatan-kegiatan yang berada di dalamnya tidak boleh digunakan untuk kegiatan-kegiatan partai politik mana pun. Larangan tersebut berlaku untuk kegiatan-kegiatan yang diindikasikan dan memiliki kaitan dengan kegiatan/kepentingan partai politik, termasuk kegiatan-kegiatan yang mengatasnamakan atau mamakai simbol-simbol keagamaan/dakwah seperti pengajian dan pembinaan keumatan, yang terkait dan memiliki hubungan dengan partai politik mana pun. Maksimalkan/optimalkan seluruh institusi milik Muhammadiyah tersebut untuk sebesar-besarnya dan sebenar-benarnya bagi kepentingan Muhammadiyah.

6. Seluruh anggota Muhammadiyah diminta untuk menghormati dan menaati Keputusan Muktamar ke-45 tahun 2005 di Malang, yang menyatakan "Menolak upaya-upaya untuk mendirikan parpol yang memakai atau menggunakan nama atau simbol-simbol Persyarikatan Muhammadiyah." (Lihat Lampiran I *Tanfidz Keputusan Muktamar Muhammadiyah Ke 45 di Malang*: Keputusan Muktamar ke-45 tentang Laporan Pimpinan Pusat Muhammadiyah Periode 2000-2005, VI. Bidang Politik poin 1).

7. Seluruh media massa yang berada di lingkungan Persyarikatan diminta untuk benar-benar menyuarakan paham, misi, dan kepentingan Muhammadiyah serta menjadi wahana untuk sosialisasi paham, pandangan, keputusan, kebijakan, kegiatan, dan syiar Muhammadiyah serta menjauhkan diri dari paham, misi, dan kepentingan organisasi/gerakan lain.

8. Sebagai langkah konsolidasi sekaligus pencegahan dan penguatan gerakan, seluruh jajaran Pimpinan Persyarikatan, Majelis/Lembaga, Organisasi Otonom, dan Amal Usaha diinstruksikan untuk melaksanakan berbagai kegiatan pembinaan keagamaan, kemuhammadiyahan, dan hal-hal yang menyangkut organisasi secara luas. Kegiatan-kegiatan tersebut antara lain sosialisasi dan pengamalan putusan-putusan Tarjih, Darul Arqam, Baitul Arqam, Gerakan Jamaah dan Dakwah Jamaah, Up-Grading, Refreshing, pengajian-pengajian umum dan khusus, pembinaan jamaah, pengelolaan kegiatan-kegiatan masjid dan mushalla, sosialisasi dan pengamalan Pedoman Hidup Islami Warga Muhammadiyah, peningkatan silaturahim, dan kegiatan-kegiatan pembinaan lainnya yang dilakukan secara sistematik, intensif, berkesinambungan, dan terorganisasi dengan sebaik-baiknya. Secara khusus ditugaskan kepada Majelis Tarjih dan Tajdid, Majelis Tabligh dan Dakwah Khusus, dan Majelis Pendidikan Kader dengan melibatkan Majelis/Lembaga, Organisasi Otonom, dan Amal Usaha terkait untuk melaksanakan kegiatan-kegiatan tersebut secara terpadu di bawah koordinasi Pimpinan Persyarikatan di masing-masing tingkatan.

9. Segenap Pimpinan Peryarikatan, Majelis dan Lembaga, Organisasi Otonom, dan Amal Usaha Muhammadiyah diinstruksikan untuk menegakkan disiplin organisasi, merapatkan barisan/langkah, dan mengokohkan ideologi serta misi Muhammadiyah sebagaimana diatur dalam AD/ART dan peraturan-peraturan organisasi serta telah menjadi prinsip-prinsip Muhammadiyah seperti keputusan Tarjih, Muqaddimah Anggaran Dasar, Kepribadian, Matan Keyakinan dan Cita-cita Hidup, Khittah Perjuangan, dan Pedoman Hidup Islami Warga Muhammadiyah serta keputusan-keputusan Muktamar Muhammadiyah.

10. Pimpinan Peryarikatan, Majelis dan Lembaga, Organisasi Otonom, dan Amal Usaha Muhammadiyah diinstruksikan untuk mengambil kebijakan dan tindakan-tindakan yang tegas dalam menegakkan misi, aturan, dan prinsip-prinsip Muhammadadiyah serta dalam mencegah dan menyelamatkan Muhammadiyah dari berbagai tindakan yang merugikan Persyarikatan sebagaimana disebutkan di atas.

Yogyakarta, 10 Zulqa'dah 1427 H
01 Desember 2006 M

Pimpinan Pusat Muhammadiyah

Ketua Umum,   Sekretaris Umum,

Prof. Dr. H. M. Din Syamsuddin, M.A.   Drs. H. A. Rosyad Sholeh

DECREE OF THE MUHAMMADIYAH CENTRAL BOARD
No. : 149/KEP/I.0/B/2006

Regarding:
POLICY OF THE MUHAMMADIYAH CENTRAL BOARD CON-
CERNING CONSOLIDATION OF ORGANIZATIONS AND
CHARITABLE ENTERPRISES WITHIN MUHAMMADIYAH

CONSIDERING:

1. That from its establishment until the present, Muhammadiyah—as an Islamic movement—has remained consistent in performing missionary and community outreach
activities through various efforts (charitable enterprises,
programs and activities) which are aimed at glorifying
the religion of Islam, so as to create a truly Muslim society;

2. That Muhammadiyah is an Islamic organization with
certain definitive principles, systems and organizational
integrity which bind its members, and which should and
must be respected by others, given that Muhammadiyah
is an organization that operates independently and has
a right to exist in this nation [Indonesia];

3. That in working to fulfill its mission, Muhammadiyah
should and must remain united in a single column,
as ordained by God in the fourth verse of the chapter
as-Saff ("The Ranks") in the Qur'an (61:4), which proclaims: "God loves those who fight in His cause united
in a single column, like the bricks in a wall";

4. That Muhammadiyah, as one of the oldest and largest
Islamic movements, reveres brotherhood, collaboration,
tolerance and mutual respect towards other elements in
society, especially other Muslim groups, and therefore
deserves the same respect from others, and has the right
to be free from intervention and/or self-interested actions by other parties that might interfere with Muhammadiyah's integrity and the performance of its responsibilities;

REFERING TO:

1. The Qur'an and Sunnah as the sources of Islamic teaching;
2. Muhammadiyah's statutes/by-laws and other related policies, which form the organization's constitutional platform;
3. The Tarjih (Legal Affairs Committee) Decree, Muhammadiyah's code of ethics, Muhammadiyah's principles and goals, Khittah, Islamic codes of ethics for Muhammadiyah followers, and other normative Muhammadiyah principles;
4. The decree of the 45th Muhammadiyah Congress held in 2005.

The decree of the Plenary Congress of the Central Board of Muhammadiyah held on Monday 22 Syawwal 1427 H / 13 November 2006

RESOLVES:

DECREE OF THE MUHAMMADIYAH CENTRAL BOARD REGARDING CONSOLIDATION OF ORGANIZATIONS AND CHARITY-BASED ENTERPRISES WITHIN MUHAMMADIYAH as follows:

1. The Muhammadiyah and all its members, leaders, charity-based enterprises, autonomous organizations, divisions, foundations, branches, offices, organizational structures and all its organizational elements must be free from sharing the beliefs, mission, and/or agenda of other parties that either directly or indirectly, in an open or veiled manner, might harm or ruin the Muhammadiyah organization.
2. In particular, all Muhammadiyah members and those who are involved in the organization's management, must be free from the influence, mission, infiltration and interests of a political party which is engaged in religious proselytizing, and (thus flies on) the wings of da'wa (proselytism), and also from the mission and

agenda of any other political organization(s), as stipulated by the 'Khittah Muhammadiyah' [a declaration of "Muhammadiyah Duty" to refrain from involving the Organization in politics, first adopted in Makassar in 1971 and renewed in 2002 in Denpassar]. This (decree) is necessitated by the fact that the afore-mentioned political party [PKS] has been conducting proselytism activities within institutions that belong to the Muhammadiyah community, such as mosques, etc., etc., as a means to accomplish its political objectives, and because these activities have caused genuine and serious divisions within the Muhammadiyah, including the ways in which Muhammadiyah members celebrate the festivals of Eid al-Fitr and Eid al-Adha. These actions have served to transform the Muhammadiyah into a mere tool of the political party in question [PKS], and furthermore, may diminish the strength, membership and unity of the Muhammadiyah Organization.

3. All Muhammadiyah members need to be aware, understand and adopt a critical attitude which recognizes that every political party in this nation—including those that claim to represent 'da'wa' or Islamic proselytism activities, such as Partai Keadilan Sejahtera (PKS)—are in fact mere political parties. Every political party is focused on the acquisition of political power. For that reason, in dealing with any political party, we must always remain committed to the true Path of the Muhammadiyah and must free ourselves from, and never engage ourselves with, the mission, interests, activities or goals of the above-mentioned political parties.

4. Every Muhammadiyah member in every division and component of the Organization, including those who are involved in charitable enterprises, are commanded to demonstrate their commitment, integrity and loyalty, and to devote their full and optimal efforts in the course of running these enterprises, to guarding and guiding the development of these institutions/enterprises in

line with the principles and interests of Muhammadiyah, and to focus their efforts on achieving the goals of the Organization. Those who have greater wealth or income, ideas, energy, relationships, networking opportunities or other good fortune derived from the grace of God should use these to increase, develop and perfect the Muhammadiyah movement, including all its charities, programs and activities, so as to help achieve Muhammadiyah's goals.

5. All institutions and divisions within Muhammadiyah, including charitable enterprises, mosques, facilities owned by the Organization, and all activities conducted within and by Muhammadiyah, are forbidden to be used for programs or activities related to any political party. This prohibition applies to programs and activities that are in any way related to the activities or agenda of, and/or which are sponsored or supported by political parties, including programs or activities that are conducted in the name of proselytism or use religious symbols, such as religious teaching or educational events that are related to political parties of any kind. Every Muhammadiyah-owned or affiliated institution, program, public service and facility must truly and completely be utilized to the maximum and optimal extent possible to advance only the goals and interests of the Muhammadiyah.

6. All Muhammadiyah members are requested to respect and obey the Decree of the 45th Congress 2005 in Malang, which stated, "Reject any efforts to establish political parties which use the name or symbols of the Muhammadiyah Organization" (See attachment).

7. All mass media associated with the Muhammadiyah Organization are requested to truly promote the views, mission and interests of the Muhammadiyah, and serve as tools to socialize its views, policies, decrees, activities and virtues, so as to help the Organization's members distance themselves and become free from the views, mission and agenda of other organizations and movements.

8. As part of this effort to consolidate and strengthen the Organization, all elements of Muhammadiyah's management, including its leaders, councils, foundations, autonomous organizations and charitable enterprises are hereby instructed to conduct various religious and other Muhammadiyah activities that involve a wide spectrum of the Organization's members. These programs and activities will socialize Muhammadiyah's decrees and policies through various means of dissemination, including Darul Arqam, the Muhammadiyah Community Movement and the Muhammadiyah Community Proselytism Program, upgrading efforts, refreshment courses, general and specific religious gatherings, the management of mosques and all activities conducted therein, and various other activities. These programs and activities [to socialize Muhammadiyah decrees and policies] shall be well-organized, held in a systemic and intensive manner, and developed to become routine and sustainable programs within society. Muhammadiyah has specially appointed several divisions within the Organization—including Tarjih (the Legal Affairs Committee) & Tajdid [the Modernization & Renewal Committee], Tabligh & Dakwah [the Proselytism Committee], Training, other autonomous organizations, and charitable enterprises— to implement these efforts and activities, under the coordination of the Organization's Central Board.

9. All leaders of the Organization, and of all Muhammadiyah councils, foundations, autonomous organizations and charitable enterprises, are hereby instructed to maintain organizational discipline, "clean up" their ranks, and strengthen the Muhammadiyah's ideology and mission, as outlined in the Organization's by-laws and various policies that have become the main principles of Muhammadiyah, such as the Tarjih Decree, the introduction of Muhammadiyah's statute, Muhammadiyah's code of ethics, Muhammadiyah's principles and goals, the Khittah Declaration, Islamic codes of ethics for Muhammadiyah followers, and the decrees

issued by periodic Muhammadiyah's Congresses.

10. All leaders of the Organization, and of all Muhammadiyah councils, foundations, autonomous organizations and charitable enterprises, are instructed to adopt policies and undertake concrete actions to promote and strengthen the Muhammadiyah's mission, rules and principles, as part of the general effort to rescue the Muhammadiyah from various actions that are damaging the Organization, as described above.

Yogyakarta, 10 Zulqa'dah 1427 H
1 December 2006 M

The Central Board of Muhammadiyah

Chairman   Secretary

Prof. Dr. H.M. Din Syamsuddin, MA.   Drs. H.A. Rosyad Sholeh

Appendix 2

Documents from the Nahdlatul Ulama Central Board Rejecting Transnational Extremist Movements and Their Ideology

Keputusan Majelis Bahtsul Masa'il Nahdlatul Ulama
Tentang Khilafah dan Formalisasi Syari'ah

3. KHILAFAH DAN FORMALISASI SYARI'AH

Deskripsi Masalah :
Wacana Islam sebagai solusi dan ideologi alternatif mengusahakan bentuk pemerintahan negara Indonesia dari negara kesatuan berformat Republik menjadi khilafah, berikut konstitusi negara sejak dari undang-undang dasar dan hukum positif diangkat dari Syari'ah Islamiyah seutuhnya. Bila mencermati fakta sejarah masa awal islam dibentuk khilafah hanya bertahan semasa Khulafa al Rasyidin dengan diwarnai tragedy pembunuhan terhadap pejabat khilafah ke 2, 3 dan 4. Hukum positif negara-negara islam masa sekarang masih mengadopsi hukum sekuler (konun maudlu'i) tatanan hukum positif di Indonesia sangat berorientasi pada keragaman agama dan budaya local serta fakta kesulitan mengganti kitab undang-undang Hukum Warisan Kolonial.

Pertanyaan :
a. Adakah tuntutan Syari'ah berbentuk dalil nash yang mengharuskan pembakuan bentuk khilafah dalam sistem ketatanegaraan islam ?

Jawaban 3 a :
Tidak ada dalil nash, karena keberadaan sistem khilafah adalah bentuk ijtihadiyyah.

Pengambilan :

١. الغيث الهامع على شرح جمع الجوامع ص : 790
قلت : مراده أنه عليه الصلاة والسلام لم يستخلف نصا أو تصريحا كما قدمته وقد قال النووى فى شرح مسلم : فيه دليل على أن النبى صلى الله عليه وسلم لم ينص على خليفة وهو إجماع أهل السنة وغيرهم.

٢. المصدر السابق. ص : 17
لقد قرر القرآن تشريعا وحدودا واحل وحرم وفرض فرائض منها ما يقوم به المرء بنفسه ومنها ما هو عمل جماعى ومنها ما يحتاج فى تنفيذه إلى من يتولى الأمر فيه وقد نص القرآن بصريح العبادة المسلمين إلى طاعة هؤلاء (يا أيها الذين آمنوا أطيعوا الله وأطيع الرسول وأولى الأمر منكم) ... كما نجد القرآن بالاستبداد والاستكبار وأثنى على الشورى والإحسان والعدل ..... ولكنه لم ينص لا على أمة الإسلام يجب أن يتطابق معها ملك الإسلام أو دولة الإسلام ولا على من يخلف الرسول فى تدبير شؤون هذه الأمة ولا حتى على ضرورة أن يكون هناك من يخلفه فى ذلك بل ترك المسئلة للمسلمين وكأنها داخلة فى قوله عليه السلام أنتم أدرى بشؤون دنياكم. إه

٣. الدين والدولة وتطبيق الشريعة لمحمد عابد الجابرى. ص : 69
ولما العنصر الثالث فهو أن الخلافة بحسب رأي أهل السنة والجماعة إنما تكون بالاختيار وليس بالنص، ذلك لأنه ما دام الصحابة قد تداولوا بعد وفاة رسول الله، لختلفوا ثم تفقوا وبايعوا أبا بكر فإن ذلك يعنى أن رسول الله لم يعهد إلى أحد بالخلافة من بعده غير أن الاختيار فى نظرية الخلافة عند أهل السنة والجماعة لا يتجاوز تقرير أن النبى لم يعهد لأى أحد من بعده. أما كيفية اختيار الخليفة فهذا موضوع تقرر فيه موازين القوى. فمن قام يطلب الخلافة لنفسه وغلب بشوكته واستطاع أن يجمع الناس حوله راضين أو مكرهين فهو الخليفة. اه.

٤. الفقه الإسلامى ج : 6 ص : 661-662
الإمامة العظمى أو الخلافة أو إمارة المؤمنين كلها تؤدى معنى واحدا وتدل على وظيفة واحدة هى السلطة الحكومية العليا وقد عرفها علماء الإسلام بتعاريف متقاربة فى ألفاظها متحدة فى معانيها تقريبا علما بأنه لا تشترط صفة الخلافة وإنما المهم وجود الدولة ممثلة بمن يتولى أمورها ويدير شؤونها ويدفع غائلة الأعداء عنها. اه.

٥. الجهاد فى الإسلام ص : 81
يلاحظ من معرفة هذه الأحكام أن تطبيق أحكام الشريعة الإسلامية ليس شرطا لاعتبار الدار دار الإسلام ولكنه حق من حقوق دار الإسلام على أعناق المسلمين، فإذا قصر المسلمون فى إجراء الأحكام الإسلامية على اختلافها فى دار هم التى أورثهم الله إياها فإن هذا التقصير لا يخرجها عن كونها دار الإسلام ولكنه يحمل المقصرين ذنوبا وأوزارا. اه.

b. Bagaimana hukum kelompok warga negara Indonesia yang berusaha mengubah bentuk dan dasar hukum negara ?

6

Jawaban 3 b :
Hukum merubah bentuk Negara Indonesia dengan bentuk yang lain maka hukumnya tidak boleh selama menimbulkan mafsadah yang lebih besar. Sedangkan merubah dasar hukum negara juga tidak diperbolehkan jika menggunakan cara yang inkonstitusional dan diperbolehkan jika menggunakan cara yang konstitusional.

Pengambilan :

1. التشريع الجنائي الاسلامي / عبد القادر عودة. ج : 2 ص : 675
... بعد ذكر تعريف الإمام وما يتعلق به .... ومع أن العدالة شرط من شروط الإمامة الا ان الرأى الراجح فى المذاهب الأربعة ومذهب الشيعة الزيدية هو تحريم الخروج على الإمام الفاسق الفاجر ولو كان الخروج للأمر بالمعروف والنهى عن المنكر لأن الخروج على الإمام يؤدى عادة إلى ما هو أنكر مما فيه وبهذا يمتنع النهى عن المنكر لأن من شروطه أن لا يؤدى الإنكار إلى ما هو أنكر من ذلك إلى الفتن وسفك الدماء وبث الفساد واضطراب البلاد وإضلال العباد وتوهين الأمن وهدم النظام. اهـ

2. التشريع الجنائي الجزء الأول ص : 237 مؤسسة الرسالة
(مدى بطلان ما يخالف الشريعة) قلنا إن ما يخالف الشريعة من قانون أو لائحة أو قرار بطلانا مطلقا لكن هذا البطلان لا ينصب على كل نصوص القانون أو اللائحة أو القرار وإنما ينصب فقط على النصوص المخالفة للشريعة دون غيرها لأن أساس البطلان هو مخالفة الشريعة فلا يمتد البطلان منطقيا لما يوافق الشريعة من النصوص ولو أنها أدمجت في قانون واحد أو لائحة واحدة أو قرار واحد مع غيرها من النصوص المخالفة للشريعة وتعتبر النصوص الموافقة للشريعة صحيحة ما دامت قد صدرت من هيئة تشريعية مختصة واستوفت الإجراءات الشكلية المقررة وإذا كان البطلان قاصرا على النصوص المخالفة للشريعة فإن هذه النصوص لا تعتبر باطلة في كل حالة وإنما هى باطلة فقط فى الحالات التى تخالف فيها الشريعة صحيحة فى الحالات التى تتفق فيها مع الشريعة وليس هذا بمستغرب ما دام أساس الصحة والبطلان راجع إلى موافقة الشريعة أو مخالفتها إذ العلة تدور مع المعلول وجودا وعدما

3. التشريع الجنائي الإسلامى الجزء الأول ص : 101
(3) الرأى الغالب فى المذاهب الأربعة أن الإمام ينعزل بالظلم والفسق وتعطيل الحقوق ومن ثم فلا يجب الخروج عليه بقصد عزله وتولية غيره لأن إباحة الخروج عليه تدعو إلى عدم الاستقرار وكثرة الفتن والثورات واضطراب أمور الناس

c. Apakah setrategi mengintegrasikan (Syari'ah) Islam secara substantif menyalahi prinsip tathbiq (penerapan) syari'ah menempuh pola tadrij (gradual) ?

Jawaban 3 c :
Tidak menyalahi prinsip tathbiq. Bahkan strategi secara tadrij sangat tepat bila diterapkan di Negara Indonesia.

Pengambilan :

1. صحيح البخارى ج : 5 ص : 201
حدثنا أبو عاصم الضحاك بن مخلد عن زكرياء بن إسحاق عن يحيى بن عبد الله بن صيفي عن أبي معبد عن ابن عباس رضي الله عنهما أن النبي صلى الله عليه وسلم بعث معاذا رضي الله عنه إلى اليمن فقال ادعهم إلى شهادة أن لا إله إلا الله وأني رسول الله فإن هم أطاعوا لذلك فأعلمهم أن الله قد افترض عليهم خمس صلوات في كل يوم وليلة فإن هم أطاعوا لذلك فأعلمهم أن الله قد افترض عليهم صدقة في أموالهم تؤخذ من أغنيائهم وترد على فقرائهم

2. مفاهيم إسلامية ج : 1 ص : 30
الإصلاح لغة : ضد الإفساد وهو من الصلاح المقابل للفساد والسيئة .... وفى القرآن الكريم (خلطوا عملا صالحا وآخر سيئا) التربة 102. (ولا تفسدوا فى الأرض بعد إصلاحها) الأعراف 56. فالإصلاح هو التغيير إلى الأفضل فالحركات الإصلاحية هى الدعوات التى تحرك قطاعات من البشر لإصلاح ما فسد فى الميادين الاجتماعية المختلفة انتقالا بالحياة إلى درجة أرقى فى سلم التطور الإنسانى.
واصطلاحا : لا يفرق بينه وبين مصطلح الثورة فى مستوى التغيير وشموله وإنما من حيث الأسلوب فى التغيير وزمن التغيير فكلاهما - إسلاميا - يعنى التغيير الشامل والعميق لكن الثورة تسلك سبل العنف غالبا والسرعة فى التغيير بينما تتم التغييرات الإصلاحية بالتدريج وكثيرا ما تعطى الثورة الأولية لتغيير الواقع بينما تبدأ مناهج الإصلاح عادة بتغيير الإنسان : وإعادة صيانة الإنسان وفق الدعوة الإصلاحية وبعد ذلك يهيئ هذا الإنسان بتغيير الواقع وإقامة النموذج الإصلاحى الجديد. ولذلك وصفت رسالات الرسل عليهم الصلاة والسلام بأنها دعوات إصلاح فيقول رسول الله شعيب عليه السلام (إن أريد إلا الإصلاح ما استطعت) هود 88.

3. قواعد الأحكام الجزء الأول ص : 77 دار الكتب العلمية
المثال السادس والثلاثون التقرير على المعاصى كلها مفسدة لكن يجوز التقرير عليها عند العجز عن إنكارها باليد واللسان ومن قدر على إنكارها مع الخوف على نفسه كان إنكاره مندوبا إليه ومشوبا عليه لأن المخاطرة بالنفوس فى إعزاز الدين مأمور بها كما يعذر بها فى قتال المشركين وقتال البغاة المتأولين وقتال ماغى يمكن تخليصهم منهم إلا بالقتال وقد قال (أفضل الجهاد كلمة حق عند سلطان جائر) جعلها أفضل الجهاد لأن قائلها قد جاد بنفسه كل الجود بخلاف من يلاقى قرنه من القتال فإنه يجوز أن يقهر ويقتله فلا يكون بذله نفسه مع تجويز سلامتها كبذل المنكر نفسه مع يأسه من السلامة

7

Ruling of the Nahdlatul Ulama's Bahtsul Masa'il
Regarding the Establishment of a Caliphate
and the Formalization of Shari'a

3. THE CALIPHATE AND FORMALIZATION OF *Shari'a*
Description of the Problem:
Public discussions that portray Islam as "the solution," and as an alternative ideology, seek to transform Indonesia's system of government from a unitary state in the form of a republic, into a caliphate, and to require that the nation's laws and constitution be based entirely upon Islamic *shari'a*. If one closely examines the facts surrounding the early history of Islam, it is evident that the caliphate lasted only a few decades, during the era of *al-Khulafâ'u al-Rashidun* [the first four "rightly-guided caliphs," who succeeded the Prophet Muhammad], whose reign was marked by tragedy and the murder of the second, third and fourth caliphs. Contemporary Muslim states have widely adopted secular laws (*konun maudlu'i*) and incorporated these in their systems of positive law. Indonesia's legal system is highly oriented towards, and colored by, local religious and cultural diversity, and by the fact that it is difficult to replace various statutes that are part of our colonial heritage.

Question:
a. Do demands for the implementation of *shari'a* constitute a "*nash*" argument [based on text in the Qur'an], requiring the establishment of a caliphate in the context of a system of government built on Islam?

Answer 3a:
There is no *nash* argument, because the caliphal system is derived from human interpretation (*ijtihad*) and is not found in the Qur'an.

Reference:

١. الغيث الجامع على شرح جمع الجوامع، ص: ٧٩٠

قلت: مراده انه عليه الصلاة والسلام لم يستخلف نصا او تصريحا كما قدمته وقد قال النواوى فى

شرح مسلم: فيه دليل على ان النبى صلى الله عليه وسلم لم ينص على خليفة وهو اجماع اهل السنة

وغيرهم

1. Al-Ghaith al-Jâmi' 'alâ Sharh Jam' al-Jawâmi, p. 790 (A Complete Analysis and Commentary upon the Compilation of Compilations), by 'Abdurrahman ibn Jadullah al-Banani (died in 1784 C.E.; Moroccan-born scholar and expert on Islamic jurisprudence).

I say: This means that I have never discovered a shred of evidence indicating that the Prophet, may God bless him and grant him peace, ever established or ordained, or provided any explanation [regarding the proper form of government]. And al-Nawawi said in his comments on the collection of hadith assembled by Imam Muslim, "Here we encounter the proposition that the Prophet, may God bless him and grant him peace, absolutely did NOT establish a caliphate. Ahlussunnah wal-jamâ'ah (Sunni Muslims) and other sects all agree upon this fact."

٢. المصدر السابق، ص: ١٧

لقد قرر القرآن تشريعا وحدودا وحلل وحرم وفرض فرائض منها ما يقوم به المرء بنفسه ومنها ما

هو عمل جماعي ومنها ما يحتاج في تنفيذه الى من يتولى الأمر فيه وقد نص القرآن بصريح العبادة

المسلمين الى طاعة هؤلاء (ياأيها الذين آمنوا أطيعوا الله وأطيعوا الرسول وأولى الأمر منكم) . . . كما

بدد القرآن بالإستبداد والإستكبار وأثنى على الشورى والإحسان والعدل . . . ولكنه لم ينص

لا على أمة الإسلام يجب ان يطابق معها ملك الإسلام او دولة الإسلام ولا على من يخلف الرسول

فى تدبير شؤون هذه الأمة ولا حتى على ضرورة ان يكون هناك من يخلفه فى ذلك بل ترك المسئلة

للمسلمين وكأنها داخلة فى قوله عليه السلام انتم ادرى بشؤون دنياكم اه .

2. Ibid, p. 17
Allah—Pure and Exalted is He!—has established *shari'a*, *hadd* (the proper limits of behavior), that which is permissible and that which is forbidden, as well as ordaining various obligations within the Qur'an, including those related to individual and social concerns, and these include obligations which require a leader; the Qur'an clearly established Muslims' religious obligations in connection with obedience to a leader: "Oh ye faithful, be obedient to God, to the Messenger (of God), and to those who are in authority over you." Thus the Qur'an has ordained and established, and praised mutual consultation, good deeds arising from a state of pure devotion (*ihsan*), and just behavior.... But the Qur'an has not ordained a duty for Muslims to establish an Islamic kingdom or other form of government. With regards to replacing one who leads a community, the Messenger of God did not ordain or establish a procedure for selecting those who manage the community's vital affairs, but rather, entrusted this to Muslims themselves, as indicated by the saying of the Prophet, may God bless him and grant him peace: "You know best about your own worldly affairs."

٣ . الدين والدولة وتطبيق الشريعة لمحمد عابد الجابرى، ص: ٦٩

واما العنصر الثالث فهو ان الخلافة بحسب رأي اهل السنة والجماعة إنما تكون بالإختيار وليس

بالنص، ذلك لأنه ما دام الصحابة قد تداولوا بعد وفاة رسول الله واختلفوا ثم اتفقوا وبايعوا أبابكر

فإن ذلك يعنى أن رسول الله لم يعهد الى احد بالخلافة من بعده غير ان الإختيار فى نظرية الخلافة

عند اهل السنة والجماعة لا يتجاوز تقرير ان النبي لم يختر لاى احد من بعده . اما كيفية اختيار

الخليفة فهذا موضوع تقرر فيه موازين القوي . فمن قام يطلب الخلافة لنفسه وغلب بشوكه

واستطاع ان يجمع الناس حوله راضين او مكروهين فهو الخليفة، اه .

3. *Al-Dîn wa al-Daulah wa Tathbîq al-Sharî'ah*, p. 69 (*Religion, Political Power and the Implementation of Sharî'a*), by Muhammad 'Abid al-Jabiri (1936 – 2010; contemporary Muslim scholar from Morocco).

There is a third element, that—in the opinion of *ahlussunnah wal-jamâ'ah* (Sunni Muslims)—the caliphate is based upon *ikhtiyar* (free choice), not *nash* (textual references from the Qur'an). Because the companions of the Prophet were scattered in different corners after his death, holding widely varied opinions, but eventually agreed to swear allegiance to Abu Bakr. In reality, the Messenger of God never promised the caliphate to anyone following his death. Thus, according to Sunni Muslims, [the companions'] exercise of free choice in establishing the caliphate does not conflict with the reality that the Prophet did not appoint anyone to follow him. Meanwhile, the actual method used to select a caliph is related to the exercise of power. Whoever feels his power in the ascendant, demands that he himself be acknowledged as caliph; if he triumphs through the exercise of strength, and is able to unite the community beneath his power—either through the people's exercise of free will, or by force—then he becomes the new caliph.

٤ . ألفقه الإسلامي، ج: ٦،ص: ٦٦١–٦٦٢

الإمامة العظمى او الخلافة او إمارة المؤمنين كلها تؤدى معنى واحد وتدل على وظيفة واحدة هي

السلطة الحكومية العليا وقد عرفها علماء الإسلام بتعاريف متقاربة فى ألفاظها متحدة فى

معانيها تقريبا علما بأنه لا تشترط صفة الخلافة وإنما المهم وجود الدولة ممثلة بمن يتولى أمورها ويدير

شؤونها ويدفع غائلة الأعداد عنها . اه .

4. *Al-Fiqh al-Islâmî wa Adillâtuh*, vol. 6, pp. 661-662 (*Islamic Juris-prudence and its Postulates*), by Wahbah Mushthafa al-Zuhayli (1932 – ; contemporary Muslim scholar from Syria).

The terms "*al-Imamah al- 'Uzhma*" ("the Supreme Leader"), "Ca-liph" or "government of the Believers" all have a single mean-ing and refer to a single arrangement, viz., the highest govern-ment power. The *ulama* have given various definitions, whose terminology and meanings are closely related, and agree that there is no need to use the term "caliphate." Rather, what is important is that there exist a [governmental] power that repre-sents those who surrender their affairs to it, which [power] will arrange their [public] affairs, and protect them from threats and dangers.

٥ . الجهاد فى الإسلام، ص: ٨١

يلاحظ من معرفة هذه الأحكام أن تطبيق أحكام الشريعة ليس شرطا لاعتبار الدار دار

الإسلام ولكنه حق من حقوق دار الإسلام فى أعناق المسلمين . فإذا قصر المسلمون فى إجراء

الأحكام الإسلامية على اختلافها فى دار هم التى أورثهم الله إياها فإن هذ التقصير لا يخرجها

عن كونها دار الإسلام ولكنه يحمل المقصرين ذنوبا وأوزارا . اه .

5. *Al-Jihâd fi al-Islâm*, p. 81 (*Jihad in Islam*), by Muhammad Sa'id Ramadhan al-Bouthi (1929 – ; contemporary Muslim scholar from Syria).

Based upon this definition of the law, the establishment of Is-lamic jurisprudence is not a requirement, in order to evaluate whether or not a state is an Islamic state. Rather, [the establish-ment of *shari'a*] delineates [and thus limits] the rights of an Islamic state vis-à-vis the Muslim community. If the Muslim community within a particular state is negligent in observing Islamic law, with all its variations, such neglect does not result in the afore-mentioned nation being excluded from the definition of an Islamic state, but rather, results in their (i.e., those who are careless or neglectful of *shari'a*) committing a sin.[1]

b. What principles of Islamic law apply to groups of Indonesian citizens who seek to alter the structure, and foundation, of this nation's legal system?

Answer 3b:
Islamic law forbids one to alter the structure of the Indonesian state and replace it with a different structure, if doing so will create a larger problem than that which it seeks to resolve. It is also forbidden to alter the foundation of national law through unconstitutional means, but permitted if constitutional methods are employed.

Reference:

١. أَلتشريع الجنائى الإسلامى، عبد القادر عودة، ج: ٢،ص: ٦٧٥

. . .بعد ذكر تعريف الإمام وما يتعلق به . . . ومع ان العدالة شرط من شروط الإمامة الا ان الرأي الراجح فى المذاهب الأربعة ومذهب الشيعة الزيدية هو تحريم الخروج على الإمام الفاسق الفاجر ولو كان الخروج للأمر بالمعروف والنهي عن المنكر لأن من شروطه ان لا يؤدى الإنكار إلى ما هو أنكر من ذلك إلى الفتن وسفك الدماء وبث الفساد واضطراب البلاد وإضلال العباد وتوهين الأمن وهدم النظام. اه.

1. *Al-Tasyrî' al-Jinâ'î al-Islâmî*, vol. 2, p. 675 (*Islamic Criminal Law*), by 'Abdul Qadir 'Audah (1921 – ; contemporary Muslim scholar from Egypt).

...After clarifying the definition of *Imam* (leader) and those things associated with it... and that justice is one of the requirements of the imamate (leadership), the firm opinion of the four

---

1. [Translator's note: According to the Nahdlatul Ulama, it is the responsibility of Muslims to follow *shari'a* (the path to God) in their personal lives, rather than formalize or embed one particular interpretation of *shari'a* (Islamic jurisprudence) in the nation's government.]

Sunni schools of Islamic jurisprudence, and of the Zaidiyah
school of Shi'ite jurisprudence, is to forbid rebellion (khurûj)
against a leader who is cruel and atheistic, even if said rebellion
is meant to enjoin the good and forbid evil (amr ma'ruf nahy
munkar), because among the rules (governing amr ma'ruf nahy
munkar) is that the rejection of evil may not be conducted in a
manner that is itself evil, and may cause civil disturbance and
bloodshed, giving rise to destruction, political chaos and leading people astray, by weakening security and social order.

٢ . ألتشريع الجنائى ،ج: ١،ص: ٢٣٧، مؤسسة الرسالة

(مدى بطلان ما يخالف الشريعة) قلنا ان ما يخالف الشريعة من قانون او لائحة او قرار بطلان

مطلقا لكن هذا البطلان لا ينصب على كل نصوص القانون او اللائحة او القرار وإنما ينصب فقط

على النصوص المخالفة للشريعة دون غيرها لأن أساس البطلان هو مخالفة الشريعة فلا يمتد

البطلان منطبقا لما يوافق الشريعة من النصوص ولو أنها أدبحت فى قانون واحد او لائحة واحدة او

قرار واحد مع غيرها من النصوص المخالفة للشريعة وتعتبر النصوص الموافقة للشريعة صحيحة

ما دامت قد صدرت من هيئة تشريعية مختصة واستوفت الإجراءات الشكلية المقررة وإذا كان

البطلان قاصرا على النصوص المخالفة للشريعة فإن هذه النصوص لا تعتبر باطلة في كل حالة وإنما

هى باطلة فقط فى الحالات التى تخالف فيها الشريعة صحيحة فى الحالات التى تتفق فيها مع

الشريعة وليس هذا بمستغرب ما دام أساس الصحة والبطلان راجع الى موافقة الشريعة او مخالفتها

إذ العلة تدور مع المعلول وجودا وعدما

2. Al-Tasyrî' al-Jinâ'î, vol. 1, p. 237 (Islamic Criminal Law), by 'Abdul
   Qadir 'Audah.

(Concerning the abrogation of anything that conflicts with
shari'a), we say that anything that conflicts with shari'a, whether
in the form of laws, regulations or [government] decisions, are
completely nullified. However, this nullification is not based
upon every decree contained within the laws, regulations or

[government] decisions, but rather, only that specific decree which conflicts with shari'a, and not others. Because the basis for nullification is the conflict [of a decree] with shari'a, the abrogation does not extend to encompass elements of the [legal] text in question that conform to shari'a, even though they may appear within the same law, regulation or [government] decision alongside the text(s) that conflict with shari'a. Any text that is in accord with shari'a is regarded as valid and legal, so long as it is derived from the spirit of shari'a, and related to the problem addressed [by the law or ruling in question]. Thus, if the nullification is limited to textual elements that conflict with shari'a, then these legal texts as a whole are not considered to be nullified, except in regard to those elements which conflict with shari'a, while the remainder of said texts are valid and legal in every respect which conforms to shari'a. There is no complete "elimination" of a law or ruling, so long as the principle of "valid" or "nullified" is based on conformity or conflict with shari'a. Thus, the law develops in accordance with these principles.

٣ . التشريع الجنائي الإسلامي، ج: ١، ص: ١٠١

(٣) الرأي الغالب في المذاهب الأربعة ان الإمام ينعزل بالظلم والفسق وتعطيل الحقوق ومن ثم فلا

يجب الخروج عليه بقصد عزله وتولية غيره لأن إباحة الخروج عليه تدعو إلى عدم الإستقرار وكثرة

الفتن والثورات والاضطراب أمور الناس .

3. Al-Tasyrî' al-Jinâ'î al-Islâmî, vol. 1, p. 101 (Islamic Criminal Law), by 'Abdul Qadir 'Audah.

(3) The general view expressed by the four schools of (Sunni) jurisprudence is that an imam (leader) will fall from power if he engages in wicked and tyrannical behavior that violates the rights of others. For this reason, it is not a religious duty to rebel (khurûj) against a ruler, with the goal of overthrowing him and replacing him with another, because such rebellion may cause civil disorder, and the emergence of unbridled conflict, violence and social chaos.

c. Does a strategy of integrating Islam (*shari'a*) in a substantive manner violate the principle of *tathbiq*, which is to accomplish tasks gradually?[2]

Answer 3c:
No, it does not violate the principal of *tathbiq*. On the contrary, it is highly appropriate to use a gradual approach in establishing the substance of Islam in the nation of Indonesia.

Reference:

۱. صحيح البخاري،ج: ٥،ص: ٢٠١

حدثنا ابو عاصم الضحاك بن مخلد عن زكرياء بن اسحاق عن يحي بن عبد الله بن صيفى عن ابى

معبد عن ابن عباس رضي الله عنهما ان النبي صلى الله عليه وسلم بعث معاذا رضي الله عنه

الى اليمن فقال ادعهم الى شهادة ان لا إله إلا الله وانى رسول الله فإن هم اطاعوا لذالك فأعلمهم ان

الله قد افترض عليهم خمس صلوات فى كل يوم وليلة فإن هم اطاعوا لذالك فأعلمهم ان الله افترض

عليهم صدقة فى أموالهم تؤخذ من أغنيائهم وترد على فقرائهم.

1. *Sahih al-Bukhari*, vol. 5, p. 201 (*The Abridged Collection of Authentic Hadith with Connected Chains Regarding Matters Pertaining to the Prophet*), by Muhammad ibn Isma'il ibn Ibrahim ibn Mughirah ibn Bardizbah al-Bukhari (9th century Persian scholar born in Bukhara, Central Asia, whose work is generally considered, by Sunni Muslims, to be the most authoritative and reliable collection of hadith, or traditions related to the Prophet Muhammad. Compiled over a period of 16 years, the work was completed around 846 C.E.)

We have been told by Abu 'Ashim al-Dlahak ibn Makhlad,

---

2. [Translator's note: "integrating Islam (*shari'a*) in a substantive manner" refers to "leavening" society with the spiritual essence of Islam, without forcing others to observe its exoteric practices, such as prayer, fasting, pilgrimage, charitable giving, abstention from pork and alcohol, etc.]

who heard from Zakariya ibn Ishaq, who heard from Yahya ibn 'Abdillah ibn Shifa, who heard from Abi Ma'bad, who heard from Ibn 'Abbas, that the Prophet, may God bless him and grant him peace, sent Mu'adz to Yemen. He said, "Invite them to bear witness that there is no god but God, and that I am His Messenger. If they follow you, tell them that God has commanded them to pray five times a day; and if they [still] follow you, let them know that God has commanded those among them who are wealthy to set aside a portion of their wealth and give it to those who are impoverished."

٢ . مفاهيم إسلامية، ج: ١، ص: ٣٠

الإصلاح لغة: ضد الإفساد وهو من الصلاح المقابل للفساد وللسيّئة . . . وفى القرآن الكريم (خلطوا عملا صالحا وآخر سيّأ) التوبة: ١٠٢. (ولا تفسدوا فى الارض بعد إصلاحها) الاعراف: ٥٦. فالإصلاح هو التغيير إلى الافضل . فالحركات الإصلاحية فى الدعوات التى تحرك قطعات من البشر لإصلاح ما فسد فى الميادين الإجتماعية المختلفة انتقالا بالحياة إلى درجة ارقى فى سلم التطور الإنسانى .

واصطلاحا: لا يفرق بينه وبين مصطلح الثورة فى مستوى التغيير وشموله وانما من حيث الاسلوب فى التغيير و زمن التغيير فكلاهما -اسلاميا- يعنى التغيير الشامل والعميق لكن الثورة تسلك سبل العنف غالبا والسرعة فى التغيير بينما تتم التغييرات الإصلاحية بالتدريج وكثيرا ما تعطى الثورة الاولية لتغيير الواقع بينما تبدأ مناهج الإصلاح عادة بتغيير الإنسان: وإعادة صيانة نفسه وفق الدعوة الإصلاحية وبعد ذلك ينهض هذا الإنسان بتغيير الواقع وإقامة النموذج الإصلاحى الجديد . ولذلك وصفت رسالات الرسل عليهم الصلاة والسلام بأنها دعوات إصلاح فيقول رسول الله شعيب عليه السلام (إن اريد إلا الإصلاح ما استطعت) هود: ٨٨ .

2. *Mafâhim Islamiyah*, vol. 1, p. 30 (*Islamic Knowledge*), by Muhammad Sa'id Ramadhan al-Bouthi.

From a linguistic perspective, *islah* (to repair, reform) is the opposite of *ifsad* (disorder, mischief), which comes from the word "error." *Islah* thus conflicts with the words *fasad* (corruption, unlawful warfare or crimes against law and order) and *sayyiah* (ugly or bad)... In the Qur'an it is said, "They intermix pious works with evil deeds" (Qur'an 9:102); "And do not ravage the earth, after improving it" (Quran 7:56). *Islah* refers to change that leads in a positive direction. Thus, social movements that are *islah* in their approach to *da'wa* (proselytism), set in motion certain aspects of human life, in order to improve that which is disordered or damaged, by transforming and elevating life to a higher level, in the course of peaceful human existence.

Although, from a linguistic perspective, *islah* is not distinguished from the term revolution, in the sense of change, it is clearly differentiated in regards to the time frame, and manner, in which change is effectuated. Both terms refer to profound and total change, but revolution refers to a path that is extreme and generally rapid, while change incurred via *islah* is effected gradually, and in stages. Most revolutions succeed in altering (social) reality at the outset, while *islah* generally begins by altering and improving human nature itself. People who succeed in changing themselves in accord with *da'wa* (proselytism) that is *islah*, can subsequently transform (social) reality by implementing reform programs that are *islah* by nature. For that reason, the sayings of all Messengers are regarded as *islah da'wa*. That is why the Messenger of God Shoaib (Jethro) said, "I only wish to reform (*islah*) in so far as I am capable (of producing it) (Qur'an 11:88).

٣. قواعد الأحكام، ج: ١، ص: ٧٧، دار الكتب العلمية

المثال السادس والثلاثون التقرير على المعاصي كلها مفسدة لكن يجوز التقرير عليها عند العجز

عن انكارها باليد واللسان ومن قدر على انكارها مع الخوف على نفسه كان انكاره مندوبا اليه

ومحثوثا عليه لأن المخاطرة بالنفوس في إعزاز الدين مأمور بها كما يعذر بها في قتال المشركين

وقتال البغاة المتأولين وقتال مانعي الحقوق بحيث لا يمكن تخليصها منهم الا بالقتال وقد قال (افضل

الجهاد كلمة حق عند سلطان جائر) جعلها افضل الجهاد لان قائلها قد جاد بنفسه كل الجود

بخلاف من يلاقى قرنه من القتال فإنه يجوز ان يقهره ويقتله فلا يكون بذله نفسه مع تجويز سلامتها

كبذل المنكر نفسه مع يأسه من السلامة .

3. Al-Qawa'id al-Ahkam fi Mashâlih al-Anam, vol. 1, p. 77 (*Principles of Islamic Law and (the Promotion of) Human Welfare*), by 'Izzuddin ibn 'Abdussalam (died 660 A.H./1262 C.E.; renowned Shafi'i scholar, whose work is noted as one of the salient contributions to the literature on legal maxims).

The 36th example is a decision based upon a fully corrupt (*mafsadah*) wickedness (*kema'siatan*), but a decision may be based upon any kind of wickedness, if one is too weak to reject evil with one's hands or tongue. It is both permissible and recommended to reject evil, even when one is in a state of fear, because fear for one's life incurred in the pursuit of ennobling religion is more praiseworthy than that encountered in war opposing the polytheists and rebels in former times, or fighting those who violate one's rights, when it is impossible to safeguard those rights except through war. The Prophet said, "The highest form of jihad is to speak the truth to a tyrannical ruler." He identified speaking the truth [to a tyrant] as the highest form of jihad, because one who does so risks his life in a manner that is different from those who step upon the field of battle. The ruler is fully capable of coercing and/or executing the critic, who thus risks his or her life opposing evil, in the hope of salvation.

Documents from the Nahdlatul Ulama Central Board
Rejecting Transnational Extremist Movements
and Their Ideology

Introduction

As the largest Muslim organization in Indonesia, and indeed the world—the Nahdlatul Ulama (NU) has published a number of official statements rejecting extremist groups that seek to establish an Islamic caliphate, or Islamic state. In November of 2007, the NU Central Board (PBNU) held a Batsul Masa'il forum at Pondok Pesantren Zainul Hasan (Zainul Hasan Islamic Boarding School) in Genggong, East Java, in order to examine the issues of an Islamic caliphate, the infiltration and seizure of NU mosques by extremist groups claiming to perform da'wa (proselytism), and various other topics.

One conclusion forwarded to the NU Central Board by this Batsul Masa'il forum was that there is no nash (text) in the Qur'an that provides any foundation for the concept of an Islamic state, or requires the establishment of such a state. Both an Islamic state and Islamic caliphate are solely the products of ijtihad, or human interpretation, conducted after the fact [of Divine revelation]. The forum declared the concept of an Islamic caliphate to be a transnational ideology that threatens the integrity of the Unitary State of the Republic of Indonesia (NKRI), and warned [the 40 million+] members of the Nahdlatul Ulama to be on guard against this dangerous movement.

The documents we have published in this appendix represent the NU Central Board's official response to the problems addressed in this book, and we have acquired these documents directly from the Nahdlatul Ulama Central Board's official website, NU Online (www.nu.or.id).

Thank you.
Editorial Staff

Viewed as Deviant, NU Mosques Confiscated
Thursday, 25 May 2006 02:11

Jakarta, NU Online
Religious life in Indonesia is growing more and more insecure. A group of people, acting in the name of Islam, have been recklessly seizing control of mosques belonging to NU followers, by accusing them of *bid'ah*,[3] and of adherence to a deviant stream of Islam.

"I've received a report that countless NU mosques, in many regions, have been seized by groups claiming that their understanding of Islam is more accurate than anyone else's. They justify their actions by claiming that the NU is expert in *bid'ah*, and a deviant stream of Islam," PBNU Vice Chairman Masdar F. Mas'udi told reporters at the Wahid Institute on Taman Amir Hamzah Street in Central Jakarta on Wednesday (24/5).

Masdar explained that these takeovers assume the form of replacing a mosque's governing board, whose trustees have always been *nahdliyyin* (NU members) ever since the mosque's founding. With the change of leadership, NU religious rituals and traditions are also cast aside.

Without hesitation, but without providing a list of the mosques in question, Masdar said that the number of NU mosques seized has already reached the hundreds. "There are many, I would guess in the hundreds," he said.

Masdar added that although the NU's name or logo is not plastered on the mosques, most of them were financed and built by

---

3. [Translator's note: *bid'ah* (innovation) is a highly inflammatory term among Muslims, when linked to religion. The word appears pejoratively in the Qur'an, and the Prophet is also reported to have strongly condemned *bid'ah* in religion. Wahhabi and Muslim Brotherhood extremists routinely accuse traditional Muslims of engaging in *bid'ah*, because of their spiritual practices and reverence for saints. Spiritual *ulama* are generally undisturbed by such accusations, due to their extensive knowledge of the Qur'an, Sunnah and Islamic law, but Muslims less educated in the traditions of Islam are unequipped to deal with such accusations, which are often accompanied by further charges of heresy and apostasy. Thus, *bid'ah* accusations are a powerful weapon in the extremists' inventory, and no effort to defeat the ideology of radical Islam can succeed without addressing the rigid, superficial concept of Islam that lies behind these accusations.]

NU members, who thus have a right to control them.

"*Nahdliyyin* do not place their names, or that of the NU, on mosques they build. This is because the NU is relaxed and inclusive, and wants to share its facilities with others. But that hospitality is being abused by [extremist] groups whose members claim to be more Islamic than anyone else," explained Masdar.

Although he did not explain in detail the identity of the group(s) behind the seizure of so many mosques, he signaled that this was being done by extremists. "I think various fundamentalist groups are behind it," he said.

Masdar strongly encouraged all NU members to retake control of the mosques in question, because they belong to the NU. "NU members should reclaim their rights," he said.

However, he added that the Nahdlatul Ulama will not use violence against those who have seized control of NU mosques. "We're not going to attack them, or assault other people. But it's clear that we'll reclaim our rights," he said firmly. (rif)

Nahdlatul Ulama National Conference
Kiai Sahal: Pancasila is Final
Friday, 28 July 2006 11:54

Jakarta, NU Online
The Nahdlatul Ulama is confident that Islamic *shari'a* can be implemented at any time and without delay, or by going through formal institutions. The NU prefers to see the essential values of *shari'a* implemented in society, rather than idealizing the institutions [of government].

"The NU has already concluded that the Unitary State of the Republic of Indonesia, with Pancasila as its foundation, represents the final form of government for our nation," said the chairman of the NU's Supreme Council, Kiai Haji Sahal Mahfudz, in his opening address to the NU's national conference, held in Kertajaya Stadium in Surabaya on Friday (27/7).

According to the head of Maslahul Huda Madrasa in Pati, Central Java, the existence of formal institutions does not guarantee that *shari'a* values will be realized in society at large. Especially given the fact that Indonesia has been destined by God—Pure and Exalted is He!—to enjoy a diverse and pluralistic society.

For that reason, the universalism of Islam [i.e., its spiritual values] need not conflict with local cultures and values that originate outside of Islam. "From its very beginning, the NU has supported the dissemination of Islamic teachings without following the path of formalization. It has never sought to "pound" its teachings into society, or forcibly restructure social reality. Instead, it has always disseminated its teachings in a highly flexible way," Kiai Sahal explained.

The NU was born and grew to maturity with its own distinct culture and patterns of behavior. It embraces an accommodative attitude toward various religious denominations. And as a mass organization, the NU displays a tolerant attitude toward local values.

Kiai Sahal emphasized that throughout its history, the NU has never considered uniting, much less eliminating, other streams of religious thought and practice. Nor, since its founding [in 1926], has the NU ever sought to cast aside local cultural values that differ from its own.

"The NU engages in acculturation and positive interaction with local cultures and traditions, wherever it goes. This acculturation process has given birth to 'Islam with a smiling face,' and a friendly demeanor towards local cultures and values, while appreciating differences in religion, traditions and belief, which represent the cultural heritage of our archipelago nation," Kiai Sahal added.

The NU itself has a rich and varied multicultural dimension. Its social policies are not specifically designed to protect local traditions or cultures, but rather, to acknowledge their existence, and their right to exist, which the NU's core understanding of Islam maintains is only right and proper.

"Because of this approach, the NU is capable of integrating teachings derived from its sacred religious texts into a "profane" cultural context. The NU thereby proves that Islamic universalism [e.g., its spiritual values] can be applied without sidelining local cultures," Kiai Sahal said. (mkf)

Take Back Nahdliyyin (NU) Mosques, LDNU[4] Assembles Islamic Study Group Councils from Throughout the Greater Jakarta Area
Thursday, 24 August 2006

Jakarta, NU Online

The Nahdlatul Ulama (NU) is concerned about the fate of mosques belonging to NU members, which have been infiltrated and seized by groups ostensibly acting in the name of Islam. In response, the Central Board of the Nahdlatul Ulama Dakwah (Proselytism) Institute (LDNU) has launched an initiative to retake mosques that belong to NU members, by gathering the heads of Islamic study group/education councils from throughout the greater Jakarta area (Jakarta, Bogor, Tangerang, Bekasi).

"On the 30th (of August) we'll assemble all chairmen of Islamic study groups from the Jakarta metropolitan region. We have to retake the mosques that have been seized by other people," LDNU general chairman Kyai Haji Nuril Huda told *NU Online* at PBNU headquarters on Jalan Kramat Raya in Central Jakarta on Thursday (24/8).

As *NU Online* has reported several times, the vice chairman of the Nahdlatul Ulama, Kyai Haji Masdar F. Mas'udi, has told of [extremist] groups using Islam as a justification to recklessly seize control of *nahdliyyin* mosques, hurling accusations that the NU is a deviant cult, engaged in *bid'ah*. They have been replacing the board members who manage these mosques—a position formerly held by NU members.

Kiai Nuril—that is his nickname—has said that the new initiative, which is a joint project involving the central leadership of the LDNU and Muslimat NU [the NU's women's auxiliary] will hold meetings at the end of each month. At this gathering, the chairmen of Islamic study groups will receive detailed knowledge

---

4. [Translator's note: Lembaga Dakwah Nahdlatul Ulama (LDNU/The NU Proselytism Institute) is institutionally responsible for disseminating NU teachings through Friday prayers, congregational study groups, etc., etc. Following publication of this book, the LDNU ordered hundreds of copies of *The Illusion of an Islamic State*, to be used by top LDNU *dais* (proselytizers) who constantly travel to deliver lectures and sermons to NU congregations throughout Indonesia.]

concerning *ahlussunnah wal-jamâ'ah* (Sunni Muslim) theology.

According to Kiai Nuril, a correct understanding of Aswaja is essential to successfully confront the [extremist] groups that have seized control of NU mosques. The problem is, the chairmen of these educational councils often do not yet fully understand *ahlussunnah wal-jamâ'ah* teachings.

In addition, added Kiai Nuril, many new religious teachings have appeared that describe themselves as *ahlussunnah*, but in fact are not representative of Sunni Islam. "A lot of ideologies are out there, claiming to be *ahlussunnah*, when in fact they're not *ahlussunnah wal-jamâ'ah*. They may claim to base their teachings on the example of the Prophet Muhammad (*ahlussunnah*), but they by no means represent the great traditions of the Sunni Muslim community (*ahlussunnah wal-jamâ'ah*). That is why the chairmen of Islamic study groups must be further educated, so they can differentiate between *ahlussunnah*, and *ahlussunnah wal-jamâ'ah*," he explained.

"The difference is, *ahlussunnah* only follow the teachings and example of the Prophet Muhammad (saw.), while *ahlussunnah wal-jamâ'ah* also follow those of the rightly guided caliphs," said Kiai Nuril.

Kiai Nuril realizes that the NU, as the largest Islamic mass organization in Indonesia, which is founded on Sunni theology, needs to immediately launch a serious movement to rescue and preserve its theological orientation, which has formed the basis of traditional Muslim belief in Indonesia for hundreds of years. If the NU neglects this task, he said, there is no guarantee that in ten years moderate Sunni teachings won't disappear, and be replaced by another [extremist] ideology.

Kiai Nuril explained that response was quite positive at the first and second meetings, which were attended by the chairmen of 162 education councils from throughout the greater Jakarta metropolitan region [which has a population of 24 million people]. In those two meetings, he said, it became clear that most of the education council chairmen did not fully understand Sunni theology, as taught by the NU since its founding.

"It's like we're going to enlighten these education council

leaders about the true and complete Sunni teachings, so they can distinguish between *ahlussunnah* [extremist] ideology and the teachings of *ahlussunnah wal-jamâ'ah*," added Kiai Nuril.

These meetings are just a start, said Kiai Nuril. The next step will expand these meetings to other regions, especially those outside the island of Java, because the phenomenon [of extremist infiltration] is occurring not only in the Jakarta metropolitan area, but throughout Indonesia.

For the next meeting (August 30), Kiai Nuril mentioned that he has already invited a female Muslim from the U.S. to speak. Her name is Mrs. Tiye Mulazim. According to Kiai Nuril, Mrs. Mulazim also embraces Sunni theology. (rif)

Hasyim Muzadi: Islamic Caliphate Is a Political, Not a Religious, Movement.
Tuesday, 5 September 2006

Jakarta, NU Online

The general chairman of the Nahdlatul Ulama's executive board (PBNU), Kyai Haji Hasyim Muzadi, has requested that all [40 million] members of the NU, and Muslims in general, to be on constant guard against discourse about an Islamic caliphate, which is being propagated by radical Islamic groups. According to Kyai Hasyim, such discourse is fundamentally part of a political, rather than religious, movement.

"An Islamic caliphate is actually a political, rather than religious, movement. Political issues are far more prominent [in talk of a caliphate] than religious aspects involving devotion and prayer. They merely focus on the system of government, not on how to help *madrasas* and mosques create prosperity and well-being for the Muslim community," said Hasyim during a friendly get-together on Tuesday (5/9) with officers of the LDNU central board at PBNU headquarters on Jalan Kramat Raya in Central Jakarta.

Hasyim—which is the familiar name of this guardian of Al Hikam Pesantren (Islamic boarding school, or *madrasa*) in Malang, East Java—stressed that in regards to the concept of an Islamic caliphate, a nation's system of government and leadership should be formed in accordance with the locally prevailing conditions in each country. "Whoever is the head of state, as established by a legal process, is—from both a religious and secular perspective—that nation's leader (caliph). There's no point in searching for other models," he stressed.

Hasyim also spoke with LDNU officers about the prolific growth of radical Islamic groups and movements in Indonesia. This, despite the fact that in most countries of the Middle East, hard line Islamic groups are denied official standing, or even forbidden. "In Europe and the Middle East, such as Jordan and Syria, they (radical Islamic groups) are denied official standing. But in Indonesia, they live freely and are spreading everywhere," he said.

The former head of the East Java chapter of the NU reminded

the LDNU leaders that the spread of radical ideology and movements is a serious matter, which must be confronted by the NU. The LDNU, he said, is the institutional vehicle responsible for preaching, and also socializing the NU's *ahlussunnah wal-jamâ'ah* (Sunni Muslim) understanding of Islam, and must be responsible for accomplishing this vital mission. If it fails to do so, the NU will be swept away by the onslaught of radical Islamic groups.

Unable to Build Their Own Mosques

Hasyim's remarks were also linked to the phenomenon of extreme "right wing" Islamic groups seizing control of mosques belonging to members of the NU. According to him, this occurs because extremists—who so readily accuse *nahdliyyin* (NU members) of practicing *bid'ah* and being infidels—are incapable of building their own mosques. Therefore, they infiltrate and seize control of mosques that were built and long managed by *nahdliyyin*, who staffed the mosques' governing boards and ensured the continuity of their religious rituals and traditions.[5]

"Since they are unable to build their own mosques, they seize other people's mosques and use them to preach their political ideology. That's their purpose. At the end of the day, it's the NU that suffers," explained Hasyim. (rif)

---

5. [Translator's note: NU mosques generally function as the center for a local community's practice of Sufi rituals (often involving music and chanting, designed to open the heart to God) and various other rites (such as those honoring the dead), which Muslim extremists harshly condemn.]

Don't Allow Other Ideologies to Infiltrate
Hasyim Warns Those Who Manage NU Mosques to be on Guard
Tuesday, 28 November 2006 12:33

Malang, NU Online

The general chairman of the Nahdlatul Ulama's administrative council (PBNU), Kyai Haji Hasyim Muzadi, announced that he has instructed all NU management personnel in regions throughout the nation to exercise greater caution, and prevent the infiltration of NU mosques by other groups.

"I have already instructed the management of various regions to protect their mosques from becoming infected by other groups' ideology," he said on Monday (27/11) at Al Hikam Pesantren in Malang, East Java.

The "other groups" to which he referred are Islamic groups that emphasize the formal aspects of religion, rather than its substance [i.e., Islamic law, rather than direct, experiential knowledge of God]. "In the past, the NU and Muhammadiyah struggled over mosques, but we no longer do that. It's finished. Only now there are new groups trying to muscle in, perhaps because their followers are not in the practice of making charitable contributions, but why should they try to occupy NU mosques? Maybe they figure that rather than build mosques, which are expensive, it's better to just take mosques that belong to other people," he explained.

Of course, Hasyim reminded NU members to be on guard against such groups, because their ideology is not compatible with NU teachings. "They're the group that's always wanting to establish an Islamic state," he explained.

Islam *rahmatan lil 'âlamin* ("a blessing for all creation") is the face of Islam that should be presented to society, not just in Indonesia, but throughout the world. To that end, Hasyim will present NU thought to the student body of Sunan Ampel Islamic State Institute (IAIN) in Surabaya this December 2nd.

On that occasion, the former chairman of the East Java chapter of the NU will receive an honorary doctorate from IAIN Sunan Ampel. Hasyim's theme will be "Islam Rahmatan Lil

'Âlamin (Islam as a Blessing for All Creation) and World Peace, from the Perspective of the NU." This oration will serve as his formal presentation, prior to receiving his doctorate.

Inspired by the NU spirit, Hasyim continues to offer the world his vision of a peaceful Islam. "Is there anyone who has embraced Islam because of war? People should not be forced to convert to Islam with a sword or cudgel, which is what's happening so often these days, in the name of God," he said.

For that purpose, as President of The World Conference of Religions for Peace, Hasyim will communicate a pacific and non-violent understanding of Islam through seminars, dialogues and conferences, involving both Muslim and non-Muslim organizations around the world. It will not be surprising if he establishes various forums, with people belonging to other groups, such as the International Conference of Islamic Scholars (ICIS) or the Islamic Supreme Council of America, which is led by Shaykh Muhammad Hisham Kabbani, a leader of the Naqshbandi Sufi brotherhood. (dtm/so)

The NU Will Stand Up and Face the 'Challenge' Posed by Hard Line Islamic Groups
Tuesday, 27 February 2007

Jakarta, NU Online
The beat of war drums has begun to resonate throughout the Nahdlatul Ulama (NU), summoning its members to confront hard line Islamic groups that have proliferated in recent years. The largest Islamic mass organization in Indonesia is preparing to confront the 'challenge' posed by radical Islamic groups, that have been causing extreme unrest among *nahdliyyin* (NU) communities.

Last Saturday, the central leadership council of the Nahdlatul Ulama's Proselytism Institute (LDNU) issued a declaration that called upon all [40 million+] *nahdliyyin* to tenaciously uphold the teachings and practices of *ahlussunnah wal-jamâ'ah* [Sunni Islam]. Eight regional LDNU chairman from throughout Indonesia signed the declaration, which constitutes a response to [extremist] accusations of religious deviance and heresy directed towards NU teachings and religious practices.

"[W]e recognize from the depths of our hearts that in recent years, ideological tendencies have developed and spread among Islamic movements (*al-harakah al-islamiyyah*), via religious practices that can eclipse the values of *ahlussunnah wal-jamâ'ah* (Sunni Islam), a la NU, and thus solemnly declare: ...To faithfully observe the charitable religious practices of *ahlussunnah wal-jamâ'ah* a la NU, and preserve the religious practices and traditions of our righteous predecessors, such as *salat sunnat* (optional prayers that may be performed by Muslims at almost any time of day), *salat tarawih* (an optional prayer performed during the month of Ramadan), with 20 *raka'ah* (prescribed cycles), *wirid* (invocations of the Divine), *salawat* (beseeching God to bless the Prophet, conducted in the form of musical chants), *qunut* (special supplications), *talqin* (a special prayer recited for the deceased, at funerals), *ziarah qubur* (pilgrimage to the tombs of prophets, saints or other revered figures), *tahlil* (recitation of the phrase, "*la ilaha ilallah*/There is no god but God"), *manaqib* (praising the virtues of Muhammad), *ratib* (a form of *dhikr*, or devotional act, performed in remembrance of God), *maulid Nabi* (celebration of the Prophet Muhammad's birth and life), *haul* (anniversary commemoration, generally for a renowned saint), and *istighâtsah* (communal prayers led by one perceived to be pure of heart); along with tolerance of cultural traditions that are compatible with Islamic values, as an integral part of *ahlussunnah wal-jamâ'ah da'wa* (proselytism) a la NU," reads one point within the aforementioned document.

The general chairman of the LDNU, Kyai Haji Nuril Huda, told *NU Online* that extremist movements have already crossed the bounds of tolerance. For they are not only infiltrating and seizing mosques that belong to NU members, but also dare to agitate and condemn the NU as a deviant sect.

"They've begun to seize NU mosques, and have published countless books that blaspheme the teachings of *ahlussunnah wal-jamâ'ah* a la NU," explained Kiai Nuril in the headquarters of the Nahdlatul Ulama on Jalan Kramat Raya in Central Jakarta on Tuesday (27/2).

Moreover, he continued, their movement has become extremely broad and is distributed throughout Indonesia, not only regions dominated by NU members. If the NU does not take serious steps to confront this threat, it is entirely possible that the religious traditions practiced by NU members [and the tolerance that accompanies these traditions] will vanish.

Not only that. What most worries the NU, according to Kiai Nuril, is that the Unitary State of the Republic of Indonesia, which is based on Pancasila and the 1945 constitution, are also under serious threat. Strong signals are radiating throughout the nation, that hard line Islamic groups intend to transform Indonesia into an Islamic state.

For this reason, in addition to strengthening the religious teachings and practices of *ahlussunnah wal-jamâ'ah* (Sunni Islam) a la NU, the memorandum also strengthens the NU's commitment and resolve to faithfully protect the Unitary State of the Republic of Indonesia. The NU does not want certain specific [extremist] parties to undermine the unity and very existence of Indonesia.

Kiai Nuril added that the next step in implementing the memorandum will be for every regional chapter of the LDNU throughout Indonesia to strengthen its barricades, in order to confront hard line Islamic groups. "We have decided to focus on five zones of consolidation for the NU. These include Sumatra, Java, Sulawesi, West Nusa Tenggara and Kalimantan. Each of these zones will gather and consolidate every regional LDNU chapter, in every province in their area," he explained.

The existence of these zones, said Kiai Nuril, will hopefully assist the LDNU accomplish its objective in far-flung regions outside the metropolitan area of Jakarta. In that way, NU mosques and the teachings and practices of the NU can be defended. "Although others' beliefs may differ from our own, it is the NU 'way' to respect and value others. Yet this must be a two-way street. There should be no more accusations that the NU is a deviant sect, and other such nonsense," he said. (rif)

PBNU Presses the Government to Halt the Spread of Transnational Ideology
Sunday, 29 April 2007

Surabaya, NU Online
The general chairman of the Nahdlatul Ulama's executive board (PBNU), Kyai Haji Hasyim Muzadi, is pressing the government to halt the infiltration of transnational ideology into Indonesia, from both the West and the [Middle] East.

"The late Mr. Ud (a nickname used for the former head of Tebuireng Pesantren in Jombang, East Java, the deceased Kyai Haji Yusuf Hasyim) once asked me to block the infiltration of transnational ideology, because it has the potential to destroy both the Nahdlatul Ulama and Indonesia," he said in Surabaya, on Sunday.

He made this statement during a speech commemorating one hundred days after the death of Kyai Haji Yusuf Hasyim in the NU's East Java regional office, which was attended by Kyai Haji Solahuddin Wahid (the current head of Tebuireng Pesantren), Kyai Haji Tholchah Hasan (Indonesia's former minister of religion), and Slamet Effendy Yusuf (former general chairman of [the NU's 10-million-member youth movement,] Ansor).

According to Hasyim, who is also the head of Al-Hikam Pesantren in Malang, East Java, the government should "sever" the infiltration of transnational ideology, because both Western liberalism and Islamic ideology from the [Middle] East are destructive.

"The government should employ Pancasila as an ideology to halt the spread of transnational ideologies, just as I have been seeking to fulfill the "dying exhortation" of Mr. Ud by constantly traveling to the East and West," he said.

The former chairman of the East Java chapter of the NU mentioned that he has visited the United States, Europe, the Middle East and other regions to campaign for the NU worldview as an alternative ideology, like the recently-deceased NU co-founder. "NU founders like Mr. Ud were exporters of ideology, not importers. I was the first Muslim leader to visit 'Ground Zero' in New York (site of the 9/11 attack on the World Trade Center) to reject the 'violence' of radical Islam," he said.

However, he said, has also visited Iraq, Iran and Palestine to condemn the violence of Western liberalism, which has embedded 'colonialism' for long enough in the Middle East.

"I visited Iraq, Iran and Palestine to promote peace. All this time they have just been 'crickets' played off against one another by foreign intelligence agencies, so that 'colonialists' can easily triumph," he explained.

Besides his visits to the East and West, he said, he also wants to demonstrate to the world that the Nahdlatul Ulama views Islam as a religion, not ideology, and to convey that all the violence in the Middle East stems not from Islam as a religion, but from Islamist ideology.

"Islamist ideological movements in the Middle East include the Muslim Brotherhood, Islamic Jihad, al-Qaeda and so forth, but their Islamist ideology is not Islam itself, because Islam as a religion does not have the characteristics of a self-interested movement, much less political characteristics," he said.

He added that he has also attempted to assemble Muslim *ulama* from throughout the world at various international Islamic conferences held in Indonesia. "Praise be to God, what the NU is doing has generated an enthusiastic response. It is has been clearly demonstrated that 85 percent of the world's Muslim population agrees with the NU, which is *tawassuth* and *tasammuh* (pursuing a middle path, that is fair and consistent), an approach that is opposed by just 15 percent of the world's Muslims, who are ideologically-driven," he said.

The service commemorating 100 days since the death of Mr. Ud was held in the NU's East Java headquarters, and attended by Kyai Haji Tholchah Hasan (former minister of religion), Slamet Effendy Yusuf (former general chairman of Ansor), Imam Nahrawi (chairman of the East Java chapter of PKB/the National Development Party), Farid Al-Fauzy (chairman of the East Java chapter of PPP/the United Development Party), and Kyai Haji Masduqi Mahfudz of the NU.

The occasion began with the reading of *tahlil* (praising God through repetition of the formula, *la ilaha ilallah*) and was lightened up when the head of Tebuireng Pesantren, Kyai Haji Solahuddin Wahid (Gus Solah) presented a book to Mr. Ud's widow, Mrs. Hajah Bariyah Yusuf Hasyim, and also by the reading of a poem in memory of Mr. Ud by Fairuz Febiyanda (Mr. Ud's first grandchild) and Taufik Ismail (a nationally-renowned cultural figure). (ant/eko)

PBNU Requests Indonesians not to Adopt Transnational Ideology
Tuesday, 15 May 2007

Jakarta, NU Online

The Nahdlatul Ulama's Executive Board (PBNU) has requested all Indonesians not to join religious movements that have a transnational ideology. This is because most of these ideologically-driven movements are not compatible with local social conditions and culture.

The General Chairman of the PBNU, Kyai Haji Hasyim, explained that most of the Islamic groups that promote transnational ideology are constantly embroiled in conflict, even in their own countries of origin. Thus, if Indonesians join such movements, we will become embroiled in their conflicts, not to mention the fact that their ideology is incompatible with our local culture.

"Hizb ut-Tahrir, al-Qaeda, the Muslim Brotherhood and so forth are, in my opinion, political movements imbued with a certain ideology, not religious movements," explained Hasyim, when he was the keynote speaker for an event designed to socialize a common policy adopted by the Ministry of Religion and the Interior Ministry at the NU headquarters building on Jalan Karamat Raya in Central Jakarta on Tuesday (15/5).

The President of The World Conference of Religions for Peace added that those political groups which "wrap themselves" in religion emerged from political conditions, and a system of government, completely different from that of Indonesia. Thus, their ideology will clearly have a different effect if applied to Indonesia.

During the meeting, which was sponsored by the Central Leadership Board of LDNU, together with the Department of Religion, Kyai Hasyim also mentioned that the Islamic groups infected by transnational ideology generally reject tolerance or an attitude of mutual respect. This can easily trigger inter-religious conflict.

"Such rejection of tolerance always leads to problems. The next thing you know, people start denigrating Islam, too, as occurred in Batu near Malang, East Java, and with the insertion of Bibles into the Qur'an in Jombang, and the distribution of cartoons of the Prophet Muhammad in Cirebon," explained Hasyim, who is also Secretary General of the International Conference of Islamic Scholars.

Movements characterized by transnational ideology appear not only within Islam, added Hasyim, but also other religions such as Christianity. He told how he was invited to attend a forum held by the World Council of Churches in Porto Alegre, Brazil, in February of 2006.

During the main conference, featuring Christian leaders from around the world, several delegations tried to persuade the forum to issue a call for Papua's independence from Indonesia. "Clearly, that was not a religious movement, but rather a political movement, although it was 'clothed' in religion," said Hasyim.

This occurrence, he added, demonstrates that ideologically-motivated transnational movements are not the sole monopoly of Islam, but characteristic of other religions as well. Therefore, he stressed, Indonesians—whatever their religion—should remember to be on guard against such movements. (rif)

RMI Assembles Pesantren (Madrasa) Heads from Throughout Indonesia to Discuss the 'Threat' of Transnational Ideology
Wednesday, 16 May 2007

Jakarta, NU Online

Rabithath al-Ma'ahid al-Islamiyah Nahdlatul Ulama (RMI NU)[6] will assemble leaders of pesantren from throughout Indonesia at the Pondok Gede Hajj Compound in Jakarta from May 18-21. One of the key agenda items at this NU all-Indonesian pesantren association meeting is to discuss the appearance of transnational ideology, which is considered a "threat" to the existence of NU pesantren themselves.

RMI NU Vice Chairman Abdul Adhim told reporters that transnational ideology, or "imported" ideology, constitutes a serious threat to national unity and to NU pesantren. This is because most of these ideologies are incompatible with our local culture and social conditions. "Indonesian Islam, which was spread by the *wali songgo* [nine Muslim saints who are regarded as having converted Java to Islam] is imbued with the spirit of tolerance and courtesy. Transnational Islamist ideology, on the other hand, arrives uninvited and without the least bit of courtesy, screaming '*Allahu Akbar!*' while shattering glass," explained Adhim, who is also chairman of the committee hosting that meeting in the Nahdlatul Ulama headquarters on Jalan Kramat Raya in Central Jakarta on Wednesday (16/5).

According to Adhim, this is why the organization—which encompasses 14,000 NU pesantren (Islamic boarding schools, or *madrasas*) throughout Indonesia—feels responsible for helping to stop the infiltration of transnational ideology, which threatens the integrity and stability of the Unitary State of the Republic of Indonesia (NKRI).

Adhim added that besides addressing the threat posed by transnational ideology, the conference—which will be opened by Vice President Jusuf Kalla—will also discuss the fate of pesantren, which

---

6. A branch of the NU responsible for addressing the interests of 14,000 NU-affiliated pesantren (*madrasas*), which at any given time enroll approximately 3 million students.

are still considered to be neglected by the national government. The meeting, which will be attended by 300 pesantren heads and by the RMI NU regional chairmen from 32 provinces throughout Indonesia, will demand that the government pay greater attention to pesantren.

For many years, he said, the government has discriminated against NU pesantren. Actually these pesantren, which constitute a vital part of Indonesia's educational system, have the same rights as other educational institutions. The degrees obtained by pesantren graduates, for example, are not recognized by the government. "Of the [14,000] pesantren that belong to RMI NU, only graduates from Sidogiri (Pasuruan) and Lirboyo (Kediri) are accredited by the government, while other pesantren graduates receive no recognition whatsoever. If we talk about the quality of education, students graduating from NU pesantren are no less prepared to succeed in life than those who have attended other educational institutions," explained Adhim.

Not only that. According to Adhim, most pesantren—which are generally situated in rural areas—do not receive proper attention from the government, especially in regard to their physical condition. "There is still very little material aid from the government, such as grants for laboratories, etc. And to the extent there have been any such grants, they were made only after the reform era dawned [with the fall of Suharto], and not before," he said.

In order to improve this situation, a separate meeting that follows the RMI NU executive meeting is scheduled, with an agenda to sign a memorandum of understanding between the central board of RMI NU and the government, as represented by various government ministers responsible for these matters. (rif)

If Transnational Ideology Succeeds, Indonesia Will be Completely Transformed
Friday, 22 June 2007

Jakarta, NU Online

We must be ever more alert to guard against political movements colored by transnational ideology. Such movements threaten the Unitary State of the Republic of Indonesia, and seek to replace Pancasila and the 1945 constitution as the twin foundations of our country.

"I think if their movement is successful, this nation will automatically be transformed; there will no longer be a unitary nation-state, and no 1945 constitution. Everything will change, because that's their agenda," said Ghozalie Said—chairman of the executive board of the NU's Batsul Masa'il (fatwa-making body)—in Jakarta on Thursday (21/6).

According to Ghozalie, if that threat becomes a reality, Indonesia will disappear, because a primary objective pursued by those adhering to said ideology is to form an Islamic government (Islamic caliphate). That concept of government seeks to dissolve the nation-state and replace it with a single government that encompasses every Muslim throughout the world.

The author of the book *The Ideology of Transnational Fundamentalist Groups in Pakistan and Egypt* defined transnational ideology as an Islamic movement that exists in Indonesia, but is controlled from abroad. For example, he mentioned that the Muslim Brotherhood's supreme leader resides in Egypt, while Hizb ut-Tahrir's leadership is Jordanian [now based in the UK], and that of Shi'ite [extremists] in Iran.

The head of An-Nur Pesantren in Wonocolo, Surabaya, East Java, hopes that the government will implement a clear policy directed against these movements, so that they will no longer threaten our nation's existence. In the Middle East, such movements are forbidden because they seek to destroy individual nation-states and replace them with a transnational Islamic government, such as the concept of an Islamic caliphate promoted by Hizb ut-Tahrir. Of course Indonesia would vanish if their goal of creating an Islamic caliphate were to become a reality.

"I think the government should develop a clear policy, and not simply allow [this kind of subversion to spread]. Or maybe the government is promoting this on purpose, and using leftists as a counterbalance," he explained.

This professor from Sunan Ampel Islamic State Institute in Surabaya explained that the transnational group in question plans to hold a global Islamic government conference in Jakarta. The plan is to invite Hizb ut-Tahrir followers from throughout the world to attend this conference.[7]

With regard to the practice of religion and *shari'a*, Ghozalie explained that the extremists are nearly all adherents of a Wahhabi worldview, which is relatively new and divorced from the traditions of Islam. Such groups dislike the traditions observed by the NU, such as *tahlil* (praising God through repetition of the formula, *la ilaha ilallah*).

Meanwhile, these groups hold a political view based on a saying of the Prophet that "Anyone who dies without having paid homage to the caliphate, has died in a state of spiritual ignorance," and is thus regarded as an infidel ("*man maata, walaisa biunukhihi baiah mata mitaatan jahiliyyah*").

The Muslim Brotherhood employs a similar tactic to elicit support from Muslims, by quoting the hadith, "*Waman lam yahkum bima anzalallah, faulaaika humul kaafiruun.*" ("Whoever does not observe the law that God revealed, is one of the infidels.")

"This is very intense from a theological perspective. They consider us to be non-Muslims, because we don't follow their ideology. I've attended many Friday sermons where this was preached, and heard it with my own ears," he said.

Ghozalie explained that the Muslim Brotherhood's doctrine is derived from Sayyid Qutb who, in his famous book *Mileposts*, asserted, along with many other claims, that if a country does not implement *shari'a*, it's a nation of infidels, lost in *jahiliyyah*

---

7. [Translator's note: held in August of 2007, the Hizb ut-Tahrir conference mentioned by Imam Ghozalie filled Indonesia's largest sports stadium with approximately 80,000 supporters, who called for the dissolution of the Indonesian nation-state and its replacement by an Islamic caliphate.]

(ignorance of Divine guidance).

"Thus their primary enemy is the head of state of whatever country they're from. Demonize and attack your own country, even before criticizing Israel. Second, [they condemn] countries that fail to implement shari'a as "jahiliyya nations," characterized by ignorance and darkness, because Islamic law is not important to jahiliyya countries," he explained.

According to Imam Ghozalie, the NU and Muhammadiyah—Islamic movements whose former leaders were among Indonesia's founding fathers—have a different spiritual nature than the aforementioned new Islamic movements, and a different role to play in Indonesia. "The difference is that NU and Muhammadiyah leaders were among the founding fathers who established Pancasila [as Indonesia's state ideology]. As a result, the NU and Muhammadiyah have a sense of spiritual unity, linked to the history and continuity of our nation. We have a moral responsibility to defend the Unitary State of the Republic of Indonesia," he stressed.

That is why NU members regard Islam and Indonesian nationalism as mutually harmonious and inseparable. "Just as a Malay is Muslim, and Muslims are Malay [in the neighboring country of Malaysia], Islam and Indonesian nationalism have long since melded, creating our culture, including the culture of mosques and various traditions that have long existed here," he said. (mkf)

Halaqoh Column[8]
If Transnational Ideology Succeeds, Indonesia Will be Completely Transformed
2 July 2007

The existence of transnational ideology has become a heated topic of discussion lately, especially in Muslim circles, due to the actions of [extremist] movements and the reaction of nationalists who perceive attempts to formalize shari'a in Indonesia as a threat to NKRI (the Unitary State of the Republic of Indonesia). What is this transnational ideology, in reality? What is its history, and what will be the consequences of its continued growth in Indonesia? Below are the views of Dr. Kyai Haji Ghozalie Said, author of "The Ideology of Transnational Fundamentalist Groups in Pakistan and Egypt," which he shared with NU Online while visiting PBNU headquarters during the middle of last month.

What is transnational Islam, really?
I did indeed author a book entitled *The Ideology of Transnational Fundamentalist Groups in Pakistan and Egypt*, which used this term. Lately, however, we find that the term is being employed by our nation's intelligence agency, apparently based on internal reports generated by members of BIN [Indonesia's National Intelligence Agency]. The term refers to Islamic movements that are active in Indonesia and are controlled by foreign entities, such as the Ikhwanul Muslimin (Muslim Brotherhood), which is controlled from Egypt. The Brotherhood's "supreme guide" (al-mursyid al-aam) resides in Egypt.

Eventually the Muslim Brotherhood spread to Indonesia, and in its long history divided into two factions. The first is the official faction, which also goes by the name Ikhwan. In other countries, its name may vary. In Sudan it's called Jamaah Islamiyah; it became a political party, because it accepted democracy and the existence

---

8. [Translator's note: *Halaqoh* refers to a system used in pesantren (*madrasas*), in which pupils sit in a cross-legged position in front of their teacher. *NU Online's* "Halaqoh Column" features interviews with religious leaders, who may present their knowledge to a wide NU audience in greater depth than is possible with the average news story.]

of the Sudanese nation-state, but this acceptance was merely a ruse enabling it to establish an Islamic government based upon *shari'a*. As I said, the movement's name varies from country to country. In Algeria it became the FIS; in Syria they had their own party, whose name I forget; in Palestine they became known as Hamas and in Indonesia they formed PKS. This is the official track, and their *mursyid al-aam* is based in Egypt.

A second, *jihad* faction also developed, which BIN describes using the term Hudaibiyah. As far as I know, this is the Hadibi faction, named after their second religious leader, Hasan Hadibi. When Hadibi became the Brotherhood's *mursyid al-aam*, there was a faction called *tandim al-khos*, which already existed during Hasan al-Banna's era, but became more radical when the *tandim al-khos* was controlled by Sayyid Qutb. To use NU language, the *tandim al-khos* is equivalent to our Banser, or paramilitary group. Of course our Banser doesn't carry weapons, but in Egypt the Brotherhood's paramilitary group was heavily armed.

Their doctrine came from Sayyid Qutb. His famous book, *Ma'alim fi-l-Tariq* (*Mileposts*) asserted, along with many other claims, that if a country does not implement *shari'a*, it's a nation of infidels, lost in *jahiliyyah* (ignorance of Divine guidance). Thus their primary enemy is the head of state of whatever country they're from. Demonize and attack your own country, even before criticizing Israel. Second, (they condemn) countries that fail to implement *shari'a* as *jahiliyya* nations, characterized by ignorance and darkness, because Islamic law is not important to *jahiliyya* countries. This view differs from that of Wahbah Zuhili, who was still young at that time.

Sayyid Qutb's Muslim Brotherhood faction established an unofficial, non-government stream of radical Islam that ultimately gave birth to the group known as Egyptian Islamic Jihad. They are anti-state and also transnational, having migrated all over the world. During the Soviet occupation of Afghanistan they received financial aid from Saudi Arabia, including Osama bin Laden, and eventually merged with bin Laden's Wahhabi faction [i.e., al-Qaeda].

Way back then people were sending groups of volunteers from Indonesia. For example, there was Amrozi, who was just a kid at the time, but already training for war.[9] Jemaah Islamiyah eventually emerged from this conflict as well. They're the group that likes to explode bombs everywhere. In distinction to these [militant, terrorist outfits], the Muslim Brotherhood's official faction is considered to be *haraqah ustadziyah* or a movement of religious teachers. They position themselves as a movement of Islamic teachers, to imply that they should be followed [by others]. But they also have relationships with other groups that are probably non-Brotherhood, although they all join in animosity towards the state.

A second movement which also originally derived from the Muslim Brotherhood is Hizb ut-Tahrir (HT). Shaykh Taqiuddin al-Nabhani had joined forces with the Muslim Brotherhood during the war against Israel in 1948. After they lost, he formed his own Islamic movement, based on his evaluation that Muslims constantly faced defeat [by Jews and the West] because they lacked an Islamic caliphate. This led him to form Hizb ut-Tahrir, which he controlled from Jordan. The Muslim Brotherhood is prohibited in Egypt, and HT in Jordan, Lebanon and Syria as well. They like to keep that a secret here, and not advertise the fact. HT's current leader is named Abu Rosta. In Indonesia the chairman of HTI (Hizb ut-Tahrir Indonesia) is actually Habib Abdurahman, but his name never appears. Instead we always see Ismail Yusanto, who's actually just a small player. In Surabaya there's Dr. Usman, but he and Yusanto are only spokespeople.

Now, HT is characterized by its absolute obedience to the organization's international policy of not accepting the existence of nation-states. So they don't wish to become a political party, because they regard the nation-state as a political system created by infidels, as is democracy. As a consequence, they practice *takfir* (branding other Muslims as *kafir/kufar*, or infidels), although they

---

9. [Translator's note: Amrozi helped organized the first Bali bombing, which killed over 200 people in October of 2002. He was subsequently convicted by an Indonesian court, and executed for his crime in November of 2008.]

generally hide this. And once others are branded as infidels, this means... Well, there are consequences and stages involved. So that's Hizb ut-Tahrir. [10]

So conflict arises when this transnational movement steals assets belonging to the NU, Muhammadiyah or other organizations?
The NU and Muhammadiyah participated in Indonesia's independence struggle, and the establishment of our nation. So you can't separate the "Islamicity" and the "nationalism" of our founding fathers. Just as a Malay is Muslim, and Muslims are Malay, and the two have become interchangeable terms [in neighboring Malaysia], Islam and Indonesian nationalism have long since melded, creating our culture, including the culture of mosques and various traditions that have long existed here. Now these new [transnational] movements don't have any traditions yet, and the fastest way [to establish themselves locally] is to infiltrate and seize any mosque that's not being closely guarded. I think we should learn from this and act decisively. If we don't, the NU will just keep sleeping [as its strength is eroded by extremist infiltration]. That's my opinion. They [extremists] actually have a program to seize control of mosques, regency by regency [throughout Indonesia], especially HTI. As for the Muslim Brotherhood, whose political party, the PKS, originates from Islamic study groups on campus, known as the *tarbiyah* movement... they're more active gnawing away at the Muhammadiyah, because so many Muhammadiyah

---

10. [Translator's note: In the Middle East and Pakistan, where *takfiris* (those who proclaim other Muslims as infidels and apostates) are much stronger and better armed than in Indonesia, their denunciation of fellow Muslims is often accompanied by suicide bombings and assassinations directed against those whom they brand as infidels. In this portion of his interview, Imam Ghozalie alludes to these facts without being explicit, because the very concept is so shocking, and blasphemous, to most Indonesian Muslims, including the readers of this column. Blasphemous, because traditional Muslims are taught that no one but God can see into the depths of a human heart, and judge whether he or she is an infidel, and also because traditional Muslims generally believe that faith is a private matter, between each individual and God. Thus, arrogating the power of life and death over others to oneself is viewed as a form of *shirk*, or idolatry, by conflating one's own ego, and judgment, with God.]

cadres have joined their movement. But the PKS also builds a lot of mosques. HTI doesn't. But the PKS does, in order to use them for their activities and advance their political agenda.

HTI also tries to infiltrate NU pesantren, don't they?
Absolutely, they're extremely active. By five o'clock in the morning they've already shown up everywhere [at local mosques and pesantren], and most of them are completely ignorant. They've just been spoon-fed HTI doctrine about an Islamic caliphate, but when they've visited me, they couldn't even tell me when this Islamic caliphate would be established. Shaykh Taqiuddin al-Nabhani said that it would take about 30 years, starting in 1952. That's more than 50 years ago, so where's the caliphate? I think it's just a romantic longing for the past, and has nothing to do with the future. The NU and Muhammadiyah are looking to the future, while HTI is yearning for the past.

Since the people who control these organizations live abroad, does this constitute a threat to the integrity of the Indonesian nation-state?
I think if their movement is successful, this nation will automatically be transformed; there will no longer be a unified nation-state, and no 1945 constitution. Everything will change, because that's their agenda. I think the government should develop a clear policy, and not simply allow [this kind of subversion to spread]. Or maybe the government is promoting this on purpose, and using leftists as a counterbalance. I've heard that on the 27th of June they plan to hold a "Caliphate Congress" in Senayan. This is no child's play they're up to, especially in terms of their financial support. Besides the money they get from local members, they also have support from rich Saudis. That's usually the case with *ahlusunnah* [extremist Sunni] groups, and there are many of them. It's different with the Shi'ites.[11] There are two Shi'ite groups in Indonesia. One is Ijabi,

---

11. [Translator's note: More than 98% of Indonesian Muslims belong to the Sunni branch of Islam. Following the Iranian revolution of 1979, a small number of Indonesians (primarily university students and academics) became Shi'ites. Because of their intellectual abilities, a number of these Shi'ite converts have become widely known and respected in Indonesian society.]

which is pluralistic and moderate, but there's also Elkap, which coordinates closely with *ahl ul-bayt* [literally "people of the house"— i.e., the family of the Prophet—but used here to refer to the *Ahl ul-bayt* World Assembly, which is a propaganda arm of the current Iranian regime], and that one's a bit fundamentalist.

If we examine this from the perspective of religious teachings, do these transnational movements have any significant teachings, or are they just pure political ideologies?
Actually, in terms of religious worship, Sunni [extremist] groups are almost all the same; they're all Wahhabi. They don't like *tahlil*. The most moderate ones aren't actively opposed to *tahlil*, but they won't practice it. The most extreme groups *are* actively opposed to *tahlil*, and all such elements of [Sunni/Sufi] religious tradition. They base their political views on a saying of the Prophet that "Anyone who dies without having sworn allegiance to the caliph, is like one who has died in a state of spiritual ignorance," and condemn such people as having died infidels (*"man maata, walaisa biunukhihi baiah mata mitaatan jahiliyyah"*). This is very intense from a theological perspective. They consider us to be infidels, because we don't follow their ideology. Now if we talk about the Muslim Brotherhood, they quote the hadith, *"Waman la yahkum bima anzalallah, faulaaika humul kaafiruun."* ("Whoever does not observe the law that God revealed, is one of the infidels.") That's their tactic for eliciting support from Muslims. I've attended many Friday sermons where this was preached, and heard it with my own ears. Of course, that's completely different from the NU understanding of Islam.

Look, the NU has to figure out how to create a suitable intellectual response to counter their ideology. This must be discussed and decided in the highest [NU] forum. If the HTI talks about creating *taqwim assakhsiyah islamiyyah*, or a fully Islamic personality, we need to create a counter-response. If HTI talks about how to observe *shari'a* without *tahlil*, this again is different from the NU [and requires a response]. Secondly, their intellectual approach is completely different. People from the NU don't like to argue, but [the extremists] love to fight with words, and call it *ghazwul fikri*, or ideological warfare.

Both of them [HTI and the Muslim Brotherhood] have *ta'amul maklumah*, or social movements. So in effect they operate on multiple levels. One is *ghazwul fikri*, or ideological warfare, while another is *ta'amul maklumah*, and a third is *istilamul hukm*, or the seizure of power. So we need to develop clear and active counter-measures within the NU, to address this threat. We must develop *fikrah nahdliyyah*, or NU ideology, and be clear on just what its goals must be.

They have been successful in recruiting campus youth and intellectuals, to the point of attracting many votes in national and local elections. What is the key to their success?
One factor is the tendency of people today to use inductive reasoning (*istidlali*). They assume that all truth and normative thought must originate from the Qur'an and/or hadith, and if something can't be traced to this source, then it must be wrong. This is a crude and simplistic way of thinking. Other groups are accustomed to using deductive reasoning [*istiqroi*], which entails observation and experimentation to ascertain reality. This style of thought requires time and a high degree of intellectuality, which inductive reasoning does not. 'Look, it's not in the Qur'an, it's *bid'ah!*' That's simple and easy to conclude. But to employ deductive reasoning to arrive at the truth [as practiced by traditional Sunni *ulama*] requires profound logical abilities.

The second reason for their success is that members of long-established Islamic organizations like the NU and Muhammadiyah have a tendency to be corrupt, in my opinion. They're enjoying their thrones, and can't mobilize economic resources very well. The NU has existed for over 80 years, but if you look at its proposals, 90 percent of them are just requesting financial aid. When you see its leaders back-stabbing each other and hopelessly corrupt, there's no way young people will find this attractive, because it's so far from ideal.

A third reason is because our constitution appears unstable and highly dependent on whoever's in power at the moment. During Sukarno's reign, he was president for life. Then Suharto played his games, and everything changed again with the reform era. This is complicated, and the 'rules of the game' keep on changing. This naturally creates disappointment in the younger generation, and makes people think, 'Wouldn't it be better if we adopt Islam as the solution?' Everywhere you look, that's their message. That, and endless talk about international [i.e., Zionist and Western] pressure that's always trying to destroy Islam, which talk evokes a desire to put up resistance.

What does the future hold? Will these transnational movements grow larger, remain stagnant, or begin to shrink in size?
That depends on their sparring partner. If the NU doesn't change or improve the level of its performance, both in terms of its activities and administration, the extremists will grow stronger. But if we become enthusiastic to improve ourselves, and our leadership renounces corruption, I don't think they [the extremists] will succeed. But look at their targets for 2009. The PKS aims to control the vice presidency in '09, and to elect a PKS candidate as president in 2014. Their next test case is the election for governor of Jakarta. Recently, in Banten, their candidate lost. What will happen in Jakarta? If they win, they'll be much closer to their goal. We need to be ready to see our constitution changed [to an Islamic state]. That's what I think.

That's the difference [between transnational groups and Indonesian Islam], because NU and Muhammadiyah leaders were among the founding fathers who established Pancasila [as Indonesia's state ideology]. As a result, the NU and Muhammadiyah have a sense of spiritual unity, linked to the history and continuity of our nation. We have a moral responsibility to defend the Unitary State of the Republic of Indonesia. But to cite a term used by Anis Matta [the PKS secretary general] when I attended one of his campaign events: "We will arrive [in power] as a party that is free of influence or control by people who have preceded us," and he read a poem to that effect. The PKB is still beneath the great shadow of the Nahdlatul Ulama; PAN is still beneath the great shadow of the Muhammadiyah. But PKS arrives without the shadow of elders. "We are the young generation, and do not recognize anyone as having come before us. We are our own predecessor." Ha ha ha....[12] (mkf)

---

12. [Translator's note: Imam Ghozali (who is relatively young himself) laughs, because traditional/Sufi Muslims generally regard guidance from elders as essential for an individual to develop spiritual wisdom and maturity. From this perspective, Anis Matta's self-adulation reflects the arrogance, and ignorance, of one who has never studied at the feet of a spiritual master. On the other hand, the PKS message of "freedom from elders" is calculated to appeal to the ego of its young cadres, who are indoctrinated to believe that their highly politicized understanding of Islam is "complete and perfect," and thus superior to that of their parents and grandparents.]

Taushiya
It's Time to Form a "Pancasila Front," to Uphold NKRI

The government is obliged to obstruct every movement that aims towards separatism, whether expressed in a symbolic form, or through action. If such actions rise to the level of armed rebellion, or secession, the state has a right, indeed an obligation, to declare war. The government, as representative of the state's executive branch, must be responsible for maintaining the nation's sovereignty.

Regarding Aceh, many people have pointed out the flaws contained within the Helsinki Accord, but the government has not wished to listen. Now, the accord is being misused by GAM (the Free Aceh Movement). As for Maluku, from the outset the NU Executive Board has stated that the ethnic conflict in Ambon/Maluku stems from separatism, not religion. As for Papua, the government is too permissive in allowing foreign intervention there.

At present, these three regions are seething, as a result of foreign involvement. It is time for the government to act and no longer twist in the wind. Indonesians must aid their government in maintaining our sovereignty, and it is time we establish a "Pancasila Front to Uphold the Unitary State of the Republic of Indonesia (NKRI)." Its purpose would be to encourage the government to be firm, while also enlightening the Indonesian public in a comprehensive manner. For contemporary threats to Pancasila/ NKRI are not limited to attacks upon our territorial sovereignty, but also consist of ideological, economic and cultural threats to our national integrity. This Front will encourage respect for the rule of law, in order to guarantee our national sovereignty.

Jakarta, 10 July 2007
General Chairman PBNU
KH. Hasyim Muzadi

PBNU: An Islamic Caliphate Would Bring Disaster to Muslim Minorities in Other Countries
Thursday, 26 July 2007 20:04

Jakarta, NU Online
The General Chairman of the Nahdlatul Ulama executive board, Kyai Haji Hasyim Muzadi, regards the idea that every Muslim is obliged to establish an Islamic government (Islamic caliphate) as completely irrational. In his opinion, this will injure minority Muslims living in other countries.

"Consider Japan, for example, where Muslims can't even meet the quorum required for Friday prayer. What if they try to establish an Islamic caliphate? It's impossible. But if they don't, they're told that they're sinners who will go to hell," he said during a "Dialogue Between Islam and State" held in the PBNU headquarters building on Jalan Kramat Raya in Central Jakarta on Thursday (26/7).

The president of The World Conference of Religions for Peace said that a number of erroneous interpretations are circulating among Muslims, regarding the term "*Islam kaffah*" (complete observance of Islam), which is understood to constitute a requirement to establish an "Islamic" government. In his opinion, *shari'a* or Islamic law should indeed be observed, but this need not occur through an Islamic government.

Muslims living anywhere in the world, he continued, are obliged to observe all of Islam's teachings. However, the establishment of an "Islamic" government is *not* one of these religious obligations. A genuine commitment to and practice of Islam does not require an Islamic caliphate. In fact, Muslims have a religious duty to acknowledge and obey whatever legitimate and sovereign government exists [ruling over them].

According to Hasyim, the two largest Muslim organizations in Indonesia, the NU and Muhammadiyah, have never wished nor intended that this nation be built upon the foundation of any one religion's teachings, including Islam.

This guardian of Al-Hikam Pesantren in Malang, East Java, believes that signs of national disintegration can already be seen, as a result of efforts to establish religious laws by force. The latest example is the plan to establish regional regulations for a "Gospel city" in Manokwari, Papua.

"If they have local *shari'a* regulations in Tanggerang, they'll have Gospel laws in Manokwari. This represents a mutual escalation," explained Hasyim, who formerly served as head of the NU's East Java chapter.

The dialogue, whose theme was "The Spirit of Religion within National Politics," was attended by Kyai Haji Ma'ruf Amin; Muhammadiyah Central Board member Yunahar Ilyas; the Deputy Head of the National Intelligence Agency (BIN), As'ad Said Ali; two officials from the Indonesian Council of Churches, Reverend Andreas A. Yewangoe (Chairman) and Reverend Richard M. Daulay (General Secretary); and the Executive Secretary of the Commission for Interreligious Relations at the Conference of Church Representatives (WKI), Father Benny Susetyo. (rif)

PBNU: The Concept of an Islamic Caliphate Has Never Been Clear
Monday, 13 August 2007

Jakarta, NU Online
The Nahdlatul Ulama's executive board (PBNU) today declared that the concept of an Islamic government (Islamic caliphate) has never been clear, in terms of the mechanisms for its establishment and how it should be structured. The only thing clear about the concept, is that those promoting it are engaged in continuous efforts to disrupt and undermine independent and sovereign nations. "This situation isn't surprising," the NU's general chairman told a reporter at PBNU headquarters on Jalan Kramat Raya in Central Jakarta (13/8). "They're doing the exact same thing in Europe, angering host nations whose state constitutions and philosophies are being undermined."

He also explained that not a single country in the entire world has a state or governmental system truly based upon Islam. Even in Muslim-majority countries, systems of government vary. "Even in the Middle East there's no caliphate, only Kingdoms like Saudi Arabia and Jordan, or Islamic Republics like Iran, Syria and Egypt. As a result, Hizb ut-Tahrir is regarded as a serious problem in the Middle East, and Australia as well," Hasyim explained.

According to the president of The World Conference of Religions for Peace, Hizb ut-Tahrir in Indonesia should be carefully monitored, because it will undoubtedly continue the behavior it has displayed elsewhere, which is to undermine and destabilize the Indonesian Republic and its secular foundation.

At the same time, Hasyim also questioned why the government is not acting firmly towards this seditious movement, which clearly poses a threat to the Unitary State of the Republic of Indonesia (NKRI). Both fundamentalism and liberalism are being allowed to run riot.

"All of this (the free rein given to fundamentalism and liberalism) will lead to the destruction of political sovereignty, economic and cultural ruin, and our capitulation to foreign nations in almost every sector," said Hasyim, who is also General

Secretary of the International Conference of Islamic Scholars. (rif)

Mbah Muchith: Our Foundational Principles are not Just for the Sake of Political Issues
Sunday, 17 August 2008 09:14

Jember, NU Online

Every time a new election season approaches, whether national or regional, the NU's foundational principles (*Khittah*) always become an issue. The context of this discussion concerns the proper relationship between the NU and politics, although in reality the NU's foundational principles are far broader.

"Our *Khittah* includes many things, and is far more important than political issues alone," said Kyai Haji Abdul Muchith Muzadi (Mbah Muchith) to *NU Online* at his residence in the Sunan Kalijaga Mosque complex in Jember on Friday (15/8).

The *Khittah* was re-formulated during the 27th NU congress through a long process, in order to help the NU continue traveling on the right track, and transform its goals and aspirations into reality, as well as to avoid constant quarreling among its members, who would thus neglect their real duties.

Strangely enough, however, the successful formulation of the NU's foundational principles was followed by intense argumentation among NU members, and especially top leaders, about how these should be applied. It's no wonder that some people say the NU's *Khittah* often obstructs the smooth functioning of the organization itself.

Mbah Muchith doesn't deny this problem. "Because most NU members don't study the NU *Khittah* seriously, they assume they already know and understand its contents, when in reality they've never read it properly and completely," explained Mbah Muchith.

"Most people have merely heard of it, and never actually read it, much less studied it carefully and deeply," said the Kyai, who is widely-regarded as an expert in the *Khittah*.

Another reason NU members often misunderstand the *Khittah* is because they merely know that the *Khittah* articulated the proper relationship between the NU and practical politics and political parties, while the scope of the NU's foundational principles are far more broad than this.

The NU's *Khittah* controls the NU as a whole, articulating the basic nature and character of moderation and balance, and enjoining good and forbidding evil. The *Khittah* also controls basic principles for understanding the Qur'an and hadith within the context of a traditional jurisprudential approach, the foundations of NU morality, public attitudes and behavior, patriotism and the NU's relationship with the state. In addition, the *Khittah* controls the proper attitude towards individual *ulama*, and the institution/existence of *ulama* in general, and so on. Issues related to politics and political parties are mentioned only briefly in the NU's foundational principles.

"The most important thing is that the NU is a religious community. Every act and step it takes [should] emerge from this religious essence," stressed Mbah Muchith.

According to this *kyai*, who was a direct student of Hadratus Shaykh Hasyim Asy'ari [founder of the NU, and grandfather of Kyai Haji Abdurrahman Wahid], what the *Khittah* says about the relationship between the NU and politics is still being widely misinterpreted. Most people think that the NU should be completely free from politics, or maintain an equal distance from all political parties. In reality, the NU's *Khittah* is not that narrow. "To properly understand the NU *Khittah*, one must also view it (and the issues it governs) within the context of time and place," said Mbah Muchith.

According to Mbah Muchith, who served as personal secretary to Kyai Haji Achmad Sudiq (who in turn authored the fundamental concepts contained in the *Khittah*), this general understanding derives from a thought pattern developed and widely disseminated by Golkar [Suharto's political party] at that time. It was Golkar that depended on this interpretation of the *Khittah*, in order to gain votes in the general election [from NU members, who constitute the single largest voting block in Indonesia]. That is where the idea came from, that the *Khittah* said it was not *wajib* (obligatory) for NU members to vote for PPP [an Islamic political party], nor *haram* (forbidden by Islam) to vote for Golkar.

"A lot of NU people adopted Golkar's way of thinking, because even before the *Khittah* was adopted and socialized by the NU to its own members, Golkar had already been systematically doing this, to the lowest grassroots level of society," explained Mbah Muchith.

In addition, at the time many top NU leaders had issues with that political party [PPP], and what became known as "the deflation of PPP" occurred on a massive scale. According to Mbah Muchith, the *Khittah* does not forbid NU members to be involved in practical politics if they wish. Because the word "not bound" can be translated elastically, sometimes the NU and its members may be closer to a certain party, and more distant from another, not always maintaining an equal distance between political parties. However, if the NU and its membership wish to maintain an equal distance from all political parties, that's ok too.

"Actually, the sentence employed in the actual text of the NU *Khittah* is extremely good, if we bother to read and understand it," stressed Mbah Muchith, who also served as chairman of the Commission to Explain the NU *Khittah* during the NU's national congress held in Bandar Lampung, Sumatra, on 23 January 1992.

At the end of the conversation, Mbah Muchtih pleaded with all NU members, and especially its top leaders, to read the NU *Khittah* once again, and seek to grasp its true meaning. Once they have understood the document, they should strive to develop a *Khittah* personality, which will be reflected in their attitude and behavior no matter where they go, or what their duty. "You shouldn't just "melt" into a new situation wherever you go, changing colors," Mbah Muchith suggested hopefully. (sbh)

Ulama Meet to Exchange Views in a Spirit of Mutual Understanding and Respect
Blocking Transnational Ideology by Strengthening Ahlussunnah wal-Jamâ'ah (Sunni) Traditions
Wednesday, 8 October 2008 11:07

Bogor, NU Online
The bright luster of transnational ideology's rapid spread in Indonesia has attracted special attention from *ulama* (religious clerics) and *habaib* (Indonesians of Arab descent who trace their ancestry to the Prophet Muhammad) in Bogor. According to them, transnational Islamist ideology is incompatible with the culture of Indonesian Muslims, most of whom embrace the *ahlussunnah wal-jamâ'ah* (Sunni Muslim) view of Islam.

That was the primary topic that emerged during a meeting of *ulama* to exchange views in a spirit of mutual understanding, friendship and respect in Pilar village, Bubulak subdistrict, in the West Bogor district of Bogor on Tuesday (7/10).

The meeting was attended by dozens of *ulama* from throughout Bogor. Among those attending were Habib Ahmad Fahmi Al-Aydrus, who is also head of the governing council of Al-Adni mosque in Ciawi, Bogor; Kyai Haji Asep Abdul Wadud, who is a famous *da'i* (Islamic proselytizer) in Bogor; Kyai Haji Ahmad Miftahuddin, who is the head of Arfah Pesantren; and Kyai Haji Yusuf Syafi'i, who serves as advisory chairman of the regional NU chapter in Bogor.

Also attending the event was the former Bogor Regency secretary, who is currently a candidate for Bogor Mayor, H. Dody Rosadi, and thousands of Muslims from local pesantren (*madrasas*) and Bogor's *ta'lim* council.

Habib Fahmi said that many kinds of transnational ideology are growing throughout Indonesia. These encompass a broad spectrum, from Islamic fundamentalism and Wahhabism to liberalism.

According to this charismatic Bogor *habib*, none of these ideologies is compatible with Bogor Muslims' traditional roots, which have always been based upon *ahlussunnah wal-jamâ'ah* (Sunni

Islam) a la NU.

For that reason, Sunni traditions need to be strengthened and preserved, so that new ideologies from abroad cannot grow and entrench themselves in Indonesian society.

Rituals such as honoring the Prophet's birthday, tahlil, isra mi'raj (commemorating the Prophet Muhammad's night journey to heaven); and haul (commemorating the memory of deceased saints), which are fading, need to be restored, because these traditions are deeply rooted in Indonesian culture.

"Traditions developed and preserved by ahlussunnah wal-jamâ'ah (Sunni) ulama have proven to be an effective way to spread Islam peacefully, throughout Indonesia. By strengthening these traditions, we can block transnational ideology [which condemns and rejects them]," he said.

Kyai Haji Asep Abdul Wahud mentioned the same thing. The former chairman of the Nahdlatul Ulama in Bogor Regency said that transnational groups, and especially those spreading Wahhabi ideology, do everything they can to attract followers. They do not even hesitate to condemn others' religious practices as bid'ah, in order to spread their own teachings.

"The methods they're using to expand do not reflect the proper conduct of Islamic proselytism, and they teach that the religious traditions embraced by the majority of Indonesian ulama are wrong," he stressed.

H. Dody Rosadi expressed the same opinion. This leading figure from Bogor is a relative of former PBNU general chairman, the late Kyai Haji Ilyas Ruchiyat. He said that society should respond to extremist infiltration by engaging in positive actions, such as re-strengthening Sunni traditions.

"We do not need to adopt less positive approaches. Let's glean wisdom from this situation, arising from the spread of new ideology. We should realize and always be on guard to preserve the traditions handed down to us by former generations of ulama, and preserve them for coming generations," he said. (hir)

IPNU-IPPNU is Requested to be on Guard Against Transnational Islamist Ideology
Wednesday, 22 October 2008 05:34

Brebes, Cenetral Java, NU Online
As a fortress of strength uniting young people in villages, the NU student organization, IPNU-IPPNU has been requested to guard against transnational Islamist movements that are seeking to interfere with the teaching of *ahlussunnah wal-jamâ'ah* (Sunni) Islam. Their actions are similar to that of worms trying to dig into and bury themselves in wet soil.

"Wherever the NU exists, they're busy transforming the landscape by infiltrating their worms into the wet fields and sucking all the nutrients from the soil," explained Imam Fadillah—a professor from Walisongo Islamic State Institute (IAIN) in Semarang—when delivering a speech at a dialogue with IPNU-IPPNU branch leaders in Brebes sub-district, and *halal bihalal* (occasion to visit and show respect to one another), held at the Department of Religion's auditorium on Tuesday (21/10).

By recruiting the NU's youth cadres, extremists are seeking to eliminate the NU's *ahlussunnah wal-jamâ'ah* teachings as well. Imam Fadillah expressed the hope that the NU's youth cadres would not be influenced by such attempts. The extremists' preaching contains a hidden agenda, which is often linked to a certain political party's activities [i.e., the PKS].

"Their cadres do not hesitate to join NU organizations, but once inside, their only objective is to recruit new adherents to their ideology, and spread slander about *bid'ah* and other allegedly deviant NU practices," he said.

Another speaker, the Chairman of the Maarif Educational Institute branch in the Subdistrict of Brebes, Syamsul Maarif, offered a solution to prevent the further spread of transnational Islamist movements. The Maarif Educational Institute intends to establish an IPNU branch in every school it manages. According to chairwoman of the local IPPNU branch, Nur Imah, a recent IPPNU committee meeting featured a discussion about edition number 23, year XVII (2008) of *Justisia* magazine, which is published by IAIN

Semarang. Present on that occasion was chief editor of *Justisia*, Moh. Nasrudin.

Approximately 150 were present for the discussion and *halal bihalal*, offering their views, each according to his or her own expertise. However, in conclusion, Nasruddin encouraged students to be cautious in choosing their friends and associates, when developing Islam in this land of Pertiwi (the Hindu earth goddess, who is often regarded as the personification of Indonesia). (was)

NU Youths Protest the PKS, for Publishing Advertisement Featuring Mbah Hasyim
Wednesday, 29 October 2008 19:41

Jakarta, NU Online
Young NU members who belong to the NU Youth Generation movement harshly criticized the Justice and Prosperity Party (PKS), for having showcased the Nahdlatul Ulama's founder, Hadratus Shaykh Kyai Haji Hasyim Asy'ari (Mbah Hasyim) in a political advertisement.

In the statement issued from the NU headquarters in Jakarta on Wednesday (29/10), NU Youth Generation—which represents the combined forces of several NU youth organizations, including PMII, IPNU, IPPNU, Ansor, and NU Fatayat—expressed their objection to the misuse of highly revered NU figures, and condemned the PKS for committing "public deception."

They stated that PKS misuse of nationalist figures in a political advertisement will diminish the progress made by these great figures [in creating a secular/nationalist state imbued with spiritual values], in the midst of an unhealthy political situation in Indonesia. "It has the potential to undermine or tarnish the image of any national figure [linked to PKS]," said Adien Jauharudin, one of the leaders of PMII's central board.

The other national heroes used by the PKS for its political advertisement were Sukarno, who proclaimed Indonesian independence from the Dutch, and Kyai Haji Ahmad Dahlan, founder of the Muhammadiyah. The NU Youth Generation demanded that the PKS immediately cease disseminating its inappropriate political advertisements.

The General Chairman of IPNU's central board, Idi Muzayyad, said that his organization will soon send a formal letter of objection to the PKS central board, asking it to stop circulating the political advertisement in question.

"Although it's obvious that the PKS is a Wahhabi movement, while Mbah Hasyim Asy'ari was a Sunni, I think there's a deliberate attempt underway by the PKS to deflect attention from this fact," he said. (min/nam)

Kang ("Older Brother") Said: Sunni Islam is a Stranger to Terrorism
Saturday, 8 November 2008 05:31

Jakarta, NU Online
Ahlussunnah wal-jamâ'ah (Sunni Islam)—the view and teachings of Islam held by the Nahdlatul Ulama—teaches Muslims to embrace tolerant behavior and to renounce violence in settling problems.

"Ahlussunnah is a stranger to violence and terrorism. We are a modern faith community, full of tolerance and moderation, and strive to set a worthy example to other communities," he said in an IPPNU meeting with First Lady Ani Yudhoyono in the Presidential Palace in Jakarta on Friday (7/11).

Kang Said, a nickname for Kyai Haji Said Agil Siradj, said that NU *ulama* are committed to defending Indonesia, as an integral part of their religious duty. Thus, the duty to help Indonesia develop is also a religious duty.

"*Ulama* who wear sarongs (i.e., NU *ulama*) have always strived to establish Indonesia as *darus salam* (a land of peace), not *darul islam* (an Islamic state). On October 22, 1945 they issued a fatwa known as the Jihad Resolution [directed against the Dutch military, which sought to re-colonize Indonesia after WWII], proclaiming that defense of our beloved nation is identical to defending religion," said Kang Said.

The meeting with the First Lady that Kang Said attended was part of the agenda for the IPPNU's Student and General Conference held in Jakarta from 6 - 9 November 2008. (nam)

PMII Requested to Join Efforts Guarding against Transnational Islam
Tuesday, 9 December 2008 07:22

Brebes, NU Online
    The [NU-based] Indonesian Islamic Students Movement (PMII) has been asked to join efforts to guard against movements that seek to undermine and destroy *ahlussunnah wal-jamâ'ah* (Sunni Muslim) faith. This is because transnational Islamist movements originating in the Middle East are very systematic and well organized.
    "As NU cadres, PMII should join efforts to guard against [extremists]," said H. M. Nasrudin—the head of Al Falah Modern Pesantren in Jatirokeh village, in the Songgom subdistrict of Brebes—during a discussion whose theme was "Guarding Against Transnational Islamist Movements," held in RSPD auditorium in Brebes Regency, Central Java, on Saturday (6/12).
    Nasrudin acknowledged that Sunni beliefs—which constitute the belief system held by most Indonesian Muslims—are facing a serious threat from other ideologies. Thus the NU, which firmly upholds Sunni principles, should be on guard against the aforementioned (transnational) movements.
    Employing a systematic and well-structured methodology, these transnational movements easily infiltrate various elements of society, including the NU. It is by no means impossible that sooner or later, a majority of Sunni followers within the NU will fall prey to extremist subversion/recruitment, and become enemies of the NU itself.
    "NU members must be on guard, including the PMII," said Nasrudin. The extremists' activities appear to be smooth and well coordinated. They're still small in number, and create an impression of being good and nice people.
    "It's clear that if anyone is attacking our faith, we must defend it," Nasrudin said, encouraging all those attending the discussion to join this effort.
    The establishment of the NU in 1926 by a number of the most respected *ulama* (religious scholars) in Indonesia was a major

step in efforts to save Sunni Islam [from Wahhabism]. These NU founders intended to prevent transnational Islamist movements, including Wahhabism, from infiltrating and putting down roots in Indonesia. "PMII must stand in the front line, to save Sunni Islam," Nasrudin said emphatically.

The chairman of the local PMII chapter in Brebes, Afifudin El Jupri, said that this discussion was intended to help remind NU cadres about the nature of Sunni principles and faith. As a key element of the Sunni Muslim community, observing and implementing its traditions, PMII has a responsibility to defend the Sunni faith.

"One of the distinguishing characteristics of transnational Islamist movements is their rejection of *tahlil*, *ziarah* (pilgrimage), *barzanji* (praise of the Prophet Muhammad), and the claim that beliefs long held by ourselves and our ancestors are mistaken," said Jupri. (was)

Kang Said: Anti-Tahlil Groups Will Not Triumph
Sunday, 11 January 2009 06:49

Jakarta, NU Online

NU Vice Chairman Kyai Haji Said Agil Siradj has declared that the teachings of Islam will not be embraced by a society, unless they take root within the local culture.

Islam is about far more than doctrine, he said. Past saints and *ulama* have implanted Islamic teachings deep within the culture of Indonesian society. They bequeathed this method of proselytism to all observant Muslims, who later joined to form the Nahdlatul Ulama (NU).

"An ideology will not endure, if divorced from local culture. If it consists only of doctrine, then that ideology or teaching will eventually disappear, or become marginalized. Doctrine must be complemented by human creativity, or what we refer to as culture," said Kang Said, when speaking with *NU Online* at his house in Ciganjur, South Jakarta, on Friday (9/1).

The power of Islam in Indonesia, said Kang Said, rests upon Islamic traditions such as *tahlil*, *haul* (commemorating the memory of saints), *ziarah* (pilgrimage to graves), *selamatan* ceremonies, and celebrating the Prophet Muhammad's birthday. "If there are no such traditions, it's going to be very quiet. Sooner or later, only small groups of people will actually practice Islam, and do so in an uncultured and inhumane manner," he said.

He mentioned that Islamic groups that oppose the traditions long practiced by Indonesian Muslims will have difficulty getting followers. "Groups that are *anti-tahlil*, *anti-Maulid*, and *anti-ziarah* will not be supported," he said.

He added that the debate about Islamic traditions in Indonesia was completely finished, until it resurfaced with a vengeance because of Muslim groups aligning themselves with transnational movements from the Middle East, who enthusiastically attack NU traditions, labeling them as deviant and *bid'ah*.

"Because there are people who want to make trouble once again, we have no choice but to revisit this problem and straighten it out. It was actually all over and done with, back when Sukarno,

Hatta, Wahid Hasyim, Maramis and other prominent figures agreed to establish Indonesia [as a secular state]. But because some Muslims have once again raised the issue of establishing an Islamic state, the relationship between state and religion has again become a hot topic," he said. (nam)

Hasyim: Religion is Often Misused as a Tool for Provocation
Thursday, 5 March 2009 20:01

Rome, NU Online
Discussions about religion and society are never-ending, and continue alongside the growth of society itself. In fact, we live in a world where religion is often misused as a tool for provocation.

The General Chairman of the NU's executive board, Kyai Haji Hasyim Muzadi, said that because religion is often misused, it is often misunderstood as well, or even deliberately misrepresented.

"We live in a world where religion is often misused as a tool for provocation. As a result, religion is often misunderstood, and Islam is no exception," said Hasyim during a speech he delivered to an interreligious dialogue held in Rome, Italy on Wednesday (4/3).

Hasyim mentioned that Islam is often misunderstood because of several factors that have surfaced within the Muslim community itself, and communities outside Islam.

Among the contributing factors from within the Muslim community, said Hasyim, is the existence of a small group of Muslims "who are not yet capable of living exemplary lives, which demonstrate the profundity of Islamic holiness and morality."

"From an external perspective, other communities (outside Islam) view the behavior of such contemporary Muslims as a reflection of Islamic teachings," he said.

The President of the World Conference of Religions for Peace also emphasized the importance of positioning religion as a key source of teachings. Especially in this multicultural world, religions must be able to walk hand-in-hand with humane principles.

Hasyim also mentioned that throughout its 82-year history, the Nahdlatul Ulama (NU) has always propagated the teachings of *ahlussunnah wal-jamâ'ah* (Sunni Islam) as a blessing for all humanity, and will continue to do so. (dar)

Be Careful with Anti-Maulid Propaganda
Monday, 9 March 2009 09:01

Jombang, NU Online

Muslims should be careful and on guard against propaganda that encourages them to stop celebrating *Maulid* (the Prophet Muhammad's birthday). This propaganda has been disseminated via numerous articles posted on the internet, proclaiming that *Maulid* is *bid'ah* and forbidden by Islam.

This was the subject of a symposium entitled "Telaah Shalawat Diba' Kampung" ["An Accurate Analysis of Village Chanting and Praise of the Prophet Muhammad"], held in commemoration of the Prophet Muhammad's birthday in As-Salam Pesantren in Peterongan, Jombang, on Sunday (8/3).

Speaking in front of the assembled students of As-Salam Pesantren, and religious teachers and other inhabitants of the district surrounding the pesantren, Yusuf Suharto—who is the head of Lajnah Ta'lif wan Nasyr NU's (LTN-NU) Jombang chapter—reminded listeners to be wary of websites created by various Muslim groups, that seek to discredit the observances and practice of Islam embraced by most Indonesian Muslims, such as commemoration of the Prophet Muhammad's birthday.

"Reading articles about *shari'a* as it applies to celebrating the Prophet's birthday, we naturally assume we'll obtain valuable additional references concerning the importance of commemorating the Prophet's birth. In fact, the exact opposite occurs, with [extremist websites] claiming that commemoration of the Prophet's birth is a horrific form of *bid'ah* (innovation)," he said.

The instructor from Denanyar Pesantren said that commemorating the Prophet's birth does indeed fall into the category of an "innovation," which did not occur during the Prophet's lifetime. In fact, the practice was still unknown even during the third century of Islam.

"If we examine how this commemoration came about, celebrating the Prophet's birthday can be categorized as a beneficial innovation, or *bid'ah hasanah*. Viewed in terms of its nature and quality, commemoration of the Prophet's birthday (*maulid*) is a positive phenomenon (*hasanah*). Thus our *ulama* have all agreed that the commemoration of the Prophet's birthday falls into the category of *mubah* (permissible) within Islamic jurisprudence, and may even be upgraded to the category of *sunnah* (recommended behavior)," he said.

He explained that commemoration of the Prophet's birthday can strengthen, cleanse and uplift Muslims' hearts—through recitation of the Prophet's life story—for he was the greatest blessing for all humanity.

Secondly, asking that God grant peace and blessings to the Prophet Muhammad (saw.) during the *maulid* celebration is consistent with God's (swt.) proclamation in verse 56 of the chapter al-Ahzab in the Qur'an: "Lo, God and His Angels shower blessings upon the Prophet. Oh ye who believe! Call for (Divine) blessings on him, and salute him with all respect."

NU Views Culture Selectively and Innovatively
Tuesday, 10 March 2009 06:21

Rome, NU Online

The General Chairman of the NU's administrative board, *Kyai* Haji Hasyim Muzadi, stated that the Nahdlatul Ulama always views cultural values in a selective and innovative manner.

According to Hasyim, Islam's historical appearance in Indonesia occurred within a cultural context in which Hinduism, Buddhism and various local belief systems were already well-established, and had been for many centuries.

He acknowledged the existence of cultural values that are entirely consistent with religious teachings, and even function as supporting factors in the dissemination of religion.

"This means that religion can enlighten a community, without having to change its original culture," said Hasyim, while addressing a meeting in Rome not long ago.

On that occasion, the General Secretary of International Conference of Islamic Scholars (ICIS) mentioned that Indonesia's multicultural reality has played an important role in shaping the character of the Nahdlatul Ulama.

Hasyim stressed that the NU's relatively lenient and adaptive attitude towards various cultural values demonstrates that it can establish good relationships with other mass organizations, and with any religion whatsoever.

He also mentioned that the NU's native land, Indonesia, constitutes a mosaic with over 200 different cultures, while in Middle East, a single (Arab) culture is divided into 32 nations. (dar)

Appendix 3

Project Description
from LibForAll Foundation's
2006 Business Plan

Wahhabi Exposé

Radical Muslims are acutely aware that they are engaged in a "battle of ideas" to convince the *ummah*, or worldwide Muslim community, that their extreme ideology is the only valid interpretation of Islam. A key component of their strategy to radicalize traditional Muslims is the establishment and support of indigenous groups that become "carriers" of Wahhabi/Salafi ideology, and seek to marginalize or destroy the more tolerant forms of Islam that have long been predominant in most parts of the Muslim world.

No concerted effort has been made within most Muslim countries to expose these Wahhabi/Salafi proselytization activities, nor to mobilize public support for an alternate, pluralistic and tolerant view of Islam that is at peace with itself and the modern world.

LibForAll Foundation's "Wahhabi Exposé" Project will accomplish exactly that in Indonesia, the nation with the world's largest Muslim population and democracy. It will do so in conjunction with Muslim opinion leaders in the fields of theology, academia, pop culture, government and business, who viscerally oppose the spread of Islamist extremism and its intolerant agenda.

The estimated cost of this 18-month project is $117,985.[1]

Our activities will focus on:

- Hiring a team of researchers from Indonesia's two most prestigious Islamic State Universities, to study the origins, ideology, activities and funding of key Wahhabi/Salafi organizations in Indonesia;
- Presenting the results of this research in the form of a book that will also contain individual chapters written by prominent Indonesian Muslims, who will interpret and put the study results into context. These renowned Muslim authorities will condemn radical ideology, and explain to the Indonesian public exactly how Wahhabi/Salafi groups are

---

1. Note: confronted by numerous difficulties, the project ultimately required two years and nine months to complete, at a cost of approximately $450,000. Extensive in-kind contributions to the project—made by renowned Muslim leaders, including President Wahid—were essential to its success. Cf. the preface by C. Holland Taylor for additional background and details, regarding the challenges LibForAll faced in executing this project.

attempting to destroy traditional Islam;

- Conduct a high-profile public relations campaign spear-headed by prominent Muslim theologians, intellectuals, pop celebrities, politicians and business leaders, designed to bring the study results to the attention of the Indonesian public at large;
- Produce a television documentary highlighting the study's results, and ensure its repeated airing on prime-time TV;
- Document the entire project and translate it into English and Arabic, to provide a role model to other Muslim countries that face a similar onslaught of radical ideology financed by Gulf petrodollars, and a template for executing similar studies in Bangladesh, Pakistan, Turkey, Nigeria, Europe, the U.S. and elsewhere.

Deliverables:
1. Help stem the tide of radical Islam in Indonesia and use it as a "launching pad" from which to stimulate opposition to the Wahhabi/Salafi agenda in the rest of the Islamic world;
2. Mobilize traditional Muslim leadership and masses, who are not yet radicalized, to consciously oppose the spread of militant Islam;
3. Expose and discredit Wahhabi/Salafi proselytization activities, which are a crucial factor in the spread of Islamist extremism worldwide;
4. Establish a proven template for discrediting Wahhabi/Salafi extremism, which can be effectively replicated in Bangladesh, Pakistan, Turkey, Morocco, Nigeria and elsewhere in the Muslim world.

Successful implementation of this project will help stem the tide of radical Islam in the world's most populous Muslim nation and democracy. It will do so by exposing and discrediting Wahhabi/Salafi organizations as enemies of traditional Islam and carriers of a deviant, "Bedouin understanding of religion" inimical to the faith of peace, brotherhood and justice that was revealed by the Qur'an.

This project will help make the Indonesian public aware of, and resist, the dangers of creeping radicalization that threaten local traditions of religious pluralism, tolerance and inter-faith harmony. The results of this project will also serve as a template for the execution of similar studies in the Middle East, South Asia, North- and Sub-Saharan Africa, Europe, North America and elsewhere.

LibForAll Foundation's "Wahhabi Exposé" project is one in a series of programs executed in conjunction with prominent Muslim artists, theologians, educators, businessmen and government leaders, designed to expose hate-filled Islamist ideology as a perversion of Islam—leading to the ultimate rejection of this ideology by the worldwide Muslim community, or *ummah*.

Appendix 4:

PKS Derailed by Wahhabi Issue

Selected News Coverage of Sequence of Events that Led to PKS Being Denied the Vice-Presidential Nomination by Incumbent Indonesian President Susilo Bambang Yudhoyono

April/May 2009

Book Exposes the PKS's Hidden Agenda
Anton Aliabbas | 4 April 2009

INILAH.COM, Jakarta – On the eve of nationwide elections, the political situation is heating up. In fact, a book is now circulating that says the PKS has a hidden agenda. The book is called *The Illusion of an Islamic State: The Expansion of Transnational Islamist Movements to Indonesia*. It was printed in April of 2009 and published by The Wahid Institute, the Bhinneka Tunggal Ika Movement, and Maarif Institute.

A banner list of famous names grace the book's cover and title page. Former President Abdurrahman Wahid is named as the editor, and the prologue was written by the Muhammadiyah's former General Chairman, Prof. A. Syafii Maarif. Ahmad Mustofa Bisri (Gus Mus), the renowned head of Pondok Pesantren Raudlatuth Thalibin in Rembang, provided the book's epilogue

In this 321 page book, the PKS is described as an agent of transnational hardline Islamist movements....

The book states that proselytization activities conducted by the Campus Proselytization Institute (LDK), which later gave birth to the PKS, enjoyed funding from Saudi Arabia. The book's researchers also obtained information that the PKS is actively seeking mosques that need renovation. Funding for said renovation is provided by Saudi Arabia, and local residents asked to support the PKS in every election cycle.

The final part of the book concludes that hardline Islamist movements in Indonesia have close ties to transnational Islamist movements from the Middle East, especially Wahhabis, the Muslim Brotherhood and Hizb ut-Tahrir. These movements' goal, in discrediting Pancasila, is to formalize religion. By using the excuse of 'moral degradation' and corruption, they intend to replace Pancasila with an Islamic state, and transform the Unified National Republic of Indonesia into an international caliphate.

iNilah.Com

INOVASI PORTAL BERITA

| inilah.com | Ekonomi | Politik | Gaya Hidup | Olahraga | Otomotif | Teknologi | Editorial |

| Wawancara | Hukum | Nasional | Sosial | Internasional | Regional |

Rabu, 27 Mei 2009

dan para legislator menuju Senayan

POLITIK

08/04/2009 - 11:26

Buku Memuat Hidden Agenda PKS Beredar

Anton Aliabbas

(Inilah.com /Wirasatria)

INILAH.COM, Jakarta - Menjelang hari H pemungutan suara, situasi politik kian memanas. Bahkan, kini beredar buku yang menyebut adanya agenda terselubung yang dimiliki PKS. Walah.

Buku tersebut bertajuk "Ilusi Negara Islam: Ekspansi Gerakan Islam Transnasional di Indonesia." Buku tersebut tercetak April 2009 yang diterbitkan oleh tiga lembaga yakni The Wahid Institute, Gerakan Bhinneka Tunggal Ika dan Maarif Institute.

Sederet nama beken tertulis dalam buku ini. Mantan Presiden Abdurrahman Wahid tercatat sebagai editor. Sementara prolog diberikan oleh mantan Ketua PP Muhammadiyah, Prof A Syafii Maarif. Sedangkan bagian epilog disajikan pemimpin pondok pesantren Raudlatuth Thalibin, Rembang, Ahmad Mustofa Bisri (Gus Mus).

Dalam buku setebal 321 halaman ini, PKS dituliskan sebagai agen kelompok garis keras Islam transnasional. Dalam melakukan kerjanya, PKS melakukan infiltrasi ke berbagai institusi yang mencakup pemerintahan dan ormas Islam antara lain Nahdlatul Ulama dan Muhammadiyah (halaman 23). Fakta yang mencengangkan adalah adanya fenomena rangkap anggota antara Muhamamdiyah dan kelompok yang disebut garis keras. Diduga hampir 75 persen pemimpin garis keras memiliki ikatan dengan Muhammadiyah.

Sajian data yang ditampilkan dalam buku ini tertulis merupakan hasil penelitian yang dilakukan selama 2 tahun terakhir. Penelitian sendiri dilakukan oleh dua tim. Tim pertama dituai oleh Abdurrahman Wahid yang merupakan peneliti konsultasi dan literatur. Sementara tim kedua yakni tim lapangan dikomandani oleh Prof Dr Abdul Munir Mulkhan (guru besar UIN Sunan Kalijaga).

Penelitian yang dilakukan di 24 kota/kabupaten yang tersebar di 17 provinsi dengan menerjunkan 27 peneliti lapangan. Tidak hanya itu, riset ini melibatkan 591 responden yang diambil dengan sengaja (purposive sampling) yang berasal dari 58 organisasi massa Islam. Profesi responden pun beragam, mulai dari pegawai negeri, dosen, mahasiswa, anggota DPRD hingga pimpinan parpol.

Buku ini menyebutkan aktivitas dakwah yang dilakukan Lembaga Dakwah Kampus (LDK) yang kemudian melahirkan PKS menikmati dana Arab Saudi. Peneliti buku ini melasir adanya informasi PKS sedang mencari masjid-masjid yang sedang direnovasi. Dana rehab tersebut diperoleh dari Arab Saudi. Syaratnya, penduduk setempat diminta mendukung PKS dalam setiap pemilihan.

Pada bagian ahir, penelitian ini menyimpulkan gerakan Islam garis keras di Indonesia memiliki hubungan dengan gerakan Islam transnasional yang berasal dari Timur Tengah terutama Wahabi, Ikhwanul Muslimin dan Hizbut Tahrir. Tujuannya, dengan mendiskreditkan pancasila, gerakan ini berusaha melakukan formalisasi agama. Dengan menggunakan alasan degradasi moral dan keterpurukan bangsa, mereka berniat mengganti Pancasila dengan negara islam dan mengubah NKRI dengan Khilafah Internasional.

Tidak hanya itu, buku ini juga menjelaskan PKAS terkesan menempuh politik bermuka dua dengan menghembuskan isu partai terbuka pada Mukernas d Bali pada tahun

On the Eve of the Election, PKS 'Attacked' by Book
Raden Trimutia Hatta | 8 April 2009

INILAH.COM, Jakarta – A book entitled *The Illusion of an Islamic State: The Expansion of Transnational Islamist Movements in Indonesia* has appeared on the eve of the 2009 elections. This phenomenon is regarded as attacking the PKS, which the book identifies as closely linked to hardline transnational Islamist movements. True?

"The PKS's hidden agenda remains the subject of sharp internal debate [within the PKS itself]. The PK [original] elements of the party truly wish to position Islam as Indonesia's state ideology. They want Indonesia to become an Islamic state," said Burhanuddin Muhtadi, a researcher from the Indonesian Survey Institute who has conducted research on the PKS, in an interview with INILAH. COM held in Jakarta on Wednesday, the 8th of April.

Clearly, that agenda is still in a process of internal transformation within the PKS, which is still debating the relationship between religion and state. But officially, the PKS regards the Unitary State of the Republic of Indonesia (NKRI) as our nation's final form of government, with the party's role being that of "enlivening the state" with the spirit of Islam.

"Many books from the PKS curriculum say that the PKS will reinstate the Jakarta Charter, the Madina Charter. They say that NKRI is final, in order to gain acceptance from the Indonesian public [which rejects calls for an Islamic state]. But if the PKS later comes to power, it is entirely possible they will reactivate that agenda," said Burhanuddin.

Burhanuddin believes that the PKS is not yet able to reveal that true agenda, which remains hidden, because the PKS still has limited power in the field of Indonesian politics. But in reality, that agenda is being revealed, in stages, by PKS cadres who have already reached positions of executive power. "They're still calculating. But they've begun to reveal their agenda. For example, the PKS governor of West Java, Ahmad Heryawan, forbid [the traditional Sudanese] Jaipong dance, and the PKS Mayor of Depok, Nur Mahmudi Ismail, has asked the people of his city to eat and drink with their right hands. Such things demonstrate that PKS cadres intend to establish Islam within the government," he said.

inilah.com | Ekonomi | Politik | Gaya Hidup | Olahraga | Otomotif | Teknologi | Editorial | Pemilu 2009

Rabu, 27 Mei 2009   KLIK! ➡   p e m i l u . i n i l a h . c o m

PEMILU 2009
08/04/2009 - 18:04

Jelang Pemilu PKS 'Diserang' Buku

Raden Trimutia Hatta

Burhanuddin Muhtadi
(dok/Pribadi)

INILAH.COM, Jakarta - Buku berjudul *Ilusi Negara Islam: Ekspansi Gerakan Islam Transnasional di Indonesia* muncul menjelang Pemilu 2009. Hal dianggap akan menyerang PKS yang disebut di buku itu sebagai bagian dari gerakan Islam garis keras transnasional. Benarkah?

"Hidden agenda PKS sampai sekarang masih terjadi perdebatan yang seru di internal. Kalau masih PK (Partai Keadilan, red) memang mereka ingin menjadikan islam sebagai ideologi Indonesia. Mereka ingin menjadikan negara Indonesia bersemangatkan Islam," ujar peneliti LSI yang pernah melakukan riset tentang PKS, Burhanuddin Muhtadi kepada *INILAH.COM* di Jakarta, Rabu (8/4).

Agenda itu, jelasnya, sampai saat ini masih bertransformasi terus di internal PKS antara agama dan negara. Tapi, sekarang ini NKRI masih dianggap final oleh PKS dengan tetap memasukan semangat Islam ke dalam negara.

"Dari buku-buku kurikulum PKS banyak menyebutkan bahwa PKS akan menghidupkan piagam Jakarta, piagam Madinah. Ini strategi dengan menyatakan NKRI final sekarang agar bisa diterima masyarakat Indonesia. Kalau misalnya nanti PKS punya kekuatan besar, bukan tidak mungkin mereka akan menghidupkan agenda itu lagi," katanya.

Burhanuddin menilai, PKS saat ini belum bisa menunjukkan agenda tersembunyinya itu. Sebab, saat ini kekuatan PKS masih minim di kancah perpolitikan Indonesia. Namun sebenarnya, secara perlahan agenda itu mulai ditunjukkan oleh kader-kader PKS yang telah menempati posisi di eksekutif.

"Mereka saat ini masih menghitung. Tapi sebenarnya perlahan agenda itu mulai ditunjukkan oleh mereka. Misalnya, saat Gubernur Jabar Ahmad Heryawan dari PKS melarang tarian Jaipong dan Walikota Depok Nur Mahmudi Ismail dari PKS yang meminta warganya untuk membiasakan makan dan minum dengan tangan kanan. Hal-hal semacam itu menunjukkan kader PKS dalam dirinya memiliki tujuan untuk menerapkan Islam dalam pemerintahan," paparnya.

Namun, hal itu dibantah keras Wasekjen PKS Fahri Hamzah. Menurutnya, PKS itu merupakan organisasi resmi yang sudah 10 tahun terbukti bersih. "Tidak benar itu. Kita tidak ada itu hidden agenda apa-apa," tegasnya. [mut/ton]

PKS Accused of Swallowing the Muhammadiyah
Djibril Muhammad | 8 April 2009

INILAH.COM, Jakarta – The PKS is engaged in massive maneuvers to expand their political base. So massive, that the PKS has been accused of snatching power in the two largest mass Islamic organizations in Indonesia, the Muhammadiyah and Nahdlatul Ulama. Is it true?

"One of the findings revealed in the book is PKS intervention in Muhammadiyah charitable institutions, such as hospitals. In the NU, the PKS is infiltrating mosques," Ahmad Suaedy, Executive Director of The Wahid Institute, explained to INILAH.COM in Jakarta on Wednesday, the 8th of April.

He explained that the object of research studied in the book *The Illusion of an Islamic State: The Expansion of Transnational Islamist Movements in Indonesia* is indeed extremist Muslim groups. This is because the public has grown disgusted by a rising tide of anarchy that stems from religious extremism.

INILAH.COM | Ekonomi | Politik | Gaya Hidup | Olahraga | Otomotif | Teknologi | Editorial | Pemilu 2009

Kamis, 28 Mei 2009   **KLIK!** ➡   p e m i l u . i n i l a h . c o m

INILAH TV   INILAH RADIO   INILAH FOTO   INILAH FORUM   INILAH ARTIS   INILAH INDIE   CITY GUIDE   INILAH KARTUN   KABAR RI

PEMILU 2009
08/04/2009 - 22:37

PKS Dituding Caplok Muhammadiyah

Djibril Muhammad

INILAH.COM, Jakarta - Manuver PKS dalam membesarkan basis politik berlangsung secara sangat masif. Begitu masifnya, sehingga PKS dituding telah mencaplok kekuatan dua organisasi massa Islam terbesar di Indonesia, Muhammadiyah dan Nahdlatul Ulama. Benarkah?

"Salah satu temuan dalam buku adalah intervensi PKS ke amal usaha Muhammadiyah seperti RS. Sedangkan di NU pada masjid-masjid," jelas Direktur Eksekutif The Wahid Institute, Ahmad Suaedy, kepada *INILAH.COM* di Jakarta, Rabu (8/4).

Ia menjelaskan obyek penelitian yang terdapat dalam buku "Ilusi Negara Islam: Ekspansi Gerakan Islam Transnasional di Indonesia" memang kelompok Islam garis keras. Sebab, masyarakat mulai resah dengan kian banyaknya anarkisme yang berlatar belakang agama. Maraknya anarkisme tersebut, kerap menyertakan massa yang besar dan mengidentikkannya dengan PKS karena PKS yang memiliki massa relatif kuat dan besar.

Dalam penelitian itu terangkum bahwa ketika salah satu unit usaha dipegang oleh kader PKS, tutur Suaedy, ada upaya pengalihan dana ke kas PKS. Namun, hal tersebut mendapat reaksi keras dari Pimpinan Pusat Muhammadiyah. "Di Muhammadiyah bahkan sudah mendapat surat teguran. Kalau di NU ada semacam reaksi kultural, walaupun ada penolakan dari masyarakat dan ulama dengan tegas," ujarnya.

Dijelaskan dia, penelitian tersebut tidak hanya dilakukan ke PKS. Tapi juga pada parpol atau ormas Islam lainnya, seperti Hizbuttahrir. Jika dibandingkan dengan parpol lainnya, seperti PPP dan PBB, PKS dinilai lebih serius dalam mengusung syariat Islam. "Secara umum orang meyakini PKS berkuasa akan mengarah perubahan radikal. Tapi tidak mengganti pancasila, karena itu mustahil. Agenda mereka secara ideologis. Itu kecerdikan mereka juga. Berbeda dengan PBB dan PPP yang secara kemampuan. Tapi secara ideologis. Selain itu, PBB dan PPP syariat Islam hanya dagangan," bebernya.

Ia mengatakan, buku tersebut sebenarnya tidak direncanakan untuk Pemilu 2009. Karena rencananya setahun lalu di-*launching*. Jika menimbulkan pro dan kontra, itu merupakan keuntungan buku tersebut. "Artinya mendapat perhatian besar. pro kontra itu biasa. Jadi, tidak ada niat sejak semula menerbitkan sebelum pemilu," ucapnya.

Buku ini merupakan hasil penelitian yang dilakukan antara The Wahid Institute, Maarif Institute dan Gerakan Bhineka Tunggal Ika. Penelitian tersebut dilakukan di 24 kota/daerah yang tersebar di 17 propinsi. Responden sebanyak 591 orang yang ditarik secara sengaja (*purposive sampling*). Penelitian dengan metode wawancara mendalam itu, dilakukan kurang lebih selama 2 tahun. [jib/ton]

PKS: The Book's Accusations are False!
Raden Trimutia Hatta | 8 April 2009

INILAH.COM, Jakarta – On the eve of political elections, the environment is not as calm as some might hope. Attacks on political opponents are still underway. One such assault is currently slamming the PKS, with the publication of a book entitled *The Illusion of an Islamic State: The Expansion of Transnational Islamist Movements in Indonesia*, which identifies the PKS as part of a hardline transnational Islamist movement.

"The accusations in that book are totally false. The PKS is an official organization that has proven itself free of corruption for the past 10 years. Why aren't they attacking other Islamic political parties whose corruption is proven?" demanded PKS Vice Secretary General Fahri Hamzah to INILAH.COM in Jakarta on Wednesday, the 8th of April.

The book's introduction, authored by Abdurrahman Wahid (Gus Dur), states that the PKS was already infiltrating the Muhammadiyah organization at the time of its congress in Malang in 2005. Agents from extremist groups such as the PKS dominated many forums, and succeeded in securing the election of hard-line movement sympathizers to the Muhammadiyah Central Board.

Rabu, 27 Mei 2009   dan para legislator menu

POLITIK
08/04/2009 - 11:35
PKS: Tuduhan Buku Itu Palsu!
Raden Trimutia Hatta

(Inilah.com /Wirasatria)

INILAH.COM, Jakarta - Masa tenang jelang pemilu, ternyata tidak setenang yang diharapkan. Aksi menyerang lawan politik masih terjadi. Salah satunya tengah mengintai PKS dengan terbitnya buku berjudul 'Ilusi Negara Islam: Ekspansi Gerakan Islam Transnasional di Indonesia' yang menyebutkan PKS sebagai bagian dari gerakan Islam garis keras transnasional.

"Tuduhan-tuduhan dalam buku itu semuanya palsu. PKS itu organisasi resmi yang sudah 10 tahun terbukti bersih. Kenapa tidak parpol Islam lainnya yang sudah terbukti tidak bersih saja yang mereka tuduh," ujar Wasekjen PKS Fahri Hamzah kepada INILAH.COM di Jakarta, Rabu (8/4).

Dalam kata pengantar buku itu yang ditulis oleh Abdurrahman Wahid (Gus Dur), memaparkan bahwa PKS telah melakukan infiltrasi ke Muhammadiyah pada Muktamar Muhammadiyah Juli 2005 di Malang. Saat itu, para agen kelompok garis keras seperti PKS mendominasi banyak forum dan berhasil memilih beberapa simpatisan gerakan garis keras menjadi Ketua PP Muhammdiyah.

Fahri membantah tulisan Gus Dur itu. Menurutnya, PKS sebagai organisasi yang legal sudah tercermin dari Anggaran Dasar dan Anggaran Rumah Tangganya yang jelas. "Kita tidak ada itu hidden agenda apa-apa. Kita dibilang telah melakukan infiltrasi ke Muhammadiyah, padahal kita ini kan resmi. Ngawur juga itu orang yang nulis bukunya," katanya.

Ia juga menyatakan bahwa tulisan-tulisan dalam buku itu tidak ada kaitannya dengan sama sekali dengan PKS. "Tolong dibuktikan kalau memang PKS seperti itu. Mereka itu takut, selama ini mereka yang menulis buku itu tapi tidak ada sama-sekali yang meminta konfrontasi dari kita," ungkapnya.

Buku tersebut diterbitkan atas kerjasama Gerakan Bhineka Tunggal Ika, the Wahid Institute dan Maarif Institute. Buku itu merupakan hasil penelitian yang berlangsung lebih dari dua tahun dan dilakukan oleh LibForAll Foundation. Yang menjadi editor dalam buku itu adalah Gus Dur dan yang menjadi penyelaras bahasanya adalah Mohammad Guntur Romli. [mut/ton]

PKS: The Book's Authors are Bush Agents
Raden Trimutia Hatta | 8 April 2009

INILAH.COM, Jakarta – The PKS is strongly rejecting a book entitled *The Illusion of an Islamic State: The Expansion of Transnational Islamist Movements in Indonesia*, which identifies the PKS as part of a hardline transnational Islamist movement. The Islamist proselytization party accuses the book's authors of being agents of former President George W. Bush of the United States.

"My guess is that funding for the book's research came from Bush. It represents Bush's final project, before his fall from power. Because Bush had a policy of waging war against terrorism," the PKS's Vice Secretary, Fahri Hamzah, told INILAH.COM in Jakarta on Wednesday, the 8th of April....

Fahri thinks that the people who wrote the book were chasing after money to buy food. "They're just searching for food, brother. I feel sorry for young people who seek to benefit by manipulating an old man like Gus Dur. Don't chase profit by pitting people against one another. Get your food in a way that's *halal* [legitimate]," he concluded.

INOVASI PORTAL BERITA

Inilah.com | Ekonomi | Politik | Gaya Hidup | Olahraga | Otomotif | Teknologi

Wawancara | Hukum | Nasional | Sosial | Internasional | Regional

Rabu, 27 Mei 2009   dan para legislator menu

POLITIK
08/04/2009 - 12:23

PKS: Penulis Buku, Antek-antek Bush

Raden Trimutia Hatta

Fahri Hamzah
(*inilah.com/ Subekti*)

INILAH.COM, Jakarta - Buku berjudul 'Ilusi Negara Islam: Ekspansi Gerakan Islam Transnasional di Indonesia' yang menyebutkan PKS sebagai bagian dari gerakan Islam garis keras transnasional ditolak oleh PKS. Partai dakwah itu menuding, para penulis buku itu merupakan antek-antek dari mantan Presiden AS George W Bush.

"Dugaan saya, dana riset buku itu didapatan dari Bush. Itu merupakan proyek terakhir Bush sebelum kejatuhannya. Karena Bush memiliki kebijakan perang melawan terorisme," ujar Wasekjen PKS Fahri Hamzah kepada INILAH.COM di Jakarta, Rabu (8/4).

Menurut Fahri, tulisan-tulisan yang ada pada buku itu masih mengacu pada framework dunia saat Bus masih jadi Presiden AS. "Padahal kan framework dunia sudah berbeda dan tuduhan-tuduhan tentang PKS itu semuanya palsu. Saat ini dunia sudah mulai tidak terlalu menyoroti isu terorisme, bahkan dunia sudah menilai Bush sebagai penjahat perang," katanya.

Fahri mengatakan, melalui buku itu antek-antek Bush di Indonesia ingin menunjukkan kepada dunia bahwa di Indonesia itu tidak aman. "Bahwa di Indonesai ini ada kekuatan yang ingin membentuk negara islam dan tidak ada lagi negara Indonesia yang demokratis. Kan ngawur itu yang nulis. Ini jelas dapat menghancurkan Indonesia di mata dunia," ungkapnya.

Fahri menilai, orang-orang yang menulis buku itu hanya mencari makan darai keuntungan yang dihasilkan. "Mereka itu cari makan mas. Kasian saya sama anak-anak muda ini yang cari makan dengan memanfaatkan orang tua seperti Gus Dur. Jangan cari makan dengan mengadu domba orang lain dong, cari makan dengan cara yang halal," pungkasnya.

Dalam kata pengantar buku itu yang ditulis oleh Abdurrahman Wahid (Gus Dur), memaparkan bahwa PKS telah melakukan infiltrasi ke Muhammadiyah pada Muktamar Muhammadiyah Juli 2005 di Malang. Saat itu, para agen kelompok garis keras seperti PKS mendominasi banyak forum dan berhasil memilih beberapa simpatisan gerakan garis keras menjadi Ketua PP Muhammdiyah.

Researcher: The PKS Doesn't Like Our Book
Raden Trimutia Hatta | 8 April 2009

INILAH.COM, Jakarta – The PKS has accused the authors of the book *The Illusion of an Islamic State: The Expansion of Transnational Islamist Movements to Indonesia* of being agents of former American President George W. Bush. But the various researchers involved in the book take said accusations in stride, and joke about them.

"If people don't like [the book], it's natural they would talk that way. But of course it's not true," said the leader of the Yogyakarta team of researchers for the book, Abdul Munir Mulkhan, while speaking with INILAH.COM in Jakarta on the 8th of April.

According to Mulkhan, field researchers encountered the fact that the Muhammadiyah has indeed objected to the presence of the PKS. For that reason, the Muhammadiyah Central Board published Decree Number 149/Kep/I.0/B/2006, to rescue the organization from organized infiltration by political parties such as the PKS.

What is written in the book are facts; before the birth of the PKS, it was Muhammadiyah members who worked in and controlled Muhammadiyah charities. Then the PKS appeared with its doctrines, and is engaged in systematic efforts to seize control of Muhammadiyah charities. Nahdlatul Ulama members also report the same phenomenon.

Munir confirmed a quote from *Voice of Muhammadiyah* magazine, which appears on page 23 of the book, and described how a calm and tranquil Muhammadiyah mosque in the remote village of Sendang Ayu was thrown into chaos because of PKS infiltration, which brought political issues into the mosque. The PKS cadres and their local sympathizers began denouncing other Muslims as infidels, and denigrating other groups, including the Muhammadiyah itself.

Munir added that the Muhammadiyah community as a whole is deeply concerned by the PKS's actions, for the extremist group has been using Muhammadiyah institutions, facilities, members and finances to serve its political interests. "No party in Indonesia has ever won an election without support from the NU and

Muhammadiyah. That's why the PKS is using the Muhammadiyah, to serve its own political interests," explained this senior professor from Sunan Kalijaga Islamic State University in Yogyakarta.

inilah.Com
INOVASI PORTAL BERITA

inilah.com | Ekonomi | Politik | Gaya Hidup | Olahraga | Otomotif | Teknologi

Wawancara | Hukum | Nasional | Sosial | Internasional | Regional

Rabu, 27 Mei 2009

dan para legislator menu

POLITIK
08/04/2009 - 16:14
Peneliti Buku: PKS Tak Suka Buku Kita
Raden Trimutia Hatta

INILAH.COM, Jakarta - PKS menuding penulis buku 'Ilusi Negara Islam: Ekspansi Gerakan Islam Transnasional di Indonesia' sebagai antek-antek mantan Presiden Amerika Serikat George W Bush. Tapi tuduhan itu ditanggapi enteng para peneliti yang terlibat dalam buku tersebut.

"Ya kalau orang yang nggak suka bisa saja mengatakan macam-macam seperti itu. Yang pasti kami tidak melakukan seperti itu," kata Ketua Tim Peneliti Yogya untuk buku itu, Abdul Munir Mulkhan saat berbincang dengan

(inilah.com/ Wirasatria)

INILAH.COM di Jakarta, (8/4).

Menurut Mulkhan, di lapangan itu ditemukan fakta bahwa di kalangan sebenarnya Muhammadiyah itu menolak keberadaan PKS. Untuk itulah, PP. Muhammadiyah sempat menerbitkan SKPP Nomor 149/Kep/I.0/B/2006 untuk menyelamatkan Persyarikatan dari infiltrasi partai politik seperti PKS.

"Yang tertulis di buku merupakan fakta, karena di lapangan sebelum lahirnya PKS warga Muhammadiyah bekerja di lingkungan amal usaha Muhammadiyah. Namun muncul doktrin PKS dan ada usaha dari PKS untuk menguasasi amal usaha Muhammadiyah. Orang NU juga katanya merasa seperti itu," ungkapnya.

Seperti dikutip dalam Suara Muhammadiyah di buku itu (hal 23), Munir menggambarkan, Masjid Muhammadiyah di desa kecil Sendang Ayu yang dulunya damai dan tenang menjadi ribut karena dimasuki PKS yang membawa isu-isu politik ke dalam masjid. Mereka gemar mengkafirkan orang lain dan menghujat kelompok lain termasuk Muhammadiyah.

Mulkhan menambahkan, warga Muhammadiyah merasa prihatin dengan keberadaan PKS sebagai kelompok garis keras yang akan menggunakan institusi, fasilitas, anggota dan sumber-sumber daya Muhammadiyah untuk kepentingan politiknya. "Karena partai di Indonesia tidak pernah menang kalau tidak ada dukungan dari NU dan Muhammadiyah. Untuk itu mereka gunakan Muhammadiyah untuk kepentingan politiknya," jelas Guru Besar UIN Sunan Kalijaga, Yogyakarta ini.

Buku setebal 321 halaman itu diterbitkan atas kerjasama Gerakan Bhineka Tunggal Ika, the Wahid Institute dan Maarif Institute. Buku itu merupakan hasil penelitian yang berlangsung lebih dari dua tahun dan dilakukan oleh LibForAll Foundation. Yang menjadi editor dalam buku itu adalah Gus Dur dan yang menjadi penyelaras bahasanya adalah Mohamad Guntur Romli.

Bagian prolog diberikan oleh mantan Ketua PP Muhammadiyah, Prof A Syafii Maarif. Sedangkan bagian epilog disajikan pemimpin pondok pesantren Raudlatuth Thalibin Rembang, Ahmad Mustofa Bisri (Gus Mus). [mut/ton]

Book Researcher: It's a Fact that the PKS is Extremist!
Raden Trimutia Hatta | 8 April 2009

INILAH.COM, Jakarta – The PKS disputes accusations that it is tied to transnational extremist Islam. Yet the lead researcher of the book entitled *The Illusion of an Islamic State: The Expansion of Transnational Islamist Movements in Indonesia* says that the book's conclusion that the PKS is extremist was derived from facts obtained in the field....

"Our conclusions are based on facts encountered in the field. It's normal that the PKS won't acknowledge this. On the one hand, it's not certain that what happens in the field is known by its central leadership. Then again, it may be part of the PKS's grand strategy," said this senior professor at Sunan Kalijaga Islamic State University in Yogyakarta....

According to Munir, Muhammadiyah members are deeply concerned by the presence of the PKS, an extremist group that is deliberately using the Muhammadiyah's institutions, facilities, members and resources to achieve its own political objectives. "Political parties in Indonesia have never won elections without support from the Nahdlatul Ulama and Muhammadiyah. That's why they're exploiting the Muhammadiyah for their own political interests," he said.

inilah.com | Ekonomi | **Politik** | Gaya Hidup | Olahraga | Otomotif | Teknologi

Wawancara | Hukum | **Nasional** | Sosial | Internasional | Regional

Rabu, 27 Mei 2009   dan para legislator **menu**

POLITIK
08/04/2009 - 14:50
Peneliti Buku: PKS Garis Keras Itu Fakta!
Raden Trimutia Hatta

(inilah.com/ Wirasatria)

INILAH.COM, Jakarta - PKS membantah tuduhan terkait Islam garis keras transnasional. Namun peneliti buku berjudul 'Ilusi Negara Islam: Ekspansi Gerakan Islam Transnasional di Indonesia' menyebutkan kesimpulan PKS garis keras didapat dari fakta di lapangan.

Hal itu diungkapkan oleh Ketua Tim Peneliti Yogya buku itu Abdul Munir Mulkhan kepada INILAH.COM di Jakarta, (8/4). Menurutnya, berdasarkan hasil penelitian timnya di lapangan, menemukan fakta bahwa PKS itu memang merupakan bagian dari gerakan Islam garis keras.

"Kalau saya itu kan menemukan fakta di lapangan. Kalau tidak diakui PKS ya biasa saja. Karena kan dilapangan belum tentu juga diketahui oleh pimpinan pusatnya. Boleh jadi itu sebagai sebuah strategi besar dari PKS," kata Guru Besar UIN Sunan Kalijaga Yogyakarta ini.

Seperti dikutip dalam Suara Muhammadiyah di buku itu (hal 23), Mulkan menggambarkan, Masjid Muhammadiyah di desa kecil Sendang Ayu yang dulunya damai dan tenang menjadi ribut karena dimasuki PKS yang membawa isu-isu politik ke dalam masjid. Mereka gemar mengkafirkan orang lain dan menghujat kelompok lain termasuk Muhammadiyah.

Menurutnya, warga Muhammadiyah merasa prihatin dengan keberadaan PKS sebagai kelompok garis keras yang akan menggunakan institusi, fasilitas, anggota dan sumber-sumber daya Muhammadiyah untuk kepentingan politiknya. "Karena partai di Indonesia tidak pernah menang kalau tidak ada dukungan dari NU dan Muhammadiyah. Untuk itu mereka gunakan Muhammadiyah untuk kepentingan politiknya," ungkapnya.

Buku tersebut diterbitkan atas kerjasama Gerakan Bhineka Tunggal Ika, the Wahid Institute dan Maarif Institute. Buku itu merupakan hasil penelitian yang berlangsung lebih dari dua tahun dan dilakukan oleh LibForAll Foundation. Yang menjadi editor dalam buku itu adalah Gus Dur dan yang menjadi penyelaras bahasanya adalah Mohamad Guntur Romli.

Bagian prolog diberikan oleh mantan Ketua PP Muhammadiyah, Prof A Syafii Maarif. Sedangkan bagian epilog disajikan pemimpin pondok pesantren Raudlatuth Thalibin Rembang, Ahmad Mustofa Bisri (Gus Mus). [mut/ton]

PKS: The Problem of a "Hidden Agenda" is an Outdated Issue
Firmansyah Abde | 9 April 2009

INILAH.COM, Jakarta – The publication of a book entitled *The Illusion of an Islamic State*, which says that the PKS has a 'hidden agenda,' has received a cold reaction from the PKS. The problem is viewed as a decrepit and outdated issue which has already been addressed, and doesn't need to be addressed any further.

Democrat and PKS Parties' Coalition Already Solid
27 April 2009

JAKARTA, KOMPAS.com – Now that several political parties have completed their national meetings, the map of party coalitions is showing a new balance. The Democrat Party, which recently 'divorced' from Golkar, is exhibiting a clearer direction through its coalition with the PKS....

Political Contract

Hilmi Aminuddin stated that the political contract is based on a common platform and agreement between the PKS and Democrat Party. The PKS team, which is led by PKS President Tifatul Sembiring, has been tasked with executing the decision of the PKS's leadership council, which was reached through consensus in a closed forum.

PKS Secretary General Anis Matta said that up to the present time, there has been no obstacle to smooth communication with the Democrat Party.

Wow! Hidayat is a Strong Candidate to Run Alongside (Indonesian president) SBY
30 April 2009

JAKARTA, KOMPAS.com – PKS Central Committee member Hidayat Nur Wahid is considered the most appropriate vice presidential candidate to run alongside Susilo Bambang Yudhoyono of the Democrat Party. This finding was derived from telepolling conducted by LP3ES on the 28th and 29th of April, in a telephone survey involving 1,118 respondents in five large cities.

"The SBY-Hidayat team was chosen by 37.9 percent of respondents, SBY-Akbar Tandjung by 13.2 percent, and SBY-Sri Mulyani by 12.5 percent. These leaders have often been mentioned as candidates to run alongside SBY," said Fajar Nursahid, the head of LP3ES's Research Division, at a discussion in the Antara Building on Thursday, the 30th of April.

Accused of Being a Wahhabi Agent
Hidayat: The PKS and I are not Wahhabis
Reza Yunanto | 29 April 2009

Jakarta – The former President of the PKS, Hidayat Nur Wahid, disputes the rumors which identify both him and the PKS as part of the Wahhabi movement. Such rumors are being used to prevent Muslims from voting for the PKS.

The PKS and I are not Wahhabis," stated Hidayat, after finishing the induction of interim members of the People's Consultative Assembly in the National Legislative Building in Jakarta on Wednesday, the 29th of April.

Telephone Text Messages (Branding) Hidayat a Wahhabi Make the Democrat Party Uneasy
Raden Trimutia Hatta | 29 April 2009

INILAH.COM, Jakarta – Secret telephone text messages saying that former PKS President Hidayat Nur Wahid is a Wahhabi are spreading throughout the general public. In fact, those text messages have already succeeded in making the Democrat Party uneasy about forming an alliance with the PKS....

Hidayat Nur Wahid has acknowledged that many people have received text messages (SMS's) slandering him as a Wahhabi, and anti-NKRI (Unitary State of the Republic of Indonesia). Hidayat has clarified the situation and stated firmly that he is not a Wahhabi. Hidayat took this step because the Democrat Party was in the process of sounding out the PKS, to request that Hidayat provide clarification concerning the text messages in question.

Hidayat: Democrat Party Asked that I Clarify SMS Defamation
Windi Widia Ningsih | 29 April 2009

INILAH.COM, Jakarta – Hidayat Nur Wahid has admitted that many people have been receiving SMS's defaming him as a Wahhabi and enemy of the Unified National Republic of Indonesia. The Democrat Party is in the process of sounding out the PKS, with the result that Hidayat was asked to issue a clarification about the text messages in question.

"I've received SMS's from a number of Democrat Party friends, asking that I address this problem," said the PKS central board member in the National Legislative Building in Jakarta on Wednesday, the 29th of April.

"Personally, I can ignore all this. But I regret if decision-makers reach a decision under the influence of slander. Feel free to make decisions, but not on the basis of character defamation and information that's not factual," said Hidayat.

Democrat Party Seeks Clarification from Hidayat about the Wahhabi Question
Wednesday, 29 April 2009

The political situation on the eve of presidential elections is growing more heated, behind the [façade of] friendly visits conducted by elite politicians. Slander is also circulating, in which one party attacks another.

Such a blow has struck down PKS Governing Board member Hidayat Nur Wahid, who has been widely regarded as a strong candidate to become the vice-presidential running mate of Democrat party leader [and incumbent president] Susilo Bambang Yudhoyono.

eramuslim
Media Islam Rujukan

| BERITA | OASE IMAN | SYARIAH | SUARA LANGIT | USTADZ MENJAWAB | KONSULTASI |

DEPAN > BERITA > NASIONAL

Demokrat Klarifikasi Hidayat Soal Wahabi

Rabu, 29/04/2009 15:08 WIB
🖨 Cetak | ✉ Kirim | 🔊 RSS

Situasi politik menjelang pemilu presiden semakin memanas, selain silaturahmi yang dilakukan para elit politik. Beredar juga SMS fitnah yang menyerang satu sama lain.

Hal ini menimpa Anggota Majelis Syuro PKS Hidayat Nur Wahid yang disebut-sebut akan menjadi pendamping kuat Capres Partai Demokrat Susilo Bambang Yudhoyono.

"Saya misalnya difitnah sebagai penganut Wahabi dan anti NKRI. Saya ingin menegaskan bahwa tidaklah semestinya fitnah-fitnah itu dikembangkan melalui SMS, atau pun melalui beragam pemberitaan," kata Hidayat usai pelantikan penggantian antar waktu anggota MPR, di Gedung MPRRI, Jakarta, Rabu (29/4).

5 TERPOPULER

Kematian Aneh Ratusan Saintis Dunia (1)

Mengapa Daging Babi Haram?

Believe it or Not?

Pejabat dan Diplomat AS Tak Bisa Seenaknya Lagi Masuk Pakistan

Aku Iri Padamu, Ukhti

5 TERBARU

Dakwah Seniman Muslim

Ooops! The Democrat Party is Correcting the PKS's Coalition Draft

Raden Trimutia Hatta | 29 April 2009

INILAH.COM, Jakarta – The PKS has submitted an envelope containing the name of vice-presidential candidates to SBY, and another envelope containing a draft coalition agreement to the Democrat Party's coalition team. At this moment, the draft coalition agreement submitted by the PKS is being corrected by the Democrats.

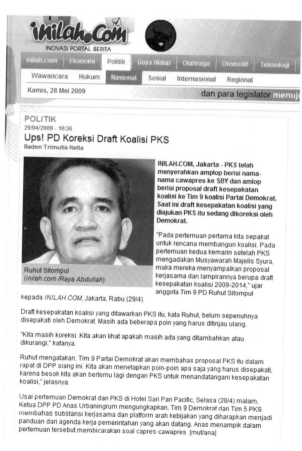

Accused of Being a Wahhabi Follower, Hidayat is Furious
Windi Widia Ningsih | 29 April 2009

INILAH.COM, Jakarta – Hidayat Nur Wahid is furious. The vice-presidential candidate proposed by the PKS as SBY's running mate has been accused of being a political follower of Wahhabism. The Speaker of the People's Consultative Assembly is aggrieved by this impolite political maneuver, which is disseminating slander via SMS's....

According to Hidayat, the slander in question is being spread by telephone text messages and various news reports. And he himself has received those defamatory SMS's in his mobile phone....

"I remind you, a remarkable (campaign) of slander has been directed towards various parties. I want to emphasize, we should not be in such a condition," added the PKS central board member.

Hidayat: Stop the Wahhabi Slanders
29 April 2009

JAKARTA – PKS Central Committee Member Hidayat Nur Wahid has asked all parties to stop the slander which claims that PKS represents an extension of Wahhabi ideology....

In an SMS (telephone text message) that *Republika* newspaper also received, the PKS is branded Wahhabi because its cadres are all Wahhabi agents. The SMS also called upon all Sunni Muslims and members of the Nahdlatul Ulama not to vote for the PKS or PKS cadres in the election. The SMS ended with a request that the recipient forward the message to 10 friends or relatives.

Don't Spread Slander for the Sake of Competition
29 April 2009

Jakarta (ANTARA News) – Hidayat Nur Wahid, Speaker of the People's Consultative Assembly of the Republic of Indonesia, requested that political competition be conducted in an elegant manner, without spreading slander about one's competitors....

"People with political interests at stake in the selection of vice president should compete in a polite and elegant manner. Don't legitimize unethical means," he said....

Hidayat stressed that he could not possibly be a Wahhabi or opposed to the Unified National Republic of Indonesia.

 ANTARANEWS

Hidayat: Jangan Sebar Fitnah Untuk Bersaing

Jakarta (ANTARA News) - Ketua MPR RI Hidayat Nurwahid meminta agar persaingan politik dilakukan dengan cara-cara yang elegan, tidak dengan menyebar fitnah terhadap pesaingnya.

Ketika menerima Ikatan Mahasiswa Muhammadiyah (IMM) di ruang kerjanya di lantai 9 Gedung MPR RI, Senayan, Jakarta, Rabu, Hidayat mengatakan, terlepas dari persoalan Partai Keadilan Sejahtera (PKS) yang mengusulkan dirinya menjadi cawapres mendampingi Susilo Bambang Yudhoyono (SBY), fitnah tidak membantu masyarakat untuk berpolitik dan berdemokrasi secara dewasa.

"Hendaknya pihak-pihak yang memiliki kepentingan terhadap kursi cawapres, bersaing dengan santun dan elegan. Tidak menghalalkan segala cara," katanya.

Ia juga mengungkapkan, terlepas dari siapa pun yang nantinya akan ditunjuk oleh SBY untuk mendampinginya sebagai cawapres, maka keputusan yang diambil basisnya bukanlah fitnah dan disinformasi.

Hidayat mengaku dirinya mendapat laporan bahwa kini banyak beredar layanan pesan singkat (SMS) ke berbagai pihak, termasuk di kalangan wartawan, yang isinya meminta agar SBY tidak memilih Hidayat Nurwahid sebagai cawapres, karena dirinya adalah tokoh Wahabi dan anti-NKRI.

Wahabi merupakan gerakan atau aliran keagamaan dalam Islam yang dikenal "keras", yang dulu pernah berkembang di Arab Saudi. Gerakan Wahabi bertujuan untuk memurnikan ajaran Islam dengan memberantas habis perbuatan kurafat (percaya tahayul), dan syirik (menyekutukan Allah) di kalangan umat Islam.

Hidayat menegaskan, tidak mungkin dirinya Wahabi dan anti-NKRI.

Dalam konteks Wahabi, katanya, Wahabi merupakan paham yang mengharamkan partai politik. "Sementara saya justru menjadi pendiri dan masih aktif dalam kegiatan partai politik, bahkan pernah menjadi Presiden PKS," katanya.

Menurut dia, fitnah seperti itu bukan sekali ini saja dihembuskan. Dalam setiap pemilihan kepala daerah, baik tingkat provinsi maupun kabupaten/kota, fitnah bahwa PKS adalah Wahabi selalu dimunculkan untuk menjegal kader atau calon yang diusung PKS.

Sementara kaitannya dengan NKRI, kata Hidayat, sebagai Ketua MPR tugasnya antara lain menyosialisasikan UUD 45 yang di dalamnya termasuk NKRI.

"Jadi saya juga ikut menyosialisasikan NKRI itu. Jadi mana mungkin saya anti-NKRI," ujarnya.

HNW: I've Been Slandered as Wahhabi and Anti-NKRI
Wednesday, 29 April 2009

Jakarta – After having recently been named as a vice-presidential candidate put forward by the PKS to run alongside Susilo Bambang Yudhoyono (SBY), Hidayat Nur Wahid has been swamped by a deluge of slander. The slander in question is being spread via telephone text messages by various parties, with distribution including journalistic circles as well. The slander aims to prevent SBY from choosing HNW as his vice-president, due to [HNW allegedly] being a Wahhabi leader and enemy of the Unified National Republic of Indonesia.

Hidayat Feels Slandered
Thursday, 30 April 2009

Jakarta, Kompas – In the run-up to the presidential election, many negative accusations are circulating, to attack political opponents. The Speaker of the People's Consultative Assembly (MPR), Hidayat Nur Wahid, also feels slandered by accusations that he is linked to the Wahhabi sect, and opposed to the Unitary State of the Republic of Indonesia [NKRI].

Hidayat made this statement when confronted by reporters after administering the oath of office to interim members of the MPR at the National Assembly Building on Wednesday (29/4).

"For example, I have been slandered as a Wahhabi, and anti-NKRI. I've received SMS's from friends in the Democrat party, asking me to clarify these rumors," he said.

According to Hidayat, the Wahhabis are a Middle East sect that forbids politics as a deviation from true Islam.

KOMPAS
AMANAT HATI NURANI RAKYAT

Berita Utama | Bisnis & Keuangan | Humaniora | International | Opini | Politik & Hukum | Sosok | Nama & Peristiwa | I
Bagian Selatan | Sumatera Bagian Utara | Jawa Barat | Jawa Tengah | Fokus | Muda | Otomotif | Musik | Foto |
Lepas | Lingkungan | Wisata | Telekomunikasi | Swara | Haji 2009 | Nasional | Teknologi Informasi | Pustakaloka | Kc

Hidayat Merasa Difitnah
Ia Diasikan dengan Wahabi dan Anti-NKRI

Kamis, 30 April 2009 | 03:03 WIB

Jakarta, Kompas - Menghadapi pemilu presiden banyak fitnah dikembangkan untuk menyerang lawan politik. Ketua Majelis Permusyawaratan Rakyat Hidayat Nur Wahid pun merasa difitnah sebagai bagian kelompok Wahabi dan juga anti-Negara Kesatuan Republik Indonesia.

Pernyataan itu disampaikan Hidayat saat ditemui pers seusai melantik anggota MPR Pergantian Antarwaktu di Gedung MPR, Rabu (29/4).

"Saya, misalnya, difitnah sebagai Wahabi dan anti-NKRI. Saya mendapat SMS dari kawan-kawan Demokrat minta tolong agar ini diklarifikasi," ujarnya.

Kelompok Wahabi, menurut Hidayat, adalah kelompok di Timur Tengah yang membidahkan dan mengharamkan politik.

Adapun dirinya adalah pendiri partai politik, bahkan pernah menjadi pimpinan partai politik, yaitu sebagai Presiden Partai Keadilan. "Di situ saja fitnah itu mengada-ada," katanya tegas.

Hidayat juga menegaskan bahwa tidak benar kalau dirinya disebut anti-NKRI. Buktinya, saat dirinya memimpin partai pernah melakukan kontrak politik dengan Susilo Bambang Yudhoyonc pada tahun 2004. Salah satu butir kontrak politik itu justru mempertahankan NKRI.

Kini, sebagai Ketua MPR, dirinya pun selalu menyosialisasikan Undang-Undang Dasar 1945 yang di antaranya menegaskan bahwa bentuk negara sebagai hal yang tidak bisa diubah.

"Sekali lagi saya menegaskan, sangatlah elok bila persaingan menuju RI-1 dan RI-2 itu dilakukan dengan cara-cara elegan," ujarnya.

Ketika ditanya siapa yang mengedarkan SMS itu, Hidayat tidak bisa menyebutkan karena dirinya pun mendapatkan SMS itu dari rekan-rekannya dan juga tidak menyebutkan sumbernya.

PKS Views Wahhabi Slander as a Form of Promotion
Raden Trimutia Hatta | 30 April 2009

INILAH.COM, Jakarta – Slandered as a follower of Wahhabi ideology through secret text messages, PKS central board member Hidayat Nur Wahid is furious. Yet the slander is actually making the PKS happy. This Islamic proselytization party even views it as a positive opportunity to promote itself....

According to PKS Deputy Chairman in the Field of Politics, Zulkieflimansyah, the view that Hidayat and the PKS are opposed to the Unified National Republic of Indonesia will generate momentum to prove whether the accusations are true or false.

Hopefully, the momentum to nominate Hidayat as SBY's Vice President will eliminate all such doubts. When SBY chooses Hidayat as his Vice President, that will be the PKS's 'arena of proof.'

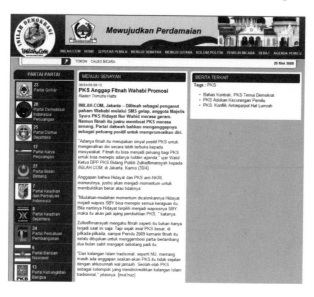

PKS Shaken by Wahhabi Accusations; Democrat Party Uneasy

Windi Widia Ningsih | 30 April 2009

INILAH.COM, Jakarta – The Wahhabi and anti-NKRI vilification that has fallen heavily upon Hidayat Nur Wahid has not only shaken the PKS, but also made the Democrat Party very nervous. In fact, Hidayat believes that the Democrats have been deeply disturbed by the SMS's in question, because he was asked (by them) to provide clarification.

"I also received SMS's from various friends in the Democrat Party who asked my assistance in providing clarification, which means that the slander has disturbed [our relationship]" said Hidayat in the National Legislative Building in Jakarta on Thursday, the 30th of April....

"The PKS is not a foreign creature that just arrived, or suddenly dropped from the sky. The PKS has been active in Indonesia for more than 10 years," he said.

Hidayat also admitted that he was informed by the Democrat Party about 3 days ago, that thousands of SMS's were warning the Democrat Party not to choose Hidayat Nur Wahid [for Vice President] or the PKS, because they follow Wahhabism and are anti-NKRI.

Inilah.com | Ekonomi | Politik | Gaya Hidup | Olahraga | Otomotif | Teknologi | Editorial | Pemilu 2009

Kamis, 28 Mei 2009   dan para legislator menuju Senayan

INILAH TV   INILAH RADIO   INILAH FOTO   INILAH FORUM   INILAH ARTIS   INILAH INDIE   CITY GUIDE   INILAH KARTUN   KABAR

PEMILU 2009
30/04/2009 - 17:59

PKS Digoyang Wahabi, Demokrat Resah
Windi Widia Ningsih

Hidayat Nur Wahid
(inilah.com/ Raya Abdullah)

INILAH.COM, Jakarta - Fitnah soal Wahabi dan anti-NKRI yang menimpa Hidayat Nur Wahid tidak hanya menggoyang PKS tapi juga meresahkan Partai Demokrat. Hidayat bahkan menilai, Demokrat sudah merasa terganggu dengan SMS tersebut, karena dia sampai diminta membuat klarifikasi.

"Saya juga mendapatkan SMS dari teman-teman PD yang meminta tolong untuk diklarifikasi, berarti fintah itu mengganggu," kata Hidayat di Gedung DPR, Jakarta, Kamis (30/4).

Hidayat mengaku merasa heran dengan beredarnya isu tersebut. Sebab, menurut anggota Majelis Syura PKS itu, PKS sudah gamblang sebagai organisasi resmi dengan AD/ART yang dibenarkan oleh hukum yang ada di Indonesia.

"PKS bukan makhluk asing yang baru datang, bukan dari langit yang nggak tahu juntrungannya. PKS sudah hadir di Indonesia lebih dari 10 tahun. Masak nggak kenal juga," ujarnya.

Hidayat juga mengaku diberitahu internal PD sekitar 3 hari yang lalu. Ada ribuan SMS yang mewarning Demokrat jangan memilih Hidayat Nur Wahid atau PKS karena menganut aliran Wahabi dan anti NKRI. [ana]

Does the PKS's Value Depend on the Wahhabi Issue?
R Ferdian Andi R | 30 April 2009

INILAH.COM, Jakarta – While political parties are busy building coalitions, the Wahhabi issue has emerged to attack the PKS. It is obvious that this issue has disrupted the PKS's plans to form a coalition with the Democrat Party. How is the PKS dealing with this?

The Wahhabi issue that has smitten the PKS is actually not a new phenomenon. But because it has now emerged again on the eve of the presidential election, the PKS views it as politically biased. All the more so since the PKS is ambitious to ensure that its cadre, Hidayat Nur Wahid, becomes Susilo Bambang Yudhoyono's vice-presidential running mate. The Wahhabi issue has the potential to severely degrade the PKS's value in the eyes of its coalition partner, the Democrat Party.

Hidayat, a member of the PKS's central board, felt it important to clarify the Wahhabi issue, which the PKS elite regard as defamation. All the more so because complaints appeared from the PKS's potential coalition partner, the Democrat Party. "I received SMS's from Democrat Party friends asking that this problem be clarified," admitted Hidayat in the National Legislative Building in Jakarta on Thursday, the 29th of April.

Not only that, but Hidayat also admitted that he was accused of being anti-NKRI. It was clear that the rumors which were milling about on the eve of a decision to form a coalition between the PKS and Democrat Party made Hidayat nervous and dismayed, both in his private capacity and as a vice-presidential candidate often mentioned as the PKS's potential running mate alongside SBY.

"Personally, I can ignore all this. But I regret if decision-makers reach a decision under the influence of slander. Feel free to make decisions, but not on the basis of character defamation and information that's not factual," said Hidayat. It was clear that these words were directed towards the leadership of the Democrat Party, so that in choosing a vice presidential candidate, SBY's judgment would not be influenced by slander....

A researcher from LSI, Burhanudin Muhtadi, thinks that the

PKS is being highly reactive in confronting the unexpected eruption of the Wahhabi issue. In his opinion, the clarifications offered by various PKS leaders are limited to their immediate political context, and do not address the essence of the public concerns raised by the SMS rumors.

Burhan explained further that if the Wahhabi rumors are believed by the public, it will curtail the acceptability of a vice-presidential candidate put forward by the PKS....

According to Burhan, who also wrote a thesis on the PKS and Social Movements at the Australian National University (ANU), the Wahhabi rumors are in fact true, if one traces the history of the PKS's founding, whose origins lay in the Tarbiyah era....

The PKS elite are naturally angry about the Wahhabi rumors, which have erupted in the middle of coalition talks with the Democrat Party. The emergence of these Wahhabi rumors may serve as a confirmation for the PKS elite, that their recent initiative to transform the PKS into a mainstream and open party have not yet succeeded. Due to these Wahhabi rumors, the value of the PKS has sharply declined. It could well be that because of this Wahhabi issue, the position of vice-presidential candidate, which is so greatly desired by PKS cadres, will fall to someone else.

Kamis, 28 Mei 2009

POLITIK
30/04/2009 - 13:43

Harga PKS Tergantung Isu Wahabi?

R Ferdian Andi R

INILAH.COM, Jakarta – Saat partai-partai politik sibuk membangun koalisi, isu wahabi menyeruak menghinggapi Partai Keadilan Sejahtera. Isu ini jelas menganggu rencana koalisi yang tengah dibangun dengan Partai Demokrat. Bagaimana PKS menyikapinya?

Isu wahabi yang menjangkiti PKS sebenarnya bukan hal baru lagi. Tapi, karena dicuatkan kembali menjelang Pemilihan Presiden, PKS melihatnya sebagai hal yang tendensius. Apalagi, PKS berambisi mengantarkan kadernya, Hidayat Nur Wahid sebagai calon wapres bagi Susilo Bambang Yudhoyono. Isu wahabi dianggap bisa menurunkan harga PKS di depan mitra koalisinya, Partai Demokrat.

Ahmad Mubarok
(inilah.com /Raya Abdullah)

Hidayat, anggota Majelis Syura PKS, merasa berkepentingan mengklarifikasi perihal isu tentang wahabi yang menurut elit PKS mengarah fitnah. Apalagi, komplain muncul dari calon mitra koalisinya, Partai Demokrat. "Saya mendapatkan SMS dari kawan-kawan Demokrat agar masalah ini bisa diklarifikasi," aku anggota Majelis Syura PKS itu di Gedung DPR, Jakarta, Kamis (29/4).

Tidak sekadar itu, Hidayat mengaku dirinya juga disebut sebagai anti-NKRI. Terang saja, rumor yang berseliweran menjelang putusan koalisi PKS dengan Partai Demokrat membuat risau Hidayat, baik dalam kapasitas pribadi maupun sebagai cawapres yang disebut-sebut diajukan PKS untuk mendampingi SBY.

"Bagi saya, itu bisa saya abaikan. Tapi saya kasihan apabila pengambil keputusan mengambil keputusan karena terpengaruh fitnah. Silakan ambil keputusan, tapi isinya jangan memfitnah dan hal-hal yang tidak faktual," imbuh Hidayat. Pernyataan ini jelas tertujukan ke pihak Partai Demokrat agar dalam menggambil cawapres SBY bukan dengan pertimbangan fitnah.

Merespon gundah gulananya Hidayat dan PKS, Wakil Ketua Umum DPP Partai Demokrat Ahmad Mubarok memastikan, jika itu muncul dari personal pengurus Demokrat. "Secara institusional (Partai Demokrat) paham siapa Hidayat Nur Wahid dan PKS. Jadi sama sekali tidak berpengaruh dengan isu wahabi itu. Saya jaminannya," katanya kepada INILAH.COM, Kamis (30/4) di Jakarta.

Meski demikian, Mubarok tidak menampik perihal aspirasi yang masuk salah satunya melalui dirinya, ada resistensi terhadap figur Hidayat jika menjadi pendamping SBY. "Wajar saja aspirasi soal resistensi terhadap figur Hidayat Nur Wahid dan PKS. Karena, gerakan reformis selalu mendapat resistensi," tegasnya.

Peneliti LSI, Burhanudin Muhtadi menilai PKS cukup reaksioner dalam menaggapi isu wahabi yang menerpa. Menurut dia, klarifikasi para petinggi PKS hanya dalam konteks politik, bukan substansi persoalan yang dirumorkan. "Saya menilai reaksi PKS terkesan reaksioner dan dalam konteks politik," katanya.

Lebih lanjut Burhan menilai, jika isu wahabi dipercaya oleh masyarakat maka akan mengurangi akseptabilitas cawapres yang diusung PKS. "Jelas jika isu wahabi dipercaya oleh publik, akan mengurangi kredibilitas dan akseptabilitas cawapres yang diusung PKS," katanya.

Sebagaimana diketahui, SBY dan Partai Demokrat telah membuat lima kriteria cawapres yang bakal mendampinginya dalam Pemilu Preisden mendatang. Lima kriteria tersebut memiliki integritas, kapabilitas, loyalitas, akseptabilitas, dan mampu meningkatkan kekokohan dan efektivitas pemerintahan.

Menurut Burhan yang juga penulis tesis PKS dan Gerakan Sosial di The Autralian National University (ANU), isu wahabi hakikatnya ada benarnya jika dirunut sejarah berdirinya PKS yang dimulai era Tarbiyyah. "Ada benarnya juga rumor tersebut, apalagi jika ditilik dalam sejarah pendirian PKS yang diawali Tarbiyah," jelasnya.

Elit PKS memang patut gusar atas isu wahabi yang santer di tengah pembicaraan koalisi dengan Partai Demokrat. Munculnya rumor wahabi ini seperti mengkonfirmasikan ke elit PKS, ikhtiar PKS beberapa waktu terakhir untuk bergeser menjadi partai tengah dan terbuka belum berhasil. Karena dengan rumor wahabi, harga PKS bakal turun. Bisa-bisa, isu wahabi ini, posisi cawapres yang diimpikan kader PKS jatuh ke pihak lainnya. [I4]

PKS's Destiny Firmly Tied to Wahhabi Issue
R Ferdian Andi R | 30 April 2009

INILAH.COM, Jakarta – In the middle of building a coalition with the Democrat Party, the Islamic proselytization party PKS was shaken by the Wahhabi issue. It is feared that accusations leveled against PKS cadre Hidayat Nur Wahid will become a stumbling block to forming such a coalition. How is the PKS dealing with this?

INOVASI PORTAL BERITA

| Inilah.com | Ekonomi | Politik | Gaya Hidup | Olahraga | Otomotif | Teknologi | Editorial | Pemilu 2009 |

Kamis, 28 Mei 2009   dan para legislator **menuju Senayan**

INILAH TV   INILAH RADIO   INILAH FOTO   INILAH FORUM   INILAH ARTIS   INILAH INDIE   CITY GUIDE   INILAH KARTUN   KABAR

PEMILU 2009
30/04/2009 - 13:45

Nasib PKS Terganjal Isu Wahabi
R Ferdian Andi R

Ahmad Mubarok.
(inilah.com /Raya Abdullah)

INILAH.COM, Jakarta – Di tengah kesibukan PKS membangun koalisi dengan Partai Demokrat, partai dakwah tiba-tiba digoyang isu wahabi. Tudingan yang mengarah pada kader PKS, Hidayat Nur Wahid, ini dikhawatirkan menjadi batu sandungan bagi koalisi itu. Bagaimana PKS menyikapinya?

Isu wahabi yang menjangkiti PKS sebenarnya bukan hal baru lagi. Tapi, karena dicuatkan kembali menjelang Pemilihan Presiden, PKS melihatnya sebagai hal yang tendensius. Apalagi, PKS berambisi mengantarkan kadernya, Hidayat Nur Wahid sebagai calon wapres bagi Susilo Bambang Yudhoyono. Isu wahabi dianggap bisa menurunkan harga PKS di depan mitra koalisinya, Partai Demokrat.

Hidayat, anggota Majelis Syura PKS, merasa berkepentingan mengklarifikasi perihal isu tentang wahabi yang menurut elit PKS mengarah fitnah. Apalagi, komplain muncul dari calon mitra koalisinya, Partai Demokrat. "Saya mendapatkan SMS dari kawan-kawan Demokrat agar masalah ini bisa diklarifikasi," aku anggota Majelis Syura PKS itu di Gedung DPR, Jakarta, Kamis (29/4).

Tidak sekadar itu, Hidayat mengaku dirinya juga disebut sebagai anti-NKRI. Terang saja, rumor yang berseliweran menjelang putusan koalisi PKS dengan Partai Demokrat membuat risau Hidayat, baik dalam kapasitas pribadi maupun sebagai cawapres yang disebut-sebut diajukan PKS untuk mendampingi SBY.

"Bagi saya, itu bisa saya abaikan. Tapi saya kasihan apabila pengambil keputusan mengambil keputusan karena terpengaruh fitnah. Silakan ambil keputusan, tapi isinya jangan memfitnah dan hal-hal yang tidak faktual," imbuh Hidayat. Pernyataan ini jelas tertujukan ke pihak Partai Demokrat agar dalam menggambil cawapres SBY bukan dengan pertimbangan fitnah.

Merespon gundah gulananya Hidayat dan PKS, Wakil Ketua Umum DPP Partai Demokrat Ahmad Mubarok memastikan, jika itu muncul dari personal pengurus Demokrat. "Secara institusional (Partai Demokrat) paham siapa Hidayat Nur Wahid dan PKS. Jadi sama sekali tidak berpengaruh dengan isu wahabi itu. Saya jaminannya," katanya kepada INILAH.COM, Kamis (30/4) di Jakarta.

Meski demikian, Mubarok tidak menampik perihal aspirasi yang masuk salah satunya melalui dirinya, ada resistensi terhadap figur Hidayat jika menjadi pendamping SBY. "Wajar saja aspirasi soal resistensi terhadap figur Hidayat Nur Wahid dan PKS. Karena, gerakan reformis selalu mendapat resistensi," tegasnya.

Peneliti LSI, Burhanudin Muhtadi menilai PKS cukup reaksioner dalam menanggapi isu wahabi yang menerpa. Menurut dia, klarifikasi para petinggi PKS hanya dalam konteks politik, bukan substansi persoalan yang dirumorkan. "Saya menilai reaksi PKS terkesan reaksioner dan dalam konteks politik," katanya.

Lebih lanjut Burhan menilai, jika isu wahabi dipercaya oleh masyarakat maka akan mengurangi akseptabilitas cawapres yang diusung PKS. "Jelas jika isu wahabi dipercaya oleh publik, akan mengurangi kredibilitas dan akseptabilitas cawapres yang diusung PKS," katanya.

Sebagaimana diketahui, SBY dan Partai Demokrat telah membuat lima kriteria cawapres yang bakal mendampinginya dalam Pemilu Preisden mendatang. Lima kriteria tersebut memiliki integritas, kapabilitas, loyalitas, akseptabilitas, dan mampu meningkatkan kekokohan dan efektivitas pemerintahan.

Menurut Burhan yang juga penulis tesis PKS dan Gerakan Sosial di The Autralian National University (ANU), isu wahabi hakikatnya ada benarnya jika dirunut sejarah berdirinya PKS era Tarbiyah. "Ada benarnya juga rumor tersebut, apalagi jika ditilik dalam sejarah pendirian PKS yang diawali Tarbiyah," jelasnya.

Elit PKS memang patut gusar atas isu wahabi yang santer di tengah pembicaraan koalisi dengan Partai Demokrat. Munculnya rumor wahabi ini seperti mengkonfirmasikan ke elit PKS, ikhtiar PKS beberapa waktu terakhir untuk bergeser menjadi partai tengah dan terbuka belum berhasil. Karena dengan rumor wahabi, harga PKS bakal turun. Bisa-bisa, isu wahabi ini, posisi cawapres yang diimpikan kader PKS jatuh ke pihak lainnya. [I4]

Democrats Understand Who the PKS Is
Ahmad Mubarok, R Ferdian Andi R | 1 May 2009

INILAH.COM, Jakarta – The Wahhabi issue has engulfed the PKS when the political party was intensely engaged in forming a coalition. As is well known, the PKS will form a coalition with the Democrat Party and submit its cadre as SBY's vice-presidential candidate. Has this issue disrupted the process?

[Note: Democrat Party Vice-Chairman Ahmad Mubarok faced intense questioning from reporters about the "Wahhabi issue" in the run up to President Susilo Bambang Yudhoyono's selection of a vice-presidential running mate, as reflected in this interview, whose questions all dealt with the Wahhabi issue.]

inilah.Com
INOVASI PORTAL BERITA

inilah.com | Ekonomi | Politik | Gaya Hidup | Olahraga | Otomotif | Teknologi

Wawancara | Hukum | Nasional | Sosial | Internasional | Regional

Kamis, 28 Mei 2009   dan para legislator menuju

WAWANCARA
01/05/2009 - 08:12
Demokrat Paham Siapa PKS
Ahmad Mubarok
R Ferdian Andi R

INILAH.COM, Jakarta - Isu wahabi menyeruak di PKS saat partai politik intensif menggalang koalisi. Sebagaimana diketahui, PKS akan berkoalisi dengan Partai Demokrat dan menyodorkan kadernya sebagai cawapres SBY. Apakah isu ini mengganggu?

Anggota Majelis Syura DPP PKS Hidayat Nur Wahid mengakui pihak Partai Demokrat meminta klarifikasi perihal isu wahabi serta anti-NKRI di tubuh PKS. Isu ini jelas membuat gusar petinggi PKS.

Namun, menurut Wakil Ketua Umum DPP Partai Demokrat Ahmad Mubarok, isu wahabi sama sekali tak merusak komunikasi politik yang kini tengah dibangun antara partainya dengan PKS.

Ahmad Mubarok
(inilah.com /Raya Abdullah)

"Kami paham siapa PKS dan Hidayat Nur Wahid. Saya tahu betul apa ideologi PKS dan apa wilayahnya," tandasnya kepada *INILAH.COM*, Kamis (30/4) di Jakarta. Berikut wawancara lengkapnya:

Anggota Majelis Syura PKS Hidayat Nur Wahid mengkhawatirkan isu soal wahabi bisa mengganggu komunikasi politik yang sedang dibangun dengan Partai Demokrat. Apakah betul pihak Partai Demokrat mengklarifikasi perihal rumor wahabi di PKS?

Itu mungkin ada personal Partai Demokrat yang belum paham. Mungkin saja, yang belum faham saja. Kalau saya faham betul bahwa Hidayat Nur Wahid bukan wahabi.

Perihal SMS dan aspirasi yang masuk ke Anda terkait dengan resistensi publik, jika Hidayat Nur Wahid menjadi cawapres SBY?

Itu wajar saja. Sosok partai militan selalu punya lawan dan kawan. Ini tidak aneh, sepanjang masa. Semua gerakan reformis selalu punya resistensi.

Jadi sama sekali isu wahabi ini tidak mempengaruhi komunikasi politik PKS-Partai Demokrat?

Tidak.

Bagaimana dengan kekhawatiran PKS jika keputusan SBY dan Partai Demokrat dalam memilih cawapres kelak berpijak pada fitnah yang beredar seperti saat ini seperti tentang wahabi?

Insya Allah tidak. Keberatan wajar saja. Bukan hanya soal Hidayat Nur Wahid. Misalnya, SMS yang mohon juru bicara Tim Sembilan jangan Hayono Isman, jangan Ruhut Sitompul, itu juga masuk. Jadi SMS seperti itu biasa saja.

Dengan isu wahabi yang menerpa PKS, apakah secara institusional partai cukup faham?

Wahhabi Issue
Dindin: Hidayat Treated Cruelly
Indra Subagja | 1 May 2009

Jakarta – Hidayat Nur Wahid has been trampled underfoot by extremely unpleasant rumors. News is spreading that he is importing Wahhabi ideology (into Indonesia). Hidayat has raised a stink about these rumors. His objections (to the rumors) are shared by Dindin Hafidudin, whom the PKS once nominated to be its presidential candidate....

Dindin explained that if the accusations were merely intended to create a negative image of Hidayat and the PKS as a whole (that would be bad enough), but it's even worse since Hidayat's name has been prominently mentioned as a potential vice-presidential nominee for SBY.

"These rumors are intended to create dissention among Muslims. That's what they did during the colonial era, to divide Muslims. Their purpose is to destroy Islamic fraternity," explained the professor from the Bandung Institute of Technology.

Jumat, 01/05/2009 10:18 WIB
Isu Wahabi

Didin: Hidayat Dizalimi

Indra Subagja - detikPemilu

Jakarta - Hidayat Nur Wahid diterjang isu tidak mengenakkan. Dia dikabarkan membawa paham wahabi. Hidayat telah menyanggahnya. Hal ini pun dikuatkan Didin Hafidudin, yang pernah dicalonkan menjadi capres oleh Partai Keadilan, cikal bakal PKS.

"Dr Hidayat dizalimi, itu isu tidak benar. Dr Hidayat sama dengan saya dan ulama yang lain. Beliau tokoh moderat, bersih, dan mempunyai toleransi yang tinggi," kata Didin yang mengaku bukan pengurus PKS ini saat dihubungi melalui telepon, Jumat (1/5/1009).

Didin menjelaskan, bila tuduhan itu hanya untuk membuat citra negatif, pada figur Hidayat dan PKS secara keseluruhan, apalagi terkait nama Hidayat yang masuk disebut-sebut masuk dalam nominasi cawapres SBY.

"Isu itu untuk memecah belah kaum muslimin. Itu masa penjajah untuk memecah belah kaum muslim. Isu itu untuk memperburuk ukhuwah islamiyah," jelas guru besar IPB ini.

Dia menegaskan bila PKS sama dengan yang lain seperti NU dan Muhammadiyah. Menurut dia, isu yang mengatakan PKS antimaulid nabi dan Isra Miraj pun tidak benar.

"PKS juga ada yang melakukan Isra Miraj dan maulid, mereka sama dengan yang lain," tutup Ketua Badan Amil Zakat Nasional ini.

Gerakan Wahabi adalah gerakan yang berkembang di Timur Tengah. Gerakan ini salah satu ciri khasnya adalah membid'ah kan dan mengharamkan partai politik. **(ndr / iy)**

Boediono Becomes SBY's Vice-Presidential Nominee
The Democrat Party's Coalition Threatens to Fall Apart; 3 Political Parties Rebel
Arifin Asydhad | 11 May 2009

Jakarta – Although the Democrat Party (PD) disputes the information, politicians who are in coalition with the Democrat Party regard news reports that SBY has chosen [Bank of Indonesia Governor] Boediono to serve as his vice presidential running mate as valid information. A number of political parties, such as PKS, PAN and PPP want to continue negotiations. But if there is no agreement, the three parties may simply abandon the coalition.

This threat emerged, because the [Islamist] political parties supporting the Democrat Party feel they were not accommodated by SBY in selecting a vice-presidential candidate. Besides, these political parties had proposed that SBY select a vice-presidential candidate from the parties supporting his coalition.

detikNews »

Senin, 11/05/2009 23:00 WIB
Boediono Jadi Cawapres SBY
Koalisi PD Terancam Pecah, 3 Parpol akan Membelot
Arifin Asydhad - detikNews

(Foto: Abror Rizki/Istana Presiden)

Jakarta - Meski Partai Demokrat (PD) sudah membantah, namun informasi dipilihnya Boediono sebagai cawapres oleh SBY diyakini para politisi yang berkoalisi dengan PD sebagai informasi yang valid. Sejumlah parpol, seperti PKS, PAN, dan PPP masih ingin ada negosiasi. Bila tidak ada kata sepakat, bisa saja tiga parpol ini keluar dari koalisi.

Ancaman ini muncul, karena parpol-parpol pendukung Demokrat merasa tidak diakomodir oleh SBY dalam penentuan cawapres. Padahal, parpol-parpol ini sudah mengusulkan agar SBY mengambil cawapres dari parpol pendukung koalisi.

"Tapi, ternyata suara parpol tidak didengar. SBY malah mengambil cawapres yang bukan parpol," kata seorang sumber **detikcom** di salah satu parpol tersebut, Senin (11/5/2009) malam.

Saat ditanya bukankah parpol-parpol pendukung SBY sudah menandatangani MoU yang menyerahkan sepenuhnya cawapres kepada SBY, sumber itu mengatakan, penekenan kesepakatan final belum dilakukan. "Kami menyerahkan kepada SBY, tapi kami minta agar cawapres diambil dari parpol," ujar dia.

Signal that PKS Will Leave the Democrat Party
Djibril Muhammad | 13 May 2009

INILAH.COM, Jakarta – The PKS is in the midst of preparing to abandon the coalition formed by the Democrat Party. One clear sign is the PKS's rejection of [SBY's vice-presidential choice] Boediono.

INOVASI PORTAL BERITA

| Inilah.com | Ekonomi | Politik | Gaya Hidup | Olahraga | Otomotif | Teknologi |

| Wawancara | Hukum | Nasional | Sosial | Internasional | Regional |

Kamis, 28 Mei 2009

dan para legislator menuj

POLITIK

13/05/2009 - 11:58

Sinyal PKS Keluar dari PD
Djibril Muhammad

INILAH.COM, Jakarta - Posisi PKS saat ini tengah bersiap-siap untuk keluar dari mitra koalisi yang digagas Partai Demokrat. Salah satu sinyal yang kian terang adalah penolakan PKS terhadap figur Boediono.

"Signal kemungkinan PKS keluar dari PD cukup besar. Sebab PKS mempertanyakan atau meragukan kemusliman Boediono dan itu sudah dipersepsikan hingga ke bawah," jelas Dosen pada Departemen Ilmu Politik Universitas Airlangga (Unair), Hariyadi dalam perbincangannya dengan INILAH.COM di Jakarta, Rabu (13/5).

PKS, menurut dia, memiliki berbagai alasan yang memungkinkan untuk keluar dari koalisi tersebut. Pertama, pasca keluarnya Partai Golkar dalam koalisi dengan PD, membuat PKS memasang harga tinggi. Yakni cawapres dan itu ditolak. Selain itu, perolehan suara PKS dalam pemilu legislatif ini begitu baik di antara mitra koalisi lainnya.

"Jika koalisi pecah terutama PAN-PKS berpotensi untuk menyempal karena kekecewaannya paling tinggi. Partai yang mendapat dukungan lumayan, punya militansi. Oleh karenanya pasang harga tinggi. Jadi 1x24 jam ini akan momen yang krisis," jelasnya.

Kendati begitu, dikatakan dia, PKS bukan partai yang bodoh untuk keluar begitu saja dari koalisi. Sebab, sebelum itu dilakukan, partai berlambang setangkai padi diapit dua bulan sabit itu, akan mempertimbangkan dengan matang.

"Mereka akan berpikir. Bahkan mereka akan menghimpun periset untuk memberikan signal apakah akan keluar atau tidak. Mereka akan melihat SBY-Boediono, kalau masih kuat mereka tidak akan kabur," tandasnya. [jib/ana]

Democrat Party/PDI-P Coalition May Save SBY-Boediono
[from defection by Islamist political parties infuriated by the selection of Boediono as SBY's vice-presidential candidate]
Elvan Dany Sutrisno | 13 May 2009

Jakarta – ....Arbi added that the Islamist parties that are now beginning to abandon the Democrat Party are in a state of chaos and confusion. If they stubbornly maintain their views, they risk losing power.

"Where do they want to run; if they run away they won't share in political power," said Arbi.

"No matter where the PKS might want to run, [political parties] are afraid of [being too closely associated with] them," he explained.

| HOME | BERITA | FOTO | PARPOL | ANGGOTA DEWAN | PETA | GUDANG DATA |

Kamis, 28 Mei 2009   Google   ○ Web   ● detikPemilu

detikPemilu » Pemilu

Rabu, 13/05/2009 07:40 WIB

Koalisi PD-PDIP Dinilai untuk Selamatkan SBY-Boediono

Elvan Dany Sutrisno - detikPemilu

Foto : dok. detikcom

Jakarta - Capres Partai Demokrat (PD), Susilo Bambang Yudhoyono (SBY), dinilai sudah mencium rencana hengkangnya beberapa partai yang menginginkan cawapres pendampingnya diambil dari parpol. Karena itulah, SBY membawa PD merapat ke PDIP untuk 'menyelamatkan' suara SBY-Boediono.

"SBY kan sudah bekerjasama dengan PDIP, sehingga kalaupun kabur, partai Islam tidak akan menjadi masalah bagi PD," tutur pengamat politik dari Universitas Indonesia (UI) Arbi Sanit saat berbincang dengan detikcom, Selasa (12/5/2009).

Menurut Arbi, PD sengaja memberikan banyak janji khusus untuk memikat PDIP. Hal inilah yang kemudian membuat PDIP rela melupakan rakernasnya dan berbalik arah mendukung PD.

"Koalisi dengan PD, PDIP jelas diuntungkan, mereka ditawari banyak hal, termasuk beberapa menteri dan ketua MPR, apa mereka mau 10 tahun menjadi oposisi?" tutur Arbi.

"Konsekuensinya memang berat, ada perdebatan internal, meskipun demikian memberikan hadiah lebih," imbuhnya.

Arbi menambahkan, partai-partai Islam yang mulai meninggalkan PD saat ini dalam keadaan kebingungan. Antara ngotot mempertahankan pendapatnya atau resiko kehilangan kekuasaan.

Does the PKS Feel that SBY Has Treated it like a Pingpong Ball?

Raden Trimutia Hatta | 13 May 2009

Boediono Alters the Coalition Map
R Ferdian Andi R | 14 May 2009 05

INILAH.COM, Jakarta – Unexpectedly, the political parties belonging to the Democrat's coalition have reacted violently to SBY's choice of [nationalist Javanese figure] Boediono as his vice-presidential candidate.

In Fahri's opinion, it is difficult for the PKS to explain Boediono selection as SBY's VP candidate to its constituents. Boediono is from nationalist circles, and the duet SBY-Boediono means there will be no Islamist element on the ticket. "We are sure that this team will damage SBY's reputation in the eyes of Islamic voters," he explained.

Like it or not, the appearance of Boediono as SBY's vice-presidential candidate will alter the national political map on the eve of the registration of presidential candidates on the 16th of May. Although the Democrats say that the [Islamist] parties' reaction is normal, if it is not handled well, the reaction may well become a boomerang for SBY's fortress.

Boediono
[inilah.com /Raya Abdullah]

MENUJU ISTANA

14/05/09 05:56

Boediono Ubah Peta Koalisi

R Ferdian Andi R

INILAH.COM, Jakarta – Di luar dugaan, reaksi keras partai politik peserta koalisi Blok Cikeas membuncah atas pilihan SBY merangkul Boediono sebagai cawapres. Reaksi ini bahkan kini memantik perubahan peta koalisi menjelang Pemilu Presiden 2009.

Reaksi keras parpol pendukung Blok Cikeas tampaknya tak main-main. PKS, PAN, dan PPP sepertinya tak tinggal diam menyikapi keputusan SBY memilih Boediono sebagai cawapres. Jika penjelasan kalangan Demokrat soal Boediono tak memuaskan, mereka pun mengancam hengkang dari Blok Cikeas.

Meski Demokrat dan SBY telah merespons perkembangan terkini dengan mengumpulkan pimpinan partai peserta koalisi di Wisma Negara, Selasa (12/5) malam, sepertinya langkah itu belum menyurutkan protes dari partai politik peserta koalisi. Absennya pimpinan PKS dalam pertemuan di Wisma Negara itu adalah sinyal kuat bahwa PKS serius dalam merepons pilihan SBY terhadap Boediono.

Wakil Sekjen DPP PKS Fahri Hamzah bahkan menilai keputusan SBY dan Demokrat memilih Boediono sebagai cawapres SBY merupakan keputusan sepihak. "Terpilihnya Boediono menjadi ujud cacatnya komunikasi di koalisi ini," tandas Fahri kepada INILAH.COM, Rabu (13/5) di Jakarta.

Menurut Fahri, sulit bagi PKS untuk menjelaskan ke konstituen perihal Boediono sebagai cawapres SBY. Figur Boediono yang dari kalangan nasionalis menjadikan duet SBY-Boediono ini absen dari unsur Islam. "Kami punya keyakinan, pasangan ini akan menjatuhkan reputasi SBY di mata pemilih Islam," terangnya.

Hal tersebut menurut Fahry, berbeda dengan pasangan JK-Wiranto yang merepresentasikan kekuatan Jawa-Non Jawa, Nasionalis-Islamis, serta sipil-militer.

PARTAI-PARTAI

23 Partai Golkar

28 Partai Demokrasi Indonesia Perjuangan

25 Partai Damai Sejahtera

17 Partai Karya Perjuangan

27 Partai Bulan Bintang

7 Partai Keadilan dan Persatuan Indonesia

8 Partai Keadilan Sejahtera

24 Partai Persatuan Pembangunan

6 Partai Barisan Nasional

13 Partai Kebangkitan Bangsa

5 Partai Gerakan Indonesia Raya

20 Partai Demokrasi Kebangsaan

PARTAI LAINNYA

BERITA TERKAIT

Tags : Boediono, SBY, Amien, Demokrat, PKS, PAN

- 'Tamparan' SBY untuk Amien Rais
- Gandeng Boediono, SBY Dinilai Pintar
- 'Boediono Tak Penuhi Kriteria Cawapres'

Appendix 5

Selected Indonesian Media/Internet Coverage of
The Illusion of an Islamic State
as the Book Went Viral
16 May – 4 June 2009

Following the Terrorist Attacks of
17 July 2009 in Jakarta

and the Book's Continuing Impact

Section 1.
Google Results

Google.com

The Indonesian title of the book, Ilusi Negara Islam, consists of a word string whose individual components are among the most common terms in the Indonesian language. Yet these terms had not been sequentially linked, in public usage, prior to the publication of this book. Thus, a Google search for "Ilusi Negara Islam" conducted prior to the book's soft launch on 2 April produced virtually no results. In the weeks that followed, several thousand links to "Ilusi Negara Islam" appeared on the internet.

Following the book's hard launch—which was attended by top religious, political, military, entertainment and media figures—publicity exploded. *The Illusion of an Islamic State* quickly became the most controversial and widely-discussed book in Indonesia, with 556,000 mentions on the internet within three weeks of its hard launch on 16 May. The image below shows Google Search results for the book title, "Ilusi Negara Islam," on 4 June 2009.

| Web History | My Account | Sign out

Google `"ilusi negara islam"` [Search] Advanced Search / Preferences

Web Show options...   Results 1 - 10 of about 556,000 for "ilusi negara islam". (0.23 seconds)

'Ilusi Negara Islam'
The book **Ilusi Negara Islam**: Ekspansi Gerakan Islam Transnasional di Indonesia, The Illusion
of an Islamic State: the Expansion of Transnational Islam.
www.indonesiamatters.com/5453/ilusi-negara-islam/ - Cached - Similar pages

Download Buku **Ilusi Negara Islam** Gratis
karodalnet.blogspot.com — Buku **Ilusi Negara Islam** yang dilucurkan oleh NU dan
Muhammadiyah atau tepatnya The Wahid Institute atau LibForAll Fundation. ...
digg.com/educational/Download_Buku_Ilusi_Negara_Islam_Gratis - Cached - Similar pages

Download Buku **Ilusi Negara Islam**
Download Buku **Ilusi Negara Islam**. indonesia.faithfreedom.org — Aktivitas Saudi di Indonesia
hanya merupakan bagian kecil dari kampanye senilai US ...
digg.com/educational/Download_Buku_Ilusi_Negara_Islam - Cached - Similar pages
More results from digg.com »

QuiGenusHumanumIngenioSuperavit's review of **Ilusi Negara Islam** ...
Ilusi Negara Islam : Ekspansi Gerakan Islam Transnaional di Indonesia by Abdurrahman Wahid
(ed.) 1618324 · QuiGenusHumanumIngenioSuperavit's review ...
www.goodreads.com/review/show/57037080 - Cached - Similar pages

4shared.com - document sharing - download **ilusi-negara-islam**.pdf
Online file hosting and sharing - 5 GB free to store and manage documents, adobe pdf files.
Multiple document upload.
www.4shared.com/file/106253311/5b89bf72/ilusi-negara-islam.html - Cached - Similar pages

hotklix | Download Buku **Ilusi Negara Islam**
Download Buku **Ilusi Negara Islam**. Friend(s) email id: (Separate multiple emails by comma).
Personalised Message. Character limit: 350. Comments. no comments ...
www.hotklix.com/redirect_link/626899 - Cached - Similar pages

'Ilusi Negara Islam' dan Teror « wiwit r fatkhurrahman's weblog - [Translate this page]
Posted by wiwit r fatkhurrahman under Islamic Studies | Tag: agama, Ahmad Syafi'i Maarif, buku,
Buya, download, download buku ilusi negara islam, e-book, ...
wiwitfatur.wordpress.com/2009/05/23/ilusi-negara-islam-dan-teror/ - Cached - Similar pages

- **Ilusi Negara Islam**. Ekspansi Gerakan Islam Transnasional di ...
Ilusi Negara Islam. Ekspansi Gerakan Islam Transnasional di Indonesia by KH Abdulrrahman
Wahid (editor). 321 p. The author writes that transnational ...
www.locjkt.or.id/application/blog/Printer_Friendly.asp?Entry=39 - Cached - Similar pages

Free File Hosting & Video Downloads, Free File Sharing, Online ...
May 21, 2009 ... ilusi-negara-islam.copy.pdf ... Link. http://www.ziddu.com/download/4835110/
ilusi-negara-islam.copy.pdf.html. Site Links ...
www.ziddu.com/download/4835110/ilusi-negara-islam.copy.pdf.html - Cached - Similar pages

Pemilu, Pilpres 2009, Kiprah PKS : Partai Keadilan Sejahtera: Buku ... - [Translate this page]
25 Mei 2009 ... Dijelaskan Zuli Qodir, isi buku '**Ilusi Negara Islam**' bukan merupakan hasil ...
Kata Zuli, tujuan penerbitan buku '**Ilusi Negara Islam**' telah ...
smsplus.blogspot.com/2009/05/buku-ilusi-negara-islam-mengadu-domba.html -
Cached - Similar pages

Goooooooooogle ▶
1 2 3 4 5 6 7 8 9 10 Next

Section 2.
Sample Download Sites

In addition to free downloads being available at the Bhinneka Tunggal Ika Movement website (www.bhinnekatunggalika.org), dozens of Indonesian websites made the book available for free download directly on their sites, demonstrating their desire to "spread the word." At one point, 45 of the top 300 Google results for "Ilusi Negara Islam" offered free downloads of the book in their opening tag line. Given that over 40,000 copies of *The Illusion of an Islamic State* were electronically downloaded from the Bhinneka Tunggal Ika website alone—which was outranked by dozens of other sites on Google and Yahoo—it is likely that hundreds of thousands of Indonesians downloaded copies of the immensely popular and controversial book.

Blog Ajaran – Indonesian blog with 101,976 visitors as of 18 May 2009

"Download the book "The Illusion of an Islamic State" 18 May 2009. In its introduction, this book—which is the result of over two years research—describes the origins, ideology and agenda of transnational extremist movements operating in Indonesia, along with recommendations for building a movement to confront and overcome these extremists in a peaceful and responsible manner."

Blog Indonesia – [Want to] Download the book *The Illusion of an Islamic State?*

Infogue

News—karodalnet.blogspot.com—The book *The Illusion of an Islamic State* was launched by the NU and Muhammadiyah, or more precisely, by the Wahid Institute and LibForAll Foundation. Although newly launched, this 321 page book has already become the subject of widespread polemic, attracting both criticism and high praise. What's really inside the book, *The Illusion of an Islamic State*? Would you like to read its contents? If you're dying of curiosity, download the book *The Illusion of an Islamic State* here. You'll receive a free download without having to pay anything!

Hotklix – Download the Book *The Illusion of an Islamic State*

The book *The Illusion of an Islamic State* was launched by the NU and Muhammadiyah, or more precisely, The Wahid Institute and LibForAll Foundation.

Digg – Download the Book *The Illusion of an Islamic State*

Indonesia.faithfreedom.org – Saudi activities in Indonesia represent just a small portion of a US $70,000,000,000 campaign from 1979 – 2003 to spread its fundamentalist Wahhabi sect throughout the world. Wahhabi proselytization *efforts*, whose funding continues to rise, constitute "the largest global propaganda campaign ever conducted...."

Infotekkom

"Download the Book *The Illusion of an Islamic State* for free. Who says that an Islamic state is only an illusion? The Muslim community is constantly striving to create an Islamic state, so it is not an illusion... The illusion will become a reality." The author and audience of this website fall into the category of "extremist." Their reading/distribution of *The Illusion of an Islamic State* demonstrates the book's effective penetration of extremist groups, who are curious to know its content.

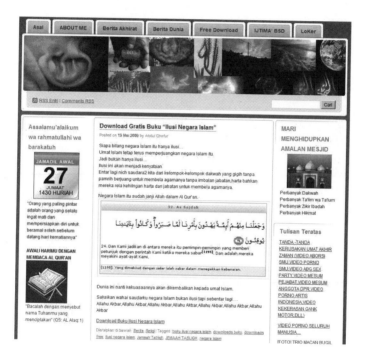

NU Online

Discussion and link to download *Ilusi Negara Islam* posted on the official website of the Nahdlutul Ulama, the world's largest Muslim organization, with 40 million members.

Nusantaraku

Long, favorable review of *Ilusi Negara Islam*, with extensive quotes from the book. "I first received information about this book from Blog Qitori, and further info from Kompas [Indonesia's largest newspaper]. The book appears to have been the subject of intense discussion for several days now, and its contents involve serious investigation of NU and Muhammadiyah circles over the past 4 years..."

Pondok Pesantren al-Badar

Free download of *Ilusi Negara Islam* offered on the website of a pesantren, or Islamic boarding school. "The book entitled *The Illusion of an Islamic State* is clear, stern and explicit in describing the nature and variants of right-wing Islamic groups, that are trying to infiltrate Indonesia. The book contains commentary by leading Muhammadiyah figure Syafii Maarif, and NU leader Kyai Haji Abdurrahman Wahid."

ppindia

"Peace. We just received word from Brother Ahmad Suaedy, Director of the Wahid Institute, that stores wanting to sell the book *The Illusion of an Islamic State* have been terrorized: receiving anonymous telephone threats that they will be attacked, and burnt." Link on a web forum to the Bhinneka Tunggal Ika website, to download the book.

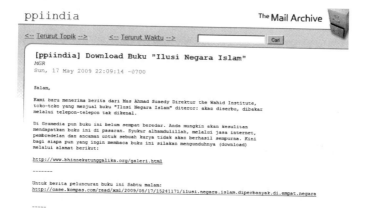

Section 3.
General Media/Internet Coverage

Antara – Book *The Illusion of an Islamic State* to Be Published in Four Nations

Indonesia's official state news agency (Antara) favorably covered the hard launch of *The Illusion of an Islamic State*, and distributed word of the event nationwide on its wire service. As a result, dozens of small and large newspapers throughout Indonesia carried the story on Sunday, 18 May, and many government, military and police websites also posted news of the book online. The Antara story confused *The Illusion of an Islamic State* with LibForAll's *Ocean of Revelations* TV/Video Series in several key regards, but without prejudice to either. The article notes the presence of top government, military and religious officials at the book/video launch.

Buku Ilusi Negara Islam Diperbanyak di Empat Negara

Sabtu, 16 Mei 2009 23:54 WIB | Hiburan | Buku/Novel | Dibaca 1399 kali

Jakarta (ANTARA News) - Buku yang berjudul Ilusi Negara Islam yang menceritakan tentang ekspansi gerakan Islam transnasional di Indonesia, akan diperbanyak di empat negara di dunia yakni Turki, Arab Saudi, Inggris dan Amerika Serikat.

"Saya menilai buku ini sangat bagus karena menceritakan Islam yang sebenarnya," kata C Holland Taylor, pendiri-bersama LibForAll Fundation, saat menghadiri peluncuran buka hasil editorial mantan Presiden RI KH Abdurrahman Wahid (Gus Dur) bersama sejumlah pimpinan Nahdatul Ulama (NU) mantan pimpinan Muhammadyah, di Jakarta, Sabtu malam.

Buku ilusi negara Islam yang merupakan hasil penelitian selama lebih dari dua tahun, mengungkap asal usul, ideologi, dana, agenda dan gerakan transnasional dan kaki tangannya di Indonesia.

Menurut Holland Taylor, buku Ilusi Islam Transnasional itu, adalah suatu ediologi Islam yang membahas tentang kehidupan Islam melalui perjuangan jihad yang diartikan bahwa Islam dengan jihad bukan merupakan kekerasan tetapi Jihad itu adalah usaha yang dilaksanakan oleh kaum muslim dengan cara yang benar tanpa melalui kekerasan.

Buku setebal 321 halaman diterbitkan PT Desantara Utama Media yang bekerja sama dengan LibForAll Fundation, sebuah lembaga non-pemerintah yang memperjuangkan terwujudnya kedamaian, kebebasan, dan toleransi di seluruh dunia yang diilhami oleh warisan tradisi dan budaya bangsa Indonesia.

Holland Taylor mengatakan, masyarakat dunia, masih banyak yang menganggap bahwa Islam itu penuh dengan kekerasan, padahal setelah dirinya mempelajari lebih dalam tentang ajaran Islam ternyata anggapan oleh sebagian orang Islam radikal maupun non Islam tidaklah begitu.

Ia mengatakan buku yang terbitkan dengan melibatkan sejumlah ulama terkemuka di Indonesia seperti, KH Ahmad Safii Maarif (mantan ketua Muhammadyah), KH Mustofa Bisri dan Azyumarrdi Azra dan Romo Franz Magnis Suseno sebagai salah satu penasihat LibForAll.

Buku tersebut menceritakan bahwa Islam sebagai "Rahmatan Lil-Alamin" itu maksudnya adalah siapa pun di seluruh dunia yang berhati baik, berkemauan baik, dan punya perhatian kuat pada usaha-usaha mewujudkan kedamaian, kebebasan dan toleransi secara kultur adalah keluarga Islam yang bersaudara.

Holland yang merupakan orang Amerika Seikat yang cukup mendalam mempelajari Islam di Tanah Air itu menganggap bahwa dengan hadirnya buku ini, akan membuka pikiran pemabacanya yang bukan hanya umat Muslim yang beraliran keras tetapi juga bagi umat non Muslim yang mau tahu tentang kehidupan Islam yang sebenarnya.

"Islam di Indonesia, kami telah membentuk sebuah jejaring para pembuat pendapat dalam bidang agama, pendidikan, budaya populer, pemerintah, bisnis, dan media yang bekerja untuk mempertahankan budaya mereka yang mendorong toleransi antar umat beragama dalam menghadapi gelombang baru ekstremisme yang melanda seluruh dunia Muslim," katanya.

Disamping itu, dengan kerjasama usaha LibForAll di Indonesia untuk mengekspor wajah Islam yang penuh senyum, dengan menghubungkan para pemimpin Muslim "moderat" "dalam sebuah jejaring mercu suar di dalam dunia Muslim yang akan mendorong terciptanya toleransi dan kebebasan berpikir dan beribadah.

Bangka Pos

Newspaper from Bangka Island, off the coast of Sumatra, describing the book's launch and its purpose, with a focus upon the prominent Muslim leaders associated with the book.

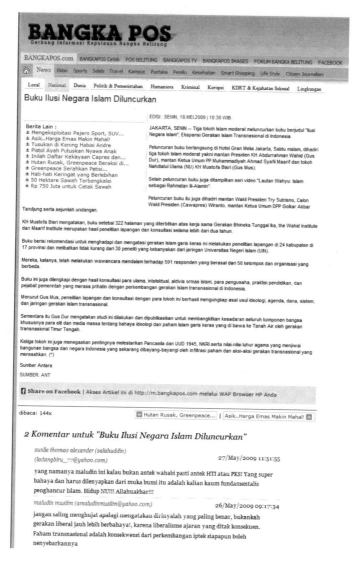

Bersama Toba

Christian publication for ethnic Bataks, whose original homeland is around Lake Toba in North Sumatra, but who now occupy positions of influence in many major cities in Indonesia.

Buntet Pesantren

Long, favorable review posted on the website belonging to a major Islamic boarding school in Cirebon, West Java, with link to electronic download of book.

detikNews – "The Illusion of an Islamic State" is the NU's and Muhammadiyah's Response to the PKS and Hizbut Tahrir

Detik.com, Indonesia's largest web portal, with over 10 million visitors a day, also serves as the country's largest press service, similar to AP or Reuters. Six separate articles appeared on detik. com about *The Illusion of an Islamic State* between 22 and 27 May.

detikNews – Terrorized, Bookstores Don't Want to Sell the Book *The Illusion of an Islamic State*

detikNews – Bookstores Deny They Have Been Terrorized

Note: Indonesia's largest bookstore chain, with over 300 outlets, bought the entire first print run of *Ilusi Negara Islam*, and asked that 10,000 additional copies be delivered ASAP, anticipating that the book would be a runaway best-seller. Within 24 hours, the head of distribution for the chain called back to apologize, stating that their firm had been threatened with physical violence if they sold the book. The company's head of retail operations also confirmed this information to LibForAll CEO Holland Taylor. Because the bookstore chain in question is owned by Christians, they feel particularly vulnerable to extremist threats of violence, while simultaneously not wishing to appear to cave in to it.

detikNews – Hizbut Tahrir: The Book *The Illusion of an Islamic State* is Intolerant

The transnational extremist group Hizbut Tahrir (HT) "regrets" the publication of *The Illusion of an Islamic State* and complains that the book does not value democracy. [Note: HT officially opposes democracy, and seeks to establish a global Islamic caliphate.] HT leader confirms the group's infiltration of the Muhammadiyah and quasi-governmental Indonesian Council of Religious Scholars, but objects to use of the term "infiltration" to describe its activities.

detikNews – Offended, Professors at Yogyakarta Islamic State University Criticize "The Illusion of an Islamic State"

Four individuals (out of more than 30) involved in the book's field research complain publicly about their names being printed in the book. Their objections range from exposure to extremist threats to alleged "manipulation" of their research, and of former Indonesian president Kyai Haji Abdurrahman Wahid, by the "foreign intelligence agent" Holland Taylor of LibForAll Foundation.

detikNews – "The Illusion of an Islamic State's" Publisher Takes Researchers' Criticisms in Stride

Ahmad Suaedy, Executive Director of the Wahid Institute, dismisses the four researchers' complaints.

Directorate General of Islamic Education

Official website of the Directorate General of Islamic Education, Department of Religion, Republic of Indonesia: "Islam is Full of Peaceful Teachings." Favorable review of the book and its launch.

Facebook – Achmad Hasyim Muzadi

Facebook page of Kyai Haji Hasyim Muzadi, current Chairman of the 40-million member Nahdlatul Ulama. Page has posting on, link to, and favorable comments about *Ilusi Negara Islam*.

Facebook – Ilusi Negara Islam

Facebook page created for *The Illusion of an Islamic State*. Note Nahdlatul Ulama Chairman Achmad Hasyim Muzadi as one of its fans.

Forum Kristen – Download

Indonesian Christian website: "Download the book 'The Illusion of an Islamic State,' which reveals the PKS's hidden agenda."

Gerakan Pemuda Ansor – Official Youth Movement of the Nahdlatul Ulama, with 10 Million Members

Ansor's home page features *The Illusion of an Islamic State*, and a link to a full review and downloadable copy of the book.

Gerakan Pemuda Ansor – Official Youth Movement of the Nahdlatul Ulama, with 10 Million Members

Favorable review of *The Illusion of an Islamic State*, with link to download the book.

Ekspresi Hati – Controversy over "The Illusion of an Islamic State"

A friend recently invited me to attend the launch of a book. Its title is *The Illusion of an Islamic State: The Expansion of Transnational Islamist Movements to Indonesia*. The book was published by the Bhinneka Tunggal Ika Movement, The Wahid Institute and Maarif Institute. The copyright is held by a foundation named LibForAll.

From the above-mentioned names, one can easily recognize that this book is being promoted by two legendary Muslim organizations: the NU and Muhammadiyah. In fact, Gus Dur acted at the book's editor (there is no need to question how Gus Dur, who has limited eyesight, could become the editor of a 324-page book)....

Asal | Ekspresi hati | FREE BOOKS ONLINE | About

EKSPRESI HATI

RSS Entri | Comments RSS · Cari

Kill Terror Day

Sehat Sinergis

SEPULUH MAKANAN PENINGKAT DAYA INGAT

Keunggulan Produk Synergy Worldwide, Pro-Argi-9

Masa Depan Bisnis di Synergy Worldwide

Gula Darah Menurun dan Luka Saya Mengering

TIDAK JADI OPERASI DAN TIDAK PERNAH TERASA SAKIT LAGI

DIABETES DAN IMPOTENSI SEMBUH

LUKA SOBEK HILANG TANPA BEKAS

STROKE DAN LUMPUH BISA BERJALAN SENDIRI KEMBALI

AMBEIEN HILANG SAMA SEKALI

LUKA SAYA MEMBAIK

Ketakinan Itu Tidak Pernah Saya Alami Lagi

Sembuh dari Sakit Typus

Alergi Gatal-gatal Ibu Saya Hilang

HIDUP KEMBALI NORMAL SEPERTI DULU

Size Otot Saya Bertambah dari XL Menjadi 2XL

Cari

HATI BERBICARA

PENINGKATAN KDRT DAN PERMASALAHANNYA

Kontroversi "Ilusi Negara Islam"

Posted on Mei 28, 2009 by pcntauli

(Postingan dari milis tetangga AIPI)

Seorang kawan akhir pekan kemarin mengajak menghadiri peluncuran sebuah buku. Judulnya, "Ilusi Negara Islam: Ekspansi Gerakan Islam Transnasional di Indonesia ". Buku tersebut diterbitkan oleh Gerakan Bhinneka Tunggal Ika, The Wahid Institute, dan Maarif Institute. Hak ciptanya dipegang oleh sebuah yayasan yang bernama LibForAll Foundation.

Dari nama-nama tersebut dengan mudah dikenali bahwa buku itu dipromotori oleh dua organisasi keagamaan legendaris: NU dan Muhammadiyah. Gus Dur bahkan bertindak sebagai editor buku (tak usah dipersoalkan bagaimana Gus Dur yang memiliki keterbatasan penglihatan, bisa menjadi editor buku setebal 324 halaman).

Mantan Ketua PP Muhammadiyah, Syafii Ma'arif dan tokoh NU KH Mustofa Bisri ikut menulis pengantar dan penutup dalam buku ini.

Saya sedang dalam proses membacanya, tetapi intisari buku tersebut adalah membeberkan adanya agenda-agenda 'terselubung' sejumlah kelompok, termasuk Partai Keadilan Sejahtera (PKS) yang disebut-sebut hendak mendirikan negara Islam. Kelompok Islam seperti PKS atau Hizbut Tahrir yang dianggap memiliki afiliasi kosmopolitanistik dengan gerakan-gerakan di luar negeri, ditengarai hendak memanfaatkan sistem demokrasi untuk mengubah konstitusi berdasarkan Islam.

Buku ini telah beredar versi soft-copy-nya dan bisa diunduh secara gratis.

Di sebuah milis, ada posting yang agak seru tentang buku ini:

"Kami baru menerima berita dari Mas Ahmad Suaedy Direktur the Wahid Institute, toko-toko yang menjual buku "Ilusi Negara Islam" diteror: akan diserbu, dibakar melalui telepon-telepon tak dikenal.

Di Gramedia pun buku ini belum sempat beredar. Anda mungkin akan kesulitan mendapatkan buku ini di pasaran. Syukur alhamdulillah, melalui jasa internet, pembredelan dan ancaman untuk sebuah karya tidak akan berhasil sempurna. Kini bagi siapa pun yang ingin membaca buku ini silakan mengunduhnya (download) melalui alamat berikut:

http://www.bhinneka tunggalika. org/galeri. html

Sebelum karut marut dalam beberapa hari ke depan, sepertinya kita (jurnalis) perlu berhati-hati menyikapi kontroversi seputar penerbitan buku ini. Di satu sisi kita perlu konsisten mendukung kebebasan akademik (karena buku ini hasil penelitian) dan kebebasan berpendapat; buku harus dibalas dengan buku, dialektika dan argumen harus dibenturkan melebihi benturan fisik.

Tapi di sisi lain, kita tetap harus skeptis terhadap 'dramatisasi' situasi sebagai bagian (misalnya) dari strategi 'pemasaran' buku.

Buku ini sendiri memang berpotensi mengunduh reaksi balik yang keras. Dalam salah satu lampirannya, misalnya, ada:

Surat Keputusan Pimpinan Pusat (SKPP) Muhammadiyah No. 149/KEP/I.0/B/2006, untuk membersihkan Muhammadiyah dari Partai Keadilan Sejahtera (PKS).

Padahal judul resmi SKPP itu adalah: Kebijakan Pimpinan Pusat Muhammadiyah Mengenai Konsolidasi Organisasi dan Amal Usaha Muhammadiyah (yang

Bahwa PKS disebut di poin 3, bunyinya juga tidak ada yang eksplisit menyatakan "membersihkan Muhammadiyah dari PKS". Saya merinding dengan diksi "membersihkan" itu. Teringat 1965: Bersihkan kabinet dari unsur-unsur PKI.

Sementara di lampiran lain, ada himbauan untuk membentuk Front Pancasila Penegak NKRI. Ini mengingatkan saya pada nama nama milisi yang dibentuk di Timor Timur, Aceh, atau daerah konflik lain. Ada aroma permusuhan yang dihembuskan secara kencang melalui pilihan kata, meski barangkali niatnya tak akan sejauh itu.

komunitas synergy world wide

Click to join komunitas_synergyworldwide

Perumahan Bumi Jati Elok

Lokasi dan keindahan Perumahan Bumi Jati Elok

Foto Salah Satu Sudut Pemandangan Perumahan Bumi Jati Elok

Lantai Dasar Rumah Tipe 23/60 Terbuat dari keramik

Beberapa Rumah yang sudah dihuni di Perumahan Bumi Jati Elok

Gambar Jalan di Lokasi Perumahan Bumi Jati Elok

Para Peminat Perumahan Bumi Jati Elok sedang Survei Rumah

Harga Jual Rumah di Perumahan Bumi Jati Elok

Sehatkah Rumah Anda?

Fasilitas Perumahan Bumi Jati Elok TANGERANG BANTEN

Elok, Strategis dan Transportasi Terjangku

Spesifikasi Semua Tipe Rumah Yang Dijual

Contoh Bangunan Rumah Tipe 23/60, DP bisa dicicil

Bagan/ Desain Rumah Tipe 23/60 Perum Bumi Jati Elok

HATI – Enlighten Your Mind

Discussion board with posts and excerpts from *The Illusion of an Islamic State*. Sample post: "Wow, the discussion in that forum is intense. I'm not going to review the book yet. I'll review my brother's novel first. If you want to download [*The Illusion of an Islamic State*], please just go to the adjacent forum [where a link is posted]."

Indonesia Matters

English language website for a domestic and international audience interested in Indonesia. Post contains details on *The Illusion of an Islamic State*, its launch, and a link to download the book.

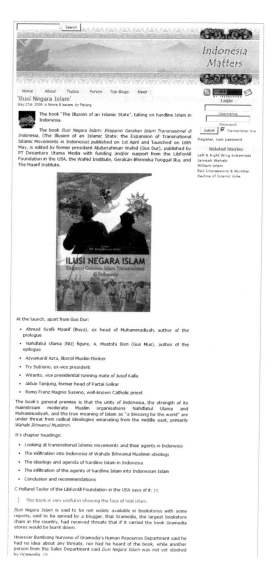

The Jakarta Post – Wahid book on Islamic state under threat

Reports in the Indonesian media about threats to bookstores selling *The Illusion of an Islamic State* found their way into the English-language *Jakarta Post*.

The Jakarta Post

Election 2009   Paper Edition   Weekender   About Us   Contact Us

Home   Headlines   Jakarta   Opinion   National   World   Business   Sports   Sci-Tech   Education   Travel

Monday, June 1, 2009 9:06 PM   Be a member & get the benefits! Register or login

Wahid book on Islamic state under threat

The Jakarta Post , Jakarta | Mon, 05/25/2009 2:38 PM | National

Wahid Institute, an NGO fighting for the enhancement of the country's pluralism, has said some Islamic radical groups have threatened bookstores not to sell a book it had co-published.

Illusion of an Islamic State was launched last week in Jakarta. It was edited by former president Abdurrahman Wahid, and published by Gerakan Bhinneka Tunggal Ika and Maarif Institute along with the Wahid Institute.

"The bookstores reported they have received phone calls threatening to burn the stores if they sell the book," said Ahmad Suaedy, executive director of the Wahid Institute.

"The distributor who has agreed to distribute our book apologized and said they would not take the book anymore."

Suaedy said they should not be afraid of any threats.

"What is really dangerous is that the threat is not coming from the government but from unidentified members of society.

"We welcome anybody who objects to the book. But they must respond in the form of a book also."

The 324-page book is subtitled Expansion of Transnational Islamic Movement in Indonesia. It contains chapters on the infiltration of Wahabi-Ikhwanul Muslimin ideology and the ideology and agenda of the hardliners movement in Indonesia, among others.

One of the book's appendices is a letter from Muhammadiyah - the country's second largest Islamic group - that asked its followers to maintain the solidity of all institutions under the group, and beware of the infiltration of other groups.

Purnama, who was eager to find the book, said after his friends told him they could not find the book in bookstores last Monday, he went directly to the bookstore at the Wahid Institute and bought eight books.

The book cannot be found in the main bookstores in Jakarta, including in Gramedia bookstores.

Bambang Muryono, human resource and public relations manager of Gramedia Publishing, however, said their company had not received any threats about stopping the sales of the Wahid Institute's book.

"We only heard that there were threats from several journalists. We have never received reports of threat from any division.

"All I know about this Islamic State Illusion book is that it hasn't arrived at the bookstores yet."

Bambang said if Gramedia cancelled selling a book in its bookstores then it would be for strong reasons.

"There are some considerations when we decide to sell a book or not. It could relate to the content."

He said the sale of many books' had been prevented before they even arrived at the stores. **(iwp)**

Jakarta Press – "The Illusion of an Islamic State," Like Slapping Water to Catch Fish

"Once again a newly published book has caused a great commotion in our country, namely, *The Illusion of an Islamic State*."

Ilusi Negara Islam, Ibarat Menepuk Air di Dulang

Jakarta Home / Berita / OPINI / [sumber: Jakartapress.com]

Jumat, 22/05/2009 | 23:03 WIB - Dibaca 655 Kali

SATU lagi buku yang menghebohkan yang terbit di tanah air, yakni "Ilusi Negara Islam". Kabarnya buku ini diterbitkan The Wahid Institute, salah satu lembaga swadaya masyarakat (LSM) yang didirikan mantan Presiden RI, KH Abdurahman Wahid (Gus Dur). Buku ini menjadi menarik karena secara langsung atau tidak telah menohok sejumlah ormas Islam, seperti Hizbut Tahir dan juga Partai Keadilan Sejahtera (PKS). Obyek penulisan buku ini adalah tentang sepak terjang kelompok-kelompok Islam yang dianggap penganut garis keras yang kemudian mulai memasuki organisasi-organisasi besar semacam Nahdlatul Ulama (NU) dan Muhammadiyah.

Untuk meyakinkan bahwa buku Ilusi Negara Islam bukanlah buku kacangan, di buku tersebut ditampilkan pendapat para tokoh ternama, seperti mantan Ketua Umum PB Muhammadiyah KH Syafi'i Maarif, KH Abdurahman Wahid, Prof Dr Azumardi Azra, dan Romo Magnis Suseno. Semua tokoh itu melihat atau memandang kehidupan berbangsa dan bernegara, serta beragama sekarang dalam kondisi yang sangat memprihatinkan. Karena munculnya Islam baru yang dianggap telah mengobok-obok kemapanan, yang jika dibiarkan dianggap dapat merusak sendi-sendi kehidupan berbhineka tunggal Ika.

Dalam satu ulasannya Syafii Maarif bahkan menguraikan, keberhasilan Nabi Muhammad SAW hijrah dari Mekah ke Madinah adalah karena adanya sinergi, terjadi harmonisasi, antara umat Islam dan non Islam. Sebagaimana kita ketahui, penduduk Madinah pada saat itu tidak semuanya beragama Islam. Di Madinah terdapat banyak suku bangsa dan banyak penganut agama yang berbeda yang dapat hidup rukun, seperti Nastrani, Yahudi dan lainnya. Ketika Islam datang ke Madinah karena desakan kaum kafir Qurays di Mekah, penduduk setempat yang multi etnis dan agama tersebut dapat menerima kehadiran saudaranya dengan tangan terbuka. Syafi Maarif sengaja mengungkit masalah ini adalah untuk menggetuk hati kita, umat Islam yang dianggapnya sekarang tengah berilusi untuk mendirikan Negara Islam.

Pertanyaan dan persoalannya adalah apakah benar tudingan para tokoh tersebut bahwa sejumlah ormas dan kelompok Islam garis keras tengah berangan-angan mendirikan Negara Islam? Adalah sebuah kewajaran, ketika orang beragama fanatik terhadap agama yang dianutnya. Yang tidak dianjurkan dan dilarang adalah jika fanatisme itu mengarah kepada radikalisme. Misalnya, ketika sekelompok orang harus menghancurkan atau memusnahkan kelompok lainnya, hanya karena pandangan yang berbeda, seperti perang bebuyutan antara Irlandia Utara dan Inggris, karena yang satu Katholik dan lainnya Kristen (Protestan). Atau juga antara kaum Syiah dan Sunni yang jarang akur, hanya karena pandangan dan asumsi yang berbeda dalam meyakini sesuatu yang sebenarnya bukanlah keyakinan pokok.

Di Indonesia, tidak terkecuali, adanya kelompok yang ingin memurnikan ajaran Islam, kita juga anggap sebagai kewajaran dan merupakan sisi lain dari kehidupan beragama yang tidak dapat kita abaikan begitu saja. Asalkan keinginan itu bukan dilakukan dengan cara pemaksaan dari satu kelompok kepada kelompok lainnya, tetapi keinginan tersebut dilakukan dengan memberi keteladanan dan contoh yang positif. Misalnya, ketika kita melihat ada musibah, dan ada saudara kita yang terkena musibah, dengan cepat kita memberikan pertolongan. Ketika ada saudara kita yang kelaparan, dengan segera kita memberikan bantuan makanan yang mereka butuhkan. Ketika ada orang yang meminta pertolongan, sesegera mungkin kita berikan pertolongan. Jika ini yang kita lakukan, maka apapun yang namanya permian agama atau lainnya pasti akan diikuti umat tanpa banyak persoalan.

BERITA TERKAIT

Belum terdapat berita yang terkait...

BERITA LAINNYA

29/05/2009 AC Milan Tanpa Kaka, Bisakah Tetap
29/05/2009 Sebagai 'Underdog', JK-Win Harus
28/05/2009 Hasil Barca Vs MU, Bukti Asumsi Bisa
28/05/2009 SBY Mesti Belajar Sejarah Bangsa
27/05/2009 Tak Perlu Heran, Koalisi Partai
26/05/2009 Kekhawatiran PKS dan Kemungkinan
25/05/2009 Usai Deklarasi, Apalagi Mau
24/05/2009 Pembelajaran dari Korsel,
23/05/2009 Peluang JK-Win Kalahkan SBY-
10/05/2009 Ketika Jusuf Kalla Pakai Blangkon

KabarIndonesia – Indonesian News

Long, favorable review of *The Illusion of an Islamic State* and its accompanying film series, *Ocean of Revelations: Understanding Islam as a Blessing for all Creation.*

Kaskus – Large Indonesian IT/Hacker Forum

Extensive discussion of *The Illusion of an Islamic State*, with hundreds of posts and links to download electronic copies of the book.

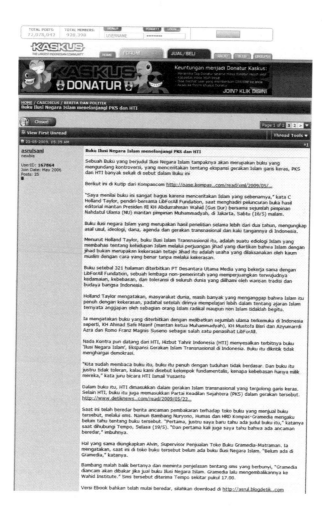

Kompas

Indonesia's largest newspaper, reporting on the publication and launch of *The Illusion of an Islamic State*.

Lampung Post – Written Work: Three Leading Islamic Figures Launch the Book, 'The Illusion of an Islamic State'

Newspaper article published in Lampung Province, Sumatra.

Library of Congress Jakarta

Library of Congress entry/brief review of *The Illusion of an Islamic State.*

musang s.x.

"Perhaps you should immediately read this book, before certain groups demand that it be banned... Fortunately, the publishers seem to have anticipated (attempts to prevent distribution of the book), and have posted it for free download at: http://www.bhinnekatunggalika.org/galeri.html"

NU Online – Official Website of the Nahdlatul Ulama, the world's largest Muslim organization, with 40 million members

Prominently placed news report on *The Illusion of an Islamic State* and its launch, with a link for downloading the book.

Politikana – Leading Indonesian political web forum

For several days following the book's launch, it became the hottest topic on politikana.com, attracting numerous articles and hundreds of comments, as seen from two such articles below ("Is the PKS a Threat to the Unified National Republic of Indonesia?" and "The Book, *The Illusion of an Islamic State*". The second article, by Roby Muhammad, is also cited by *Tempo*, Indonesia's largest weekly newsmagazine, on a different page of this appendix.

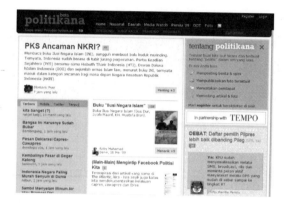

PPIUK – Association of Indonesian Students/United Kingdom Branch: "Why be afraid of a book… *The Illusion of an Islamic State*[?]"

Thoughtful posting meant to dissipate Muslim students' fears that *The Illusion of an Islamic State* will "give rise to problems threatening the existence of Islam or the existence of our own identity." Indonesian students in Europe, the Middle East and North America quickly became aware of, and often deeply engaged in, debates concerning the content of this book.

Republika Online – Transnational Movements and Their Responsibilities

Thoughtful editorial published in *Republika* newspaper by a professor at a leading Indonesian university. It analyzes the controversy generated by *The Illusion of an Islamic State*, including xenophobic accusations directed towards LibForAll, and asserts the inevitability of transnational movements—which, he states, should be judged by their positive or negative impact upon Indonesia—and their legitimacy, if they support the authenticity and integrity of local culture and values.

Republika Koran | Republika Photo | Republika E-paper | Syiar | Bisnis Syariah

Home | Sakinah | Kesehatan | Pendidikan | Trend Teknologi | Olahraga | Senggang | Pemilu

Koran » Opini

Sabtu, 30 Mei 2009 pukul 01:55:00

Gerakan Transnasional dan Tanggung Jawabnya

Zainal Abidin Bagir
(Pengajar Program Studi Agama dan Lintas Budaya, Pascasarjana UGM)

Kontroversi penerbitan buku *Ilusi Negara Islam: Ekspansi Gerakan Islam Transnasional di Indonesia* beserta protes sebagian peneliti yang pernah terlibat di dalamnya (*Republika*, 26 Mei 1009) memang cukup runyam. Kerunyaman menjadi makin rumit karena ada yang memanfaatkan buku itu untuk menunjukkan bahaya 'Islam garis keras' di Indonesia, sementara yang lain memanfaatkan protes sebagian peneliti itu untuk menyerang kredibilitas kelompok yang disimplifikasi sebagai 'Muslim liberal'.

Tapi, kalau mau sedikit berterus terang, mungkin kerunyaman ini bisa mulai diurai dan kontroversi ini memberikan banyak pelajaran penting. Setidaknya, kita bisa melihat dua hal yang terpisah, namun juga bisa terkait di sini: mengenai gerakan transnasional yang menjadi isu utama buku ini dan kualitas penelitian yang dikeluhkan para peneliti itu.

Dalam *Ilusi Negara Islam*, sifat transnasional dengan tepat dilekatkan pada beberapa organisasi Islam yang disebut sebagai gerakan 'garis keras'. Kritiknya tentu adalah pada 'garis keras'-nya. Sifat transnasional dilekatkan pada gerakan tersebut untuk menunjukkan bahwa ini adalah isu besar dan serius. Bahkan, karena melibatkan dana asing, besar kemungkinan agendanya adalah agenda asing yang tak relevan dengan lokalitas Indonesia dan dianggap mengancam Indonesia. Menarik bahwa Hizbut Tahrir Indonesia, yang menjadi salah satu tertuduh utama di buku itu, tidak menampik tuduhan transnasional itu. Bahkan, mereka meneguhkannya: bukahkah Islam sendiri adalah transnasional? Jadi, apa yang salah? Beberapa peneliti yang merasa namanya dicatut untuk kepentingan buku ini sesungguhnya juga secara implisit menisbahkan ke-transnasional-an upaya melawan gerakan Islam garis keras itu. Mereka menyebut campur tangan terlalu jauh pihak LibForAll dari Amerika Serikat yang mendanai penelitian dan penerbitan buku ini sebagai salah satu sumber pelanggaran etis pencatutan nama mereka. Ini terlepas dari penegasan mereka tentang kekhawatiran yang sama pada tumbuh berkembangnya kelompok-kelompok garis keras itu.

Di era globalisasi ini, ke-transnasional-an tak bisa dihindari. Dan, sebetulnya, sama sekali tak punya konotasi negatif, justru sebagian besar positif. Semua gerakan demokratisasi ataupun anti-demokrasi, gerakan lingkungan dan gerakan perempuan, gerakan fundamentalis ataupun pluralis yang ada dalam Islam, agama-agama lain, atau yang tak membawa label agama makin kuat dan bersaing melampaui batas-batas negara.

Ide Khilafah atau Kristen Pantekosta dan hak asasi manusia atau kesetaraan gender terlalu besar untuk bisa dibatasi oleh batas-batas negara. Gerakan transnasional pun, jika berhasil, dampaknya bisa sangat signifikan. Keberhasilan gerakan kemerdekaan Timor Timur, misalnya, bukan hanya merupakan hasil tekanan negara-negara besar, tapi juga gerakan masyarakat sipil transnasional yang menjadikan isu lokal itu terlihat dalam dunia internasional. Karena dampak ide atau gerakan dalam suatu komunitas bisa mengenai komunitas lain, itu sah saja jika orang atau kelompok asing punya kepedulian.

Berkat kebebasan yang muncul mengikuti Reformasi 1998, ladang Indonesia pun menjadi makin subur dan menyatu dengan dunia internasional sehingga menjadi lahan persaingan beragam kelompok itu. Jika transnasionalitas tak terelakkan, lalu apa persoalannya? Ini menjadi persoalan jika pohon dari luar hendak ditanam di lahan sendiri secara paksa. Ide bisa datang dari mana saja. Penting diakui bahwa tanah kita bukanlah tanah ideal yang tak bisa diperkaya lagi. Namun, memang tak selalu jelas perubahan mana yang akan membawa perbaikan atau justru merusak identitas (baik itu identitas 'Islam Indonesia, Islam yang murni/sebenarnya', maupun yang lain). Identitas pun sebetulnya sifatnya cair, tak statis, serta bisa bahkan selalu berubah kandungannya demi pencapaian apa yang dianggap ideal. Yang lalu menjadi persoalan tampaknya adalah autentisitas dan integritas. Di sini, isunya bisa terkait dengan persoalan sumber dana. Dana asing menjadi buruk jika itu mengorbankan autentisitas dan integritas. Secara lebih konkret, persoalannya adalah akuntabilitas. Untuk sebuah penelitian, seperti buku *Ilusi Negara Islam* (yang sesungguhnya cukup serius karena berasal dari penelitian dua tahun), akuntabilitas salah satunya terletak pada pertanggungjawaban akademik, pertanggungjawaban atas klaim-klaim yang dibuat, atau pengakuan karya seperti yang disinggung para pemrotes.

Sinar Indonesia – Terrorized, Bookstores Refuse to Sell "The Illusion of an Islamic State"

Newspaper from the third-largest Indonesian city, Medan, in North Sumatra.

Tempo Interaktif – "The Illusion of an Islamic State" Widely Debated; Gramedia Bookstores Deny Having Been Threatened

The largest weekly news magazine in Indonesia reports on the controvery that surrounds publication of the book: "Earlier, on http://politikana.com, various discussions of the book became the top news items on that website devoted to politics. One guest author, Roby Muhammad, shared an address where readers could download the book, and over 140 visitors have already posted comments in response."

HOME | 22 MEI 2009 | ENGLISH

TEMPO|interaktif **Metro**

T Majalah Tempo | E English Edition | Koran Tempo | PDAT | Photostock | U-Mag | Ruang Baca | Blog

Nasional Metro Bisnis Olahraga Teknologi Gaya Hidup Seni & Hiburan

Jakarta **Kriminal** Kota Layanan Publik Index Pemilu 2009

'Ilusi Negara Islam' Diperdebatkan, Gramedia Bantah Diancam

Selasa, 19 Mei 2009 | 18:10 WIB

TEMPO Interaktif, Jakarta: Penerbitan buku berjudul Ilusi Negara Islam, tampaknya akan menuai kontroversi. Saat ini telah beredar berita ancaman pembakaran terhadap toko buku yang menjual buku tersebut, melalui sms.

Namun Bambang Nuryono, Humas dan HRD Kompas-Gramedia mengaku belum tahu tentang buku tersebut. "Pertama, justru saya baru tahu ada judul buku itu," katanya saat dihubungi Tempo, Selasa (19/5). "Dan pertama kali juga saya tahu bahwa ada ancaman beredar," imbuhnya.

Hal yang sama diungkapkan Alvin, Supervisor Penjualan Toko Buku Gramedia-Matraman. Ia mengatakan, saat ini di toko buku tersebut belum ada buku Ilusi Negara Islam. "Belum ada di Gramedia," katanya.

Bambang malah balik bertanya dan meminta penjelasan tentang sms yang berbunyi, "Gramedia diancam akan dibakar jika jual buku Ilusi Negara Islam. Gramedia lalu mengembalikannya ke Wahid Institute." Sms tersebut diterima Tempo sekitar pukul 17.00.

Ditanya mengenai antisipasi yang akan dilakukan Gramedia terhadap ancaman itu, Bambang mengatakan pihaknya belum bisa membayangkan langkah yang akan ditempuh. "Kami belum bisa membayangkan akan ngapain sebab baru dengar kabar ini pertama kali," katanya. "Terima kasih juga atas informasinya," pungkas Bambang.

Sebelumnya, di situs http://politikana.com, pembahasan mengenai buku ini menjadi berita utama website tentang politik tersebut. Penulis tamu di situs itu, Roby Muhammad berbagi alamat tempat mengunduh buku Ilusi Negara Islam. Sejauh ini, tanggapan terhadap tulisan tersebut sudah mencapai 140 komentar.

Buku Ilusi Negara Islam berisi hasil penelitian yang antara lain melibatkan oleh Abdurrahman Wahid atau Gus Dur, Syafii Maarif, KH. Mustofa Bisri ini membahas tentang gerakan Islam ekstrim global yang harus diwaspadai.

Twitter Gandrasta

Twitter social networking site, informing others that "gandrasta" has read the electronic version of *The Illusion of an Islamic State*.

Twitter Kakilangit

Twitter social networking site, pointing readers to a website where they can download the electronic version of *The Illusion of an Islamic State.*

Twitter Syahrani

Another twitter social networking site, pointing readers to a website where they can download the electronic version of *The Illusion of an Islamic State.*

Viva News Forum

Online forum notifying readers of the publication of *The Illusion of an Islamic State*, and pointing them to the Bhinneka Tunggal Ika website, where they can download the book.

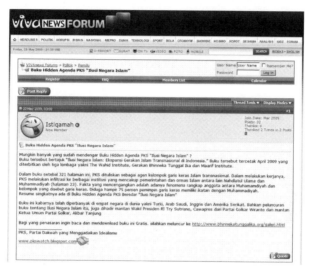

Wahid Institute – Gus Dur: Indonesian Islam is Tolerant

Report on the book launch posted on The Wahid Institute's website.

Yahoo News Indonesia – Terrorized, Bookstores Refuse to Sell *The Illusion of an Islamic State*

Yahoo version of article from Indonesian wire service detik. com.

Yahoo Answers Indonesia – Congratulations! Finally Someone Has Bellowed Out the Truth About the PKS

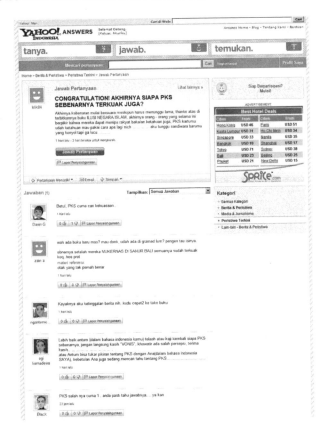

Section 4.
Negative Reactions to *The Illusion of an Islamic State*

Agung Yulianto – The Book 'The Illusion of an Islamic State' Seeks to Provoke Conflict Among Muslims

Website belonging to a PKS politician.

Hizbut Tahrir – Offended, Professors at Yogyakarta Islamic State University Criticize "The Illusion of an Islamic State"

Official Hizbut Tahrir website reprints detik.com article about 4 researchers' complaints regarding *The Illusion of an Islamic State*. Photo is of LibForAll Foundation delegation that visited Israel and Palestine in December of 2007, with an Israeli rabbi, in order to imply that the various Muslim leaders associated with LibForAll are "Zionist" agents.

Hizbut Tahrir – *The Illusion of an Islamic State?* Islamic Law (Shari'a) Is Dangerous Because It Threatens the Colonialism of Western Capitalism

Official Hizbut Tahrir website posts an article attacking the Bhinneka Tunggal Ika Movement, Wahid Institute and Maarif Institute as Zionist agents and enemies of Islam.

Irfan Syauqi Beik – Criticism of the Book *The Illusion of an Islamic State*

Long article defending PKS and calling *The Illusion of an Islamic State* "propaganda."

Al-Jamaah (The Community) – Here is the Book from that Accursed Satanic Network. Read, Study and Anticipate. This is the link (to download it):

Further evidence that extremists themselves are reading *The Illusion of an Islamic State*. Hardline website apparently linked to, or sympathetic with, the terrorist organization Jema'ah Islamiyah, whose 17 July 2009 bombings of the Marriott and Ritz-Carlton hotels in Jakarta precipitated an enormous, second wave of publicity for the issues raised in *The Illusion of an Islamic State* (see sections 5 and 6 of this appendix).

Nahimunkar (Forbidding Evil) – The Book *The Illusion of an Islamic State*: Screams of the Syphilitic Crowd

Long, harsh and crude attack upon *The Illusion of an Islamic State*, and those associated with its publication. Sample text: "There is a new book from the Syphilitic [secularism, religious pluralism and liberalism] School of Thought that perhaps has not yet found its way into your hands.... In order to save Muslims the trouble of reading the book (and indeed, perhaps there is no need to read it at all), nahimunkar.com has summarized everything you need to know about this book."

Buku Ilusi Negara Islam Teriakan Sia-sia Kaum Sepilis

May 20, 2009 9:56 pm admin Artikel

Buku *Ilusi Negara Islam*
Teriakan Sia-sia Kaum Sepilis

Kaum Sepilis melontarkan aneka kecaman kasar lewat buku. Hamper dapat dipastikan: Simpati yang mau diraih kaum Sepilis tidak tercapai, sedang makin bertambahnya jumlah yang memusuhi mereka sudah pasti. Itulah kerja sia-sia terbaru kaum Sepilis yang melibatkan para dedengkotnya. Bahkan bukan sekadar sia-sia, namun rugi besar, masih pula menunjukkan jati diri mereka yang kurang bisa membawa diri, hingga jatuhlah harga diri mereka.

Pengantar: Ada buku dari "perguruan" Sepilis (sekulerisme, pluralisme agama, dan liberalisme) yang mungkin belum sampai ke tangan Anda. Buku yang berjudul *Ilusi Negara Islam* itu diluncurkan pada hari Sabtu tanggal 16 Mei 2009. Di dalamnya ada pengantar atau tulisan-tulisan orang yang dikenal nyeleneh bahkan kadang berkata kasar terhadap Islam atau Ummat Islam, di antaranya: Gus Dur, Ahmad Syafi'I Ma'arif, dan A Mustofa Bisri.
Untuk membantu Ummat Islam agar tidak usah berpayah-payah (dan mungkin memang tidak perlu) membaca buku itu, maka nahimunkar.com menyajikan tanggapan seperlunya mengenai buku itu. Namun sebelumnya kami mohon kesabarannya, perlu kami sajikan lebih dulu buku produk mereka yang lebih tebal yakni 1000-an halaman namun tampaknya tidak laku di pasaran, hingga daripada *menuh-menuhi* gudang, tampaknya kemudian dibagi-bagikan. Berikut ini ulasannya. Terimakasih. **(Redaksi nahimunkar.com).**

Buku *Negara Tuhan*

Pada tahun 2004, pernah diluncurkan sebuah buku berjudul *Negara Tuhan: The Thematic Encyclopaedia* yang diterbitkan oleh SR-Ins Publishing — Jogjakarta. Penulisnya (atau yang tercantum namanya, ikut menulis di situ) keroyokan (SR-Ins Team), yaitu Abd Salam Arif, A. Yani Abeveiro, Hamim Ilyas, N.A. Abafaz, A. Maftuh Abegebriel, M. Ishom El-Saha, Mukhlas Syarkun, W. Ghorara, Ibida Syitaba, Muhammad Iqbal Ahnaf, Murba Abu, dan Machasin.

Buku setebal 1000 halaman itu, menyoroti tentang bahaya gagasan negara Islam, bahaya wacana penegakan syari'ah Islam dan khilafah Islam, bahaya fundamentalisme Islam, terorisme Islam yang direpresentasikan melalui Jama'ah Islamiyah. Ketika itu, yang disoroti adalah MMI (Majelis Mujahidin Indonesia), HTI (Hizbut Tahrir Indonesia), dan JI (Jama'ah Islamiyah).

Secara khusus, pada Bab 10 buku tersebut, diulas tentang MMI dan HTI, dengan judul *MMI dan HTI; The Image of The Others* yang ditulis oleh Muhammad Iqbal Ahnaf. Sedangkan mengenai JI diulas pada Bab 13 dengan judul *Ada Apa Dengan Dokumen JI? Sebuah Penghampiran Hermeneutik* yang ditulis oleh A. Maftuh Abegebriel, sang komandan.

Saat itu, PKS (Partai Keadilan Sejahtera) sama sekali luput dari pembahasan buku Negara Tuhan. Meski di tahun 2004 perolehan suara PKS naik secara signifikan dibanding

Republika Online – Statement Regarding the Book *The Illusion of an Islamic State*

Republika newspaper reports on four Yogyakarta researchers' complaints about *The Illusion of an Islamic State*, including the accusation that Holland Taylor and LibForAll are pursuing a foreign political agenda through publication of the book.

Swara Muslim (The Voice of Muslims) – Through its Book *The Illusion of an Islamic State*, LibForAll Has Backed [Radical] Islam into a Corner

Long article containing detailed attack on LibForAll Foundation and its CEO, Holland Taylor, for promoting a pluralistic understanding of Islam, and opposing "good" Muslims such as Laskar Jihad, or the Warriors of Jihad, who killed thousands of Indonesian Christians in the Maluku Islands from 1999 – 2002 (a reference to LibForAll's earlier work with Indonesian rock star Ahmad Dhani, whose album *Laskar Cinta* (Warriors of Love) inspired millions of Muslim youth to proclaim, "Yes to the Warriors of Love! No to the Warriors of Jihad!).

Syabab (Youth) – Hizb ut-Tahrir Indonesia Reveals the Illusions, Hatred and Provocations Contained in the Book, "The Illusion of an Islamic State"

"First, Islam is tolerant, but the strange thing is, in their extreme narcissism, the authors of this book are intolerant of their fellow Muslims, as evidenced by their continuous attacks [on Muslim extremists], stigmatizing their fellow Muslims as close-minded literalists, in addition to other pejorative attacks. On the other hand, while they themselves are incapable of behaving in a tolerant manner towards their fellow Muslims, they call for tolerance towards infidels, using the justification that they, too, are muslim [i.e., "surrendered to God"]. Indeed, they reinterpret Qur'anic verses and sayings of the Prophet Muhammad which command [us] to wage war against them [i.e., infidels], in accordance with their own intentions. As a result, the logical argument contained within this book is extremely clear, and completely inconsistent with [the author of this article's understanding of] the true message of Islam."

Hizbut Tahrir Indonesia Mengungkap Ilusi, Kebencian dan Provokasi Buku "Ilusi Negara Islam"

TUESDAY, 26 MAY 2009 12:35

Syabab.Com - Buku "Ilusi Negara Islam: Ekspansi Gerakan Islam Transnasional di Indonesia", yang diluncurkan beberapa waktu lalu itu sebenarnya tidak layak dibaca apalagi ditanggapi. Meski diklaim sebagai karya ilmiah, dan konon merupakan hasil penelitian selama dua tahun, namun semuanya itu tidak bisa menutupi fakta, bahwa buku ini sangat tidak ilmiah dan jauh dari obyektivitas sebuah penelitian. Demikian ditegaskan oleh Hizbut Tahrir Indonesia dalam pernyataan sikapnya.

Alih-alih bersikap obyektif, buku ini justru dipenuhi dengan ilusi, kebencian dan provokasi penyusunnya. Jubir Hizbut Tahrir Indonesia Ismail Yusanto menegaskan, "Inilah yang mendorong kami untuk menanggapi buku ini, khususnya yang berkaitan dengan Hizbut Tahrir."
Beberapa tanggapan atas buku tersebut diantaranya:

Dari aspek metodologi: *Pertama*, dari sisi referensi: Buku ini sama sekali tidak menggunakan referensi utama (primer), yaitu buku-buku resmi Hizbut Tahrir. Satu-satunya referensi resmi yang digunakan adalah booklet Selamatkan Indonesia dengan Syariah, itu pun tampaknya hanya dicomot judulnya. Selebihnya, pandangan dan sikap penyusun buku tersebut tentang Hizbut Tahrir didasarkan pada kesimpulan-kesimpulan yang dibangun oleh Zeno Baran dalam bukunya, Hizb ut-Tahrir: Islam's Political Insurgency (Washington: Nixon Center, 2004) dan Ed. Husain dalam bukunya, The Islamist (London: Penguin Books, 2007).

"Mereka tidak tahu atau pura-pura tidak tahu, bahwa baik Zeno Baran yang berdarah Yahudi maupun Ed. Husain adalah sama-sama bukan orang yang ahli tentang Hizbut Tahrir. Ed. Husain yang diklaim sebagai salah seorang pimpinan Hizb terbukti bohong, yang memang sengaja dibangun untuk menunjukkan kredibilitas karyanya, yang sesungguhnya tidak kredibel," katanya Ismail.

Dari sini saja, lanjutnya lagi, sebenarnya cukup untuk membuktikan, bahwa buku Ilusi Negara Islam ini sebenarnya tidak ilmiah dan jauh dari obyektivitas. Karena itu, kesimpulan-kesimpulan yang dibangun di dalamnya tidak lebih dari ilusi penyusunnya. Bahkan, buku ini juga sangat narsis, karena kebencian dan provokasi yang ditaburkan di dalamnya mulai dari awal hingga akhir. Tampak jelas, bahwa buku ini disusun dengan target, bukan sekedar untuk mengemukakan pandangan, tetapi untuk memobilisasi perlawanan.

Kedua, cara menarik kongklusi: Kongklusi di dalam buku ini banyak ditarik dengan menggunakan analogi generalisasi (qiyas syumuli), sehingga menganggap semua kelompok dan organisasi yang nyata-nyata berbeda, seperti DDII, MMI, PKS dan HTI sebagai sama.

"Ini adalah bukti, bahwa buku ini tidak obyektif. Lebih-lebih ketika, sejak pertama kali, penyusun buku ini sudah melakukan monsterisasi terhadap Wahabi, kemudian mengeneralisasi bahwa semua organisasi Islam yang tidak sepaham dengan-nya dicap Wahabi."

Section 5.
Coverage Following the 17 July 2009
Jakarta Terrorist Attacks

A. M. Hendropriyono – Terrorism in Light of Analytical/ Philosophical Research: Its Relevance to National Defense

General A. M. Hendropriyono is a retired four-star general, who served as chief of Indonesia's National Intelligence Service from 2001 – 2004. In the wake of the terrorist attacks of 17 July 2009, General Hendropriyono ignited a nationwide firestorm of controversy, by linking the terrorist attacks to transnational Wahhabi/Muslim Brotherhood ideology. This document from Gen. Hendropriyono's website is from a summary of the dissertation he recently authored at Gadjah Mada University in Yogyakarta, Indonesia. It specifically references *The Illusion of an Islamic State*, and acknowledges the top Muslim leaders associated with LibForAll Foundation, who have summoned Indonesians—Muslim and non-Muslim alike—to resist the spread of radical Islam.

"Indonesian Islam considers the identification of Islam with fundamentalism, or hard line ideologies a la Wahhabism and the Muslim Brotherhood, to be the most serious threat [facing our nation]. Indonesia's top Muslim leaders are fully aware of efforts to annihilate the culture and traditions of Indonesia, and replace these with an alien, Wahhabi-flavored culture and tradition, which claims to be the culture and tradition of Islam itself. This will only subordinate the people of Indonesia to a global network of Wahhabi/ Muslim Brotherhood extremists, whose views are virtually identical to those of Osama bin Laden. What most concerns [Indonesia's top Muslim leaders] about this phenomenon are the extremists' efforts to infiltrate Indonesia's institutions of government, in order to accomplish their objectives. For this reason, Abdurrahman Wahid and the Nahdlatul Ulama (NU) have called upon the Indonesian people to actively resist Wahhabi extremist movements—which have already succeeded in infiltrating Indonesia and are driving towards their goal with the assistance of local accomplices, in order to pervert the nobility and honor of Islam, which they have sullied—and at the same time, to rescue Pancasila and the Unified National Republic of Indonesia (Wahid, *The Illusion of an Islamic State*, 2009).... If we allow Wahhabism to continue to spread unchecked in Indonesia, it will lead to the dissolution of our national unity, and of our secular constitution."

Beranda | Kontak | Berita | Links

Cari

A M Hendropriyono
★ ★ ★ ★

Jayalah Negeriku

Beranda ■ Pemikiran ■ Terorisme Dalam Kajian Filsafat Analitika: Relevansinya dengan Ketahanan Nasional

Terorisme Dalam Kajian Filsafat Analitika: Relevansinya dengan Ketahanan Nasional

PDF PRINT

Ditulis Oleh Administrator
Monday, 24 August 2009

Terorisme kembali menjadi topik pembahasan dunia sejak serangan sangat dahsyat terhadap menara kembar WTC di New York dan Pentagon Amerika Serikat pada tanggal 11 September 2001. Sebagai tertuduh pelaku (subjek) mega-terorisme tersebut adalah jaringan organisasi transnasional al-Qaeda pimpinan Osama bin Laden. Secara eksplisit ideologi para teroris yang menyerang Twin Towers dan Pentagon pada 11 Sept 2001 ialah penolakan atas modernitas dan sekularisasi, yang di dalam tradisi filsafat diasosiasikan dengan 'Konsep Pencerahan'. Di dalam filsafat, 'Pencerahan' menggambarkan bukan hanya sebuah periode spesifik, yang secara historis bertepatan dengan abad ke-18, melainkan juga afirmasi atas demokrasi dan pemisahan kekuasaan politik dari kepercayaan keagamaan yang dijadikan fokus oleh Revolusi Perancis dan juga Revolusi Amerika Serikat (Borradori, 2003). Terhadap sistem demokrasi itu, pemimpin jaringan organisasi transnasional 'al-Qaeda', Osama bin Laden, menyatakan sebagai berikut :

- They have chosen democracy, the faith of ignorants. Those who obey their King or scholars·······in permitting what God has prohibited, through becoming members of Legislative councils, or prohibiting God has permited such as Jihad for the sake of God·······they have thus made them their Lord rather than obey God (Osama bin Laden, 18 Oktober 2003) (Berner, 2006). ["Mereka telah memilih demokrasi, keyakinan dari orang-orang tolol! Mereka yang taat kepada Raja atau kaum cendekiawannya·······dengan mengijinkan apa yang dilarang Tuhan menjadi anggota Legislatif, atau melarang apa yang diijinkan Tuhan seperti ber-jihad demi Tuhan·······mereka berarti telah memper-Tuhan diri mereka sendiri, bukan taat kepada Tuhan" (Osama bin Laden, 18 Oktober 2003)(Berner, 2006)]

Osama bin Laden menggugat keabsahan sistem demokrasi, yang kini telah merupakan paham politik universal, yang secara realitas telah dapat diterima dalam beraneka ragam perspektif. Filsafat demokrasi telah digandrungi oleh sejumlah masyarakat non-Barat sejak permulaan abad ke-20. Berbagai koloni negara-negara Barat di benua Asia dan Afrika telah bangkit untuk membangun nilai-nilai demokrasi, di dalam masyarakatnya masing-masing. Dengan sistem politik demokrasi yang diperoleh dari pendidikan politik dan perubahan sistem ekonomi negara-negara kolonialisnya sendiri, para pemimpin dan para tokoh masyarakat di berbagai wilayah-wilayah koloni (jajahan) secara fenomenal mulai mengembangkan nilai-nilai filsafat demokrasi, untuk keperluan membebaskan diri dari belenggu kolonialisme. Dalam konteks Indonesia yang dulu disebut Hindia Belanda, fenomena tersebut dikenal dalam sejarah sebagai 'Kebangkitan Nasional'. Paham-paham politik Barat yang lain seperti Nasionalisme, Pan-Islamisme, Sosialisme atau Komunisme adalah juga yang membuka perspektif bagi emansipasi kaum pribumi dari para kolonialisnya. Paham-paham Barat itu sekaligus juga memungkinkan pembebasan bangsa-bangsa pribumi dari 'kurungan besi' feodalisme, dengan melalui pembentukan partai-partai politik serta serikat-serikat kerja modern. Mereka yang merupakan lulusan pendidikan Barat adalah para kader bangsa yang sudah siap ketika kekalahan Jepang, untuk kemudian membuka peluang historis mengisi kemerdekaan negaranya. Oleh karena itu negara-negara bangsa (Nation States) termasuk Republik Indonesia, dulu telah didirikan oleh para pemimpin patriotik dan kelompok kekuatan politik 'pribumi', yang lahir dalam modernitas intelektual dan pandangan-pandangan serta juga transformasi-transformasi yang distrukturkan oleh Barat (Suseno,2006). Kini berbagai derivatif yang diharapkan dari pelaksanaan demokratisasi adalah munculnya komitmen untuk suatu proses demokratisasi yang damai, tanpa kekerasan dan tidak 'berlumuran darah'. Namun ternyata konsep teoritis demokrasi, bukan teori politik yang begitu saja dapat dikatakan etis (Nurtjahjo, 2006). Menurut Bung Karno (1958) ideologi Kapitalisme di dalam praktek adalah demokrasi tetapi juga agresi, dua hal yang paradoksal. Di masa sedang berjaya (Kapitalisme im aufstieg) mereka menggunakan etika politik, sedangkan di kala posisinya sedang menurun (Kapitalismus im niedergang) mereka melakukan agresi. Juga komitmen damai dari filsafat demokrasi, tidak selalu hadir di dalam praksisnya (Nurtjahjo, 2006). Hal ini merangsang kebangkitan fundamentalisme Islam melawan alternatif penerapan kekuasaan keras (Hard Power) yang diambil oleh Amerika Serikat ketika di bawah administrasi Presiden George Walker Bush dan fihak Barat. Kekuatan perlawanan kaum fundamentalis tersebut dibangun secara semesta, dengan menggunakan dalih patriotisme dan spirit keagamaan. Dengan keyakinan terhadap kebenaran kekuatan yang dibangun itu, maka artikulasi politik yang santun yang mendahulukan dialog, negosiasi dan kompromi tidak lagi mendapatkan tempat (Arubusman,2006).

Pada puncak dari perkembangan keadaan global yang saling berhadapan ini, terletak terorisme yang menilai jiwa manusia sedemikian rendah, seolah-olah tidak ada bedanya dengan batu. Betapapun baik msalnya tujuan dari sesuatu konsep, tetapi jika kekerasan yang dipilih untuk mencapainya, maka secara keseluruhan konsep itu tidak akan mendapat legitimasi sebagai sebuah kebenaran. Terorisme yang merebak sejak menjelang dan awal abad ke-21 merupakan alternatif dari komunikasi yang terdistorsi secara resiprokal, antara Osama bin Laden dengan George Walker Bush, yang masing-masing berlaku sebagai sampel yang representatif dari dua kutub yang saling berhadap-hadapan. Bahasa yang digunakan dalam terorisme, walaupun masuk akal, namun saling tidak dapat dimengerti oleh para komunikannya. Bahasa disebut masuk akal karena digunakan oleh manusia, sedangkan yang tidak masuk akal adalah bahasa yang tidak digunakan oleh manusia, misalnya bahasa hewan. Bahasa terorisme tersebut hanya dapat diberi makna oleh lingkungan hidup atau habitat terorisme itu sendiri, yaitu masyarakat fundamentalis. Fundamentalisme yang melahirkan terorisme adalah suatu ideologi politik, bukan agama Islam yang secara sinis kerap dikaitkan oleh fihak Barat dengan ideologi tersebut. Fundamentalisme adalah ketaatan manusia terhadap keyakinannya dengan cara pandang politis. Dalam beberapa hal aktivis politik tersebut tidak tertarik pada etika agama dan etika kebudayaan. Membedakan antara Islam sebagai keimanan dengan ideologi politik Islam sebagai fundamentalisme agama, merupakan hal penting untuk menolak klaim para teroris sebagai representasi Islam (Tibi, 1988).

Kajian terhadap terorisme ini menggunakan objek formal filsafat analitika bahasa. Filsafat analitika Bahasa Wittgenstein menjelaskan, tentang praktek penggunaan ungkapan bahasa dalam kehidupan manusia. Ungkapan bahasa dalam pengertian ini bukanlah bahasa secara harfiah, melainkan ungkapan di dalam realitas kehidupan manusia. Sebagaimana halnya seniman sastra menciptakan karya sastra, sajak, novel; protes atau demo merupakan ungkapan bahasa dalam kehidupan politik; menguji hipotesis dan melakukan analisis adalah ungkapan bahasa dalam kehidupan ilmiah; menari adalah ungkapan bahasa dalam kehidupan seni tari dan berbagai bahasa dalam kehidupan lainnya. Menurut Wittgenstein, ungkapan bahasa yang digunakan dalam konteks kehidupan itu sangat beragam, bahkan tak terbatas banyaknya, bahkan yang lama telah hilang dalam kehidupan masyarakat, untuk kemudian muncul dalam konteks kehidupan yang baru, dengan menggunakan ungkapan bahasa tertentu di bawah rule of the game yang tertentu pula (Wittgenstein, 1983).

MENU UTAMA

Beranda
Biografi
Aktivitas
▶ Pemikiran
Galeri Foto
Cari
Links
Amh
Republik Indonesia
Republik Indonesia

Administrator

Kompas – Hendropriyono: There are Certain Groups Sheltering Terrorists

Indonesia's largest circulation daily newspaper reports that "Islamic teachings in Indonesia have truly emphasized harmony, moderation and tolerance. However, there has been infiltration by extremists. The public should not remain silent about this. They should actively prevent the establishment of new 'habitat' [for radicals]," said Hendropriyono."

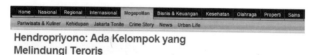

Home | Nasional | Regional | Internasional | Megapolitan | Bisnis & Keuangan | Kesehatan | Olahraga | Properti | Sains
Pariwisata & Kuliner | Kehidupan | Jakarta Tonite | Crime Story | News | Urban Life

Hendropriyono: Ada Kelompok yang Melindungi Teroris

Hendropriyono

KOMPAS/AGUS SUSANTO

KAMIS, 23 JULI 2009 | 20:53 WIB
Laporan wartawan KOMPAS Wisnu Dewabrata

JAKARTA, KOMPAS.com — Mantan Kepala Badan Intelijen Negara (BIN) AM Hendropriyono menilai, Indonesia, khususnya aparat intelijen, bukanlah satu-satunya pihak yang harus merasa kebobolan akibat serangan peledakan bom di Hotel JW Marriott dan Ritz-Carlton.

Kecolongan, menurut Hendropriyono, juga dirasakan seluruh masyarakat dunia lantaran mengingat aksi teror yang dilancarkan pelakunya adalah jaringan teroris global. Seolah gurita, jaringan teroris global tersebut memang punya banyak tentakel, yang tersebar di banyak negara di dunia ini.

Artikel Terkait:
> Turis Asing di Banyumas Tak Khawatir Dampak Terorisme
> Benarkah Ibrahim Telah Diamankan?
> Ahmad Jenggot, Penghubung Jaringan Teroris Cilacap-Sumatera
> Pria Berinisial A Itu Bernama Ahmady
> TNI Waspadai Teroris Melintasi Perbatasan

Pernyataan itu disampaikan Hendropriyono, Kamis (23/7), saat dihubungi *Kompas* per telepon. Menurutnya, jaringan teroris yang beroperasi di banyak negara tadi hanya bisa tuntas diberantas jika bagian otaknya bisa dihancurkan.

"Dunia telah mengakui kemampuan aparat intelijen kita, mulai dari BIN, Polri, dan TNI, pascapengungkapan teror Bom Bali I dan II. Namun sayang, bantuan yang diberikan oleh negara maju tidak berimbang dan sifatnya sekadar pelatihan teknis, penandatanganan MoU, atau pemberian bantuan dana yang terkesan hanya seperti basa basi," ujar Hendropriyono.

Bagaimana tidak, sejak tahun 2002 sampai sekarang, praktis negara maju tidak pernah bersedia menginisiasi atau bahkan menggelar pola operasi intelijen bersama dengan pihak Indonesia. Bahkan, menurut Hendropriyono, intelijen negara maju hanya mau meminta akses dan informasi yang mereka perlukan tanpa mau berbagi hal sama yang mereka miliki.

North Sumatra Post – Noordin M. Top is Behind the Terrorist Bombings

This newspaper from Indonesia's third largest city, Medan, reports that "Hardline movements, like Wahhabism, represent the most suitable environment for terrorism. 'Those movements have begun to infiltrate the psychology of many Indonesian Muslims,' said [Hendropriyono]. According to Hendropriyono, all terrorist actions, including those recently committed in Indonesia, are the 'implementation' of their perpetrators' way of thinking.... Terrorism stems from ideology, rather than from self-interest. The only way to stop it is to change the way people think."

Banjarmasin Post – Noordin M. Top's Network Ready to Spread Terrorism!

This newspaper from one of the major cities in Kalimantan (Borneo) reports that "the spread of terrorist networks is greatly facilitated by extremist groups. Hendropriyono himself believes that these radical groups are part of a transnational movement that is being driven by Wahhabi followers. 'Maybe some people don't agree, but I call it 'transnational extremist movements' or 'Wahhabism,' he said."

Detik News – Hendropriyono: It's Enough Just to Monitor Proselytization During Ramadan

Indonesia's largest web portal reports former intelligence chief Hendropriyono as saying that "in order to defeat global terrorism, Muslim nations must unite and work together to cleanse themselves of fundamentalist influence. This is a prerequisite to neutralizing the environment that serves as a habitat for terrorism, allowing it to regenerate again and again."

Senin, 24/08/2009 17:48 WIB

Hendropriyono: Dakwah Ramadan Cukup Dimonitor Saja

Bagus Kurniawan - detikNews

dok detikcom

Yogyakarta - Kegiatan dakwah atau pengajian selama bulan Ramadan tidak perlu diawasi dengan ketat. Dakwah Ramadan cukup dimonitor saja terutama para penceramahnya.

"Bulan puasa memang efektif untuk memonitor masuknya paham terorisme sehingga perlu diawasi. Paham terorisme itu kan masuk lewat pendidikan, sehingga ini penting untuk dimonitor juga," kata Mantan Kepala Badan Intelijen Indonesia (BIN) A.M. Hendropriyono, usai ceramah di Fakultas Filsafat Universitas Gadjah Mada (UGM), di Bulaksumur Yogyakarta, Senin (24/8/2009).

Hendro juga mendesak pemerintah segera menerapkan UU anti kekerasan untuk mengatasi terorisme. UU tersebut untuk menangkal fundamentalisme atau aliran keras keagamaan.

"UU anti kekerasan diperlukan saat ini bagi Indonesia, sehingga yang ikut mazhab, pikiran atau idealisme yang identik dengan kekerasan tidak bisa berlaku di negeri ini," kata Hendro.

Menurut dia, fundamentalisme atau aliran keras transnasional Wahabisme kontemporer merupakan aliran keras yang sudah mulai menginfiltrasi sebagian pikiran umat Islam Indonesia. Munculnya aliran fundamentalisme merupakan lingkungan yang kondusif bagi berkembangnya terorisme di Indonesia.

Suara Pembaruan (The Voice of Renewal) – Don't Underestimate Radicalism

A major daily newspaper reports that "Governor Mulyadi of the National Defense Institute gave a speech to new postgraduate students at Padjadjaran University in Bandung, West Java on Monday (24/8). In his opinion, ulama (religious scholars) have an important role to play in preventing terrorist acts.

"Fundamentalism and radicalism, as fostered by Wahhabi groups, represent an extreme movement that has already begun to infiltrate Indonesian Muslim society. For that reason, rather than adopt repressive measures, as the police normally do [when countering terrorists], preventative measures are required."

MEMIHAK KEBENARAN

| Home | E-Paper | SP Minggu | Indeks 2005-2008 | Index 2009 | Edisi PILPRES 2009 | Search | About Us |

Jangan Remehkan Radikalisme

SP/Adi Marsiela

Gubernur Lembaga Pertahanan Nasional (Lemhanas) Muladi (kiri) memberikan kuliah perdana untuk mahasiswa baru pascasarjana Universitas Padjadjaran tahun ajaran 2009/2010 di Graha Sanusi Hardjadinata, Bandung, Jawa Barat, Senin (24/8). Menurutnya, peran ulama penting untuk mencegah aksi teroris.

[YOGYAKARTA] Fundamentalisme dan radikalisme, yang digagas kelompok wahabi, merupakan aliran keras yang sudah mulai menginfiltrasi sebagian pikiran umat Islam di Indonesia. Karena itu, selain tindakan represif, seperti yang sudah dilakukan polisi, dibutuhkan pula upaya preventif.

"Pada 2009 ini merupakan tahapan keempat dari infiltrasi ini. Jadi, kelompok ini tidak bisa dianggap remeh," ujar mantan Kepala Badan Intelijen Indonesia (BIN) AM Hendropriyono di Universitas Gadjah Mada (UGM) Yogyakarta, Senin (24/8).

Oleh karena itu, menurutnya, Indonesia harus segera memberlakukan UU Antikekerasan. Dia meminta ketegasan pemerintah untuk segera menerapkan UU itu dalam mengatasi kegiatan terorisme.

Hendropriyono meyakinkan, UU Antikekerasan merupakan salah satu cara untuk menangkal masuknya radikalisme dan paham wahabi yang menganggap Indonesia sebagai ladang subur bagi berkembangnya terorisme.

"Dengan UU Antikekerasan, mazhab, pikiran, dan idealisme yang identik dengan radikalisme tidak bisa berkembang leluasa di negeri ini," ujarnya.

Dia juga menyinggung tentang sulitnya aparat melacak jejak gembong terorisme Noordin M Top. Warga negara Malaysia itu, katanya, mendapatkan perlindungan dari pengikat organisasi wahabi yang tumbuh subur di Indonesia. "Noordin bersembunyi dalam habitat yang senang kekerasan," ujarnya.

Namun, selain menangkal secara internal, Hendropriyono juga meminta agar negara-negara Islam bekerja sama membersihkan pengaruh fundamentalisme tersebut dari kaidah agama.

Gubernur Lembaga Pertahanan Nasional (Lemhannas) Muladi menyatakan, peran ulama dengan pemikiran moderat dalam pemberantasan terorisme sangat penting. "Tidak bisa hanya ceramah di televisi. Harus langsung di masjid- masjid," katanya di Bandung, kemarin.

Menurutnya, pemantau dakwah di masjid-masjid yang rencananya akan dilakukan polisi harus dilakukan secara diam-diam, tanpa diumumkan ke masyarakat. Kalau memang ada orang menghasut untuk melakukan kekerasan, polisi harus langsung menangkapnya dengan mengacu pada Kitab Undang-undang Hukum Pidana (KUHP).

Official Muhammadiyah Website – It's Important for the Muhammadiyah to Closely Monitor Transnational Islamist Movements

The official website of the world's second-largest Muslim organization reports that Professor Sunyoto Usman from the Social and Political Science Department at Gadjah Mada University in Yogyakarta advised the Muhammadiyah to closely monitor transnational movements such as the Muslim Brotherhood and Hizb ut-Tahrir. Sunyoto spoke at a Ramadan gathering held by the Muhammadiyah's central board on 29 August 2009.

Sunyoto explained that "Although many people who monitor extremists say that they do not form a unified front, they do have a common enemy, the West [and anyone they accuse of supporting a Western agenda]." Earlier, Sunyoto had said that the Muhammadiyah itself is an Islamic movement that regards the United National Republic of Indonesia [with its secular constitution] as final. For that reason, transnational Islamist movements obviously object to the Muhammadiyah establishment.

"It's enough to cite the involvement of a Muhammadiyah school teacher in Temanggung in the recent terrorist attacks, to recognize that the Muhammadiyah needs to pay more attention to the infiltration of extremist ideology into its lower ranks," said Sunyoto. For this reason, the Muhammadiyah needs to develop a systematic policy so that its rank-and-file cadres and all levels of the organization will be secure from transnational movements' intervention and influence.

Persyarikatan

Muhammadiyah
www.muhammadiyah.or.id

today IS | nov 11 2009

cari... | search | INFORMASI ∨ | PROFIL ∨ | ORG. OTONO

Agu
29
2009

Gerakan Islam Trans Nasional Penting Menjadi Perhatian Muhammadiyah

Arif Nur Kholis

Yogyakarta - Prof. Sunyoto Usman, dari Fakultas Ilmu Sosial dan Politik Univ. Gadjah Mada Yogyakarta menyarankan kepada Muhammadiyah untuk memberikan perhatian kepada gerakan trans nasional seperti Ikhwanul Muslimin dan Hisbut Tahrir. "Saat ini Muhammadiyah atau NU baru sampai tahap international relation belum sampai trans national practices "kata Sunyoto pada pengajian Ramadhan PP Muhammadiyah, Sabtu (29/08/2009) di Kampus UM Yogyakarta.

Sunyoto menerangkan bahwa masuknya pengaruh gerakan Islam Transnasional ini merupakan buah dari keterbukaan pasca orde baru. "Gerakan-gerakan memperoleh ruang gerak melakukan kegiatan politik maupun pergulatan pemikiran alternatif yang tidak mungkin dilakukan pada jaman orde baru" lanjut Sunyoto.

Lebih lanjut Sunyoto menerangkan bahwa karakteristik gerakan Islam transnasional ini definisi ummatnya secara riil bisa berbeda dengan Muhammadiyah dan NU. "Definisi ummat di Muhammadiyah mungkin hanya ummat Islam di Indonesia saja" seloroh Sunyoto kemudian. "Sedangkan definisi ummat gerakan trannasional ini tidak dibatasi oleh negara bangsa, salah satunya dengan usulan konsep khilafah" lanjutnya.

Ideologi gerakan trans nasional ini adalah memerangi barat dengan agen-agennya, bahkan dengan satu asumsi bahwa saat ini dunai sudah rusak karena pengaturan oleh orang-orang sekuler, maka mereka berfikir harus ada perubahan sitem yang memungkinkan pengaturan Tuhan bisa menggantikannya.

Yang menarik, menurut Sunyoto implikasi kelembagaannya menjadi bagian dari kelompok internasional dengan sistem komando.Sedangkan implikasi finansialnya, mereka memperoleh dukungan dana secara Internasional, dan dialirkan oleh agen-agen yang tidak mudah dilacak sebagai implikasi globalisasi. "Namun mereka kemudian mengabaikan konsep negara bangsa" terang Sunyoto. Selain itu mereka juga berfokus pada kekuasaan politik, demokrasi dianggap bertentangan dengan Islam. "Walaupun banyak pengamat menyatakan bahwa sebenarnya mereka tidak kompak, namun memiliki musuh bersama , Barat" lanjut Sunyoto.

Sebelumnya, Sunyoto menerangkan bahwa Muhammadiyah sendiri adalah gerakan Islam yang menganngap bahwa Negara Kesatuan Republik Indonesia adalah sesuatu yang sudah final. Karena itu gerakan Islam Tran Nasional in tentu akan bisa bermasalah dengan pendirian Muhammadiyah tersebut.

Kaskus – The Indonesian Council of Holy Warriors re. Hendropriyono!

A post from Indonesia's largest online community (1,198,296 members as of 10 November 2009), quoting a news story from the mainstream press. "The Indonesian Council of Holy Warriors (MMI) strenuously object to the attitude and behavior of a group of former police chiefs who have stigmatized [radical Islam] by saying that terrorism is born from [terrorists'] understanding of Islamic teachings. MMI disputed the analysis put forward by the former head of Indonesia's National Intelligence Agency (BIN), A. M. Hendropriyono; the head of the Coordinating Desk for Combating Terrorism, Police Chief Arsyad Mbai; the former commandant of [counter-terrorist task force] Detachment 88, Brigadier General Suryadarma Salim; and Police Staff Expert Brigadier General Anton Tabah.

Three pages of posts follow, including a reference to the media frenzy accompanying this news: "TV One's ratings shot through the roof."

DetikForum – Destroy Wahhabi Movements in Indonesia

A user forum on Indonesia's largest web portal, which receives millions of visitors. The opening post reads: "Let's destroy Wahhabi movements, that have long been murdering Indonesians and our guests. For too long they've been massacring innocent people and trying to overthrow the Indonesian government. Come on, Indonesia[ns], defend NKRI (the Unitary State of the Republic of Indonesia)!!! Defend our 1945 constitution and Pancasila. Don't allow our nation to be colonized once again [this time, by Wahhabi extremists]!!!!! Come on, Indonesia! Come on, come on!!!!!!

The second post reads: "....It's extremely comfortable and easy for terrorists to operate in Indonesia because they have many fans [i.e., Wahhabi sympathizers]."

The third post reads, "I agree. Their fans include a lot of politicians. In fact, a former vice president once supported the head of Jemaah Islamiyah. Fortunately, his party is no longer relevant."

Another post reads: "Hendropriyono (former head of BIN) yesterday declared in a TVOne interview that the people pulling the strings behind terrorists in Indonesia are extremists, that is, Wahhabis and the Muslim Brotherhood."

Another posting reads: "Yeah yeah, if they don't support violence, why do they give moral support to thugs? DESTROY ALL THE WAHHABI ORGANIZATIONS IN INDONESIA. Hey you Wahhabis, take your war somewhere else. If you're brave enough, go to afghanistan, iraq or israel."

The postings go on for 5 pages, and become an open forum for debate between those supporting and defending Wahhabism.

detikForum

DETIKFORUM | FORUM INET | FORUM BANDUNG | FORUM SURABAYA -- Basic Blue

DetikForum > Politik & Peristiwa > Politik
Hancurkan Gerakan Wahabi di Indonesia

User Name [User Name] Remember Me?
Password [ ] Log in

18th July 2009, 09:11 #21

DJ_Eko
Addict Member

Join Date: May 2009
Posts: 293

Quote:

> Originally Posted by **danyto**
> *salah satu mentri di kabinet bersatu juga pernah mengunjungi ketua FPI waktu di penjara log, semacam memberi moral support apa memang supporter untuk gerakan itu??*

Ya iyah lah, kalau dia tidak mendukung kekerasan, ngapain dia kasih moral support kepada preman?

HANCURKAN ORMAS ORMAS WAHABI DI INDONESIA

Woi orang Wahabi, bawa perang mu ke negara lain. Kalau lo berani, pergi ke afganistan, iraq atau israel.

---

hihihi.... suka JIL karena mempermudah misi jamaah anda y.... dari bujang_sumatra

Quote

18th July 2009, 09:19 #22

skeptic
Registered Member

Join Date: Jul 2009
Posts: 34

apa dan siapa wahabi sih? kok gak ada penjelasannya, kalo mau mengalahkan kan harus tahu dulu apa dan siapa yang dianggap musuh, think like enemy then you can destroy them

Quote

18th July 2009, 14:09 #23

Suporter
Registered Member

Join Date: Jul 2009
Posts: 99

Kenapa wahaby seharusnya oknumnya yg ditangkep karena yang bikin reseh kan individunya

Quote

19th July 2009, 21:45 #24

cn-235
Addict Member

Join Date: Oct 2008
Posts: 136

Quote:

> Originally Posted by **DJ_Eko**
> *Hancurkan gerakan Wahabi yg sudah terlalu lama bunuh rakyat Indonesia dan tamunya. Sudah lama mereka bunuh wong cilik dan mau jatuhkan pemerintah Indonesia.*
>
> *Ayo Indonesia, pertahankan NKRI!!! Pertahanakan UUD 45 dan Pancasila. Jgn mau lagi negara kita di jajah oleh orang lain!!!!!*
>
> *Maju Indonesia, Maju Indonesia, Maju Indonesia!!!!!!*

Henrdopriyono (Mantan Ka. BIN) kemaren wawancara dengan TVOne projam Jalur Polisi, dengan tegas mengatakan bahwa dalang terrorist di indonesia adalah 2 aliran keras, yaitu Wahabi dan Ikhwanul Muslimin.

Jangan jual NKRI atas nama apapun

Quote

19th July 2009, 23:09 #25

anakchumie
Registered Member

Join Date: Aug 2008
Posts: 65

Quote:

> Originally Posted by **DJ_Eko**
> *Ya iyah lah, kalau dia tidak mendukung kekerasan, ngapain dia kasih moral support kepada preman?*
>
> *HANCURKAN ORMAS ORMAS WAHABI DI INDONESIA*
>
> *Woi orang Wahabi, bawa perang mu ke negara lain. Kalau lo berani, pergi ke afganistan, iraq atau israel.*

ke iran juga kali ya..sekalian perang dgn kaum syiah bedebah

Quote

Jakarta Post – Terrorism Feared, Jema'ah Tabligh Members Expelled

The Jakarta Post reports that hundreds of extremist proselytizers have been told to leave the region of south-central Java near Cilacap, by local inhabitants concerned about their possible relationship with terrorism. The shocking news is the sheer number of Jema'ah Tabligh members who were in the region proselytizing and harassing locals to adhere to their fundamentalist interpretation of Islam, prior to the nation-wide firestorm of controversy about Wahhabism gave local inhabitants the courage to expel them.

The Jakarta Post

| Home | Headlines | Jakarta | Opinion | National | World | Business | Sports | Sci-Tech |

Wednesday, November 11, 2009 10:08 PM

Terrorism feared, Jama'ah Tabligh members expelled

Agus Maryono , The Jakarta Post , Banyumas | Wed, 08/19/2009 1:22 PM | The Archipelago

The current intensive police hunt for wanted terrorist Noordin M. Top and followers of his organization Jamaah Islamiyah has prompted residents to be more vigilant of Islamic groups.

Central Java residents have refused to allow members of Jama'ah Tabligh to stay at their mosque. Members of Jama'ah Tabligh, an Islamic sect originated from India, move from one mosque to another, preaching. Male members of the group usually wear Pakistani-style attire and have beards while its female members wear face veils, and thus they are often believed to be linked to radical groups, including to Noordin and his group.

The exclusion of Jama'ah Tabligh members has happened in several regencies in the province, including Purbalingga, Cilacap and Banyumas.

"Their presence made us uncomfortable. They "the members of Jama'ah Tabligh" slept, ate and took a bath in our mosque. Residents feared that they were part of a terrorist group. So we did not allow them to stay here," Rojikin, one of the mosque's board members, said Tuesday.

Rojikin said the residents reported the group members to the police because they were reluctant to leave the Nurul Huda mosque in Sidakangen village, Kalimanah district, Purbalingga.

Twelve members of Jama'ah Tabligh were then taken to the Purbalingga police station.

The members, who had stayed at the mosque for two weeks, told police they had only asked the residents to perform sholat prayers, rejecting the accusation that they were a terrorist group.

"We don't teach violence. We just ask people to pray together," Hamid, one of the members, said.

Police released the members, residents of Sulawesi, and asked them to move on to the group's center of operations in Purwokerto, Central Java.

The head of the Unitary Nation and People's Protection Agency in Cilacap regency, Yayan Rusiawan, said his agency had asked hundreds of Jama'ah Tabligh members to leave the regency in the past two weeks.

"Residents reported they felt uncomfortable with the presence of the group members. The members had to leave the mosques," Yayan said Tuesday.

He said the group members admitted that they came from Jakarta, Bengkulu and various West Java cities, however, some of the expelled members could still be seen in Majenang, Dayuehluhuer and Kawunganten and western Cilacap areas.

Pujiono, 40, one of the Jama'ah Tabligh activists from Purwokerto defended the group, saying they just preached from one mosque to another.

"We just ask people to liven up their mosques."

He claimed many members of Jama'ah Tabligh were also members of Nahdlatul Ulama and Muhammadiyah, the country's two largest Muslim organizations which are known for their moderate stances.

"We are not a different sect," he added.

Section 6.
Extremist Response to the Deluge of Negative Publicity Generated in the Indonesian Media Regarding Wahhabism and Other Transnational Islamist Movements

Hidayatullah Magazine – It's the West that Benefits Most from Stigmatizing Wahhabism

Interview with Dr. Anis Malik Thoha (Mustasyar of the Nahdlatul Ulama's Special Branch in Malaysia)

Since the explosion of the bombs in Kuningan [Jakarta] in July of 2009, the terms Wahhabism and transnationalism have suddenly been on everyone's lips. Many national television stations and other mass media outlets have been quoting a number of leading national figures about the relationship between terrorist bombs and Wahhabism.

Whether this is intentional or not, one thing is certain: the assistance of media (especially TV) has caused the term Wahhabi to become a new stigma that is terrorizing many [extremist] Muslim organizations. It may be that those behind the spread of this stigma hope to divide Indonesian Muslims and turn them against each other....

"The people behind this are identical to those who were behind the book *The Illusion of an Islamic State....* I can't stop thinking about LibForAll (which financed and published this project) and how it claims to be liberal and promoting liberalism, but in reality is extremely conservative, sectarian and exclusive, unwilling to tolerate differences [i.e., extremist interpretations of Islam]."

HOME   BERITA   KOLOM   KONSULTASI   OPINI   KAJIAN & IBRAH   CERMIN & FEATURE

Barat Paling Diuntungkan Stigma Wahabi

"Apa logikanya, membenarkan gerakan trans-nasional non-Islam (Barat) leluasa merangsek ke masyarakat kita, sementara gerakan-gerakan trans-nasional yang Islam malah tidak boleh?"

Dr. Anis Malik Thoha: **"Barat Paling Diuntungkan Stigma Wahabi"**
(Mustasyar NU Cabang Istimewa Malaysia)

Hidayatullah.com--SEJAK peristiwa bom Kuningan Juli 2009, istilah Wahabi dan trans-nasional tiba tiba dibicarakan banyak orang. Berbagai stasiun televisi nasional dan media massa sibuk mengutip ucapan beberapa tokoh tentang hubungan teror bom dengan Wahabi.

Entah sengaja atau tidak, yang jelas dengan bantuan media (khususnya TV) istilah Wahabi tiba-tiba muncul menjadi stigma baru untuk meneror banyak organisasi Islam. Boleh jadi, penyebar stigma ini berharap kaum Muslim Indonesia terpecah belah.

Apa dan mengapa stigma Wahabi ini dimunculkan? Dan siapa yang untung dengan kasus ini? Kali ini, Hidayatullah mewawancarai Dr Anis Malik Thoha, *Khatib 'Aam Syuriah* NU Cabang Istimewa Malaysia.

Pria yang masih punya ikatan kekerabatan dengan KH Sahal Mahfudz, Rais Aam Pengurus Besar Nahdlatul Ulama (PBNU) ini menyelesaikan S1 di Universitas Islam Madinah. Menyelesaikan gelar masternya di *University of the Punjab* dan PhD (bidang *Comparative Religion*) di International Islamic University Islamabad, Pakistan.

Kini, selain menjadi dosen tetap di *International Islamic University Malaysia* (IIUM), pria yang juga dikenal sebagai pakar pluralisme agama ini sering diundang di berbagai forum internasional guna membicarakan masalah Islam.

Tempo Interaktif: Infidels May Not Be Killed... [as long as they don't oppose radical Islam]

Indonesia's largest news magazine featured an interview with the former head of the terrorist group Jemaah Islamiyah, Abu Bakar Ba'asyir, whose public statements constitute incitement to murder. "Infidels may not be killed if they don't oppose [radical] Islam. We can live alongside them. But people who are involved with movements that oppose Islam, even on the level of thought, not only may be killed, but should and must be."

HOME | 11 NOVEMBER 2009 | ENGLISH

TEMPO|interaktif Nasional

| Nasional | Metro | Bisnis | Olahraga | Teknologi | Gaya Hidup | Internasional |

+ Besar − Kecil A Normal

Abubakar Ba'asyir : Orang Kafir Tak Boleh Dibunuh

Kamis, 23 Juli 2009 | 05.41 WIB

TEMPO *Interaktif*, Jakarta - Kemarin siang Pesantren Al-Mukmin di Ngruki, Sukoharjo, lebih ramai daripada biasanya. Puluhan wartawan dari dalam dan luar negeri berdatangan ke pesantren itu. Mereka mencari kabar seputar Nur Said, lulusan Ngruki yang diduga terkait dengan pengeboman Hotel JW Marriott dan Ritz-Carlton di Mega Kuningan, Jakarta.

Meski membenarkan bahwa Nur Said pernah *mondok* di pesantren yang didirikannya, Abubakar Ba'asyir mengaku tak pernah mengenal bekas santri yang kini dicari-cari polisi itu. Berikut ini petikan wawancara sejumlah wartawan, termasuk Ahmad Rafiq dari *Tempo*, dengan Abubakar.

Bekas santri Anda, Nur Said, disebut-sebut terlibat pengeboman?
Itu kan baru dugaan. Belum tentu benar. Menurut saya, tidak semudah itu orang keluar-masuk hotel yang penjagaannya ketat. Kalaupun itu benar, saya yakin ada pihak-pihak yang menunggangi. Seperti pada kasus bom Bali. Yang percaya bom Bali buatan Muchlas hanya orang idiot.

Anda mengenal Nur Said?
Tidak. Memang dia pernah menjadi santri di sini dan lulus pada 1994, namun waktu itu saya masih di Malaysia, tak pernah bertemu dengannya. Setelah dia lulus, kami belum pernah bertemu. Mendengar namanya saja juga baru kemarin. Kalau Muchlas, memang saya pernah bertemu.

Jadi, menurut Anda, peledakan bom di Mega Kuningan itu....
Saya curiga peledakan itu rekayasa oleh lawan-lawan Islam. Tujuannya, memfitnah umat Islam, agar pemerintah bertindak represif terhadap umat Islam. Misalnya agar para mubalig ditangkapi.

Anda percaya Noor Din M. Top berada di balik peledakan bom tersebut?
Kalau sudah tidak senang, orang cenderung langsung menuduh. Padahal bukti-buktinya belum ada. Saya justru menduga Amerika berada di balik kejadian tersebut. Rekayasa sengaja dibuat untuk memojokkan Islam. Namun ini baru praduga.

Sabili – Ideological Warfare is More Powerful, and Dangerous, Than Bombs

In the wake of the 17 July 2009 terrorist bombings of the Marriott and Ritz-Carlton Hotels in Jakarta, a second enormous wave of publicity swept Indonesia, linking the terrorists to the transnational ideology of Wahhabism identified in *The Illusion of an Islamic State*. The extremist magazine *Sabili* dedicated an entire issue in August of 2009 to defending Wahhabism and denying its alleged role in terrorism, including this 4-page article about *The Illusion of an Islamic State*, excerpts of which appear below:

Like the change of seasons, heavy rain always begins with an initial shower. The enemies of Islam never cease in their efforts to destroy the Muslim community. They use not only physical methods, but ideological warfare as well. They regard this methodology as more inexpensive and effective. Just look at what happened before the bombing of the J.W. Marriott and Ritz Carlton hotels. A couple months earlier we were "treated" to the book *The Illusion of an Islamic State*, which attacks political Islam.

The afore-mentioned book was published jointly by the Bhinneka Tunngal Ika [Oneness Amid Diversity: Indonesia's national slogan] Movement, the Wahid Institute and the Maarif Institute. The book represents the result of more than two years' research by LibForAll Foundation. The book's editor was [former Indonesian president] Gus Dur, and its proof-reader Mohamad Guntur Romli.

The book—whose full title is *The Illusion of an Islamic State: The Expansion of Transnational Islamist Movements to Indonesia*—identifies the PKS as part of a hard-line transnational Islamist movement. The PKS rejected this claim and said that the book's authors are all tools of former U.S. president George W. Bush. In the editor's introduction written by Abdurrahman Wahid (Gus Dur), he states that the PKS infiltrated the Muhammadiyah during its Congress in July of 2005 in Malang. At the time, the agents of hard-line movements such as PKS dominated many forums and succeeded in electing a number of extremist movement sympathizers to the Muhammadiyah's central board....

History tells the world that radicalism is constantly nurtured, to serve colonial interests that always alternate players. Thus, loud statements about [an alleged] Wahhabi [threat] are truly more powerful and dangerous than bombs.

Ghazwul Fikri Lebih Dahsyat dari Bom

Rabu, 12 Agustus 2009 06:29

Ibarat musim, hujan lebat selalu dimulai dengan gerimis terlebih dulu. Usaha musuh-musuh Islam untuk menghancurkan umat Islam tak pernah kendor.

Tak hanya fisik, ghazwul fikri pun ditempuh. Cara ini dipandang lebih efektif dan murah. Lihatlah, sebelum terjadi pengeboman di JW Marriot dan Ritz Carlton. Bulan sebelumnya kita disuguhkan dengan buku Ilusi Negara Islam. Buku ini menyerang Islam politik.

Buku tersebut diterbitkan atas kerjasama Gerakan Bhineka Tunggal Ika, the Wahid Institute dan Maarif Institute. Buku itu merupakan hasil penelitian yang berlangsung lebih dari dua tahun dan dilakukan oleh LibForAll Foundation. Yang menjadi editor dalam buku itu adalah Gus Dur dan yang menjadi penyelaras bahasanya adalah Mohamad Guntur Romli.

Buku berjudul lengkap Ilusi Negara Islam: Ekspansi Gerakan Islam Transnasional di Indonesia yang menyebutkan PKS sebagai bagian dari gerakan Islam garis keras transnasional. PKS membantah dan mengatakan, para penulis buku itu merupakan antek-antek dari mantan Presiden AS George W Bush.

Dalam kata pengantar buku itu yang ditulis oleh Abdurrahman Wahid (Gus Dur), memaparkan bahwa PKS telah melakukan infiltrasi ke Muhammadiyah pada Muktamar Muhammadiyah Juli 2005 di Malang. Saat itu, para agen kelompok garis keras seperti PKS mendominasi banyak forum dan berhasil memilih beberapa simpatisan gerakan garis keras menjadi Ketua PP Muhammdiyah.

"Dugaan saya, dana riset buku itu didapatkan dari Bush. Itu merupakan proyek terakhir Bush sebelum kejatuhannya. Karena Bush memiliki kebijakan perang melawan terorisme," ujar Wasekjen PKS Fahri Hamzah.

Menurut Fahri, tulisan-tulisan yang ada pada buku itu masih mengacu pada framework dunia saat Bus masih jadi Presiden AS. "Padahal kan framework dunia sudah berbeda dan tuduhan-tuduhan tentang PKS itu semuanya palsu. Saat ini dunia sudah mulai tidak terlalu menyoroti isu terorisme, bahkan dunia sudah menilai Bush sebagai penjahat perang," katanya.

Adapun tuduhan terhadap Hizbut Tahrir sebagai kelompok yang membahayakan Indonesia, adalah sebuah kebohongan besar. Hizbut Tahrir dengan perjuangan syariah dan Khilafah justru bertujuan untuk menyelamatkan Indonesia dari keterpurukan akibat Sekularisme, Liberalisme, Kapitalisme dan penjajahan modern di segala bidang.

Menurut Ismail Yusanto, Jurubicara HTI, Liberalisme dan Sekularisme yang selama ini mereka propagandakan itulah yang telah nyata-nyata merusak dan menghancurkan Indonesia. Atas dasar Liberalisme pula, mereka mendukung aliran sesat (Ahmadiyah, Lia Eden, dll) legalisasi aborsi, menolak larangan pornografi dan pornoaksi, mendukung penjualan aset-aset strategis.

"Maka, merekalah yang sesungguhnya harus diwaspadai, karena mereka menghalangi upaya penyelamatan Indonesia dengan syariah, dengan tetap mempertahankan Sekularisme dan penjajahan asing di negeri ini," tegas Ismail Yusanto.

Dalam masalah Bom di JW Marriot dan Ritz Carlton, HTI Menyerukan kepada semua pihak, khususnya kepolisian dan media massa, untuk bersikap hati-hati menanggapi spekulasi yang mengaitkan bom JW Marriot dan Ritz Carlton ini dengan kelompok, gerakan atau organisasi Islam. Dari sekian kemungkinan, bisa saja peledakan bom itu sengaja dilakukan oleh orang atau kelompok tertentu untuk mengacaukan situasi keamanan di masyarakat dan negara ini demi mendiskreditkan organisasi Islam.

Setelah pelaku bom bunuh diri di Hotel JW Marriott Jakarta, Jumat (17/7), berhasil diungkap Kepolisian. Kontroversi teror bom masih mengganggu benak umat muslim Indonesia. Kedekatan pelaku dengan Noordin M Top dan Jamaah Islamiyah (JI) seolah-olah kembali menggiring opini publik jika Islam di Indonesia identik dengan kekerasan meski tanpa bukti dan fakta yang nyata. Sehingga menyebabkan antipati publik terhadap Islam. Padahal, selama ini Islam selalu hidup damai, terbuka dan toleran.

Sabili – Radicalism Is Being Cultivated Intentionally

This four-page cover story floats the theory that "foreign intelligence agencies" and other "enemies of Islam" are deliberately maintaining terrorist groups, so that "whenever the plans of those who wish to destroy Muslims and Indonesia are ripe, they simply click their fingers and launch a deadly terrorist strike."

Radikalisme Sengaja Dipelihara

RABU, 12 AGUSTUS 2009 06:34

Setelah sekian lama tiarap, bom kembali diledakkan. Hasil dari memelihara radikalisme?

Pagi itu, Jumat (17/7/09), kawasan Mega Kuningan, Jakarta Selatan, masih sejuk dan segar. Di kawasan inilah Hotel JW Marriot dan The Ritz Carlton berdiri berdampingan. Lalu lintas di pusat bisnis ini pun masih lengang. Tak heran jika di beberapa sudut jalan setapak di kawasan ini, terlihat beberapa orang sedang berolahraga, lari pagi atau jalan cepat.

Jarum jam baru menunjuk angka 07.30 WIB, ketika di JW Lounge, lantai 1 Hotel JW Marriott, suasana sedikit berbeda. Di restoran yang berdekatan dengan lobby hotel ini, berkumpul 18 petinggi perusahaan multinasional dan nasional. Ada Timothy Mackay (Presiden Direktur Holcim Indonesia), Kevin Moore (Presiden Direktur Husky Oil), Dave Potter (Direktur Eksplorasi Freeport Indonesia), Adrianto Machribie (Penasihat Senior Presiden Direktur PT Freeport Indonesia), dan Noke Kiroyan (Presiden Direktur Kiroyan Partners).

Di situ juga bergabung James Castle, mantan Presiden Kamar Dagang Amerika Serikat di Indonesia. Saat ini, ia menjabat chairman dan pendiri Castle Asia, perusahaan konsultan yang didirikan di Jakarta pada 1980. Perusahaan ini bergerak di bidang strategi advokasi kebijakan, proyeksi ekonomi, resiko politik, dan market-entry. Oleh sejumlah kalangan, James Castle dipercaya sebagai pelobi ulung bagi perusahaan asing yang akan atau sedang berinvestasi di Indonesia.

Acara kumpul para eksekutif ini merupakan perhelatan rutin tiap Jumat pagi yang digelar oleh Castle Asia. Sebelum masuk acara utama, yang akan membahas perkembangan bisnis minyak dan pertambangan, para ekspatriat ini beramah tamah sambil sarapan pagi terlebih dulu. Sedianya, pengamat ekonomi Umar Juoro dijadwalkan sebagai pembicara utama, tapi yang bersangkutan berhalangan hadir. Mereka menempati meja panjang dengan 18 kursi.

Acara belum dimulai, para peserta masih menikmati sarapannya sambil menyeruput minuman hangat. Jarum jam menunjuk angka 07.45 WIB, ketika tiba-tiba terdengar ledakan dasyat. Bom pertama meledak di Hotel JW Marriott. Sepuluh menit kemudian, bom juga menghancurkan Lobby Hotel Ritz Carlton yang berdiri bersebelahan dengan JW Marriott.

Jakarta seakan terhenti sesaat, tapi tak lama. Pasalnya, telunjuk aparat dan siapapun yang mendengar berita pengeboman ini, langsung mengarahkan pada lima huruf sakral 'Islam' sebagai pelaku sekaligus dalang intelektualnya. Dalam tempo singkat, kepolisian langsung menetapkan bahwa bom yang meledak di dua hotel itu adalah 'bom bunuh diri.' Orang yang diduga sebagai pelaku bom bunuh diri pun segera dilansir. Bukti berupa rekaman CCTV pun ditayangkan sejumlah stasiun televisi.

Sabili – Jemaah Islamiyah Didn't Do It

Another article in the 13 August 2009 issue of *Sabili* featured a six-page interview with a former commander of the terrorist group responsible for the July 2009 bombings in Jakarta. "Abu Rusydan... received his military training at Camp Mujahaddin Afghanistan in Sadda, Pakistan. His position in Jemaah Islamiyah was as the head of Military Region III, which exercised authority over a number of districts including the Indonesian and Malaysian areas of Borneo, Sulawesi and the southern Philippines. He has also been identified as having functioned day-to-day as the operational head of Jemaah Islamiyah. A court sentenced him to 3 years and 6 months in prison for having sheltered Mukhlas, in conjunction with the first Bali bombing.

"It isn't easy to meet this 47-year-old man born in Kudus. The stigma that attaches itself to anyone accused of being a terrorist is crude and terrifying. However, when Eman Mulyatman from *Sabili* met with Abu Rusydan in his home in Kudus, Central Java, that image completely vanished. Abu Rusydan was friendly, and even humorous.... Without requesting that anything be off the record or hidden in any way, he spoke openly with our reporter."

During the interview, Abu Rusydan remarks: "*The Illusion of an Islamic State* really scourged Wahhabism, only it didn't directly state that Jemaah Islamiyah is part of the Wahhabi movement. But the [Muslim Brotherhood-affiliated] Justice and Prosperity Party (PKS) fell victim and was gravely wounded [by the book's publication]."

[Note: contrary to Abu Rusydan's assertion that *The Illusion of an Islamic State* did not link Jemaah Islamiyah to the Wahhabi movement, chapter 2 of this book ("The Infiltration of Wahhabi/Muslim Brotherhood Ideology in Indonesia") describes the extensive links between the terrorist group Jemaah Islamiyah and al-Qaeda, with its Wahhabi/Muslim Brotherhood ideology.]

CYBERSabili.com

Bukan JI Pelakunya

Jumat, 31 Juli 2009 07:21

itu tendensius sekali persoalan jadi tidak jelas

Tokoh Jamaah Islamiyah Abu Rusydan

Abu Rusydan, dalam catatan polisi ustadz yang satu ini juga memiliki beberapa nama alias, Thoriquddin alias Hamzah. Lelaki yang satu ini, pernah mendapat pendidikan militer di Kamp Mujahidin Afghanistan, di Sadda, Pakistan.

Jabatannya dalam Jamaah Islamiyah adalah Ketua Mantiqi III yang memiliki otoritas di beberapa wilayah seperti Kalimantan, Sabar dan Sarawak, Sulawesi termasuk juga Filipina Selatan.

Namanya juga pernah disebut sebagai Pelaksana Harian tugas Amir Jamaah Islamiyah (JI). Pengadilan memberikan vonis 3 tahun 6 bulan padanya karena dianggap melindungi Mukhlas, dalam peristiwa Bom Bali I.

Tak mudah bertemu pria kelahiran Kudus 47 tahun silam ini. Stigma yang sudah melekat pada setiap sosok yang dituduh teroris, adalah kasar dan menyeramkan. Tapi, ketika Eman Mulyatman dari Sabili bertemu dengan Abu Rusydan di rumahnya, Kudus Jaw Tengah, image tersebut langsung pudar.

Abu Rusydan ramah, bahkan cenderung humoris. "Nanti antum rugi kalau jauh-jauh dari Jakarta tidak foto sama ana," selorohnya saat mengajak Sabili foto bersama.

Berikut petikan wawancaranya:

Setelah peristiwa bom, lagi-lagi umat Islam menjadi sasaran?

Sebetulnya, tidak ada pengamat, intel, bekas intel maupun aparat keamanan yang menyebutnya. Tidak secara langsung menyebut umat Islam, bahkan mereka juga agak segan menyebut nama JI terlibat dalam aksi-aksi itu. Mereka selalu menggunakan istilah, Kelompok Nordin.

AM Hendropriyono (Mantan Kepala BIN) menyebut Wahabi Radikal?

Itu tendensius sekali, Wahabi itu apa, jadi tidak jelas. Kalau yang dimaksud gerakan Syekh Muhammad Abdul Wahab, tapi dari kitab-kitab dan hujjah-hujjah yang kita pelajari itu benar. Nah sekarang yang dimaksud Wahabi itu apa, justru dengan lontaran semacam itu, persoalan jadi bertambah ruwet.

Apa targetnya?

Sekali lagi statemen itu tendesius. Wahabi itu memang gerakan agama sekaligus gerakan politik. Jadi kita mewarisi gerakan Wahabi bukan dalam rangka gerakan politiknya. Tapi, bagaimana tulisan-tulisan beliau yang sesuai dengan al-Qur'an, As-Sunnah dan Salafusshalih, itu yang kita ambil.

Apakah pernyataan itu semacam test the water?

Tidak tahu. Tapi jelas tendensius dan ada semacam sentimen anti Wahabi. Buku Ilusi Negara Islam, jelas menghantam Wahabi, hanya tidak disebut langsung bahwa JI sebagai bagian dari Wahabi. Tapi justru Partai Keadilan Sejahtera (PKS) yang menjadi korban.

Jangan-jangan yang mengucapkan tidak mengerti?

Ya silakan ditanyakan sendiri. Yang jelas ucapan itu sering diucapkan oleh orang-orang yang tidak suka dengan gerakan pemurnian akidah.

Semacam propaganda begitu?

Jadi sebenarnya cap buruk kepada Wahabi itu warisan penjajah Barat. Jadi kalau ini perang propaganda, maka harus dihadapi dengan propaganda pula. Tapi, kalau itu dimaksudkan untuk perbaikan bangsa, mari kita jujur. Jadi harus jelas maksudnya apa, agar tidak kontraproduktif.

Sabili – Wahhabism: Stigma, or [Genuine] Extremism?

A four-page article in the same issue of *Sabili* defends Wahhabism, explaining that "Wahhabism is employed as a stigma by those who don't want Islam to assume a political role in Indonesia," and exhorting readers: "Don't let 'Wahhabism' become a stigma like 'communism' and 'the Communist Party of Indonesia' during the Suharto regime...."

Sabili – Watch Out for Attempts to Discredit Islam!

Another four-page article warns readers: "After the bombs exploded in Kuningan, Jakarta, Muslim leaders warned the public not to allow this incident to 'corner' Islam. There are some who believe that the bombings were actually planned to discredit and destroy Islam."

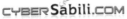

Home ⁞ Berita ⁞ Indonesia Kita ⁞ Awas Mendiskreditkan Islam

Awas Mendiskreditkan Islam!
RABU, 12 AGUSTUS 2009 06:24

Setelah bom meledak di bilangan Kuningan Jakarta, tokoh-tokoh Islam menyatakan jangan sampai peristiwa ini menyudutkan Islam. Ada yang berpendapat peristiwa ini seperti sudah direncanakan memang untuk menjatuhkan Islam.

Cerahnya pagi hari seharusnya berarti keceriaan. Dari hari sebelumnya dia adalah pembaharuan. Tapi tidak demikian. Pagi yang cerah penuh kesedihan. Rakyat Indonesia di waktu itu penuh tangisan, menyaksikan puluhan orang menjadi korban ledakan.

Penyebabnya sama dengan tragedi Bali 2002 dan 2005, serta tragedi JW Marriot 2003. Bom lagi-lagi menumpahkan darah manusia. Tempatnya pun tidak berbeda, JW Marriot. Bahkan kali ini, hotel tetangganya, Ritz Carlton, juga jadi sasaran ledakan pada Jumat 17 Juli.

Kedua hotel itu memiliki sistem keamanan yang sangat ketat. Sehari-hari, belasan petugas keamanan bersenjata lengkap siap sedia. Kendaraan tidak sembarangan bisa parkir di basement. Untuk melewati portal menuju parkiran, sebuah mobil tidak lepas dari sorotan mata 10 petugas keamanan.

Kalau sudah terparkir, mobil pun akan dicek, entah bagian bawahnya, atau bagasinya. Untuk masuk ke lobi saja, seseorang masih kena pemeriksaan lagi. Jika membawa tas, maka tas tersebut akan dibuka, untuk diketahui apa isinya.

Pengamanan yang sudah ketat begitu saja masih bisa bobol. Tidak tanggung-tanggung, bom langsung meledakkan ruang restauran Syailendra hotel JW Marriot dan restauran Airlangga hotel Ritz Carlton.

Pernyataan Umat Islam

Pada tanggal yang sama, Ismail Yusanto, jurubicara Hizbut Tahrir, mengutuk pelaku tindakan keji ini sebagai tindakan zalim luar biasa. Dia juga mengimbau pihak kepolisian dan media masa untuk berhati-hati menanggapi spekulasi yang mengaitkan pemboman ini dengan kelompok, gerakan, atau organisasi Islam tertentu.

"Bisa saja pelakunya adalah orang atau kelompok tertentu untuk mengacaukan situasi keamanan demi kepentingan politik mereka sambil mendiskreditkan organisasi Islam." Jika ini terjadi, maka dia mensinyalir hal tersebut sebagai rekayasa sistematis serta provokasi keji untuk menyudutkan Indonesia sebagai sarang teroris.

Hidayatullah Magazine Interview – Asep Sobari: the Terms "Transnational Islam" and "Wahhabi" have been Pirated

Another major extremist magazine, *Hidayatullah*, also devoted an August cover story and several articles to the subject of Wahhabism, and *The Illusion of an Islamic State's* role in generating massive public rejection of Wahhabi/radical ideology, as seen below:

The NU and Muhammadiyah [Indonesia's two largest Muslim organizations] have also been influenced by transnationalism. Their founders had relationships with ulama in Mecca and the Hijaz.

Hidayatullah.com – The terms Wahhabi and transnational have become overnight sensations. Yes, without wind or rain, they have suddenly become linked [in the public imagination] with terrorist bombs. The strange thing is, those who launched the term Wahhabi [as an ideological weapon] have never been intensely associated with Islam. Even more disturbing, the mass media has joined this campaign to stigmatize Wahhabism and transnational Islam, without understanding the true meaning of these terms, or the effect of their current usage. "A form of pirating has occurred in recent months, through the appropriation of the terms 'transnational Islam' and 'Wahhabi'," said Asep Sobari.

This week, www.hidayatullah.com interviews a researcher in the history of Islam from the Institute for the Study of Islamic Thought and Civilizations (INSISTS), Asep Sobari, LC (33 years old). A graduate of Darussalam Gontor Modern Islamic Boarding School in Ponogoro (1994), he is recognized as an expert in Islamic history. He continued his studies at the Islamic University of Medina (1999), which is dedicated to developing the religious thought of Shaykh Muhammad Abdullah bin Wahab. Asep explained at length to hidayatullah.com what lies behind the stigmatization of "Wahhabism" and "transnational Islam," which everyone [in Indonesia] has been talking about for months.

The term "Wahhabi" has become the subject of intense polemic in recent months, among a wide variety of groups. Can you explain the background of this term?

Wahhabi is a term that appeared in conjunction with the movement founded by Shaykh Muhammad Abdullah bin Wahab in Saudi Arabia. In my opinion, from the perspective of *mazhab* [schools of Islamic jurisprudence], Shaykh Abdullah bin Wahab was a follower of the Hanbali School of Law. That particular school is one of four recognized by all [Muslim] nations. That includes the NU, which adheres to *ahlussunnah wal-jamaah* [Sunni Islam]. In terms of morality, there is nothing new or deviant about Wahhabism. It's simply a revival of Ibn Tamiyah's teachings. Pure moral views. Thus it is known for purifying *tauhid* [monotheism].

Then why are people linking the term Wahhabi to terrorism?

Exactly. What is there even extreme about it? Much less to tie Wahhabism to extremism and terror. That's impossible! Where are these accusations coming from?

In your opinion, where does the term Wahhabi originate?

In reality, Shaykh Muhammad Abdullah bin Wahab and his group did not use that term themselves; it was a label imposed on them by leaders from other (rival) groups. The question is, why did those people proclaim that Shaykh Abdullah bin Wahab founded a "Wahhabi" movement, when he himself never claimed to have done so? Well, we should ask those who are using the term. In their opinion, what is Wahhabism, and who are its followers? What is the movement and what are its objectives? All these issues can be discussed in an objective, scientific manner, through academic channels [rather than the nationwide uproar over Wahhabism currently underway in Indonesia]. A great deal of literature exists, explaining the concepts of Abdullah bin Wahab. From this study we can ascertain whether Wahhabism propagates an aroma of terrorism and extreme behavior, as claimed by many people who have a false understanding [of Wahhabism].

What were Shaykh Abdullah bin Wahab's views regarding violence, for example?

According to historical records, he himself had absolutely no thoughts or agenda like that. He never permitted anyone to be killed. He forbade the killing of Muslims, and also of non-Muslims. Thus, once again, he had absolutely no views that could rightly cause his movement to be identified as extremist.

What about Arab tribal conflict and civil wars?

There is a history of war, as virtually every nation has a history of conflict or war. But it's weird that this should be linked to terrorism. And what does any of that have to do with Shaykh Abdullah bin Wahab? Once again, I'm still confused: what is the term Wahhabi supposed to mean? Try to get those who hurl such accusations to explain themselves. Are they talking about people who live in Saudi Arabia, or follow the religious beliefs of Shaykh Abdullah bin Wahab?

So what really happened, to give birth to the term Wahhabi?

Those who created the term Wahhabi were individuals and/ or groups who did not follow the religious teachings of Shaykh Abdullah bin Wahab, and were unhappy with his movement. History records the existence of rival political movements linked to the Ottoman dynasty, governing the Hijaz, and a number of differences of opinion between Abdul Wahab's school of law and ulama [Muslim scholars] living in the Hijaz. As a result, there emerged a stigmatization of Abdullah bin Wahab, in order to discredit him. However, he himself straightened out these matters. Thus, in reality, the name or term Wahhabi was not self-generated, but imposed upon the new movement from the outside, in order to stigmatize it. To heighten the effectiveness of this stigma, leaders of various other movements have become identified as "Wahhabi movements," when in reality they have no relationship whatsoever with Abdullah bin Wahab in Saudi Arabia.

So this is all a distortion of history, is that right?

Yes, right. It's a distortion of historical facts. A huge number of Muslim groups exist at present. Some of them have adopted the thoughts of Shaykh Abdullah bin Wahab. But it is by no means certain that they represent the true or original religious teachings of Shaykh Abdullah bin Wahab himself. They may be non-representative. Just like with the term "transnational" that's being talked about so much these days.

What exactly do they mean by the term transnational? There is no clear definition. They seem to be using this term to distinguish between Islamic movements indigenous to Indonesia and a "foreign" Islam. That's too superficial. Because fundamentally, Islam does not distinguish between "local" and "international." Islam does not recognize territory or state, all are the same to Islam. All is fundamentally transnational. No matter where they are from, Muslim leaders study Islam in the Middle East, including the NU's leadership. *Rahmatan lil 'âlamin* ["a blessing for all creation"] is transnational. The very phrase indicates [that Islam is] a blessing for *all* creation. Thus, in my opinion, there's been a pirating of terminology, followed by a new and specific definition given to the term [transnational], in order to promote specific interests. We adhere to Islam as a blessing for ALL creation, not a "local" Islam. The same is true of the NU and Muhammadiyah. And if there is a "local" Islam, that's just an alias for *bid'a* [deviant and heretical innovations]. [The five times daily] prayer is one [for all Muslims], and the basic belief system of Islam is one.

So distinguishing between national and transnational Islam leads to religious deviance and heresy?

Yes. I'll give you a specific example. There's a book entitled *The Illusion of an Islamic State.* It has given rise to enormous polemics [within Indonesia], which is precisely what they intended. All kinds of people are now following the lead of [the book's authors, former Indonesian president and NU chairman] Gus Dur and [former Muhammadiyah chairman] Syafii Maarif [criticizing Wahhabism and transnational Islamist movements]. But what is clear is that this book was created by LibForAll, a foreign NGO operating in Indonesia. In my opinion, this is transnationalism in spades. They are attacking "transnational Islam," using deep-rooted local power structures [in Indonesia]. And yet LibForAll itself is not local. This should be criticized.

The NU and Muhammadiyah have also been influenced by transnationalism. Their founders had relationships with ulama in Mecca, the Hijaz and elsewhere. Leading NU figures in Indonesia had close ties to the recently deceased [Sufi master and leading exponent of the Maliki school of Islamic jurisprudence] Shaykh Alawi al-Maliki in Mecca. Thus the NU is not a purely local school of Islamic jurisprudence. In addition, Imam Shafi'i [founder of the Shafi'i school of jurisprudence, practiced in Indonesia] was born in Gaza and raised in Mecca. Later he studied in Egypt and his school of jurisprudence is followed in Indonesia, including by the NU. And yet no one has ever found fault with this, much less viewed it as "transnationalism."

If the definition of transnational Islam is a movement that is affiliated with ulama in the Middle East, whether in terms of *mazhab* [school of jurisprudence] or thought, then every single Islamic movement in Indonesia is transnational. Don't forget, the founders of these two mass organizations (the Muhammadiyah and NU) studied in the Middle East and adhere to a school of jurisprudence that originated in the Middle East.

Then what about the definition various individuals are giving to Wahhabism and its [alleged] ties to terrorism?

In recent months there has been a pirating of the terms "transnational Islam" and "Wahhabism." Especially when these terms are given a negative connotation, [and identified] as movements involved in the spread of terrorism. The creation and/or redefinition of such terminology has occurred in order to serve specific interests. I do not deny that some people are attracted to violence. Perhaps there is such a thing as terrorism. But terrorism is not caused by any single factor. There may be people who commit violent acts, but one shouldn't discuss or attribute their actions to a specific school of Islamic jurisprudence [such as Wahhabism]. That is unwise. In my opinion, it constitutes stigmatization and is a very serious error. At present, by imposing this stigma, even to the point of mentioning physical characteristics—for example, those who wear trousers cut above their ankles, beards and other features [typical of Wahhabis]—people are directly stigmatizing a particular target. In essence, organized efforts are underway to cause Muslims to lose their identity [i.e., reject Wahhabism]. Organized efforts are underway to trap Muslims, and inspire fear in those who follow the path of Islam [i.e., Wahhabis and their allies]. Even though following the example [of the Prophet Muhammad] is noble. What's wrong with wearing a beard and expressing our love for the Messenger of God, by wearing clothes that are more Islamic, and from the perspective of morality and politeness clearly embody the values of Islam?

Is there a foreign entity intervening and giving rise to this stigmatization of Wahhabism and transnational [Islam]?
    The book *The Illusion of an Islamic State* represents a concrete form of transnational [intervention].

Who benefits from this case?
    Those who have interests. There is no need to say who in particular. This stigma has arisen because of a conflict between two powers. The dominant power that wants stability [and a continuation of its dominance]. If it has no strength of argument, then it resorts to stigmatization. In the history of the Prophet's struggle [to promote Islam], this strategy was often employed by the Quraish infidels. They knew that the Messenger of God was knowledgeable, that the Messenger enjoyed inner peace and gratitude to God, but because he brought new teachings stigmatization arose, with people claiming that the Prophet was a black magician, a plagiarist and other such things. Because the Quraish could not defeat him through argument.
    They [the power(s) behind *The Illusion of an Islamic State*] are afraid [of change] and seek to maintain their power through stigmatizing things derived from the example of the Messenger of God. Westerners have researched Islam for hundreds of years. They know exactly what they're doing [with this book and its stigmatization of Wahhabism]. Although they're committing these corrupt acts, Islam is too strong [to be destroyed by the West]. Their efforts can always be defeated, even if [they're so strong and effective that] Muslims retreat [at first]. But Westerners know that Muslims have a power that, once consciously awakened, cannot be defeated [by the West]. Thus, they hope that their [campaign of] stigmatization will cause Muslims to lose confidence and feel inferior, and lack immunity [to such attacks].

What about accusations leveled by the former head of Indonesia's national intelligence agency Hendropriono or the commander of Detachment 88 [Indonesia's elite counter-terrorism unit], Suryadarma Salim, who say that there is a relationship between [terrorist] bombs and the establishment of an Islamic State?

You should ask them to clarify their statements and explain what they mean by Wahhabism, before you pay any further attention [to their claims]. Is their definition identical with that of Shaykh Abdullah bin Wahab? They keep talking about an Islamic state. But in Saudi Arabia itself, there is no issue concerning an Islamic state, much less any organized effort to overthrow the official [Saudi] state, so long as it is not 100% infidel by nature. It is forbidden for people in Saudi Arabia even to demonstrate. Why? Because such behavior is considered a prelude to open rebellion. Thus it is truly strange if Wahhabism is linked to efforts to establish an Islamic state [in Indonesia]. When they talk about Wahhabis, it isn't clear who they're talking about. [Syaiful Anshor/cha/www.hidayatullah.com]

Asep Sobari: Ada Pembajakan Istilah "Islam Transnasional" dan "Wahabi"

Hidayatullah.com—Istilah Wahabi dan transnasional mendadak terkenal. Tanpa ada angin dan hujan, ia, tiba-tiba dikaitkan dengan teror bom. Uniknya, yang melancarkan istilah Wahabi bukan orang yang selama ini dikenal intens ada sangkut-pautnya dengan Islam. Lebih merepotkan, media ikut andil mengkampanyekan stigma itu tanpa mengerti benar apa arti sesungguhnya istilah itu berikut dampaknya. "Ada semacam pembajakan istilah 'Islam transnasional' dan 'Wahabi' akhir-akhir ini." kata Asep Sobari.

Kali ini, www.hidayatullah.com, mewawancarai peneliti sejarah Islam pada *Institute for the Study of Islamic Thought and Civilizations (INSISTS)* Asep Sobari, Lc (33). Lulusan Pesantren Modern Darussalam Gontor Ponogoro (1994) dikenal pengamat sejarah Islam. Ia pernah melanjutkan studi di Univ. Islam Madinah (1999), tempat pemikiran Muhammad Syeikh Abdullah bin Wahab berkembang. Kepada www.hidayatullah.com secara panjang lebar menjelaskan ada apa dibalik stigma

Istilah wahabi, akhir-akhir ini seolah menjadi polemik oleh sejumlah golongan. Bisakah antum menjelaskan latar belakang istilah itu?

Istilah Wahabi ini istilah yang dimunculkan dari dikaitkan dengan gerakan Muhammad Syeikh Abdullah bin Wahab di Arab Saudi. Menurut saya, dari segi mazhab, sebenarnya Syeikh Abdullah bin Wahab juga menganut mazhab Hambali. Di mana mazhab ini adalah merupakan salah satu dari 4 mazhab lainnya yang diakui oleh seluruh negara. Termasuk NU yang menganut *ahlussunnah Wajamaah* (ASWAJA). Dalam masalah akidah tidak ada sesuatu yang baru dan melenceng darinya. Yang ada cuma penyegaran dari Ibnu Taimiyah. Pandangan akidanya murni. Makanya dikenal dengan memurnikan tauhid.

Tapi mengapa dikaitkan dengan teror?

Ya itu dia. Jadi letak ekstrim nya di mana? Apalagi dikait-kaitkan dengan ekstrimis dan teroris. Kok bisa, dari mana?

Menurut Anda, dari mana penyebutan istilah Wahabi itu?

Sebenarnya istilah ini bukan dinamakan oleh mereka sendiri (Syeikh Muhammad Abdullah Bin Wahab atau kelompoknya), melainkan justru dari pihak golongan luar. Masalahnya, kenapa orang luar yang mengatakan Syeikh Abdullah bin Wahab adalah gerakan Wahabi? Padahal ia sendiri tidak mengatakan demikian. Nah, kita patut mempertanyakan kepada yang memberi sebutan itu. Menurut mereka Wahabi itu sebenarnya siapa dan apa? Apa gerakannya apa gerakannya? Semua itu bisa diskusikan secara ilmiah dan melalui jalur akademis. Sudah banyak literatur yang membahas gagasan-gagasan Abdullah Bin Abdul Wahab. Setidaknya, dari situ bisa mengetahui, apa benar Wahabi itu menebarkan aroma teror dan tindakan ekstrimisme sebagaimana disebutkan beberapa orang yang tak mengerti benar.

Bagaimana pandangan Syeikh Abdullah bin Wahab tentang kekerasan, misalnya?

Menurut catatan sejarah, beliau sendiri tidak memiliki gagasan maupun pemikiran seperti itu. Beliau tidak pernah membolehkan pembunuhan. Janganlah pembunuhan terhadap Muslim, di luar Muslim juga diharamkan untuk dibunuh. Jadi, sekali lagi, tidak ada pandangan beliau yang mengidentifikasi sebagai gerakan ekstrimisme.

Bagaimana kasus konflik suku dan perang saudara di Arab?

Adapun sejarah perang, praktis semua Negara punya sejarah konflik atau perang. Tapi aneh saja bisa dikaitkan dengan kasus terorisme. Dari apa kaitannya dengan Syeikh Abdullah bin Wahab. Lagi pula saya masih bingung istilah Wahabi itu apa? Coba yang melontarkan pernyataan itu menjelaskan. Apakah orang yang ada di Saudi atau yang mengikuti pemikiran Syeikh Abdullah Bin Wahab.

Jadi apa sebenarnya yang terjadi dengan munculnya istilah Wahabi itu?

Yang membuat istilah Wahabi sebenarnya adalah orang ataupun golongan di luar kelompok penganut pemikiran Syeikh Abdullah Bin Wahab yang tidak senang dengan gerakannya. Dalam sejarah, ada gerakan rival politiknya, berkaitan dengan Dinasti Ustmaniyah, pemerintah di Hijaz, dan sejumlah perbedaan paham antara mazhab Abdul Wahab dengan ulama Hijaz. Kemudian, munculah stigma-stigma yang dimunculkan untuk mendeskriditkan Abdullah Bin Wahab. Namun hal itu pernah dilunaskan oleh beliau. Jadi, sebelumnya, nama atau istilah Wahabi itu bukan dari dalam, melainkan dari luar dengan mengatakan gerakan itu. Untuk lebih menarik, kemudian tokoh gerakan itu dikenalah menjadi gerakan Wahabisme, yang pada dasarnya, tidak memiliki keterkaitan dengan Abdullah bin Wahab di Arab Saudi.

Jadi semacam ada pendistorian sejarah ya?

Ya benar. Ada semacam pendistorsian fakta sejarah. Sekarang ini banyak kelompok gerakan Islam sangat ekstis. Sebagian memakai pemikiran Syeikh Abdullah bin Wahab. Namun belum tentu mewakili orisinalitas pemikiran Syeikh bin Abdul Wahab sendiri. Bisa tidak representative. Sama dengan istilah transnasional yang sering didengung-dengungkan sekarang ini.

Mereka menyebut istilah transnasional maksudnya apa? Itu definisi yang tidak jelas. Mendefinisikan ada keterkaitan pola-pola gerakan Islam Indonesia dengan Islam di luar negeri itu terlalu dangkal. Karena pada dasarnya Islam tidak mengenal pembedaan lokal atau internasional. Islam tidak mengenal territorial dan Negara, semua sama. Semuanya dasarnya transnasional. Tokoh-tokoh Islam di manapun, pernah belajar Islam di Timur Tengah. Termasuk tokoh-tokoh NU. Rahmatan lilalamin itu transnasional. Namanya juga *rahmatan lilalamin*. Jadi menurut saya, ada pembagian terminologi. Kemudian didefinisikan tertentu untuk kepentingan tertentu. Kita ini Islam rahmatan lil'alamin bukan Islam lokal. NU dan Muhammadiyah juga seperti itu. Justru kalau ada Islam lokal, malah nggak jelas alias bid'ah. Shalat kan satu dan dasar-dasar pemikirannya kan satu.

Jadi pembagian istilah nasional dan transnasional itu menyesatkan gitu?

Ya. Contoh nyata. Ada buku berjudul *"Ilusi Negara Islam"*. Buku yang menjadi polemik karena sumbernya mereka sendiri. Ada sih yang merujuk Gus Dur dan Syafii Maarif. Tapi yang jelas, buku ini didukung Libforaal, sebuah LSM asing di Indonesia. Menurut saya, ini adalah transnasional paling nyata. Menyebut dengan Islam transnasional dengan kekuatan lokal. Libforaal itu bukan lokal, jadi ini harus dikritisi.

NU dan Muhammadiyah juga terpengaruh transnasional. Pendirinya NU ada hubungan dengan transnasional. Para kiai ada hubungan dengan ulama di Mekah, hijaz dan lainnya. Tokoh-tokoh NU di Indonesia itu punya keterkaitan dengan (jam) Syeikh Alawi Al-Maliki di Mekkah. Jadi tidak murni mazhab lokal. Selain itu, secara resmi Imam Syafii lahir di Gaza dan besar di Mekah. Lalu belajar di Mesir dan kemudian dipakai di Indonesia. Termasuk NU. Toh tidak pernah dipermasalahkan. Apalagi dianggap transnasional.

Liberation Youth – Ideological Warfare is More Powerful, and Dangerous, than Bombs

Articles supporting and opposing LibForAll's thesis that radical Islam underlies and animates terrorism spread virally through the internet, with a single article often posted on scores or even hundreds of sites. Here a *Sabili* article—which characterizes LibForAll's "ideological warfare" as a "cheaper and more effective means than physical attacks" to "destroy Islam and Muslims"—is reposted on a youth-oriented extremist site, one of at least several dozen websites that reposted this particular article.

LIBERATIONYOUTH

HOME   KAMI   ARTIKEL   BERITA   SASTRA   FORUM   ZINE

Ghazwul Fikri Lebih Dahsyat dari Bom

THURSDAY, 13 AUGUST 2009 07:59

Ibarat musim, hujan lebat selalu dimulai dengan gerimis terlebih dulu. Usaha musuh-musuh Islam untuk menghancurkan umat Islam tak pernah kendor.

Tak hanya fisik, ghazwul fikri pun ditempuh. Cara ini dipandang lebih efektif dan murah. Lihatlah, sebelum terjadi pengeboman di JW Marriot dan Ritz Carlton. Bulan sebelumnya kita disuguhkan dengan buku Ilusi Negara Islam. Buku ini menyerang Islam politik.

Buku tersebut diterbitkan atas kerjasama Gerakan Bhineka Tunggal Ika, the Wahid Institute dan Maarif Institute. Buku itu merupakan hasil penelitian yang berlangsung lebih dari dua tahun dan dilakukan oleh LibForAll Foundation. Yang menjadi editor dalam buku itu adalah Gus Dur dan yang menjadi penyelaras bahasanya adalah Mohamad Guntur Romli.

Buku berjudul lengkap Ilusi Negara Islam: Ekspansi Gerakan Islam Transnasional di Indonesia yang menyebutkan PKS sebagai bagian dari gerakan Islam garis keras transnasional. PKS membantah dan mengatakan, para penulis buku itu merupakan antek-antek dari mantan Presiden AS George W Bush.

Jihad and Dakwah (Proselytization) – Asep Sobari: The Terms "Transnational Islam" and "Wahhabi" Have been Pirated

Another example of articles being reposted, this on an explicitly jihadist website.

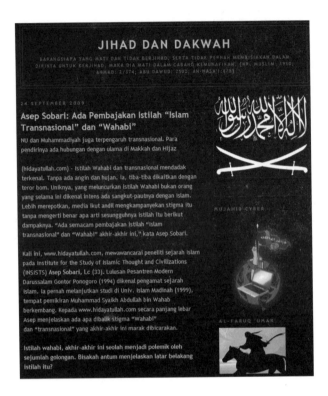

Section 7.
Coverage of the Book's Continuing Impact

Kompas – Openness a la PKS

Indonesia's largest circulation newspaper reports that on 17 June 2010, the PKS's governing board amended its bylaws to allow party membership by non-Muslims. "The experience of three general elections has caused the PKS to recalculate its political strategy. By adopting the slogan, 'PKS for all,' the Islamist party is beginning to open itself to all groups and religions.... But according to Professor Abdul Munir Mulkhan of Sunan Kalijaga Islamic State University in Yogyakarta [who was the head of field research for *The Illusion of an Islamic State*], 'This does not indicate that PKS's ideology is fading, but rather, that they're adopting a new political strategy.' According to Munir, this aligns with the thought of Yusuf Qaradawi, who has inspired many political parties around the world that have adopted Muslim Brotherhood ideology, including the PKS. Under certain conditions, an Islamist party may behave pragmatically—such as accepting democracy, non-Muslims and the leadership of women—as long as this is merely a strategy to achieve its ideal, long-term goals.

"Munir is certain that if the PKS accommodates non-Muslims within the party, they will nonetheless be excluded from its governing board, which makes all key policy decisions. "If the governing board ever has non-Muslim members, that will indicate that PKS's ideology has truly changed," said Munir. Thus, although the PKS has publicly declared itself to be an 'open party' that accepts non-Muslims, it continues to guard its [Islamist] ideology."

KOMPAS.com

MUNAS II

Keterbukaan ala PKS

Editor: Glo

Jumat, 18 Juni 2010 | 11.40 WIB

Tribun Pekanbaru/ Melvinas Priananda

Kampanye PKS di Pekanbaru.

Oleh: Anita Yossihara dan M Zaid Wahyudi

KOMPAS.com — Pengalaman tiga kali pemilihan umum cukup untuk membuat Partai Keadilan Sejahtera (PKS) menghitung ulang strategi politiknya. Melalui semboyan "PKS untuk semua", partai Islam itu mulai membuka diri kepada semua golongan dan agama.

TERKAIT:

- PKS Pertegas Komitmen
- Presiden Ajak Kader PKS Terdepan
- PKS Pertegas Koalisi dengan Demokrat
- PKS Targetkan Tiga Besar pada 2014
- Presiden SBY Buka Munas PKS

Setelah lebih dari satu dasawarsa berkiprah di kancah politik Indonesia, PKS mulai mempertimbangkan untuk melegalformalkan keanggotaan kalangan non-Muslim. Masalah keanggotaan non-Muslim itu menjadi salah satu usulan yang dibahas dalam Sidang Majelis Syura PKS, Rabu lalu.

Usulan itu membuat persidangan Majelis Syura dengan agenda amandemen anggaran dasar/anggaran rumah tangga (AD/ART) berjalan cukup alot. Salah seorang panitia Musyawarah Nasional (Munas) II PKS, Mahfudz Shiddiq, menuturkan, sidang sesi ke-2 yang dimulai pukul 14.00 baru selesai sekitar pukul 23.00. Usulan keanggotaan non-Muslim itu memang baru dibahas dalam sidang sesi ke-2.

Sidang itu berjalan lambat lantaran masih ada anggota Majelis Syura yang keberatan dengan usulan keanggotaan non-Muslim. Mereka khawatir, pembukaan ruang bagi kalangan non-Muslim akan berimbas terhadap basis massa PKS yang berasal dari kalangan Muslim. "Mereka hanya ingin berhati-hati saja. Tapi, setelah dijelaskan bahwa Islam bersifat terbuka dan berorientasi untuk mendatangkan kemaslahatan umat, semua anggota Majelis Syura akhirnya sepakat," katanya.

Namun, klausul keanggotaan non-Muslim itu tidak secara eksplisit diatur dalam AD/ART baru. Tidak ada kalimat yang menjelaskan secara gamblang bahwa kalangan non-Muslim bisa menjadi anggota PKS.

PKS hanya membagi keanggotaan menjadi dua kategori, yakni kader dan anggota. Kader adalah anggota yang terikat penuh dengan AD/ART partai dan terikat penuh dengan sistem kaderisasi yang berbasis keislaman. Sedangkan mereka yang masuk kategori anggota adalah semua warga negara Indonesia yang terikat penuh kepada organisasi. Anggota bersifat lebih umum dan terbuka bagi siapa pun dari golongan serta agama apa pun.

Pada AD/ART sebelumnya, PKS hanya mengenal anggota saja. Anggota harus terikat penuh dengan AD/ART serta mengikuti kaderisasi yang berbasis keislaman dengan mengawali sebagai anggota mula, kemudian naik menjadi anggota muda, madya, dewasa, ahli, dan purna.

Legalisasi keanggotaan non-Muslim itu didasari pertimbangan semakin banyak pendukung PKS dari kalangan non-Muslim, seperti di Papua dan Nusa Tenggara Timur. Apalagi kini PKS memiliki 20 anggota legislatif dari kalangan non-Muslim. Sebagian besar merupakan anggota Dewan Perwakilan Rakyat Daerah di Papua.

Bukan hanya kalangan non-Muslim, PKS juga mulai mendekati basis massa tradisional Islam. Pada Pemilu 2009, PKS mulai mendapat dukungan dari masyarakat pedesaan yang juga merupakan basis massa gerakan Islam tradisional, seperti Nahdlatul Ulama (NU). PKS pun memperoleh kursi DPR dari daerah basis NU, seperti Pasuruan dan Madura.

PKS juga memperoleh dukungan dari warga Muhammadiyah. Pada Pemilu 2004, banyak suara warga Muhammadiyah, yang merupakan basis massa tradisional Partai Amanat Nasional, beralih ke PKS.

Kaskus (Large Indonesian IT/Hacker Forum) – 'PKS for All'

Extensive discussion of the PKS's new slogan and its purported move to the political center, as a nationalist rather than Islamist party. The news attracted hundreds of posts, including:

"Your sales pitch failed last time, PKS... why should anyone believe you have a new product now?" "So are they prepared to boot the Muslim Brotherhood from the PKS?" "They're just trying to get more votes." "This is getting more and more weird." "Why don't they just disband the party instead of thinking they can somersault like this?"

The response from PKS supporters ranged from acute disappointment to assumptions that the party has cleverly adopted a diversionary tactic, to achieve its ultimate goal: "The PKS has lost its precious glow. I'm leaving it." "I'm disappointed with you, PKS. Come back to the true path.... I feel sorry for all the students who've followed PKS for so long. The bow of its ship has already turned, turned, turned." "Establishing *shari'a* requires a 'safe' path, and if the path isn't safe, [we] can be accused of being terrorists."

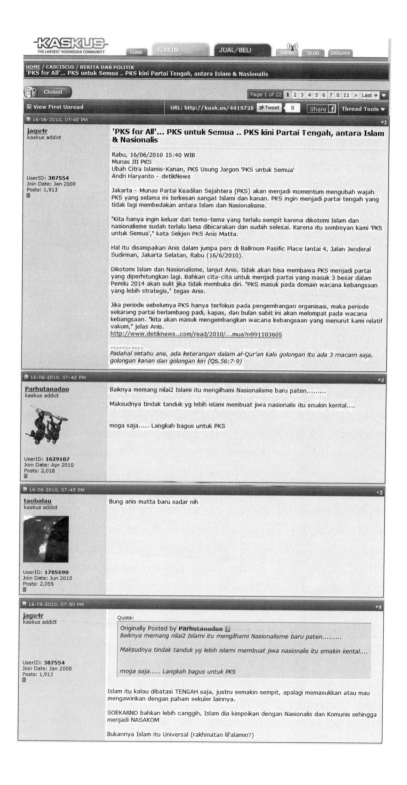

KASKUS
THE LARGEST INDONESIAN COMMUNITY
HOME   FORUM   JUAL/BELI   RADIO   BLOG   GROUPEE

HOME / CASCISCUS / BERITA DAN POLITIK
'PKS for All'... PKS untuk Semua .. PKS kini Partai Tengah, antara Islam & Nasionalis

Closed   Page 1 of 22 1 2 3 4 5 6 7 8 11 > Last »

☑ View First Unread   URL: http://kask.us/4419728   Tweet   0   Share   Thread Tools ▾

■ 16-06-2010, 07:40 PM   #1

jagu4r
kaskus addict

UserID: 387554
Join Date: Jan 2008
Posts: 1,913

'PKS for All'... PKS untuk Semua .. PKS kini Partai Tengah, antara Islam & Nasionalis

Rabu, 16/06/2010 15:40 WIB
Munas III PKS
Ubah Citra Islamis-Kanan, PKS Usung Jargon 'PKS untuk Semua'
Andri Haryanto - detikNews

Jakarta - Munas Partai Keadilan Sejahtera (PKS) akan menjadi momentum mengubah wajah PKS yang selama ini terkesan sangat Islami dan kanan. PKS ingin menjadi partai tengah yang tidak lagi membedakan antara Islam dan Nasionalisme.

"Kita hanya ingin keluar dari tema-tema yang terlalu sempit karena dikotomi Islam dan nasionalisme sudah terlalu lama dibicarakan dan sudah selesai. Karena itu semboyan kami 'PKS untuk Semua'," kata Sekjen PKS Anis Matta.

Hal itu disampaikan Anis dalam jumpa pers di Ballroom Pasific Place lantai 4, Jalan Jenderal Sudirman, Jakarta Selatan, Rabu (16/6/2010).

Dikotomi Islam dan Nasionalisme, lanjut Anis, tidak akan bisa membawa PKS menjadi partai yang diperhitungkan lagi. Bahkan cita-cita untuk menjadi partai yang masuk 3 besar dalam Pemilu 2014 akan sulit jika tidak membuka diri. "PKS masuk pada domain wacana kebangsaan yang lebih strategis," tegas Anis.

Jika periode sebelumya PKS hanya terfokus pada pengembangan organisasi, maka periode sekarang partai berlambang padi, kapas, dan bulan sabit ini akan melompat pada wacana kebangsaan. "kita akan masuk mengembangkan wacana kebangsaan yang menurut kami relatif vakum," jelas Anis.
http://www.detiknews...com/read/2010/...mua?n991103605

Padahal setahu ane, ada keterangan dalam al-Qur'an kalo golongan itu ada 3 macam saja, golongan kanan dan golongan kiri (QS.56:7-9)

■ 16-06-2010, 07:42 PM   #2

Parhutanadao
kaskus addict

UserID: 1629107
Join Date: Apr 2010
Posts: 2,018

Baiknya memang nilai2 Islami itu mengilhami Nasionalisme baru paten.........

Maksudnya tindak tanduk yg lebih islami membuat jiwa nasionalis itu smakin kental....

moga saja..... Langkah bagus untuk PKS

■ 16-06-2010, 07:45 PM   #3

taobalau
kaskus addict

UserID: 1785690
Join Date: Jun 2010
Posts: 2,055

Bung anis matta baru sadar nih

■ 16-06-2010, 07:50 PM   #4

jagu4r
kaskus addict

UserID: 387554
Join Date: Jan 2008
Posts: 1,913

Quote:

Originally Posted by **Parhutanadao**
Baiknya memang nilai2 Islami itu mengilhami Nasionalisme baru paten.........

Maksudnya tindak tanduk yg lebih islami membuat jiwa nasionalis itu smakin kental....

moga saja..... Langkah bagus untuk PKS

Islam itu kalau dibatasi TENGAH saja, justru semakin sempit, apalagi memasukkan atau mau mengawinkan dengan paham sekuler lainnya.

SOEKARNO bahkan lebih canggih, Islam dia kimpoikan dengan Nasionalis dan Komunis sehingga menjadi NASAKOM

Bukannya Islam itu Universal (rakhmatan lil'alamin?)

Titus Jonathan's Stories (blog site) – The PKS for All? Oh Come On!

The new motto of the Prosperous Justice Party (PKS) that was recently announced at the party's national congress in Jakarta was a surprise to all of us. The motto states "The PKS for All" and is intended to woo all elements of this nation to join the party. The motto constitutes an advertisement that the party is ready to switch from exclusivity to a more inclusive party.

Interestingly, the congress invited US Ambassador to Indonesia Cameron Hume to speak about "The US view of Islam". The PKS admitted bilateral relations between Indonesia and the US were strategic and benefited both countries. This is a rare occasion, but "surprising progress" since the PKS' political stance is deemed anti-Western.

[A]s the fourth-ranked party in the 2009 election, the PKS has a chance to go one step higher and snatch the third rank in 2014. However, it will not be as simple as flipping the palm because of the conservative principles label that has been stuck on the party. The PKS was known for a long time as the staunch promoter of upholding shari'a in Indonesia. The party, since it was established, has several achievements to its credit such as the controversial pornography law, and many other "shari'a- nuanced" bylaws in particular regions that are headed by the party's members.

Another stumbling block that may hamper the "PKS for All" probably are several leaders within the party who are connected to a tendency to religious sentiments. We remember shortly after President Susilo Bambang Yudhoyono (SBY) picked Boediono as his running mate in the 2009 presidential election, the then PKS president Tifatul Sembiring blatantly questioned Boediono's faith in Islam. Tifatul claimed, at that time, that the fact Boediono regularly attended Friday prayers at Bank Indonesia's mosque was not enough to consider him a devout Muslim....

The PKS may have made progress when they launched the "PKS for All" motto, however, if they are still reluctant to do a simple thing like greeting people over Christmas or on other religious occasions, is the party really for all? Oh, come on!

TITUS JONATHAN'S STORIES

SUNDAY, JUNE 20, 2010

The PKS for All? Oh Come On!

(published by The Jakarta Post on 22 June 2010. Click here)

The new motto of the Prosperous Justice Party (PKS) that was recently announced at the party's national congress in Jakarta was a surprise to all of us. The motto states "The PKS for All" and is intended to woo all elements of this nation to join the party. The motto constitutes an advertisement that the party is ready to switch from exclusivity to a more inclusive party.

Interestingly, the congress invited US Ambassador to Indonesia Cameron Hume to speak about "The US view of Islam". The PKS admitted bilateral relations between Indonesia and the US were strategic and benefited both countries.

This is a rare occasion, but "surprising progress" since the PKS' political stance is deemed anti-Western.

The party secretary-general, Anis Matta, said the party aimed to reach 2 million members from the current 800,000 members, and to pursue the top three parties in the 2014 election. Apparently, the PKS realized there was no history that parties with Islamic-based ideologies ever won elections. Although Indonesia is the country with the largest Muslim population in the world, nationalist-based parties gained the most votes.

Nevertheless, as the fourth-ranked party in the 2009 election, the PKS has a chance to go one step higher and snatch the third rank in 2014. However, it will not be as simple as flipping the palm because of the conservative principles label that has been stuck on the party. The PKS was known for a long time as the staunch promoter of upholding *sharia* in Indonesia. The party, since it was established, has several achievements to its credit such as the controversial pornography law, and many other "*sharia*-nuanced" bylaws in particular regions that are headed by the party's members.

Another stumbling block that may hamper the "PKS for All" probably are several leaders within the party who are connected to a tendency to religious sentiments. We remember shortly after President Susilo Bambang Yudhoyono (SBY) picked Boediono as his running mate in the 2009 presidential election, the then PKS president Tifatul Sembiring blatantly questioned Boediono's faith in Islam. Tifatul claimed, at that time, that the fact Boediono regularly attended Friday prayers at Bank Indonesia's mosque was not enough to consider him a devout Muslim

The second time, Tifatul (now the Communications and Information Technology Minister) gave a controversial statement was when he compared a sex tape scandal involving Ariel Peterpan, Luna Maya and Cut Tari look-alikes to the theological debate between Christians and Muslims about the death of Jesus Christ.

STORIES CATEGORY

characters (9)
economy (2)
education (2)
family (2)
law (4)
music and film (2)
politics (27)
religion (12)
social (32)
sport (2)
terrorism (3)
travelling (1)

BLOG ARCHIVE

▶ 2011 (4)
▼ 2010 (21)
  ▶ December (2)
  ▶ November (1)
  ▶ October (2)
  ▶ September (1)
  ▶ August (1)
  ▶ July (1)
  ▼ June (3)
    The PKS for All? Oh Come On!
    The Celebrity Look-alikes
    A Good Neighbor Should Not Kill The Other's Dog
  ▶ May (2)
  ▶ April (2)
  ▶ March (2)
  ▶ February (3)
  ▶ January (1)
▶ 2009 (30)
▶ 2008 (15)

ABOUT ME

TITUS JONATHAN

This blog is written based on my experiences, my feelings, my thoughts, what I've seen, what I've heard and what I've felt. You may hate or love the articles. It's ok. The words can be the best friends or the worst of enemies, said Rene J. Cappon. Life is beautiful, and also simple.

Jakarta Post – Assessing PKS's new look

One of the Prosperous Justice Party (PKS) leaders Mahfudz Siddiq, as quoted by Pandaya, acknowledges it is not easy to erase the image of being an "exclusive party", because in it was founded by proponents of an Islamic state. (See: "Moving closer to the West a high-stake gamble for PKS", The Jakarta Post, 18 June 2010).

The party's new tagline, "PKS for all", which was expected to help re-brand the Islamic-based party to be more inclusive is likely not enough. The PKS is still viewed with suspicion by some critics for not only its alleged links to the Muslims brotherhood movement but also for its failure to prove its pluralistic attitude when faced by sociological tests.

Fadjroel Rachman, director of the Research Institute for Democracy and Prosperous State, for instance, said the PKS would be unable to convince the public unless its leaders dared to break conservatism by, among others, greeting other believers on their religious holy days. "How could you expect to be pluralist party if both your former and current president [Luthfi Hasan Ishaaq] refuse to greet people of other religions on their religious holidays?" Fadjroel said, referring to an incident in which Tifatul refused to greet Christians on Christmas....

In April, Tifatul tweeted a quote from Nazi leader Adolf Hitler. He wrote, "The union between two children, when both of them complete each other, this is magic—Adolf Hitler". There is no prohibition to quote wise words from anywhere, but when he quoted it from the perpetrator of war crimes, Hitler, the question is whether he idolized him. It can be interpreted as the minister's lack of respect for the millions of people killed in the genocide perpetrated under Nazi leadership during World War II.

The Jakarta Post

OPINION

Assessing PKS' new look

Nurrohman, Bandung | Tue, 06/22/2010 9:49 AM | Opinion

One of the Prosperous Justice Party (PKS) leaders Mahfudz Siddiq, as quoted by Pandaya, acknowledges it is not easy to erase the image of being an "exclusive party", because in it was founded by proponents of an Islamic state. (See: "Moving closer to the West a high-stake gamble for PKS", The Jakarta Post, June 18, 2010).

The party's new tagline, "PKS for all", which was expected to help re-brand the Islamic-based party to be more inclusive is likely not enough. The PKS is still viewed with suspicion by some critics for not only its alleged links to the Muslims brotherhood movement but also for its failure to prove its pluralistic attitude when faced by sociological tests.

Fadjroel Rachman, director of the Research Institute for Democracy and Prosperous State, for instance, said the PKS would be unable to convince the public unless its leaders dared to break conservatism by, among others, greeting other believers on their religious holy days. "How could you expect to be pluralist party if both your former and current president [Luthfi Hasan Ishaaq] refuse to greet people of other religions on their religious holidays?" Fadjroel said, referring to an incident in which Tifatul refused to greet Christians on Christmas.

Tifatul was also criticized for comparing the sex tape controversy to the theological debate between Christian and Muslims about the death of Jesus Christ. A Catholic priest from the Indonesian Bishop Council, Father Beny Susetyo, said that as a public official, Tifatul Sembiring should not compare a pornography scandal to the crucifixion of Jesus Christ, because it could hurt the feelings of believers.

"There is no connection between pornography and the crucifixion of Jesus Christ at all," he told The Jakarta Post. criticizing the minister for showing a lack of appreciation for beliefs other than his own in such a diverse country as Indonesia.

In April, Tifatul tweeted a quote from Nazi leader Adolf Hitler. He wrote, "The union between two children, when both of them complete each other, this is magic — Adolf Hitler". There is no prohibition to quote wise words from anywhere, but when he quoted it from the perpetrator of war crimes, Hitler, the question is whether he idolized him. It can be interpreted as the minister's lack of respect for the millions of people killed in the genocide perpetrated under Nazi leadership during World War II.

Mahfudz Siddiq makes an ambiguous stance when commenting on qanun jinayat Aceh, which stipulates that a person convicted of committing adultery must be buried neck deep before the public is permitted to stone them to death.

While Usman Hamid, the coordinator of the Commission for Missing Persons and Victims of Violence, firmly said, "Stoning is constitutionally baseless. Such punishment is cruel, inhumane and degrades the value of humanity", Mahfudz said that punishment needed to be introduced to society. "This idea needs to be elaborated further. The Aceh administration needs to talk with other fellow civil organizations," he said "It should be proven that the law positively impacts on the society before it is passed," he said. (See The Jakarta Post, Sept. 12, 2009)

In Indonesia's history, the idea of an Islamic state has had a negative image since it always related to theocratic, exclusive, discriminatory components and was negligent to the rights of women and non-Muslims.

The Indonesian experience also reveals that parties involved in establishing an Islamic state eventually use violence or armed struggle in order to achieve their goal. Look at what is said by Ubaid, one of the terrorist suspects arrested in Aceh. Ubaid said the military training facility had been established to provide human resources to transform Indonesia into an Islamic state by military force.

In 2008, its law-making body had affirmed that this party supported Pancasila as the state ideology, but the question is whether this acceptant is final or temporary. PKS will be recorded in history if it is successfully transforming Islamic state into welfare state or, in the word of PKS, prosperous justice state, among other by eliminating negative elements embedded in the old concept of Islamic state and replacing it with the new one with more suitable with the demand of democracy and human rights.

As the party founded by proponents of the Islamic state, the PKS actually has an opportunity to persuade its fellow Muslims who are still trapped in the utopian idea of the Islamic state that is contrary to Pancasila, the constitution and the principle of democracy. From an ideological perspective, the PKS is the most close to Muslims engaged in the jihadi movement.

The concept of Islamic state or Islamic politics should be treated as an open concept based on universal ideas such as freedom, equality, justice and brotherhood.

The idea of Islamic politics actually like the idea of Islamic economics or Islamic banking that can be operated by both Muslims as well as non-Muslims. The late Nurcholish Madjid said that the triumph of Islam is actually the triumph of Islamic ideas but not automatically the triumph of those of Muslims.

After all, corruption is still the largest Indonesian enemy, so in order to make a welfare state, the PKS motto as clean, caring and a professional party needs to be supported by all of us.

Muslim Daily (website) – Farewell PKS, Farewell Da'wa (Proselytism) Party, Farewell Islamic Party!

A major blog devoted to the PKS announced that it was discontinuing publication in response to the PKS's decision to "move to the center," as expressed by its new slogan, "PKS for All."

I began the blog PKSwatch on 26 October 2005, motivated by concern at the behavior of this *da'wa* (proselytism) movement that I loved, which had begun to go off the rails and was heading for a wreck, although not many of its passengers seemed to realize this. In less than 2 months, I had posted 83 articles and attracted thousands of comments from readers, on what quickly become a hit blog....

Many [Muslim] Brothers said they were aware of this blog (PKSwatch), but many were also angry and disagreed with it, and asked me to stop. I told them that I would stop this blog if and when either of two conditions developed, namely:

First, that the PKS returned to the straight path, at least as articulated at the time the PK was founded [in 1998], or

Second, if the PKS was irretrievably broken, or no longer an Islamic party....

Today, the PKS national congress has just ended. Right from the decision to hold the event in a super-luxurious hotel [the Ritz-Carlton], it was clear that the PKS aimed to change its image, and this was confirmed by various naked political maneuvers that occurred, and were clearly visible to the public.

The PKS General Secretary, Anis Matta, proclaimed that they wanted to "abandon narrow themes," in the context of changing their Islamist image, by adopting the slogan, "PKS for All"....

Thus a proselytism mission such as purifying our faith in God's Oneness, and establishing the values of *shari'a*, are no longer relevant to the PKS, and dismissed as "narrow themes." I ask forgiveness from God, for did not Allah send all the prophets and messengers for no purpose other than this? Yet apparently the PKS is now insisting that this mission is no longer relevant....

Because they are impatient to grow large, the party image must move "to the center," so it no longer gives the impression of being an Islamist party. But if it has now become a centrist or nationalist or open party, how is it different from PDI-P, the Democrat Party or Golkar? They're all the same. Most members of those parties are Muslim, too, our brothers in faith.

With this realization, things became more clear to me. The PKS is now an open party, while I have been critiquing it all these years out of my love for it as a *da'wa* (proselytism) party. Now that PKS has become an open party and abandoned its *da'wa* mission, its original reason for existence has vanished, along with any reason for me to continue critiquing it....

I say to all [my] Muslim Brothers, do not lose hope, or your zeal to proselytize. Look upon the PKS's behavior as a test from God. A test to which hundreds, and even thousands of groups have been subjected in the past. Some pass the test and are saved, but many fail, because the temptation to enjoy worldly pleasures (which has struck down the PKS) is truly more difficult to withstand than most. *Da'wa (proselytism) must go on, with or without the PKS.* There are still many other vehicles for conducting *da'wa.*

Venting somewhat, I have been quite depressed this past week. I felt a great loss, like when my late father passed away (although not quite that bad). Yes, depressed at the loss of the *da'wa* vehicle I have loved and embraced all these years, having endowed it with my hopes and dreams. Then, a few days ago, I became aware that God alone determines all things... and realized my great error all these years, in having placed my hopes and dreams in the PKS. This was a mistake. For I am to place my hope in none but God alone. Only God will not disappoint us.

Now, praise God, I have begun to free my heart and mind from the PKS, and feel greatly relieved. Farewell, PKS. Thinking and talking about the PKS is no longer the least bit attractive for me. It's just like talking about any other political party. With a heart rooted in certainty, and uttering the name of God—the great, the glorious!—I hereby announce that I am shutting down this blog.

7 Rajab 1431 Hijriyah, 21 June 2010, 00:30.

Home » Opini » Selamat Tinggal PKS, Selamat Tinggal Partai Dakwah, Selamat Tinggal Partai Islam !!!

Selamat Tinggal PKS, Selamat Tinggal Partai Dakwah, Selamat Tinggal Partai Islam !!!

Diposting pada Senin, 21-06-2010 | 09:11:55 WIB

Sesungguhnya segala puji hanya bagi Allah Subhanahu wa Ta'ala, kita memujiNya, minta tolong padaNya, mohon ampun padaNya dan bertaubat hanya padaNya. Shalawat dan salam untuk *qudwah* kita Muhammad Rasulullah *shallaLlahu 'alaihi wassalam*, beserta keluarganya, para sahabatnya dan orang-orang yang setia kepadanya hingga hari kiamat.

26 Oktober 2005, ketika saya memulai blog PKSWatch untuk pertama kalinya, didasari dengan sebuah rasa keprihatinan atas sepak terjang gerakan dakwah yang saya cintai, yang saya lihat mulai keluar dari rel dan celakanya tidak banyak disadari oleh para penghuninya. Ada total 83 tulisan dan ribuan komentar dari para pembaca, hingga saya memutuskan untuk membekukannya pada tanggal 25 Desember 2006, ketika hit blog sedang tinggi-tingginya.

Ketika saya mulai pertama kali, saya menggunakan nada tulisan yang keras terutama pada 2-3 bulan pertama, dengan maksud untuk menyentak pemikiran, tapi saya salah karena yang terjadi malah sikap antipati yang berlebihan meskipun setelah berjalan beberapa bulan nada tulisan sudah jauh berubah. Namun demikian beberapa tulisan yang keras tersebut tetap ada sehingga pembaca yang baru mengikuti cenderung untuk bersikap antipati pula. Selain itu kebijakan sensor komentar juga sangat liberal, sehingga suasana diskusi terkadang sangat panas. Atas beberapa pertimbangan, saya memutuskan untuk membekukan blog itu (blog PKSwatch_red) terlebih dahulu.

Dalam perjalanannya, periode di atas itu saya sebut blog **PKSWatch versi 1**.

Pertengahan 2007, beberapa ikhwah kader di Jakarta menghubungi saya, menasehati dan meminta saya untuk mengaktifkan lagi blog PKSWatch sebagai sarana kontrol kepada jama'ah. Akhirnya tanggal 12 November 2007, saya mulai kembali blog PKSWatch (versi 2). Dengan tulisan yang lebih kuat pada referensi ilmiah, dalam perjalanannya ada 77 tulisan dengan total ribuan komentar pembaca hingga tanggal 9 Juni 2009. Sebagian tulisan tersebut dibuat oleh *asatidz* yang juga prihatin terhadap PKS, ada tulisan mereka yang memang sudah tersedia di ranah publik, ada pula tulisan yang memang baru dimuat di blog PKSWatch.

Kemudian sempat vakum karena saya sempat merasa amat "mual" melihat polah politik PKS pada waktu itu, terutama menjelang pemilu presiden 2009. Sampai kemudian saya mulai lagi pada tanggal 17 Desember 2009. Kali ini hanya ada tiga tulisan hingga saya membuat tulisan ini. Mood saya untuk menulis tidak seperti dulu lagi, mungkin karena sudah malas melihat PKS semakin jauh dari yang saya bayangkan, dari rel yang semestinya PKS berada di atasnya.

Padahal sangat banyak data dan informasi masuk kepada saya, sebagian lengkap dengan bukti-bukti, yang bisa saya gunakan untuk membuat tulisan, tapi saya sudah seperti kehilangan minat kepada PKS. Dulu, saya membuat blog ini karena saya yakin bahwa PKS bisa tetap dijaga agar tetap berada di atas relnya.

Banyak ikhwah yang mengakui bahwa mereka tersadarkan oleh keberadaan blog ini (blog PKSwatch_red), tapi juga banyak yang jengkel dan tidak setuju dengan blog ini (blog PKSwatch_red), lalu meminta saya untuk menghentikan blog ini. Kepada mereka, saya menjawab bahwa saya akan menghentikan blog ini (blog PKSwatch_red) kalau ada satu dari dua kondisi sudah tercapai, yaitu:

Jakarta Post – Support for sharia law is in the minority—and declining

by Debnath Guharoy

Wednesday, 28 July 2010 – The army is in the barracks. The press is free. The constitution is alive. But from the way many elected leaders continue to behave, voter may well think politicians were put in office by divine intervention.

The mayor of Bekasi, eager to follow in the footsteps of the mayor of Tangerang, has now declared that he too would like to introduce sharia law. If the mayors believe they are acting in the name of the people who put them in power and enforcing the will of the electorate, then they are both wrong.

True to form, the politicians are again displaying the arrogance of ill-informed bullies who are eager to force their individual whims on a growing majority who reject narrow religious rules.

If both mayors believe they are acting in the name of the voting public, enacting into law what they believe has a groundswell of popular support, they would do well to look at the facts....

In the last 12 months alone, there has been a palpable hardening in the attitude of Indonesians against sharia law. From April 2009 to March 2010, the number of people who said "Islamic sharia law should be introduced in my area" declined from 43 to 36 percent of the population. That's one in three people, not what an elected mayor could call a majority.

Expressions of support for sharia law have even less support. A year ago, 38 percent of the population believed "thieves should have their hands cut off". By March of 2010, that number had slipped to 32.

"Those committing adultery should be whipped to death in public" also lost steam, with an almost identical decline during the same period.

Communications and Information Minister Tifatul Sembiring would do well to take note, not just members of religious political parties such as the Prosperous Justice Party (PKS), of which he is a former leader.

Always a delicate subject, sharia law is increasingly being rejected, not embraced, by growing numbers of Muslims around the country. Even people unfamiliar with Islam know that sharia is a way of life for all believers, not a set of laws.

When asked the question, most Muslims would understandably have difficulty separating sharia from Islam. Rejecting the imposition of sharia law in that sense is an act of courage, a choice made consciously. In much the same way, a practicing Christian might be troubled if asked whether the Virgin Mary was indeed a virgin.

In this world's Muslim majority nation, steadily growing numbers of moderate Muslims are looking at tomorrow's Indonesia, differently. The purists and the fundamentalists are in the minority, and shrinking.

The politicians are reading the signs and even religious parties are seeking to redefine themselves.

Only opportunists are using the religious card for political gain, by ignoring the popular view and promoting the incendiary actions of the fundamentalist fringe instead.

The bigots and their political supporters have yet to buckle under the popular winds of change. Sabres drawn, they are the defenders of a faith they share with only their diminishing ranks. They aren't exactly keen to go with the flow.

In the minority, they are the elected leaders who provide protection to lawless groups like the Islam Defenders Front (FPI), imposing their will on a peaceful, moderate, gentle majority eager to see a modern Indonesia blossom.

The economy is in good shape, consumer confidence is running high. But the meaningless distractions created by elected leaders are just that, distractions and meaningless.

In a country where religions have lived side by side for centuries, where the constitution endorses plurality, the views of a diminishing minority being imposed on a growing majority has a surreal air, similar to the days of Idi Amin in Uganda.

Will the president of this republic please take note? And let the people know which side he is on?

Focusing on the runaway mayors of Tangerang and Bekasi, the picture is similar. Undoubtedly, they are imposing the minority will on the majority. Like the rest of the nation, that includes the majority of Muslims in their jurisdictions.

Only 38 percent of Muslims in Tangerang think "Islamic sharia law should be implemented in my area."

In the past, its mayor had neither the authority nor mandate to impose his beliefs on the majority.

In Bekasi, only 42 percent of the population and 42 percent of Muslims agree. Who is the mayor of Bekasi aiming to please, in the future? The majority of voters everywhere, not just in Bekasi, would like the President to throw the book at him. The constitutional book, that is. Everybody who loves Indonesia must be wondering what's stopping him.

By shrugging off these wanton acts, by allowing them to mold a society against its own will, the silent majority will hurt itself for generations to come. A people capable of defining modern Islam should not allow themselves to be hijacked by a diminishing fundamentalist minority. A nation capable of influencing the balance of power in the 21st century cannot allow itself to be ridiculed on the world stage. Now is not the time for silent acquiescence.

Any attempt to challenge the research on which these conclusions are based, is a waste of time. With more than adequate numbers of respondents, the margin of error is insignificant. This is not a flimsy one-off poll conducted on the web with a handful of interviews. The opinions are based on Roy Morgan Single Source, country's largest syndicated consumer survey with over 25,000 respondents annually. Interviews are conducted face-to-face each week, continuously, with results released every quarter. The findings are projected to reflect over 85 percent of the population, 14 years of age and older.

HEADLINES

Support for sharia law is in the minority — and declining

Debnath Guharoy, Contributor, Jakarta | Sun, 07/25/2010 12:21 PM | Headlines

The army is in the barracks. The press is free. The constitution is alive. But from the way many elected leaders continue to behave, voter may well think politicians were put in office by divine intervention.

The mayor of Bekasi, eager to follow in the footsteps of the mayor of Tangerang, has now declared that he too would like to introduce sharia law. If the mayors believe they are acting in the name of the people who put them in power and enforcing the will of the electorate, then they are both wrong.

True to form, the politicians are again displaying the arrogance of ill-informed bullies who are eager to force their individual whims on a growing majority who reject narrow religious rules.

If both mayors believe they are acting in the name of the voting public, enacting into law what they believe has a groundswell of popular support, they would do well to look at the facts. Not anywhere else, just in their cities, where ignorance is bliss. That both cities are integral parts of the Republic of Indonesia warrants mention, lest basic truths are forgotten. Indonesia, rather than with Indonesians, is a good place to begin looking for the truth.

In the last 12 months alone, there has been a palpable hardening in the attitude of Indonesians against sharia law. Form April 2009 to March 2010, the number of people who said "Islamic sharia law should be introduced in my area" declined from 43 to 36 percent of the population. That's one in three people, not what an elected mayor could call a majority.

Expressions of support for sharia law have even less support. A year ago, 38 percent of the population believed "thieves should have their hands cut off". By March of 2010, that number had slipped to 32.

"Those committing adultery should be whipped to death in public" also lost steam, with an almost identical decline during the same period.

Communications and Information Minister Tifatul Sembiring would do well to take note, not just members of religious political parties such as the Prosperous Justice Party (PKS), of which he is a former leader.

Always a delicate subject, sharia law is increasingly being rejected, not embraced, by growing numbers of Muslims around the country. Even people unfamiliar with Islam know that sharia is a way of life for all believers, not a set of laws.

When asked the question, most Muslims would understandably have difficulty separating sharia from Islam. Rejecting the imposition of sharia law in that sense is an act of courage, a choice made consciously. In much the same way, a practicing Christian might be troubled if asked whether the Virgin Mary was indeed a virgin.

In this world's Muslim majority nation, steadily growing numbers of moderate Muslims are looking at tomorrow's Indonesia, differently. The purists and the fundamentalists are in the minority, and shrinking.

The politicians are reading the signs and even religious parties are seeking to redefine themselves.

Only opportunists are using the religious card for political gain, by ignoring the popular view and promoting the incendiary actions of the fundamentalist fringe instead.

The bigots and their political supporters have yet to buckle under the popular winds of change. Sabres drawn, they are the defenders of a faith they share with only their diminishing ranks. They aren't exactly keen to go with the flow.

In the minority, they are the elected leaders who provide protection to lawless groups like the Islam Defenders Front (FPI), imposing their will on a peaceful, moderate, gentle majority eager to see a modern Indonesia blossom.

The economy is in good shape, consumer confidence is running high. But the meaningless distractions created by elected leaders are just that, distractions and meaningless.

In a country where religions have lived side by side for centuries, where the constitution endorses plurality, the views of a diminishing minority being imposed on a growing majority has a surreal air, similar to the days of Idi Amin in Uganda.

Will the president of this republic please take note? And let the people know which side he is on?

Focusing on the runaway mayors of Tangerang and Bekasi, the picture is similar. Undoubtedly, they are imposing the minority will on the majority. Like the rest of the nation, that includes the majority of Muslims in their jurisdictions.

Only 38 percent of Muslims in Tangerang think "Islamic sharia law should be implemented in my area."

In the past, its mayor had neither the authority nor mandate to impose his beliefs on the majority.

In Bekasi, only 42 percent of the population and 42 percent of Muslims agree. Who is the mayor of Bekasi aiming to please, in the future? The majority of voters everywhere, not just in Bekasi, would like the President to throw the book at him. The constitutional book, that is. Everybody who loves Indonesia must be wondering what's stopping him.

By shrugging off these wanton acts, by allowing them to mold a society against its own will, the silent majority will hurt itself for generations to come. A people capable of defining modern Islam should not allow themselves to be hijacked by a diminishing fundamentalist minority. A nation capable of influencing the balance of power in the 21st century cannot allow itself to be ridiculed on the world stage. Now is not the time for silent acquiescence.

Any attempt to challenge the research on which these conclusions are based, is a waste of time. With more than adequate numbers of respondents, the margin of error is insignificant. This is not a flimsy one-off poll conducted on the web with a handful of interviews. The opinions are based on Roy Morgan Single Source, country's largest syndicated consumer survey with over 25,000 respondents annually. Interviews are conducted face-to-face each week, continuously, with results released every quarter. The findings are projected to reflect over 85 percent of the population, 14 years of age and older.

The writer is regional director-Asia for Roy Morgan Research. He is also a columnist and speaker at investment forums overseas and a frequent visitor to Indonesia. He can be contacted at debnath.guharoy@roymorgan.com

Appendix 6:
Excerpts from

Preventing Violent Radicalization and Terrorism: The Case of Indonesia

by Dr. Magnus Ranstorp
of the Center for Asymmetric Threat Studies
at Sweden's National Defense College

Preventing Violent Radicalization and Terrorism

The Case of Indonesia

Magnus Ranstorp

CATS
Center for Asymmetric Threat Studies

Preface (from page v of the report)

This document – written by Dr. Magnus Ranstorp, Research Director at CATS – addresses the effects and relevance of measures to counteract radicalization and terrorism. The document presents the conclusions from a previous project that our Center for Asymmetric Threat Studies undertook and submitted to Sida (Swedish International Development Cooperation Agency) in 2009 involving an in-depth case study of Indonesia which was carried out in the southeast Asian region.

The underlying idea of this study was, from an overall point of view, to describe and analyze the various efforts undertaken to marginalize extremist elements within Indonesia with relevant differences and similarities from European experiences as a reference point. Indonesia was chosen since the country has frequently been described as a major success story. As one of the largest Muslim countries in the world, Indonesia has successfully stemmed widespread development of violent radicalization as well as marginalized Jemmah Islamiyyah, an indigenous terrorist movement with regional and transnational tentacles. However, very little has been written on the relatively systematic efforts on the part of the Indonesian government and various societal actors towards these ends. Issues that the study attempts to elucidate include: How did they successfully marginalize these extremist forces? Which means and methods have been used? Are there any lessons that can be applied to other countries where Sida is active?

This document only addresses the conclusions of the above-mentioned project. It presents a spectrum of ideas for different methods that can be used to prevent radicalization with regards to religious extremism and generic countermeasures. On the whole, these may be applicable to several operational and programme areas of development cooperation aimed at preventing this type of development.

Lars Nicander
Center for Asymmetric Threat Studies, CATS
Stockholm, October 2009

1. Introduction

1.1 Background (from page 1)

Generic understanding of conditions conducive for terrorism and various means and methods that can be used to prevent these conditions are of great importance in terms of developing policy aimed at promoting peace and security. The OECD-DAC's (Organisation for Economic Co-operation and Development – Development Assistance Committee) guidelines *Helping Prevent Violent Conflict* and *A Development Co-operation Lens on Terrorism Prevention: Key Entry Points for Action* offer points of departure for using development cooperation as an instrument to counteract terrorism. Analytical and method support are important in terms of investigating, potentially developing and determining to what extent, within the framework of aid targets, development cooperation can serve as an instrument to reinforce a country's indigenous ability to counteract terrorism.

For a number of years, the Center for Asymmetric Threat Studies (CATS) at the Swedish National Defence College has performed advanced analytical work and government-funded research on countering various forms of terrorism. The research is primarily focused on ascertaining functioning tools and the best practices for settings where ideological (in the form of 'violent radicalization'), religious and cultural factors exist individually or together.

2. Conclusions and Relevance for Development Cooperation and Recommendations for Sida's Work

2.1 Analysis of Methods to Combat Radicalization (from pages 5-6)

A central element of the Indonesian model involves working through networks of individuals who have religious credibility, are well established and greatly respected within the various groups that have far-reaching impact on the society. The largest religious organizations in Indonesia have a popular character and thus constitute important channels for actors promoting countermeasures. The LibForAll Foundation (LibForAll) is a particularly interesting non-governmental actor that is able to create networks and promote effective messages and initiatives in various constellations.

A relatively original way of reaching young people involves identifying popular artists who then communicate crafted messages aimed at counteracting radical currents. Music productions with lyrics about tolerance as a countermeasure to radicalism, violence and terrorism have quickly become popular all over Southeast Asia (with best-selling albums topping the charts on MTV Asia).

2.2 Strategic Level (from page 8)

The key to success on a strategic level – according to LibForAll's founder Charles Holland Taylor – involves mobilizing Muslim public opinion on all social levels to unite behind the message that extremists are ideological 'emperors without clothes.' Calling attention to the fact that extremist interpretations of Islam lack a theological basis is a prerequisite in terms of mobilizing the quiet majority of Muslims to reject extremism and to marginalize extremists.

This is not a matter of merely taking the position of watchman over moderate forces where subversive political agendas, infiltration attempts into moderate Muslim organizations/institutions or external financing to extremists are exposed. Success is primarily based on actual organizational capacity in terms of forming horizontal and vertical networks of moderate forces. This is also combined with the ability to find new and innovative ways of communicating the 'counterrmessage'. A combination of a credible and effective message on the one hand and the 'right' messenger on the other makes this happen.

2.2.2 Popular Culture as an Effective Tool (from pages 11-13)

LibForAll has been exceptional in a regional context for issues involving innovative forms and communicating the message of anti-extremism. One guiding star in these efforts has been selecting methods with maximum impact and that reach the largest possible audience. Thus, it was natural to promote the Indonesian pop star

Ahmed Dani and the song *Lashkar Cinta* ('love soldiers'). Doing so created chasms within and a reaction from extremist forces, which could then subsequently be marginalized after they had been enticed to react and reveal themselves. LibForAll says that 6-7 million copies of the album were sold, and that the concerts were covered by the national media. Over 90 concerts were held, and over 10,000 people attended each one. Furthermore, three songs with anti-extremist messages reached the top of the radio charts and were aired on MTV Asia, which generated months of publicity for the anti-extremist message....

Both the LibForAll and Yeh Hum Naheen projects, which aim to independently disseminate and internationalize their Muslim and cultural movements across language and cultural barriers, are worth supporting *indirectly*. The credibility of these projects is largely based on the initiative of entrepreneurs on local levels; these should be stimulated and supported in different ways.

Even if the ambition is to create a global Muslim cultural movement that propagates religious tolerance and that is the direct opposite of extremism, the projects' generic basic principles and focus can be applied and inspired on a more local level in other contexts that struggle with the same problems. One prioritized aspect might be to examine which cultural forms are the most effective in local contexts such as Bangladesh, Somalia or Kenya. Are there any positive cultural forces in these countries that can help build a broad and credible network and that can reinforce a nation as well as mobilize positive counterbalances to extremism? A survey of potential 'gap bridgers' and cultural personalities and a careful analysis of effective forms and means would constitute the first step towards a more sustained and massive initiative.

LibForAll has also achieved success through Lautan Wahu "Ocean of Revelation" – a widespread TV campaign that consists of 26 video episodes that discredit extremist arguments. References are made to scholarly and respected imams who have preferential right of interpretation within Islam.

The first six episodes are primarily based on the Indonesian perspective but contain the appearance of the Grand Mufti from the Egyptian Al-Azhar Mosque and University which is opposed to extremism and terrorism in the name of *jihad*. Even if focus is on an Indonesian audience, LibForAll aims to produce an additional 20 episodes based on other legitimate voices from across the globe that stand united against extremism. The planned episodes will be filmed in Sweden, the Netherlands and Germany with the aim of creating positive voices on the topic of Islam and Muslims.

One important aspect of the LibForAll video project is how the balance between active Indonesian religious figures and credible voices in the Arab world can be reinforced; this will help bridge the gap between Indonesia and the rest of the Muslim world. How can the most influential imams in the Arab world be persuaded to stand behind the project? Creating a video series that is perceived as relevant outside Indonesia as well requires a great deal more work. One aspect that can be called into question is why the LibForAll video production is not primarily focused on Southeast Asia where it can be possibly most effective.

This type of TV campaign is far from new in the battle against extremism. Even if it has primarily dealt with the repressive aspects related to combating terrorism where TV confessions outline the mistakes terrorists have made and how they have been manipulated to commit acts of violence (as exemplified by the classic Egyptian approach), LibForAll's campaign has a decidedly positive focus. There is scope for examining how the message can be communicated most effectively in terms of reaching young people via innovative pop culture. Besides pop artists, comics have been used to reach out to young people with anti-extremist messages.

2.2.3 Exposing the Extent of Extremism and Its 'True Colours' (from pages 14-15)

LibForAll's publication of *The Illusion of an Islamic State: The Expansion of Transnational Islamist Movements to Indonesia* had a considerable impact on domestic policy. It primarily contributed to neutralizing one candidate's bid for vice president in the 2009 national election campaign, who had ties to the Muslim Brotherhood. It also helped drive a wedge between President Susilo Yudhoyono, who was running for re-election, and the PKS party's candidate, which had been his coalition partner for the previous five years. PKS has played a double role – it has supported the government the past five years on the one hand and continued to promote radicalization on the other. Yudhoyono nominated a strong nationalist candidate as vice president instead.

According to Charles Holland Taylor, LibForAll's founder, the PKS party was put on a defensive and reactive path for the first time in ten years. PKS often negotiates on various minister portfolios, with a particular focus on the Department of Education as it can spread its influence on the local levels most effectively. PKS was apparently so surprised by and unprepared for the antiextremist campaign that it only defended itself by stating that the controversial book was funded by George W. Bush as one of his final political decisions.

Publication of the controversial book was a calculated risk that managed to marginalize extremist political forces. Translation of the book received support from the Swedish Ministry for Foreign Affairs. Not only did it create breathing space, it also created the necessary prerequisites for follow-up initiatives such as debates and other networks to further counterbalance extremism.

On 16 May 2009, for example, the Bhinneka Tunggal Ika ('*Oneness in Diversity*') movement was created by Wahid (the former president), Syafii Maarif (the former chairman of Muhammadiyah), Kyai Haji Mustofa Bisri (a leading Nahdlatul Ulama leader) and Charles Holland Taylor. The aim of the initiative was to organize leading members of the Indonesian elite and society as a whole to actively prevent the spread of radical Islam on all levels and with all available means.

There were also reports of an extensive SMS text message campaign before the national elections being sent to the general public that claimed that the former PKS president Hidayat Nur Wahid was a Wahabi follower; it also discredited a government coalition with PKS. This led *de facto* to political distrust and PKS being prevented from influencing the minister portfolio. [Note: although politically damaged by LibForAll's campaign, the PKS managed to preserve its relationship with President Susilo Bambang Yudhoyono and acquire ministerial posts in his second administration.]

Despite LibForAll's success, the organisation has been criticized for its polarized rhetoric on Islam since it uses provocation strategies to divide Muslims (and Muslim countries) into 'good' and 'ill-intentioned' Muslims instead of offering a modulated view on the different trends within Islam. However, the most recent political successes indicate that provocation is effective in terms of marginalizing PKS.

Indonesia is certainly unique with its coalitions of various strategic players that simultaneously act individually and collectively on different levels against extremism. However, the model of exposing and attempting to marginalize extremist forces additionally through widespread publication initiatives is an interesting tool to study and possibly support for other types of social tensions. In general, the model is based on forcing reactions that are then actively addressed on many different fronts in a structured, controlled and pre-determined manner.

2.2.4 Creating 'Positive' Counterbalances to Extremism (from pages 15-16)

LibForAll has also utilized Rahmatan lil Alamin's network that allows the scope of the programme to extend beyond Indonesia's borders. For example, LibForAll organized a religious summit on Bali. Participants condemned the forces that deny the existence of the Jewish holocaust and emphasized 'religious tolerance as a blessing for all beings' in conjunction with Iranian President Ahmadinejad's holocaust conference in Teheran in February 2007. The conference was organized together with the Simon Wiesenthal Center as a means of emphasizing tolerance between religions.

LibforAll's demonstration of strength involves creating a cross-sector network that is based on a five-level integration of the following: religious leaders (*ulama*) who have garnered widespread public support and who can address radical backlash; religious scholars and teachers who can garner the requisite intellectual and theological support for a pluralistic and tolerant interpretation of Islam; pop idols who have massive support from young people; government leaders who are able to address social factors as an underlying factor of extremism; as well as business leadership that can offer requisite financial support.

One expression of 'positive counterbalance' is the wealth of books and articles that aim to influence Muslim ideological circles. The guiding star of this work is large-scale distribution with the aim of reaching as many people as possible as exemplified by the Wahid Institute which distributes 500,000 newsletters on a grass roots level. The aim of the publications is to reinforce the theological interpretations that oppose violence motivated by faith and to reinforce arguments for separation of religion and state since mixing them undermines Islam and its fundamental values.

Initiatives aim to create a cultural, intellectual and theological mustering of strength that supports a pluralistic and tolerant interpretation of Islam. Identification, mobilization and support of the appropriate public opinion leaders in the Muslim society are decisive to these efforts.

2.2.5 Promoting Democracy (from page 16)

One decisive initiative was Muhammidiyah's decision to issue a ban on outside influence or activities that were in conflict with the organization's principles according to its charter and against the spirit of democracy. Nahdlatul Ulama has also issued an official decree stating that Muslims are not theologically required to establish a khalifa or oppose democracy. Warnings pertaining to imported ideology and activities that are contrary to the government ideology of *pancasila* have also been issued.

2.2.6 Promoting 'Mainstream' Religious Education (from page 17)

LibForAll has also established the Institute of Qur'anic Studies, which has its seat in Leiden. The aim is to create a renaissance within Islam with impetus towards pluralism, tolerance and critical thinking and to develop democracy and safeguard universal human rights.

2.2.7 Capacity-Building Initiatives for Muslim Movements and Activists on a Grass Roots Level (from page 17)

Even if LibForAll's strategy involves working from a top-down perspective, other institutes also contribute by focusing on the grass roots level. The different focuses complement one another. The work is in part focused on denying extremists opportunity, and in part on reinforcing local communities on a social level by combating poverty.

3. Concluding Comments (from page 23)

Violent radicalization is a complex societal phenomenon. Broad approaches are needed both to prevent and counteract anti-democratic forces that propel extremism and violence forward. Addressing these forces from a strategic perspective often demands the presence of forceful leadership and enthusiasts within the various public authorities. At the same time, strong individuals within civic communities are needed who carry on creative and constructive dialogs via non-profit associations and who also, from time to time, coordinate various initiatives and measures on national and local levels.

The development of extremism in Indonesia has been successfully stemmed by cultural factors (*pancasila*) and a strategically coordinated initiative, primarily promoted by LibForAll, including goal-oriented activities on tactical and strategic levels. The main achievement has involved mobilizing counterforces to extremism by creating a robust defence of the principle of separation of state and religion in Indonesia. The Bhinneka Tunggal Ika (*Oneness Amid Diversity*) movement has also been established; this movement actively works to defend the *pancasila* government ideology and the 1945 constitution. One of the most distinguishing conclusions from this study involves the decisive importance of popular movements, which can serve as a counterforce to extremism by coordinating various initiatives on national, regional and local levels. Even if the possibilities for exporting the Indonesian model are limited and linked to context, our study shows that it is possible to identify different useful and generic tools and approaches to prevent and address different kinds of extremism.

Indonesia stands out as a global leader in the ideological struggle against violent radicalization and extremism. Unfortunately, many Indonesian attempts to link its own successful experiences to the Middle East have been overshadowed and received a relatively chilly reception in the region. LibForAll constitutes, however, an interesting phenomenon in terms of bridging the gap against extremism both within and between regions. The organization has also, in an experimental manner, used various means and forums to reach out to as large a segment of society as possible by using credible messengers and new technological platforms. The study primarily shows that LibForAll's coordinated media strategy has had a decisive political effect in terms of curbing political parties with an extremist agenda. Exposing the true nature of the parties has enabled marginalization of corrosive, subversive forces.

Finally, different Indonesian tools and lessons can probably be applied to areas of Southeast Asia where extremism appears to be on the rise: primarily in Malaysia and the Philippines, as well as outside the region in areas such as Bangladesh. The Indonesian approach of preventing and addressing extremism can potentially be used in other regions as well. One example might be parts of Africa where Islam does not have the same historical roots as in other regions and where extremism is often an exogenous phenomenon.

Newsweek

"The Jihad Against the Jihadis," by Fareed Zakaria, cites the CATS study and, without naming LibForAll, refers to its decisive role in helping to counter radicalization: "Perhaps the most successful country to combat jihadism has been the world's most populous Muslim nation, Indonesia. In 2002 that country seemed destined for a long and painful struggle with the forces of radical Islam. The nation was rocked by terror attacks, and a local Qaeda affiliate, Jemaah Islamiah, appeared to be gaining strength. But eight years later, JI has been marginalized and main-stream political parties have gained ground, all while a young democracy has flowered after the collapse of the Suharto dictatorship.

"Magnus Ranstorp of Stockholm's Center for Asymmetric Threat Studies recently published a careful study examining Indonesia's success in beating back extremism. The main lesson, he writes, is to involve not just government but civil society as a whole, including media and cultural figures who can act as counterforces to terrorism."

BIBLIOGRAPHY

A. Books

'Abdul Wahhab, Sulaiman ibn (2006). *Al-Shwâ'iq al-Ilâhiyyah fî alradd 'alâ al-Wahhâbiyyah* (*A Strong Warning from Allah to Reject Wahhabi Ideology*), First edition published during the formative period of the Wahhabi movement; reprinted together with *Al-Tsaurat al-Wahhabiyah* ('Abdullah al-Qasimi, 2006). Köln, Germany: Al-Kamel Verlag.

A'la, Abdul (2008). *Genealogi Radikalisme Muslim Nusantara: Akar dan Karakter Pemikiran dan Gerakan Padri dalam Perspektif Hubungan Agama dan Politik Kekuasaan* (*The Genealogy of Muslim Radicalism in the Indonesian Archipelago: The Character and Roots of Radical Thought and the Padri Movement, from the Perspective of the Relationship Between Religion and Political Power*). Unpublished paper and speech delivered during investment ceremony, installing the author as a full professor at Sunan Ampel Islamic State Institute in Surabaya, East Java.

Abdullah, Taufik (1987). *Islam dan Masyarakat: Pantulan Sejarah Indonesia* (*Islam and Society: Reflections on Indonesia's History*). Jakarta: LP3ES.

Abdullah, Taufik and Mohammad Hisyam (2003). *Sejarah Umat Islam Indonesia* (*The History of Indonesia's Muslims*). Jakarta: MUI and Yayasan Pustaka Umat.

Abou El Fadl, Khaled M. (2001). *Melawan "Tentara Tuhan"* (*Fighting Against "God's Army"*). Jakarta: Serambi.

⸻, (2003). *Atas Nama Tuhan: dari Fikih Otoriter ke Fikih Otoritatif* (*In the Name of God: from the Authoritarian System of Jurisprudence to an Authoritative System of Jurisprudence*), translated from *Speaking in God's Name: Islamic Law,*

Authority and Women. Jakarta: Serambi.

Aburish, Said K. (2005). *The Rise, Corruption and Coming Fall of the House of Saud.* London: Bloomsbury.

Abuza, Zachary (2009), "Jemaah Islamiyah Adopts the Hezbollah Model" in *Middle East Quarterly*, Winter 2009.

Al-Darimi, Abu Muhammad 'Abdullah ibn 'Abdurrahman ibn al-Fadll ibn Bahram (tt.). *Sunan al-Dârimî.* Cairo: Mauqi'al-Wizârat al-Auqâf al-Mishriyah.

Algar, Hamid (2002). *Wahhabism: A Critical Essay.* New York: Islamic Publications International.

Al-Isbahânî, Abû Nu'ain Ahmad ibn 'Abdillah (1405). *Hilyat al-Auliyâ'.* Beirut: Dâr al-Kutub al-'Arabî.

Allen, Charles (2006). *God's Terrorists, The Wahhabi Cult and the Hidden Roots of Modern Jihad.* Cambridge, MA: Da Capo Press.

Almond, Gabriel A., R. Scott Appleby, and Emmanuel Sivan (2003). *Strong Religion: The Rise of Fundamentalism Around the World.* Chicago and London: The University of Chicago Press.

Al-Rasheed, Madawi (2002). *A History of Saudi Arabia.* Cambridge: Cambridge University Press.

Al-Râzî, Fakhruddin (tt.). *Mafâtih al-Ghaib.* Cairo: Mauqi' al-Tafâsir.

Al-Syaukânî (tt.). *Fath al-Qadîr.* Cairo: Mauqi' al-Tafâsir.

Amal, Taufik Adnan and Samsu Rizal Panggabean (2004). *Politik Syariat Islam: Dari Indonesia hingga Nigeria (The Politics of Islamic Shari'a: From Indonesia to Nigeria).* Jakarta, Alvabet.

Anwar, M. Syafi'i (1995). *Pemikiran dan Aksi Islam Indonesia: Sebuah Kajian Politik tentang Cendekiawan Muslim Orde Baru (Indonesian Islamic Thought and Action: a Political Study of Muslim Intellectuals During the New Order).* Jakarta, Paramadina.

Asfar, M (2003). *Islam Lunak – Islam Keras (Soft Islam – Hard Islam).* Surabaya: JP Press.

Ausop, Asep Zainal, (2005). "NII: Ajaran dan Gerakan (1992-2002)" ("NII: The Movement and Its Teaching (1992-

2002)"). Doctoral dissertation, PPS, UIN Jakarta.

Azra, Azyumardi (1994). *Jaringan Ulama: Timur Tengah dan Kepulauan Nusantara Abad XVII dan XVIII* (*Networks of Middle Eastern and Malay-Indonesian 'Ulama in the Seventeenth and Eighteenth Centuries*). Bandung: Mizan.

———, (2000). "The Islamic Factor in Post-Soeharto Indonesia" in Chris Manning & Peter van Diermen (eds.), *Indonesia in Transition: Social Aspect of Reforms and Crisis.* Canberra & Singapore: Research School of Pacific and Asian Studies, Australian National University & Institute of Southeast Asian Studies, 309-19.

———, (2002a). "The Globalization of Indonesian Muslim Discourse: Contemporary Religion-Intellectual Connections between Indonesia and the Middle East" in Johan Meuleman (ed.), *Islam in the Era of Globalization: Muslim Attitudes towards Modernity and Identity.* London: Routledge Curzon, 31-50.

———, (2002b). *Konflik Baru Antar-Peradaban: Globalisasi, Radikalisme & Pluralitas* (*The New Clash of Civilizations: Globalization, Radicalism & Pluralism*). Jakarta: Raja Grafindo Persada.

———, (2003a). "The Megawati Presidency: The Challenge of Political Islam", in Hadi Soesastro, Anthony L. Smith & Han Mui Ling (eds.), *Challenges Facing the Megawati Presidency.* Singapore: ISEAS.

———, (2003b). "Bali and Southeast Asian Islam: Debunking the Myths", in Kumar Ramakrishna & See Seng Tan (eds.), *After Bali: The Threat of Terrorism in Southeast Asia.* Singapore: World Scientific & IDSS.

———, (2004). *The Origins of Islamic Reformism in Southeast Asia.* Crownest, Aust., Honolulu, Leiden: AAAS & Allen & Unwin; University of Hawaii Press; KITLV Press.

———, (2006), *Indonesia, Islam and Democracy; Dynamics in a Global Context.* Jakarta & Singapore: Solstice-Equinox, ICIP & The Asia Foundation.

——— and Arskal Salim (2003). *Shari'a and Politics in Modern Indonesia.* Singapore: ISEAS.

Baidhawy, Zakiyuddin and Mutohharun Jinan (2003). *Agama*

dan Pluralitas Budaya Lokal (Religion and the Pluralism of Local Culture). Surakarta: University of Muhammadiyah Surakarta.

Bamualim, Chaider S. et al, (2001). Laporan Penelitian Radikalisme Agama dan Perubahan Sosial di DKI Jakarta (Research Report on Religious Radicalism and Social Change in Jakarta). Jakarta: Center for Language and Culture & Council of Regional Development Planner.

⸺, Dick van der Meij and Karlina Helmanita, eds. (2003). Islam and the West: Dialogue of Civilizations in Search of a Peaceful Global Order. Jakarta: PBB UIN Jakarta and Konrad Adenauer Stiftung.

⸺, ed., (2005). A Portrait of Contemporary Indonesian Islam. Jakarta: Center for Language and Culture UIN Jakarta and Konrad Adenauer Stiftung.

Baran, Zeyno (2004). Hizb ut-Tahrir: Islam's Political Insurgency. Washington: Nixon Center.

Barton, Greg (2005). Jemaah Islamiyah, Radical Islamism in Indonesia. Singapore: Ridge Books.

Benda, Harry J. (1958). The Crescent and the Rising Sun: Indonesian Islam under the Japanese Occupation. The Hague & Bandung: van Hoeve.

Bisri, A. Mustofa (2009). Lautan Wahyu: Islam sebagai Rahmatan lil 'Âlamîn (Ocean of Revelations: Understanding Islam as a Blessing for All Creation), (DVD), ©LibForAll Foundation 2009.

Bisyr, 'Utsman ibn 'Abdullah ibn (tt.), Unwân al-Majd fî Târîkh al-Najd.

Boland, B. J. (1982). The Struggle of Islam in Modern Indonesia. Leiden: The Hague-Martinus Nijhoff.

Bukhari, Imam, Shahih al-Bukhari.

Burr, J. Millard and Robert O. Collins (2006). Alms for Jihad: Charity and Terrorism in the Islamic World. New York: Cambridge University Press.

Crouch, Harold (2002). "The Recent Resurgence of Political Islam in Indonesia" in Anthony L. Smith, ed., Islam in Southeast Asia: Analysing Recent Developments. Singapore: ISEAS.

Dahlan, Sayyid Ahmad ibn Zaini (2006). *Al-Durar al-Sunniyyah fi al- Radd 'alâ al-Wahhâbiyyah* (*The Sunni Diamond's Rejection of Wahhabi Ideology*), printed together with *Al-Tsaurat al-Wahhabiyah* (*The Wahhabi Rebellion*) ('Abdullah al-Qasimi, 2006). Köln, Germany: Al-Kamel Verlag.

Damanik, Ali Said (2002). *Fenomena Partai Keadilan: Transformasi 20 Tahun Gerakan Tarbiyah di Indonesia* (*The Justice Party Phenomenon: Transformation Through 20 Years of the Tarbiyah Movement in Indonesia*). Jakarta: Teraju.

Dhume, Sadanand (2005), "Indonesian Democracy's Enemy Within: Radical Islamic party threatens Indonesia with ballots more than bullets," in the *Far Eastern Economic Review*, May 2005.

———, (2008). *My Friend the Fanatic: Travels with an Indonesian Islamist*. Melbourne: Text Publishing Company.

Directorate of Islamic Higher Education, General Directorate of Islamic Institutions, Department of Religion (2004). *Jejakjejak Islam Politik: Sinopsis Sejumlah Studi Islam Indonesia* (*The Footsteps of Political Islam: a Synopsis of Several Studies on Indonesian Islam*). Jakarta: Ditpertais.

The Economist (2003), "Nigeria's Muslim – Christian Riots: Religion or Realpolitik," 17 January 2003.

Effendy, Bahtiar (1998). *Islam dan Negara: Transformasi Pemikiran dan Praktik Politik Islam di Indonesia* (*Islam and the State: The Transformation of Islamic Political Thought and Practice in Indonesia*). Jakarta: Paramadina.

Esposito, John L. (1987). *Islam and Politics*. Syracuse: Syracuse University Press.

Fananie, Zainuddin, Atika Sabardila & Dwi Purnanto, (2002). *Radikalisme Agama & Perubahan Sosial* (*Religious Radicalism & Social Change*). Surakarta: Muhammadiyah University Press & The Asia Foundation.

Fathurrahman, Oman (2003). *Syatariah Brotherhood in the Malay-Indonesian World: a Study of its Dynamics and Development Through Manuscripts from West Sumatra*, dissertation from the Literature postgraduate program at the University of Indonesia, Jakarta 2003 (unpublished), p. 164, as quoted by Abdul A'la, Ibid., p.14.

Federspiel, Howard M., (1970). *Islamic Unitary: Islamic Reform in Twentieth Century Indonesia.* Ithaca, NY: Cornell University Modern Indonesia Project.

Furkon, Aay Muhammad (2004). *Partai Keadilan Sejahtera: Ideologi dan Praksis Politik Kaum Muda Muslim Indonesia Kontemporer* (*The Justice and Prosperity Party: Ideology and Political Practices of Contemporary Indonesian Muslim Youth*). Bandung: Teraju.

Gatra magazine, "Gertak Mati Pengawal Akidah" ("Threatening to Murder in the Name of Islamic Morality"), edition 14, 13 February 2004.

Gatra magazine, "Kebijakan Daerah Bernuansa Syari'ah" ("Regional Policies Have a Shari'a Nuance"), 29 November 2007.

Geertz, Clifford, 1968 (orig. 1960). *The Religion of Java.* New York: The Free Press (orig. New Haven & London: Yale University Press).

Hassan, Noorhaidi (2005). *Laskar Jihad: Islam, Militancy, and the Quest for Identity in Post-New Order Indonesia.* Dissertation. Leiden, Utrecht University, The Netherlands.

———, (2007), "Islamic Militancy, Sharia, and Democratic Consolidation in Post-Soeharto Indonesia," Working Paper No. 143, S. Rajaratnam School of International Studies (Singapore, 23 October 2007).

Hawwa, Sa'id (2005). Foreword to Abu Ridho, *Membina Angkatan Mujahid: Studi Analisis atas Konsep Dakwah Hasan al-Banna dalam Risalah Ta'lim* (*Training a Generation of Holy Warriors: Analysis of Hasan al-Banna's Concept of Proselytism in His Ta'lim Treatise*). Solo: Intermedia.

Hidayat, Komaruddin and Ahmad Gaus AF, eds. (2006). *Menjadi Indonesia: 13 Abad Eksistensi Islam di Bumi Nusantara* (*Becoming Indonesia: 13 Centuries of Islam in the East Indies Archipelago*). Jakarta, Mizan and Yayasan Festival Istiqlal.

Higgins, Andrew (2010). "Indonesia steps up pressure on Islamist militants," in the *Washington Post*, 13 May 2010.

Hizbut Tahrir Indonesia (2006). *Selamatkan Indonesia dengan*

Syari'ah (Rescue Indonesia With Shari'a). Jakarta: HTI Press.

Hourani, Albert (1983). *Arabic Thought in the Liberal Age, 1798 – 1939*. Cambridge: Cambridge University Press.

Husain, Ed. (2007). *The Islamist* (London: Penguin Books, 2007), (Translated into Bahasa Indonesian with title: *Matinya Semangat Jihad: Catatan Perjalanan Seorang Islamis*. Jakarta: Pustaka Alvabet, 2008).

Ibn Hanbal, Abu 'Abdillah Ahmad ibn Muhammad (tt.), *Masnad Ahmad*. Cairo: Mauqi' Wizârat al-Auqâf al-Mishriyyah.

Ibn Manzhur al-Ifriqi al-Mishri, Muhammad ibn Mukrim (tt.), *Lisân al-'Arab*. Beirut: Dâr al-Shâdir.

ICG (International Crisis Group), October (2001). *Indonesia: Violence and Radical Muslims*. Jakarta/Brussels.

————, August (2002). *Al-Qaeda in Southeast Asia: The Case of the "Ngruki Network" in Indonesia*. Jakarta/Brussels.

————, December (2002). *Indonesia Backgrounder: How the Jemaah Islamiyah Terrorist Network Operates*. Jakarta/Brussels.

————, September (2004). *Indonesia Backgrounder: Why Salafism and Terrorism Mostly Don't Mix*. Southeast Asia/Brussels.

The Jakarta Globe (2009), "Stoning, Caning Are Now the Law in Aceh, Local Legislator Says," 15 October 2009.

The Jakarta Post (2007), "Caliphate not part of Koran: NU," 25 November 2007.

The Jakarta Post (2008), "Govt defies calls to review sharia bylaws," 16 February 2008.

The Jakarta Post (2008), "Review sharia bylaws, say scholars," 1 March 2008.

The Jakarta Post (2009), "NU states opposition to sharia bylaws," 29 July 2009.

Jamhari & Jahroni Jajang, eds., (2004). *Gerakan Salafi Radikal di Indonesia (Radical Salafi Movements in Indonesia)*. Jakarta: Rajawali Press.

Kamil, Sukron and Chaider S. Bamualim, eds., (2007). *Syariah Islam dan HAM: Dampak Perda Syariah terhadap Kebebasan Sipil, Hak-hak Perempuan, dan Non-Muslim (Islamic Shari'a and Human Rights: The Impact of Regional Shari'a Regulations*

Upon Civil Liberty, Women's Rights and Non-Muslims). Jakarta, CSRC-UIN Jakarta and Konrad Adenauer Stiftung.

Kepel, Gilles (2002). *Jihad: The Trial of Political Islam.* Cambridge, Massachusetts: Harvard University Press.

Kompas (2006), "Fraksi PKS Diingatkan Tak Paksakan Ideologi Partai" ("PKS Faction Reminded Not to Impose Party Ideology"), 18 December 2006.

Kompas (2008), "PKS Serukan Bangkitkan Semangat Kebangsaan" ("PKS Encourages Raising the Spirit of Nationalism"), 4 February 2008.

Maarif, Ahmad Syafii (2001), "Pertimbangkan Dampak yang Akan Timbul" ("Imagine the Consequences that will Ensue") in Kurniawan Zein and Saripuddin HA, *Shari'a Islam Yes, Shari'a Islam No: Dilemma of Jakarta Charter in the 1945 Amendment to the Constitution.* Jakarta: Paramadina.

Machmudi, Yon (2005). *Partai Keadilan: Wajah Baru Islam Politik Indonesia (Justice Party: The New Face of Indonesian Political Islam).* Bandung: Harakatuna Publishing.

Madjid, Nurcholish (1999). *Cita-cita Politik Islam Era Reformasi (The Goals of Islamic Politics in the Era of Reformation).* Jakarta, Paramadina.

————, (2003). *Indonesia Kita (Our Indonesia).* Jakarta: Paramadina University.

Mahmud, Ali Abdul Halim (2004). *Perangkat-perangkat Tarbiyah Ikhwanul Muslimin (The Muslim Brotherhood's Tarbiyah Agents).* Solo: Intermedia.

Mahmud, Ali Abdul Halim (tt.). *Ikhwanul Muslimin: Konsep Gerakan Terpadu (Muslim Brotherhood: The Concept of an Integrated Movement) (Minhaju al-Tarbiyah 'inda al-Ikhwan al-Muslimin).* Jakarta: Gema Insani Press.

Majelis Pertimbangan Pusat PKS (2007). *Platform Kebijakan Pembangunan Partai Keadilan Sejahtera (Policy Platform [to Ensure] Development of the Justice and Prosperity Party).* Jakarta, Majelis Central Consideration PKS.

Mas'udi, Masdar F. (2006). *Membangun NU Berbasis Masjid dan Umat (Building the NU on the Basis of Mosques and*

Congregations). Jakarta: Lajnah Takmir Masjid Nahdatul Ulama, Pesantren Development Association and Masyarakat (P3M).

Mulkhan, Abdul Munir (2006). "Sendang Ayu: Pergulatan Muhammadiyah di Kaki Bukit Barisan" ("Sendang Ayu: Muhammadiyah Battle at the Foot of Barisan Mountain") in *Voice of Muhammadiyah*, 2 January 2006.

Muzadi, K.H. Hasyim, et al. (2004). *Gerakan Radikal Islam di Indonesia dalam Sorotan* (*Indonesia's Radical Islamic Movements in the Spotlight*). Jakarta: ASEAN Youth and Student Network.

Muzadi, Hasyim (2006). "Khilafah Islamiyah bukan Gerakan Agama, tapi Gerakan Politik" ("The Islamic Caliphate is a Political Movement, not a Religious One"), in *NU Online*, Tuesday, 5 September 2006.

Nashir, Haedar (2007). *Manifestasi Gerakan Tarbiyah: Bagaimana Sikap Muhammadiyah?* (*Manifestation of the Islamic Education Movement: How Should the Muhammadiyah Respond?*) 5th edition, Yogyakarta: Voice of Muhammadiyah.

————, (2007). *Kristalisasi Ideologi & Komitmen Bermuhammadiyah* (*The Crystallization of Muhammadiyah Ideology and Commitment*). Yogyakarta: Voice of Muhammadiyah.

————, (2007). *Gerakan Islam Syariat: Reproduksi Salafiyah Ideologis di Indonesia* (*Islamic Shari'a Movements: The Reproduction of Ideological Salafism in Indonesia*). Jakarta: Center for Religious Study and Civilization (PSAP) Muhammadiyah.

Noer, Deliar (1980). *Gerakan Modern Islam di Indonesia, 1900 – 1942* (*Modern Islamic Movements in Indonesia 1990 – 1942*). Jakarta: LP3ES.

NU Online (2007), "PBNU Desak Pemerintah Cegah Ideologi Transnasional" ("NU Central Board Presses the Government to Halt Transnational Ideology"), 29 April 2007.

Nursalim, Muh., (2001). *Faksi Abdullah Sungkar dalam Gerakan NII Era Orde Baru* (*The Abdullah Sungkar Faction Within the NII* ("*Indonesian Islamic State*") *Movement During the New*

Order Era), MA thesis, University of Muhammadiyah Surakarta.

Partai Keadilan Sejahtera (2004). *Kurikulum Tarbiyah: Panduan LIQA' Anggota Pemula PK Sejahtera (Islamic Education Curriculum: Guide for New Members of the PKS*). Yogyakarta: Muliya Press.

Patmono SK (2006). "Aspirasi Islam dalam Konteks Negara Bangsa" ("Islamic Aspirations within the Context of the Nation State"), in Komaruddin Hidayat and Ahmad Gaus AF (eds.), *Becoming Indonesia: 13 Centuries of Islamic Existence in Bumi Nusantara*. Jakarta: Mizan and Yayasan Festival Istiqlal.

Puti Reno Raudha Thaib, "Sejarah Istana Pagaruyung" ("The History of Pagaruyung Palace") see http://groups.yahoo.com/group/RantauNet/message/61114

Qashîmî, 'Abdullah al- (2006). *Al-Tsaurah al-Wahhâbiyyah* (first edition in 1936). Köln, Germany: Al-Kamel Verlag.

Rahmat, M. Imdadun (2005). *Arus Baru Islam Radikal: Transmisi Revivalisme Islam Timur Tengah ke Indonesia (A New Tide of Radical Islam: The Transmission of Islamic Revivalism from the Middle East to Indonesia*). Jakarta: Erlangga Publisher.

Ramli, Andi Muawiyah (ed.) (2006). *Demi Ayat Tuhan: Upaya KPPSI Menegakkan Syari'ah Islam (For the Sake of God's Verses: The KPPSI's Efforts to Implement Islamic Shari'a*). Jakarta: OPSI.

Rashid, Ahmed (2000). *Taliban: Militant Islam, Oil, and Fundamentalism in Central Asia*. New Haven: Yale Nota Bene, Yale University Press.

"Regulasi Syari'ah di Kalimantan Selatan," in *Reform Review: Jurnal untuk Kajian dan Pemetaan Krisis* ("Shari'a Regulations in South Kalimantan," in *Reform Review: Journal for Studying and Mapping the Crisis*), Vol. I No. 1, April-June 2007.

Reid, Anthony, (1988) Vol I. *Southeast Asia in the Age of Commerce, 1450 – 1680*. New Haven & London: Yale University Press; 1993 (Vol. II).

Republika (2008), "PKS Mukernas Recomendasikan Tiga Agenda" ("PKS Congress Recommends Three Agendas"), 4

February 2008.

Reuters News Service 10 July 2008, "Indonesian Islamist party eyes polls and presidency".

Ricklefs, M.C., (1998). *The Seen and the Unseen Worlds in Java: History, Literature and Islam in Court of Pakubuwana II, 1726 – 1749.* Canberra: AAAS & Allen Unwin.

"Risalah PKS untuk Mengokohkan Ukhuwah dan Ishlah" ("PKS Treatise to Strengthen Muslim Fraternity and Reconciliation"), (27 September 2007).

Robbins, Thomas (1998). *Cult, Convert, and Charisma: The Sociology of New Religious Movements.* London: Sage.

Roy, Olivier (1996). *The Failure of Political Islam,* translated by Carol Volk. Harvard: Harvard University Press (published in Indonesia, *The Failure of Islamic Politics.* Jakarta: Serambi).

———, (2004). *Globalized Islam: The Search for a New Ummah.* New York: Columbia University Press.

Salim, Arskal and Azyumardi Azra (2003), "The State and Shari'a in the Perspective of Indonesian Legal Politics," Introduction to the book *Shari'a and Politics in Modern Indonesia.* Singapore: ISEAS.

Schwartz, Stephen Sulaiman (2002). *The Two Faces of Islam: Saudi Fundamentalism and Its Role in Terrorism.* New York: Doubleday (published in Indonesian as *Dua Wajah Islam: Moderatisme vs Fundamentalisme dalam Wacana Global,* Jakarta: LibForAll Foundation, the Wahid Institute, Center for Islamic Pluralism, and Blantika).

Setiawan, Farid (2006). "Ahmad Dahlan Menangis (Tanggapan terhadap Tulisan Abdul Munir Mulkhan)" ("Ahmad Dahlan in Tears (Reflections on an Article by Abdul Munir Mulkhan)"), in *Voice of Muhammadiyah,* 20 February 2006.

———, (2006). "Tiga Upaya Mu'allimin dan Mu'allimat" ("Three Actions (to Improve the Muhammadiyah's) Male and Female Teachers Schools"), in *Voice of Muhammadiyah,* 3 April 2006.

Setiawan, Zudi (2007). *Nationalism NU (NU Nationalism).* Semarang:

CV. Aneka Ilmu.

Shihab, Habib Rizieq (2002). "Jika Syari'ah Islam Jalan, Maka Jadi Negara Islam" ("If Shari'a is Enacted, an Islamic State Will Come into Being"). Tashwirul Afkar. Edition No. 12, 2002.

Siba'i, Hani al- (2005). *Balada Jamaah Jihad* (*The Story of the Jihad Community*) (translated by Sarwedi M. Hasibuan). Solo: Jazera.

Simanjuntak, Togi (2000). *Premanisme Politik* (*Political Thuggery*). Jakarta: ISAI.

Simuh (1996). *Tasawuf dan Perkembangannya dalam Islam* (*Sufism and Its Development in Islam*). Jakarta: Rajawali Pers.

Smith, Anthony L., ed., (2002). *Islam in Southeast Asia: Analyzing Recent Developments*. Singapore: ISEAS.

Stephens, Bret, "The Arab Invasion: Indonesia's Radicalized Muslims Aren't Homegrown," see: http://www.libforall. org/news/Wall-Street-Journal_The-Arab-Invasion.pdf).

⸺, "The Exorcist: Indonesian man seeks to create an Islam that will make people smile'," see http://www.libforall.org/ news/Wall-Street-Journal_The-Exorcist.pdf

Suaedy, Ahmad. "MUI Bungker Islam Radikal" ("MUI as a Bunker of Radical Islam"), http://www.wahidinstitute. org/Program/Detail/?id=47/hl=id/MUI_Bunker_ Islam_Radikal

⸺, (2006). Foreword: "Fatwa MUI dan Problem Otoritas Keagamaan" ("MUI Fatwas and the Problem of Religious Authoritarianism"), in *When Fatwa Becomes a Prison*. Jakarta: The Wahid Institute.

Subhani, Syaikh Ja'far (1989). *Tawassul, Tabarruk, Ziarah Kubur, Karamah Wali termasuk Ajaran Islam, Kritik atas Faham Wahabi* (*Drawing Near to God, Seeking Blessings from the Prophet, Visiting Saints' Graves and the Sanctity of God's Friends are Legitimate Islamic Teachings; Critique of Wahhabi Ideology*), (translated from Arabic to Indonesian by Zahir). Jakarta: Pustaka Hidayah.

Suratmin (1982). *Nyai Ahmad Dahlan Pahlawan Nasional: Amal dan Perjuangannya* (*Mrs. Ahmad Dahlan, a National Hero:*

Her Good Deeds and Struggle). Yogyakarta: Publisher PP. Aisyiyah.

Suryadi, *The Padri Controversy: If Not For Tuanku Nan Renceh*, as quoted by Abdul A'la, Ibid., p. 14.

Syadid, Muhammad (2003). *Manhaj Tarbiyah: Metode Pembinaan dalam al-Qur'an* (*Islamic Education: Training Methods from the Qur'an*). Jakarta: Robbani Press.

Taylor , C. Holland (2008). "Unfriendly Fanatics," in the *Asian Wall Street Journal*, 24 June 2008.

Thalibi, Abu Abdirrahman al- (2006). *Dakwah Salafiyah Dakwah Bijak: Meluruskan Sikap Keras Dai Salafi* (*Salafi Proselytism, Wise Proselytism: Correcting the Harsh Behavior of Salafi Proselytizers*). Jakarta: Hujjah Press.

The WAHID Institute 2008, *Pluralisme Beragama Berkeyakinan di Indonesia: "Menapaki Bangsa yang Kian Retak"* (*Religious Pluralism in Indonesia: "Contemplating an Increasingly Fractured Nation"*).

Turmudi, Endang and Riza Sihbudi (2005). *Islam dan Radikalisme di Indonesia* (*Islam and Radicalism in Indonesia*). Jakarta: LIPI Press.

US News & World Report (2003), "How Billions in Oil Money Spawned a Global Terror Network," 7 December 2003.

Van Cleef, Jabez L. (2008). *The Tawasin Of Mansur Al-Hallaj, In Verse: A Mystical Treatise On Knowing God, & Invitation To The Dance.* Self-published.

Vision of the Justice and Prosperity Party (PKS), see www.pk-sejahtera. org, "Visi dan Misi" ("Vision and Mission").

Wahid, K.H. Abdurrahman (1999). *Islam, Negara, dan Demokrasi* (*Islam, State, and Democracy*). Jakarta: Erlangga.

————, (1999). *Mengurai Hubungan Agama dan Negara* (*Disentangling the Relationship Between Religion and State*). Jakarta: Grasindo.

————, (2006). *Islamku Islam Anda Islam Kita* (*My Islam, Your Islam, Our Islam*). Jakarta: The Wahid Institute.

————, (2006). "Kongkow bersama Gus Dur" ("Chatting with Gus Dur") Commemorate the Day of National Awakening on Radio Utan Kayu, Jl Utan Kayu No. 68 H, Jakarta,

20 May 2006.

————, (2006). "Extremism Isn't Islamic Law," in the *Washington Post*, 23 May 2006.

————, (2006). "Penerapan Perda Syari'ah Mengkudeta Konstitusi" ("Establishing Regional Shari'a Regulations Constitutes a Coup d'Etat Against the Constitution"), see www.gusdur.net.

Waluyo, Sapto (2005). *Kebangkitan Politik Dakwah: Konsep dan Praktik Politik Partai Keadilan Sejahtera di Masa Transisi (The Rise of Missionary Politics: The Justice and Prosperity Party's Concept and Practice of Politics During a Time of Transition)*. Bandung: Harakatuna Publishing.

Woodward, Mark R., (1989). *Islam in Java: Normative Piety and Mysticism in the Sultanate of Yogyakarta*. Tucson: The University of Arizona Press.

————, ed. (1999). *Jalan Baru Islam: Memetakan Paradigma Mutakhir (Islam's New Path: Mapping the Latest Paradigms)*. Bandung, Mizan

Yunanto, S. (2004). *Gerakan Militan Islam (Militant Islamic Movements)*. Jakarta: Ridep.

Zada, Khamami, (2002). *Islam Radikal: Pergulatan Ormas-ormas Islam Garis Keras di Indonesia (Radical Islam: The Struggle of Hard Line Islamic Mass Organizations in Indonesia)*. Jakarta: Teraju.

Zastrouw (2007). *Gerakan Islam Simbolik (Symbolic Islamic Movements)*. Yogyakarta: LKiS.

Zein, Kurniawan and Saripuddin HA, eds. (2001). *Syariat Islam Yes, Syariat Islam No! Dilema Piagam Jakarta dalam Amandemen UUD 1945 (Islamic Shari'a Yes, Islamic Shari'a No! The Jakarta Charter Dilemma, in Amending the 1945 Constitution)*. Jakarta, Paramadina.

B. Websites

- www.asianews.com ("Catholic students forced to wear the Islamic veil").
- www.gatra.com ("PKS Reject the Decision to Refuse Shari'a Regional Regulations," 14 June 2006).

- www.gusdur.net ("The Application of Shari'a Regional Regulations a Coup d'Etat Against the Constitution").
- www.wahidinstitute.org
- www.nu.or.id/page.php
- www.pk-sejahtera.org
- www.ndi.org/indonesia
- www.libforall.org/news/Wall-Street-Journal_The-Arab-Invasion.pdf
- www.libforall.org/news-WSJ-the-exorcist.html

Biographical Information

ABOUT THE AUTHORS

T-shirts featuring Abdurrahman Wahid, Syafii Maarif and A. Mustofa Bisri were distributed to journalists who attended the launch of *The Illusion of an Islamic State*, and the images posted online for free download by the public at large.

**Translation of text on t-shirt featuring the three *resis* (sages)
who presented the book to the Indonesian public on
16 May 2009:**

"Although a ruler has the body of a human,
he or she should have the characteristics of a Divine Being,
armed with the sacred trident (honest, grounded in Truth,
and free of egotistical self-interest); be obedient to holy sages
(*resis*), whose unshakable grip upon the sacred trident
is embedded in their very souls;
and live to serve the people."

~ Motto of the Bhinneka Tunggal Ika Movement,
inspired by the Old Javanese text,
Serat Jongko Joyoboyo

"If the government does not listen to religious leaders who,
just like hermits [*resis*] come down the mountain to give moral
lessons, who will they listen to?"

~ Dr. A. Syafii Maarif, quoted in *The Jakarta Post*,
11 January 2011, speaking on behalf of interfaith religious leaders
calling for government accountability

H.E. Kyai Haji Abdurrahman Wahid

Translation of text on t-shirt:
"Always be honest and open; there's no need for us to be afraid."

Indonesia's first democratically-elected president (1999 – 2001), long-time head of the world's largest Muslim organization, the Nahdlatul Ulama (1984 – 1999), and co-founder and patron of LibForAll Foundation (www.libforall.org) and The Wahid Institute (www.wahidinstitute.org), Abdurrahman Wahid (1940 – 2009) has been acclaimed as "the single most influential religious leader in the Muslim world" and "easily the most important ally the West has in the ideological struggle against Islamic radicalism" (*Wall Street Journal*, "The Last King of Java," by Bret Stephens).

Recipient of the 2003 Friends of the United Nations Global Tolerance Award, and of the Simon Wiesenthal Center's Medal of Valor in 2008, Abdurrahman Wahid consistently used his influential position, and mass following, to promote religious tolerance, pluralism and democracy. On numerous occasions, he sent members of his Muslim organization to defend Christian churches and congregations—with their lives, if necessary—from attack by Islamist radicals.

It was typical of President Wahid's greatness that even when religious extremists attacked and reviled him, he remained self-confident and experienced a deep, inner joy, derived from the knowledge that he was performing God's work, and serving humanity. Although, in his own words, he has now "vanished from the face of the earth," his enormous influence remains—a testament to God's infinite love, mercy and compassion, and the noble heights to which the human spirit may attain.

"[A] product of Indonesia's traditionally tolerant and humane practice of Islam, he took that tradition to a higher level and shaped it in ways that will last long after his death" (*Wall Street Journal*, "Wahid and the Voice of Moderate Islam," by Paul Wolfowitz).

Ahmad Syafii Maarif

Translation of text on t-shirt:
"Absolute Truth belongs only to God.
We must strive to reach It, although we may never
succeed in doing so."

Dr. Ahmad Syafii Maarif is the former Chairman (1998 – 2005) of the world's second largest Muslim organization, the Muhammadiyah, with 30-million followers. Under his leadership, the Muhammadiyah demonstrated a strong commitment to a pluralistic, tolerant and peaceful understanding of Islam, and to the nation of Indonesia.

Dr. Maarif received his Master's degree from Ohio University, and a Ph.D. in History from the University of Chicago in the field of Middle Eastern Languages and Civilizations. At the University of Chicago, Dr. Maarif studied with the renowned Islamic reformer Dr. Fazlur Rahman, together with his fellow Indonesian Nurcholish Madjid. Along with Kyai Haji Abdurrahman Wahid, their thought was formative in building Indonesian civil society during the 1980s and '90s, and preparing Indonesia for its successful transition to democracy after the fall of Suharto in 1998.

Dr. Maarif is a 2008 recipient of the Ramon Magsaysay Award

(often considered Asia's Nobel Prize) in the category of Peace and International Understanding. The award specifically honored him for "guiding Muslims to embrace tolerance and pluralism as the basis for justice and harmony in Indonesia and in the world at large."

Dr. Maarif is a prolific writer and speaker, whose prominent works include *The Dynamics of Islam* and *Islam, Why Not?* He is the founder and chairman of Maarif Institute (www.maarifinstitute.org), a non-profit, non-governmental organization that promotes the values of Islam, humanity and Indonesian culture, and a co-founder and patron of LibForAll's International Institute of Qur'anic Studies.

Kyai Haji Achmad Mustofa Bisri

Translation of text on t-shirt:
"Only God's Truth is truly Real and Valid."

Kyai Haji A. Mustofa Bisri is often called "Sang Kyai Pembela-jar"—the Great Religious Scholar Devoted to Learning—by members of the Nahdlatul Ulama (NU). Widely revered as an *'alim* (Muslim religious scholar), poet, novelist, painter and public intellectual, "Gus Mus" (Brother MUStofa) is often called the "President of Poets," and celebrated for his courage in defending artistic and religious freedom in the face of radical onslaughts.

Descended from a long line of charismatic religious leaders, Gus Mus heads the prestigious Pondok Pesantren Raudlatuth Tholibin (*madrasa*) in Rembang, Central Java, where he was born in 1944. He received a thorough education in Islamic studies from his father and other leading Muslim scholars—all of whom encouraged artistic development and critical thought among their young students—and at al-Azhar University in Cairo, where he established a life-long friendship with Kyai Haji Abdurrahman Wahid, who was studying there at the same time.

K. H. Mustofa Bisri currently serves as Deputy Chairman of

the Nahdlatul Ulama's Supreme Council, and as senior advisor to LibForAll Foundation and its International Institute of Qur'anic Studies. Gus Mus's personal philosophy can be seen in the Mata Air ("Living Spring") Community that he heads, whose membership is open to all who share its essential values: "Worship God; respect elders; treat those who are younger with loving kindness; open your heart to all humanity."

"One of the most influential liberal Islamic scholars worldwide."

~ *Der Spiegel*, "German University Starts Seminars for Imams," by Anna Reimann

C. Holland Taylor

Educated at the University of North Carolina – Chapel Hill and Princeton University, Mr. Taylor is co-founder, chairman and CEO of LibForAll Foundation, which he established in 2003 with his close friend, the former Indonesian president H.E. Kyai Haji Abdurrahman Wahid (1940 – 2009). Under their leadership, LibForAll has grown into the leading NGO developing and operationalizing successful counter-extremism strategies worldwide.

An expert on Islam and the process of Islamization in Southeast Asia, Mr. Taylor has lived, studied and worked in the Muslim world, from Iran to Indonesia, over a period of more than four decades. Although his knowledge of Islam pales in comparison with that of the renowned Muslim leaders who form the backbone of LibForAll Foundation, Mr. Taylor's unique combination of experience in the fields of international business, strategy and the forging of cross-cultural relationships has enabled LibForAll to become "a model of what a competent public diplomacy effort in the Muslim world should look like" (*Wall Street Journal*) and "the world's most potent and innovative anti-extremism network" (*The Weekly Standard*).

Mr. Taylor's work with LibForAll follows a career as a successful entrepreneur and global telecom executive, during which he served as CEO of USA Global Link, and was credited by numerous leading publications as one of the essential catalysts in the deregulation of the global telecommunications industry.

Kyai Haji Hodri Ariev

Kyai Haji Hodri Ariev is LibForAll Foundation's director of programs, Southeast Asia. A highly-trained *kyai*, or *'alim* (religious scholar), Mr. Ariev was born in Jember, East Java and hails from a Nahdlatul Ulama pesantren (*madrasa*) background closely affiliated with LibForAll co-founder Kyai Haji Abdurrahman Wahid. Kyai Ariev's father, grandfather, and great-grandfather were all respected *ulama*, or religious scholars, trained in Islamic law and spirituality.

In 1926—in the wake of the Saudi/Wahhabi conquest of Mecca and Medina—Kyai Ariev's great-grandfather carried the newly established Nahdlatul Ulama's flag to Islamic boarding schools throughout East Java, on behalf of President Wahid's grandfather, summoning traditional *ulama* to awaken and unite in the face of extremist threats to the Sunni Muslim understanding, and practice, of Islam.

Kyai Ariev completed his Bachelors degree in Islamic Law (Shari'a) at the Annuqayah Islamic Sciences College on Madura Island in East Java, graduating cum laude, and his Masters degree in Islamic Philosophy and Mysticism at the prestigious Syarif Hidayatullah Islamic State University in Jakarta. His areas of expertise include Islamic law, philosophy, mysticism and Qur'anic exegesis.

Kyai Ariev has served as interim Rector (President) of Annuqayah Islamic Sciences College, handling the process of development and succession within the College, which together with its affiliated boarding school has approximately 8,000 students. He continues to lecture on Arabic and English textual studies at Annuqayah, and is also the head of Pondok Pesantren Bahrul Ulum ("Ocean of Knowledge Madrasa") in Jember, East Java, which was founded by his father, the late Kyai Haji Arifurrahman, in 1958.

Kyai Ariev has translated numerous books from Arabic and English into Indonesian, and is a producer (responsible for theological content) of LibForAll's *Ocean of Revelations* film series.

Dr. Ratno Lukito

Dr. Ratno Lukito is Deputy Director of Post-Graduate Studies at Sunan Kalijaga Islamic State University (UIN) in Yogyakarta, Indonesia. An internationally-recognized expert on Islamic and traditional law (*fiqh* and *adat*), Dr. Lukito is also a member of the Muhammadiyah organization's Tarjih (Legal Affairs) Committee, and has worked closely with LibForAll Foundation and its International Institute of Qur'anic Studies for several years.

Dr. Lukito has extensive experience developing and assessing academic programs; conducting field research in his area of specializations; and continues to teach Islamic Law at UIN. At Yogyakarta's Muhammadiyah University, Dr. Lukito was responsible for developing a doctoral program in Islamic Studies, and serves as the secretary of this program. At Gadjah Mada University in Yogyakarta, Dr. Lukito is a member of the teaching staff in the American Studies postgraduate school where he lectures Masters students in religion and state in America and the American legal system. He has held positions of national trainer and central committee secretary on basic education projects sponsored by the Indonesian Ministry of Religious Affairs and the Asian Development Bank. He serves as an assessor for the Indonesian National Board of University Accreditation and is a member of the International Commission on Folk Law and Legal Pluralism.

Dr. Lukito is the author of 9 books and over 30 articles on Islamic Law, especially as it relates to the Indonesian context. His 2008 book on conflicts between religious and secular law, and their resolution in the Indonesian context, was distributed by the Supreme Court of Indonesia to judges throughout the country.

Born in Yogyakarta, Indonesia, Dr. Lukito holds a BA from the Islamic State University in Yogyakarta, Indonesia, and both an MA in Islamic Studies and a Ph.D. in Civil Law (DCL) from McGill University, Montreal, Canada.

Explanation of the Book's Cover

Statue of Indonesian founding fathers Soekarno and Muhammad Hatta, proclaiming the nation's independence on 17 August 1945—establishing the new nation as a multi-religious and pluralistic state, while explicitly rejecting calls for an Islamic State.

Background text on the front cover is the actual text of the Independence proclamation, signed by Soekarno and Hatta.

Red and white are the colors of the Indonesian flag.

Eagle with spread wings, shield and motto is Indonesia's national symbol (Garuda). The national motto, *Bhinneka Tunggal Ika*, means "Oneness Amid Diversity."

Green symbol to the left, above Soekarno's shoulder (featuring nine stars and an image of the globe) is that of the Nahdlatul Ulama—the world's largest Muslim organization, with over 40 million followers.

Green symbol to the right (above Muhammad Hatta's shoulder) is that of the Muhammadiyah, the world's second-largest Muslim organization, also based in Indonesia.

Masked figures "beneath the feet" of Sukarno and Hatta are affiliated with the extremist group Front for the Defense of Islam (FPI), which on 1 June 2008 attacked an assembly of peaceful demonstrators gathered at Indonesia's national monument in Jakarta, to express their support for religious minorities and the nation's tradition of pluralism and tolerance.

Back cover shows the smoking ruins of the World Trade Center shortly after 9/11. In *The Illusion of an Islamic State*, President Wahid condemned the brutal acts of "thugs, [who] wish to convince others that the extremist views they scream at the top of their lungs and try to force on everyone else represent the true message of Islam, for which all must struggle. Yet in reality they are damaging the religion of Islam... [a]nd the rest of us, as Muslims, should be deeply ashamed of their actions."